Creativity and Mental Illness

Are creative people more likely to be mentally ill? This basic question has been debated for thousands of years, with the "mad genius" concept advanced by such luminaries as Aristotle. There are many studies that argue the answer is "yes," and several prominent scholars who argue strongly for a connection. There are also those who argue equally strongly that the core studies and scholarship underlying the mad genius myth are fundamentally flawed. This book re-examines the common view that a high level of individual creativity often correlates with a heightened risk of mental illness. It expands conventional wisdom that links creativity with mental illness, arguing that the relationship is complicated; there are some ways in which creativity is associated with mental illness, other ways in which it is associated with positive mental health, and other ways in which the two traits are simply not associated. With contributions from some of the most exciting voices in the fields of psychology, neuroscience, physics, psychiatry, and management, this is a dynamic and cutting-edge volume that will inspire new ideas and studies on this fascinating topic.

JAMES C. KAUFMAN is Professor of Educational Psychology in the Neag School of Education at the University of Connecticut.

Creativity and Mental Illness

Edited by

James C. Kaufman

University of Connecticut
Storrs, CT

CAMBRIDGE
UNIVERSITY PRESS

CAMBRIDGE
UNIVERSITY PRESS

University Printing House, Cambridge CB2 8BS, United Kingdom

Cambridge University Press is part of the University of Cambridge.

It furthers the University's mission by disseminating knowledge in the pursuit of
education, learning and research at the highest international levels of excellence.

www.cambridge.org
Information on this title: www.cambridge.org/9781107021693

© Cambridge University Press 2014

First published 2014

A catalogue record for this publication is available from the British Library

ISBN 978-1-107-02169-3 Hardback

For my brother
David S. Kaufman
(1968–2004)

Of all sad words of tongue or pen,
The saddest are these: "It might have been."
(John Greenleaf Whittier)

Contents

Figures

Tables

Contributors

ANNA ABRAHAM, PhD, is an associate professor in the Department of Community Medicine and Behavioural Sciences at the Faculty of Medicine in Kuwait University. She is also scientifically affiliated to the Department of Clinical Psychology at the Justus Liebig University of Giessen in Germany. She is a psychologist and a cognitive neuroscientist whose research revolves around the neurocognitive study of imagination, encompassing domains such as creativity, mental time travel, mental state reasoning and the reality–fiction distinction.

NEUS BARRANTES-VIDAL obtained an MS degree in child and adolescent clinical psychopathology, an MS in adult clinical psychology, and a PhD in psychology, as well as being a licensed clinical psychologist. She is an associate professor at the Department of Clinical Psychology at the Universitat Autònoma de Barcelona (Spain), adjunct associate professor at the University of North Carolina at Greensboro (USA), researcher at the Spanish Ministry of Health Network on Mental Health Research (CIBERSAM), and research consultant at the Sant Pere Claver Health Foundation. She is currently a member of the Advisory Board of the Spanish Agency for the Assessment of Scientific Research (ANEP) and holds a research distinction awarded by the Catalan Institution for Research and Advanced Studies (ICREA).

ROGER E. BEATY is a graduate student in psychology at the University of North Carolina at Greensboro. His research broadly focuses on the cognitive processes underlying creative behavior. In addition to figurative language production, Roger is also interested in the neuroscience of creativity. Using functional magnetic resonance imaging and functional connectivity analysis, he is interested in the complex interactions between multiple neural networks in the brain. He also uses these methods to study musical performance, such as jazz improvisation.

MELANIE L. BEAUSSART is a psychology researcher and writer whose research focus is primarily in the areas of social psychology and human evolution. Her empirical work is somewhat eclectic. In particular, she is interested in sexual strategies theory and what variables influence humans to engage in one-night stands or serial monogamy. She also has an interest in sexual selection's relationship to creativity and intelligence. Part of this research has led her to explore the attributes that influence creativity, such as mental health and personality.

GEORGE BECKER is an associate professor of sociology at Vanderbilt University. He holds degrees from Columbia University (MA in modern European history), Illinois Institute of Technology (MS in sociology of education), and Stony Brook University (PhD in sociology). His research interests include historical sociology, the sociology of religion, the sociology of science and knowledge, and the sociology of mental illness. His contributions to the latter include a book, *The mad genius controversy*, and a number of articles. He is currently at work on another book entitled *Creativity and psychopathology: The social construction of illness*.

SHELLEY CARSON, PhD, is an associate of the Department of Psychology and lecturer in extension at Harvard University, where she conducts research and teaches courses on creativity, abnormal psychology, and resilience. Her work on creativity has been published in national and international peer-reviewed science journals, and has been highlighted in national media, including the Discovery Channel, CNN, and National Public Radio. She is also author of the award-winning book *Your creative brain: Seven steps to maximize imagination, productivity, and innovation in your life* and coauthor of *Almost depressed: Is my (or my loved one's) unhappiness a problem?*.

MAJA DJIKIC, PhD, is a senior research associate and the Director of the Self-Development Lab at the Rotman School of Management, University of Toronto. She is a psychologist specializing in the field of personality development. She has been a post-doctoral fellow at the Desautels Centre for Integrative Thinking (Rotman School of Management) and the Psychology Department at Harvard University. Her research has been published in *Journal of Research in Personality*, *Psychological Science*, *Creativity Research Journal*, *New Ideas in Psychology*, *Journal of Adult Development*, and many others.

JOHN T. DOMBROWSKI recently completed his thesis and MA in experimental psychology at the College of William and Mary. In the future, he is looking to turn his interest toward education in elementary and secondary schools, and to bridge the gap between laboratory psychology and applied settings in the classroom and through administration.

He credits his professors both within psychology and from other disciplines for his desire to pursue a professional interdisciplinary future focused on education, psychology, and community implementation.

MARIE J. C. FORGEARD is a doctoral candidate in clinical psychology at the University of Pennsylvania. Her research program investigates whether and how creative thinking enhances well-being. She is particularly interested in the role of motivation, mastery, meaning making, and cognitive flexibility. Marie's work earned her the 2013 Frank X. Barron Award from the Society for the Psychology of Aesthetics, Creativity, and the Arts (Division 10 of the American Psychological Association).

AMANDA K. FULLER started her research career working with disadvantaged youth in low-income neighborhoods in Virginia and moved on to study anxious solitary children in urban areas of North Carolina. Her focus then turned to creativity, inspiration, and motive congruence while working with Dr. Todd Thrash at the College of William and Mary. Currently a Master's candidate at Peabody College, Vanderbilt University, Amanda is focused on positive youth development and the promotion of positive physical and mental health in adolescents. She has become a strong advocate for applied research and hopes to impact policy through research.

DIONE HEALEY's broad research area is in childhood attention-deficit/hyperactivity disorder (ADHD). She is currently assessing the effectiveness of a novel early intervention program that she has developed along with colleagues in New York, *ENGAGE: Enhancing Neurobehavioral Gains with the Aid of Games and Exercise.* The program is focused on developing self-control skills in hyperactive preschoolers. She is currently a senior lecturer in the Department of Psychology at the University of Otago. She is the recipient of the NZ Psychological Society's Goddard Award for Achievement and Excellence in Research and Scholarship; and the University's Early Career Award for Distinction in Research.

ERANDA JAYAWICKREME is an assistant professor of psychology at Wake Forest University. He received his PhD in positive and political psychology from the University of Pennsylvania in 2010, and is broadly interested in questions related to well-being and personality. He graduated with summa cum laude honors from Franklin & Marshall College in 2005, and was awarded the Henry S. Williamson

Medal, the college's highest student award presented annually to the outstanding senior of the graduating class. His awards include grants from the John Templeton Foundation, the Asia Foundation/USAID, the Penn Program on Democracy, Citizenship, and Constitutionalism, a Mellon Refugee Initiative Fund Fellowship, and numerous academic awards from Franklin & Marshall College.

JAMES C. KAUFMAN is a professor of educational psychology at the University of Connecticut. He is the author or editor of twenty-eight books and more than 200 papers. He is the President of the American Psychological Association (APA)'s Division 10 and the founding editor of the APA journal *Psychology of Popular Media Culture*. He received the 2003 Daniel E. Berlyne Award and the 2012 Paul Farnsworth Award from APA's Division 10, the 2008 E. Paul Torrance Award from the National Association of Gifted Children, the 2009 Early Career Research Award from the Western Psychological Association, and Mensa's 2011–2012 Award for Excellence in Research.

SCOTT BARRY KAUFMAN is the Scientific Director of the Imagination Institute and a researcher in the Positive Psychology Center at the University of Pennsylvania, where he investigates the nature, measurement, and development of imagination. In his book, *Ungifted: Intelligence redefined*, he presents a holistic approach to achievement that takes into account each person's ability, engagement, and personal goals. Kaufman is also cofounder of *The Creativity Post*, and he writes the blog Beautiful Minds for *Scientific American Mind*.

ASTRID KAUFMANN obtained her PhD (1988) from the University of Bergen, Norway. She is an associate professor of organizational psychology at BI Norwegian Business School and at the University of Bergen where she lectures in clinical psychology. She is a specialist in clinical psychology and has a special interest in bipolar diseases. Her research interests also include the fields of antisocial behavior and the relationship between personality and creativity. She has published books in her special fields and won teaching awards.

GEIR KAUFMANN obtained his PhD (1975) from the University of Bergen, Norway. He has been a professor of cognitive psychology at the University of Bergen, and is now Professor of Organizational Psychology at BI Norwegian Business School. His major research interest is the relationship between emotion and cognition, and he takes a special interest in the effect of mood on creative problem solving. He has published a large number of scientific articles and books in his special field, and is a winner of the Emerald Award, 2005, for Citation of Excellence in the field of creativity and innovation.

JOSEPH U. KIM is a doctoral student in clinical psychology at Vanderbilt University. His current research interests include examining the interplay between affect and core cognitive functions. He utilizes magnetic resonance imaging (MRI), human lesion studies, and repetitive transcranial magnetic stimulation (rTMS) to better understand these interactions.

DENNIS K. KINNEY, PhD, is a senior research psychologist at McLean Hospital, Belmont, MA. He recently retired as an associate professor in the Department of Psychiatry at Harvard Medical School, and he now teaches psychology part-time at the University of Massachusetts, Lowell. He has directed research about, and authored many papers on, creativity and its relation to psychiatric disorders and the liability for those disorders.

AARON KOZBELT is Professor of Psychology at Brooklyn College and the Graduate Center of the City University of New York. His research examines creativity and cognition in the arts, focusing on the nature of the creative process in visual art, life span creativity trajectories in classical composers, and the psychological basis of skilled artistic drawing. He is the author of over sixty journal articles and book chapters on these and other topics and serves on several editorial boards. He has been the recipient of several national and international awards, and his research has been funded by the National Science Foundation.

JUSTIN J. LACASSE is an adult psychiatry resident at Tufts Medical Center in Boston, MA. Justin's primary interests center around the relationship between culture and psychopathology as well as the study of mental health in refugee populations based in the United States and abroad.

MICHAEL J. LOWIS ("Mike") is a chartered psychologist in the UK. He was a lecturer at the University of Northampton and at the Open University and, although now retired, currently holds an honorary academic position with the University of the Highlands and Islands, Inverness, Scotland. His research interests include the psychology of humor, religion, music, and later life, and he has been able to bring all these areas into his chapter. Mike is the author of over fifty peer-reviewed papers, and he is regularly called upon by journalists and television producers to comment on a range of issues within his areas of experience. He also presents talks to community groups and runs humor workshops.

ANNE C. MECKLENBURG is a first-year PhD student in the English Department at the University of Michigan. Until recently, she was a research coordinator at the Positive Psychology Center at the University of Pennsylvania. She is particularly interested in how the psychology of creativity can inform the study of literature, and vice versa.

EMIL G. MOLDOVAN graduated cum laude from the Ohio State University with a BS in psychology. At the College of William and Mary, Emil is working towards an MA in experimental psychology. He is interested in factors that precipitate implicit–explicit motive congruence. Two such factors are body awareness and the words that people use to explicate their feelings. He is also interested in the consequences of motive congruence for well-being.

EMILY C. NUSBAUM is a graduate student in psychology at the University of North Carolina at Greensboro. Her main research focuses on creativity, cognition, and personality: who has creative ideas, and how do they come up with them? Similarly, another main focus of her research looks at personality and cognitive factors involved in humor production and sense of humor. Her other research interest involves aesthetic chills in response to music – broadly, who gets them and why do they happen? – and the autonomic nervous system activity that accompanies them.

KEITH OATLEY is Professor Emeritus of Cognitive Psychology at the University of Toronto, where he has taught courses on cognitive psychology (which included topics of expertise and creativity), on the psychology of emotions, and on the psychology of imaginative literature. He has published more than 200 articles in journals and as book chapters. He is the author of seven books on psychology, most recently *The passionate muse*, and three novels, the first of which, *The case of Emily V.*, won a Commonwealth Writers Prize for Best First Novel. His most recent novel is *Therefore choose*. He is a fellow of the Royal Society of Canada, the British Psychological Society, and the Association of Psychological Science.

LUZ H. OSPINA is a current psychology doctoral student at the Graduate Center of the City University of New York (CUNY). Her current research projects include the effects of emotional valence, physiological arousal, and individual differences on aspects of cognitive functioning. She has previously worked on neuropsychiatric and genetic studies focusing on the etiology of autism and schizophrenia, which includes animal models as well as the administration of tests assessing development, motor coordination, anxiety, and depression.

MARK PAPWORTH is a consultant clinical psychologist and the course director for the low intensity cognitive behavior therapy training course that is based at Newcastle University. He has worked clinically in the UK National Health Service for some 25 years treating adults with mental health problems. He also trained as a fine artist and has exhibited in the UK. In this way, Mark has developed an interest in art and mental health that includes but extends beyond an academic perspective.

ADAM PULLARO graduated with honors from the California State University at San Bernardino.

RUTH RICHARDS, MD, PhD, is an educational psychologist and board-certified psychiatrist, serving as professor of psychology, Saybrook University, and lecturer, Department of Psychiatry, Harvard Medical School. She has studied creativity in education, clinical settings, social action, and spirituality, publishing numerous papers and the two edited books *Eminent creativity, everyday creativity and health* (with Mark Runco) and *Everyday creativity and new views of human nature.* Dr. Richards is listed in *Who's Who in America* and was honored to win the Rudolf Arnheim Award from the Division of Aesthetics, Creativity, and the Arts of the American Psychological Association for Outstanding Lifetime Achievement.

JUDITH SCHLESINGER, PhD, is a psychologist, writer, jazz critic, musician, and producer. Author of a Humphrey Bogart biography and contributor to *Stephen Sondheim: A casebook*, her work has appeared in *American Psychologist* and the *British Journal of Psychiatry*, among other journals. A member of the National Association of Science Writers, and columnist and music reviewer for www.allaboutjazz.com since 2002, Schlesinger spent three decades as a university professor and psychotherapist. In 2012, she combined years of scholarship with her clinical and artistic experiences into *The insanity hoax: Exposing the myth of the mad genius.*

PAUL J. SILVIA is an associate professor of psychology at the University of North Carolina at Greensboro. He is interested in creativity assessment, particularly for cognitive processes related to divergent thinking, humor, and metaphor. He is the author of *How to write a lot: A practical guide to productive academic writing* and *Exploring the psychology of interest*, among many other publications.

DEAN KEITH SIMONTON is Distinguished Professor of Psychology at the University of California, Davis. His honors include the William

James Book Award, the Sir Francis Galton Award for Outstanding Contributions to the Study of Creativity, the Rudolf Arnheim Award for Outstanding Contributions to Psychology and the Arts, the Distinguished Scientific Contributions to Media Psychology Award, the George A. Miller Outstanding Article Award, the Theoretical Innovation Prize in Personality and Social Psychology, the E. Paul Torrance Award for Creativity, three Mensa Awards for Excellence in Research, and the Joseph B. Gittler Award for significant contributions to "the philosophical foundations of Psychology."

JAMES E. SWAIN is an assistant professor of psychiatry and psychology at the Center for Human Growth and Development at the University of Michigan (adjunct assistant professor at the Yale Child Study Center). He is a clinically active child and adolescent psychiatrist with a PhD background in basic neurophysiology. He employs multiple biological and psychological approaches to understand human thoughts and behaviors in mental health and illness – especially with a developmental perspective. This has led to studies of the brain-basis and psychology of parenting and child development in mental health, illness, and resilience toward improved risk identification and interventions.

JOHN D. SWAIN trained as an experimental particle physicist whose recent research work has been at CERN in Geneva, Switzerland, and at the Pierre Auger Observatory in Argentina. In addition to teaching as a faculty member at Northeastern University, he also works extensively in theoretical physics, including theoretical particle and nuclear physics, astrophysics, foundations of quantum mechanics, biophysics, loop quantum gravity, and other fields. He is also a member of the National Association of Science Writers, writes a monthly column for the *CERN Courier*, and appears frequently on the Discovery Channel in Canada.

TODD M. THRASH received a PhD in personality and social psychology from the University of Rochester in 2003. He is presently an associate professor at the College of William and Mary and an associate editor of *Journal of Personality*. He is a fellow of the Society of Experimental Social Psychology and principal investigator on a National Science Foundation grant. His research interests span diverse areas of personality, motivation, and emotion. Specific research interests include approach–avoidance processes, implicit–explicit motive congruence, inspiration, creativity, and "the chills."

DEBORAH J. WALDER is an associate professor of psychology at Brooklyn College and the Graduate Center of the City University of New

York (CUNY). Her research emphasizes the study of neurodevelopmental factors that precede mental health problems such as psychosis, with consideration of sex effects. She is currently funded by a NARSAD grant through the Brain and Behavior Research Foundation to study neuroanatomic, genetic, environmental (stress), and behavioral factors during adolescence that may increase risk of depression. She is a coprincipal investigator on a National Science Foundation grant aimed at immersing diverse undergraduates in innovative clinical, cognitive, and behavioral neuroscience research.

ARIELLE E. WHITE is a second-year Master's student in the Social Psychology Program at San Francisco State University. Her research interests include prejudice and discrimination toward groups marginalized on the basis of gender, sexual orientation, gender identity, and race/ethnicity. She is interested both in the dominant group perceptions of minority groups and the real-life implications for those who are marginalized within the US socio-political atmosphere.

Preface

Are creative people more likely to be mentally ill? This basic question has been debated for thousands of years, with the "mad genius" concept advanced by such luminaries as Aristotle (Runco and Albert, 2010). One of the first researchers to study creativity did so as a way of addressing this question (Lombroso, 1894). By the year 1800, according to Simonton (1994), this stereotype had become dogma. Most people today still accept this connection as a truth (Plucker *et al.*, 2004).

Yet is it true? Is creativity associated with mental illness? There are many studies that argue the answer is "yes" (e.g., Andreasen, 1987; Ludwig, 1995; Post, 1994), and several prominent scholars who argue strongly for a connection (Jamison, 1993). There are also those who argue equally strongly that the core studies and scholarship underlying the mad genius myth are fundamentally flawed (Rothenberg, 1990; Schlesinger, 2009).

More recently, researchers have explored exactly what we mean by "creativity" and "mental illness" (Silvia and Kaufman, 2010). New areas of psychology have impacted the eternal debate, as scholars from positive psychology and neuroscience have addressed this key issue. There are numerous recent studies and theories that have advanced this question. Yet most discussions of the creativity–mental illness relationship continue to cite the same decades-old work.

The goal of this book is to collect together some of the most exciting voices in the field to create a dynamic and cutting-edge edited volume that will inspire new ideas and studies on this fascinating topic. In compiling these essays, I realized that the relationship between creativity and mental illness was an international phenomenon. Studies have been conducted all across the globe, and the authors in this book represent eight countries (the United States, Canada, England, Scotland, Norway, Spain, Germany, and New Zealand).

Part I of the book begins with four chapters that set up the state of the field. George Becker tracks the history of how creativity and mental illness have been. Next, Dean Keith Simonton highlights the historiometric approach to studying the topic. Melanie Beaussart, Arielle White, Adam Pullaro, and I then cover more traditionally empirical studies. Finally, Judith Schlesinger offers an important cautionary chapter about flaws in classic papers.

Part II offers cognitive and neuroscientific perspectives on the issue. Anna Abraham discusses underlying neurocognitive mechanisms of creativity, based on studies of mental illness. Aaron Kozbelt, Scott Barry Kaufman, Deborah Walder, Luz Ospina, and Joseph Kim take an evolutionary genetics viewpoint, and then James Swain and John Swain analyze the creativity–mental illness connection using concepts from physics and brain research. Finally, Mark Papworth uses an approach based on principles from cognitive behavioral therapy.

Essays that cover the wide spectrum of mental illness comprise Part III of the book. Neus Barrantes-Vidal presents a sweeping review of creativity's relationship to both clinical and subclinical disorders. Geir Kaufmann and Astrid Kaufmann analyze the complex relationship that creativity has with mood (both positive and negative), and then Dione Healey writes about the connection creativity may have with attention-deficit/hyperactivity disorder.

Part IV examines possible commonalities that creativity and mental illness may share beyond a straightforward causal relationship. Shelley Carson begins with a chapter on her shared vulnerability model. Maja Djikic and Keith Oatley discuss the "precarious triad" that may end up harming artists. Finally, Dennis Kinney and Ruth Richards review evidence from many studies for increased creativity as compensatory advantage to genes that increase liability for schizophrenia and bipolar disorder. This creative advantage may help keep liability genes in the population, with practical implications for therapists and teachers, and patients and their families.

In Part V, research from the alternate perspective is presented – that creativity may be linked with positive mental health. Marie Forgeard, Anne Mecklenburg, Justin Lacasse, and Eranda Jayawickreme cover the growing area of creativity and posttraumatic growth. Todd Thrash, Emil Moldovan, Amanda Fuller, and John Dombrowski discuss the role of inspiration in the creative process, and then Michael Lowis uses the concept of psychoneuroimmunology to analyze how coping, humor, and creativity are linked.

In Part VI, Emily Nusbaum, Roger Beaty, and Paul Silvia integrate the many voices and perspectives in this volume as they offer a rumination on creativity and mental illness. Finally, I offer my own last thoughts on this issue.

References

Andreasen, N. C. (1987). Creativity and mental illness: Prevalence rates in writers and their first-degree relatives. *American Journal of Psychiatry*, 144, 1288–1292.

Jamison, K. R. (1993). *Touched with fire: Manic-depressive illness and the artistic temperament.* New York: Free Press.

Lombroso, C. (1894). *The man of genius.* London: Scott.

Ludwig, A. M. (1995). *The price of greatness.* New York: Guilford Press.

Plucker, J. A., Beghetto, R. A. and Dow, G. T. (2004). Why isn't creativity more important to educational psychologists? *Educational Psychologist*, 39, 83–96.

Post, F. (1994). Creativity and psychopathology: A study of 291 world-famous men. *British Journal of Psychiatry*, 165, 22–34.

Rothenberg, A. (1990). *Creativity and madness.* Baltimore, MD: Johns Hopkins University Press.

Runco, M. A. and Albert, R. A. (2010). Creativity research: A historical view. In J. C. Kaufman and R. J. Sternberg (Eds.), *The Cambridge handbook of creativity* (pp. 3–19). New York: Cambridge University Press.

Schlesinger, J. (2009). Creative mythconceptions: A closer look at the evidence for the "mad genius" hypothesis. *Psychology of Aesthetics, Creativity, and the Arts*, 3, 62–72.

Silvia, P. J. and Kaufman, J. C. (2010). Creativity and mental illness. In J. C. Kaufman and R. J. Sternberg (Eds.), *The Cambridge handbook of creativity* (pp. 381–394). New York: Cambridge University Press.

Simonton, D. K. (1994). *Greatness: Who makes history and why.* New York: Guilford Press.

Acknowledgments

Many thanks to my students for their help in the compilation of this book, most notably Alex McKay, Winter Meyer, Heather Roessler, and – especially – Harold Thomas. Thanks also to Anne Abel Smith for her fantastic copy-editing job, and to everyone at Cambridge University Press.

As always, love and gratitude to my family (parents Alan and Nadeen Kaufman, wife Allison, sons Jacob and Asher, and everyone else) and to my circle of friends and colleagues. I submit this manuscript to the publisher as I transition from California State University at San Bernardino to the University of Connecticut. I am thrilled at the adventures to come and grateful for the memories that have been.

Part I

Creativity and mental illness:
the state of the field

1   A socio-historical overview of the creativity–pathology connection: from antiquity to contemporary times[1]

George Becker

Writing around the turn of the middle of the twentieth century, the renowned literary critic Lionel Trilling (1945/1950, pp. 160–161) published an essay, "Art and neurosis," in which he sought to expose as an insidious "myth" what he called "one of the characteristic notions of our culture," the idea of an intimate connection between artistic creation and mental illness. However, like two noteworthy earlier critiques, Charles Lamb's (1826) *The sanity of true genius* and George Bernard Shaw's (1895/1909) *The sanity of art*, Trilling's essay remains little more than a footnote in the rapidly expanding literature on the topic of creativity and psychopathology. Indeed, the belief in a close connection between genius or, more generally, creativity and illness has sprung ever deeper roots in the cultural fabric of Western society, a development that received new impetus from the weight of support from both clinical and non-clinical studies published over the course of the past three decades. Before then, few of the studies expounding a pathology position were focused on clinical diagnosis. Most of them, based primarily on biographical and anecdotal accounts of those viewed as geniuses, produced highly conjectural findings. However, starting in the 1980s, one witnesses the continuing use of historical sources regarding the eminent, in addition to clinical studies in the form of psychiatric and psychometric approaches. These clinical studies involved comparisons of living creative with living non-creative individuals. Notwithstanding dissenting views, the combined force of the most recent studies has led to something resembling a consensus, one that views the link between creativity and illness as a genuine, pervasive, and timeless phenomenon with decided biological roots that most often takes the form of manic-depressive illness or related types of mood disorders.

This study locates current thinking regarding the relation between creativity and psychopathology in the historical context of the changes in

---

[1] This chapter is a revised and expanded version of ideas originally proposed in Becker (2001).

3

the intellectual assumptions regarding the nature of creative individuals and of the creative process more generally. As this examination will show, the association of creativity with clinical madness is a decidedly modern phenomenon. Far from having been a source of concern over the course of many centuries in Western society, as supporters of the pathology position tend to assume, this association does not predate the 1830s. Even though speculations regarding the mental state of individuals during the act of creation predate this point in time by centuries, they typically fell short of the verdict of clinical insanity.

It was the Romantic movement in literature, it will be shown, that provided the single most powerful impetus to the establishment of this medical verdict. By selectively adopting and redefining certain cultural axioms from the past, the Romantics produced not only a logical connection between creativity and madness but also one in which madness was simultaneously a piteous and exalted condition that stood in sharp contrast to what they regarded as dreaded normality. These redefinitions, although they tended to benefit the Romantics by providing them with a new and clearer sense of their own identity, simultaneously invited a system of logic that precluded the possibility of total health and sanity on the part of creative individuals. As such, it left them defenseless against the label of clinical madness. This logic proved so compelling, in fact, that many Romantics, in departure of the behavior of creative individuals during previous centuries, openly testified to spells of mental affliction, expressed concern over the possibility of becoming clinically ill, and attested to manifestations of madness in their midst. While many of these pronouncements were of a vague and general nature and frequently expressed by reference to "divine mania," melancholia, and other concepts derived from antiquity, members of the medical profession tended to treat the Romantics' "admissions" as evidence of a decidedly serious mental condition. As this examination will show, it was the medical profession, equipped with what then were regarded as the latest clinical concepts and diagnostic categories in conjunction with its reliance on the Romantics' pronouncements regarding their mental condition, that over the course of the latter part of the nineteenth century helped to establish the connection between creativity and psychopathology as medical fact. As noted, recent research has served to strengthen belief in this connection.

Given that contemporary thinking on the nature of creative individuals has roots in concepts dating back to antiquity, I open with a brief overview of relevant conceptions during three periods of Western history: Greek antiquity, the Italian Renaissance, and the Age of Enlightenment. In regard to the latter, I devote particular attention to the introduction of a new model of the creative individual, the man of genius, and the prevailing view regarding the operations of his mind. Next, I examine the Romantics' reformulation of historically antecedent ideas as well as the concept of genius and the functions these changes tended to serve. I proceed to examine the reception of the Romantics' changes in the field of philosophical–psychological speculation and the rising medical specialty of psychiatry up to the middle of the twentieth century. From there I examine some of the recent contributions to the literature. I conclude with discussion of some of the implications of this historically informed overview for current debates concerning creativity and attendant mental conditions.

Reflections on the mental state of creative individuals before the Romantic age

The ancient Greeks were the first in Western society to reflect on the nature of creative individuals. Given the Greeks' disdain for physical labor, their reflections typically excluded sculptors, painters, and others who created with their hands, and instead were narrowly focused on seers, poets, and those given to cerebral expression. As we shall see, the examination of the Greeks' pronouncements on the nature of the creatively gifted in their larger cultural context leads us to question the common practice of citing these observations as evidence of a long-standing recognition, dating back to antiquity, of an intimate connection between creativity and clinical madness.

Critical to an understanding of the ancient Greeks' ruminations regarding the nature of the creative process are the concepts of demonic possessions and melancholia. The "demon," which the Greeks conceived as a semi-deity that presided over a person, a locality, or some other discrete entity, was believed to be endowed with powers to shape the destiny of each in either a positive or negative fashion. Somewhat different from this general view of the term, in the Socratic conception the demon was regarded as a divine gift granted to a few select individuals only. According to this view, the poet, priest, philosopher, and sage communicated with the gods through the intervention of their demon. It is in this sense that Socrates called on his demon and attributed most of his knowledge to intimations from it (Cahan, 1911). This conception of demons as the benevolent agents of the gods was generally endorsed by Plato and others and found support in Plato's doctrine of divine madness, or *enthousiasmos*. In this view, the poet, who himself is devoid of talent, is seen as divinely inspired, as an agent or servant of the gods. Inspiration and the gift of prophecy, however, were attainable only during particular states of mind, such as the loss of consciousness due to sleep or a mind affected by illness or possession (Rosen, 1969). Importantly, to Socrates, Plato, and other contemporaries, the divine disturbance that invited prophetic or poetic activity was clearly distinguished from clinical insanity. Unlike the latter, the inspired madness of seers and poets was conceived as a virtue, a state of mind greatly desired. To quote from Plato (1974), "Madness, provided it comes as a gift from heaven, is the channel by which we receive the greatest blessings... [It] is a nobler thing than sober sense... madness comes from God, whereas sober sense is merely human" (pp. 46–47). Sharply distinguished from its dreaded clinical counterpart, Plato's divine madness is conceived as a temporarily granted blessing from the heavens.

Another claim frequently encountered on behalf of the idea of a long-standing recognition of a creativity–pathology connection involves an assertion, attributed to Aristotle, that extraordinary talent is characterized by a melancholic temperament. Aristotle's reference to melancholia has its origins in the then current humoral theory. This theory, closely identified with Hippocrates, the father of Western medicine, stipulated that disease resulted from imbalances in the four basic bodily fluids, or humors: blood, black bile, yellow bile, and phlegm. Each humor, in turn, was believed to be endowed with variable basic qualities such as heat, cold, dryness, and moistness. If the humors and the corresponding qualities were properly balanced, the person was deemed healthy. When internal or external factors produced an excess or deficiency of one or more of these humors, disease would result. Significantly, in the humoral theory, differences in human temperament were similarly determined by an individual's composition of humors. Accordingly, a preponderance of blood in the human body was believed to engender sanguine types: of phlegm, phlegmatic types; of yellow bile, choleric types; and of black bile, melancholic types.

Building on Hippocrates' theory, it was Aristotle who was first to postulate a connection between the melancholic type and profound creativity. The often quoted reference to Aristotle frequently involves a shortened, declaratory version of the author's opening question on the subject. "Why is it," the author (1984) asks in the original, "that all those who have become eminent in philosophy or politics or poetry or the arts are clearly of an atrabilious [i.e., melancholic] temperament...?" (pp. 1498–1499). Clearly, the author views the connection between the creative and the melancholic temperament as a given. However, in the same way that not all or even most or many of those individuals seen as belonging to one of the three other types of temperament were seen as subject to the mental or bodily afflictions associated with these types, Aristotle's linkage of creativity with melancholia was not meant to suggest that all melancholic individuals were subject to the mental illness of melancholia. Indeed, as Aristotle (1984) argues, "To sum up, owing to the fact that the effect of black bile is variable, atrabilious persons also show variation . . . And since it is possible for a variable state to be well tempered and in a sense a favorable condition . . . the result is that all atrabilious persons have remarkable gifts, not owing to disease but from natural causes" (p. 1502). In short, a closer reading strongly suggests that to Aristotle the attribution of melancholia was simply descriptive of a type of individual, the homo melancholicus, who, depending on the particular combination of his fluid substances, could be either a sane person of distinction or a clinically afflicted individual (see Wittkower and Wittkower, 1963).

Quite different from the subsequent Roman era and the Middle Ages, when there was little attention devoted to creative individuals, the Italian Renaissance produced a renewed interest in persons esteemed most highly in a wide range of creative endeavors. Unlike the Greeks who devalued manually created efforts, the Renaissance embraced the sculptor and painter along with the poet and philosopher as worthy of admiration and reflection. For these possessors of superior creative ability, the term *genio* was reserved. However, creativity was thought of primarily in terms of an imitation of the established masters and of nature. Unlike the modern conception of the genius, one that stresses originality as the distinguishing feature of the creative individual, the standard of the humanistic tradition involved the *imitatio-ideal*. Although some, like Leonardo and Vasari, insisted that the *genio* should not be just imitatively creative but newly creative (Lange-Eichbaum, 1930/1932), these attacks on the *imitatio-ideal* did not become commonly accepted during the late Renaissance (Zilsel, 1926).

Similar to the Greek descriptions of the poet, philosopher, and sage, the unique attributes of the Renaissance *genio* commonly were described in terms of melancholia and *pazzia*, or madness. Again, a distinction was maintained between the sane melancholics capable of rare accomplishments and those condemned to insanity. The Florentine Ficino, who popularized the Aristotelian idea of melancholy, regarded this type of temperament in its application to distinguished men as a divine gift that constituted a metonymy for Plato's divine mania. Accordingly, only the melancholic temperament was considered capable of creative enthusiasm. Hence, assessments of scholars and artists in terms of *pazzia* were generally not intended to convey the notion of insanity. When applied to great people, the term referred to qualities associated with the melancholic temperament, such as eccentricity, sensitivity, moodiness, and solitariness. Far from being regarded as negative qualities, emulating these manifestations of melancholic behavior was turned into a fad in sixteenth-century Europe (Babb, 1951; Wittkower and Wittkower, 1963). Reflective of this development is Dürer's melancholia engraving, which provides us with a moving self-revelation of the artist in the form of a brooding *melancholicus*.

What was initially a fashionable affectation that conferred prestige became toward the end of the sixteenth century a subject of criticism and derision. Typical of such critiques are the reactions of a painter, Giovan Battista Armenini, who observes:

An awful habit has developed among common folk and even among the educated, to whom it seems natural that a painter of the highest distinction must show signs of some ugly and nefarious vice allied with a capricious and eccentric temperament...And the worst is that many ignorant artists believe themselves to be very exceptional by affecting melancholy and eccentricity. (In Wittkower and Wittkower, 1963, p. 92)

As a result of criticisms such as this, by the seventeenth century, the fashion of the melancholic artist was supplanted by the new image of the conforming gentleman artist and the belief that artists should merge unobtrusively with the intellectual and social elites. More than simply an ideal, this new conception was reflected in the actual behavior of artists. As Wittkower (1973) observes, since the Renaissance concept of the *melancholicus* has been supplanted by this newer image, "none of the great seventeenth-century masters – Rubens and Bernini, Rembrandt and Velasquez – was ever described as melancholic...It was not until the romantic era...that melancholy appears once again as a condition of mental and emotional catharsis" (p. 309).

Before turning our attention on the Romantics, it is necessary to examine developments associated with the Enlightenment. It was during the eighteenth century that the term *genius* was introduced in reference to individuals who displayed a high degree of creative ability (Lange-Eichbaum, 1927/1935; Tonelli, 1973; Zilsel 1926). Different from the Renaissance *genio* and the associated *imitatio-ideal*, the Enlightenment genius was defined as one who was in possession of an innate power that manifested itself in works of great imaginative creation in which the decisive characteristics were profound novelty and the originally creative. Although most commentators on genius acknowledged certain sub-rational components, the leitmotiv most frequently encountered stressed the rational processes of the mind (Fabian, 1966; Tonelli, 1973). Closely tied to the Enlightenment's emphasis on reason along with its conception of a harmoniously functioning universe subject to immutable timeless laws, the mental processes of genius were stipulated in terms of forces standing in balance and harmony to each other.

Perhaps the model exposition of the Enlightenment conception of genius is Gerard's (1774/1966) *An essay on genius* (see Fabian, 1966, p. xi; Wittkower, 1973, p. 306). Defined as the faculty of invention "by means of which a man is qualified for making new discoveries in science, or for producing original works of art" (Gerard, 1774/1966, p. 8), the creative power in genius was conceived as originating in an active imagination. Asserting that an unbridled imagination constitutes a capricious and irresponsible faculty, Gerard stipulated that it must be "subject to established laws" (p. 70). True genius, to him, was only possible as a result of a synthesis or subtle interplay of four powers: (a) imagination, (b) judgment, (c) sense, and (d) memory. He argued:

Mere imagination will not constitute genius . . . As fancy [imagination] has an indirect dependence both on sense and memory, from which it received the first elements of all its conceptions, so when it exerts itself in the way of genius, it has an immediate connexion with judgment, which must constantly attend it, and correct and regulate its suggestions. This connexion is so intimate, that a man can scarce be said to have invented till he has exercised his judgment. (Gerard, 1774/1966, pp. 36–37)

Gerard was not alone in viewing genius as an interplay of different mental powers. To Kant (1790/1957), the requisites of genius rested on the harmonious workings among the faculties of imagination, understanding, creative spirit, and taste. Concerned over the inherent dangers of an unbridled imagination, he posited the relation between the imagination and understanding as follows:

Abundance and originality of Ideas are less necessary to beauty than the accordance of the Imagination in its freedom with the law of the Understanding. For all the abundance of the former produces in lawless freedom nothing but nonsense; on the other hand, the Judgment is the faculty by which it is adjusted to the Understanding. (Kant, 1790/1957, p. 432)

Weighing the importance of the imagination relative to the judgment, Kant (1790/1957, p. 433) deemed it best to "sacrifice the freedom and wealth" of the former "than permit anything prejudicial" to the latter.

Despite differences in nomenclature regarding the operative mental faculties or powers, the rational, or Enlightenment, conception of genius stressed the measured, harmonious interplay among these powers. To Duff, it was a balance of imagination, judgment, and taste; to Voltaire, imagination worked in conjunction with memory and judgment; to Moses Mendelssohn, genius corresponded to a state of perfection of all mental powers working in harmony; and to Shaftesbury, although he stressed the irrational traits of genius in terms of revelation and enthusiasm, a true genius did not infringe on the rules of art – he needed knowledge and good sense (see Tonelli, 1973).

The prevailing Enlightenment conception of genius did, therefore, recognize certain natural or sub-rational components rooted primarily in the creative imagination. However, it pointedly established judgment, or reason, as a counterweight to these components and buttressed judgment with memory, taste, sense, sensibility, and so forth. Judgment was not only capable of averting caprice and extravagance but also made madness a virtual impossibility for genius. As Gerard (1774/1966, p. 73) observed, "a perfect judgment is seldom bestowed by Nature, even on her most favored sons; but a very considerable degree of it always belongs to a genius." Endowed with a powerful faculty of judgment, true genius was most unlikely to succumb to madness, either of the clinical or the inspired variety.

The Romantics' redefinition of genius and the functions it served

The late eighteenth and early nineteenth centuries, under the impact of the Romantic movement, saw a profound change in the prevailing conception of genius. This change had a number of causes. Among these was the Romantics' reaction against the Enlightenment idea of a universe that, in conformity to immutable natural laws, functioned with the mechanistic exactitude of a timepiece. In place of this mathematical world of Newtonian physics, the Romantics opted for a more mysterious view of the universe, one that found expression in what aptly has been called "Romantic science." This development, closely tied to the discoveries in the fields of electricity and chemistry during this period, gave expression, in the words of Richard Holmes (2008, p. viii), to a "softer 'dynamic' science of invisible powers and mysterious energies, of fluidity and transformations, of growth and organic change." Reflective of these changes in the conception of science and the universe, the Enlightenment concept of a genius whose mental powers operated in balanced harmony with each other was now supplemented by one that stressed the unbridled supremacy of the faculty of imagination in conjunction with such elements as spontaneity, enthusiasm, childish naiveté, divine inspiration, and the reckless pursuit of truth, beauty, and knowledge.

Critically important to our understanding of this change from the rational to the romantic conception of genius were developments intimately tied to the precarious state of existence of the Romantic poets and men of letters. It should be recalled that the application of the term *genius* to select individuals during the eighteenth century marked the arrival of a new model for man. Generally deprived of wealth or privileged status, men of genius, or those who aspired to be such, tended to challenge the existing hierarchical order by substituting innate creative ability as a superior criterion for the evaluation of men. D'Alembert (1967), an Enlightenment spokesperson for the man of letters, recognized three factors separating people: birth, wealth, and intelligence; but only intelligence was deemed worthy of true esteem. Unlike the others, he argued, intelligence is a dependable national "resource," by its nature inexhaustible and incapable of being "taken" from its possessors (p. 354). De Saint-Simon (1803/1964), writing a few years after the demise of the Ancien Régime, was less guarded in his vision of the future society; it was to be dominated by men of genius: scientists, artists, men of ideas. In fact, he cautioned the power holders and the propertied classes not to impede the geniuses' quest for power, "great prestige," and money. Failure to comply with this warning, he feared, would lead to the almost certain extinction of the ruling elites: "To be convinced of the truth of what I have said, you have only to reflect on the course of events in France since 1789" (p. 3).

The period of reaction to all "revolutionary" ideas initiated by Napoleon's defeat and the creation of the Quadruple Alliance meant, of course, that prospects of establishing intelligence as a foremost legitimate criterion for the ranking of men had received a serious setback. The Metternich era refused to comply with the demands of this new, self-appointed intellectual aristocracy. Indeed, the events of the late eighteenth and early nineteenth centuries made the position of this aspiring group rather precarious. The disappearance of the traditional "sponsor" class, the nobility and the aristocratized bourgeoisie, and the subsequent hazards of commercialization and the modern marketplace, left the status of the man of genius in question (see Graña, 1964). Compounding the quest for fame and stable employment was an overproduction of university-trained individuals in a number of European countries, and especially in the German states (Gerth, 1976; La Vopa, 1988), which in conjunction with the oppressive constraints imposed by the academies on literacy and artistic expression (White and White, 1965) left many in a state of despair. Commenting on the impact of crushing disappointments, the poet and dramatist Achim von Arnim wrote in 1815 that "It would make terrible reading to count off all the beautiful German souls who surrendered to madness or suicide or to careers they detested" (in Coetzee, 2006, p. 69).

Generally impoverished and deprived of fame and political power throughout this period, the aspiring artist and person of ideas felt engulfed by the anonymous masses. Although the idea of genius may have commanded a degree of respect, even reverence, the men of genius themselves, faced with a practical world, lacked the special sense of identity necessary to separate themselves effectively from the masses.

It was the idea of a special kind of madness that could serve as a distinguishing factor, one that could mark a person as separate, unique, and even divinely chosen. The Romantic artists and men of letters, in particular, revived the classical notion of divine mania or inspiration and established it as a defining mark of the extraordinary individual. It was the aura of mania that endowed the genius with a mystical and inexplicable quality that differentiated him from the typical man, the bourgeois, the philistine, and the merely talented. It established the genius as the modern heir of the ancient Greek poet and seer and, like the classical counterpart, enabled the genius to claim some of the powers and privileges granted the "possessed" prophet. In this role, the man of genius could counsel kings and blaspheme with impunity. Importantly also, the idea of mania conveyed to the Romantics the notions of possession, suffering, and *weltschmerz*, or a mood of sentimental sadness, and the display of these qualities confirmed an individual's identity as a true genius. The theme of the blessedness of some special kind of madness is clearly reflected in Poe's *Eleanora*:

I am come from a race noted for vigor of fancy and ardor of passion. Men have called me mad; but the question is not yet settled, whether madness is or is not the loftiest intelligence; whether much that is glorious, whether all that is profound, does not spring from disease of thought. (As cited in Marks, 1926, p. 22)

Similarly, the poet Wieland spoke of the "amiable insanity of the muses" (as cited in Hirsch, 1897, p. 71), and the clergyman Beecher commented on the desirability of at least some degree of madness on the part of poets (as cited in Sanborn, 1886, p. 188).

The desire of the Romantics for an affirmed identity, however, constituted only one of their aspirations; a second, closely connected goal was to establish their intellectual independence from the past. Although the conception of the innately creative genius did much to advance the cause of originality in intellectual life, those engaged in literature and the arts remained tied to the authority of the academies and the ancient masters. Therefore, the Romantics' attempt to appropriate certain supposed qualities of the ancients had to be effected without assuming a subservient role to traditional authority. This necessitated a redefinition of genius.

Before the eighteenth century, it was commonly accepted that the human imagination constituted a capricious and dangerous element in the lives of men. Recognized as the fountainhead of original creativity, it was simultaneously admired and feared. Pascal (1670/1968), writing in the mid-seventeenth century, reflected this ambivalence clearly:

> Imagination – it is this dominant part in man, this mistress of error and falsity, and more often trickster than not . . . But being most often false, it gives no mark of its quality, marking the true and the false with the same nature. (pp. 362–363)

To benefit from imagination and yet contain its great potential for disaster and evil meant, as Pascal (1670/1968, p. 363) cautioned the "wisest of men," that one had to consciously "resist" its intoxicating powers with all one's strength. It is not surprising, therefore, that during the eighteenth century, when the genius first became recognized by many as a model of a superior person, the nature of genius was defined in a way that virtually precluded victimization by one's own imagination. As we have seen, in the typical Enlightenment explication of genius, the imagination was seen as constrained by a number of powers or faculties that were particularly developed in the great person. Indispensable to the harmonious interplay of mental powers was the faculty of judgment, or reason, which, in conjunction with memory, taste, and sense, averted not only caprice and extravagance but also, as Gerard (1774/1966, pp. 73–74) observed, made "madness and frenzy" a near impossibility for genius.

The Enlightenment view of the genius as an educated individual whose abundant imagination was properly tempered by good taste, training in the classics, and an appreciation of the masters proved unacceptable to the romantic spirit. To create a new independence, genius could no longer be seen in the Enlightenment terms of balance, proportion, and a synthesis of mental powers. The Romantics, therefore, granted the imagination a clear predominance over those faculties traditionally seen as the rational counterweights to the imagination. Like the Schlegels, Lessing, and others (see Cahan, 1911, pp. 32–38; also Nordau, 1892/1900, p. 73), Schiller proposed that the deliberate application of the faculty of reason, far from being beneficial, would serve to obstruct the imagination and bind the potential for profound creativity:

> It is not well in works of creation that reason should too closely challenge the ideas that come thronging to the doors. Taken by itself, an idea may be highly unsuitable, even venturesome, and yet in conjunction with others, themselves equally absurd alone, it may furnish a suitable link in the chain of thought. Reason can not see this . . . In a creative brain reason has withdrawn her watch at the doors, and ideas crowd in pell-mell. (As cited in Hirsch, 1897, p. 31)

To suspend the "laws of rationally thinking reason" meant, as the Schlegels observed, to be transported "into the lovely vagaries of fancy and the primitive chaos of human nature" (as cited in Nordau, 1892/ 1900, p. 73).

Psychology, physician–psychiatrists, and the clinical association of genius and madness

The Romantics' redefinition of genius in terms of the imagination reigning supreme satisfied two goals simultaneously. Through its stress on the spontaneous and irrational imagination, it made possible the appropriation of mania from the past, but it did so while ensuring intellectual independence in the present. There was, however, a critical by-product: Although the new definition liberated the Romantics from the past, it also disassociated them from the very qualities that previously had been seen as establishing and safeguarding sanity. Given the commonality of the belief concerning the relation of sanity to the balance of mental faculties, the Romantic reformulation of genius, which removed this balance, established a logical foundation for the association of genius and madness. Most ironically, perhaps, the Romantics, trapped by their premises and system of logic, began to suspect that clinical madness was indeed a likely if not inevitable end of the condition of genius.

The need of the Romantics, then, for a sense of identity and for their own intellectual and artistic independence led them to adopt a system of premises that left them defenseless against the label of madness. Trapped by their own logic, they came to see their madness as inevitable. Accordingly, the Romantic people of genius were among the first to suggest (e.g., Lamartine, Schopenhauer, Wieland, Poe, and others), in reference to themselves and other eminent individuals, that the ancients were indeed correct in their assessment: the "demon of madness" was more than just a stranger among their ranks. Although many of these confessions or pronouncements on the nature of genius were expressed in more general than specific terms and referred to the "inspired" madness of the ancients, some testified, quite clearly, to the fear of clinical insanity. Coleridge, for example, commented specifically on the dire consequences of a suspended judgment or reason:

The reason may resist for a long time . . . but too often, at length, it yields for a moment, and the man is mad forever . . . I think it was Bishop Butler who said that he was all his life struggling against the devilish suggestions on his senses, which would have maddened him if he had relaxed the stern wakefulness of his reason for a single moment. (As cited in Sanborn, 1886, p. 139)

Similarly, Byron, although often appearing to revel in a professed madness, nevertheless spoke with considerable apprehension about his future:

"I picture myself slowly expiring on a bed of torture, or terminating my days like [Jonathan] Swift – a grinning idiot" (as cited in Sanborn, 1886, p. 126).

It would be erroneous to assume, however, that such trepidations and self-admissions on the part of geniuses were sufficient to establish as a medical fact the connection between genius and madness. For such to occur, there had to exist a close correspondence between the intellectual grounds on which these trepidations were based and the specialized knowledge claims associated with the rising fields of psychology and the medical–psychiatric profession. It should be noted in passing that at least one dominant philosophical–psychological tradition was unfavorably disposed and frequently hostile to the romantic conception of the extraordinary individual. The psychological empiricism of Hobbes, Locke, and Hume (which, in the hands of Hartley, Bentham, and James and John Stuart Mill, was transformed into psychological associationism) was unalterably opposed to the view that knowledge is in some way innate to humans or the result of inherent dispositions. Instead, these empiricists stressed the extrinsic nature of all human knowledge. The support the Romantics needed to help articulate and legitimate their view of the extraordinary individual and the workings of the individual's mind was located in a highly speculative psychological tradition that predated the critical empiricism of Locke and Hume (see Boring, 1950).

Before 1700, Western scholars attempted to understand the nature of the mind, learning, and creativity from a modified Aristotelian position. This position recognized the existence of some half dozen more or less distinct mental components or "faculties," which, to some degree, were subject to improvement through their exercise (Coladarci, 1968). The belief in mental faculties was gradually expanded and formalized during the eighteenth and nineteenth centuries and, through the writings of Wolff, Reid, Sully, and others, became established as a school of thought known as "faculty psychology" (see Boring, 1950; Robinson, 1976). In Reid's reformulation of this perspective, for example, the number of components of the mind was expanded to twenty-four but retained such traditionally recognized intellectual powers as perception, judgment, memory, and moral taste (Boring, 1950). Although Reid and other faculty psychologists concurred that the mental powers could be improved through training, they believed that a pronounced display of strength in any faculty was rooted, overwhelmingly, in a powerfully endowed instinct or native disposition (Robinson, 1976). Accordingly, an individual distinguished by an extraordinary ability to memorize facts was seen to possess an unusually vigorous instinct or faculty of memory (Boring, 1950). The belief in inherent mental dispositions supported not only the inception of the genius ideal but also its subsequent Romantic reformulation.

Unlike the school of psychological empiricism, therefore, the faculty psychology of Reid, Wolff, and others, with its stress on innate powers and inherent mental dispositions, was sufficiently vague and mystical to accommodate most of the Romantics' assertions regarding the transcendental nature of profound creativity. Importantly, also, faculty psychology even concurred with the Romantics' position that the genius' dependence on an "overcharged" and highly impulsive imagination constituted a form of madness, divine or otherwise. It had long been an established principle, particularly for faculty psychologists, that an excessive stimulation of any faculty of mind was incompatible with perfect health and mental adjustment (see Sully, 1885, p. 326).

Whether or not, however, the supposed infirmities of genius constituted clinical pathology, rather than a divine gift or mania, remained, until the middle of the nineteenth century, a matter more of philosophical speculation than of supposedly scientific fact. The individuals, overwhelmingly, who were to establish the verdict of clinical madness as a medical fact were those who, as I argued elsewhere (Becker, 1978), had earned a medical degree and are classifiable under the general category of physician–psychiatrist. These specialists, engaged with what then were regarded as the latest clinical concepts and diagnostic categories, relied quite heavily on their determination of genius as clinically mad on the self-admissions of illness on the part of the "gifted" (Becker, 1978, pp. 67–74). Although many of these self-admissions were expressed in terms of the inspired madness of the ancients, these physician–psychiatrists took the people of genius at their words; they decidedly were not like ordinary, healthy humans.

The first examination of genius as a purely medical problem may be dated to Lélut (1836, pp. 97–98), a French psychiatrist, who in 1836 scandalized the world of letters with the first clinical history of genius in which he claimed that Socrates' inclination "to take the inspirations of his conscience from the voice of a supernatural agent [his demon]" was evidence of a "most undeniable form of madness." Other psychiatrists and scholars soon followed suit with their own views and analyses of other gifted persons (e.g., Galton, 1869/1962; Lombroso, 1863/1891; Maudsley, 1886/1908; Moreau, 1859; Stekel, 1909/1917), with the result that within a century such works numbered in the hundreds (see Lange-Eichbaum, 1927/1935). As my survey of this literature for the period from 1836 to 1950 revealed (Becker, 1978, pp. 46–51), the judgment of genius as pathological was the dominant position on the issue, one that derived its overwhelming support from members of the medical and the developing psychiatric professions. As one anonymous supporter (1912) of the pathology position argued:

The insanity of genius is a phenomenon of which the literatures of every country and of every epoch have furnished abundant examples . . . In many instances it is no longer a question as to whether a certain genius was insane or not. The modern query is, "From what form of insanity did he suffer?" (Anonymous, 1912, p. 161)

Those who projected the image of sickness distinguished themselves from each other by identification of different types of mental illness, largely in step with the rise and fall of diagnostic categories in psychiatry then currently in favor. Foremost among these were diagnostic labels such as psycho–physical disequilibrium, monomania, degeneracy, neurasthenia, and neurosis. Those challenging the genius–madness association, a decided minority in my sample, were disproportionally psychologists who promulgated the idea that it was physical and emotional stability, rather than illness, that had close association with genius. The majority of these psychologists based their conclusion on their examinations of living "gifted" children, or "young" geniuses.

The decades of the mid-twentieth century witnessed a sharp decline of interest in the question of genius and madness. The paucity of publications during this period resulted in part from a growing ambivalence toward eugenics, a movement closely identified with a number of supporters of the pathology position (i.e., Galton, 1869/1962; Hirsch, 1931), as well as the growing participation of psychologists in the debate, along with a shift in focus whereby environmental explanations tended to supersede the former biological–determinist views. As such, in place of Galton's and Lombroso's emphasis on the hereditary nature of genius, there was a growing tendency to stress the "sociological" causes and determinants of genius as exemplified by the works of Faris (1940), Lehman (1947), and others. This change from a biological to a sociological focus, though relatively short-lived, was accompanied by a gradual shift in terminology whereby many of the issues traditionally associated with genius became increasingly addressed under the headings of creativity, ability, intelligence, and achievement motivation, a change that continues to the present.

As previously noted, the late 1980s witnessed a resumption of the debate under the new rubric of creativity and psychopathology. This renewed interest and the attendant weight of support on behalf of the pathology position is traceable, in large measure, to the recent shift in the psychiatric profession from psychoanalysis and other types of "talk" therapy, approaches that enjoyed considerable professional acceptance during the middle decades of the twentieth century, to a decidedly phys-iological and genetic orientation regarding the etiology of mental illness with attendant pharmaceutical solutions to afflictions. Three types of research have contributed to this shift in focus. In addition to historio-metric research where biographic materials of deceased creative individ-uals are analyzed to discern the presence of symptoms of mental disorder (e.g., Jamison, 1993; Ludwig, 1995), two types of clinical studies with a focus on living individuals were brought to bear. Whereas the psychiatric approach examines the incidence of clinical diagnosis and therapeutic treatment in samples of contemporary creative and non-creative individ-uals (e.g., Andreasen, 1987; Jamison, 1989), the psychometric approach applies standard assessment instruments (e.g., the Minnesota Multi-phasic Personality Inventory [MMPI]) to two types of populations: the creative and a control group of non-creative participants (e.g., Carson, this volume; Carson *et al.*, 2003; Eysenck, 1995). Notwithstanding dis-senting views (e.g., Schlesinger, 2009, this volume; Waddell, 1998), the combined impact of these studies has produced something resembling a consensus. The dominant view tends to posit the existence of an intimate connection, regardless of time, place, or cultural difference, between orig-inal creativity and mental illness. Such a connection is assumed to have a biological link or some unspecified inherent disposition and is believed to be especially pronounced on the part of those who excel in the fields of literature, music, painting, and other creative arts in the form primarily of manic-depressive illness or related types of mood disorders.

It is worth noting that the bipolarity captured by the concept of manic-depressive illness has striking similarity to terminology from Greek antiq-uity in its application to creative individuals. The mania component has its counterpart in the ancients' references to such states of mind as divine mania and demonic possession. Similarly, the depressive component bears close resemblance to the Greeks' attribution of the melancholic temperament in reference to the gifted. As this examination has argued, however, the ancients' use of these terms was intended to convey much desired, positive attributes rather than pathological states of mind.

Some implications for the contemporary debate

As we have seen, the Romantic poets and men of letters were among the first to suggest, in referring to themselves and other eminent individuals, that the ancients were indeed correct in their assessment. The demon of madness was hardly a stranger in their ranks. As previously noted, these pronouncements, while they entailed distortions of the intended meanings of the ancients, played an integral part in the past in the determination of the genius as clinically afflicted. This tendency to take the gifted at their word regarding their own condition also applies equally to contemporary examinations of the issue. Jamison (1993), a foremost spokesperson for the pathology position, provides demonstrations of this fact in her book, *Touched with fire: Manic-depressive illness and the artist temperament*. Jamison built a clinical connection between creativity and manic-depressive illness by allowing scores of artists, composers, and writers from across time in Western society to reflect on their own changes of mood ranging from melancholic states to feelings of euphoria, their obsessions and fears of going mad, their thoughts about suicide, and their addictions to alcohol and drugs: those and other behaviors and mental states, in other words, were identified as symptomatic of mood disorders.

One of the problems of treating such self-admissions as essentially reliable descriptions of mental illness is that it tends to overlook one critical fact: These pronouncements on the part of the creative individuals may involve self-serving descriptions and projections of images that were made in the context of cultural assumptions often quite different from those of contemporary society. In light of these facts, it remains unclear what meaning should be attached to the tendency on the part of many poets and other creative persons to admit to a "touch" of madness.

Two examples will have to suffice as illustrative of the difficulties involved in the interpretations of such admissions. The first concerns an excerpt of a poem from Michael Drayton, a poem written in praise of another poet, Drayton's friend Henry Reynolds:

> His raptures were
> All air, and fire, which made his verses clear,
> For that *fine madness* [italics added] still he did retain,
> Which *rightly should possess* [italics added] a poet's brain.
> (Cited in Jamison, 1993, p. 1)

This excerpt is open to a number of interpretations that include the reference to the divine mania of the ancients, a condition, as previously noted, that was not synonymous with clinical madness. Rather, it was a state of mind greatly desired. Given this fact, are we justified in treating this excerpt (as Jamison did) as an essentially reliable description of illness, or is it not equally possible that Drayton's reference to the presence of a "fine madness" on the part of Reynolds had little if nothing to do with clinical illness and was intended as the ultimate compliment a poet could be paid, one that confirmed his membership of the tribe of truly eminent poets?

Similarly, what are we to make of Coleridge's pronouncement when, in a defense of Swedenborg, he proposed that, unlike ordinary madness, his was the madness of genius: "a madness, indeed celestial, and glowing from a divine mind" (as cited in Sanborn, 1886, p. 154). Is it not likely, as Kretschmer (1931) argued, that pronouncements such as these are confirmation of the fact that "many men of genius themselves prize madness and insanity as the highest distinction of the exceptional man"? After all, Kretschmer observed, "the mentally normal man is, according to the conception itself, identical with the typical man, the average man, the philistine" (1931, p. 6).

Consistent with this line of argument, the association of creativity and madness may essentially be seen as a kind of role expectation, appropriate for artists and writers, that originated in antiquity and received powerful reinforcement as a result of the Romantics' redefinitions of the nature of genius. In the way that contemporary scientists, accountants, and engineers are expected to display attributes of objectivity, reason, and emotional stability, for poets, writers, and artists the expectations involve manifestations of intuitiveness, a fanciful imagination, sensitivity, temperament, and emotional expressiveness – in short, a manifestation of a kind of madness. It is not at all unreasonable to assume that to the extent that these expectations continue to be part of a professional ideology of what it means to be truly creative, even contemporary writers and artists, far from disavowing the label of madness, may actually invite it. Indeed, they may even inadvertently volunteer evidence of madness in diagnostic and psychological examinations. Moreover, is it not possible that these expectations may involve the elements of a self-fulfilling prophecy? In a rephrasing of a line from Orwell (1953), "they are wearing a mask, and their faces grow to fit it" (p. 152).

Such possibilities have implications for the issues of creativity and psychopathology. Indeed, they may invite conclusions at odds with the conventional association regarding these two variables. One of such conclusions is associated with the existentialist philosopher Jaspers (1926), who maintained that the greater manifestation of mental illness in geniuses was the result of society's selective granting of fame. To Jaspers, in other words, the term *genius* was a socially applied label primarily reserved for those talented individuals who displayed certain attributes of sickness closely tied to the role expectations noted previously. He did not believe that the notion of the "mad genius" was applicable to all historical periods. Rather, what distinguishes the nineteenth and twentieth centuries from the seventeenth and eighteenth, Jaspers (1926, pp. 148–149) reasoned, is a general mood or inclination in Western society that craves the mysterious, the unusual, the undefinable, and the blatantly diseased. Accordingly, although the Enlightenment tended to reward creative individuals who were healthy and rational with the distinction of genius, the nineteenth and twentieth centuries (since the time of Romanticism, that is) have shown a distinct preference for those creative individuals who are diseased and, specifically, schizophrenic. It should be noted that Lange-Eichbaum (1927/1935) provided an interesting variation of this type of argument.

All of this is not to suggest that the display of symptoms of mental illness on the part of the creative are the result of nothing more than deliberate role playing and adherence to role expectations deemed appropriate for artists and writers. Rather, it is a reminder that examinations regarding the relation of creativity to mental illness must take full measure of relevant historical and sociocultural developments as well as their impact on contemporary conceptions regarding the nature of creative individuals and the creative process. To the extent that these conceptions find expression in a pervasive societal belief in the existence of a close connection between the creative arts and some form of madness, as is the case in Western society, they are likely to be of consequence and become intimately tied to the acknowledged mind–body connection in the causation of genuine illness. As such, they are indispensable to a thorough understanding regarding the relationship between creativity and mental health.

References

Andreasen, N. (1987). Creativity and mental illness: Prevalence rates in writers and their first-degree relatives. *American Journal of Psychiatry*, 144, 1288–1292.

Anonymous (1912). Literary genius and manic-depressive insanity. *The Woman's Medical Journal*, xxii, 161.

Aristotle (1984). Problems connected with practical wisdom, intelligence, and wisdom (E. S. Foster, Trans.). In J. Barnes (Ed.), *The complete works of Aristotle* (Vol. 2) (pp. 1498–1502). Princeton University Press.

Babb, L. (1951). *The Elizabethan malady*. East Lansing, MI: Michigan State College Press.

Becker, G. (1978). *The mad genius controversy: A study in the sociology of deviance.* Beverly Hills, CA: Sage.

Becker, G. (2001). The association of creativity and psychopathology: Its cultural-historical origins. *Creativity Research Journal*, 13, 45–53.

Boring, E. G. (1950). *A history of experimental psychology.* New York: Appleton-Century-Crofts.

Cahan, J. (1911). *Zur kritik des geniebegriffs* [Toward a criticism of the concept of genius]. Bern, Switzerland: Scheitlin.

Carson, S. H., Peterson, J. B. and Higgins, D. M. (2003). Decreased latent inhibition is associated with increased creative achievement in high functioning individuals. *Journal of Personality and Social Psychology*, 85, 499–506.

Coetzee, J. M. (2006). The poet in the tower. *New York Review of Books*, October 19, 69–75.

Coladarci, A. P. (1968). Educational psychology. In D. L. Sills (Ed.), *International encyclopedia of the social sciences* (Vol. 4) (pp. 533–539). New York: Macmillan.

d'Alembert, J. L. (1967). *Oeuvres completes de d'Alembert* [Complete works of d'Alembert]. Geneva, Switzerland: Slatkine.

de Saint-Simon, H. (1803/1964). Letters from an inhabitant of Geneva to his contemporaries. In *Social organization, the science of man and other writings* (pp. 1–11). New York: Harper & Row.

Eysenck, H. J. (1995). *Genius: The natural history of creativity*. New York: Cambridge University Press.

Fabian, B. (1966). Introduction. In *An essay on genius* (pp. 1–48). Munich, Germany: Fink Verlag.

Faris, R. E. L. (1940). Sociological causes of genius. *American Sociological Review*, 5, 689–699.

Galton, F. (1869/1962). *Hereditary genius: An inquiry into its laws and consequences*. Cleveland, OH: Meridian.

Gerard, A. (1774/1966). *An essay on genius*. Munich, Germany: Fink Verlag.

Gerth, H. H. (1976). *Bürgerliche intelligenz um 1800: zur soziologie des deutschen frühliberalismus* [Bourgeois intellectuals around 1800: Toward a sociology of early German liberalism]. Göttingen, Germany: Vandenhoech and Ruprecht.

Graña, C. (1964). *Bohemian versus bourgeois: French society and the French man of letters in the nineteenth century*. New York: Basic Books.

Hirsch, N. D. (1931). *Genius and creative intelligence*. Cambridge, MA: Sci-Art Publishers.

Hirsch, W. (1897). *Genius and degeneration: A psychological study*. London: Heinemann.

Holmes, R. (2008). *The age of wonder: How the romantic generation discovered the beauty and terror of science*. New York: Pantheon Books.

Jamison, K. R. (1989). Mood disorders and patterns of creativity in British writers and artists. *Psychiatry: Interpersonal and Biological Processes*, 52, 125–134.

Jamison, K. R. (1993). *Touched with fire: Manic-depressive illness and the artistic temperament*. New York: Free Press.

Jaspers, K. (1926). Strindberg und Van Gogh [Strindberg and Van Gogh]. *Philosophische forschungen*, 3, 8–151.

Kant, I. (1790/1957). Critique of judgement. In T. M. Greene (Ed.), *Kant selections*. New York: Scribner's.

Kretschmer, E. (1931). *The psychology of men of genius*. New York: Harcourt Brace Jovanovich.

Lamb, C. (1826). *The sanity of true genius: The last essays of Elia* (Vol. vii). London: Oxford University Press.

Lange-Eichbaum, W. (1927/1935). *Genie: Irrsin und ruhm* [Genius: Madness and fame]. Munich, Germany: Reinhardt.

Lange-Eichbaum, W. (1930/1932). *The problem of genius*. New York: Harcourt Brace Jovanovich.

La Vopa, A. J. (1988). *Grace, talent, and merit: Poor students, clerical careers, and professional ideology in eighteenth-century Germany.* Cambridge, UK: Cambridge University Press.

Lehman, H. (1947). National differences in creativity. *American Journal of Sociology,* 52, May, 475–488.

Lélut, L. F. (1836). *Du demon de Socrate* [The demon of Socrates]. Paris: Trinquart.

Lombroso, C. (1863/1891). *The man of genius.* New York: Scribner's.

Ludwig, A. M. (1995). *The price of greatness: Resolving the creativity and madness controversy.* New York: Guilford Press.

Marks, J. (1926). *Genius and disaster: Studies in drugs and genius.* New York: Adelphi.

Maudsley, H. (1886/1908). *Heredity, variation and genius.* London: John Bale, Sons & Danielsson.

Moreau, J. J. (1859). *La psychologie morbid dans ses rapports avec la philosophie de l'histoire* [Abnormal psychology in its relation to the philosophy of history]. Paris: Masson.

Nordau, M. (1892/1900). *Degeneration.* New York: Appleton-Century-Crofts.

Orwell, G. (1953). Shooting an elephant. In *A collection of essays* (pp. 148–156). New York: Harcourt Brace.

Pascal, B. (1670/1968). *Pensées et opuscules* [Reflections and small works]. Paris: Classiques Hachette.

Plato (1974). *Phaedrus and the seventh and eighth letters* (W. Hamilton, Trans.). Middlesex, UK: Penguin.

Robinson, D. N. (1976). *An intellectual history of psychology.* New York: Macmillan.

Rosen, G. (1969). *Madness in society: Chapters in the historical sociology of mental illness.* New York: Harper & Row.

Sanborn, K. (1886). *The vanity and insanity of genius.* New York: Coombes.

Schlesinger, J. (2009). Creativity mythconceptions: A closer look at the evidence for the "mad genius" hypothesis. *Psychology of Aesthetics, Creativity, and the Arts,* 3, 62–72.

Shaw, G. B. (1895/1908). *The sanity of art.* New York: B. R. Tucker.

Stekel, W. (1909/1917). Nietzsche und Wagner: Eine sexualpsychologische studie zur psychogenese des freundschaftsgefühles und des freundschaftsverrates [Nietzsche and Wagner: A sexual-psychological study to the psychological genesis of friendship and the betrayal of friends]. *Zeitschrift für sexualwissenschaft und sexualpolitik,* 4, 22–65.

Sully, J. (1885). *Outlines of psychology.* New York: Appleton-Century-Crofts.

Tonelli, G. (1973). Genius from the Renaissance to 1770. In P. P. Weiner (Ed.), *Dictionary of the history of ideas* (pp. 293–298). New York: Scribner's.

Trilling, L. (1945/1950). Art and neurosis. In *The liberal imagination: Essays on literature and society* (pp. 160–180). New York: Viking.

Trilling, L. (1950). *The liberal imagination: Essays on literature and society.* New York: Viking.

Waddell, C. (1998). Creativity and mental illness: Is there a link? *Canadian Journal of Psychiatry,* 43, 166–172.

White, H. C. and White, C. A. (1965). *Canvases and careers: Institutional change in the French painting world.* New York: John Wiley & Sons, Inc.

Wittkower, R. (1973). Genius: Individualism in art and artists. In P. P. Weiner (Ed.), *Dictionary of the history of ideas* (pp. 297–312). New York: Scribner's.

Wittkower, R. and Wittkower, M. (1963). *Born under Saturn.* London: Shenval.

Zilsel, E. (1926). *Die entstehung des geniebegriffes* [The origin of the genius concept]. Tübingen, Germany: Mohr.

2   The mad (creative) genius: what do we know after a century of historiometric research?

Dean Keith Simonton

On November 19, 1909, Frederick A. Woods, a geneticist at the Massachusetts Institute of Technology (MIT), coined a "new name for a new science." This he called *historiometry*, which covers when "the facts of history of a personal nature have been subjected to statistical analysis by some more or less objective method" (p. 703). Woods (1911) later identified historiometry not just as a science but an "exact science" and claimed that the technique was particularly well suited for the scientific "psychology of genius." In the original article, Woods (1909) also listed a dozen examples of historiometric inquiries that appeared before the method had acquired a formal name. The list included Francis Galton's (1869) *Hereditary genius*, Alphonse de Candolle's (1873) *Histoire des sciences et des savants depuis deux siècles*, James McKeen Cattell's (1903) "A statistical study of eminent men," and Havelock Ellis' (1904) *A study of British genius*. Although Wood intended his list to be comprehensive, he actually overlooked the first bona fide historiometric study published by Adolphe Quételet (1835/1968) more than a third of a century before Galton's (1869) book (cf. Galton, 1865). Of course, Woods' (1909) bibliography could not possibly encompass examples of historiometric research published in the century or so since the method acquired a name. Even so, among the most notable examples are Lewis M. Terman (1917), Catharine Cox (1926), Edward L. Thorndike (1950), and R. B. Cattell (1963). It is noteworthy that many historiometricians are themselves noteworthy, and some could themselves count as genuine geniuses – but I will not name names.

If historiometry is truly useful in the scientific study of genius, then it must be able to address some of the central questions in the psychology of genius (Simonton, 2009a). Is genius born or made? Is genius generic or domain specific? Is genius isolated or necessarily situated in a sociocultural context? Is genius mad? Because this chapter is part of a volume devoted to creativity and mental illness, it is the last question that I address here. What do historiometric investigations tell us about the relation between genius and madness – and especially the relation between *creative* genius and madness? But before I can review the main empirical results dealing with this question, I first must give a brief overview of the methods involved.

Methods

Historiometry has advanced considerably since Woods (1909) first named the science, and it has even progressed considerably since the first book-length treatment of the technique (Simonton, 1990; cf. Simonton, 2009a). Thus, I can do no more than outline the core features of the methodology. In a nutshell, it consists of the following four steps.

First, the researcher specifies one or more *nomothetic hypotheses* that can be subjected to empirical test. By "nomothetic" is meant hypotheses that apply generally across a large group of individuals rather than just a single individual. For example, the hypothesis that genius-level creativity is positively associated with psychopathology is a nomothetic hypothesis. In contrast, the hypothesis that Van Gogh cut off part of his ear to give to a prostitute because of some specific condition or experience cannot be a nomothetic hypothesis (cf. Runyan, 1981).

Second, the investigator must gather a representative sample of cases to test the hypotheses. Because historiometry concentrates on the "psychology of genius," this sample does not consist of college students, nor is it made up of a random sample of the general population. Instead, the cases are usually chosen precisely because they are the most eminent figures in a given domain of achievement (Simonton, 1990). This sampling criterion is what sets historiometric research apart from mainstream research in the behavioral sciences. Whereas the samples in most studies consist of anonymous undergraduates, the samples in historiometric studies tend to contain subjects with recognizable names – names that have "gone down in history." The figures constitute unequivocally "significant samples" (Simonton, 1999).

Third, biographical and historical data pertaining to these significant samples are then quantified in order to measure the variables relevant to an empirical test of the nomothetic hypotheses. For instance, to test the "mad genius" hypothesis, it is necessary to establish an objective and quantifiable measure of mental illness in a historic figure. However, a strictly scientific test must do more. Besides the assessment of "substantive" variables, the investigator must also quantify requisite "control" variables to enable corrections for potential statistical artifacts or spurious relations. To the extent possible, the investigator should establish the reliability and validity of the resulting measures, an obligation that is not always followed.

Fourth and last, the resulting measures must be subjected to quantitative analyses most appropriate to testing the given nomothetic hypothesis or hypotheses. These analyses are most often statistical, albeit occasionally the investigator may strive to fit mathematical models to the historiometric dataset (Simonton, 1990). The statistical analyses themselves may assume a tremendous variety of forms, including multiple regression, factor analysis, structural equation modeling, and time-series analysis – as well as more elementary statistics like bivariate correlations and chi-square tests.

Results

Although scientific research on the mad genius issue is often said to date from Lombroso (1891), his work does not qualify as an instance of historiometry: His analytical approach was too qualitative, subjective, and anecdotal. The first genuine historiometric study germane to this topic was Ellis' (1904) *A study of British genius*, which is based on 1,030 men and women of sufficient importance to have been honored with entries in a prestigious biographical dictionary. Ellis' goal was to discover the main characteristics of this distinguished group, including such factors as ethnicity, socioeconomic class, family pedigree, childhood and educational experiences, marriage and family, life expectancy, and various physical attributes. Even so, he did note that 4.2 percent of his sampled geniuses exhibited insanity at some time in their lives, 8.3 percent displayed melancholy, and 6.6 percent showed pronounced, even pathological, "shyness and timidity." It is hard to know what to make of these statistics because Ellis' sample is extremely heterogeneous with respect to both the magnitude of eminence and the domain of achievement – indeed, a very large percentage of his sample could not be properly identified as creative geniuses.

In this chapter, therefore, I emphasize more recent historiometric studies that present sufficient statistics for us to be able to make some comparative statements about how psychopathology varies across domains of creative achievement. Based on their sample characteristics, such inquiries can be grouped into three general categories: all kinds of geniuses, creative geniuses only, and literary geniuses only.

All kinds of geniuses

After Cox (1926) published her classic historiometric investigation, she continued to study her sample of creators and leaders under her married name, Catherine Cox Miles. Having already assessed these geniuses on intelligence and personality, she decided to examine their childhood mental and physical health as well. Although she published a partial analysis of her findings (Miles and Wolfe, 1936), she never conducted a complete study (Simonton, 2010a). Fortunately, she deposited the raw data for the 282 geniuses in the Archives of the History of American Psychology at the University of Akron. Simonton and Song (2009) discovered these data and subjected them to a proper statistical analysis. From the standpoint of this chapter, the most interesting results were the domain contrasts in mental health: Political leaders and composers exhibited superior mental health to the rest, whereas imaginative writers displayed more mental illness than the others did. The intriguing feature of this finding is that the psychopathology of literary geniuses was already present before they attained adulthood – the only inquiry to address this possibility.

The original Cox (1926) sample consisted of geniuses born between 1450 and 1849. Goertzel *et al.* (1978) examined 317 historic figures who were born much later and thus defined a non-overlapping sample (cf. Goertzel and Goertzel, 1962). Like Ellis (1904) long before, their primary interest was a host of biographical variables, with only a partial interest in psychopathology. Nonetheless, the statistical analyses yielded some useful contrasts when the figures were grouped into four areas of achievement: political (politicians and officials, military figures, revolutionaries, reformers, etc.), literary (fiction writers, dramatists, poets, non-fiction writers, etc.), artistic (painters, sculptors, dancers, composers, film directors, actors, etc.), and miscellaneous (a residual conglomerate of science, business, athletics, mysticism, religion, etc.). Most notably, the literary figures, when compared with the rest, were much more likely to attempt or attain suicide – by a factor of two! The literary geniuses were also much more likely to have had alcoholic parents.

Two far more focused historiometric inquiries were conducted and published about the same time: by Felix Post in 1994 and Arnold Ludwig in 1995.

Post's (1994) 291 world-famous creators and leaders   Based on available biographical materials, Post collected a sample of highly eminent politicians, scientists, thinkers (and scholars), (creative) writers, composers, and (visual) artists. He then scored each member of his sample on a psychopathology index that had four levels: none, mild, marked, and severe. The corresponding percentages of figures that received each score are shown in Table 2.1. A few useful conclusions can be drawn from this table. First, like what the Goertzels (1978) reported, the creative

Table 2.1 *Percentages of eminent figures displaying different degrees of psychopathology*

Achievement domain	None	Mild	Marked	Severe	n
Politicians	15.2	26.1	41.3	17.4	46
Scientists	31.1	24.4	26.7	17.8	45
Thinkers	10.0	28.0	36.0	26.0	50
Writers	2.0	10.0	42.0	46.0	50
Composers	17.3	32.7	19.2	30.8	52
Artists	14.6	29.1	18.8	37.5	48

Note. Percentages are taken from Table 1 in Post (1994, p. 25).

writers exhibited higher levels of psychopathology, noticeably higher than the composers and artists. Indeed, 88 percent of the literary geniuses scored either "marked" or "severe." Second, the scientists scored the lowest in psychopathology, even lower than the politicians did. In fact, almost one-third of the scientific geniuses had no psychopathology whatsoever. Finally, the thinkers fell roughly between the scientists and the three kinds of artistic geniuses – the writers, composers, and visual artists.

Post (1994) also conducted a more detailed breakdown according to diagnostic categories and to whether the instances of illness were episodic or chronic. In addition, he scrutinized the rates of substance abuse, suicide, and other unhealthy behaviors. The results are rather too complex to report here, except to say that the findings closely parallel what is shown in Table 2.1 – for instance, that writers have the highest rates of depression, alcoholism, and incapacitating personality disorders.

Ludwig's (1995) 1,004 modern creators, leaders, and celebrities
Ludwig began by collecting a rather large sample of eminent figures in a diversity of achievement domains (see also Ludwig, 1992a). Although the sample included both creators and leaders, all were active in the late nineteenth and/or early twentieth centuries, thus minimizing the overlap with Post's (1994) contemporaneous inquiry. Ludwig's luminaries were then assigned to the following domains: natural sciences, social sciences, architecture, visual art, poetry, fiction, non-fiction, drama, musical composing, musical performance, exploration, business, social figure, companion (of the famous), sports, military, and public office. Ludwig then determined the presence of psychopathology, but made a dichotomous yes–no decision rather than using an ordinal scale like Post (1994) did.

In any event, the highest rates of any lifetime disorder were exhibited by the poets (87%), followed by the fiction writers (77%), dramatists (74%), visual artists (73%), non-fiction writers (72%), musical composers (60%), and architects (52%). In contrast, the eminent natural scientists had a rate less than half as high as the composers did (28%), albeit the social scientists were at about the same level as the architects (51%). For the most part, the creators exhibited more psychopathology than those from other areas of achievement. The military figures were only at 30 percent and the eminent in public office 35 percent. Clearly, creative geniuses are far more prone toward mental illness than any other type of genius. Furthermore, among the creators, artistic geniuses (in the inclusive sense) are at the highest risk for some kind of psychopathology. The same geniuses are more likely to have parents and siblings who display substantial mental illness, with special risk for alcoholism, drug abuse, and depression.

The picture becomes much more complex when Ludwig (1995), like Post (1994), broke down the domain contrasts according to specific syndromes or symptoms. In a sense, every kind of creative genius had its own "favorite" mental illness: Alcoholism was most common among those in drama (60%), a group that also had the highest incidence of mania (17%); drug abuse was favored by music performers (36%); non-fiction authors had the highest rate of anxiety (16%); and poets, not to be outdone by anyone, dominated with respect to psychosis (17%), suicide rate (20%), and depression (77%) – thereby illustrating how poetic genius is most susceptible to some kind of mental disorder. Poets have too many pathology favorites.

Admittedly, these comparisons across creative domains do not specifically address whether the overall frequency and intensity of psychopathology are higher in creative geniuses. Nevertheless, it is obvious that many of these percentages exceed what would be expected in the general population. More than three-quarters of the latter are not subject to severe depression.

Besides the foregoing findings, Ludwig (1995) also investigated whether psychopathology exhibited a positive correlation with overall creative achievement. According to his statistical analyses, various indicators of psychopathology were positively associated with higher scores on the Creative Achievement Scale (Ludwig, 1992b). He concluded that "the presence of psychological 'unease,' potentially but not necessarily produced by any mental illness that is not too incapacitating, contributes to the realization of true greatness" (Ludwig, 1995, p. 194). He adds that this "unease" must be accompanied by other critical traits that ameliorate potential negative consequences.

Creative geniuses only

Ludwig published follow-ups on his 1995 historiometric inquiry. One investigation concentrated on leadership (Ludwig, 2002) and the other focused on creativity (Ludwig, 1998). The latter has the most obvious relevance to this chapter, and I discuss that first. Afterward, I close this section on a set of miscellaneous inquiries.

Ludwig's (1998) follow-up and a sequel   Here Ludwig was most interested in conducting a more fine-grained analysis of the creativity–psychopathology relationship. The relation could hold not only across domains but also within domains, depending on the specific nature of the creativity required. More specifically, Ludwig (1998) showed that creative geniuses in domains "that require more logical, objective, and formal forms of expression" tend to feature less psychopathology than those active in domains "that require more intuitive, subjective, and emotive forms" (p. 93). This principle operates not only across domains, but within domains and sub-domains, generating what Ludwig called a "fractal pattern" of "self-similarity." To be specific, (a) artists display more psychopathology than do scientists; (b) within the sciences, social scientists display more psychopathology than do natural scientists; (c) within the arts, artists in the expressive arts (e.g., the visual arts and literature) have higher psychopathology rates than those in the performing arts (e.g., dance and music) who in their turn have higher rates than those in the formal arts (e.g., architecture); (d) within a particular expressive art like literature, poets exhibit higher rates of psychopathology than do fiction writers who in their turn have higher rates than do non-fiction writers; and (e) within any given artistic domain (e.g., sculpture or painting), those who create in an emotive style exhibit higher psychopathology rates than those creating in a symbolic style, and the latter exhibit yet higher rates than those creating in a formal style.

These findings have two interesting applications, the first in the arts and the second in the sciences.

1. Martindale (1990) has extensively documented stylistic changes in the arts. An example is the shift from Neo-Classical to Romantic styles in most artistic media (see also Hasenfus *et al.*, 1983). Given Ludwig's (1998) results, we would predict that these stylistic changes should be accompanied by corresponding changes in the psychopathology rates of the creative geniuses involved. For example, Romantic poets should display more psychopathology than do Neo-Classical poets. This conjecture is certainly testable empirically.

2. Kuhn (1970) distinguished between two kinds of scientists operating within paradigmatic disciplines. Paradigmatic sciences are those that enjoy a strong consensus on theory and methodology, a consensus that provides the basis for the choice of research problems and the evaluation of results. A practitioner of "normal science" is someone who strives to develop and extend the received paradigm. However, some scientists aspire to overthrow the paradigm and replace it with a new one that can explain otherwise inexplicable "anomalies." These latter individuals are the scientific revolutionaries. Because revolutionary scientists have fewer paradigmatic constraints on their creativity, they can "regress" toward more "artistic" ways of thinking (Simonton, 2009b). In Max Planck's (1949) words, such scientists "must have a vivid intuitive imagination, for new ideas are not generated by deduction, but by an artistically creative imagination" (p. 109). If so, then psychopathology should be more common among revolutionary scientists than among normal scientists.

Unlike the first implication, the second actually has empirical endorsement in a fascinating historiometric study of 82 scientific geniuses in the natural (paradigmatic) sciences (Ko and Kim, 2008). They first classified these eminent scientists into two groups, the "paradigm-preserving contributors" (or "normal scientists") and the "paradigm-rejecting contributors" (or "revolutionaries"). The scientists were also assessed regarding differential eminence (using Murray, 2003) and psychopathology, the latter represented by four levels: none, personality disorders, mood disorders, and schizophrenic disorders. The results were striking: For paradigm-preserving contributors eminence was negatively related to the level of mental illness, but for paradigm-rejecting contributors the eminence–pathology relation became positive – a classic "cross-over" interaction effect.

Miscellaneous (but still important) inquiries   Before turning to the final category of studies, I should mention six diverse investigations that belong properly to this section.

1. Raskin (1936) studied 120 eminent scientists and 123 eminent writers, all from the nineteenth century. Although her focus was on biographical variables, she reported that the scientific geniuses scored higher than did the literary geniuses on "cheerfulness," "sociability," and "modesty" whereas the literary geniuses scored higher than the scientific geniuses on "persistence," "emotionality," and "evidence of neuroses." This reinforces the repeated contrast between creative geniuses in the arts and those in the sciences. The "persistence" trait of the creative writers may reflect the greater determination that is

required to make it in the literary world. The typical writer probably receives more rejection slips than the typical scientist receives advice to "revise and resubmit."

2. Juda's (1949) study is a curious methodological hybrid, combining historiometric research with psychiatric interviews of contemporary geniuses. Because the published version was an English-language abstract of a much larger German manuscript, it is sometimes difficult to decipher the details. Nevertheless, she apparently compared 181 scientists and 113 artists, where the latter term encompassed architects, sculptors, painters, poets, and composers. Juda again showed that the scientists had less psychopathology than did the artists, and that among the artistic geniuses it was poets who fared the worst in terms of mental health. Unlike the other studies discussed thus far, the creative geniuses in her sample came exclusively from German-speaking nations (mainly Germany, Austria, and Switzerland). Because most other historiometric studies are strongly biased toward the English-speaking world, Juda's study provides a valuable independent confirmation of those results.

3. Karlsson's (1970) study was also confined to a specific non-English-speaking nationality, only in this case, Iceland. This inquiry also used a mixed methodology, combining a historiometric measure of achieved eminence (an entry in a "who is who" reference work) with an objective archival record of actual psychopathology (as stored in the nation's only mental hospital). The researcher used these two sets of data to address a relevant yet novel issue: whether highly eminent Icelanders were more likely to have had close relatives who were psychotic. In line with the investigator's hypothesis, having a psychotic close relative doubled a person's likelihood of attaining distinction as a novelist, poet, painter, composer, or performer. This finding suggests that inheriting a certain propensity toward psychopathology – without necessarily manifesting psychopathology – may be conducive to creative genius.

4. R. B. Cattell (1963) used biographies to rate a sample of scientific geniuses on his 16 Personality Factors. He carried out this retrospective "at-a-distance" assessment before he had the opportunity to administer the same personality instrument to 140 eminent contemporary scientists. Nonetheless, he obtained corroborating results. Of special interest to our current concerns are two findings. First, scientific geniuses rate high in schizothymia – that is, they are "withdrawn, skeptical, internally preoccupied, precise, and critical" (p. 121). Second, creative geniuses in science score high in desurgency, signifying that they are disposed toward "introspectiveness, restraint, brooding,

and solemnity of manner" (p. 123). We have noted multiple times that scientific genius is much less likely to display psychopathology than is artistic genius. Yet combining the two sets of schizothymic and desurgent traits, we cannot conclude that such scientists are just like the rest of us! A scientific genius as a neighbor or office-mate would be reclusive, remote, and even offensive to a degree contrary to the expected decorum. While technically "normal," the scientific genius is still a bit "off" or, to be more generous perhaps, "eccentric."

5. Ludwig (1990) scrutinized the relation between creative output and alcohol consumption in 34 twentieth-century writers, artists, and composers or performers who were notorious for their heavy drinking. His goal was to determine alcohol's impact. In more than three-quarters of these artistic creators, alcohol undermined productivity, a detrimental effect that was particularly strong in the later stages of their drinking lives. Even so, there were instances when alcohol had a positive effect as well as examples when creativity led to increased alcohol assumption. In brief, the relations were too complex to permit simple generalizations.

6. Mark Schaller's (1997) historiometric study was designed to test a specific hypothesis: When geniuses become famous, they become increasingly self-conscious, and the latter leads to drinking or drugs to relieve the unpleasant state. The hypothesis was tested in three case studies: Kurt Cobain, the former singer–songwriter for Nirvana; Cole Porter, the Broadway songwriter and composer; and John Cheever, the novelist and short-story writer. Archival data and content analyses supported the hypothesis. Becoming famous can indeed lead to psychopathology!

Although these investigations are rather diverse in purpose and design, they do enhance our understanding of the creativity–psychopathology relation.

Literary geniuses only

Given that literary geniuses tend to outscore all other forms of creative genius in psychopathological leanings, it should come as no surprise that they have received so much attention in historiometric research. As an early instance, Colin Martindale (1972) focused solely on eminent poets, twenty-one English (born between 1670 and 1809) and twenty-one French poets (born between 1770 and 1909). These forty-two were the same poets used in a series of content analytical studies that culminated in his classic (1990) *Clockwork muse* (see also Martindale, 1975).

Taking advantage of biographical materials, Martindale gauged the poets' mental health at three levels: normal, symptomatic, and psychotic. A poet was symptomatic if he or she displayed alcoholism, suicide, phobias, or mental "crises" or "breakdowns," whereas a poet was psychotic if he or she was committed to an asylum or exhibited recurring symptoms such as hallucinations. According to this scaling, 15 percent of the poets had psychotic episodes at some time in their lives, and nearly 50 percent had some type of psychopathological symptoms. Although the exact statistics differ from what was reported earlier, poetic geniuses are clearly not always of sound mind.

Because Martindale's (1972) study lacks a comparison group, his results have to be supplemented by a historiometric study that Kaufman (2005) conducted using a sample of 826 Eastern European authors, including poets, playwrights, fiction writers, and non-fiction writers. When compared with each other, mental illness was appreciably higher in the poets and noticeably lower in the fiction writers, with the playwrights and non-fiction writers falling between.

In some respects, however, Kaufman's (2000–2001) earlier investigation was even more fascinating: He wanted to determine whether literary creativity was positively associated with psychopathology. It is one thing to claim that literary creators feature more psychopathology, and quite another to assert that the greater creators display more psychopathology than do less creative writers. To address this question, he conducted two historiometric inquiries, one using a sample of 986 writers from the twentieth century, the other a sample of 889 authors confined to the United States but active from the seventeenth to twentieth centuries. The gauge of literary genius was a major award, whether the Nobel Prize or Pulitzer Prize. In both investigations, those who won major prizes experienced more mental illness than did less honored writers. Furthermore, Nobel laureates had a particular problem with alcoholism. These findings were certainly consistent with Ludwig's (1995) general conclusion that creative achievement was positively associated with some degree of mental or emotional disturbance.

In yet another study, Kaufman (2001) tackled the matter of gender differences. This question is perhaps of particular significance given that literature has attracted the highest proportion of female geniuses than any other domain of creative achievement (Murray, 2003). This feminine presence is apparent not just in Western literatures but also in Eastern literatures, such as the Japanese (Simonton, 1992). Kaufman conducted two studies. The first analyzed 1,629 writers to determine indicators of psychopathology. Not only were the female poets at a higher risk for mental illness, but their risk was elevated relative to both female fiction writers and male writers in any genre. The second study looked at 520 women who had attained eminence in literature, the visual arts, acting, or politics. Again, the female poets once more displayed more psychopathology. Having replicated the finding across both samples, Kaufman styled it the "Sylvia Plath effect" after the female poet whose suicide perhaps most dramatically illustrates the phenomenon.

Plainly, suicidal personalities have lowered life expectancies. Even in the absence of outright suicide, psychopathology can lead to unhealthy lifestyles, such as alcoholism, an illness that is certainly prominent among literary creators (Post, 1996; see also Ludwig, 1990). At any rate, Kaufman (2003) determined the "cost of the muse" in 1,987 creative writers from America, China, Turkey, and Eastern Europe. Overall, the poets in the sample had lower life expectancies than the fiction writers, playwrights, and non-fiction writers. Simonton (1975) likewise found in a transhistorical and cross-cultural sample that poets died 6 years younger than other literary geniuses, albeit Simonton (1997) found a somewhat different pattern in Japanese literature, where it was the fiction writers who had the shortest life span. Even so, Japanese writers still had lower life expectancies than geniuses in non-literary domains.

Evaluation

It would seem that the connection between creativity and psychopathology has been established beyond reasonable doubt. Nonetheless, some observers remain highly skeptical (e.g., Schlesinger, 2009). Accordingly, I now discuss the cons and pros associated with historiometric research.

Cons

Although historiometric research has been around since 1835 – longer than any other method for studying the question at hand – it certainly cannot be considered a mainstream method. No doubt, the technique can be criticized on methodological grounds. Consider the following three complaints.

First, historiometric research must depend on the reliability of the biographical data. How much faith can we place in a retrospective diagnosis carried out decades after a creator's death? This problem may be especially acute in older investigations that use outdated diagnostic standards. To illustrate, Martindale (1972) included homosexuality among his criteria for psychopathology, a decision that could not be justified today. Still, it should be noted that many of the diagnoses are founded on objective behaviors that do not even require a skilled therapist to discern. On that basis, it would be absurd to say that Van Gogh had a perfectly healthy mind: Besides the self-mutilation episode, his letters to his brother, his sojourn in an asylum, and his probable suicide all reveal a very troubled soul. In addition, the diagnostic attributions are often reinforced by other objective facts. To give an example, the contrast between scientific and artistic geniuses in susceptibility to psychopathology parallels a similar contrast in the homes in which they grew up: Scientists are more likely to come from stable and conventional families while artists are more prone to emerge from unstable and unconventional families (Simonton, 2009b).

Second, even if we take assessment reliability on face value, how do we know that a sampling bias does not intrude such that those creative geniuses who are mentally ill are more likely to have biographies written about them – a criterion often used in defining historiometric samples? After all, the lives of crazy creators make more interesting stories than the lives of normal creators. In support of this concern, it is interesting that the plays by William Shakespeare that are the most popular tend to be those in which a main character becomes mad, or at least feigns madness (Simonton, 1986). The biographies of Robert Schumann, Friedrich Nietzsche, and Vincent Van Gogh thereby feature dramatic appeal! In response, a study's vulnerability to this criticism depends on the sampling strategy. Some investigators do indeed define their samples according to the availability of biographies (e.g., Ludwig, 1995). Yet other researchers use objective criteria, such as receiving a major prize or having an entry in an encyclopedia or biographical dictionary (e.g., Kaufman, 2000–2001).

Third, historiometric studies are inherently correlational, and thus they are always vulnerable to spurious relations owing to the impact of extraneous "third variables." The only route around this is to introduce numerous control variables and to implement multivariate data analyses that take advantage of those controls. Sad to say, the vast majority of historiometric inquiries fail to introduce these advanced statistical procedures. As a case in point, almost every conclusion that Ludwig (1995) makes is based on simple bivariate comparisons without controls. Of the three criticisms, this one is the most serious – and one that I hope will be heeded in future research. The full potential of historiometric work has yet to be realized fully.

Pros

The foregoing cons are counterweighed by the following two pros.

First, historiometric research enjoys high face validity when it comes to defining creative genius (Simonton, 1999). The "subjects" in such studies include the most notable creators in any domain. If creativity bears some relation with psychopathology, then the relation should be most obvious for the most eminent creators – including creators now long deceased! Although researchers can sometimes recruit contemporary creators to participate in their psychometric or psychiatric inquiries, this recruitment is relatively rare, and the participants are often not as eminent as seen in historiometric inquiries (e.g., Barron, 1963; MacKinnon, 1978). Furthermore, these more mainstream approaches introduce their own methodological problems (Simonton, 1999). For example, reliance on a person's willingness to become a research subject probably introduces a sampling bias of a different kind. The J. D. Salingers of the world will reject invitations out of hand! The upshot would likely be a sample biased in favor of mental health (see, e.g., Csikszentmihályi, 1997).

Second, the conclusions drawn from historiometric research do not differ in any substantial way from those arrived at using alternative methods (see Simonton, 2010b, for a review). In particular, the relation between creativity and psychopathology shows up in psychometric, psychiatric, epidemiological, and behavior-genetic investigations. Because different methods have distinct advantages and disadvantages, this congruence is crucial. The diverse sources of artifact thus cancel out, reinforcing the general conclusion. Even more important, these alternative methods help researchers flesh out the reasons for the connection – as well as why creative genius is by no means synonymous with madness. This point is well made in Shelley Carson's (2011; also this volume) "shared vulnerability model." Highly creative people are distinguished by some of the same psychological variables as the mentally ill – such as cognitive disinhibition – that in isolation would make creators equally vulnerable. Yet the highly creative enjoy compensatory strengths – such as superior intelligence – that convert a possible disability into an exceptional ability. Creative geniuses thus acquire the capacity to generate original combinations of ideas and to notice novelties in their environment that would be missed by more "normal minds."

To be sure, from time to time these vulnerabilities may spill over into overt psychopathology. An asset becomes a deficit – perhaps even resulting in yet another historic but tragic suicide. Yet if such is the "price of greatness," it may remain a good deal.

References

Barron, F. X. (1963). *Creativity and psychological health: Origins of personal vitality and creative freedom.* Princeton, NJ: Van Nostrand.

Candolle, A. de (1873). *Histoire des sciences et des savants depuis deux siècles* [History of science and scientists for two centuries]. Geneve: Georg.

Carson, S. H. (2011). Creativity and psychopathology: A shared vulnerability model. *Canadian Journal of Psychiatry*, 56, 144–153.

Cattell, J. M. (1903). A statistical study of eminent men. *Popular Science Monthly*, 62, 359–377.

Cattell, R. B. (1963). The personality and motivation of the researcher from measurements of contemporaries and from biography. In C. W. Taylor and F. Barron (Eds.), *Scientific creativity: Its recognition and development* (pp. 119–131). New York: Wiley.

Cox, C. (1926). *The early mental traits of three hundred geniuses*. Stanford University Press.

Csikszentmihályi, M. (1997). *Creativity: Flow and the psychology of discovery and invention*. New York: HarperCollins.

Ellis, H. (1904). *A study of British genius*. London: Hurst & Blackett.

Galton, F. (1865). Hereditary talent and character. *Macmillan's Magazine*, 12, 157–166, 318–327.

Galton, F. (1869). *Hereditary genius: An inquiry into its laws and consequences*. London: Macmillan.

Goertzel, M. G., Goertzel, V. and Goertzel, T. G. (1978). *300 eminent personalities: A psychosocial analysis of the famous*. San Francisco, CA: Jossey-Bass.

Goertzel, V. and Goertzel, M. G. (1962). *Cradles of eminence*. Boston, MA: Little, Brown.

Hasenfus, N., Martindale, C. and Birnbaum, D. (1983). Psychological reality of cross-media artistic styles. *Journal of Experimental Psychology: Human Perception and Performance*, 9, 841–863.

Juda, A. (1949). The relationship between highest mental capacity and psychic abnormalities. *American Journal of Psychiatry*, 106, 296–307.

Karlsson, J. I. (1970). Genetic association of giftedness and creativity with schizophrenia. *Hereditas*, 66, 177–182.

Kaufman, J. C. (2000–2001). Genius, lunatics and poets: Mental illness in prize-winning authors. *Imagination, Cognition and Personality*, 20, 305–314.

Kaufman, J. C. (2001). The Sylvia Plath effect: Mental illness in eminent creative writers. *Journal of Creative Behavior*, 35, 37–50.

Kaufman, J. C. (2003). The cost of the muse: Poets die young. *Death Studies*, 27, 813–821.

Kaufman, J. C. (2005). The door that leads into madness: Eastern European poets and mental illness. *Creativity Research Journal*, 17, 99–103.

Ko, Y. and Kim, J. (2008). Scientific geniuses' psychopathology as a moderator in the relation between creative contribution types and eminence. *Creativity Research Journal*, 20, 251–261.

Kuhn, T. S. (1970). *The structure of scientific revolutions* (2nd edn.). University of Chicago Press.

Lombroso, C. (1891). *The man of genius*. London: Scott.

Ludwig, A. M. (1990). Alcohol input and creative output. *British Journal of Addiction*, 85, 953–963.

Ludwig, A. M. (1992a). Creative achievement and psychopathology: Comparison among professions. *American Journal of Psychotherapy*, 46, 330–356.

Ludwig, A. M. (1992b). The Creative Achievement Scale. *Creativity Research Journal*, 5, 109–124.

Ludwig, A. M. (1995). *The price of greatness: Resolving the creativity and madness controversy*. New York: Guilford Press.

Ludwig, A. M. (1998). Method and madness in the arts and sciences. *Creativity Research Journal*, 11, 93–101.

Ludwig, A. M. (2002). *King of the mountain: The nature of political leadership*. Lexington, KY: University Press of Kentucky.

MacKinnon, D. W. (1978). *In search of human effectiveness*. Buffalo, NY: Creative Education Foundation.

Martindale, C. (1972). Father absence, psychopathology, and poetic eminence. *Psychological Reports*, 31, 843–847.

Martindale, C. (1975). *Romantic progression: The psychology of literary history*. Washington, DC: Hemisphere.

Martindale, C. (1990). *The clockwork muse: The predictability of artistic styles*. New York: Basic Books.

Miles, C. C. and Wolfe, L. S. (1936). Childhood physical and mental health records of historical geniuses. *Psychological Monographs*, 47, 390–400.

Murray, C. (2003). *Human accomplishment: The pursuit of excellence in the arts and sciences, 800 B.C. to 1950*. New York: HarperCollins.

Planck, M. (1949). *Scientific autobiography and other papers* (F. Gaynor, Trans.). New York: Philosophical Library.

Post, F. (1994). Creativity and psychopathology: A study of 291 world-famous men. *British Journal of Psychiatry*, 165, 22–34.

Post, F. (1996). Verbal creativity, depression and alcoholism: An investigation of one hundred American and British writers. *British Journal of Psychiatry*, 168, 545–555.

Quételet, A. (1968). *A treatise on man and the development of his faculties*. New York: Franklin. (Reprint of 1842 Edinburgh translation of 1835 French original.)

Raskin, E. A. (1936). Comparison of scientific and literary ability: A biographical study of eminent scientists and men of letters of the nineteenth century. *Journal of Abnormal and Social Psychology*, 31, 20–35.

Runyan, W. M. (1981). Why did Van Gogh cut off his ear? The problem of alternative explanations in psychobiography. *Journal of Personality and Social Psychology*, 40, 1070–1077.

Schaller, M. (1997). The psychological consequences of fame: Three tests of the self-consciousness hypothesis. *Journal of Personality*, 65, 291–309.

Schlesinger, J. (2009). Creative mythconceptions: A closer look at the evidence for the "mad genius" hypothesis. *Psychology of Aesthetics, Creativity, and the Arts*, 3, 62–72.

Simonton, D. K. (1975). Age and literary creativity: A cross-cultural and trans-historical survey. *Journal of Cross-Cultural Psychology*, 6, 259–277.

Simonton, D. K. (1986). Popularity, content, and context in 37 Shakespeare plays. *Poetics*, 15, 493–510.

Simonton, D. K. (1990). *Psychology, science, and history: An introduction to historiometry*. New Haven, CT: Yale University Press.

Simonton, D. K. (1992). Gender and genius in Japan: Feminine eminence in masculine culture. *Sex Roles*, 27, 101–119.

Simonton, D. K. (1997). Achievement domain and life expectancies in Japanese civilization. *International Journal of Aging and Human Development*, 44, 103–114.

Simonton, D. K. (1999). Significant samples: The psychological study of eminent individuals. *Psychological Methods*, 4, 425–451.

Simonton, D. K. (2009a). Historiometry in personality and social psychology. *Social and Personality Psychology Compass*, 3, 49–63.

Simonton, D. K. (2009b). Varieties of (scientific) creativity: A hierarchical model of disposition, development, and achievement. *Perspectives on Psychological Science*, 4, 441–452.

Simonton, D. K. (2010a). The curious case of Catharine Cox: The 1926 dissertation and her Miles-Wolfe 1936 follow-up. *History of Psychology*, 13, 205–206.

Simonton, D. K. (2010b). So you want to become a creative genius? You must be crazy! In D. Cropley, J. Kaufman, A. Cropley and M. Runco (Eds.), *The dark side of creativity* (pp. 218–234). New York: Cambridge University Press.

Simonton, D. K. and Song, A. V. (2009). Eminence, IQ, physical and mental health, and achievement domain: Cox's 282 geniuses revisited. *Psychological Science*, 20, 429–434.

Terman, L. M. (1917). The intelligence quotient of Francis Galton in childhood. *American Journal of Psychology*, 28, 209–215.

Thorndike, E. L. (1950). Traits of personality and their intercorrelations as shown in biographies. *Journal of Educational Psychology*, 41, 193–216.

Woods, F. A. (1909). A new name for a new science. *Science*, 30, November 19, 703–704.

Woods, F. A. (1911). Historiometry as an exact science. *Science*, 33, April 14, 568–574.

3 Reviewing recent empirical findings on creativity and mental illness

Melanie L. Beaussart, Arielle E. White, Adam Pullaro, and James C. Kaufman

Given that the entire book is devoted to creativity and mental illness, we view this chapter as a chance to highlight key work on the topic and raise some of the questions that will be addressed later in these pages. The historical antecedents of the debate have already been discussed (Becker, this volume), and the previous chapter highlighted the extensive historiometric studies conducted on this topic. Here, therefore, we will primarily focus on empirical research. Many of the studies discussed here are by scholars who have also contributed to this volume; similarly, other chapters have covered specific topics in great detail. We will only briefly allude to this work and instead send interested readers to the relevant parts of this book.

Conceptual issues

Conceptions of creativity

The connection between creativity and mental illness has been widely debated, both in creativity research and across many other disciplines. One of the biggest sources of variability and conflicting results is the problem of *definitions*: What exactly do we mean by creativity? Standard definitions of creativity often specify novelty and task-appropriateness (Amabile, 1996; Barron, 1955). Some also include a third concept, such as whether something is surprising (Simonton, 2013) or of high quality (Sternberg *et al.*, 2003). Yet such broad conceptions invariably raise more questions than they answer. In order to interpret empirical results cohesively, there must be a way in which studies of creativity and mental illness define creativity. Certainly, such studies do not consistently highlight how they operationally define creativity (similar to most papers on creativity; see Plucker *et al.*, 2004). Beyond definitions, there are many theories on how to measure creativity, from divergent thinking to remote associations to consensual assessment (Kaufman *et al.*, 2012). Countless further dimensions may be derived from these measures, such as fluency, flexibility, unusual responses, originality, novelty, functionality, aesthetics, or remoteness of associations.

A further distinction is how creativity may vary across different domains. Many theorists believe that creativity varies by domain, to at least some extent (see essays in Kaufman and Baer, 2005). Furthermore, being creative in one field (such as music) does not necessitate creativity in another field (such as painting). Researchers have argued that the different cognitive processes required for creativity are discipline dependent, such that artistic creativity and scientific creativity may be connected with different types of psychological disorders (Greenberg, 2004).

Conceptions of mental illness

Just as creativity can be expressed in writing, art, or many other domains, so too can mental illness mean schizophrenia, bipolar disorder, depression, or a combination of numerous other diagnoses. Thus, simply saying that creativity is associated with mental illness is like saying in a broad far-reaching statement that "food is associated with feelings." Although you may think that you understand the connection between food and feelings, to appreciate the intricacies of the association you would need to ask a very basic question: "In what way are they connected?" To discover that the smell of peanut butter makes people furious is very different from finding that the taste of popcorn induces sadness – yet studies of famous poets and depression are lumped together with research on college students' divergent thinking performance and anxiety.

The issue of mental health is a controversial topic across all fields of psychology (i.e., Caplan, 1996); within creativity research, it is also a source of general disagreement. Who should be considered mentally ill? One way is to study people who have been diagnosed with a specific mental illness (e.g., Richards et al., 1988) or who are patients at a hospital (e.g., Ghadirian et al., 2001). Another way is to give clinical interviews to possible participants (Andreasen, 1987). Others rely on historiometric methods (see Simonton, this volume) or (as will be discussed later in this chapter) psychometric measures.

As mentioned, "mental illness" is an incredibly broad term. The most work has likely been conducted on people with bipolar disorder or manic depression (see Barrantes-Vidal, this volume; Kaufmann and Kaufmann, this volume). Other frequently studied diagnoses include schizophrenia (see Barrantes-Vidal, this volume; Carson, this volume; Kozbelt et al., this volume), attention-deficit/hyperactivity disorder (see Healey, this volume), unipolar depression (see Djikic and Oatley, this volume), anxiety disorders (see Barrantes-Vidal, this volume), and many others.

Studies of specific populations

Studies of creative people

Some of the most publicized work has measured creativity via group membership. In other words, these creative people may have gone down in history as having contributed to the world or they may be in an occupation traditionally considered creative (such as being an artist or writer). One such technique is using the historiometric method – namely, using biographical information available from historical, literary, or public records to statistically analyze for retrospective data. These studies have the ability to measure a large number of people and look at those with very high levels of creative ability (see Simonton, this volume, for a full review).

Given that creative writers represent one type of noted group, another stream of research is to analyze the writing itself. Thomas and Duke (2007) categorized word usage of eminent authors. They found that the poets showed significantly more cognitive distortion than the fiction writers, hypothesizing that poets were more apt to accept depressive thinking. Similarly, suicidal poets were likely to use words associated with the self (as opposed to the collective) in their poetry, compared with non-suicidal poets (Stirman and Pennebaker, 2001).

The relationship between linguistic patterns and psychopathology is not limited to just poets; some research has found that creative writers in general used more emotion-related words and – specifically – more negative-emotion words such as those related to anger, anxiety, or depression compared with non-writers (Djikic *et al.*, 2006). By that same token the linguistic patterns of eminent writers who were either bipolar or unipolar revealed that bipolar writers used more death-related words than unipolar (Forgeard, 2008). These findings do not necessarily mean that creative people feel these emotions more, but that their choice of words reflects certain emotional patterns.

Studies that test actual members of creative groups are rarer. The most commonly cited work of this nature is by Andreasen (1987; Andreasen and Glick, 1988) and Jamison (1989). Andreasen used structured interviews to analyze 30 creative writers and 30 matched controls. The writers had a higher rate of mental illness as diagnosed from the clinical interview, with a particular tendency toward bipolar and other affective disorders. Based on information from the interviews with the writers and controls, Andreasen also diagnosed first-degree relatives and assessed their creativity (based on any accomplishments or pursuing a "creative" occupation). She concluded that the writers' first-degree relatives were more likely to both be creative and have affective disorders than those of the controls.

Jamison is best known for her popular book *Touched with fire* (1993), which includes some historiometric work. She also did an empirical study on creative groups; she interviewed 47 British artists and writers and found that a significantly higher percentage of them suffered from some form of mental illness, particularly from affective disorders (such as bipolar), than would be expected from population rates (Jamison, 1989).

It is important to note that other researchers have specifically challenged the work of both Andreasen and Jamison (Rothenberg, 1990, 1995). Schlesinger (this volume) highlights many of the arguments against these studies.

More recent work has included large-scale studies of occupation and mental illness (Kyaga *et al.*, 2011, 2012). These studies used Swedish registries to examine the possible connection between creativity and mental illness. "Creative" occupations consisted of jobs in either the arts or science. Kyaga *et al.* (2011) found that people with bipolar disorder and (healthy) relatives of people with schizophrenia or bipolar were more likely to have creative occupations. In a second, larger study, Kyaga *et al.* (2012) found that only bipolar disorder was associated with creative occupations while diagnoses, such as schizophrenia, depression, anxiety, alcoholism, and autism, were not. The only specific occupation to be associated with a wide array of diagnoses was writing.

Other work has also focused on specific occupations. In the Staltaro (2003) study of 43 published poets, she found that, although poets did not score significantly higher than the norm on a measure of current depression, approximately one-third had a history of at least one psychiatric condition and more than half had been in therapy; these figures were notably higher than population rates. Nettle (2006) examined poets, mathematicians, visual artists, and everyday people, finding higher levels of schizotypy in poets and visual artists and lower levels in mathematicians. Another study that found domain-based differences among creative professionals was Rawlings and Locarnini (2008), which gave measures of subclinical psychosis and autism to artists and scientists. For artists, creativity was linked to schizotypy and hypomania. For scientists, these connections were not found; however, a slight connection was found between creativity and autistic tendencies.

Studies of people with mental illness

Empirical studies of people with clinical-level mental illness (like studies of creative professionals) are comparatively rare. Many such studies are discussed in detail in the pages that follow, and we will only highlight a few here (see Kinney and Richards, this volume, for a more complete discussion). Ghadirian *et al.* (2001) compared two groups of hospitalized patients with varying illness severity to test the hypothesis that severity of illness would correlate with level of creativity. They also hypothesized that patients diagnosed with bipolar disorder would score higher on creativity tasks than patients with other mental disorders (such as depression, schizophrenia, and personality disorders). Although no statistical difference in creativity was found between the two groups, there was a difference in creativity by illness severity. Patients diagnosed as severely ill had the lowest levels of creativity, patients who were moderately ill produced the highest creativity scores, and patients in recovery or mildly ill scored in the middle. A different recent study (Soeiro-de-Souza *et al.*, 2011) found that when participants discontinued their medications and were assessed for their current state of bipolar – whether depression, mania, or mixed – those in the manic and mixed stages scored significantly higher in creativity than the depressed participants.

Considerable research into the relationship between psychopathology and creativity has provided evidence that creativity is associated with both schizophrenia spectrum disorder and the other aforementioned affective disturbance (see Barrantes-Vidal, this volume, for a review). These findings may be why some of the early research into the relationship between creativity and psychopathology focused on exacting a relationship with schizophrenia (e.g., Sass and Schuldberg, 2001). However, more recent research suggests that creative ability – in particular, divergent thinking – is lower in those with full-blown schizophrenia (Rodrigue and Perkins, 2012).

Subclinical spectrum models: studies of everyday people

Everyday people are those who are not professionals in their creative domain (though they may be novices or students), nor are they specifically suffering from any mental illness. This population has been heavily studied primarily because of its ease of access – most research participants tend to be college students, and this area is no different. Most of the associations, then, are between subclinical (i.e., clinically insignificant) levels of mental illness and everyday creative performance. These studies can nonetheless give insight into how these larger constructs interrelate.

Creativity has been shown to relate to several mild forms of mental illness. Some studies have examined creative traits in everyday people and "lesser" subclinical disorders, such as hypomania (Furnham *et al.*, 2008) and schizotypy (Abraham and Windmann, 2008; Karimi *et al.*, 2007;

Nettle, 2006; see also Abraham, this volume). Hypomania, as Furnham *et al.* (2008) and Lloyd-Evans *et al.* (2006) argue, is a disorder that is related to bipolar depression – there are periods of elevated mood, but these are less intense and shorter – yet does not necessarily lead to a diagnosis of "mentally ill." People with minor hypomania may be more creative, whereas people with extreme bipolar disorder may be less creative (Richards and Kinney, 1990; see also Kinney and Richards, this volume). Vellante *et al.* (2011) found that undergraduates with traditionally creative majors scored higher on cyclothymic, hyperthymic, and irritable affective temperaments, but not on current psychological distress; they also reported greater involvement in creative activities than those in non-creative disciplines.

Depression and bipolar disorder often coexists with other mental and somatic disorders. Pathological anxiety is one disorder in particular that is commonly comorbid with major depression and is found in about half of those patients with a primary diagnosis of major depression (Barbee, 1998). Given these findings, anxiety's impact on creativity is somewhat surprising. Research on creativity and its relationship to anxiety has shown a positive relationship (Carlsson, 2002); people who are more creative tend also to be more anxious (Carlsson *et al.*, 2000).

There are also many studies on schizotypy, a disorder that is closer to a personality trait than a mental illness (Kwapil *et al.*, 2008; see also Barrantes-Vidal, this volume). Most people at risk for schizophrenia will not develop the disorder, but may nonetheless exhibit some of the symptoms, mannerisms, and features of people with schizophrenia. It has been suggested that there are certain dimensions of schizotypy that are associated with patterns of cognitive and emotional functions (e.g., divergent thinking, heightened emotion) that are common to both creativity and psychopathology (Fisher *et al.*, 2004). Perhaps this is why research has focused on schizotypy, with dimensions such as "aberrant perceptions and beliefs," "cognitive disorganization," "introvertive anhedonia" (the inability to feel pleasure), and "asocial behavior," and how each relates to creativity (Batey and Furnham, 2008). Researchers have found that low levels of schizotypy are related to creativity (Batey and Furnham, 2008). Although research suggests that schizotypy does predict creativity, it may be more of a proxy for certain personality factors such as openness to experience (Miller and Tal, 2007).

Because it is easier to recruit non-clinical samples, researchers can expand the range of variables they assess and recruit larger samples. With many measures and a big sample, researchers can then analyze latent-variable relationships between creativity and symptoms (Silvia and Kimbrel, 2010). One valuable direction for creativity and mental illness research is to explore the full spectrum of disordered symptoms, not just the extreme and more clinically interesting levels (Schuldberg, 2001). Dimensional models of mental illness propose that disorders usually appear as a dimension of adjustment, not as exclusive normal/disordered classes; thus, people can be located on a spectrum instead of being classified as disordered or healthy (Widiger and Lowe, 2007).

Biological and genetic connections

The role of genetics and evolution in mental illness

The roots for many psychological phenomena are found in the complex interplay of nature and nurture, or genetics and the environment in which those genetics are shaped. Susceptibility to depression, schizophrenia, and other mental afflictions are strongly grounded in biology and are triggered by environmental factors. Only in recent years have researchers begun to parse apart the many factors that make up "biological" influences. Kéri (2009) took a genetic approach to studying how the biologic factors of mental illness might correlate with creativity. Kéri assessed intelligence, creativity, and schizotypy in participants who had achieved scientific or artistic importance and who did not have specific psychiatric disorders. He then extracted a sample of blood for genetic testing to compare the relationship between genotypes and creativity scores. The results showed that the neuregulin 1 gene, previously known to be associated with increased risk for psychosis, was also related to higher creativity. Based on his results, Kéri argued that, although the traits linked to mental illness may be maladaptive, the mutation that causes the mental illness may also bring beneficial traits; and he found that high-achieving, creative individuals were the most creative if they had a genetic mutation linked to both brain structure formation and psychosis.

Other studies have found a higher prevalence of mental disorders in relatives of creative individuals, and elevated creative interests in close relatives of psychiatric patients (see Kinney and Richards, this volume, for a review). The highest level of creativity may manifest itself in relatives who are themselves free of psychopathology (Heston, 1966). Some researchers have theorized that the underlying heritable factors responsible for mental illness are also associated with an increase in creativity (Karlsson, 1984), and that the characteristics of certain pathologies (intense focus, outgoingness, introspection, etc.) may enhance creativity.

In addition, a twin study assessing the heritability of certain personality traits that play a role in creative achievement provided support for the relationship between certain traits and achievement (Schermer *et al.*, 2011). Although most research on personality and creativity finds the strongest support for the role of openness to experience, other traits are more or less prominent in different domains. Regardless, the researchers found 44 percent heritability for aggression and 65 percent heritability for extraversion, suggesting a remarkable genetic influence on personality and its subsequent influence on creative and practical ability. These results may suggest that the relationship between creativity and mental illness confers those with creative ability advantages for the genes associated with psychopathology and thus the negative fitness effects are counterbalanced.

Evolutionarily speaking, if a trait has no beneficial adaptation, it should be selected out of the gene pool (see Kozbelt *et al.*, this volume, for a review). Over the past decade, Miller (1998, 2000) has argued that creativity evolved because of conscientious mate choice for cultural displays (e.g., painting, poetry, architecture, etc.). His premise is that the creative products are the results of one's effort to broadcast courtship displays indicative of that person's genetic fitness. Hypothetically, people who are more creative should have more sex partners – yet studies have shown that people with mental illness have fewer sex partners (Avila *et al.*, 2001; Bassett *et al.*, 1996). If one takes the perspective that mental illness enhances creativity, how would this connection influence the number of sexual partners a person has?

An increase in mating success would certainly confer a genetic advantage for the possession of mental illness. By exploring a sample representative of the general population and a targeted sample of artists and poets, Nettle and Clegg (2006) found that the number of sexual partners positively correlated with certain dimensions of schizotypy. These results were also found in non-artistic men (but not women) with higher creative ability and higher symptoms of schizotypy (Beaussart *et al.*, 2012). The schizotypy dimension of unusual experiences was found to have a positive impact on creative activity, which in turn led to a positive effect on the number of partners, while impulsive non-conformity only had a significant positive effect on the number of partners. However, cognitive disorganization had no significant bearing on creativity or number of sexual partners, and introvertive anhedonia had an inhibiting effect on both.

The biological relationship between creativity and mental illness does not exist in a vacuum; certain environmental factors can also influence creativity. For example, Akinola and Mendes (2008) looked at how biological vulnerability, measured as a baseline level of the adrenal steroid DHEAS (dehydroepiandrosterone-sulfate, a neurochemical associated with depression), interacted with the experience of being socially rejected or accepted to influence artistic creativity, and found that persons with lower baseline adrenal steroid experiencing social rejection produced the most creative products (as judged by artists). Participants were screened for baseline DHEAS levels. The authors hypothesized that lower baseline DHEAS levels would increase the negative affect brought about by social rejection. Experimental manipulation was conducted by assigning participants to social acceptance or social rejection groups. Participants' creativity was assessed by local artists' critique of a collage that participants were asked to make after the social acceptance or rejection condition. Results indicated that participants in the social rejection condition produced significantly more creative collages than social acceptance and control conditions. Additionally, participants lower in baseline DHEAS, and thus more susceptible to depression, produced more creative products than participants with higher DHEAS levels, demonstrating that both biology and environment play a role in the link between depression and creativity.

Brain illness and creativity

Even though many studies have focused on the correlates of creativity with mental illness from a cognitive perspective, the creative products produced by patients with brain illness can present an excellent opportunity for understanding not only the underlying mechanisms of cerebral dysfunction but also provide useful information about the creative processes. The degeneration in crucial areas of the brain is characteristic of a category of diseases referred to as frontotemporal dementia. While frontotemporal dementia comes with a long list of negative symptoms, from memory loss to paralysis, in some it also manifests an increased desire to be creative.

The brain regions that correlate with the developing artistic creativity in frontotemporal dementia patients are to a certain extent vague. Case reports have shown that, when frontotemporal dementia is restricted to the anterior temporal lobe and when the integrity of the right prefrontal cortex, posterior temporal, and parietal areas are moderately intact, a new passion for art, music, and even photography has been seen (Midorikawa et al., 2008; Miller and Hou, 2004; Miller et al., 1998, 2000). It has also been shown that lesions in the right medial prefrontal cortex impaired creative originality, whereas lesions in the left parietotemporal cortex were associated with high levels of creative originality (Shamay-Tsoory et al., 2011). Patients with cortical damage in the left hemisphere developed interests in producing creative products; however, their creative ability was limited to nothing more than rudimentary-level creations (Liu *et al.*, 2009).

The brain correlate of the developing artistic creativity in frontotemporal dementia patients is unclear. The disease begins when spindly neurons in the cortex start to die and the brain becomes filled with holes. The frontal and temporal lobes inhibit the creative impulses of the right posterior brain; however, when these brain areas deteriorate, the disease can allow multisensory data such as colors, sounds, and spatial awareness that are in the temporal lobe to be suddenly unleashed into conscious cognition. Thus, the disintegration of inhibitory neural circuits appears to uninhibit activity in other areas. In addition, the result of damage to one part of the brain can stimulate other parts to remodel and become stronger. The culmination is that, in some reported cases, these illnesses can increase interest in creative endeavors but the extent to which dementia patients show creativity depends on the neurological and neuropsychological pattern of the disease (see Palmiero *et al.*, 2012, for a review).

In essence, the disruption of neural networks can lead to the emergence of new artistic talent seemingly overnight. One might wonder then if this emergence of artistic ability observed in these patients is real creativity. De Souza *et al.* (2010) argue that the emergence of artistic talent in dementia patients is by the presence of involuntary behaviors, rather than by the development of creative thinking. In this direction, Rankin *et al.* (2007) revealed that dementia patients did not show a pronounced level of creativity in their art production. However, Schott (2012) suggests that the evidence for creativity is in the creation itself. Regardless, due to the minuscule numbers of the existence of these frontotemporal dementia patients with increased artistic ability, it is likely that these case studies may be the exception rather than the rule (Rankin *et al.*, 2007).

Possible explanations: mediating factors

The impact of personality and related factors

Another approach to study creativity and mental illness is to look at which personality traits may underlie both constructs. Much work has been conducted on personality and creativity, with openness to experience traditionally being most associated (see Feist, 1998, and Djikic and Oatley, this volume, for reviews). Personality has also been studied as it relates to mental illness. For example, a review of empirical work on the effects of bipolar disorder on personality found five recurring positive personality traits, one of which was creativity (Galvez *et al.*, 2011). Other scholars who have looked at the link between bipolar disorder and creativity contend that the two are linked by the common personality traits of openness to experience and impulsivity (Murray and Johnson, 2010). A different study found that both substance abusers and professional actors were higher on both creativity and the psychoticism personality trait compared with a control group of university students (Fink *et al.*, 2012).

Others have proposed different common personality factors. One study of bipolar patients argued that cognitive flexibility and emotionality were the determining factors (Strong *et al.*, 2007). Verhaeghen *et al.* (2005) tested Kaufman and Baer's (2002) hypothesis that creativity may be linked to depression via self-reflective rumination. They found that self-reflective rumination was a stronger correlate to both originality and elaboration than current depression. The researchers suggested that it is not the current mood disorder that contributes most to an individual's creativity but dwelling on past experiences.

Shared vulnerabilities theory

Just as some work has focused on shared personality dimensions, other work has focused on how cognitive traits may mediate creativity and mental illness. Carson (this volume) proposes that this relationship is described by a model of shared biological vulnerability in which some people with an altered mental state have access to cognitive material that other people would normally filter out of their consciousness. Such cognitive traits may protect the individual from the most severe consequences of mental disorder (Fink *et al.*, 2012; Simonton, 2012). In other words, creative individuals tend to not screen things out from conscious awareness that other people would consider to be irrelevant, and are therefore said to have selective attention deficits (Takeuchi *et al.*, 2011).

One of these shared vulnerabilities where schizophrenia and creativity overlap is with latent inhibition, which is defined as an individual's ability to ignore irrelevant input based on previous experience (Lubow, 1989). Schizophrenics and those suffering from schizophrenic-type disorders tend to have lower levels of latent inhibition. In other words, they are less likely to self-censor and monitor unneeded information. One study suggests that low latent inhibition in highly intelligent individuals correlates with higher levels of creativity (Peterson *et al.*, 2002). This finding makes sense in light of the relationship of fluency (being able to come up with many different possible responses) to divergent thinking and creativity. Someone with high levels of latent inhibition would score lower on measures of fluency.

The "mad genius" trap

The relationship between mental illness and creativity has been studied extensively; can public awareness of this work be an impacting factor? Schlesinger (2003) contends that creative people (in her sample, jazz musicians) are aware of the myth yet choose to not focus on it. Romo and Alfonso (2003), however, studied Spanish painters and found that one of the implicit theories that they held about creativity involved the role of psychological disorders. This theory stated that isolation and personal conflicts were at the heart of art. These associations do not necessarily mean that artists desire such a connection. Others have suggested that creators acknowledge the connection and use their art as a form of self-therapy, trying to heal themselves as they express their feelings (e.g., Spaniol, 2001; see also Lewis, this volume).

Kaufman *et al.* (2006) examined how everyday people's own creative ability might be associated with their beliefs in the creativity–mental illness stereotype. They found that people who specifically agreed or disagreed with the myth rated themselves as more creative than did people with a neutral opinion. Yet those with higher measured creativity were more likely to endorse the stereotype. If (as argued by Schlesinger, this volume) the creativity–mental illness stereotype helps non-creative people feel better about their lives, it may also enable some creative people to idealize being mentally ill.

Conclusion

Earlier in this chapter we asked the reader to think about the relationship between creativity and mental illness and in what way the two constructs might be connected. Occam's razor is a key principle in science that argues for parsimony – the simplest explanation is usually the correct one. One negative side effect, however, is that people can see causation where none exists. A common example is the idea that ice cream sales impact crime rates – indeed, when sales go up, so do crime rates. The true connection is a third variable: the weather. In hotter temperatures, people are more likely to buy ice cream – and leave their windows open, inviting in burglars. Another example is the story of when Britain began converting ovens to use natural gas in the 1970s. Suicide rates dropped by a third, and they have stayed at this lower level since. The simplest explanation may be that natural gas makes people happier (or less depressed). Yet the actual connection was that a common method of suicide was gassing – the old coal-based ovens made the process quite simple. The newer ovens emitted fewer fatal fumes (Anderson, 2008). These types of issues are real concerns when it comes to research on creativity and mental illness.

Much of the difficulty in understanding the association of creativity and mental illness lies in the basic problems of comprehensively defining each construct. The underlying phenomena of creativity and mental illness are multifaceted and interwoven. The nature of creativity, with varying domains, measures, and levels of eminence, and the nature of mental illness, with spectrums of severity and difficulty in exact diagnoses, makes it an unwieldy topic to study, akin to a sack full of squirming, two-headed kittens. We doubt there will ever be a final, one-size-fits-all, "mad genius" conclusion. The other chapters in the book approach this key question from many different approaches and perspectives, and shed more light on the question. If we cannot hope to conclusively solve a debate, then there is still the promise of moving ever closer to an answer.

References

Abraham, A. and Windmann, S. (2008). Selective information processing advantages in creative cognition as a function of schizotypy. *Creativity Research Journal*, 20(1), 1–6.

Akinola, M. and Mendes, W. B. (2008). The dark side of creativity: Biological vulnerability and negative emotions lead to greater artistic creativity. *Personality and Social Psychology Bulletin*, 34(12), 1677–1686.

Amabile, T. M. (1996). *Creativity in context*. Boulder, CO: Westview Press.

Anderson, S. (2008). The urge to end it all. *New York Times*, July 6. www.nytimes.com/2008/07/06/magazine/06suicide-t.html, last accessed March 15, 2014.

Andreasen, N. C. (1987). Creativity and mental illness. *American Journal of Psychiatry*, 144(10), 1288–1292.

Andreasen, N. C. and Glick, I. D. (1988). Bipolar affective disorder and creativity: Implications and clinical management. *Comprehensive Psychiatry*, 29(3), 207–217.

Avila, M., Thaker, G. and Adami, H. (2001). Genetic epidemiology and schizophrenia: A study of reproductive fitness. *Schizophrenia Research*, 47(2), 233–241.

Barbee, J. G. (1998). Mixed symptoms and syndromes of anxiety and depression: Diagnostic, prognostic, and etiologic issues. *Annals of Clinical Psychiatry*, 10(1), 15–29.

Barron, F. (1955). The disposition toward originality. *Journal of Abnormal and Social Psychology*, 51(3), 478.

Bassett, A. S., Bury, A., Hodgkinson, K. A. and Honer, W. G. (1996). Reproductive fitness in familial schizophrenia. *Schizophrenia Research*, 21(3), 151–160.

Batey, M. and Furnham, A. (2008). The relationship between measures of creativity and schizotypy. *Personality and Individual Differences*, 45(8), 816–821.

Beaussart, M. L., Kaufman, S. B. and Kaufman, J. C. (2012). Creative activity, personality, mental illness, and short-term mating success. *The Journal of Creative Behavior*, 46(3), 151–167.

Caplan, P. J. (1996). *They say you're crazy: How the world's most powerful psychiatrists decide who's normal*. Cambridge, MA: Da Capo Press.

Carlsson, I. (2002). Anxiety and flexibility of defense related to high or low creativity. *Creativity Research Journal*, 14(3–4), 341–349.

Carlsson, I., Wendt, P. E. and Risberg, J. (2000). On the neurobiology of creativity: Differences in frontal activity between high and low creative subjects. *Neuropsychologia*, 38(6), 873–885.

de Souza, L. C., Volle, E., Bertoux, M., Czernecki, V., Funkiewiez, A., Allali, G. and Dubois, B. (2010). Poor creativity in frontotemporal dementia: A window into the neural bases of the creative mind. *Neuropsychologia*, 48(13), 3733–3742.

Djikic, M., Oatley, K. and Peterson, J. B. (2006). The bitter-sweet labor of emoting: The linguistic comparison of writers and physicists. *Creativity Research Journal*, 18(2), 191–197.

Feist, G. J. (1998). A meta-analysis of personality in scientific and artistic creativity. *Personality and Social Psychology Review*, 2(4), 290–309.

Fink, A., Slamar-Halbedl, M., Unterrainer, H. F. and Weiss, E. M. (2012). Creativity: Genius, madness, or a combination of both? *Psychology of Aesthetics, Creativity, and the Arts*, 6(1), 11.

Fisher, J. E., Mohanty, A., Herrington, J. D., Koven, N. S., Miller, G. A. and Heller, W. (2004). Neuropsychological evidence for dimensional schizotypy: Implications for creativity and psychopathology. *Journal of Research in Personality*, 38(1), 24–31.

Forgeard, M. (2008). Linguistic styles of eminent writers suffering from unipolar and bipolar mood disorder. *Creativity Research Journal*, 20(1), 81–92.

Furnham, A., Batey, M., Anand, K. and Manfield, J. (2008). Personality, hypomania, intelligence and creativity. *Personality and Individual Differences*, 44(5), 1060–1069.

Galvez, J. F., Thommi, S. and Ghaemi, S. N. (2011). Positive aspects of mental illness: A review in bipolar disorder. *Journal of Affective Disorders*, 128(3), 185–190.

Ghadirian, A., Gregoire, P. and Kosmidis, H. (2001). Creativity and the evolution of psychopathologies. *Creativity Research Journal*, 13(2), 145–148.

Greenberg, N. (2004). The beast at play: The neuroethology of creativity. In R. Clements and L. Fiorentino (Eds.), *The child's right to play: A global approach* (pp. 309–327). Westport, CT: Praeger Press.

Heston, L. L. (1966). Psychiatric disorders in foster home reared children of schizophrenic mothers. *British Journal of Psychiatry*, 112(489), 819–825.

Jamison, K. R. (1989). Mood disorders and patterns of creativity in British writers and artists. *Psychiatry: Interpersonal and Biological Processes*, 52(2), 125–134.

Jamison, K. R. (1993). *Touched with fire: Manic depressive illness and the artistic temperament*. New York: Free Press.

Karimi, Z., Windmann, S., Güntürkün, O. and Abraham, A. (2007). Insight problem solving in individuals with high versus low schizotypy. *Journal of Research in Personality*, 41(2), 473–480.

Karlsson, J. L. (1984). Creative intelligence in relatives of mental patients. *Hereditas*, 100(1), 83–86.

Kaufman, J. C. and Baer, J. E. (2002). I bask in dreams of suicide: Mental illness, poetry, and women. *Review of General Psychology*, 6(3), 271–286.

Kaufman, J. C. and Baer, J. E. (2005). *Creativity across domains: Faces of the muse.* Mahwah, NJ: Lawrence Erlbaum Associates.

Kaufman, J. C., Bromley, M. L. and Cole, J. C. (2006). Insane, poetic, lovable: Creativity and endorsement of the "mad genius" stereotype. *Imagination, Cognition and Personality*, 26(1), 149–161.

Kaufman, J. C., Plucker, J. A. and Russell, C. M. (2012). Identifying and assessing creativity as a component of giftedness. *Journal of Psychoeducational Assessment*, 30(1), 60–73.

Kéri, S. (2009). Genes for psychosis and creativity: A promoter polymorphism of the neuregulin 1 gene is related to creativity in people with high intellectual achievement. *Psychological Science*, 20(9), 1070–1073.

Kwapil, T. R., Barrantes-Vidal, N. and Silvia, P. J. (2008). The dimensional structure of the Wisconsin schizotypy scales: Factor identification and construct validity. *Schizophrenia Bulletin*, 34(3), 444–457.

Kyaga, S., Landén, M., Boman, M., Hultman, C. M., Långström, N. and Lichtenstein, P. (2012). Mental illness, suicide and creativity: 40-year prospective total population study. *Journal of Psychiatric Research*. doi:10.1016/j.jpsychires.2012.09.010

Kyaga, S., Lichtenstein, P., Boman, M., Hultman, C., Långström, N. and Landén, M. (2011). Creativity and mental disorder: Family study of 300,000 people with severe mental disorder. *British Journal of Psychiatry*, 199(5), 373–379.

Liu, A., Werner, K., Roy, S., Trojanowski, J. Q., Morgan-Kane, U., Miller, B. L. and Rankin, K. P. (2009). A case study of an emerging visual artist with frontotemporal lobar degeneration and amyotrophic lateral sclerosis. *Neurocase*, 15(3), 235–247.

Lloyd-Evans, R., Batey, M. and Furnham, A. (2006). Bipolar disorder and creativity: Investigating a possible link. *Advances in Psychology Research*, 40, 111–142.

Lubow, R. E. (1989). *Latent inhibition and conditioned attention theory* (Vol. 9). New York: Cambridge University Press.

Midorikawa, A., Fukutake, T. and Kawamura, M. (2008). Dementia and painting in patients from different cultural backgrounds. *European Neurology*, 60(5), 224–229.

Miller, B. L. and Hou, C. E. (2004). Portraits of artists: Emergence of visual creativity in dementia. *Archives of Neurology*, 61(6), 842.

Miller, B. L., Boone, K., Cummings, J. L., Read, S. L. and Mishkin, F. (2000). Functional correlates of musical and visual ability in frontotemporal dementia. *British Journal of Psychiatry*, 176(5), 458–463.

Miller, B. L., Cummings, J., Mishkin, F., Boone, K., Prince, F., Ponton, M. and Cotman, C. (1998). Emergence of artistic talent in frontotemporal dementia. *Neurology*, 51(4), 978–982.

Miller, G. F. (1998). How mate choice shaped human nature: A review of sexual selection and human evolution. In C. Crawford and D. Krebs (Eds.), *Handbook of evolutionary psychology: Ideas, issues, and applications* (pp. 87–129). Mahwah, NJ: Lawrence Erlbaum.

Miller, G. F. (2000). *The mating mind: How sexual selection shaped the evolution of human nature.* New York: Doubleday.

Miller, G. F. and Tal, I. R. (2007). Schizotypy versus openness and intelligence as predictors of creativity. *Schizophrenia Research*, 93(1), 317–324.

Murray, G. and Johnson, S. L. (2010). The clinical significance of creativity in bipolar disorder. *Clinical Psychology Review*, 30(6), 721–732.

Nettle, D. (2006). The evolution of personality variation in humans and other animals. *American Psychologist*, 61(6), 622.

Nettle, D. and Clegg, H. (2006). Schizotypy, creativity and mating success in humans. *Proceedings of the Royal Society B: Biological Sciences*, 273(1586), 611–615.

Palmiero, M., Di Giacomo, D. and Passafiume, D. (2012). Creativity and dementia: A review. *Cognitive Processing*, 13(3), 193–209.

Peterson, J. B., Smith, K. W. and Carson, S. (2002). Openness and extraversion are associated with reduced latent inhibition: Replication and commentary. *Personality and Individual Differences*, 33(7), 1137–1147.

Plucker, J. A., Beghetto, R. A. and Dow, G. T. (2004). Why isn't creativity more important to educational psychologists? Potentials, pitfalls, and future directions in creativity research. *Educational Psychologist*, 39(2), 83–96.

Rankin, K. P., Liu, A. A., Howard, S., Slama, H., Hou, C. E., Shuster, K. and Miller, B. L. (2007). A case-controlled study of altered visual art production in Alzheimer's and FTLD. *Cognitive and Behavioral Neurology: Official Journal of the Society for Behavioral and Cognitive Neurology*, 20(1), 48.

Rawlings, D. and Locarnini, A. (2008). Dimensional schizotypy, autism, and unusual word associations in artists and scientists. *Journal of Research in Personality*, 42(2), 465–471.

Richards, R. and Kinney, D. K. (1990). Mood swings and creativity. *Creativity Research Journal*, 3(3), 202–217.

Richards, R., Kinney, D. K., Benet, M. and Merzel, A. P. (1988). Assessing everyday creativity: Characteristics of the Lifetime Creativity Scales and validation with three large samples. *Journal of Personality and Social Psychology*, 54(3), 476–485.

Rodrigue, A. L. and Perkins, D. R. (2012). Divergent thinking abilities across the schizophrenic spectrum and other psychological correlates. *Creativity Research Journal*, 24(2–3), 163–168.

Romo, M. and Alfonso, V. (2003). Implicit theories of Spanish painters. *Creativity Research Journal*, 15(4), 409–415.

Rothenberg, A. (1990). *Creativity and madness: New findings and old stereotypes.* Baltimore, MD: Johns Hopkins University Press.

Rothenberg, A. (1995). Creativity and mental illness. *American Journal of Psychiatry*, 152(5), 815–816.

Sass, L. A. and Schuldberg, D. (2001). Introduction to the special issue: Creativity and the schizophrenia spectrum. *Creativity Research Journal*, 13(1), 1–4.

Schermer, J. A., Johnson, A. M., Vernon, P. A. and Jang, K. L. (2011). The relationship between personality and self-report abilities: A behaviour-genetic analysis. *Journal of Individual Differences*, 32(1), 47–53.

Schlesinger, J. (2003). Issues in creativity and madness. Part three: Who cares? *Ethical Human Sciences and Services*, 5(2), 149–152.

Schott, G. (2012). Pictures as a neurological tool: Lessons from enhanced and emergent artistry in brain disease. *Brain*, 135(6), 1947–1963.

Schuldberg, D. (2001). Six subclinical spectrum traits in normal creativity. *Creativity Research Journal*, 13(1), 5–16.

Shamay-Tsoory, S., Adler, N., Aharon-Peretz, J., Perry, D. and Mayseless, N. (2011). The origins of originality: The neural bases of creative thinking and originality. *Neuropsychologia*, 49(2), 178–185.

Silvia, P. J. and Kimbrel, N. A. (2010). A dimensional analysis of creativity and mental illness: Do anxiety and depression symptoms predict creative cognition, creative accomplishments, and creative self-concepts? *Psychology of Aesthetics, Creativity, and the Arts*, 4(1), 2–10.

Simonton, D. K. (2012). Creative genius as a personality phenomenon: Definitions, methods, findings, and issues. *Social and Personality Psychology Compass*, 6(9), 691–706.

Simonton, D. K. (2013). What is a creative idea? Little-c versus Big-c creativity. In K. Thomas and J. Chan (Eds.), *Handbook of research on creativity* (pp. 69–83). Cheltenham, UK, and Northampton, USA: Edward Elgar Publishing.

Soeiro-de-Souza, M. G., Dias, V. V., Bio, D. S., Post, R. M. and Moreno, R. A. (2011). Creativity and executive function across manic, mixed and depressive episodes in bipolar I disorder. *Journal of Affective Disorders*, 135(1), 292–297.

Spaniol, S. (2001). Art and mental illness: Where is the link? *The Arts in Psychotherapy*, 28(4), 221–231.

Staltaro, S. O. (2003). *Contemporary American poets, poetry writing, and depression*. Unpublished doctoral dissertation, Alliant International University at Fresno.

Stirman, S. W. and Pennebaker, J. W. (2001). Word use in the poetry of suicidal and nonsuicidal poets. *Psychosomatic Medicine*, 63, 517–522.

Sternberg, R. J., Kaufman, J. C. and Pretz, J. E. (2003). A propulsion model of creative leadership. *The Leadership Quarterly*, 14(4), 455–473.

Strong, C. M., Nowakowska, C., Santosa, C. M., Wang, P. W., Kraemer, H. C. and Ketter, T. A. (2007). Temperament–creativity relationships in mood disorder patients, healthy controls and highly creative individuals. *Journal of Affective Disorders*, 100(1), 41–48.

Takeuchi, H., Taki, Y., Hashizume, H., Sassa, Y., Nagase, T., Nouchi, R. and Kawashima, R. (2011). Failing to deactivate: The association between brain activity during a working memory task and creativity. *Neuroimage*, 55(2), 681–687.

Thomas, K. M. and Duke, M. (2007). Depressed writing: Cognitive distortions in the works of depressed and nondepressed poets and writers. *Psychology of Aesthetics, Creativity, and the Arts*, 1(4), 204.

Vellante, M., Zucca, G., Preti, A., Sisti, D., Rocchi, M. B. L., Akiskal, K. K. and Akiskal, H. S. (2011). Creativity and affective temperaments in non-clinical professional artists: An empirical psychometric investigation. *Journal of Affective Disorders*, 135(1), 28–36.

Verhaeghen, P., Joormann, J. and Khan, R. (2005). Why we sing the blues: The relation between self-reflective rumination, mood, and creativity. *Emotion*, 5(2), 226–232.

Widiger, T. A. and Lowe, J. R. (2007). Five-factor model assessment of personality disorder. *Journal of Personality Assessment*, 89(1), 16–29.

4   Building connections on sand: the cautionary chapter

Judith Schlesinger

There is a widespread and long-running belief that great talent and great psychopathology are closely related; it dictates that no one receives the gift of genius without the curse of depression, and probably mania as well. But the truth is this: There is no hard proof that highly creative people are more susceptible to mental disorder than anybody else. Despite centuries of professional attention, the link between creativity and madness (C&M) remains more stereotype than science.

In the absence of compelling empirical evidence, C&M advocates have had to assemble their argument from other sources. These include weak studies that are cited more often than they are read, and acquire their clout from repetition, rather than valid results; the (mis-)reported opinions of Greek philosophers; melodramatic literary accounts of creative ecstasy and anguish; and lists of geniuses who are diagnosed after death, mostly from second- and third-hand reports from their contemporaries (data which, in other settings, would be known simply as "gossip").

C&M do have basic things in common: they each involve behavior that differs from the norm, and each is intuitively recognized by observers whenever they appear. Unfortunately, they also share an ambiguous and confusing nature. This chapter will discuss why the connection between them is so flimsy, why it is likely to remain so, and why the science finally doesn't matter, because the notion of the "mad genius" – the artist who is both brilliant and doomed – is too popular to ever disappear.

Definition dilemma: "C"

There are so many different ideas of creativity that "those in the field become estranged from each other over semantic issues and those outside the field become distanced because it appears no one in the field can even define creativity" (Plucker and Makel, 2010, p. 48). One reaction to the confusion is to organize it, such as filing the theories into ten major categories; but even these authors choose to omit the theories that involve mental illness, personality, biology, and cultural differences (Kozbelt *et al.*, 2010). Another approach is to detour around the problem by not defining creativity at all, and nobody seems to mind.

But the effort to decode creativity continues. This keeps numerous fundamental issues in play, such as where its most crucial determinants might be found. Some say they are internal, in personality and thought, while others point to external influences like incentives, competition, and environment. There is general agreement about the importance of "novelty," "usefulness," and "quality," but not about who gets to judge these things. Should they be experts? Peers? And by what criteria (see Kaufman and Baer, 2012)? Besides, is it even possible to standardize the evaluation of such ephemeral variables? The relative contributions of talent, experience, and mentors are also on the table, together with still-unproven genetic speculation and psychodynamic explanations, like Freud's belief that creativity is just a compensation prize for the sexually frustrated.

This broad range of variables has generated an impressive array of assessments to match. There are numerous personality scales, activity checklists, drawing exercises, teacher rating instruments, attitude indicators, measures of independence and confidence, and tests of divergent thinking and remote associations. When surveying the ever-multiplying options of topics and tools, it is hard to remember that only one phenomenon – creativity – is the target.

Definition dilemma: "M"

The "M" side of the equation presents a similar problem. Despite the world's extensive reliance on the *Diagnostic and Statistical Manual of Mental Disorders* (*DSM*) (APA, 2013) to classify all troublesome human behaviors, psychiatric categories are fully as hypothetical as any aspect of creativity. The truth is that, despite the authority implicit in its quasi-medical language, diagnosis has always been an impressionistic enterprise. Long an open secret in the profession itself, this has not been general knowledge until fairly recently.

A major shift occurred in 2003, when the American Psychiatric Association (APA) publicly conceded that they could not verify a single biological cause for any *DSM* disorder (APA, 2003; Schlesinger, 2012). They still cannot, but this has not slowed the proliferation of new ones, all of which seem to require pharmaceutical remedies. In fact, the troublesome intimacy between psychiatry and the drug companies has been the subject of a growing journalistic chorus in the past decade (see Schlesinger, 2012, pp. 41–46).

Traditionally, the "madness" most commonly tied to creativity has been bipolar disorder, which, when first proposed nearly two centuries ago, was considered as debilitating as schizophrenia. Over time its definition has gradually become so elastic, with so many possible levels and gradations, that it captures virtually anyone who's ever had a mood. But there is no test for it, or any other disorder, for that matter: "in truth, the biological underpinnings of madness remain as mysterious as ever" (Whitaker, 2002, p. 285). As Szasz puts it, "psychiatrists do not even perform physical examinations . . . their claim that they treat brain diseases is manifestly absurd" (2001, p. 84). Instead, clinicians use observational criteria to decide whether the verdict will be "bipolar" or one of its milder variants – "cyclothymic personality," perhaps, or some shade of "spectrum disorder" or "shadow syndrome."

Without physiological detection, the decision turns on the subjective appraisal of clients' current level of distress and impairment, as well as the retroactive analysis of qualifying behavior they may have shown at any time in the past. There may be paperwork and family members to consult, although written records are only other people's judgment calls, and family members may well have agendas of their own. The diagnostic challenge, already formidable, automatically escalates when clinicians must evaluate someone they are meeting for the first time, which often happens, particularly in hospital and emergency settings when there is no time to spare.

In recent years, the flexibility of psychiatric classification has facilitated some abrupt spikes in population rates of psychopathology. Such "false epidemics" have occurred with attention deficit disorder (ADD) and autism as well as bipolar disorder (Frances, 2009). These have sent culture-watchers scurrying for explanations in childrearing practices and food additives, when the more likely cause is the overgenerous application of diagnostic guidelines – and too often for personal gain. For instance, it is hard to trust the validity of a disorder when one psychiatrist was responsible for the 4,000 percent increase in pediatric diagnoses, and was handsomely paid for it by the company that makes the remedy (Carey, 2007; Harris, 2008; *What Killed Rebecca Riley?* [2007]).

As the APA prepared the newest revision of its manual, the *DSM-5* (APA, 2013), many mental health professionals, including the psychiatrists who guided the previous two editions, were publicly warning that the proposed lowering of diagnostic thresholds would sweep even more normal people over the doorway into pathology. Resounding from the halls of the "other" APA (i.e., the American Psychological Association), there were impassioned calls for petitions, boycotts, and independent reviews of the manual before it went to press in May of 2013. None of those inspired confidence in the "science" of psychiatry.

Problems linking C&M

With all the conjecture about C&M definition and measurement, all researchers are free to follow their hunches and seek their answers in a different place. This has naturally resulted in a jumble of experimental variables, designs, populations, and methodologies. One solution is to pile all the mismatched studies together and claim the result is cumulative, and "points to" a common outcome. While this may be the best shot at clarity, it's not the same thing as actual proof.

Another way to shore up C&M is to condense creativity into a single, powerful force, which helps underscore its similarity to madness. Unfortunately, this simplification implies that writing a play requires the same mechanisms as inventing a computer game or composing a symphony, which seems reductionist, at best. It also negates the important psychological differences that probably exist among playwrights, techies, and musicians. Psychiatrist William Frosch (1996) puts it well: "The impulse to create and the skills necessary to each of the tasks are likely to differ. It may be that we are linking many kinds of acts because they are special and mystifying, not because they are the same" (p. 507).

One practical response has been to split creativity into "domain general" and "domain specific." Although these territories are still being mapped, at least the "specific" model reflects the growing recognition that creativity is not a one-size-fits-all phenomenon. There is also increasing interest in the "everyday" variety, which dials down the abilities of genius to more humble levels, and provides less serious mental disorders to match (Richards, 2009). Apparently, psychopathology of some sort must always be included.

But such gradations are lost on those who believe that all highly creative individuals live approximately the same emotional life, and must therefore suffer the same fate. This conviction is regularly reinforced by the ongoing media parade of the talented and doomed; there seems to be no end to the procession, the spectators who line up to watch it, or the pundits who reliably pronounce how predictable it is. No one would expect all teachers or dentists to feel and behave the same way, but then their psychological travails are less romantic, and rarely draw the spotlight.

Another simplistic C&M belief is that great creativity is a continuous wellspring that is always available to those who are blessed with it; this makes it inconceivable that it would not be flowing all the time. From this perspective, creative idleness never comes from anything so mundane as a temporary lack of inspiration; rather, any lapses in productivity must be caused by involuntary interference – most probably, some crippling underlying pathology. Moreover, portraying "C" as mysterious and uncontrollable makes it seem more like "M," and thereby chalks up one more argument for their connection.

The chosen "M" is bipolar disorder because its defining mood vacillations so neatly accommodate the alternating joys and frustrations of artistic effort. But fitting a particular client's history to the diagnosis is a much messier procedure. Given the lack of quantifiable variables, all judgments must pass through the intricate, idiosyncratic filter of each clinician's training, experience, and theoretical bias, with unpredictable input from their personalities, values, and even their own mood at the time of assessment. As noted earlier, some decisions may be even influenced by the financial incentives for finding a particular "M."

With all this amorphous complication, it's no wonder that inter-clinician agreement is not known to be high (Beutler, 2000; Eysenck, 1995; Faust and Ziskin, 1988; Sleek, 1996). Furthermore, even if bipolar disorder is firmly decreed, it is still difficult to predict, because its course will fluctuate from one person to another. Treatments can vary widely as well, because some people benefit from the usual drugs, some do not, and still others manage to improve or even recover with no medication at all.

Among other disparate variables, research has focused on gender, age at first episode, use of marijuana, and the role of the family in affecting the progression of the disorder. For example, it is no surprise that, when people hospitalized for bipolar disorder return home, their future stability is imperiled by a hostile and critical family (Miklowitz, 2007). But it was only in 2009 that an international task force produced guidelines for describing bipolar course and outcome – before that, researchers lacked standardized nomenclature even for purposes of discussion (Tohen *et al.*, 2009). All of this argues against viewing bipolar disorder as any kind of reliable and standardized entity.

In sum, considering all the guesswork involved with both C&M, forging a scientific link between them is like trying to get two clouds to stick together. (This is even harder when the person in question has been dead for two hundred years, as we will soon see.) But that hasn't stopped anyone from trying.

The wobbly tripod

Most C&M researchers maintain that a solid empirical foundation already exists, pointing to the efforts of psychiatrists Nancy Andreasen and Arnold Ludwig, and psychologist Kay Redfield Jamison. Virtually everything written in the past generation begins with references to these three people, although, as we will see, their contributions are much less definitive than their popularity would suggest. One explanation is that, rather than reading this work for themselves, many psychologists are only passing the citations along, trusting that someone else, earlier in the chain, has already checked them for flaws.

The first to be published was Andreasen's (1987) exploration of mood disorders at the Iowa Writers' Workshop. Often referred to as the "landmark" study, it is mentioned frequently in the popular and professional press as a pivotal moment in the quest to equate C&M. So is Jamison's 1989 article, which claims that artists and writers are more prone to pathology than everyone else; this was such welcome news that it was announced in *Time Magazine* 5 years before the study appeared in a more professional setting (Leo, 1984). Both these studies are invoked over 20 years later because nothing equally compelling has appeared in the interim; their conclusions have become so dogmatic that they completely obscure all their flaws in methodology and design.

And there are many such flaws, as discussed elsewhere (see Schlesinger, 2009, 2012). For now, a summary would include: using too few participants for meaningful results; enlisting people who are personally known to the sole interviewer and judge; relying on idiosyncratic measurements of mood disorders; and generalizing the results from highly specialized samples to the population at large. Andreasen, who took 15 years to complete her study of thirty people, developed her own interview to assess pathology, but did not publish it with her article. For Jamison's group of forty-seven, her identification of mood disorder was simply the participants' word that he was treated for it (they were all male); aside from being a unique definition, this assumes a perfect correspondence between complaint and diagnosis that is unreliable, at best (see Lish *et al.*, 1994).

To her credit, Andreasen has freely admitted her lack of significant results, but insists that this pales before the fact that two of her participants committed suicide (Andreasen, 1986, 1987). While tragedy does add some clinical urgency to the discussion, it does not trump the need for scientific rigor – arguably, it even increases it. In Jamison's case, there was no control group at all; this prevented her from using conventional statistics, such as tests of significance, forcing her to report only simple percentages instead.

Ironically, this more primitive method led to Jamison's most celebrated conclusion: that fully 50 percent of poets have bipolar disorder. But unless you read the original study, which is extremely difficult to find, you'd never know that this 50 percent represents only *nine* people. Similarly, the reported 12.5 percent of visual artists who rely on mood-disorder medication actually refers to just *one* person. Neither of these facts is reported by the media – either because they have no idea, or because it blunts the sensational impact of the study's results.

Such empirical drawbacks are too often overlooked by C&M researchers as well. One exception is Harvard psychiatrist Albert Rothenberg, who, along with his team, spent 25 years directly studying highly creative people, and personally clocked over 2,000 hours of interviews. Working with the head reference librarian at Yale, he catalogued nearly 10,000 scientific writings on creativity from 1566 to 1973 (Rothenberg and Greenberg, 1974); his later book, published in 1990, was also one of the first to comprehensively tackle the C&M mythology.

In this later book, Rothenberg criticizes Andreasen for her "inexplicit and misleading creativity criteria" and Jamison for her "questionable" sample selection and hypothesis testing. Their numbers, he writes, are "far too small to draw adequate conclusions." He also points out how the eagerness of C&M advocates gives these studies more credence than they deserve: "The need to believe in a connection between creativity and madness appears to be so strong that affirmations are welcomed and treated rather uncritically" (Rothenberg, 1990, pp. 150–153). In the quarter century of his own research, Rothenberg found that creative people reliably shared just one psychological characteristic: the motivation to create. Not a mood disorder in sight (Schlesinger, 2012).

The third leg of the C&M tripod has serious weaknesses as well. This is Arnold Ludwig's book, *The price of greatness: Resolving the creativity and madness controversy* (1995), another source that seems to be cited far more often than it is read. In this instance, people may not feel any need to read it, because the case is made right on the cover: The title confirms that people must pay for their exceptional gift, while the subtitle promises that this is the book that puts the issue to rest. Certainly its title appears more often in the literature than any discussion of its contents.

But any researcher who does acquire a copy will be impressed by its fifty-five pages of charts and graphs – so long as they are not examined too closely. A careful look reveals that, in seeking the common denominators of greatness in 1,004 celebrity biographies – all of which are presumably unbiased and accurate – Ludwig invents his own collection of intangible factors such as "anger at mother" and "oddness" with no explanation of how these variables might be detected and defined (Ludwig, 1995, pp. 260, 268). Finally, it is problematic that Ludwig lumps together labor leader Samuel Gompers and politician Winston Churchill together with magician Harry Houdini and musician Marvin Gaye, as if their psychological dynamics were interchangeable.

Ludwig (1995) contains some confusing contradictions as well. One is the report that musical entertainers are "relatively free from depression," which is followed, two sentences later, by the claim that they're also "more likely to attempt suicide" (for more details, see Schlesinger, 2009, pp. 68–69). But perhaps the most baffling assertion is Ludwig's straight-forward pronouncement that "mental illness does not seem necessary for exceptional achievement" (p. 157). If this is indeed what he discovered, why is his book always cited as proof of the opposite position? Once again, perhaps too few people are getting past the triumph implicit in the title.

Historical precedent

At this point, the question becomes "What keeps the C&M link so central on the public stage if it's so full of holes?" But any stereotype can be sustained indefinitely on a small grain of truth, particularly when it carries a message as comforting as this one: You may not have these people's talent, but at least you don't share their awful burdens.

The fear that creativity can be dangerous owes much of its power from its longevity, because it dates all the way back to ancient Athens as well as early mythical warnings about punishing humans who reach too high (Schlesinger, 2012). Quoting Plato and Aristotle provides an aura of timelessness and prestige, which makes it seem that the connection between C&M has always been "known." But enlisting these sages requires twisting their original intent.

For example, it is common to conflate Plato's "divine" madness with the "clinical" kind we refer to today. Plato was describing a lucky drop-in by the muses that inspired artists and enabled them to create. This was a longed-for event, not negative or crazy in any way. It was also temporary, because, once the product was done – the poem written, the song composed – the gods would disappear, with no guarantee they would ever return (Kris and Kurz, 1979; Padel, 1995; Plato, 2002). Yet over the centuries, this privileged selection changed into an inherent vulnerability. In the Middle Ages, when any kind of altered state was suspect, it was easy to turn this "divine visitation" into "demon possession." Later, it was another short step for this diabolical creative excitement to turn into "mental illness."

A similar distortion occurred with Aristotle's "melancholia," which did not mean "depressed" in his original use of the term. The word lit-erally means "black bile," and refers to one of the four vital saps that flow through the body; in ancient Greece, significant imbalances among these fluids could cause disease, but a bit more of one kind than the oth-ers simply created temperament. For Aristotle, the melancholic variety provided the ideal launching pad for genius.

He describes an optimal melancholic state – a kind of Goldilocks compromise in which the black bile is neither too hot nor too cold, but just right. In his *Problemata*, he explains that these lucky melancholics "have more practical wisdom and are less eccentric and in many respects superior to others" (Schlesinger, 2012, p. 59; Aristotle, 1984, book 30, page 1501, lines 39–41, and book 30, page 1502, lines 30–40; Northwood, 2010, n.d.).

It took centuries for Aristotle's benign melancholia to darken into depression. One milestone that moved it along was the new translation of the classics that was supplied by Ficino, the Renaissance scholar. He identified melancholia as not only depression but a sure sign of genius as well. It was no coincidence that Ficino himself was depressed; just to assure his anointing, he further insisted that all geniuses were born under the sign of Saturn, as he was (Radden, 2000; Wittkower and Wittkower, 1963).

In 1621, Ficino's self-serving interpretations were reinforced in the best-selling *The anatomy of melancholy* (Burton, 1621). In this nearly 1,000-page tome, British author Robert Burton wrote voluminously about his own depression, claiming that only his creative efforts kept his sadness at bay. The C&M link got a huge boost from these two creative individuals, both of them driven by the need to glorify their own depression – a motivation that continues in many quarters today.

Another brick in the foundation came from the Romantic period of nineteenth-century Europe, where the mad genius became a glamorous cultural icon. The flamboyant accounts of poets and writers have been used ever since to "prove" that art demands passionate extremes of its creators, requiring a kind of emotional whiplash between ecstasy and despair. For example, when the English poet Lord Byron writes, "We of the craft are all crazy," it becomes "evidence" that this is true of every other creator, even though Byron was notorious for his dramatic posturing and exaggerations.

All this wild emotionality flourished for about 50 years until the early scientists made it into something suspect. As the century turned, the word was that geniuses, criminals, and the insane were all physiologically related, and these traits traveled together down the generations. One influential voice belonged to the Italian criminologist Cesare Lombroso, who claimed that people of high ability were pasty, emaciated, and sexually sterile, with "prominent ears and inadequate beard" (1895, pp. 5–37, vi). Lombroso is cited today to establish a long "scientific" pedigree for C&M, but the specific nonsense he actually wrote is rarely revealed (Schlesinger, 2012, pp. 77–81).

The hostility that informs the research of Lombroso and his contemporaries still echoes in our time, and probably for the same reason: Condescending to genius helps neutralize any jealousy their talents provoke. Moreover, bringing our icons down also brings them closer – even Zeus, king of the gods, was forever changing his lovers into animals to avoid the wrath of his wife. His anxieties made him more familiar, and his power less threatening (Schlesinger, 2002b, p. 140). Making the creatives "less than" helps to blunt the envy of genius with the distancing and diminishing mechanisms of pathology and pity (Schlesinger, 2002b, p. 141; see also "genius envy," Schlesinger, 2012, pp. 143–148).

There is new experimental evidence for the intuitive notion that the more insecure people feel about their own lives, the more they will resent those who are exceptional (Mueller et al., 2012). Envy also pollutes social attitudes toward "giftedness," a concept that rivals creativity in its number of synonyms and definitions (Subotnik et al., 2011, pp. 8–9). Here, the myth that great talent is magical, and requires little effort, helps feed the perception that gifted children can make it on their own, and therefore need no special programs to help them.

Questionable techniques

As already noted, diagnosing bipolar disorder is difficult enough when client and clinician share a time and place – imagine the struggle when the client has been dead for centuries. Now clinicians must conduct their retrospective examination, or "psychological autopsy," by gathering up the few facts they can find, and using their imagination to fill in the rest.

Given that helpful medical reports are rare, the clinical evidence is usually derived from three main sources: (1) letters to, from, and between the person's relatives, especially those who express anxiety about the target's behavior; (2) the person's own journals, which are quoted without knowing the true context of any entry; and (3) the creative products themselves, which are used to infer the mental health of those who made them.

This is a tenuous business. For example, legendary classical composers have been pronounced "bipolar" mostly because they wrote both happy pieces and sad ones, and their disorder is then "demonstrated" by playing the two in sequence (Jamison, 1988). It often seems that the major justification for pinning a pathological label on the long-deceased is just the autopsists' determination to do so.

Moreover, whether this look-back assessment is called "psychological autopsy" or "historiometry," it requires applying the psychiatric conventions and cultural expectations of the twentieth or twenty-first century to scraps of information from the seventeenth, eighteenth, and nineteenth. At this point, it is fair to ask: Is it even possible to discover the true psychology of people who are so long in their graves?

The possibilities further diminish when factoring in how many people in that time period may have suffered from advanced syphilis, which was not curable until 1943. This is a very real and protracted disease whose symptoms mimic the contours of bipolar disorder, complete with erratic mood swings and psychosis. One famous sufferer was composer Robert Schumann. Always a favorite of C&M advocates because of his well-documented asylum stay, he is often evoked to support the C&M connection.

But in 2007, John Worthen translated Schumann's original medical records into English and made a very compelling case for syphilis. This definitive biography reveals Schumann's decades of relevant physical complaints as well as the results of his brain autopsy. Other likely sufferers include Beethoven, Nietzsche, and Van Gogh, all of whom have been called bipolar (Hayden, 2003). One wonders how psychological autopsists can be so sure, centuries later, that they are looking at one, and not the other.

The most popular collection of autopsy subjects is in Jamison's 1993 book, *Touched with fire: Manic-depressive illness and the artistic temperament.* Appendix B is her selection of 166 dead writers, artists, and composers with "probable cyclothymia, major depression, or manic-depressive illness," although the "probable" qualifier tends to slide off whenever the list is mentioned.

This list is often evoked to demonstrate the pervasiveness of the C&M link, although readers who wonder why these 166 were chosen must sort through eighty-two single-spaced pages of notes for the answer, and not always successfully. More often than not, as with Michelangelo, people are included with little or no explanation at all. Certainly there are enough strange and unsupported choices to suggest that many of the selections were simply arbitrary. For example, the famously serene Ralph Waldo Emerson gets the bipolar label because he had an unnamed first-degree relative who was "seriously affected" (Jamison, 1993, p. 236), and wrote about his frustration with writer's block (Jamison, 1993, p. 248). Another designate is jazz composer Cole Porter, whose legs were crushed in a riding accident in 1937. Despite thirty futile operations and constant pain over the next three decades, he managed to create the dazzling music and witty lyrics that are still enjoyed today. Although Porter's medical traumas are never specified, he appears in a subgroup of list members who had physical ailments but whose mood symptoms "predated their other conditions" or actually existed "independently" of them, as if such things were possible to determine among the deceased (Jamison, 1993, p. 268).

There's also an ethics problem with this whole procedure. In 1964, responding to a survey in FACT magazine (Boroson, 1964), 2,000 psychiatrists who never met him pronounced Arizona Senator Barry M. Goldwater unfit to be president, ascribing to him pejorative labels like "paranoid" and "psychotic." After Goldwater sued the magazine, holding psychiatric practice up to public ridicule, the APA introduced a new "Goldwater rule" into its official principles, making it "intellectually dishonest" as well as unethical to diagnose people without personally examining them. Although psychologists are not technically bound by this rule, they should also be wary of the pitfalls that are associated with such judgments (Friedman, 2011; Slovenko, 2000).

There are other research obstacles that get in the way of a definitive C&M link. One that looms large is the fact that, although most of the primary literature is dominated by white, middle-aged, male, and English-speaking writers, conclusions derived from this population are freely applied to people all around the world, regardless of age, race, gender, and creative pursuit. Such generalizations are inappropriate at best.

Another problem is the widespread dependence on self-report instruments, which are notoriously unreliable but so easy to administer that their weaknesses are often overlooked. When people are asked to describe their creative experiences or mood fluctuations, their replies can be affected by undetectable factors like false memory, the need to buttress their self-image, and – especially with captive and grade-dependent undergraduates – the desire to please the examiners by confirming their hypotheses. Moreover, design effects themselves can be extremely subtle; the answers can even be affected by the order of the questions. Finally, the field in general suffers from a lack of replication, the gold standard of research; unfortunately, it seems that neither professional journals nor the public media are very interested in publishing "old" news. In any case, few explorers want to plant a flag on anyone else's mountain.

What is to be gained?

The field of psychology grew out of philosophy, and continues to be nourished by those common roots. Both disciplines must deal in abstractions, where truth is created by the best logic, shaped by the most compelling argument, and formalized by the greatest consensus. Except for the direct brain measures of neuropsychology, no mental health concept will ever be as tangible as the book you're holding right now. But it is still worthwhile to pursue those truths and strive for that consensus, especially if this will relieve human suffering in any way.

And this brings us to the most crucial questions of all: What is to be gained by striving so hard to link creativity and madness? Will it comfort or inspire creative people to learn that they face a lifetime of pathology? True, there will always be artists who use bipolar disorder as a shield from the world's demands, and those who embrace any psychiatric label in order to justify their irresponsible behavior ("What can you expect of me? I'm an artiste!"). There are also people who embrace the "M" associated with "C," believing this diagnosis entitles them to some of the stardust of genius, whether they are exceptionally creative or not.

But the sad truth is that, even in our supposedly enlightened age, people can still be harmed by a psychiatric diagnosis. They may be penalized by banks and landlords and prospective in-laws who consider them bad risks (Schlesinger, 2009). The label alone can be pernicious, because the public stigmatizes those who are said to be mentally ill, even if they see them doing nothing abnormal (Ben-Zeev et al., 2010).

So, as this chapter draws to a close, ask yourself this: Is Beethoven's music more enjoyable when you picture him as a tortured human being? Do Van Gogh's vibrant colors fade when you learn that somebody else sliced off his ear? There's also this paradox to consider: If great art requires some degree of psychopathology to create, how can audiences truly appreciate it without having comparable disorders of their own?

The fact that society has long been fascinated with a C&M link does not mean it has any scientific justification. This research has long been distinguished by too little clarity and too much jumping to conclusions – and chances are it always will be. In the meantime, psychology has more urgent things to do than pin unverifiable labels on history's most exceptional minds. We would all do better if great creativity were celebrated, rather than diagnosed.

References

American Psychiatric Association (APA) (2003, September 26). Statement on diagnosis and treatment of mental disorders. Press release, #03–39.

American Psychiatric Association (APA) (2013). *Diagnostic and statistical manual of mental health disorders* (5th edn.). Washington, DC: Author.

Andreasen, N. C. (1986). Mood disorders and their effect on creativity. Presentation at Michael A. Axinn Memorial Conference, North Shore University Hospital, Manhasset, New York, May 2.

Andreasen, N. C. (1987). Creativity and mental illness: Prevalence rates in writers and their first degree relatives. *American Journal of Psychiatry*, 144, 1288–1292.

Aristotle (1984). Problemata. In J. Barnes (Ed.), *The complete works of Aristotle: The revised Oxford translation* (Vol. 2) (pp. 1319–1527). Princeton University Press.

Ben-Zeev, D., Young, M. and Corrigan, P. (2010). DSM-V and the stigma of mental illness. *Journal of Mental Health*, 19(4), August, 318–327.

Beutler, L. (2000). David and Goliath: When empirical and clinical standards of practice meet. *American Psychologist*, 55(9), 997–1007.

Boroson, W. (1964). FACT, September–October, 1, 5, 24–64.

Burton, R. (1621/2001). *The anatomy of melancholy: What it is, with all the kinds, causes, symptoms, prognostickes, and severall cures of it.* A New York Review Book, introduction by William H. Gass. New York: New York Review of Books.

Carey, B. (2007). Bipolar illness soars as diagnosis for the young. *New York Times*, September 4. www.nytimes.com/2007/09/04/health/04psych.html, last accessed March 14, 2014.

Eysenck, H. (1995). *Genius: The natural history of creativity.* New York: Cambridge University Press.

Faust, D. and Ziskin, J. (1988). The expert witness in psychology and psychiatry. *Science*, 241, 31–35.

Frances, A. (2009). A warning sign on the road to *DSM-5*: Beware of its unintended consequences. *Psychiatric Times*, 26. www.psychiatrictimes.com/print/article/1016/1425378, last accessed March 14, 2014.

Friedman, R. A. (2011). How a telescopic lens muddles psychiatric insights. *New York Times*, May 24, D5.

Frosch, W. A. (1996). Creativity: Is there a worm in the apple? *Journal of the Royal Society of Medicine*, 89, September, 506–508.

Harris, G. (2008). Top psychiatrist didn't report drug makers' pay. *New York Times*, October 4. www.nytimes.com/2008/10/04/health/policy/04drug.html, last accessed March 14, 2014.

Hayden, D. (2003). *Pox: Genius, madness, and the mysteries of syphilis.* New York: Basic Books.

Jamison, K. R. (1988). *Moods and Music.* Sixty-minute video featuring the works of composers with [alleged] bipolar illness. Performed by the National Symphony Orchestra at the John F. Kennedy Center for the Performing Arts, Washington, DC. Executive producer and writer. Public Broadcasting Service television special. National broadcast, November.

Jamison, K. R. (1989). Mood disorders and patterns of creativity in British writers and artists. *Psychiatry*, 52, 125–134.

Jamison, K. R. (1993). *Touched with fire: Manic-depressive illness and the artistic temperament.* New York: Free Press.

Jamison, K. R. (1995). *An unquiet mind: A memoir of moods and madness.* New York: Alfred A. Knopf.

Kaufman, J. C. and Baer, J. (2012). Beyond new and appropriate: Who decides what is creative? *Creativity Research Journal*, 24, 83–91.

Kaufman, J. C. and Sternberg, R. J. (Eds.) (2010). *The Cambridge handbook of creativity*. New York: Cambridge University Press.

Kozbelt, A., Beghetto, R. A. and Makel, M. C. (2010). Theories of creativity. In J. C. Kaufman and R. J. Sternberg (Eds.), *The Cambridge handbook of creativity* (pp. 20–47). New York: Cambridge University Press.

Kris, E. and Kurz, O. (1979). *Legend, myth and magic in the image of the artist: A historical experiment*. New Haven, CT: Yale University Press.

Leo, J. (1984). The ups and downs of creativity: Genius and emotional disturbance are linked in new study. *Time Magazine*, 124, October, 76–77.

Lish, J. D., Dime-Meenan, S., Whybrow, P. C., Price, R. A. and Hirschfeld, R. M. A. (1994). The National Depressive and Manic-Depressive Association (DMDA) survey of bipolar members. *Journal of Affective Disorders*, 31, 281–294.

Lombroso, C. (1895). The man of genius. *Contemporary Science Series* (Havelock Ellis, Ed.). London: Walter Scott; Whitefish, Montana: Kessinger's Publishing Rare Reprints.

Ludwig, A. M. (1995). *The price of greatness: Resolving the creativity and madness controversy*. New York: Guilford Press.

Medin, D. (2012). Rigor without rigor mortis: The APS board discusses research integrity. *Observer*, 25(2), 5–8.

Miklowitz, D. J. (2007). The role of the family in the course and treatment of bipolar disorder. *Current Directions in Psychological Science*, 16(4), 192–196.

Mueller, J., Melwani, S. and Goncalo, J. (2012). The bias against creativity: Why people desire but reject creative ideas. *Psychological Science*, 23(1), 13–17.

Northwood, H. (2010). Personal communication, July 28–29.

Northwood, H. (n.d.) *The melancholic mean: The Aristotelian problema XXX.1. Paideia: Ancient philosophy*. www.bu.edu/wcp/Papers/Anci/AnciNort.htm, last accessed March 14, 2014.

Padel, R. (1995). *Whom the gods destroy: Elements of Greek and tragic madness*. Princeton University Press.

Plato (2002). *Phaedrus* (R. Wakefield, Trans.). New York: Oxford University Press.

Plucker, J. A. and Makel, M. C. (2010). Assessment of creativity. In J. C. Kaufman and R. J. Sternberg (Eds.), *The Cambridge handbook of creativity* (pp. 48–73). New York: Cambridge University Press.

Radden, J. (Ed.) (2000). *The nature of melancholy from Aristotle to Kristeva*. New York: Oxford University Press.

Richards, R. (2009). *Everyday creativity and new views of human nature: Psychological, social, and spiritual perspectives*. Washington, DC: American Psychological Association.

Rothenberg, A. (1990). *Creativity and madness: New findings and old stereotypes*. Baltimore, MD: Johns Hopkins University Press.

Rothenberg, A. and Greenberg, B. (1974). *The index of scientific writings on creativity. General: 1566–1974*. Hamden, CT: Archon Books.

Schlesinger, J. (2002a). Issues in creativity and madness. Part one: Ancient questions, modern answers. *Ethical Human Sciences and Services: An International Journal of Critical Inquiry*, 4(1), 73–76.

Schlesinger, J. (2002b). Issues in creativity and madness. Part two: Eternal flames. *Ethical Human Sciences and Services: An International Journal of Critical Inquiry*, 4(2), 139–142.

Schlesinger, J. (2004). Creativity and mental health. *British Journal of Psychiatry*, 184 (February), 184–185.

Schlesinger, J. (2009). Creative mythconceptions: A closer look at the evidence for the "mad genius" hypothesis. *Psychology of Aesthetics, Creativity, and the Arts*, 3(2), 62–72.

Schlesinger, J. (2010). Mad and genius are separate states of mind. *National Psychologist*, 19(3), 13.

Schlesinger, J. (2012). *The insanity hoax: Exposing the myth of the mad genius*. New York: Shrinktunes Media.

Sleek, S. (1996). Ensuring accuracy in clinical decisions: Psychologists explore ways to make their diagnoses and assessments as accurate as possible. *APA Monitor*, April, 30.

Slovenko, R. (2000). Ethics and legality of psychiatric opinion without examination. *Journal of Psychiatry and Law*, 28, 103–143.

Subotnik, R. F., Olszewski-Kubilius, P. and Worrell, F. C. (2011). Rethinking giftedness and gifted education: A proposed direction forward based on psychological science. *Psychological Science in the Public Interest*, 12 (1), 3–54.

Szasz, T. (2001). *Pharmacracy: Medicine and politics in America*. Westport, CT: Praeger Publishers.

Tohen, M., Frank, E., Bowden, C. L., Colom, F., Ghaemi, S. N., Yatham, L. N., Malhi, G. S., Calabrese, J. R., Nolen, W. A., Vieta, E., Kapczinski, F., Goodwin, G. M., Suppes, T., Sachs, G. S., Chengappa, K. N. R., Grunze, H., Mitchell, P. B., Kanba, S. and Berk, M. (2009). The International Society for Bipolar Disorders (ISBD) Task Force report on the nomenclature of course and outcome in bipolar disorders. *Bipolar Disorders*, 11, 453–473.

What Killed Rebecca Riley? (2007). 60 Minutes DVD. CBS Broadcasting.

Whitaker, R. (2002). *Mad in America: Bad science, bad medicine, and the enduring mistreatment of the mentally ill*. Cambridge, MA: Perseus Publishing.

Wittkower, R. and Wittkower, M. (1963). *Born under Saturn: The character and conduct of artists*. New York: W.W. Norton.

Worthen, J. (2007). *Robert Schumann: Life and death of a musician*. New Haven, CT: Yale University Press.

Part II

Cognitive and neuroscientific perspectives on creativity and mental illness

5   Neurocognitive mechanisms underlying creative thinking: indications from studies of mental illness

Anna Abraham

> Creative people who can't but help explore other mental territories are at greater risk, just as someone who climbs a mountain is more at risk than someone who just walks along a village lane.
>
> – R. D. Laing

> One must still have chaos in oneself to be able to give birth to a dancing star.
>
> – Friedrich Nietzsche

The magnetic appeal of the nexus between madness and creativity has persevered over centuries. The ubiquity of this fascinating idea is no doubt primarily due to the greater incidence of mental illness associated with professions that purportedly involve a high degree of creativity (e.g., Post, 1994). However, its remarkable persistence can be attributed, at least in part, to the shared characteristics of mental illness and creativity. Both are associated with a high tolerance for ambiguity, the ability to go beyond generic conceptual connections, and the adoption of alternative perspectives. Despite the considerable interest in this theme and concerted efforts to demystify the ineffability surrounding it, the precise manner in which enhanced creative abilities can be related to mental illness has remained a difficult one to pin down.

There are several reasons for this. One is that creativity itself is an extremely multifaceted and heterogeneous construct for which few comprehensive or unifying information-processing frameworks have been proposed (Dietrich, 2004). In addition, while several measures have been developed to assess creative thinking, most do not specify which particular facets of creativity are assessed within the tasks because related psychometric work is lacking (Arden *et al.*, 2010). For example, clarifications about the manner in which any creativity measure is comparable to or differentiable from other creativity tasks are usually absent. Moreover, unlike in the case of personality tests, for instance, the lack of comprehensive reliability or validity indices accompanying creativity tests makes it difficult to estimate the efficacy of, not just the measures in question, but also their associated concepts. So making clear claims about creative thinking in relation to almost any variable is extremely challenging.

This picture is further complicated by the fact that critical issues also surface when investigating information-processing biases in mental illness. Several ideas are in circulation about which specific types of mental illness are associated with enhanced creative abilities. Mood disorders and schizophrenia spectrum disorders have received the bulk of the focus so far (e.g., Abraham *et al.*, 2007; Andreasen and Powers, 1975; Dykes and McGhie, 1976; Soeiro-de-Souza *et al.*, 2011). But other psychiatric disorders, such as autism spectrum disorders and attention-deficit/hyperactivity disorder (ADHD), have also been discussed in relation to enhanced creativity skills (Abraham *et al.*, 2006; Healey, this volume; Healey and Rucklidge, 2006; Pring *et al.*, 2012).

What still remains largely unknown, however, is the nature of these information-processing differences between the disorders. Do such widely varied clinical conditions overlap in some way with regard to creative cognition? Given their rather distinct cognitive and behavioral profiles, is it at all possible to argue for an underlying cognitive bias that is common to all of these disorders? In what manner is the cognitive bias during creative thinking in bipolar disorder related to that of ADHD, for instance? Can information-processing biases during creative cognition be predicted from the well-documented biases in normative cognition that are associated with each of the mental disorders? These are some of the many questions that need to be explored to be able to gain precise insights about the dynamics of the relation between creativity and mental illness.

Can information-processing biases lead to advantages in creativity?

The core idea behind investigations on creativity and mental illness is that each of the psychiatric conditions in question is associated with one or more insufficiencies in information processing during normative cognition (negative biases) that may be advantageous in the context of creative cognition (positive biases). Factors such as reduced top-down control, defocused attention, flat associative hierarchies, and cognitive disinhibition have been proposed as underlying the roots of such information-processing biases (Carson, 2011; Eysenck, 1995; Kasof, 1997; Mednick, 1962; Mendelsohn, 1974; Snyder, 2009; Thompson-Schill *et al.*, 2009).

The relevance of defocused attention in creative thinking, for instance, was highlighted by Mendelsohn (1974). Defocused attention refers to a widened attentional capacity and can best be understood with reference to the metaphor of the attentional spotlight. To arrive at a creative idea, conceptual elements that are available within one's attentional focus need to be combined. From a statistical standpoint, an increase in the number of elements present within one's attentional stream would result in an exponential surge in the number of potential combinations of elements. For instance, if one's attention spotlight is extremely focused and one is only able to attend to two conceptual elements (A, B) at the same time, only one combination would arise (AB). If, however, one's attentional focus is comparatively less focused and there are three elements within one's attentional stream (A, B, C), then four permutations would be possible (AB, BC, AC, ABC). So, according to this view, the manner in which information from one's conceptual networks can be accessed (focused versus defocused) has a direct effect on the amount of information available within one's stream of attention, and, consequently, the number of potential conceptual combinations that can be generated. This has a crucial impact on creative output because the greater the number of conceptual combinations available in one's attentional focus, the higher the likelihood of unique combinations occurring.

This idea can be readily aligned to other prominent hypotheses, such as that of cognitive disinhibition (Carson, 2011), that link enhanced creative abilities with insufficiencies in select aspects of information processing. Notwithstanding their differences, each of these hypotheses has been proposed as the missing link that would allow one to align the greater incidences of mental illness among practitioners of ostensibly creative professions (such as artists and poets) with the presence of cognitive and behavioral deficits that typify the very same mental illnesses. Such ideas set the stage for a number of debates about the "upside" of having a mental illness including the proposal that the propensity for mental illness must confer some evolutionary advantage for humankind or else it would have been weeded out through processes such as natural selection. This evolutionary advantage has been posited to take the form of enhanced creative potential (Crespi et al., 2007; Karlsson, 1970).

So there are several influential ideas that postulate the presence of some kind of positive bias in creative thinking in association with certain mental illnesses. While the general thrust of such hypotheses carries considerable intuitive appeal, they have received only limited direct or indirect support (e.g., Andreasen and Powers, 1975; Carson et al., 2011; Soeiro-de-Souza et al., 2011). In some of the earliest empirical work on this topic, in comparison to healthy control participants, a group of patients with schizophrenia and a group of highly creative individuals were both found to exhibit poor performance on a divided attention task along with superior performance on a creative thinking task (Dykes and McGhie, 1976). Almost four decades later, in investigations of subclinical populations with a high degree of schizotypal traits, Carson and her colleagues (2003) reported related evidence that showcased advantages in creative output in association with a higher propensity for mental illness alongside concurrent disadvantages in cognitive inhibition.

In addition to schizophrenia, mood disorders and specific childhood disorders have also been linked empirically and theoretically to superior creative abilities (Abraham et al., 2006; Andreasen, 2008). However, as mentioned earlier, few studies have explicitly addressed key issues such as what aspects of creative thinking would be positively affected by information-processing biases typical of any disorder, and which other facets of creativity would be unaffected or negatively influenced by the very same biases. The fact that no mental disorder is known to be unequivocally associated with greater creativity is a clear sign that any potential bias in information processing that hampers some distinctive aspect of normative cognition is likely to be extremely specific in terms of which particular facet of creative cognition would be enhanced as a result.

How is creative cognition related to normative cognition?

In order to estimate the specificity associated with positive versus negative consequences of information-processing biases, it is necessary to first understand how creative and normative cognition are linked to one another. Surprisingly, this issue has only seldom been explicitly addressed in the literature. Most cognitive-based investigations of creativity attempt to characterize what differentiates high and low creative individuals. Within the domain of cognitive neuroscience, for instance, neuroimaging investigations mainly seek to clarify the neural basis for individual differences in creative thinking (Dietrich and Kanso, 2010). However, most studies do not openly address in what manner creative thinking is similar to or distinguishable from non-creative or normative thinking. In fact, there is a latent assumption that creative thinking is somehow qualitatively different from normative thinking (Panels A and B of Figure 5.1). But are we correct in making such an assumption?

The only researchers to have broached this issue head on were the proponents of the Geneplore model who adopted the creative cognition approach (Abraham and Windmann, 2007; Finke et al., 1996; Ward et al., 1995). According to this framework, it is unlikely that there are mental operations that are exclusively in place for creative cognition. The information-processing "toolboxes" would be expected to be one and

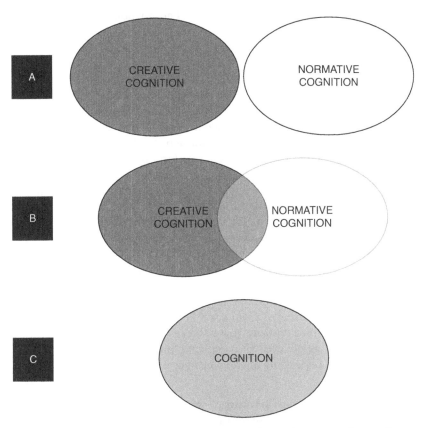

Figure 5.1 The relationship between information-processing toolboxes of creative cognition and normative cognition can be conceived of as mutually exclusive (A), partially overlapping (B), or undifferentiated (C) (adapted from figure as originally published in Abraham [2013])

the same for both creative and normative cognition (Panel C of Figure 5.1). The essential difference between creative and normative cognition, though, lies in the kind of situations in which our information-processing toolboxes need to be applied. The situational factors during creative cognition are open-ended or unclear, whereas the situational factors during normative cognition are concrete or predictable. A situation that is open-ended and involves the generation of novel responses to reach a solution would necessitate creative cognition.

The creative cognition framework has only been explored to a limited extent so far using neuroscientific techniques (Abraham *et al.*, 2012;

Kröger *et al.*, 2012; Rutter *et al.*, 2012). The relation between normative and creative cognition in terms of brain function has mainly been
informed through behavioral investigations of psychiatric (Abraham *et al.*,
2006, 2007) and subclinical populations (Abraham and Windmann,
2008; Abraham *et al.*, 2005; Karimi *et al.*, 2007). In each of these studies,
diverse aspects of creative cognition were assessed including the ability
to extend conceptual boundaries when forming new ideas (conceptual
expansion task) (Ward, 1994) or when generating new uses for common
objects (alternate uses task) (Wallach and Kogan, 1965), originality and
practicality when generating new objects within a predetermined category
(creative imagery task) (Finke, 1990), the ability to overcome constraints
imposed by recently activated knowledge (constraints of examples task)
(Smith *et al.*, 1993), and overcoming functional fixedness during analytical reasoning (insight problem-solving tasks) (Weisberg, 1995). Adopting
a comprehensive creative cognition approach enables one to establish not
only whether there is evidence of cognitive biases during creative thinking associated with any clinical or subclinical population, but also allows
one to determine which aspects of creative cognition these biases are
restricted to, and how the biases in one population (e.g., ADHD) parallel
and/or can be differentiated from another population (e.g., schizophrenia). Indeed, the insights from these studies indicate that information-
processing biases associated with a specific mental disorder exert a dis-
cerning influence depending on the type of creative operation in question.

Specificity of information-processing biases in creative cognition: attention-deficit/hyperactivity disorder

Diverse aspects of creative cognition were investigated in adolescents
with ADHD, for instance, and the findings indicated that, for the most
part, the clinical group performed comparably to the matched healthy
control group on almost all the tested measures of creativity (conceptual
expansion, fluency and originality in the alternate uses task, originality in
creative imagery, insight problem solving) (Abraham *et al.*, 2006). Two
creative cognition measures were, however, associated with significant
and, at first glance, seemingly opposing findings.

On the constraints of examples task, which requires the generation of a
novel response (inventing a new toy) following exposure to salient distractors (examples of three novel toys that were engineered to have three core
features in common), the ADHD group outperformed the healthy control group in that they were more successful at inventing new toys that did
not have features in common with the examples. But their information-
processing advantage, which was discussed as the positive consequence

of being highly distractible, was only limited to this particular facet of creative cognition. The ADHD adolescents, in fact, concurrently demonstrated a significant disadvantage on an alternate facet of creative thinking. The creative imagery task requires that participants invent objects that fall into a pre-specified category (e.g., transport) using three geometrical figures (e.g., cube, cone, handle). The inventions are assessed in terms of their originality (unusualness or novelty) and practicality (relevance or appropriateness). While the ADHD participants were no different from the control participants in the degree of originality associated with the inventions, they were far less able to generate inventions that were functional, practical, or usable. This finding was attributed to the impulsive tendencies that are characteristic of ADHD. Hasty or erratic responses and the resulting lack of appropriate goal-directed planning in this type of generative situation could have resulted in the creation of inventions that were less functional and practical than otherwise.

These findings showcased the importance of assessing different facets of creativity in the same sample. For instance, had the ADHD group only been assessed on a single creativity task, one would have attained only a limited understanding about the specificities underlying their performance, which may have even led to erroneous conclusions (e.g., generally low creative ability in ADHD based on their poor performance on the creative imagery measure). Including a wide range of tasks that tap different operations associated with creativity allows one to also make more specific claims about which aspects of creativity are affected in a particular group and whether these can be related to the cognitive insufficiencies associated with that population.

ADHD is a disorder that is known to be associated with deficits of the top-down frontostriatal system in the brain that manifest in the form of high levels of distractibility, impulsivity, and poor inhibitory control (Bradshaw and Sheppard, 2000; Cherkasova and Hechtman, 2009; Dickstein et al., 2006). It is not difficult to imagine why such factors have been considered to potentially confer specific advantages during creative thinking. For instance, in a working memory task when salient information must be maintained over time in the service of an active goal, it would be imperative to exert optimal inhibitory control to avoid being misled by distractors. The opposite is true in the case of the constraints of examples task when salient information that is highly relevant to the task at hand must be actively inhibited in order to generate a creative response. Healthy participants have difficulties inhibiting salient information because a functional attentional system is optimized to automatically focus on information that is salient or relevant in a particular context. As a result, these semantic distractors interfere with and exert a strong influence on the ability of the healthy participants to generate a novel idea. The ADHD group would be less affected by the pre-exposure to relevant semantic information because their increased distractibility causes their attention to be readily diverted away from any particular focus. This ordinarily detrimental factor in their overall cognitive functioning translates to an advantage in the constraints of examples task, thereby enabling the ADHD group to outperform healthy participants.

So the constraints of examples task provides a unique context in which the ordinarily negative bias of poor attentional control and increased distractibility associated with ADHD can be advantageous. While this finding is interesting in itself, the next step that can be, or indeed must be, explored at such a juncture is to determine why this advantage is only specific to this particular task. What sets the constraints of examples task apart from the other tasks of creativity? The creative cognition approach would emphasize a consideration of the contextual factors to determine the differences. To follow from that perspective then, in what manner is the context within the constraints of examples task different from that of other creativity tasks, such as the conceptual expansion task? To abet the discussion of the issue of context further, it will be useful to first briefly explore other findings in association with the constraints of examples task in comparison to other creative cognitive measures.

Specificity of information-processing biases in creative cognition: schizophrenia

Following the study on adolescents with ADHD, a more extensive investigation of creative cognition was carried out on adults with chronic schizophrenia relative to healthy matched control participants (Abraham *et al.*, 2007). Schizophrenia is an exceedingly heterogeneous disorder that, like ADHD, is characterized by poor top-down attentional and cognitive control. But the magnitude of the insufficiencies is far more comprehensive in the case of schizophrenia. Hallmark deficits associated with this condition are in the domains of executive function, working memory, inhibitory control, and fluency, particularly in the presence of negative and thought disorder symptoms (Kalkstein *et al.*, 2010; Lesh *et al.*, 2011).

A number of questions were explored in the study. Would the results of the schizophrenia study parallel those of the ADHD study, given that both disorders demonstrate some overlap in the negative information-processing biases particularly in the domain of frontostriatal function that subserves cognitive control? Or was it necessary to take a new factor into account in the equation – namely, the degree of severity of the information-processing biases? For instance, do the predictions concerning directional influence of information-processing biases during creative thinking necessarily vary as a function of the severity of the deficits? In fact, can this be taken one step further to determine to what degree executive dysfunction in schizophrenia modulates performance on the creative cognition variables?

The findings of the study revealed that except for the constraints of examples task, when they fared comparably to the healthy control group, the schizophrenia group performed worse on all other creative cognition measures. So, here again, the constraints of examples task stands out distinctly from the other creativity tasks. Moreover, a high degree of thought disorder symptoms among the schizophrenics was associated with poorer performance across all the executive function measures but better performance on the constraints of examples task. The negative bias in this case of executive dysfunction may be the very same grounds for the relative cognitive advantage associated with thought disorder on this task. Thought disorder is characterized by conceptual disorganization and the tendency to be continually diverted from an intended direction in thinking (Payne, 1973). This kind of disorderly "digressive" thinking, or the inability to stick to a logical train of thought because of involuntary access to irrelevant conceptual representations, would more easily enable the overriding of the conceptual restrictions actively posed by the constraints of examples task. A similar logic was applied earlier to explain the ADHD group's superior performance on the same task.

The next issue was to determine to what degree the schizophrenics' poor performance on the creativity measures could be explained by their deficits on frontal lobe measures of top-down executive function and cognitive control. The findings revealed a most fascinating dissociation in that a partial or full mediation by executive function measures was found only on some measures of creative cognition (insight problem solving, practicality in creative imagery, fluency in the alternative uses task) but not on others (conceptual expansion, originality in creative imagery, originality measure in the alternate uses task).

An ad hoc examination of the contextual differences between the tasks was carried out with a view to dissociate the creativity measures in terms of the extent to which they draw on the defining components of creativity such as originality and relevance. A response is customarily defined to be creative in the extent that it is original (novel/unique) as well as relevant (appropriate/fitting) to a given end (Hennessey and Amabile, 2010; Runco, 2004). While the schizophrenics exhibited suboptimal function across almost all facets of creativity, performance differences on the creativity measures that assessed the originality of generated responses were not linearly modulated by performance on the executive function tasks. The opposite was true of measures that assessed the relevance and fluency components of creativity, such as the propensity to make functional responses (practicality – creative imagery), generate a large number of responses (fluency – alternate uses), or employ effective strategies to overcome functional fixedness (insight – problem solving).

So the findings suggested that impairments at the level of executive function are accountable for deficits on select facets of creative cognition such as fluency and relevance, which require functional goal-directed thinking for optimal responses, but not in contexts that require originality. The issue of context and its effects on the influence of information-processing biases surfaces once again here and it is one that will be explored in more detail within the next section.

Contexts: types and influences

The modulatory role played by different types of contexts in the top-down control on information processing has yet to be comprehensively addressed in cognitive psychology. David Hemsley (2005) highlighted a number of distinctions that beg clarification in addressing the issue of context due to the sheer variety in the types of contextual input: temporal or spatial, tonic or phasic, inhibitory or facilitatory, and arising due to contextual priming or executive control. The last category bears some parallels to the concept of cognitive contexts in contrast to socioaffective or perceptual contexts in an alternative classification of contexts (Park et al., 2003). One type of cognitive context includes contextual effects provided by stored representations in long-term memory, and which can be direct or indirect and explicit or implicit. An example of the workings within this kind of context would be in a semantic priming task when past experience and associations between stored representations in memory would influence the readiness to respond on a lexical decision task. Another type of cognitive context is the kind provided by task-relevant information that is actively held in working memory. An example for the effects of this type of context is the AX-type continuous performance task, in which the subject is presented with a series of letters and is required to respond to an X only if an A preceded it.

In order to understand the contextual differences between the creative cognitive measures tested in the aforementioned studies, it would be useful to relate the operations involved in the tasks using the general framework of Park et al. (2003). For instance, the conceptual expansion task and the constraints of examples task are similar in that both assess the degree to which people are constrained in their responses when explicitly instructed to create something novel. However, the essential difference between the tasks lies in the kind of contextual processing that both necessitate. By providing examples of novel toys with common fundamental elements before allowing participants to generate a novel toy, the constraints in the examples task are highly salient and actively interfere with the ability to generate a new toy. This is because it is difficult to overcome or inhibit explicitly pertinent information that is directly relevant to the task at hand. This kind of active inhibition of concrete and relevant information that is called for within the constraints of examples task gives rise to qualitatively different contextual processing demands compared with the conceptual expansion task.

In the latter, the contextual constraints are imposed by the extent to which one's existing knowledge in the form of stored conceptual structures (e.g., concept of an animal) influence the capacity to generate an original response (e.g., create a novel kind of animal). So the contexts that are implicated in the conceptual expansion task are those generated from long-term memory information retrieval. Although the activated schemas regulate and delimit the extent to which one can expand concepts, the contextual effects do not actively impinge on one's ability to widen conceptual structures to the extent that it does during the constraints of examples task. So while the constraints of examples task is primarily influenced by "active" or explicitly salient contexts in short-term memory, the conceptual expansion task appears to be mainly influenced by implicit or "passive" contextual effects in the form of stored representations of concepts in memory.

Just as in the case of the conceptual expansion task, passive contexts also exert a modulatory influence on other measures of creativity such as the creative imagery and alternate uses tasks. There is an underlying commonality between these three measures. All assess the capacity to make original or unusual responses albeit in different generative situations and with differing degrees of abstraction. There is far less active intrusion of interfering, salient, and recently activated representations in any of the tasks. In the case of the creative imagery task, the passive contextual processing is directed by the predetermined categories that limit the nature of the conceptual structures that are activated. Within the alternate uses task, passive contextual constraints are posed not only by the prepotent use for the objects, but also by the properties of the objects themselves, such as their weight, shape, size, flexibility, and so on. Indeed, performance on the conceptual expansion task is positively correlated with performance on the originality dimensions of the creative

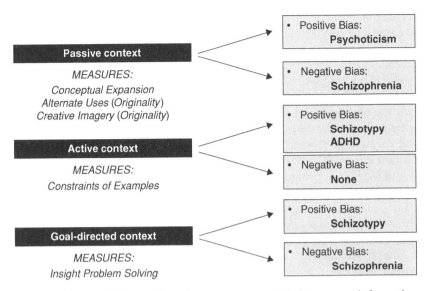

Figure 5.2 Types of top-down or contextual influences on information processing during creative idea generation and their associated findings related to positive versus negative biases

imagery task and the alternate uses task (Abraham *et al.*, 2005, 2006, 2007). This is indicative of underlying similarities between the cognitive operations that are employed when performing these tasks.

So this classification of active versus passive contexts in the top-down control of information processing during creative thinking was proposed to explain contextual influences during divergent creative thinking, when active contexts refer to conditionally salient representations in short-term memory, and passive contexts refer to implicitly activated generic representations from long-term memory (Abraham and Windmann, 2007) (Figure 5.2). While this differentiation plausibly explained some of the differences between the contextual factors involved in many of the creative cognition measures, this was not true of all the tasks that were assessed. The process of insight during creative problem solving was a specific exception to this case.

Insight is held to be a phenomenon that goes hand in hand with creativity and it is said to occur when a solution to a problem appears suddenly as a result of a perspective shift or after overcoming functional fixedness. It is typically assessed by means of the remote associates task or problems of analytical reasoning (Bowden and Jung-Beeman, 2003; Weisberg, 1995). What makes insight tasks different from other measures of creative thinking is that insight problems involve convergent thinking given that there is only one ostensibly correct or viable solution to the problem. In contrast, the aforementioned creativity measures involve divergent thinking when the problem is open-ended with an unlimited number of potential solutions to solve it. Unlike the case of the divergent creativity measures, both the means state and the goals state are clear in the case of the insight problems and participants have to work their way through the operations state in order to reach the prescribed goal. As the contextual factors in insight problem-solving tasks are not entirely comparable to the other tasks of creativity cognition, a third kind of context – namely, the goal-directed context – is introduced to explain the contextual factors that exert an influence in this situation. The link between creativity and mental illness will be explored next from the perspective of the influence of different contexts on information-processing biases.

The relationship between mental illness and creativity

In order to determine the accuracy of the idea that the propensity for mental illness confers a specific cognitive advantage in terms of creative ability, it is vital to integrate the findings from the previously discussed neuropsychological findings on the clinical groups (schizophrenia and ADHD) with the findings from related behavioral investigations on subclinical populations (schizotypy and psychoticism). Assessments of subclinical samples are widely carried out in an effort to evaluate whether high-risk healthy populations (e.g., high schizotypy individuals), who exhibit a high degree of psychosis-relevant personality traits, also display the same information-processing biases as their related clinical group (e.g., schizophrenia). Indeed there is evidence of parallels between information-processing biases in the form of reduced negative priming and latent disinhibition seen in clinical groups like schizophrenia and subclinical populations such as high psychoticism or schizotypy groups (e.g., Minas and Park, 2007; Vink *et al.*, 2005).

The constructs of psychoticism and schizotypy are similar in that both concepts stem from a dimensional approach whereby psychosis and normalcy are viewed as two ends of a continuum and varying degrees of each of these personality traits are experienced along this continuum (Claridge, 1997). So the idea is that studying healthy individuals who possess a high degree of such traits, and in doing so display some degree of predisposition for the clinical disorder, allows us to understand the workings of the information-processing biases related to the disorder without the burden of having to control for the kind of variables that can exert major confounding effects in clinical studies such as medication, comorbidity, etc. Schizotypy is explicitly related to traits typically found in the schizophrenia spectrum of disorders, whereas psychoticism, which emerged from H. J. Eysenck's *Einheitpsychose* conception of mental illness, is related to traits typical of psychosis in general. Not only have high psychoticism and high schizotypy trait individuals been reported to exhibit similar, albeit subtler, information-processing biases that have also been reported in schizophrenia, there is abundant evidence to show that they also display superior creativity skills compared with their low trait counterparts (e.g., Carson *et al.*, 2003; Folley and Park, 2005; Gibson *et al.*, 2009; Stavridou and Furnham, 1996).

But the question of specificity also arises in this situation. To which select creative operations are the information-processing biases limited to in the case of psychoticism and schizotypy? Do the differences between the performances of the high psychoticism and schizotypy groups relative to the schizophrenic and ADHD groups reveal hints about the neurocognitive mechanisms underlying these biases? After all, there is considerable variation in the degrees of disruption in top-down information processing that manifests as suboptimal attentional and cognitive control associated with each of these populations. The severity of the cognitive deficits is severe in the case of schizophrenia, moderate in the case of ADHD, and only mild in the case of psychoticism and schizotypy (Figures 5.2 and 5.3). How does this varying degree of top-down dysfunction affect the influence of these information-processing biases during creative thinking? The investigations that have assessed different creative cognition measures as a function of psychoticism and schizotypy indicate that such populations are not associated with any disadvantages in creative thinking. The fact that the ADHD and schizophrenia groups were in fact associated with disadvantages in creative performance on some measures indicates that the "degree" of reduced top-down to executive control has a direct bearing on creative performance.

That does not explain the whole story though, because the information-processing advantages associated with psychoticism and schizotypy do not overlap with one another (Figure 5.2). While psychoticism was associated with better performance on the conceptual expansion task (passive context) and the originality measure of the creative imagery task (passive context), schizotypy was associated with superior performance on the constraints of examples task (active context) and during insight in problem solving (goal-directed context). So it seems necessary to consider a second factor when interpreting the findings – namely, the "type" of top-down control in terms of the differences in the contextual processing demands of the tasks in question. To briefly recapitulate the findings related to advantages and disadvantages in generating

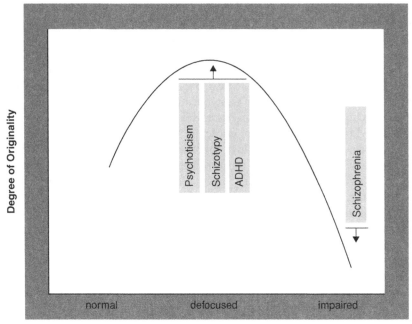

Degree of Top-Down Control on Information Processing

Figure 5.3 The relation between the propensity to generate original responses during creative thinking and the degree of functionality in top-down control of information processing associated with clinical and subclinical populations

original responses during creative idea generation, the ADHD group exhibited only an active contextual processing advantage during creative idea generation. The schizophrenics exhibited goal-related and passive contextual processing deficits but displayed no impairments in active context processing nor advantages otherwise. High levels of schizotypy were associated with advantages in processing involving active contexts and goal-directed contexts, whereas passive contextual processing advantages were related to the presence of high psychoticism traits. Such findings indicate that the constructs of psychoticism and schizotypy indeed appear to represent discrete facets within the dimensional conception of schizophrenia.

So both the "type" of affected top-down context as well as the "degree" of reduced top-down control have an impact on creative performance. The global picture that emerges from the integration of these disparate findings indicates that the simplest way of understanding the effects of alterations in top-down control on creativity is in terms of an inverted-U-shaped function (Figure 5.3). Defective top-down control, as seen in schizophrenia, is accompanied by markedly poor performance across most measures of originality in creativity. On the other hand, defocused top-down processing that is characteristic of a moderately impaired clinical group like ADHD, and is also present to a milder extent in the presence of a high degree of schizotypy and psychoticism traits, is associated with higher originality in creative idea generation. So while diffuse or defocused top-down activation confers some degree of cognitive advantage on select processes of creative cognition, too much top-down control (customary levels) or too little top-down control (completely disrupted or impaired top-down control) may pose a hindrance or even be detrimental to the same.

In demonstrating the role played by both the degree and type of contextual or top-down influences in creative idea generation, the aforementioned findings have not only allowed for a deeper understanding of the relation between creativity and mental illness. They also provide enough fodder to allow for viable predictions to be made regarding the neural underpinnings of creative cognition and individual differences in creative ability. These ideas will be explored in the final section of this chapter.

Neural correlates of creativity: predictions

Relating creative cognition to brain function has been the subject of electrophysiological research for several decades now, but the recent past has seen a great surge in brain-related investigations on creative thinking in the form of neuroimaging (for a review, see Dietrich and Kanso, 2010) and neuropsychological studies (Reverberi et al., 2005; Shamay-Tsoory et al., 2011). The study of creativity and brain function has primarily focused on issues such as enhanced creative or artistic ability following, or as a function of, brain damage (Miller et al., 1996; Seeley et al., 2008), left versus right brain contributions to creativity (Carlsson et al., 2000; Seger et al., 2000), and the brain basis of high or exceptional creativity in intact brains (Fink et al., 2009; Limb and Braun, 2008). Bringing together the insights from these studies is a highly challenging endeavor. This is because such an undertaking requires making generalizations concerning the neurocognitive mechanisms underlying creative thinking, but what is still lacking in the literature are theoretical frameworks that can guide us in doing so (Abraham, 2012). The problem is compounded by the fact that a wide range of creativity tasks, which are difficult to compare with one another, have been employed in neuroscientific studies on creativity (Arden et al., 2010) and few authors have attempted to assess the differences and similarities between the employed tasks and the cognitive operations they necessitate.

So can we use the previously discussed insights from the performances of the clinical and subclinical groups on the creative cognition measures to aid us in formulating predictions for the brain basis for creativity? The commonality between the cognitive profile associated with schizophrenia and ADHD is that, although the insufficiencies are far more severe in the case of schizophrenia, the frontostriatal system of executive and cognitive control is compromised in both clinical disorders. The brain areas that are especially relevant for executive function and cognitive control are those that belong to the frontostriatal system and include a network of regions in the lateral prefrontal cortex, anterior cingulate cortex, and the subcortical structures within the basal ganglia (Badre, 2008; Chow and Cummings, 2006). What are the predictions that can be made with regard to the specific role of the frontostriatal system in creative thinking, such as in the case of neurological damage to brain areas within this system?

The findings from the schizophrenia study provide important clues in this context. The results indicated that the degree of intact executive function fully or partially modulated performance on creativity tasks that assessed fluency and relevance, but did not exert a significant influence on tasks that primarily included a strong originality component. So although poor executive function was related to poor performance on relevance- and fluency-based creativity tasks, it did not fully explain poor performance on originality-dominant creativity tasks. Damage to the frontostriatal system could therefore be expected to be accompanied by poorer performance on measures of relevance and fluency, such as practicality in creative imagery and fluency in the alternate uses task, as well as on tasks that require goal-directed thinking, such as in the insight problem-solving tasks. On the other hand, the insights from the findings of the ADHD study suggest that insufficiencies at the level of the frontostriatal system would also be expected to be associated with better performance on creativity tasks that are marked by active contextual demands, such as in the constraints of examples task. This is because the increased distractibility and poor attentional control that result from damage to this neural circuit are the very factors that can abet performance on this task.

Because the capacity to generate original responses, particularly in the case of passive contextual processing tasks, was not fully mediated by executive function, other candidate regions in the brain also need to be considered. Generating an original response requires the activation of distantly or weakly connected conceptual nodes in the semantic knowledge network. The uniqueness of generated responses could therefore depend on how semantic networks are organized in the anterior temporal lobes and accessed through related structures in the semantic cognition system, such as the ventrolateral prefrontal cortex and the superior temporal cortex (Turken and Dronkers, 2011; Wong and Gallate, 2012). Damage to regions belonging to the semantic network of the brain would be expected to compromise the ability to generate original responses during idea generation as well as affect fluency during creativity.

Given that the generation of creative ideas involves not only the access and selection but also the integration of previously unrelated conceptual knowledge, the frontopolar cortex would also be expected to play a critical role. The frontopolar cortex is involved in many aspects of higher-order cognition where its overarching role is to integrate information from two or more separate cognitive operations (Ramnani and Owen, 2004). This brain region, which is located in the anteriormost part of the prefrontal cortex, is singular from the point of view of hominid evolution in that it has increased greatly not only in size but also in connectivity with other higher-order association areas in the brain (Semendeferi *et al.*, 2001). It is no wonder then that this region is purported to exert the highest level of cognitive control at the level of abstract representations (Badre, 2008) and is therefore likely to be extremely relevant in the context of creative thinking.

Conclusions

Studies that have explored the link between creativity and mental illness indicate that the differences between the type of contextual influences as well as the degree of cognitive dysfunction fundamentally influence our capacity to be creative. These insights are particularly valuable because neuroscientific investigations of creative thinking using neuroimaging or electrophysiological techniques are fraught with problems, both conceptual and methodological, that pose considerable limitations on the degree to which hypotheses can be optimally tested (Abraham, 2012; Sawyer, 2011). Investigations of creativity and mental illness therefore not only inform us about the dynamics of this fascinating association, they also offer a unique backstage pass to unravel the cognitive and neurocognitive mechanisms that underlie creative thinking.

References

Abraham, A. (2012). The neuroscience of creativity: A promising or perilous enterprise? In D. A. P. Alejandre and M. M.-L. Garrido (Eds.), *Creativity and cognitive neuroscience* (pp. 15–24). Madrid: Fundación Tomás Pascual y Pilar Gómez-Cuétara.

Abraham, A. (2013). The promises and perils of the neuroscience of creativity. *Frontiers in Human Neuroscience*, 7, 246. doi:10.3389/fnhum.2013.00246

Abraham, A. and Windmann, S. (2007). Creative cognition: The diverse operations and the prospect of applying a cognitive neuroscience perspective. *Methods* (San Diego, CA), 42(1), 38–48. doi:10.1016/j.ymeth.2006.12.007

Abraham, A. and Windmann, S. (2008). Selective information processing advantages in creative cognition as a function of schizotypy. *Creativity Research Journal*, 20(1), 1–6. doi:10.1080/10400410701839819

Abraham, A., Pieritz, K., Thybusch, K., Rutter, B., Kröger, S., Schweckendiek, J., Stark, R., Windmann, S. and Hermann, C. (2012). Creativity and the brain: Uncovering the neural signature of conceptual expansion. *Neuropsychologia*, 50(8), 1906–1917. doi:10.1016/j.neuropsychologia.2012.04.015

Abraham, A., Windmann, S., Daum, I. and Güntürkün, O. (2005). Conceptual expansion and creative imagery as a function of psychoticism. *Consciousness and Cognition*, 14(3), 520–534. doi:10.1016/j.concog.2004.12.003

Abraham, A., Windmann, S., McKenna, P. and Güntürkün, O. (2007). Creative thinking in schizophrenia: The role of executive dysfunction and symptom severity. *Cognitive Neuropsychiatry*, 12(3), 235–258. doi:10.1080/13546800601046714

Abraham, A., Windmann, S., Siefen, R., Daum, I. and Güntürkün, O. (2006). Creative thinking in adolescents with attention deficit hyperactivity disorder (ADHD). *Child Neuropsychology: A Journal on Normal and Abnormal Development in Childhood and Adolescence*, 12(2), 111–123. doi:10.1080/09297040500320691

Andreasen, N. C. (2008). The relationship between creativity and mood disorders. *Dialogues in Clinical Neuroscience*, 10(2), 251–255.

Andreasen, N. J. and Powers, P. S. (1975). Creativity and psychosis: An examination of conceptual style. *Archives of General Psychiatry*, 32(1), 70–73.

Arden, R., Chavez, R. S., Grazioplene, R. and Jung, R. E. (2010). Neuroimaging creativity: A psychometric view. *Behavioural Brain Research*, 214(2), 143–156. doi:10.1016/j.bbr.2010.05.015

Badre, D. (2008). Cognitive control, hierarchy, and the rostro-caudal organization of the frontal lobes. *Trends in Cognitive Sciences*, 12(5), 193–200. doi:10.1016/j.tics.2008.02.004

Bowden, E. M. and Jung-Beeman, M. (2003). Normative data for 144 compound remote associate problems. *Behavior Research Methods, Instruments and Computers: A Journal of the Psychonomic Society, Inc.*, 35(4), 634–639.

Bradshaw, J. L. and Sheppard, D. M. (2000). The neurodevelopmental frontostriatal disorders: Evolutionary adaptiveness and anomalous lateralization. *Brain and Language*, 73(2), 297–320. doi:10.1006/brln.2000.2308

Carlsson, I., Wendt, P. E. and Risberg, J. (2000). On the neurobiology of creativity: Differences in frontal activity between high and low creative subjects. *Neuropsychologia*, 38(6), 873–885.

Carson, S. H. (2011). Creativity and psychopathology: A shared vulnerability model. *Canadian Journal of Psychiatry [Revue Canadienne De Psychiatrie]*, 56(3), 144–153.

Carson, S. H., Peterson, J. B. and Higgins, D. M. (2003). Decreased latent inhibition is associated with increased creative achievement in high-functioning individuals. *Journal of Personality and Social Psychology*, 85(3), 499–506. doi:10.1037/0022-3514.85.3.499

Cherkasova, M. V. and Hechtman, L. (2009). Neuroimaging in attention-deficit hyperactivity disorder: Beyond the frontostriatal circuitry. *Canadian Journal of Psychiatry [Revue Canadienne De Psychiatrie]*, 54(10), 651–664.

Chow, T. W. and Cummings, J. L. (2006). Frontal-subcortical circuits. In B. L. Miller and J. L. Cummings (Eds.), *The human frontal lobes: Functions and disorders* (2nd edn.) (pp. 25–43). New York: Guilford Press.

Claridge, G. (Ed.) (1997). *Schizotypy: Implications for illness and health* (1st edn.). New York: Oxford University Press.

Crespi, B., Summers, K. and Dorus, S. (2007). Adaptive evolution of genes underlying schizophrenia. *Proceedings. Biological Sciences/The Royal Society*, 274(1627), 2801–2810. doi:10.1098/rspb.2007.0876

Dickstein, S. G., Bannon, K., Castellanos, F. X. and Milham, M. P. (2006). The neural correlates of attention deficit hyperactivity disorder: An ALE meta-analysis. *Journal of Child Psychology and Psychiatry, and Allied Disciplines*, 47(10), 1051–1062. doi:10.1111/j.1469-7610.2006.01671.x

Dietrich, A. (2004). The cognitive neuroscience of creativity. *Psychonomic Bulletin & Review*, 11(6), 1011–1026.

Dietrich, A. and Kanso, R. (2010). A review of EEG, ERP, and neuroimaging studies of creativity and insight. *Psychological Bulletin*, 136(5), 822–848. doi:10.1037/a0019749

Dykes, M. and McGhie, A. (1976). A comparative study of attentional strategies of schizophrenic and highly creative normal subjects. *British Journal of Psychiatry*, 128, 50–56.

Eysenck, H. (1995). *Genius: The natural history of creativity*. New York: Cambridge University Press.

Fink, A., Graif, B. and Neubauer, A. C. (2009). Brain correlates underlying creative thinking: EEG alpha activity in professional vs. novice dancers. *NeuroImage*, 46(3), 854–862. doi:10.1016/j.neuroimage.2009.02.036

Finke, R. A. (1990). *Creative imagery: Discoveries and inventions in visualization*. Hillsdale, NJ: L. Erlbaum Associates.

Finke, R. A., Ward, T. B. and Smith, S. M. (1996). *Creative cognition: Theory, research, and applications* (1st paperback edn.). Cambridge, MA: MIT Press.

Folley, B. S. and Park, S. (2005). Verbal creativity and schizotypal personality in relation to prefrontal hemispheric laterality: A behavioral and near-infrared optical imaging study. *Schizophrenia Research*, 80(2–3), 271–282. doi:10.1016/j.schres.2005.06.016

Gibson, C., Folley, B. S. and Park, S. (2009). Enhanced divergent thinking and creativity in musicians: A behavioral and near-infrared spectroscopy study. *Brain and Cognition*, 69(1), 162–169. doi:10.1016/j.bandc.2008.07.009

Healey, D. and Rucklidge, J. J. (2006). An investigation into the relationship among ADHD symptomatology, creativity, and neuropsychological functioning in children. *Child Neuropsychology: A Journal on Normal and Abnormal Development in Childhood and Adolescence*, 12(6), 421–438. doi:10.1080/09297040600806086

Hemsley, D. R. (2005). The schizophrenic experience: Taken out of context? *Schizophrenia Bulletin*, 31(1), 43–53. doi:10.1093/schbul/sbi003

Hennessey, B. A. and Amabile, T. M. (2010). Creativity. *Annual Review of Psychology*, 61, 569–598. doi:10.1146/annurev.psych.093008.100416

Kalkstein, S., Hurford, I. and Gur, R. C. (2010). Neurocognition in schizophrenia. *Current Topics in Behavioral Neurosciences*, 4, 373–390.

Karimi, Z., Windmann, S., Güntürkün, O. and Abraham, A. (2007). Insight problem solving in individuals with high versus low schizotypy. *Journal of Research in Personality*, 41(2), 473–480. doi:10.1016/j.jrp.2006.03.008

Karlsson, J. L. (1970). Genetic association of giftedness and creativity with schizophrenia. *Hereditas*, 66(2), 177–181. doi:10.1111/j.1601-5223.1970.tb02343.x

Kasof, J. (1997). Creativity and breadth of attention. *Creativity Research Journal*, 10(4), 303–315. doi:10.1207/s15326934crj1004_2

Kröger, S., Rutter, B., Stark, R., Windmann, S., Hermann, C. and Abraham, A. (2012). Using a shoe as a plant pot: Neural correlates of passive conceptual expansion. *Brain Research*, 1430, 52–61. doi:10.1016/j.brainres.2011.10.031

Lesh, T. A., Niendam, T. A., Minzenberg, M. J. and Carter, C. S. (2011). Cognitive control deficits in schizophrenia: Mechanisms and meaning. *Neuropsychopharmacology: Official Publication of the American College of Neuropsychopharmacology*, 36(1), 316–338. doi:10.1038/npp.2010.156

Limb, C. J. and Braun, A. R. (2008). Neural substrates of spontaneous musical performance: An fMRI study of jazz improvisation. *PloS One*, 3(2), e1679. doi:10.1371/journal.pone.0001679

Mednick, S. A. (1962). The associative basis of the creative process. *Psychological Review*, 69, 220–232.

Mendelsohn, G. A. (1974). Associative and attentional processes in creative performance. *Journal of Personality*, 44, 341–369.

Miller, B. L., Ponton, M., Benson, D. F., Cummings, J. L. and Mena, I. (1996). Enhanced artistic creativity with temporal lobe degeneration. *Lancet*, 348(9043), 1744–1745.

Minas, R. K. and Park, S. (2007). Attentional window in schizophrenia and schizotypal personality: Insight from negative priming studies. *Applied and Preventive Psychology*, 12(3), 140–148. doi:10.1016/j.appsy.2007.09.003

Park, S., Lee, J., Folley, B. and Kim, J. (2003). Schizophrenia: Putting context in context. *Behavioral and Brain Sciences*, 26(1), 98–99. doi:10.1017/S0140525X03380021

Payne, R. W. (1973). Cognitive abnormalities. In H. J. Eysenck (Ed.), *Handbook of abnormal psychology* (pp. 193–261). London: Pitman.

Post, F. (1994). Creativity and psychopathology: A study of 291 world-famous men. *British Journal of Psychiatry*, 165(2), 22–34.

Pring, L., Ryder, N., Crane, L. and Hermelin, B. (2012). Creativity in savant artists with autism. *Autism: The International Journal of Research and Practice*, 16(1), 45–57. doi:10.1177/1362361311403783

Ramnani, N. and Owen, A. M. (2004). Anterior prefrontal cortex: Insights into function from anatomy and neuroimaging. *Nature reviews neuroscience*, 5(3), 184–194. doi:10.1038/nrn1343

Reverberi, C., Toraldo, A., D'Agostini, S. and Skrap, M. (2005). Better without (lateral) frontal cortex? Insight problems solved by frontal patients. *Brain: A Journal of Neurology*, 128(Part 12), 2882–2890. doi:10.1093/brain/awh577

Runco, M. A. (2004). Creativity. *Annual Review of Psychology*, 55, 657–687. doi:10.1146/annurev.psych.55.090902.141502

Rutter, B., Kröger, S., Stark, R., Schweckendiek, J., Windmann, S., Hermann, C. and Abraham, A. (2012). Can clouds dance? Neural correlates of passive conceptual expansion using a metaphor processing task: Implications for creative cognition. *Brain and Cognition*, 78(2), 114–122. doi:10.1016/j.bandc.2011.11.002

Sawyer, K. (2011). The cognitive neuroscience of creativity: A critical review. *Creativity Research Journal*, 23(2), 137–154. doi:10.1080/10400419.2011. 571191

Seeley, W. W., Matthews, B. R., Crawford, R. K., Gorno-Tempini, M. L., Foti, D., Mackenzie, I. R. and Miller, B. L. (2008). Unravelling Boléro: progressive aphasia, transmodal creativity and the right posterior neocortex. *Brain: A Journal of Neurology*, 131(Part 1), 39–49. doi:10.1093/brain/awm270

Seger, C. A., Desmond, J. E., Glover, G. H. and Gabrieli, J. D. (2000). Functional magnetic resonance imaging evidence for right-hemisphere involvement in processing unusual semantic relationships. *Neuropsychology*, 14(3), 361–369.

Semendeferi, K., Armstrong, E., Schleicher, A., Zilles, K. and Van Hoesen, G. W. (2001). Prefrontal cortex in humans and apes: A comparative study of area 10. *American Journal of Physical Anthropology*, 114(3), 224–241. doi:10.1002/1096-8644(200103)114:3<224::AID-AJPA1022>3.0.CO;2-I

Shamay-Tsoory, S. G., Adler, N., Aharon-Peretz, J., Perry, D. and Mayseless, N. (2011). The origins of originality: The neural bases of creative thinking and originality. *Neuropsychologia*, 49(2), 178–185. doi:10.1016/j.neuropsychologia.2010.11.020

Smith, S. M., Ward, T. B. and Schumacher, J. S. (1993). Constraining effects of examples in a creative generation task. *Memory & Cognition*, 21(6), 837–845.

Snyder, A. (2009). Explaining and inducing savant skills: Privileged access to lower level, less-processed information. *Philosophical Transactions of the Royal Society of London. Series B, Biological Sciences*, 364(1522), 1399–1405. doi:10.1098/rstb.2008.0290

Soeiro-de-Souza, M. G., Dias, V. V., Bio, D. S., Post, R. M. and Moreno, R. A. (2011). Creativity and executive function across manic, mixed and depressive episodes in bipolar I disorder. *Journal of Affective Disorders*, 135(1–3), 292–297. doi:10.1016/j.jad.2011.06.024

Stavridou, A. and Furnham, A. (1996). The relationship between psychoticism, trait-creativity and the attentional mechanism of cognitive inhibition. *Personality and Individual Differences*, 21(1), 143–153. doi:10.1016/0191-8869(96)00030-X

Thompson-Schill, S. L., Ramscar, M. and Chrysikou, E. G. (2009). Cognition without control: When a little frontal lobe goes a long way. *Current Directions in Psychological Science*, 18(5), 259–263. doi:10.1111/j.1467-8721.2009.01648.x

Turken, A. U. and Dronkers, N. F. (2011). The neural architecture of the language comprehension network: Converging evidence from lesion and connectivity analyses. *Frontiers in Systems Neuroscience*, 5, 1. doi:10.3389/fnsys.2011.00001

Vink, M., Ramsey, N. F., Raemaekers, M. and Kahn, R. S. (2005). Negative priming in schizophrenia revisited. *Schizophrenia Research*, 79(2–3), 211–216. doi:10.1016/j.schres.2005.05.004

Wallach, M. A. and Kogan, N. (1965). *Modes of thinking in young children: A study of the creativity–intelligence distinction*. New York: Holt, Rinehart & Winston.

Ward, T. B. (1994). Structured imagination: The role of category structure in exemplar generation. *Cognitive Psychology*, 27, 1–40.

Ward, T. B., Finke, R. A. and Smith, S. M. (1995). *Creativity and the mind: Discovering the genius within*. Cambridge, MA: Perseus Publishing.

Weisberg, R. W. (1995). Prolegomena to theories of insight in problem solving: A taxonomy of problems. In R. J. Sternberg and J. E. Davidson (Eds.), *The nature of insight* (pp. 157–196). Cambridge, MA: MIT Press.

Wong, C. and Gallate, J. (2012). The function of the anterior temporal lobe: A review of the empirical evidence. *Brain Research*, 1449, 94–116. doi:10.1016/j.brainres.2012.02.017

6 The evolutionary genetics of the creativity–psychosis connection

Aaron Kozbelt, Scott Barry Kaufman, Deborah J. Walder, Luz H. Ospina, and Joseph U. Kim

> Why is it that all those who have become eminent in philosophy or politics or poetry or the arts are clearly melancholics?
>
> – Aristotle

> Nothing in biology makes sense except in the light of evolution.
>
> – Dobzhansky (1973)

Introduction

Schizophrenia, a debilitating mental illness affecting roughly 1 percent of the population worldwide, is widely accepted as being highly genetically influenced (Cardno *et al.*, 1999; Gershon *et al.*, 1988; Kendler and Diehl, 1993). Schizophrenia is often marked by distortions of reality, disorganized thought, emotional blunting, and/or social isolation that may interfere with optimal functioning (Cornblatt *et al.*, 2012). Schizophrenia may be associated with creativity, although research findings are mixed (e.g., Andreasen, 2011; Kyaga *et al.*, 2013). Evidence also points to adverse effects on fertility and reproductive success among (particularly) males with schizophrenia (Svensson *et al.*, 2007), in part accounted for by marital status (McCabe *et al.*, 2009), suggesting potential biological and social influences. Collectively, this raises an intriguing potential evolutionary puzzle: *How does schizophrenia persist in the population at a stable prevalence rate too high to be explained by simple random mutation?* (Doi *et al.*, 2009; see also Del Giudice *et al.*, 2010). Among various hypotheses, including in the context of the emerging field of evolutionary epidemiology, schizophrenia may represent "one extreme of a sexually selected fitness factor" (Shaner *et al.*, 2004).

One possibility, which we explore in this chapter, is that schizophrenia remains in the human population (in part via the gene pool) because of shared genetic linkages to creativity (Andreasen, 2011; Carson, 2011), with acknowledgment of likely concurrent environmental (e.g., epigenetic) influences. Available evidence – particularly from twin studies – suggests that both creativity and schizophrenia have a heritable basis (Barron and Parisi, 1977; Vinkhuyzen *et al.*, 2009). Moreover, schizotypal thinking is often viewed as sharing features with creative thought, such as cognitive flexibility and divergent thinking via unusual but meaningful associations. These commonalities, coupled with the observed heritability of both constructs, suggest that there may be genetic factors common to both creativity and schizophrenia. Such genetic factors may be expressed along a continuum and thus vary with respect to serving protective or risk functions. Moreover, there may be genetic and environmental influences that discourage the expression of severe forms of schizophrenia (and other mental illnesses), whereby the results of unusual thought processes may be guided by "executive control" over these thoughts, so that they are put to their most productive use.

As a preliminary, we note that the general question of the relationship between creativity and mental health concerns (including schizophrenia) remains *highly* contentious, with some arguing for strong links (e.g., Andreasen, 1987; Jamison, 1993; Kottler, 2005; Ludwig, 1995; Nettle, 2001), others for basically no relation (e.g., Sawyer, 2006; Weisberg, 2006), and others occupying either a middle ground (Eysenck, 1993; Kyaga *et al.*, 2011, 2013; Simonton, 1994) or focusing on pointing out significant methodological and conceptual limitations in much research to date (e.g., Schlesinger, 2009; Silvia and Kaufman, 2011). Many aspects of this debate are explored throughout this volume, and we will not attempt to resolve it in this chapter. Here we entertain the possibility that there may be overlap in some aspects of creativity and psychosis – particularly thought patterns and genetic links – and we explore the genetic evidence bearing on this possible connection, as well as the implications of this evidence for our thinking about the relation between mental illness and creativity.

Specifically, in this chapter, we cautiously explore an evolutionary genetics approach in attempting to understand the possible connection between schizophrenia and creativity. We first discuss some general perspectives on the evolutionary persistence of genes associated with schizophrenia, emphasizing complex *polygenic* influences (i.e., the idea that schizophrenia and other mental disorders reflect an inevitable mutational load on the thousands of genes underlying human behavior – see Keller and Miller, 2006), together with environmental influences. At a finer grain, we then detail some of the specific genetic factors that have been implicated in schizophrenia spectrum disorders and in creativity. We next explore the nature of the association between creativity and mental illnesses (particularly schizophrenic spectrum disorders), in terms of shared cognitive processes and mechanisms, as well as potential genetic linkages. Finally, we close by noting that, while this research converges onto a more or less theoretically coherent gene's-eye perspective linking psychosis and creativity, its explanatory power may ultimately be limited, particularly when applied to understanding very high levels of creative achievement.

Perspectives on the evolutionary persistence of schizophrenia

In line with a dimensional model (Meehl, 1962, 1990), there is increasing evidence that psychotic and psychotic-like symptoms and presentation (associated with schizophrenia) fall along a continuum spanning the non-clinical (e.g., schizotypy and psychotic-like experiences, or PLEs) and the clinical (e.g., hallucinations; schizophrenia) ranges (e.g., Daly et al., 2012; Walder, Statucka et al., 2012). The generally adverse impact of schizophrenia across various functional domains together with evidence of reduced fecundity (e.g., McGrath et al., 1999) and high rates of the non-clinical phenotype collectively render the relatively stable, cross-cultural persistence of schizophrenia in the population an evolutionary puzzle.

Despite initial excitement in the field about the possibility of identifying major specific gene effects, recent escalating evidence instead suggests schizophrenia involves complex (i.e., diagnostically non-specific) polygenic influences (see Walder, Ospina et al., 2012). Some have argued that there may be shared genetic variation between illness and non-clinical psychotic-like symptom expression, and that the relatively high prevalence of the non-clinical phenotype may "mask" identification of these critical genes when comparing diagnostic groups – and that such genes may carry an evolutionary advantage (Kelleher et al., 2010). This perspective argues for the import of conducting studies more closely examining genetic and behavioral variation among individuals in the general population who experience PLEs, towards uncovering schizophrenia etiology (see Daly et al., 2012; Walder, Statucka et al., 2012). For example, some traits may have an optimal level of expression that is advantageous within the general population, beyond which the trait has adverse consequences for the individual.

The question regarding what processes maintain the persistence of high heritable variation in relatively disadvantageous traits – such as schizotypy (and in its extreme form, schizophrenia) – in the general population remains a universal challenge across the domains of Darwinian psychiatry, psychiatric genetics, and evolutionary genetics (Keller and Miller, 2006). To date, several evolutionary theories have been proposed using the Darwinian paradigm of selective advantage as a frame to account for the evolutionary persistence of psychosis (see the review by Kelleher *et al.*, 2010). For instance, Crow's (1997) "speciation hypothesis" argued that language developed at the price of psychosis. Burns' (2004) "costly-by-product" hypothesis posited that schizophrenia emerged as a by-product of social cognition, and argued for a paradigm shift including a "new philosophy of mind" towards an integrated "socio-neurologically" based understanding of mental disorders. Nesse's (2004) "cliff-edge" fitness theory contended that particular traits enhance fitness until a critical threshold, beyond which fitness diminishes. Dodgson and Gordon (2009) suggested that some hallucinations are evolutionary by-products of cognitive threat-detection systems reflecting an evolutionary bias towards the propagation of genes that promote false positives over false negatives (e.g., hypervigilance hallucinations) among a few members of society; while at times disadvantageous at the individual level, this may be advantageous at the group level. In yet another view, Crespi and Badcock (2008a, 2008b; see also Del Giudice *et al.*, 2010) hypothesized that psychotic spectrum presentations (as with the autism spectrum) represent pathological extremes of individual differences in the cognitive dimensions defining the human "social brain." They emphasized the role of a diametrical genetic process underlying psychosis; namely, the conflict between maternally and paternally expressed imprinted genes. Specifically, Crespi and Badcock argued that psychosis is characterized by overexpression of maternally expressed genes, a view in line with the kinship theory of genomic imprinting (Burt and Trivers, 2006), which represents an evolutionary-genetic extension of kin selection and parent–offspring conflict models, whereby imprinted genes contribute (albeit not exclusively) to the origin of psychosis as well as to individual variation in schizotypy. In this way, variability in genetic sequences and epigenetic patterns of imprinting at the same genetic loci may underlie heritable individual differences.

Sexual selection through mate choice, a perspective most closely associated with Miller and colleagues (see Geher and Kaufman, 2011; Miller, 2001), represents another broad, evolution-based hypothesis accounting for the persistence of psychosis-proneness in the human gene pool. According to Miller, our more recently evolved capacities for creativity (e.g., art, music, humor, language, and so on) are analogous to the peacock's ornate tail or the lion's mane, which do not serve any function directly relevant to the organism's survival; rather, they serve the function of attracting mates by acting as fitness indicators – revealing "good genes" and "good parent" traits. (Of course, it is now well known that genes are not uniformly "good" or "bad," as the influence of genes depends on gene expression, which is in part contingent on neurobiological and environmental context.) In this view, individuals who can demonstrate verbal fluency, divergent thinking, and looseness of associations in a productive, meaningful way demonstrate that they have other fitness-enhancing protective factors that support such displays of creativity. Some researchers argue that schizophrenia, on the other hand, represents the low-fitness extreme of cognitive processes that are normally distributed in the general population and are associated with creative production (Shaner et al., 2008). As detailed by Del Giudice et al. (2010), some have posited that moderate schizotypy in the absence of severe mental disorder may carry a reproductive advantage beyond the potential "costs" that may accompany subsequent illness (Nettle, 2001). Specifically, the benefits of positive (versus negative) schizotypy arguably are accounted for by their association with creativity, which may enhance attractiveness and courtship success. Indeed, some research has found a higher number of sexual partners among artists (Clegg et al., 2011; Nettle and Clegg, 2006), with higher levels of mating success among creative individuals mediated by milder forms of schizophrenia. A more recent study also found that schizotypy was indirectly related to short-term mating success (through engagement in creative activity), although the findings only held for males (Beaussart et al., 2012).

There has been healthy debate about these hypotheses. While some researchers claim that there tends to be an association between schizotypy and creativity (e.g., Batey and Furnham, 2008), others argue that general intelligence and openness to experience serve as better predictors of creativity than do schizotypal traits (Miller and Tal, 2007). Thus, in line with Shaner et al.'s (2004, 2008) consideration of psychotic spectrum disorders as a disadvantageous extreme of a sexually selected fitness indicator, schizotypal traits hold potential for both maximizing mating success while also increasing the risk for psychosis, rendering high positive schizotypy a high-risk strategy that is expected to be found among males more than females. This dynamic would help account for the continued propagation of genes associated with schizophrenia, despite some relative disadvantages, over the course of human evolution.

Notably, Miller (2010) has recently challenged equilibrium models like fitness neutrality, balancing selection, and pleiotropic mutations for understanding the genetic variation of traits, arguing that human traits are unlikely to have been at evolutionary equilibrium for the past several hundred generations. Miller posits the need for a novel evolutionary genetics model that appreciates the value of ongoing post-Pleistocene human evolution characterized by strong selective sweeps (i.e., relatively rapid increases in frequency of new fitness-increasing alleles) due to factors such as increased population density (Hawks *et al.*, 2007) and more selective assortative mating (Miller, 2001). Miller and colleagues highlight, at the molecular genetics level, the potential role of overall mutation load (Keller and Miller, 2006), as opposed to the more traditionally considered allelic variants targeted in genome-wide association studies (or GWAS). At the neurogenic level, they point to overall mutation load as influencing neurodevelopmental stability (Prokosch *et al.*, 2005), versus particular allele effects on specific cortical regions, neurotransmitter systems, or fiber tracts. This perspective shows promise in light of increasing evidence of complex, polygenic influences in the etiology of a range of psychiatric disorders, including schizophrenia, as opposed to previously considered major specific gene effects – and the absence of convergence in identifying particular risk alleles (e.g., in GWAS studies). At the psychometric level, Miller argues for consideration of a hierarchical structure of reliably measured psychological traits that supersedes aspects of psychological functioning such as cognition, emotion, motivation, and consciousness. Finally, at the sociological level, he points out that mutation load and selection are relevant to explaining human psychodiversity. In sum, while Miller seems to advocate for an evolutionary genetics approach, he offers caution with an eye on the potential limitations of existing evolutionary genetics models and their far-reaching potential implications, which need to be carefully considered.

Thus, all told, researchers have postulated a diverse and sophisticated set of perspectives and mechanisms detailing how the evolutionary persistence of mental illnesses like schizophrenia might be explained. These explanations are not mutually exclusive, but they remain the subject of vigorous debate and empirical analysis, extending over a range of methodologies. Notably, common to many of the explanations is a link between creative and psychotic thought patterns, whose positive benefits may outweigh or at least mitigate the obvious negative effects of a psychotic disorder like schizophrenia. With this set of evolutionary genetic principles in mind, we next turn to empirical findings on specific genes associated with schizophrenic spectrum disorders, and then to genes associated with creative thought.

Genes associated with schizophrenia spectrum disorders

In line with the diathesis-stress model of schizophrenia (see Walker and Diforio, 1997; Walker *et al.*, 2004), family and twin studies have demonstrated upwards of a ten-fold increased risk of developing a psychotic disorder compared with the general population (Cardno and Gottesman, 2000). As reviewed by Walder, Ospina *et al.* (2012), however, the precise genetic contributions to psychosis remain contentious. Despite recent literature on candidate gene approaches and GWAS initially seeming to suggest small-to-moderate gene effects in the development of psychotic disorders (Keller and Miller, 2006; Wang *et al.*, 2005), these cumulative approaches have proven largely inconclusive. Thus, major individual genes with small or moderate effects (examined via early linkage and candidate association studies) are unlikely to be responsible for susceptibility to – or the onset of – psychosis. Rather, schizophrenia spectrum disorders – or SSDs – are probably far more likely accounted for by a *polygenic* model, whereby some gene variants (including in combination) and more recently explored rare point mutations (e.g., copy-number variants, or CNVs) contribute small effects, as well as other genetic (e.g., epigenetic) factors (see Gebicke-Haerter, 2012). A number of reviews have explored some of the major individual candidate genes initially believed to contribute to a polygenic model of SSDs and more recent evidence pointing to genetic factors beyond GWAS and CNVs (Rodriguez-Murillo *et al.*, 2012; for a brief overview see Walder, Ospina *et al.*, 2012). In this section, we summarize this line of research and point to additional, more recent findings examining DNA methylation and histone modifications.

The earliest genetic studies aimed at identifying genes underlying psychosis included linkage studies, which assess the tendency of certain loci to be inherited together. These studies demonstrated inconsistent results, though a recent meta-analysis of 32 linkage studies revealed a number of significant linkages, particularly on chromosomes 2q and 5q (Ng *et al.*, 2009). Other approaches such as positional candidate gene studies, which prioritize genes in known linkage regions, have been more successful in discovering promising susceptibility genes (Ross *et al.*, 2006). These genes include *dysbindin* (*DTNBP1*), *D amino acid oxidase activator* (*DAOA*), *DISC1*, and *neuregulin 1* (*NRG1*). *DTNBP1* was first identified as a gene associated with schizophrenia through linkage on the chromosome 6p (Straub *et al.*, 2002) and is thought to influence glutamate neurotransmission (Numakawa *et al.*, 2004). Chromosome 13, which includes the *DAOA* gene, has strong linkage regions to schizophrenia (Detera-Wadleigh and McMahon, 2006); *DAOA* activates D amino acid oxidase, which is a coagonist at NMDA glutamate receptors. *DISC1*, found on chromosome 1, has been implicated in schizophrenia, bipolar disorder, and other major mental illnesses (Hennah *et al.*, 2006). Although its molecular mechanism is unknown, *DISC1* is thought to be involved in brain development and adult neuronal functioning such as neuronal migration and maturation, and synaptic transmission and plasticity. *NRG1* was identified as a candidate gene via fine-mapping of a locus on chromosome 8 (Harrison and Law, 2006) and has been subsequently linked with schizophrenia. Finally, *NRG1* encodes many types of mRNA and proteins that influence cell signaling, axon guidance, synaptogenesis, glial differentiation, myelination, and neurotransmission (Corfas *et al.*, 2004). The mechanisms by which altered *NRG1* function might lead to schizophrenia remain unclear, however.

More recently, the creation of the entire human genome-wide map of 3.1 million single nucleotide polymorphisms (SNPs) has allowed researchers to conduct GWAS (Frazer *et al.*, 2007). GWAS have the ability to detect small effect genes while not requiring the knowledge of specific pathogenesis. One such study based on pooled DNA sampling reported a significant association to the *REELIN* gene, believed to encode a protein involved in neuronal positioning and neuronal development (Shifman *et al.*, 2008). GWAS based on individual genotyping have implicated genes such as *colony stimulating factor 2 receptor alpha (CSF2RA)*, which is thought to regulate granulocytes and macrophages, and *short stature homeobox isoform b (SHOX)*, which is a transcription factor whose involvement is still unknown (Lencz *et al.*, 2007). Interestingly, another GWAS based on individual genotyping for schizophrenia revealed a significant result for the *zinc finger protein 804A* gene (*ZNF804A*) only when the phenotype was expanded to include bipolar disorder (O'Donovan *et al.*, 2008). Therefore, *ZNF804A* is very likely a susceptibility locus for both schizophrenia and bipolar disorder, which share similar clinical symptomatology (and which have been associated with creativity; e.g., Eysenck, 1993; Jamison, 1993). Later, we discuss potential shared genetic factors implicated in both psychosis and creativity.

GWAS technology also allows for the assessment of CNVs, which are stretches of genomic deletions and duplications ranging from 1 Kb to several Mb that can vary between individuals. One of the most consistent findings using CNV analysis is the role of chromosome 22q11; a deletion of chromosome 22q11 increases the risk for schizophrenia approximately 25-fold (Murphy *et al.*, 1999). With regards to individual CNVs implicating specific genes, Kirov *et al.* (2008) identified a rare deletion affecting part of the gene *NRXN1*, which has been previously implicated in autism and mental retardation (Szatmari *et al.*, 2007). They also observed a *de novo* duplication of *amyloid beta A4 precursor protein-binding (APBA2)*, a protein that interacts with *NRXN1*. Together, *NRXN1* and *APBA2* are believed to play a role in synaptic development and function.

Most recent GWAS studies have failed, however, to demonstrate convergence of findings across investigations. Environmental effects also contribute to the etiology of psychotic disorders through epigenetic means. Epigenetics is the study of heritable – but reversible – changes in gene expression that occur without any changes in the genomic DNA sequence such as DNA methylation (Pidsley and Mill, 2011). Growing evidence for DNA methylation in schizophrenia mainly involves candidate genes associated with neurotransmitter function such as *REELIN* (Abdolmaleky *et al.*, 2004). Altered function of serotonin has also been implicated in the increased susceptibility of a number of psychiatric disorders, including schizophrenia (Gaddum and Hameed, 1954). Methylation of a serotonin-related allele (*HTR2A* C102) has been found to correlate with *DNMT1* expression levels (Polesskaya *et al.*, 2006). DNA methylation analyses of *COMT* (believed to play a role in schizophrenia) have discovered respective reductions in the promoter in approximately 50 percent of patients (Abdolmaleky *et al.*, 2006). These results demonstrate that DNA methylation provides a viable option for better understanding the development of psychotic disorders.

In sum, despite the complexity of polygenic models of gene expression, in which a large number of genes contribute small-to-moderate effects for developing a disorder, and the fact that the study of the genetic basis of psychosis and other mental disorders is in its infancy, researchers have identified a fair number of genes that appear to be associated with SSDs. However, their complex inter-relationships and roles remain ambiguous.

Genes associated with creative thought

The methodological and conceptual complications inherent in the study of the genetic basis of psychosis are echoed and perhaps even intensified in the study of the genetic basis of creative thought. Creativity itself has only been the subject of scientific investigation in the last 60 years or so (see Guilford, 1950), with a notable acceleration in the past two decades. There is broad agreement that creativity involves the ability to generate novel and useful ideas and behaviors, which are then implemented in everyday life. However, assessments of novelty and value occur against the backdrop of sociocultural factors (Csikszentmihalyi, 1988; Sawyer, 2006), which can be construed as largely subjective. Indeed, the whole enterprise of understanding creativity from neurological or genetic perspectives is rife with controversy. For instance, as Gardner (2001) argued, "You could know every bit of neurocircuitry in somebody's head, and you still would not know whether or not that person was creative" (p. 130). Sawyer (2006) bluntly stated, "We can't look to genetics for the explanation of creativity" (p. 94).

However, the notion that there is a heritable aspect of at least some aspects of high ability (including creativity) is a venerable one, going back at least to Francis Galton's book *Hereditary genius* (1869). Earlier studies of monozygotic versus dizygotic twins, which provide an estimate of genetic heritability, yielded somewhat mixed results. For instance, Barron (1972) found evidence for heritability of aspects of creative thought like adaptive flexibility and aesthetic judgment of visual displays, but no evidence of heritability for the ability to generate numerous ideas or original ideas; Vandenberg (1968) and Reznikoff *et al.* (1973) found no evidence for the heritability of divergent thinking or other putative aspects of creative thought. However, more recent research by Vinkhuyzen *et al.* (2009) looking at both normal and high levels of ability in diverse (and plausibly creative) domains like music, art, writing, language, chess, mathematics, and sports, as well as in memory and knowledge, have revealed high heritability rates – ranging from .32 to .71 for aptitude measures and .50 to .92 for talent measures in these domains. Thus, the extent to which aspects of creativity, or at least creative potential, has some genetic basis remains at the very least an open question, with recent results suggesting a relatively strong association.

If this is the case, then what are the genetic variations associated with cognition, personality, and behavior that bestow on an individual more creative capacity than the average person and, thus, perhaps render him or her more reproductively successful? This is not a question with a simple answer. Analogous to the polygenic view that multiple genes jointly confer a probabilistic risk for developing complex mental illnesses on the individual (Hyman, 2000), recent studies in creativity research similarly demonstrate the existence of several genes that appear to contribute to individuals' creative abilities (Reuter *et al.*, 2005). This is understandable given that it is highly likely that creative behaviors involve a widely distributed network of brain regions (Chávez-Eakle, 2007), and also that genes and complex behaviors (such as creativity) are unlikely to have direct, simple links with these regions (Kandel, 1998).

This polygenic perspective on creativity is indispensable in our discussion of genetic bases of creativity, because creativity is not a unitary or homogenous entity but rather involves a conglomeration of cognitive components (Amabile, 1996; Sternberg and Lubart, 1995). Among the more prominent components are: ideational or cognitive *fluency*, in which (many) raw ideas are generated or conceptually combined; the ability to devise *original* or novel ideas, typically defined in terms of their statistical infrequency; cognitive *flexibility*, or facility in switching attentional focus from one domain to another (Guilford, 1967; Torrance, 1969); and the ability to *discern* promising ideas from those that are unlikely to lead to creative final outcomes (Silvia, 2008). This is by no means an exhaustive list; moreover, such processes are unlikely to be exclusively associated with creative cognition. The multiplicity inherent in creative thought is also evident when considering that creative achievement across various domains often draws on different sets of cognitive abilities and behavioral skills (Kaufman and Baer, 2005).

Despite the daunting variability in the cognitive and behavioral components that constitute creative abilities, some research has begun to investigate the genetic basis of creativity. In particular, dopamine (DA) receptor genes, which are related to the brain's dopaminergic functioning, have been targeted. Notably, dopamine receptor genes are simultaneously relevant to psychopathology and creativity, because several studies have pointed to the importance of intact dopaminergic signaling for normal and efficient prefrontal functioning necessary for working memory (Sawaguchi and Goldman-Rakic, 1991) and attention (Nieoullon, 2002). Additionally, there is some evidence to suggest that personality traits associated with creative behavior are affected by dopaminergic signaling (Reuter *et al.*, 2005). In particular, a tendency for novelty seeking has been generally found to be associated with D4 receptor gene (*DRD4*) polymorphisms (Epstein *et al.*, 1996). Such research findings have sparked interest in trying to find a link between dopamine-related genes and creative thought processes. One positron emission tomography (PET) imaging study found a negative correlation between divergent-thinking abilities and D2 receptor densities in the thalamus region (de Manzano *et al.*, 2010), further supporting the idea that dopamine availability has important influence on creative thought processes.

Interestingly, in schizophrenia, abnormal dopaminergic functioning in the thalamic region has been previously associated with psychotic symptoms and genetic risks of psychosis (Bucksbaum *et al.*, 2006; Talvik *et al.*, 2003). A specific allele (A1+) of the D2 receptor gene (*DRD2*) has also been linked with verbal creativity, whereas the A allele of the *TPH1* gene was associated with figural and numerical creativity (Reuter *et al.*, 2006). In regards to a more behavioral manifestation of creativity, *AVPR1a* and *SLC6A4* gene polymorphisms were found to be associated with creative dance performance (Bachner-Melman *et al.*, 2005).

In the same family of dopamine-related genes, there has been some demonstration of a link between dopamine (DA) transporter genetic polymorphisms and an important component of creative thinking ability – namely, attentional cognitive flexibility. Studies have shown that individuals homozygous for the 9-repeat allele of the *DAT1* dopamine transporter gene have a greater advantage over those without a 9-repeat allele in one's ability to detect task novelty (Garcia-Garcia *et al.*, 2010) and also greater cognitive readiness to be attentionally flexible (Colzato *et al.*, 2010). Presumably such a difference is accounted for by the variability in *DAT1* polymorphism that affects individuals' striatal DA availability. This association influences individuals' adeptness at changing their focus of attention, which may in turn mediate a creative thinking process of rapidly shifting attentional focus and making original connections between unrelated objects or items. Interestingly, one study (White and Shah, 2006) has shown that adults diagnosed with attention-deficit/hyperactivity disorder (ADHD) could generate more items in a divergent-thinking task (i.e., an unusual uses task, in which participants are asked to think of many possible alternative uses of a common object), demonstrating a cognitive advantage in terms of ideational fluency (although it should be noted that ADHD-diagnosed participants also showed compromised convergent thinking and inhibitory control in other tasks).

Due to its functional significance in dopaminergic functioning, the *catechol-O-methyl-transferase (COMT)* gene and its polymorphisms have also been a focus of active research in the past decade. While the general body of behavioral genetics literature points to the finding that reduced *COMT* activity related-genotypes (i.e., Val158Met polymorphism) are associated with higher general intelligence measures (Goldman *et al.*, 2009), studies more specifically investigating their link to creativity have found no association between *COMT* genotypes and measures of creativity (Lu and Shi, 2010; Reuter *et al.*, 2006).

While the aforementioned genes relevant to dopaminergic functioning have undoubtedly been in the spotlight of behavioral genetics research in creativity, other non-DA-related genes associated with cognitive functioning have also received interest in their potential linkage to creative thinking and behavior. In one study, 5-HTTLPR polymorphism of the serotonin (5-HTT) transporter gene was associated with verbal and figural creativity, in that participants who had short/short (s/s) alleles and short/long (s/l) alleles showed greater verbal creativity than those with long/long (l/l) alleles of the genetic polymorphism (Volf *et al.*, 2009). The same study additionally reported that the s/s type had greater figural creativity compared with both the s/l and s/s types. Interestingly, individuals with the short allele of the 5-HTTLPR polymorphisms are also considered to have lower transcriptional efficiency in the promoter region of the serotonin gene compared with those with the long allele of the polymorphism (Lesch *et al.*, 1996), and this seems to confer on them disproportionate risk toward developing depression under stressful life experience (Caspi *et al.*, 2003) – although recent evidence (Pluess *et al.*, 2010) on the "differential sensitivity" hypothesis suggests that, with positive developmental experiences, such individuals are also more likely to experience positive outcomes (e.g., reduced neuroticism). Adding to this indirect evidence of the link between serotonergic functioning and creativity is that some psychiatric patients who receive selective serotonin reuptake inhibitor (SSRI) treatment complain of emotional blunting (Opbroek *et al.*, 2002) and diminished creativity (Bolling and Kohlenberg, 2004) associated with the intake of SSRI medication. Research on the cognitive and behavioral relevance of serotonergic functioning in relation to creativity is still scarce, and further research will be needed to clarify the connection between them.

In sum, despite ongoing controversy about the relevance of genetics to understanding the phenomenon of creativity, there appears to be at least some direct preliminary evidence linking aspects of creative thought to specific genes. Moreover, these genes appear to be related to brain systems often invoked in discussions of creativity – as well as some types of psychopathology. In the next two sections, we make explicit some alleged linkages between mental illness and creativity, both in terms of cognitive and personality factors, and at the genetic level.

General links between mental illness and creativity

As suggested by the Aristotle quotation that serves as this chapter's epigraph, there is a long anecdotal history of associating mental illness and creativity. Indeed, in this chapter, our argument thus far has implicitly assumed that there exists some kind of connection between at least some aspects of mental illness (specifically, psychosis) and some aspects of creativity. But to what extent does this alleged association withstand rigorous scientific scrutiny? Researchers and scholars interested in this issue have implemented a variety of methodologies in pursuing it. These include anecdotal and biographical case studies of creative persons – either individually or as part of larger samples – as well as measures of intelligence and personality, laboratory tests of other cognitive constructs, and functional neuroimaging. Given the complexity and multidimensionality of mental illness and creativity, in order to obtain reliable information about the association between the two, it is necessary to narrow the scope of investigation to very particular aspects of each construct (Silvia and Kaufman, 2011), regardless of the method used. Since this level of clarification is rarely achieved, a key point in this section is that definitive answers about the association between mental illness and creativity are still rather elusive. However, on our particular topic of the relation between general creative thought processes and the thought processes associated with schizotypy, the available empirical research suggests some likely patterns of association.

In this section, we first briefly review some more general lines of evidence on the association between mental illness and creativity. Case studies represent perhaps the most venerable line of research in this vein. Biographical accounts of eminent creative historical figures often describe the presence of mental disorders such as mood disorders (major depression and bipolar spectrum disorders) as well as episodes of psychosis and other SSDs. Among the many famous cases of alleged mood disorders are Vincent van Gogh, Martin Luther, Ernest Hemingway, Winston Churchill, and Theodore Roosevelt (see Andreasen, 2008). Others are known for also having family members with mental illness (bolstering the case for a genetic link), such as James Joyce, whose daughter had schizophrenia and schizotypal traits; Albert Einstein, whose son had schizophrenia with schizotypal and eccentric traits; and Bertrand Russell, who had many relatives with schizophrenia/psychosis (Andreasen, 2011). However, as Silvia and Kaufman (2011) noted, such case studies suffer from a number of intrinsic limitations, including generalizability across creators as well as judges. That is, many case study reports involve a single judge (usually the author of the case study), who had specific reasons for picking the subject, thereby focusing on the traits and life experiences of the creator that support their conclusion. Therefore, in many case studies, participant and judge are confounded.

Indeed, rigorous research designed to examine the association of creativity with mental illness is laced with multiple challenges, such as identifying the optimal sample and comparison group, as well as defining the nature of the sample and even defining the terms "creativity" and "mental illness" (Andreasen, 2008). In an effort to empirically test the creativity–psychosis hypothesis, some researchers have studied more global patterns by examining larger samples of creative individuals. Several empirical investigations have been conducted on historically important creative individuals. For example, Ludwig (1995) reviewed information on 1,004 individuals considered to be influential in the twentieth century and reported high rates of alcoholism, schizophrenia, and mood disorders. Andreasen's (1987) study of currently living highly creative individuals, conducted at the University of Iowa during the 1970s and 1980s, was rooted in empirical evidence of famous cases coupled with a theoretical underpinning based on the possibility that the frequently observed cognitive trait among individuals with psychosis – namely, a capacity to see the world in a novel and original way – may be shared by creative people who likewise can see things that others cannot (Andreasen, 2011). Andreasen's study did not reveal a link between creativity and psychosis, although she did report an elevated level of mood disorders among creative writers. Others (Jamison, 1993; Ludwig, 1995) have reported concordant results using personal interviews of participants towards determining diagnosis using modern conceptualizations of depression and bipolar disorder. Along similar lines, Post (1996) studied 291 British and American creative achievers and reported similarly high incidences of mood and SSDs in participants and their family members.[1]

This research led to the second Iowa study of creative genius, still ongoing, which uses a case-control comparison design (Andreasen, 2011). This neuroimaging study attempts to compare highly creative individuals, defined as those who have won a major award in their field (e.g., Nobel or Pulitzer prizes), with "non-creative" controls on measures of intelligence and personality as well as functional neuroimaging. The latter uses a paradigm that activates the association cortices, those most active when engaged in free-ranging and uncensored thought. Preliminary findings have revealed that brain activations in these areas are stronger among creative individuals, and comparable between artists and scientists. However, limited sample size to date precludes conclusions about creativity differences as a function of mental illness.

In sum, while such studies are interesting and suggestive, the precise nature of the association between creativity and mental illness remains difficult to delineate, and as yet there is no general-purpose answer (Silvia and Kaufman, 2011). There are different levels of creative achievement (e.g., little-c versus Big-C: Kaufman and Beghetto, 2009), different aspects of creative cognition (e.g., conceptual combination, divergent thinking, latent inhibition), and different degrees and kinds of illness expression (e.g., schizophrenia, positive schizotypy, negative schizotypy), which do not necessarily map onto each other in a uniform manner. For instance, while schizophrenia tends to be marked by debilitating symptoms across positive, negative, and disorganized symptom domains, artists who demonstrate schizotypal traits tend to experience positive symptoms (e.g., unusual perceptual experiences, magical beliefs) more so than negative or disorganized trait dimensions (Nelson and Rawlings, 2010), while mathematical and scientific creativity tends to be associated with negative schizotypal traits (e.g., physical and social anhedonia, introversion) (Nettle, 2006; Rawlings and Locarnini, 2008). As Silvia and Kaufman highlight, researchers attempting to investigate the nature of the relation between mental illness and creativity need to specify the various levels of creative achievement, aspects of creative cognition, and illness expression under investigation.

Because, in this chapter, our focus is primarily on general creative thought processes and the thought processes associated with schizotypy (characterized by eccentricity, magical thinking, and unusual

---

[1] Importantly, however, see Schlesinger's (2009) strong methodological critique of this whole line of inquiry, which in her view casts considerable doubt on the strength of the popular "genius–madness" association.

experiences), we now focus on research investigating links between these constructs. In recent years, a number of theorists and empirical studies have explored possible linkages between creative cognition and schizotypy, with some suggestive findings. For example, Eysenck (1993) argued that certain aspects of cognition associated with high scores on a psychotic personality dimension (e.g., overinclusive thinking) might facilitate originality and, under optimal circumstances, creative thinking. One study examining 100 students found a significant correlation between intensity of psychoticism and creativity, as measured using divergent-thinking tasks (Woody and Claridge, 1977). O'Reilly *et al.* (2001) reported that creative art students scored higher on creativity measures as well as on the unusual experiences dimension of schizotypy compared with students in the humanities. Burch *et al.* (2006) also demonstrated higher rates of schizotypy in a sample of visual arts students compared with students in other academic departments. A more recent study (Nelson and Rawlings, 2010) found interesting linkages between the positive symptoms of schizotypy and normally varying personality traits: in a sample of 100 artists, positive schizotypal traits were the strongest predictors of aspects of the creative experience, including absorption and power/pleasure. Further research suggests that absorption is aligned with the personality trait Openness to Experience distinctly from Intellect. For instance, DeYoung *et al.* (2011) found that the Openness/Intellect domain of personality comprised a simplex of traits, with Openness at one end and Intellect at the other. Absorption was one of the best markers of Openness, while a traditional measure of intelligence was one of the best markers of Intellect.

What cognitive mechanisms underlie schizotypy? DeYoung *et al.* (2011) argued that positive schizotypy is in large part due to the false detection of patterns through an overfiring of causal connections, known as apophenia. Accordingly, positive schizotypy involves an overactive implicit learning system. In support of this, recent research has found a correlation between Openness to Experience and implicit learning ability (Kaufman *et al.*, 2010). In the latter study, implicit learning was not related to Intellect, further suggesting that the cognitive mechanisms that underlie positive schizotypy specifically also underlie Openness to Experience.

Another plausible cognitive mechanism associated with both schizotypy and creative cognition is the construct of latent inhibition. Latent inhibition is a gating mechanism that screens from conscious awareness information previously tagged as irrelevant. Carson *et al.* (2003) found that reduced latent inhibition was associated with creative achievement among a high-IQ sample. They proposed that decreased latent inhibition increases creativity by allowing irrelevant stimuli to enter one's conscious awareness, thereby increasing the number of novel and useful combinations of stimuli.

Taken together, these studies suggest that: (1) creative persons (particularly artists) have higher levels of positive schizotypy and a propensity for psychosis, and (2) milder symptoms are more conducive to creativity than more severe forms of SSDs. With these preliminary associations in mind, we next look at common genetic linkages between these creative mental processes and schizotypy.

Genetic links between creativity and schizophrenia spectrum disorders

Despite the provocative links between psychosis and creativity outlined in the previous sections of this chapter, and the apparent heritability of both constructs, few empirical studies have been conducted to directly assess or identify genes that potentially undergird both psychosis and creativity. While such research is in its earliest stages, several notable findings have emerged.

For instance, Kéri (2009) argued that the neuroregulin 1 gene (*NRG1*) is linked to both increased risk for psychosis (see Mei and Xiong, 2008) and creative achievement, particularly in individuals with high intellectual and academic achievement (see also Venkatasubramanian and Kalmady, 2010). Kéri focused on a particular polymorphism of *NRG1*, SNP8NRG243177/rs6994992 (C versus T), where the T/T phenotype is associated with an increased risk for psychosis and lower premorbid IQ (Hall *et al.*, 2006), lower working memory capacity (Stefanis *et al.*, 2007), and neurodevelopment and synaptic plasticity (Harrison and Law, 2006). Participants were administered measures of schizotypy and creativity, and genomic DNA was extracted. Kéri discovered that individuals with the T/T phenotype demonstrated significantly higher divergent-thinking scores (e.g., originality, flexibility, and fluency) compared with the other phenotypes. While no direct link was made between creativity and a risk for developing psychosis in the study sample, this line of research suggests that *NRG1* may be simultaneously related to psychopathology and creativity. This is one of the first studies suggesting that a genetic polymorphism linked to mental illness may confer an advantage in psychological functioning by means of higher creative, intellectual functioning.

A common area of interest with regards to overlap among mental illnesses and creativity concern genes that code for neurotransmitters and neurotransmission. For example, dopamine (D2) receptor sensitivity, a neurotransmitter highly associated with psychosis, has been linked with decreased latent inhibition (Wang *et al.*, 2004), that is, the inability to filter extraneous and potentially distracting information from the environment, an individual-difference variable that has been linked to creativity (Carson *et al.*, 2003; see also Carson, this volume). As mentioned previously, the gene *COMT*, which is involved in the regulation of dopamine levels, has also been implicated in psychotic disorders and as contributing to various cognitive processes. For instance, the Val allele of the Val158Met polymorphism allows for greater expression of *COMT* (and therefore lower levels of dopamine) in the prefrontal areas (Honea *et al.*, 2009). While the Val+ allele has been linked with SSDs (Egan *et al.*, 2001), the Val– allele has been associated with higher IQ, working memory, and cognitive flexibility, a common characteristic of creative behavior (Joober *et al.*, 2002; Malhotra *et al.*, 2002). There is also recent evidence of *COMT* modulation of neuroendocrine (hypothalamic-pituitary-adrenal) activity (e.g., cortisol) among adolescents at risk for psychiatric disorders, including psychosis (Walder *et al.*, 2010).

As in psychotic disorders, serotonin has also been implicated in creative ability, as discussed earlier. The gene *SLC6A4* (also called *5HTT*), which is thought to regulate synaptic levels of serotonin, has been associated with personality constructs of creativity, such as increased scores on assessments of Openness to new experiences (Stoltenberg *et al.*, 2002). More recently, the short *SLA6A4* promoter region polymorphism has been associated with creative dancing ability, such that altered serotonin levels are theorized to increase ability for imagery and attention to stimuli (Bachner-Melman *et al.*, 2005). Along similar lines, Volf *et al.* (2009) found that individuals with the short allele of the 5-HTTPR polymorphism of the *5HTT* gene demonstrated significantly higher levels of verbal creative ability than individuals with an l/l configuration, and individuals with an s/s genotype demonstrated higher figural creativity scores compared with carriers of the L allele. Other evidence for the influence of serotonin levels on creativity includes the *A779C* polymorphism of the *TPH1* gene, which influences the enzyme that regulates levels of 5-HT, which has been linked to schizophrenia and suicide (Abbar *et al.*, 2001; Zaboli *et al.*, 2006). Reuter *et al.* (2006) discovered that carriers of the A allele of *A779C* polymorphism scored higher on measures of figural and mathematical creativity compared with carriers of the C allele in a group of university students.

Further creativity research focusing on specific positional candidate genes has revealed a genetic influence of *AVPR* polymorphism. Again, Bachner-Melman *et al.* (2005) revealed an association with the *SLC6A4* polymorphism and creative dance; however, they also discovered an association with creative dance and the *AVPR1A* polymorphism. The AVP (or arginine vasopressin) receptor 1A is coded by the *AVPR* receptor 1A gene and has been observed to influence the AVP hormone in the brain, which is thought to affect social, emotional, and behavioral traits such as aggression (Thompson *et al.*, 2004), parenting (Hammock and Young, 2006), and love (Zeki, 2007). Also, Ukkola *et al.* (2009) assessed the genetic influences on musical creativity and discovered a significant relationship with musical ability and the haplotype RS1 + RS3 of the *AVPR1A* polymorphism. Finally, Reuter *et al.* (2006) ambitiously set forth to discover the first candidate genes for creativity, focusing particularly on polymorphisms of *COMT*, *DRD2*, and *TPH1* genes, because they have been implicated in executive cognitive functioning. They discovered no relationship between *COMT* and creativity measures, while the *DRD2* TAQ 1A allele was associated with verbal creativity and the *TPH1* A779 allele was associated with figural creativity.

In sum, despite limited direct support, there is converging evidence of some shared genetic underpinnings of psychosis and creativity. This result is in line with long-standing anecdotal speculation about the relation between mental illness and creativity, as well as more recent cognitive research identifying loose, flexible mental processes that play out in similar (if not identical) ways in schizotypal and creative thought.

Limits of these explanations

The conceptualization in the preceding sections is clearly preliminary, relying on early genetic studies of creativity and SSDs that have been conducted only in recent decades, and is thus presented with caution. Surely, future research techniques elucidating these issues will increase in sophistication, scope, and detail. Nevertheless, it is impressive how much progress has been made so far, both at the levels of theories and specific empirical results, in producing a coherent genetic perspective linking aspects of psychosis and creativity. Thus far, the key elements in this perspective have focused on the activity (including interaction) of several genetic factors (in the context of environmental influences), including genes that code for neurotransmitters like dopamine and serotonin. If we imagine the likely improvements in technology and measurement that will be applied to this question in the coming years and decades, it may be useful to consider some of the potential limitations of this approach.

On the theory side, our current understanding of all of the issues raised in this chapter is limited by the way in which the relevant constructs have been conceptualized up to the present time. This point applies to the action of genes and possible mechanisms relating genes to cognitive processes and behaviors, general evolutionary models (including sexual selection models) explaining the evolutionary persistence of seemingly disadvantageous traits, as well as mental illnesses and our understanding of the nature of human creativity. Indeed, as detailed by Miller (2010), evolutionary genetics is an emerging field that is in flux, as is our understanding of the genetic factors contributing to mental illnesses and creative ability. Thus, theoretical considerations must continue to evolve in tandem with new knowledge gained in the field. As each of these bodies of theoretical work evolves and is constrained by emerging empirical findings (and the associated technological advances allowing such findings), we might expect some aspects of our basic understanding of these issues to change, maybe quite radically.

Similar issues pertain to the scientific study of creativity. As noted by Silvia and Kaufman (2011), many basic questions about the relation between mental illness and creativity simply remain unanswered, largely because the questions have not been asked with sufficient specificity or addressed with sufficient methodological rigor. Thinking even more broadly, it is probably fair to state that many issues about the fundamental nature of creativity remain poorly understood; these lacunae have almost certainly colored our understanding of how creativity may be related to psychosis and other mental illnesses. For instance, throughout this chapter, we have characterized the loose, disorganized thought patterns evident in schizotypal thinking as being closely associated with mental processes like divergent thinking and distant conceptual combinations that are traditionally regarded as essential to creativity.

However, such idea-generating cognitive processes typically represent only the very beginning of the creative process. Many sophisticated models of creativity (e.g., Martindale, 1990; Simonton, 1984; Ward et al., 1999) posit two fundamental regimes of creative thought: a largely unconscious process of generating ideas, followed by a largely conscious, goal-directed process of elaborating them into finished creative products. Currently, such models typically show a peculiar bias whereby generating ideas is given priority as *the* essential engine of creativity, while idea elaboration is often underemphasized and undervalued (Kozbelt, 2009). However, mounting evidence (e.g., Fayena-Tawil et al., 2011; Kozbelt, 2006, 2007, 2008; Silvia, 2008) suggests that the kinds of evaluative and goal-directed cognitive processes typical of idea elaboration play a far more important role in creative productivity than has been traditionally recognized.

Elaborative processes are certainly critical for the creation of complex, domain-specific Big-C creative achievements, such as symphonies and novels – a process virtually always rife with revision and rethinking. The main links between psychosis and creativity, however, have almost exclusively emphasized idea generation rather than idea elaboration (Kozbelt, 2009). Reconceptualizing the general nature of creativity to give greater weight to elaborative processes has the potential to shift the balance away from the potential psychosis–creativity association, at least for instances of very high levels of creative achievement. The extent to which any genetic basis might be identified for such complex cognitive and socioculturally informed processes is difficult to assess, particularly because, as with evolutionary genetic models of schizophrenia, such an alternative framework of creativity has yet to be worked out in detail.

Despite potential limitations towards understanding these complex issues, the nature and origins of a possible association of creativity with psychosis may slowly become clearer as the field gains an increasingly sophisticated understanding of the complexity of polygenic influences on the mind, brain, and behavior – including the importance of gene sequencing and the role of epigenetics (including environmental influences). Importantly, rather than vying for a singular explanation, a healthier and sounder approach likely will be more integrative. From an evolutionary perspective, an optimistic appraisal of the outcome of this line of research would be something like a multilevel synthesis of theoretical approaches that integrates, as one possible explanation, sexual selection with evolutionary genetics. Potentially, this would move the dynamic of scholarly discussion and debate away from the current surfeit of (albeit non-mutually exclusive) models described early in the chapter toward a more integrated and parsimonious position. Such a model would need to account for several key findings (among others): (1) the evolutionary persistence of psychosis in the population worldwide; (2) tentative (although not consistent nor conclusive) evidence of possibly higher likelihood of psychiatric disorders (including across the schizophrenia spectrum) among highly creative individuals; (3) a link between creative professions and first-degree relatives of schizophrenia patients (see Kyaga et al., 2013); and (4) the modest (albeit not uniform) evidence of an association of creativity with psychotic-like experiences (in the non-clinical range) in the general population (see Kyaga et al., 2013). Providing a sound, integrative genetic, and environmentally informed explanation for the evolutionary enigma of the persistence of schizophrenia, and the nature of its relation to creativity, is an enormous challenge – but one which, if the past decade of research is any indication, may well be scientifically tractable.

References

Abbar, M., Courtet, P., Bellivier, F., Leboyer, M., Boulenger, J. P., Castel-hau, D., Ferreira, M., Lambercy, C., Mouthon, D., Paoloni-Giacobino, A.,

Vessaz, M., Malafosse, A. and Buresi, C. (2001). Suicide attempts and the tryptophan hydroxylase gene. *Molecular Psychiatry*, 6, 268–273.

Abdolmaleky, H. M., Cheng, K. H., Faraone, S. V., Wilcox, M., Glatt, S. J., Gao, F., Smith, C. L., Shafa, R., Aeali, B., Carnevale, J., Pan, H., Papageorgis, P., Ponte, J. F., Sivaraman, V., Tsuang, M. T. and Thiagalingam, S. (2006). Hypomethylation of MB-COMT promoter is a major risk factor for schizophrenia and bipolar disorder. *Human Molecular Genetics*, 15, 3132–3145.

Abdolmaleky, H. M., Smith, C. L., Faraone, S. V., Shafa, R., Stone, W., Glatt, S. J. and Tsuang, M. T. (2004). Methylomics in psychiatry: Modulation of gene–environment interactions may be through DNA methylation. *American Journal of Medical Genetics Part B: Neuropsychiatric Genetics*, 127(1), 51–59.

Amabile, T. M. (1996). *Creativity in context*. Boulder, CO: Westview.

Andreasen, N. C. (1987). Creativity and mental illness: Prevalance rates in writers and their first-degree relatives. *American Journal of Psychiatry*, 144(10), 1288–1292.

Andreasen, N. C. (2008). The relationship between creativity and mood disorders. *Dialogues in Clinical Neuroscience*, 10(2), 251–255.

Andreasen, N. C. (2011). A journey into chaos: Creativity and the unconscious. *Mens Sana Monographs*, 9(1), 42–53.

Aristotle (1984). *The complete works of Aristotle: The revised Oxford translation* (Vol. 2) (E. S. Foster, Trans.; J. Barnes, Ed.). Princeton University Press.

Bachner-Melman, R., Dina, C., Zohar, A. H., Constantini, N., Lerer, E., Hoch, S., Sella, S., Nemanov, L., Gritsenko, I., Lichtenberg, P., Granot, R. and Ebstein, R. P. (2005). AVPR1a and SLC6A4 gene polymorphisms are associated with creative dance performance. *PLoS Genetics*, 1(3), e42.

Barron, F. (1972). *Artists in the making*. New York: Seminar Press.

Barron, F. and Parisi, P. (1977). Twin resemblances in expressive behavior. *Acta geneticae medicae et gemellologiae*, Spring.

Batey, M. and Furnham, A. (2008). The relationship between measures of creativity and schizotypy. *Personality and Individual Differences*, 45, 816–821.

Beaussart, M. L., Kaufman, S. B. and Kaufman, J. C. (2012). Creative activity, personality, mental illness, and short-term mating success. *Journal of Creative Behavior*, 46, 151–167.

Bolling, M. Y. and Kohlenberg, R. J. (2004). Reasons for quitting serotonin reuptake inhibitor therapy: Paradoxical psychological side effects and patient satisfaction. *Psychotherapy and Psychosomatics*, 73(6), 380–385.

Buchsbaum, M., Christian, B. and Lehrer, D. (2006). D2/D3 dopamine receptor binding with [F-18]fallypride in thalamus and cortex of patients with schizophrenia. *Schizophrenia Research*, 85, 232–244.

Burch, G. S. J., Pavelis, C., Hemsley, D. R. and Corr, P. J. (2006). Schizotypy and creativity in visual artists. *British Journal of Psychology*, 97, 177–190.

Burns, J. K. P. (2004). An evolutionary theory of schizophrenia: Cortical connectivity, metarepresentation and the social brain. *Behavioral and Brain Sciences*, 27, 831–885.

Burt, A. and Trivers, R. (2006). *Genes in conflict: The biology of selfish genetic elements*. Cambridge, MA: Belknap.

Cardno, A. G. and Gottesman, I. I. (2000). Twin studies of schizophrenia: From bow-and-arrow concordances to star-wars Mx and functional genomics. *American Journal of Medical Genetics*, 97, 12–17.

Cardno, A. G., Marshall, E. J., Coid, B., Macdonald, A. M., Ribchester, T. R., Davies, N. J., Venturi, P., Jones, L. A., Lewis, S. W., Sham, P. C., Gottesman, I. I., Farmer, A. E., McGuffin, P., Reveley, A. M. and Murray, R. M. (1999). Heritability estimates for psychotic disorders: The Maudsley twin psychosis series. *Archives of General Psychiatry*, 56(2), 162–168.

Carson, S. H. (2011). Creativity and psychopathology: A shared vulnerability model. *Canadian Journal of Psychiatry*, 56, 144–153.

Carson, S. H., Peterson, J. B. and Higgins, D. M. (2003). Decreased latent inhibition is associated with increased creative achievement in high-functioning individuals. *Journal of Personality and Social Psychology*, 85, 499–506.

Caspi, A., Sugden, K., Moffitt, T. E., Taylor, A., Craig, I. W., Harrington, H., McClay, J., Mill, J., Martin, J., Braithwaite, A. and Poulton, R. (2003). Influence of life stress on depression: Moderation by a polymorphism in the 5-HTT gene. *Science*, 301, 386–389.

Chávez-Eakle, R. A. (2007). Creativity, DNA, and cerebral blood flow. In C. Martindale, P. Locher and V. M. Petrov (Eds.), *Evolutionary and neurocognitive approaches to aesthetics, creativity, and the arts* (pp. 209–224). Amityville, NY: Baywood.

Clegg, H., Nettle, D. and Miell, D. (2011). Status and mating success amongst visual artists. *Frontiers in Psychology*, 2, 1–4.

Colzato, L. S., Pratt, J. and Hommel, B. (2010). Dopaminergic control of attentional flexibility: Inhibition of return is associated with the dopamine transporter gene (DAT1). *Frontiers in Human Neuroscience.* doi:10.3389/fnhum.2010.00053

Corfas, G., Roy, K. and Buxbaum, J. D. (2004). Neuregulin 1-erbB signaling and the molecular/cellular basis of schizophrenia. *Nature Neuroscience*, 7, 575–580.

Cornblatt, B. A., Carrión, R. E., Addington, J., Seidman, L., Walker, E. F., Cannon, T. D., Cadenhead, K. S., McGlashan, T. H., Perkins, D. O., Tsuang, M. T., Woods, S. W., Heinssen, R. and Lencz, T. (2010). Risk factors for psychosis: Impaired social and role functioning. *Schizophrenia Bulletin*, 38(6), 1247–1257.

Crespi, B. and Badcock, C. (2008a). Psychosis and autism as diametrical disorders of the social brain. *Behavioral and Brain Sciences*, 31, 241–261.

Crespi, B. and Badcock, C. (2008b). The evolutionary social brain: From genes to psychiatric conditions. *Behavioral and Brain Sciences*, 31, 284–296.

Crow, T. J. (1993). Sexual selection, Machiavellian intelligence, and the origins of psychosis. *The Lancet*, 342, 594–598.

Crow, T. J. (1995). A Darwinian approach to the origins of psychosis. *British Journal of Psychiatry*, 167(1), 12–25.

Crow, T. J. (1997). Is schizophrenia the price that Homo sapiens pays for language? *Schizophrenia Research*, 28, 127–141.

Crow, T. J. (2008). The "big bang" theory of the origin of psychosis and the faculty of language. *Schizophrenia Research*, 102, 31–52.

Csikszentmihalyi, M. (1988). Society, culture, and person: A systems view of creativity. In R. J. Sternberg (Ed.), *The nature of creativity: Contemporary psychological perspectives* (pp. 325–339). New York: Cambridge University Press.

Daly, M. P., Afroz, S. and Walder, D. J. (2012). Schizotypal traits and neurocognitive functioning among nonclinical young adults. *Psychiatry Research*, 200, 635–640.

Del Giudice, M., Angeleri, R., Brizio, A. and Elena, M. R. (2010). The evolution of autistic-like and schizotypal traits: A sexual selection hypothesis. *Frontiers in Psychology*, 1, 41.

de Manzano, Ö., Cervenka, S., Karabanov, A. and Farde, L. (2010). Thinking outside a less intact box: Thalamic dopamine D2 receptor densities are negatively related to psychometric creativity in healthy individuals. *PloS ONE*, 5(5): e10670.

Detera-Wadleigh, S. D. and McMahon, F. J. (2006). G72/G30 in schizophrenia and bipolar disorder: Review and meta-analysis. *Biological Psychiatry*, 60(2), 106–114.

DeYoung, C. G., Grazioplene, R. G. and Peterson, J. B. (2011). From madness to genius: The Openness/Intellect trait domain as a paradoxical simplex. *Journal of Research in Personality*, 46, 63–78.

Dobzhansky, T. (1973). Nothing in biology makes sense except in the light of evolution. *The American Biology Teacher*, 35, 125–129.

Dodgson, G. and Gordon, S. (2009). Avoiding false negatives: Are some auditory hallucinations an evolved design flaw? *Behavioural and Cognitive Psychotherapy*, 37, 325–334.

Doi, N., Hoshi, Y., Itokawa, M., Usui, C., Yoshikawa, T. and Tashikawa, H. (2009). Persistence criteria for susceptibility genes for schizophrenia: A discussion from an evolutionary viewpoint. *PloS ONE*, 4: e7799.

Egan, M. F., Goldberg, T. E., Kolachana, B. S., Callicott, J. H., Mazzanti, C. M., Straub, R. E., Goldman, D. and Weinberger, D. R. (2001). Effect of COMT Val108/158 Met genotype on frontal lobe function and risk for schizophrenia. *Proceedings of the National Academy of Sciences USA*, 98, 6917–6922.

Epstein, R., Novick, O., Umansky, R. and Priel, B. (1996). Dopamine D4 receptor (D4DR) exon III polymorphism associated with the human personality trait of Novelty Seeking. *Nature Genetics*, 12, 78–80.

Eysenck, H. J. (1993). Creativity and personality: Suggestions for a theory. *Psychological Inquiry*, 4(3), 147–178.

Fayena-Tawil, F., Kozbelt, A. and Sitaras, L. (2011). Think global, act local: A protocol analysis comparison of artists' and non-artists' cognitions, metacognitions, and evaluations while drawing. *Psychology of Aesthetics, Creativity, and the Arts*, 5, 135–145.

Fett, A. K., Viechtbauer, W., Dominguez, M. D., Penn, D. L., van Os, J. and Krabbendam, L. (2011). The relationship between neurocognition and social cognition with functional outcomes in schizophrenia: A meta-analysis. *Neuroscience & Bio-behavioral Reviews*, 35(3), 573–588.

Frazer, K., Ballinger, D., Cox, D., Hinds, D., Stuve, L., Gibbs, R. *et al.* (2007). A second generation human haplotype map of over 3.1 million SNPs. *Nature*, 449(7164), 851–861.

Gaddum, J. H. and Hameed, K. A. (1954). Drugs which antagonize 5-hydroxytryptamine. *British Journal of Pharmacology*, 9(2), 240–248.

Galton, F. (1869). *Hereditary genius: An enquiry into its laws and consequences.* London: Macmillan.

Garcia-Garcia, M., Barceló, F. and Clemente, I. (2010). The role of DAT1 gene on the rapid detection of task novelty. *Neuropsychologia,* 48, 4136–4141.

Gardner, H. (2001). Creators: Multiple intelligences. In K. H. Pfenninger and V. R. Shubik (Eds.), *The origins of creativity* (pp. 117–143). New York: Oxford University Press.

Gebicke-Haerter, P. J. (2012). Epigenetics of schizophrenia. *Pharmacopsychiatry,* 45, Supplement 1, S42–S48.

Geher, G. and Kaufman, S. B. (2011). Mating intelligence. In R. J. Sternberg and S. B. Kaufman (Eds.), *The Cambridge handbook of intelligence* (pp. 603–622). Cambridge, UK: Cambridge University Press.

Gershon, E. S., DeLisi, L. E., Hamovit, J., Nurnberger, J. I., Maxwell, M. E., Schreiber, J., Dauphinais, D., Dingman, C. W. and Guroff, J. J. (1988). A controlled family study of chronic psychoses: Vs schizophrenia and schizoaffective disorder. *Archives of General Psychiatry,* 45(4), 328–336.

Goldman, D., Weinberger, D. R., Malhotra, A. K. and Goldberg, T. E. (2009). The role of COMT Val158Met in cognition. *Biological Psychiatry,* 65(1), e1–2.

Guilford, J. P. (1950). Creativity. *American Psychologist,* 5, 444–454.

Guilford, J. P. (1967). *The nature of human intelligence.* New York: McGraw-Hill.

Hall, J., Whalley, H. C., Job, D. E., Baig, B. J., McIntosh, A. M., Evans, K. L., Thomson, P. A., Porteous, D. J., Cunningham-Owens, D. G., Johnstone, E. C. and Lawrie, S. M. (2006). A neuregulin 1 variant associated with abnormal cortical function and psychotic symptoms. *Nature Neuroscience,* 9, 1477–1478.

Hammock, E. A. and Young, L. J. (2006). Oxytocin, vasopressin and pair bonding: Implications for autism. *Philosophical Transactions of the Royal Society of London B. Biological Sciences,* 361, 2187–2198.

Harrison, P. J. and Law, A. J. (2006). Neuregulin 1 and schizophrenia: Genetics, gene expression, and neurobiology. *Biological Psychiatry,* 60(2), 132–140.

Hawks, J., Wang, E. T., Cochran, G. M., Harpending, H. C. and Moyzis, R. K. (2007). Recent acceleration of human adaptive evolution. *Proceedings of the National Academy of Sciences,* 104(52), 20753–20758.

Hennah, W., Thomson, P., Peltonen, L. and Porteous, D. (2006). Genes and schizophrenia. Beyond schizophrenia: The role of *DISC1* in major mental illness. *Schizophrenia Bulletin,* 32(3), 409–416. doi:10.1093/schbul/sbj079

Honea, R., Verchinski, B. A., Pezawas, L., Kolachana, B. S., Callicott, J. H., Mattay, V. S., Weinberger, D. R. and Meyer-Lindenberg, A. (2009). Impact of interacting functional variants in COMT on regional gray matter volume in human brain. *Neuroimage,* 45, 44–51.

Hyman, S. (2000). Mental illness: Genetically complex disorders of neural circuitry and neural communication. *Neuron,* 28(2), 321–323.

Jablensky, A., Sartorius, N., Ernberg, G., Anker, M., Korten, A., Cooper, J. E., Day, R. and Bertelsen, O. (1992). *Schizophrenia: Manifestations, incidence and course in different cultures. A World Health Organization ten-country study.* New York: Cambridge University Press.

Jamison, K. R. (1993). *Touched with fire: Manic-depressive illness and the artistic temperament.* New York: Simon & Schuster.

Joober, R., Boksa, P., Benkelfat, C. and Rouleau, G. (2002). Genetics of schizophrenia: From animal models to clinical studies. *Journal of Psychiatry and Neuroscience*, 27, 336–347.

Kandel, E. R. (1998). A new intellectual framework for psychiatry. *American Journal of Psychiatry*, 155(4), 457–469.

Kaufman, J. C. and Baer, J. (Eds.) (2005). *Creativity across domains: Faces of the muse.* Mahwah, NJ: Erlbaum.

Kaufman, J. C. and Beghetto, R. A. (2009). Beyond big and little: The four c model of creativity. *Review of General Psychology*, 13, 1–12.

Kaufman, S. B., DeYoung, C. G., Gray, J. R., Jimenez, L., Brown, J. B. and Mackintosh, N. (2010). Implicit learning as an ability. *Cognition*, 116, 321–340.

Kelleher, I., Jenner, J. A. and Cannon, M. (2010). Psychotic symptoms in the general population: An evolutionary perspective. *The British Journal of Psychiatry*, 197, 167–169. doi:10.1192/bjp.bp.109.076018

Keller, M. and Miller, G. F. (2006). An evolutionary framework for mental disorders: Integrating adaptationist and evolutionary genetics models. *Behavioral and Brain Sciences*, 29, 429–452.

Kendler, K. S. and Diehl, S. R. (1993). The genetics of schizophrenia: A current, genetic-epidemiologic perspective. *Schizophrenia Bulletin*, 19, 261–285.

Kéri, S. (2009). Genes for psychosis and creativity: A promoter polymorphism of the neuregulin 1 gene is related to creativity in people with high intellectual achievement. *Psychological Science*, 20(9), 1070–1073.

Kirov, G., Gumus, D., Chen, W., Norton, N., Georgieva, L., Sari, M., O'Donovan, M. C., Erdogan, F., Owen, M. J., Ropers, H.-H. and Ullman, R. (2008). Comparative genome hybridization suggests a role for *NRXN1* and *APBA2* in schizophrenia. *Human Molecular Genetics*, 17(3), 458–465.

Kottler, J. (2005). *Divine madness.* San Francisco, CA: Jossey-Bass.

Kozbelt, A. (2006). Dynamic evaluation of Matisse's 1935 "Large Reclining Nude." *Empirical Studies of the Arts*, 24, 119–137.

Kozbelt, A. (2007). A quantitative analysis of Beethoven as self-critic: Implications for psychological theories of musical creativity. *Psychology of Music*, 35, 147–172.

Kozbelt, A. (2008). Longitudinal hit ratios of classical composers: Reconciling "Darwinian" and expertise acquisition perspectives on lifespan creativity. *Psychology of Aesthetics, Creativity, and the Arts*, 2, 221–235.

Kozbelt, A. (2009). Ontogenetic heterochrony and the creative process in visual art: A précis. *Psychology of Aesthetics, Creativity, and the Arts*, 3, 35–37.

Kyaga, S., Landén, M., Boman, M., Hultman, C., Langstrom, N. and Lichtenstein, P. (2013). Mental illness, suicide and creativity: 40-year prospective total population study. *Journal of Psychiatric Research*, 47, 83–90.

Kyaga, S., Lichtenstein, P., Boman, M., Hultman, C., Langstrom, N. and Landén, M. (2011). Creativity and mental disorder: Family study of 300,000 people with severe mental disorder. *British Journal of Psychiatry*, 199, 373–379.

Lencz, T., Morgan, T., Athanasiou, M., Dain, B., Reed, C., Kane, J., Kucherlapati, R. and Malhotra, A. (2007). Converging evidence for a pseudoautosomal cytokine receptor gene locus in schizophrenia. *Molecular Psychiatry*, 12(6), 572–580.

Lesch, K. P., Bengel, D., Heils, A., Sabol, S. Z., Greenberg, B. D., Petri, S., Benjamin, J., Müller, C. R., Hamer, D. H. and Murphy, D. L. (1996). Association of anxiety-related traits with a polymorphism in the serotonin transporter gene regulatory region. *Science*, 274(5292), 1527–1531.

Lu, L. and Shi, J. (2010). Association between creativity and COMT genotype. *National Natural Science Foundation of China*, 30670716, 1–4. IEEE.

Ludwig, A. M. (1995). *The price of greatness: Resolving the creativity and madness controversy*. New York: Guilford Press.

McCabe, J. H., Koupil, I. and Leon, D. A. (2009). Lifetime reproductive output over two generations in patients with psychosis and their unaffected siblings: The Uppsala 1915–1929 Birth Cohort Multigenerational Study. *Psychological Medicine*, 39(10), 1667–1676.

McGrath, J. J., Hearle, J., Jenner, L., Plant, K., Drummond, A. and Barkla, J. M. (1999). The fertility and fecundity of patients with psychoses. *Acta Psychiatrica Scandinavica*, 99, 441–446.

Malhotra, A. K., Kestler, L. J., Mazzanti, C., Bates, J. A., Goldberg, T. and Goldman, D. (2002). A functional polymorphism in the COMT gene and performance on a test of prefrontal cognition. *American Journal of Psychiatry*, 159, 652–654.

Martindale, C. (1990). *The clockwork muse: The predictability of artistic change*. New York: Basic Books.

Meehl, P. E. (1962). Schizotaxia, schizotypy, schizophrenia. *American Psychologist*, 17, 827–838.

Meehl, P. E. (1990). Toward an integrated theory of schizotaxia, schizotypy, and schizophrenia. *Journal of Personality Disorders*, 4, 1–99.

Mei, L. and Xiong, W. C. (2008). Neuregulin-1 signaling in neural development, synaptic plasticity and schizophrenia. *Nature Reviews Neuroscience*, 9, 437–452.

Miller, G. F. (2001). *The mating mind: How sexual choice shaped the evolution of human nature*. New York: Anchor.

Miller, G. F. (2010). Are pleiotropic mutations and Holocene selective sweeps the only evolutionary-genetic processes left for explaining heritable variation in human psychological traits? In D. M. Buss and P. H. Hawley (Eds.), *The evolution of personality and individual differences* (pp. 376–399). New York: Oxford University Press.

Miller, G. F. and Tal, I. (2007). Schizotypy versus intelligence and openness as predictors of creativity. *Schizophrenia Research*, 93(1–3), 317–324.

Murphy, K. C., Jones, L. A. and Owen, M. J. (1999). High rates of schizophrenia in adults with velo-cardio-facial syndrome. *Archives of General Psychiatry*, 56, 940–945.

Nelson, B. and Rawlings, D. (2010). Relating schizotypy and personality to the phenomenology of creativity. *Schizophrenia Bulletin*, 36, 388–399.

Nesse, R. M. (2004). Cliff-edged fitness functions and the persistence of schizophrenia (commentary). *Behavioral and Brain Sciences*, 27, 862–863.

Nettle, D. (2001). *Strong imagination: Madness, creativity and human nature*. Oxford: Oxford University Press.

Nettle, D. (2006). Schizotypy and mental health amongst poets, visual artists, and mathematicians. *Journal of Research in Personality*, 40, 876–890.

Nettle, D. and Clegg, H. (2006). Schizotypy, creativity, and mating success in humans. *Proceedings of the Royal Society*, 273, 611–615.

Ng, M. Y., Levinson, D. F., Faraone, S. V., Suarez, B. K., DeLisi, L. E., Arinami, T. *et al.* (2009). Meta-analysis of 32 genome-wide linkage studies of schizophrenia. *Molecular Psychiatry*, 14(8), 774–785.

Nieoullon, A. (2002). Dopamine and the regulation of cognition and attention. *Progress in Neurobiology*, 67(1), 53–83.

Nuechterlein, K. H., Subotnik, K. L., Ventura, J., Green, M. F., Gretchen-Doorly, D. and Asarnow, R. F. (2012). The puzzle of schizophrenia: Tracking the core role of cognitive deficits. *Developmental Psychopathology*, 24(2), 529–536.

Numakawa, T., Yagasaki, Y., Ishimoto, T., Okada, T., Suzuki, T., Iwata, N., Ozaki, N., Taguchi, T., Tatsumi, M., Kamijima, K., Straub, R. E., Weinberger, D. R., Kunugi, H. and Hashimoto, R. (2004). Evidence of novel neuronal functions of dysbindin, a susceptibility gene for schizophrenia. *Human Molecular Genetics*, 13(21), 2699–2708.

O'Donovan, M. C., Craddock, N., Norton, N., Williams, H., Peirce, T., Moskvina, V. *et al.* (2008). Identification of loci associated with schizophrenia by genome-wide association and follow-up. *Nature Genetics*, 40, 1053–1055.

Opbroek, A., Delgado, P. and Laukes, C. (2002). Emotional blunting associated with SSRI-induced sexual dysfunction: Do SSRIs inhibit emotional responses? *The International Journal of Neuropsychopharmacology*, 5, 147–151.

O'Reilly, T., Dunbar, R. and Bentall, R. (2001). Schizotypy and creativity: An evolutionary connection? *Personality and Individual Differences*, 31, 1067–1078.

Pidsley, R. and Mill, J. (2011) Research highlights: Epigenetic changes to serotonin receptor gene expression in schizophrenia and bipolar disorder. *Epigenomics*, 3(5), 521–523.

Pluess, M., Belsky, J., Way, B. M. and Taylor, S. E. (2010). 5-HTTLPR moderates effects of current life events on neuroticism: Differential susceptibility to environmental influences. *Progress in Neuro-Psychopharmacology & Biological Psychiatry*, 34, 1070–1074.

Polesskaya, O. O., Aston, C. and Sokolov, B. P. (2006). Allele C-specific methylation of the 5-HT2A receptor gene: Evidence for correlation with its expression and expression of DNA methylase DNMT1. *Journal of Neuroscience Research*, 83(3), 362–373. doi:10.1002/jnr.20732.

Post, F. (1996). Verbal creativity, depression, and alcoholism: An investigation of one hundred American and British writers. *British Journal of Psychiatry*, 168, 545–555.

Prokosch, M. D., Yeo, R. A. and Miller, G. F. (2005). Intelligence tests with higher *g*-loadings show higher correlations with body symmetry: Evidence for a general fitness factor mediated by developmental stability. *Intelligence*, 33, 203–213.

Rawlings, D. and Locarnini, A. (2008). Dimensional schizotypy, autism, and unusual word associations in artists and scientists. *Journal of Research in Personality*, 42, 465–471.

Reuter, M., Panksepp, J., Schnabel, N., Kellerhoff, N., Kempel, P. and Hennig, J. (2005). Personality and biological markers of creativity. *European Journal of Personality*, 19, 83–95.

Reuter, M., Roth, S. and Holve, K. (2006). Identification of first candidate genes for creativity: A pilot study. *Brain Research*, 1069(1), 190–197.

Reznikoff, M., Domino, G., Bridges, C. and Honeyman, M. (1973). Creative abilities in identical and fraternal twins. *Behavior Genetics*, 3(4), 365–377.

Rodriguez-Murillo, L., Gogos, J. A. and Karayiorgou, M. (2012). The genetic architecture of schizophrenia: New mutations and emerging paradigms. *Annual Review of Medicine*, 63, 63–80.

Ross, C. A., Margolis, R. L., Reading, S. A., Pletnikov, M. and Coyle, J. T. (2006). Neurobiology of schizophrenia. *Neuron*, 52(1), 139–153.

Rothenberg, A. (1990). *Creativity and madness*. Baltimore, MD: Johns Hopkins University Press.

Sawaguchi, T. and Goldman-Rakic, P. (1991). D1 dopamine receptors in prefrontal cortex: Involvement in working memory. *Science*, 251(4996), 947–950.

Sawyer, R. K. (2006). *Explaining creativity: The science of human innovation*. New York: Oxford University Press.

Schlesinger, J. (2009). Creative mythconceptions: A closer look at the evidence for the "mad genius" hypothesis. *Psychology of Aesthetics, Creativity, and the Arts*, 3(2), 62–72.

Shaner, A., Miller, G. and Mintz, J. (2004). Schizophrenia as one extreme of a sexually selected fitness indicator. *Schizophrenia. Research*, 70(1), 101–109.

Shaner, A., Miller, G. and Mintz, J. (2008). Mental disorders as catastrophic failures of mating intelligence. In G. Geher and G. Miller (Eds.), *Mating intelligence: Sex, relationships, and the mind's reproductive system* (pp. 193–223). New York: Psychology Press.

Shifman, S., Johannesson, M., Bronstein, M., Chen, S. X., Collier, D. A., Craddock, N. J., Kendler, K. S., Li, T., O'Donovan, M., O'Neill, F. A., Owen, M. J., Walsh, D., Weinberger, D. R., Sun, C., Flint, J. and Darvasi, A. (2008). Genome-wide association identifies a common variant in the Reelin gene that increases the risk of schizophrenia only in women. *PLoS Genetics*, 4(2), e28. doi:10.1371/journal.pgen.0040028

Silvia, P. J. (2008). Discernment and creativity: How well can people identify their most creative ideas? *Psychology of Aesthetics, Creativity, and the Arts*, 2, 139–146.

Silvia, P. J. and Kaufman, J. C. (2011). Creativity and mental illness. In J. C. Kaufman and R. J. Sternberg (Eds.), *The Cambridge handbook of creativity* (pp. 381–394). New York: Cambridge University Press.

Simonton, D. K. (1984). Creative productivity and age: A mathematical model based on a two-step cognitive process. *Developmental Review*, 4, 77–111.

Simonton, D. K. (1994). *Greatness: Who makes history and why*. New York: Guilford Press.

Stefanis, N. C., Trikalinos, T. A., Avramopoulos, D., Smyrnis, N., Evdokimidis, I., Ntzani, E. E., Ioannidis, J. P. and Stefanis, C. N. (2007). Impact of schizophrenia candidate genes on schizotypy and cognitive endophenotypes at the population level. *Biological Psychiatry*, 62, 784–792.

Sternberg, R. J. and Lubart, T. I. (1995). *Defying the crowd: Cultivating creativity in a culture of conformity.* New York: Free Press.

Stoltenberg, S., Twitchell, G., Hanna, G., Cook, E., Fitzgerald, H., Zucker, R. and Little, K. (2002). Serotonin transporter promoter polymorphism, peripheral indexes of serotonin function, and personality measures in families with alcoholism. *American Journal of Medical Genetics*, 114(2), 230–234.

Straub, R. E., Jiang, Y., MacLean, C. J., Ma, Y., Webb, B. T., Myakishev, M. V., Harris-Kerr, C., Wormley, B., Sadek, H., Kadambi, B., Cesare, A. J., Gibberman, A., Wang, X., O'Neill, F. A., Walsh, D. and Kendler, K. S. (2002). Genetic variation in the 6p22.3 gene DTNBP1, the human ortholog of the mouse dysbindin gene, is associated with schizophrenia. *American Journal of Human Genetics*, 71(2), 337–348.

Svensson, A. C., Lichtenstein, P., Sandin, S. and Hultman, C. M. (2007). Fertility of first-degree relatives of patients with schizophrenia: A three generation perspective. *Schizophrenia Research*, 91(1), 238–245.

Szatmari, P., Paterson, A., Zwaigenbaum, L., Roberts, W., Brian, J., Liu, X. *et al.* (2007). Mapping autism risk loci using genetic linkage and chromosomal rearrangements. *Nature Genetics*, 39(3), 319–328.

Talvik, M., Nordström, A. and Olsson, H. (2003). Decreased thalamic D2/D3 receptor binding in drug-naive patients with schizophrenia: A PET study with [11C]FLB 457. *The International Journal of Neuropsychopharmacology*, 6(4), 361–370.

Thompson, R., Gupta, S., Miller, K., Mills, S. and Orr, S. (2004). The effects of vasopressin on human facial responses related to social communication. *Psychoneuroendocrinology*, 29, 35–48.

Torrance, E. P. (1969). *Creativity: What research says to the teacher.* Washington, DC: National Education Association.

Tsuang, M. T. (2000). Schizophrenia: Genes and environment. *Biological Psychiatry*, 47(3), 210–220.

Tunbridge, E. M., Harrison, P. J. and Weinberger, D. R. (2006). Catechol-*o*-Methyltransferase, cognition, and psychosis: Val158Met and beyond. *Biological Psychiatry*, 60, 141–151.

Ukkola, L. T., Onkamo, P., Raijas, P., Karma, K. and Järvelä, I. (2009). Musical aptitude is associated with AVPR1A-haplotypes. *PLoS ONE*, 4(5): e5534.

Vandenberg, S. G. (Ed.) (1968). *Progress in human behavior genetics.* Baltimore, MD: Johns Hopkins University Press.

Van Os, J., Linscott, R. J., Myin-Germeys, I., Delespaul, P. and Krabbendam, L. (2008). A systematic review and meta-analysis of the psychosis continuum: Evidence for a psychosis-proneness-persistence-impairment model of psychotic disorder. *Psychological Medicine*, 8, 1–17.

Venkatasubramanian, G. and Kalmady, S. V. (2010). Creativity, psychosis and human evolution: The exemplar case of *neuregulin 1* gene. *Indian Journal of Psychiatry 2010*, 52, 282.

Vinkhuyzen, A. A. E., van der Sluis, S., Posthuma, D. and Boomsma, D. I. (2009). The heritability of aptitude and exceptional talent across different domains in adolescents and young adults. *Behavioral Genetics*, 39(4), 380–392.

Volf, N., Kulikov, A. and Bortsov, C. (2009). Association of verbal and figural creative achievement with polymorphism in the human serotonin transporter gene. *Neuroscience Letters*, 463, 154–157.

Walder, D. J., Ospina, L., Daly, M. P., Statucka, M. and Raparia, E. (2012). Early neurodevelopment and psychosis risk: Role of neurohormones and biological sex in modulating genetic, prenatal and sensory processing factors in brain development. In X. Anastassiou-Hadjicharalambous (Ed.), *Psychosis: Causes, diagnosis and treatment* (pp. 44–78). Hauppauge, NY: Nova Science.

Walder, D. J., Statucka, M., Daly, M. P., Axen, K. and Haber, M. (2012). Biological sex and menstrual cycle phase modulation of cortisol levels and psychiatric symptoms in a non-clinical sample of young adults. *Psychiatry Research*, 197, 314–321.

Walder, D. J., Trotman, H., Cubells, J., Brasfield, J. and Walker, E. F. (2010). Catechol-O-Methyltransferase (COMT) modulation of cortisol among adolescents at high-risk for psychopathology and healthy controls. *Psychiatric Genetics*, 20(4), 166–170.

Walker, E. and Diforio, D. (1997). Schizophrenia: A neural diasthesis-stress model. *Psychological Review*, 104, 667–685.

Walker, E., Kestler, L., Bollini, A. and Hochman, K. M. (2004). Schizophrenia: Etiology and course. *Annual Review of Psychology*, 55, 401–430.

Wang, H., Ng, K., Hayes, D., Gao, X., Forster, G., Blaha, C. and Yeomans, J. (2004). Decreased amphetamine-induced locomotion and improved latent inhibition in mice mutant for the M5 muscarinic receptor gene found in the human 15q schizophrenia region. *Neuropsychopharmacology*, 29, 2126–2139.

Wang, W. Y., Barratt, B. J., Clayton, D. G. and Todd, J. A. (2005). Genome-wide association studies: Theoretical and practical concerns. *Nature Reviews Genetics*, 6, 109–118.

Ward, T. B., Smith, S. M. and Finke, R. A. (1999). Creative cognition. In R. J. Sternberg (Ed.), *Handbook of creativity* (pp. 189–212). New York: Cambridge University Press.

Weisberg, R. W. (2006). *Creativity: Understanding innovation in problem solving, science, invention, and the arts.* Hoboken, NJ: Wiley.

White, H. A. and Shah, P. (2006). Uninhibited imaginations: Creativity in adults with attention deficit/hyperactivity disorder. *Personality and Individual Differences*, 40(6), 1121–1131.

Woody, E. and Claridge, G. (1977). Psychoticism and thinking. *British Journal of Social and Clinical Psychology*, 16(3), 241–248.

Zaboli, G., Gizatullin, R., Nilsonne, A., Wilczek, A., Jonsson, E. G., Ahnemark, E., Asberg, M. and Leopardi, R. (2006). Tryptophan hydroxylase-1 gene variants associate with a group of suicidal borderline women. *Neuropsychopharmacology*, 31(9), 1982–1990.

Zeki, S. (2007). The neurobiology of love. *Federation of European Biochemical Societies Letters*, 581, 2575–2579.

7   Non-linearity in creativity and mental illness: the mixed blessings of chaos, catastrophe, and noise in brain and behavior

James E. Swain and John D. Swain

The emergent capacity for creative abstraction allows humans to alter our concepts and behaviors quickly and have new ones that might not be an easy extension of current ideas. We can model some of the consequences of our actions in the dramatic workplace of our imagination, and generate new ideas. However, principles of overproduction, error, and culling still apply, in the realm of creative abstraction: Many of our ideas are fatal, larger proportions still are significantly out of touch with reality or insane, and those that are neither fatal nor insane are generally impractical. Indeed, the vast majority of new inventions do not reach the marketplace and most new businesses fail within 10 years (Shane, 2008). Perhaps it is for this fundamental reason that creativity and insanity appear linked by eternal intuition: In the hunt for a solution, more ideas are better, but most ideas are still bad. The conservative strategy may therefore be to avoid new ideas altogether, and that is a common approach. Many people appear neither intelligent nor open enough to be genuinely creative, and only a small proportion of those few who manifest creativity are also sufficiently disciplined and emotionally stable to see their ideas realized. The typical best strategy may therefore be to do whatever everyone else does. This is what animals generally do, and it generally works (Kaufman *et al.*, 2011). Nonetheless, stasis also presents its dangers. Because situations change, creativity is necessary and valued to accommodate new circumstances, despite its dangers.

So we may ask such questions as: Where do new ideas come from?; Who generates them?; and How are they generated? Some answers may be forthcoming from the fields of artificial intelligence that attempt to model human creativity. Human beings are constrained and low-capacity processors. Our perceptions are necessarily low-resolution representations of an almost infinitely high-resolution reality. Likewise, our concepts are mere shadows of our perceptions. The informational array that constantly presents itself to us can be simplified, for pragmatic purposes, just as a low-resolution photograph can stand as a substitute for a high-resolution photograph (which can, in turn, stand as a substitute for the thing it represents). Thus, the same "thing-in-itself" can be perceived in many different ways, none of which are necessarily more or less accurate than any other (except insofar as they serve, or fail to serve, some motivated purpose). This means that the real object always contains additional information, available to the imaginative or diligent searcher (Peterson and Flanders, 2002). Indeed the information may even refer to external objects, with the image suggesting a leap to a new idea or the examination of a new object. Our ideas, lacking one-to-one correspondence with the world they represent, instead serve primarily pragmatic purposes: We wish to live, and to gratify our desires while doing so. The fundamental constraint placed on ideation is therefore functional utility: Can we get from a less desirable point A to a more desirable point B, using our simplified representations of the world? If so, those representations are good enough. If not, our goal-directed actions fail, and the world confronts us with the evidence of our insufficiency, and the information we have heretofore avoided processing. This confrontation can be frightening to a pathological degree. The emergence of the unexpected is rapidly equated with danger by specialized brain systems, including the hippocampus, amygdala, anterior cingulate cortex, and the reticular activating system (Flaherty, 2011). When plans fail, it is best to first be cautious. However, an extreme response of limbic and cortical novelty-detection systems may bring ongoing goal-directed behavior to a halt when the unexpected emerges, disinhibiting the production of negative emotion: anxiety, shame, guilt, and emotional pain. If nothing additionally unexpected or negative occurs in the aftermath of the first failure, then protective negative emotion may recede, and the dopaminergic psychomotor exploratory systems, with their origin in the hypothalamus (Swanson, 2000), govern perception and behavior. The emergence of the unexpected is dangerous, but promising. Pragmatic failure means that there was more to the thing-in-itself than originally suspected. The unmapped portion of that thing may pose a threat, but may also offer possibility for the expansion of competence. Exploration generates the information from which new possibilities are born.

Of course there is no realistic model of how the brain works in sufficient detail to sensibly talk about the emergence of thought or consciousness, but, remarkably, there are radically simplified models that do offer a framework that is motivated by biology. For example, connectionist computational models have been used to explain the acquisition of complex cognitive skills (Leech *et al.*, 2008). Errors in such models may also help explain unusual brain activity such as in creativity – as well as in mental illness, including childhood onset problems with problematic social behaviors in autism, the inability to maintain focus in attention-deficit/

hyperactivity disorder (ADHD), and the lack of motivation of depressive disorders (Swain and Swain, 2008).

Any link between creativity and mental illness must, at the present stage of human understanding of the brain and mind, be speculative. That said, there are several concepts in modern physics and mathematics that at least are very suggestive of processes akin to what one might think of as "creativity," and which, as suitable parameters are varied, naturally allow for processes that one might think of as mental illness.

We will now suggest how the brain processes that underlie creativity are all linked fundamentally to the idea of non-linearity. After reviewing the difference between linear and non-linear systems, we will argue that non-linearity is only generic in the nature of the brain, but in fact that non-linear systems are concretely realized in the brain both intrinsically and in connectionist models such as neural networks. Perception is an example of such non-linearity, although perhaps any kind of creative thought process is also non-linear. We now look at how, depending on parameters such as environment, non-linear phenomena show many behaviors that are reminiscent of both creativity and madness.

Linear versus non-linear systems

A linear system is, by definition, one in which the response to the sum of two inputs is the sum of the responses to the inputs taken separately and for which the response to the input multiplied by some constant (c) is the output multiplied by that same constant. In equations, for inputs A and B and any constant c, the response R should satisfy:

$$R(A + B) = R(A) + R(B) \text{ and } R(cA) = cR(A).$$

Linearity is very often taken as a convenient model for many physical phenomena, partly because it often provides a very good approximation, and partly because the mathematical tools we have for linear systems are very well developed. Many physical "laws" are, in fact, merely linear approximations, which happen to work very well a large fraction of the time. For example, Ohm's "law," which states that the current that flows through a system is proportional to the voltage applied across it, works very well over many orders of magnitude for most common materials. However, it is actually far from a law. For instance, for a spark gap, one might find that for a voltage of 6,000 volts almost no current flows, and the same for a voltage of 9,000 volts, but when 15,000 volts are applied a spark forms and a large current flows. That is, the current produced by 6,000 volts, or 9,000 volts, is almost zero, while the current produced by 15,000 volts is quite large. In fact, any system involving a threshold is intrinsically non-linear – there is no response until a certain threshold input is reached (Pippard, 1985).

It is well known that perception has similar non-linear properties. For example, there is a minimum threshold for light to be seen at all (at the level of a few photons at a time), and then again another threshold for color to be perceived, using rods as well as cones. Neural circuitry is also based on thresholds being reached for the release of neurotransmitters at a synapse, or for an action potential (Kandel *et al.*, 2012). Simple connectionist models (so-called "artificial neural networks") are based on artificial neurons connected by weights, which represent synaptic strengths and which "fire" when the total weighted input to them is above some threshold. Due to the threshold behavior involved, they are intrinsically non-linear systems, modeling the non-linear behavior of neurons in the brain in a drastically simplified way, and yet capable of learning to recognize patterns and generalize trends in data. They follow earlier attempts, like the perceptron, to produce linear systems able to perform interesting cognitive-like tasks but were quickly realized to fail at the computation of the simple "exclusive OR" function – a function returning "1" if one of the other inputs is "1" and the other is "0," and "1" otherwise. In this case a very small input ("0" and "0") produces a zero, a larger input (a "0" and a "1") produces a large output, but then a still larger input (two "1"s) produces a zero again – so there's no chance of this being linear (Rosenblatt, 1958).

The allowance for non-linearity in the artificial neurons allows essentially any function of the inputs to produce essentially any output, and here we see the start of what could be a link to both creativity and madness, but first let us consider some generic features of the behavior of non-linear systems. (For a good introduction and review, see Pippard, 1985.)

We note that, for our purposes, the word "neuron" can be replaced by any collection of neurons, or any substructure of the brain. The arguments we will make are essentially of a very general nature, which do not reply on the details of the systems, which are connected, but merely on the fact that their responses are not linear. (Indeed, linearity or response is never a property of any physical system, but rather a property of simplified models, largely for mathematical convenience and successful only to the extent that linearity is often a good approximation over some range of parameters for most systems.)

Generic features of the behavior of non-linear systems

Let us consider a generic system (which we will later identify with the brain or mind) with inputs "I" and outputs "R" and some number of control parameters "c."

In general, the output will be some function of the inputs and the control parameters:

$$R = f(I, c)$$

If R is a non-linear function of the inputs, we can expect a number of possible behaviors that will depend on both the inputs and the control parameters.

Approximately linear behavior may be exhibited, in which case responses will typically be proportional to inputs and the difference between responses to slightly different inputs. The closeness of responses to similar inputs allows for a good deal of predictability. To take physical examples, drop a ball and then drop it again from a slightly different place – the trajectories followed in both cases will be quite similar and one could make a reasonable prediction that the trajectory would be similar again were the ball to be dropped from yet another nearby location. Weather, on the other hand, is typically non-linear on time scales of a few days, meaning that small differences in conditions today can lead to dramatically different weather in a week's time – a phenomenon popularly referred to as the "butterfly effect," with the idea being that the flapping of a butterfly's wings could conceivably make a significant difference to later weather somewhere else on the earth (Bradbury, 2005).

Much of sane and not particularly creative thought involves responses of the linear kind. For example, one commonly speaks of "overreaction" of an unbalanced person, meaning that a small perturbation to the conditions in which a person finds themselves, or the challenges of transitions for children with autism, gives rise to dramatic changes in behavior. It is important to note that the qualitative behavior of a non-linear response need not be pathological. For example, one has the well-known "straw that broke the camel's back," where cumulative small perturbations finally reach some threshold that triggers a change in behavior.

There are at least two ways in which a non-linear response can occur, and both will be of interest to us in considering creativity: The first is that of "chaos" in which a system in response to a perturbation moves far from its original state over time, but continuously, an example being the "butterfly effect." The second is that of "catastrophes," in which a perturbation causes a sudden and discontinuous change, such as "the straw that broke the camel's back."

With the basic idea in place that the brain must be a non-linear system – as argued both from the physiology of threshold effects and the ability to perform cognitive tasks such as the "exclusive OR" function – and the fact that qualitative behaviors such as chaos and catastrophes are generically expected, we now move on to connections to creativity.

Creativity, madness, and non-linearity

We make the case that the properties of both creativity and madness are manifest in non-linear systems and that there are concrete reasons to think of them as similar. As noted at the outset, creativity is a notoriously difficult term to make precise. That said, we feel that it would generally be agreed on that creativity involves arriving at a thought (brain state or state of mind) that is not close to that reached by most people from the same starting point. For example, one might consider many people seeing some common problem and thinking about it, but arriving at states of mind similar to their original states, leaving the problem unsolved, and apparently no creativity involved. On the other hand, if one person found himself or herself in a mental state that differed significantly, they might be said to have been "creative" – in the sense of having created a mental state, possibly a solution or a novel way of looking at the problem – which was not present before their rumination.

Such a "creative" act, viewed simply as winding up far from the common initial state of mind, might be reached at by a gradual process leading far from the initial state via what one could term a "chaotic" route, or might be achieved as a sudden "gestalt" by what one could term a "catastrophic" route. Note the fact that these sorts of transitions to a state far from the original one, for at least some people, are quite generically expected in non-linear systems and, as we have argued, the brain or mind must be considered as non-linear in their behavior. That is, it should be expected that, at least sometimes, "unexpected" behavior – which we might call creativity – would arise. This prediction is quite robust and based on nothing more than non-linearity that we know must be present.

Transitions to chaotic behavior or to potentially catastrophic behavior (or not) are in general controlled by parameters of the system, which we have lumped together as "c" earlier. In the case of the brain, they might include neurotransmitter levels, drugs, other physiological parameters such as temperature, thirst, etc., as well as preset brain parameters such as memories and habits. This may all sound quite generic, but herein lies the strength of these ideas because it suggests applications and tests as we describe later.

Now, what about mental illness? Remarkably, much of mental illness may then seem quite similar: A mentally ill person presented with the same situation as a sane one winds up, much like a creative person, with a radically different perception and associated behavior. As an extreme example, consider schizophrenia. Here normal events or objects are perceived not just "as they are" according to normal people, but connected to things that are "far away," either by a chain of increasingly bizarre associations (via a chaotic route) or suddenly being seen as something other than what they are to normal people (via a catastrophic route). It is remarkable in this context that many neuroleptic drugs seem to produce effects that resemble a "slowing down" or limiting of the range over which thoughts can go. These effects and the critical parameters may be quite different for different illnesses and different developmental periods. For example, in attention-deficit/hyperactivity disorder (ADHD), children's behavior can appear quite chaotic with apparently catastrophic shifts. Stimulants may worsen schizophrenia's symptoms, but serve to improve cognitive regulation and focus with associated improvements in behavior in ADHD.

The difference, it seems, between creativity and mental illness is very much one of how much control one has over the non-linear wanderings of the mind to places – either via a chaotic route drifting farther and farther away, or a catastrophic route, making sudden transitions to new states for which we offer the following examples.

It has been said that Thomas Edison tried thousands of materials before finding one suitable for light bulb filaments. Is this a case of obsessional thinking bordering on the pathology of obsessive–compulsive disorder? If so, one would be hard put to make that charge. But a less stable mind could well have got lost trying material after material and losing one's way. The wandering through thousands of tries may be fine as long as one comes back.

The great inventor Nikola Tesla had visions of his inventions so clear that he would work without blueprints. Indeed, the visions were so clear that apparently at times he had trouble distinguishing them from reality, and could visualize flicking a switch and turning them on to see how they ran. Perhaps he was experiencing chronic hallucinations akin to those of schizophrenia, or perhaps dissociative symptoms with uncanny control (Roguin, 2004). It appears that, some of the time at least, we could manage them and still function in the world.

Akin to this, the prominent German organic chemist Friedrich August Kekulé von Stradonitz described how the chemical structure of benzene – a hugely important advance in the understanding of aromatic compounds – came to him after having a reverie or daydream of a snake seizing its own tail (Rocke, 1985). Without appropriate control over daydreams, we would no doubt meet the diagnostic criteria of some psychotic or dissociative disorder.

Albert Einstein was led to the theory of special relativity by imagining what it would be like to ride on a beam of light. This turned out to be a fruitful line of thought that allowed him to make progress in physics that many could not, but not a useful one to follow indefinitely. At some point, one has to come back to earth and ride a normal train.

The brilliant mathematician Srinivasa Ramanujan claimed to receive his mathematical insights in dreams from the goddess Namagiri with scrolls of mathematics unrolling before his eyes. Would one call these delusions? Again, the difference between creativity and madness seems to be in dealing with going to faraway states of mind, precisely as one would expect to be possible and indeed generic in non-linear systems, but managing and incorporating them in normal life.

Note that in each of the cases just outlined, there are seemingly mad thoughts: questing through thousands of candidate materials when there was no reason to believe that a suitable one would be found, daytime hallucinations competing with reality, imagination of wildly impossible events, and dreams with knowledge presented by a supernatural being. All of these involve states of mind wildly far from the norm, and yet we do not classify them as cases of madness because of the ability of the people involved to understand them for what they are, and come back to, and function in, normal consensus reality. This seems to be achieved by some balance between brain regions associated with drives, and higher executive mental functions that can decide what to do with these mental states. Perhaps the study of some meditative states and people who develop this capacity to choose mental states – such as shamans in traditional cultures where they are often seen to manage, rather than suppress, unusual thought processes – would be informative to our brain models of creativity (Brune, 2004).

Excessive stability and mental illness

So far we have considered how creativity, seen as a manifestation of non-linear behaviors of brain and mind, shares traits with many sorts of mental illness. We also point out that lack of sufficient non-linearity can also produce aspects of pathology. For example, a depressed person apparently remains close to the state in which they find themselves with a kind of emotional "inertia." Despite large stimuli (happy events, etc.), depressed individuals can neither gradually cheer up (wind up in a very different mental state via the chaotic route) nor "snap out of it" (wind up in a very different mental state via the catastrophic route). This notion of being "stuck" can arise within a close-to-normal state and perhaps manifest as anhedonia, or it may come in a sad or apathetic state and manifest as depression.

States in which a non-linear system can get "stuck" need not be time independent. Other possibilities include cyclic attractors, when a cyclic sequence of states is passed through (similar to someone stuck in a repeating loop of thoughts), or chaotic attractors, when a chaotic sequence of states is passed through (similar to someone stuck rambling incoherently from topic to topic and state of mind to state of mind).

A few words about noise

Noise, in the physical sense, is ubiquitous and inescapable. It sets important constraints on our senses: were our hearing much more acute, we would hear a constant rustling due to fluctuations in the ambient air pressure. Similarly, were our eyes a little more sensitive to light, we might find small background fluctuations (including thermal excitations of photoreceptors) a constant annoyance.

However, noise could also play a number of important useful roles in living systems. For example, a small amount of noise can raise an undetectably low signal to an observable threshold – a phenomenon known as "stochastic resonance" (Moss et al., 2004). Similarly, in connectionist models of brain activity, noise can play an important role in shifting the model brain from one state to another, with the typical example being "Boltzmann machines" and their relatives, which use an analog of thermal annealing ("simulated annealing") to find the best global solutions to problems without getting stuck in "local minima" – approximate good solutions that are still not the best overall (Rumelhart, 1987).

Here again, non-linearity has an essential role to play as non-linearity must be present for the noise to do anything interesting: a linear function f(signal+noise) is just f(signal)+f(noise).

For the purposes of creativity and connections to mental illness, one might ask both how much noise one might inject into a system to produce an interesting change and how intrinsically sensitive to noise that system might be. The changes could correspond to creative insights in a healthy, creative patient, but excesses or lack of such changes could both result in symptoms of mental illnesses. Creativity might require a certain ease of being pulled out of a particular state of mind to move to another. This could be facilitated with noise, which might come from external environmental sources, or perhaps be a product of normal physiological processes. Too much noise, or too much response to it, might lead to a pathological inability to focus and perhaps something akin to ADHD. Conversely, too little noise might lead to an inability to shift out of a given state – in extreme cases, perhaps even catatonia.

Applications and tests

Once one accepts the idea that the brain and mind act non-linearly, one readily sees models for both creativity and a variety of mental illnesses, as well as for a link between creativity and some forms of mental illness. Thus some of the ideas presented here are testable as follows.

If one thinks of the brain as a "black box" with some control parameters, and inputs and outputs, one has the full spectrum of techniques to study non-linear systems. These are very generic and essentially topological in nature – plots of some quantities versus others can be studied for signs of chaotic behavior in a very model-independent fashion. Some work along these lines can be found in Basar (1990), but there is no need for the data to be restricted. For example, to monitor electroencephalogram (EEG) and functional magnetic resonance imaging (fMRI) signals, anything measurable can be used, including data obtained from asking a subject questions. This leaves the field very much wide open.

For control parameters, one has the full spectrum of variables controllable in psychiatry, including measured levels of endogenous substances, administered drugs, and environmental factors, including early-life and developmental factors. Mapping out how these control parameters affect the chaotic or catastrophic behavior, which we propose is measurable, would be an enormous field, but could start to show how one could use them to control and influence both creativity and mental illness from a unified viewpoint. There could also be an interesting blurring of the line between therapeutic protocols and ones designed to provide enhancements to creativity and cognition.

Some conditions might require a damping of non-linearities (e.g., this might be how a neuroleptic drug helps a schizophrenic from wandering too far away in thought). It may also be that control of some higher executive function of the mind via talk therapy could allow creative aspects of the schizophrenic mental process to be usefully incorporated into a useful life. (It seems unlikely that Edison, Tesla, Kekulé, Einstein, or Ramanujan would have chosen to forfeit their unusual modes of thinking.)

Almost paradoxically, it may also be that some increase in non-linearity might be needed in states that involve being "stuck," either in depression or in obsessional or psychotic thoughts.

We offer here one simple example of a control parameter: dopamine, which, when manipulated, shows some evidence for the line of thought presented here. Low dopamine levels can be associated with depression, higher levels with elevated mood and optimism, and still higher levels with hallucinations (Galletly, 2009). Could this be a simple model of only one response in a depressed state having more responses in a happy state, and having too many (and perhaps not realizing it) in a state of hallucination?

With respect to the relevance of noise, it would be interesting to study the degree to which different subjects (sane and mentally ill) perform better (i.e., via stochastic resonance in the case of perception, or finding creative multiple solutions to problems in the case of thought) in response to added noise (Mehta *et al.*, 2012), drugs, or psychotherapy (Majani, 2011), which might usefully reduce or increase focus of attention (Fox, 2011).

Conclusions

We have argued that non-linearity is likely of importance in perception and thought and that non-linear phenomena behave in ways that are at the very least strongly suggestive of both creative thought and a variety of pathological processes. This suggests new ways of looking for links between creativity and mental illness – both are unusual modes of thought with characteristics that can be tracked to the generic behavior of non-linear systems. More detailed studies, such as looking for chaotic behavior in mental and physiological processes or evidence for catastrophes in transitions in thought or behavior, are a very much open field. With quantitative measurements, one might find new ways to make diagnoses and to study the effects of drugs or other therapies. Finally, we hope that some of the ideas presented could allow one to think of aspects of exceptional functioning such as creativity and madness perhaps as more or less desirable aspects of common non-linearities necessary for both states.

References

Basar, E. (1990). *Chaos in brain function*. Berlin: Springer-Verlag.

Bradbury, R. (2005). *A sound of thunder and other stories* (reprint edition). New York: William Morrow Paperbacks.

Brune, M. (2004). Schizophrenia – an evolutionary enigma? *Neuroscience and Biobehavioral Reviews*, 28(1), 41–53. doi:10.1016/j.neubiorev.2003.10.002

Flaherty, A. W. (2011). Brain illness and creativity: Mechanisms and treatment risks. [Review.] *Canadian Journal of Psychiatry*, 56(3), 132–143.

Fox, D. (2011). Neuroscience: Brain buzz. [Historical Article News.] *Nature*, 472(7342), 156–158. doi:10.1038/472156a

Galletly, C. (2009). Recent advances in treating cognitive impairment in schizophrenia. [Review.] *Psychopharmacology (Berl)*, 202(1–3), 259–273. doi:10.1007/s00213-008-1302-9

Kandel, E. R., Schwartz, J. H., Jessell, T. M. and Siegelbaum, S. A. (2012). *Principles of Neural Science* (5th edn.). New York: McGraw-Hill Professional.

Kaufman, A. B., Butt, A. E., Kaufman, J. C. and Colbert-White, E. N. (2011). Towards a neurobiology of creativity in nonhuman animals. *Journal of Comparative Psychology*, 125(3), 255–272. doi:10.1037/a0023147-2011-09977-001 [pii]

Leech, R., Mareschal, D. and Cooper, R. P. (2008). Analogy as relational priming: A developmental and computational perspective on the origins of a complex cognitive skill. *Behavioral and Brain Sciences*, 31(4), 357–378.

Majani, G. (2011). Positive psychology in psychological interventions in rehabilitation medicine. *Giornale Italiano di Medicina del Lavoro ed Ergonomia*, 33(1 Suppl A), A64–68.

Mehta, R., Zhu, R. and Cheema, A. (2012). Is noise always bad? Exploring the effects of ambient noise on creative cognition. *Journal of Consumer Research*, 39(4), 784–799. doi:10.1086/665048

Moss, F., Ward, L. M. and Sannita, W. G. (2004). Stochastic resonance and sensory information processing: A tutorial and review of application. [Research Support, Non-US Government Research Support, US Government, Non-P.H.S. Review.] *Clinical Neurophysiology*, 115(2), 267–281.

Peterson, J. B. and Flanders, J. L. (2002). Complexity management theory: Motivation for ideological rigidity and social conflict. *Cortex*, 38(3), 429–458.

Pippard, A. B. (1985). *Response and stability: An introduction to the physical theory.* New York: Cambridge University Press.

Rocke, A. J. (1985). Hypothesis and experiment in the early development of Kekule Benzene theory. *Annals of Science*, 42(4), 355–381. doi:10.1080/00033798500200411

Roguin, A. (2004). Nikola Tesla: The man behind the magnetic field unit. *Journal of Magnetic Resonance Imaging*, 19(3), 369–374. doi:10.1002/jmri.20002

Rosenblatt, F. (1958). The perceptron: A probabilistic model for information storage and organization in the brain. *Psychological Review*, 65(6), 386–408.

Rumelhart, D. E. (1987). *Parallel distributed processing: Explorations in the microstructure of cognition foundations (Vol. I).* Cambridge, MA: Bradford Books.

Shane, S. (2008). *The illusions of entrepeneurship.* New Haven, CT: Yale University Press.

Swain, J. E. and Swain, J. D. (2008). Creativity or mental illness: Possible errors of relational priming in neural networks of the brain. *Behavioral and Brain Sciences*, 31(4), 398–399.

Swanson, L. W. (2000). What is the brain? *Trends in Neurosciences*, 23(11), 519–527.

8 Artists' vulnerability to psychopathology: an integrative cognitive perspective

Mark Papworth

Introduction

Many highly creative individuals have been noted to experience mental health problems. Since the 1960s, the cognitive-behavioral therapy (CBT) model has become pivotal in the understanding and treatment of psychological difficulties. However, it is rarely considered by creativity researchers who more usually focus upon psychoanalytic, personality, contextual, or biological factors. This chapter explores commonalities between the cognitive styles observed in both the creative and those who are psychologically vulnerable. In doing so, it offers new insights into the relationship between creativity and some forms of psychopathology. I begin by introducing CBT, before investigating similarities between the cognitive styles that are (a) considered to underlie mental health difficulties – which are more common in the highly creative – and (b) implicated in the creative process. The chapter ends by examining two strands of research that investigate whether these similarities exist within creative samples.

CBT has arguably become the foremost psychological treatment for many of those suffering with mental health difficulties. The approach has revolutionized mental health care. By way of illustration, the UK's National Institute of Health and Care Excellence (NICE) has determined, by systematically reviewing the evidence base, that it should be a core component of treatment for those suffering from one of many disorders. These include depression (2009), panic disorder and generalized anxiety disorder (2007), posttraumatic stress disorder (2005a), obsessive–compulsive/body dysmorphic disorder (2005b), and also schizophrenia (2002). Consequently, as part of the largest scheme of its type to date, the government is committed to train and employ a further 3,600 new CBT therapists to practice within the English National Health Service in an attempt to improve access to psychological therapy in England (Clark *et al.*, 2009).

The CBT model assumes that psychological difficulties are primarily driven by dysfunctional patterns of cognition and behavior. In this context, cognition refers to patterns of thoughts, interpretations, and images the individual constructs about themselves and their environment. Dysfunctional cognitive patterns are characterized by bias or distortion, and have been found to be pivotal in the development and maintenance of mental health difficulties. In some conditions, bias often additionally occurs in other levels of appraisal – for instance, in "core beliefs" that are shaped by childhood experience, linked assumptions about situations that then determine coping responses, and also meta-cognitive processes (interpretations of cognitive experience). Examples of these phenomena are described later.

Surveys of creative individuals have found the artistically creative to experience a greater prevalence of psychological problems including mood-related difficulties such as depression, mania, and suicidal tendencies, as well as addiction (Andreasen and Canter, 1974; Ludwig, 1992, 1994, 1998; Murphy *et al.*, 1989; Post, 1994, 1996; Schildkraut *et al.*, 1994; Stack, 1996). Additionally, links have been found between creativity and psychotic or schizotypal disorders (the latter having common features with psychosis; Dykes and McGhie, 1976; Karlsson, 1970; Keefe and Magaro, 1980; Schuldberg, 2001; Schuldberg *et al.*, 1988; Weinstein and Graves, 2001). For example, the prevalence of depression within groups of successful, professional artists has often been observed to be within a 30–60 percent range (Andreasen, 1987; Andreasen and Canter, 1974; Post, 1994; Schildkraut *et al.*, 1994). This level is similar to or greater than that observed for acknowledged vulnerable groups that have been highlighted by the UK government for preventive intervention (Department of Health, 1998), such as lone mothers (Brown and Moran, 1997) or the unemployed (Artazcoz *et al.*, 2004). Here I describe some of the salient cognitive characteristics of these psychological disorders before looking at some similarities between these and creative styles of thinking.

Key cognitive features of selected mental health difficulties

Arguably the most influential figure in CBT is acknowledged to be Aaron Beck. His cognitive model of depression (Beck *et al.*, 1979) states that dysfunctional beliefs (e.g., "My value as a person depends on what others think of me") contribute to a cognitive bias when information is processed in an unrealistically negative manner. This negatively biased pattern of cognition, in turn, escalates negative mood, which can eventually result in a depressive episode. In addition, depressed individuals have an increased tendency to display biases (such as "overgeneralizing") in their thought processes and draw global negative conclusions about themselves or their lives on the basis of insufficient or no evidence (for instance, concluding they are worthless after their boss fails to acknowledge them when they pass them in the corridor). Research has suggested that these cognitive biases may increase individuals' depressed mood at any given moment and are also generally retained over time as an enduring feature of their mental state (Beevers and Miller, 2004; Zuroff et al., 1999). The latter trait component imbues the individual with a degree of vulnerability to the development of disorder.

In addition, cognitive biases can impact upon problem-solving performance, which has also been reported to profoundly affect mood (Williams, 1996). Poor problem-solving skills may lead to either avoidance of decision making or an adoption of negative choices/strategies that may, in turn, increase the impact that life events have on the individual. As such, studies have noted a relationship between problem-solving deficits and depression (Dobson and Dobson, 1981; Gotlib and Asarnow, 1979), suicidality (Orbach et al., 1990), and psychosis (Platt and Spivack, 1972; Simpson and Done, 2004).

While the application of the CBT model is less well established in regard to mania, cognitive processes have been implicated in mood swings in those who experience this condition (Mansell and Lam, 2003; Mansell et al., 2007). As in the model for depression, dysfunctional beliefs (e.g., "When I am energized I know that I am important") are shaped by early life experience such as failure events. Manic episodes then escalate out of a triggering event, which prompts a change in internal state (such as towards excitement). These changes in internal state are then appraised in a self-relevant, biased, and both extremely positive and negative conflicting fashion, with a deeply personal meaning. For instance, they might be characterized by both an imminent catastrophe and personal success (e.g., "I am making a fool of myself" and "I have the energy to do anything I want"). These appraisals trigger immediate efforts to maximize the chances of a positive outcome that interfere with the individual's ability to reappraise their internal state or resolve their conflicting appraisals. Efforts are characterized as being either "ascent" (increasing activation levels; e.g., increased involvement in activity, risk taking, and extended wakefulness) or "descent" in nature (decreasing activation levels; e.g., social withdrawal, rumination, and self-critical thinking), and are often counter-productive, resulting in an escalation in symptoms.

Cognitive biases have also been proposed as a means of explaining some aspects of the development and maintenance of psychosis (Bentall et al., 1994; Chadwick and Birchwood, 1994; Garety et al., 2001; Morrison, 2001). Perceptions are dependent on some interaction between incoming sensory stimuli (bottom-up processing) and stored memories of sensory inputs. The latter help the individual in the formation of expectancies and regularities (top-down processing) in order to make sense of current stimuli. In contrast, those suffering with schizophrenia fail to establish these expectations, often resulting in an intrusion of irrelevant material that would normally be excluded from conscious awareness. In fact, it is this lack of top-down guidance in the interpretation of auditory or visual perceptions that is considered to be fundamental to the psychotic condition (Garety et al., 2001; Hemsley, 1993). Cognitive biases may lead to a false attribution of intruding internal thought processes as being caused externally (for instance, thoughts may be experienced as voices) and may indeed be threatening to the individual (triggering cognitions such as: "I am losing my mind"; Morrison, 2001). Similarly, an individual's self-monitoring of intentions and actions may be disrupted to such an extent that they are not recognized as the person's own and are therefore experienced as alien (Frith, 1992; Garety et al., 2001). Some evidence suggests that these cognitive processes, which contribute to symptom formation, are also likely to contribute to the maintenance of the disorder (Freeman et al., 2000; Garety et al., 1997; Maher, 1974).

Cognitive style has also been found to be involved in the formation and maintenance of addictions (which are often comorbidly prevalent with other mental health difficulties; Kessler et al., 1994; Regier et al., 1990). Beck et al. (1993) describe how dysfunctional beliefs (such as, "I don't have the power to stop," or "I can't be happy unless I can use") undermine self-efficacy, fuel craving, and can be an obstacle to cessation, while termination of the habit can be interpreted as being characterized by threat or deprivation. One example of bias that has been observed in addicts is associated with the expectation linked to substance use. Individuals typically inflate expectancies associated with positive outcomes related to their habit and deflate expectancies associated with negative outcomes. Levels of consumption, treatment outcomes, and abstinence survivorship have all been shown to have a relationship with belief bias (Christiansen et al., 1989; Connors et al., 1993; Jones and McMahon, 1996; Sher et al., 1996; Stacy et al., 1991). Beliefs subsequently inform distorted cognitions that are additionally involved in the process. For instance, an acute stressor might activate the belief, "If I use, I can handle life better," which may result in cognitions such as, "I can use this just this once," which would result in relapse. Often individuals experience an internal "battle" involving patterns of cognition associated with craving and permission giving that are in conflict with other patterns that are linked to ideas about self-control.

Finally, some cognitive differences have an impact across conditions, resulting in trans-diagnostic effects. With psychosis, it has been noted that a reduced level of "cognitive inhibition" is integral to the disorder. This is the reduced ability to exclude less relevant experience from experience (as described earlier). This phenomenon has also been implicated in rumination, which is a common symptom observed in both depression and obsessive–compulsive disorder. An attenuation of cognitive inhibition results in difficulty in disengaging from negative stimuli or information, resulting in a reduced ability to prevent this cognition from entering and remaining in working memory (the ruminative process). This subsequently increases the consolidation of this material into long-term memory (Enright and Beech, 1993; Joormann et al., 2007).

As well as being reflected in self-report methods of assessment, patterns of biased cognition are observed in patients on a more fundamental level in laboratory-based tasks. Consistently, those with forms of psychological disorder have been found to respond in different ways to control participants. With depression, early work suggested that depressed individuals might be more realistic in their probability judgments (Alloy and Abramson, 1979). However, more recent and ecologically valid work demonstrated a negative bias in their self-evaluations of performance on prediction tasks (predictions were regarding how others perceived them and how they performed on a vocabulary task). This effect was observed despite depressed individuals performing as equally well as non-depressed participants on the tasks themselves (Strunk and Adler, 2009).

Patients experiencing mania have been found to have an increased impulsivity in their decision making. Strakowski et al. (2009) found that their performance differed from controls in the predicted fashion in that the patients were more impulsive in their decision making (as assessed by a stop-signal task), less able to delay gratification (to their disadvantage on a monetary-based task), and poorer at a number-based attention task. The decision-making processes in individuals diagnosed as having psychosis have similarly been investigated. In a probability task, participants were required to judge whether a bead was drawn from one of two possible hidden jars containing two types of colored bead in differing ratios. It was established that, in comparison to normal controls, participants experiencing psychosis make this decision earlier or "jump to conclusions" (Dudley and Over, 2003; Garety et al., 1991; Huq et al., 1988; Moritz and Woodward, 2005). Similarly, the cognitive processes of addicts (problem drinkers, smokers, and compulsive gamblers) were assessed using the Stroop Test. Here, individuals are presented with a succession of words written in colored ink and are required to name the color of the ink as quickly as possible. Addicts experienced performance deficits with words that had salience for them in terms of being semantically relevant to their addiction (Gross *et al.*, 1993; Johnson *et al.*, 1994; McCusker and Gettings, 1997; McCusker *et al.*, 1995). Likewise, performance on reaction time tasks, when individuals were exposed to task-irrelevant auditory stimuli, was selectively poorer in addicts when these stimuli were related to some aspect of their habit (Sayette and Hufford, 1994; Sayette *et al.*, 1994). Addicts also display a positive bias in memory in regard to their addictive behavior as assessed by associative tasks that measure positive and negative endorsements associated with their habit, together with endorsement reaction times (Armstrong, 1997). Finally, individuals experiencing addiction displayed this memory bias in semantic priming tasks when participants were required to generate activities associated with positive and negative outcomes or states. In this instance, the positive condition tended to prime more drug-related representations in the addicts (Ames and Stacy, 1998; Stacy, 1997; Stacy *et al.*, 1996; Weingardt *et al.*, 1996).

In summary, cognitive processes are integral to the development, experience, and maintenance of many mental health conditions. These are characterized by bias in thoughts and beliefs, as well as meta-cognitive processes (which are more prevalent in psychosis). These broader macro-level differences are reflected in more fine-grained, micro-level deficits where fundamental biases have been observed in evaluation, reasoning, attention, and recall processes in those who are either vulnerable to or experience mental health problems.

Key cognitive processes involved in creative activities

In this section, I outline selected cognitive processes that are considered to be important to the creative process. In particular, these have been linked to the artistically creative – this group having been observed to experience a greater prevalence of mental health difficulties (Ludwig, 1998). In particular, divergent and associational cognitive styles are discussed, together with related forms of inhibition.

The "divergent" cognitive style is considered to be pivotal to artistic creation (Barron and Hetherington, 1981; Guilford, 1967; Hudson, 1966; Ludwig, 1998). In a pioneering series of studies involving British schoolboys, Hudson (1966) found that those who specialized in the sciences tended to excel at tests of logic relations perception that required a *convergence* on the correct answer. In contrast, those who chose arts had strengths over measures that required the individual to *diverge* or think fluently or tangentially, without evaluating a particular line of reasoning in detail. This divergent style is characteristically distinct in terms of the production of a greater quantity of responses to tasks requiring creativity, with these being typically more original and of less "repressive" quality in comparison to a convergent style (typically generating more data with fantastic content; Dudek, 1968; Freud, 1933; Guilford, 1967; Hudson, 1966; McCrae, 1987; Walker et al., 1995). Additionally, Hudson (1966) found divergers to be able to more comfortably tolerate ambiguity in their cognition. Rothenberg (1979) echoed this latter perspective, characterizing the creative as having a *penchant* for thinking in terms of polar extremes. This is illustrated by a phrase from the poem "The monkey puzzle" by Marianne Moore (1951): "The lion's ferocious chrysanthemum head," where the lion's ferocity is countered with the fragility of the flower.

An alternative but not unrelated form of cognition that is considered to underlie creativity is linked to the associative combinations that are made by the individual. Mednick (1962) defines the creative thinking process as the "forming of associative elements into new combinations which either meet specified requirements or are in some way useful" (p. 221). This perspective suggests that an aspect of creative cognition involves the bringing together of elements in novel and creative ways. For example, in *The persistence of memory* (1931), Salvador Dali uniquely combined the pocket watch with the concept of flexibility to produce the novel concept of a floppy timepiece. More usually, "watch" might be linked to other objects such as "clock" or concepts such as "time." According to Mednick (1962), patterns of cognition that are characterized by an ability to make more unusual associations underlie creativity; associative theories have also been proposed by a number of other authorities (Koestler, 1964; Maltzman, 1960, 1962; Wallach, 1970, 1971).

More recently, deficits in regard to forms of inhibition have been observed in the creative. Carson (this volume) investigated levels of "latent inhibition." This is the capacity for the brain to filter or screen out irrelevant information from attention. As our natural environment is hugely complex, organisms are hypothesized to use a perceptual gating system that allows them to ignore stimuli of more limited value. This allows them rather to focus attention on more important, novel stimuli. This concept has similarities with "cognitive inhibition" (see earlier), but has its roots in animal studies rather than in clinical psychology. A reduced capacity for latent inhibition was found to correlate with a number of measures of creativity as well as creative achievement. As a result, Carson et al. (2003) assumed that the creative are "privileged to access a greater inventory of unfiltered stimuli during early processing, thereby increasing the odds of original recombinant ideation" (p. 505). In this way, latent inhibition might be seen as one possible cognitive basis for both divergent and associative means of creativity. The reduced capacity to filter out stimuli means that the individual has a greater range of experience to draw upon, which would facilitate a greater variety of responses as well as a broader range of conceptual connections. This is possibly reflected in a need for a number of creative historical figures to eliminate, where possible, extraneous stimuli. For example, Charles Darwin's need for "extreme quietness" led to his move to his highly secluded home in Down (Pickering, 1974), Marcel Proust lined his bedroom with cork as a means of soundproofing (Barker, 1958), and Thomas Carlyle also constructed a sound-proofed room in his house (Halliday, 1950).

Bristol and Viskontas (2006) describe how reduced levels of inhibition can facilitate the production of creative associative combinations through influencing recall and creative (rather than perceptual) processes in both real-world and laboratory situations. For example, they note the findings of Anderson *et al.* (1994) where participants were exposed to word pairs – one of which was a "category cue" for an "exemplar" (for instance, "orange" would be the exemplar for the category of "fruit"). Individuals were then exposed to a category-cued retrieval phase where the first two letters of only a selection of the exemplars for just some of the categories were presented with the cue, the participants' task being to recall the exemplar word. Finally, after some 20 minutes, a second retrieval test occurred where all of the categories were presented and participants were required to recall the full range of the exemplars that were linked to them. It was found that the first retrieval phase resulted in inhibited recall in the second phase (in comparison to the control exemplars and categories that were not presented during the first retrieval phase) for the unpracticed exemplars that were part of a practiced category. In this way, the act of retrieval of some words inhibited the subsequent retrieval of conceptually similar words within this laboratory task. This is illustrative of how levels of inhibition underlie "retrieval-induced forgetting." This is a phenomenon where a greater use and reliance upon a concept or strategy will result in a reduced ability to construct novel approaches to the same or a similar task. In this way, levels of inhibition are directly linked to creativity and the quality of associative combinations.

These inhibitory and associative cognitive processes may be seen to be at least partially connected through the more general concept of "breadth of attention." This refers to the number and range of stimuli experienced at any one time by an individual (Mendelsohn, 1976). Those who have a chronically wide focus in their attention are more aware of erroneous or irrelevant stimuli. This wider breadth of attention increases the probability of creative activity through an increased potential to bring together disparate ideas. Kasof (1997) explored the relationship between these processes by asking participants to do a creative task (write a poem), with individuals being assessed in terms of their breadth of attention (via self-report), while being exposed to forms of distracting audio stimuli (which were hypothesized to have a bigger impact on those with a wider breadth of attention). Creativity was found to be associated with a wider breadth of attention, with noise affecting these individuals more profoundly than those who displayed a more focused pattern of attention.

The cognitive biases noted in the two previous sections of this chapter might all be categorized as differences in cognitive appraisal. In this context, appraisal is taken to refer to logical-evaluative, recall, and perceptual processes; mechanisms that "make sense" of external stimuli as well as the thought processes themselves. These may arise at different levels of processing. For instance, in the depressed, the interpretation of complex social situations may be shaped by a rich tapestry of previous experiences, whereas the phenomenon of latent inhibition has been associated with more basic processes at a perceptual level (which might, in turn, underlie differences in higher-level processes). This raises a question about the link between mental illness and creativity: Can it at least partially be explained by common patterns in cognitive processing? Given the profound implications of this hypothesis, the minimal attention that it has received in both the empirical (see Kaufman, 2001) and the review literature (Lauronen et al., 2004; Waddell, 1998) warrants remediation. I summarize two strands of this literature below.

The links over the cognitive domain

Earlier, conceptual similarities in cognition were outlined between the creative and the psychologically distressed. A limited number of studies have explicitly investigated these similarities through simultaneously investigating aspects of creative and clinical cognition within creative samples. Other studies have investigated similarities within general samples. For the most part, the latter are not outlined here because surveys have found these effects to be more prominent in the creative (Ludwig, 1998; Post, 1994). The studies next outlined explore these links through examining the basic cognitive mechanisms of attention and latent inhibition, and then probabilistic reasoning and broader characteristics of cognitive distortion.

Dykes and McGhie (1976) investigated cognitive attentional strategies in both creative individuals and those with a diagnosis of schizophrenia.

They hypothesized that both of these groups would perceive a wider and more intensive sampling of environmental stimuli in comparison to less creative, healthy controls. Additionally, a reduced ability to process this information was hypothesized to distinguish those with a psychosis from the creative. This was assessed through use of a card-sorting task and additionally a dichotic-shadowing task (where individuals needed to repeat audio material on one headphone channel while ignoring material in another) that had a linked visual word recognition task. Both of the experimental groups (creative individuals and those with a diagnosis of schizophrenia) scored highly on a divergent-thinking task. Participants with a diagnosis did less well than both the creative and control groups on the card-sorting task. This suggests that creative individuals have an increased ability, in comparison to those with a diagnosis, to inhibit irrelevant material from their attention. Finally, performance across all three groups on the dichotic-shadowing task displayed some similarities but individuals with schizophrenia had an overall increased tendency to switch to the irrelevant channel within the task. The highly creative participants differed in their performance from the less creative controls under the more extreme conditions of the task, with an increased tendency to switch to the irrelevant channel in these instances. Likewise, a greater recognition of irrelevant material was found in the creative individuals in comparison to the low creative participants on the word recognition task, the performance of individuals with psychosis falling between the creative and control groups over this domain. These results are suggestive of similar patterns of attention within both the creative participants and those experiencing schizophrenia, this finding being in keeping with theories that describe commonalities in patterns of latent inhibition across both groups.

Carson *et al.* (2003) hypothesized that high levels of intelligence may moderate this process, representing cognitive abilities that protect against the development of mental health difficulties for some creative individuals. In a two-staged study, they initially assessed levels of latent inhibition, creativity, and IQ in a creatively diverse, high IQ sample of Harvard students (see Carson, this volume). The latent inhibition task consisted of both a pre-exposure phase and a test phase. The former involved an auditory discrimination task requiring individuals to attend to nonsense syllables while bursts of white noise were randomly superimposed onto the audio recording. Participants in a non-exposed comparison condition received similar instructions in the pre-exposure phase, but were not asked to attend to a particular syllable. Latent inhibition is elicited by the test in that those who have been in the active pre-exposure phase will take longer to pinpoint the target syllable in the test phase – pre-exposure triggering attentional inhibition in the later test. Members of a low creative achievement group showed a significant difference over exposed and non-exposed conditions, whereas members of a high creative achievement group did not, indicating attenuated latent inhibition in the latter. An additional finding was that negative latent inhibition scores and high IQ scores were jointly greater predictors of creative achievement than latent inhibition scores alone.

In a second analysis using a subsample of eminent creative achievers, Carson *et al.* (2003) found that these individuals were seven times more likely to have low rather than high latent inhibition scores. Once again, with this sample, negative latent inhibition scores and high IQ scores were predictors of creative achievement, accounting for some 33 percent of the variance over this domain. This study, together with the earlier investigation by Dykes and McGhie (1976), is supportive of the presence of common cognitive appraisal patterns within both the creative and also those who experience mental health problems. In particular, these patterns are evident in psychosis as well as psychotic-prone individuals (Lubow *et al.*, 1992), but additionally involved in both depression and obsessive–compulsive presentations (see earlier).

I move now to the second strand of research. A depression-prone attributional style is a broader form of distortion in cognitive appraisal that was identified by Peterson and Seligman (1984). Those who are more vulnerable to depression are negatively biased in their interpretations regarding the cause of negative events, tending to see them to be internal rather than externally caused (e.g., exam failure being due to personal inability rather than poor teacher performance), stable rather than unstable (perceiving failure as also occurring over previous and future exams rather than this being an isolated occasion), and global rather than specific (failure reflecting a lack of ability over a variety of domains rather than being limited to a single one). DeMoss *et al.* (1993) investigated attributional style in a sample of school children through use of self-report questionnaires. Intriguingly, mixed results were obtained. For female participants, high verbal creativity scores were linked to a positive attributional style, whereas, for both sexes, a relationship existed between high figural creativity scores and this depressogenic attributional style.

Papworth and James (2003) and then later Papworth *et al.* (2008) expanded upon this approach over two studies that investigated differences between arts and science university students. This was over the following dimensions: (1) mood, (2) levels of cognitive distortion (as assessed by an inventory that asks participants to report how they would interpret a number of situations), (3) probabilistic reasoning (using the bead task [see earlier], and a random number task that estimates logical reasoning by noting the number of times the same digit is listed twice consecutively within a participant-generated list), (4) practical problem-solving ability (through use of a written problem-solving task), and (5) perceptions of problem-solving ability (through use of a self-report inventory). As well as scoring more highly on a divergent-thinking test, art students reported lower mood than their science peers. Also, their responses indicated a greater number of depressive and distorted appraisals of everyday situations. Art students reached decisions on the bead task after fewer draws and displayed fewer pairs on the random number task. These latter findings are indicative of less probabilistic accuracy within their reasoning and a more "hasty" decision-making style. Finally, artists produced more ineffective responses to the problem-solving task and, perhaps accurately, displayed more negative self-appraisals of their problem-solving abilities.

Papworth and James (2003) additionally performed an unpublished subanalysis that compared expressive (fine artists) and formal artists (musicians) over a selection of these domains. Surveys that have used large posthumous samples of acknowledged creative figures have noted *within-arts* differences with respect to prevalence rates (Ludwig, 1998; Post, 1994). Those artists showing fewer difficulties were from fields involving more formal, objective, rational, precise, or performance-based modes of artistic expression (such as music and architecture), whereas those eliciting the greatest prevalence of problems were involved in fields requiring more expressive, emotive, or intuitive modes (such as the visual arts and literature). As expected, the expressive arts group performed better on divergent-thinking measures but reported lower mood. Similarly, greater levels of cognitive distortion were evident in the expressive artists and these participants also displayed poorer problem-solving abilities.

Together, these latter studies suggest that cognitive appraisal differs for creative artists (and even more so in the expressive artists) over a variety of processes. On a more fundamental level, their reasoning appears to be less probabilistic. In fact, this effect was predicted by Hudson (1966), who noted that logical reasoning would be likely to be an area of difficulty for divergers. Perhaps undermined by this deficit, higher-level differences were noted in terms of reduced problem-solving ability, greater distortion in interpretations of situations, and also lower mood. These cognitive appraisal differences are in keeping with phenomena observed in a variety of mental health conditions, but more commonly in psychosis and depression (see earlier). In this way, these two strands of research both confirm the presence of common cognitive processes within both the creative and those with specific mental health difficulties, the assumption being that the processes are facilitative to creativity but also imbue some individuals with certain vulnerabilities.

Issues and future directions

This chapter has highlighted theoretical similarities in cognitive appraisal processes across the artistically creative and those who experience some mental health difficulties. Latterly, two veins of research have been examined that support this position. I close by exploring some associated issues and, in doing so, suggest avenues for further exploration.

First, more investigation into the genesis of this relationship is required. Due to the "correlational" nature of this research, we cannot determine whether there is a common pattern to its development and, if so, the factors that are causal and resultant. As Ludwig (1995) and also Richards and Kinney (2000) note, there are various possibilities associated with this. One is that clinical or subclinical phenomena may facilitate aspects of creativity. In this way, preexisting patterns of experience will have an impact on cognition, which, in turn, will then have a beneficial effect upon creativity. Naturally, this causal link would be unlikely to be solely cognitive based. For instance, the mood experience itself could have a beneficial impact on creativity. Some artists (for instance, Virginia Woolf) have seen depression as an intense inner experience that they can later draw on while creating. Additionally, some of the finest works of literature draw on the experience of suffering and despair (such as the soliloquies of Hamlet and Keats' "Ode to melancholy"). Similarly, the increased energy and flight of ideas that occur during hypomanic periods may directly result in an increase in creative activity. For example, Poincaré described discovering the nature of Fuchsian functions during a "wild night of excitement."

Another possibility is that the ongoing artist role and linked habitual cognitive processes subsequently result in changes in patterns of cognition that imbue the individual with a greater vulnerability to distress. Thus, individuals might engage in increasingly extreme forms of thinking as their ideas develop or as they aim to maintain originality over time. As their cognition becomes more unusual in terms of content and/or process, so vulnerability increases. Here again, other factors are likely to be mediators. For example, some paint pigments are toxic. Before the invention of the paint tube, artists were required to grind pigments and mix paint by hand. It has been suggested that Van Gogh experienced (among other conditions) poisoning from the lead pigment contained in the large amount of white paint he used in his paintings (Santiago, 2006). Additionally, some creative individuals have experimented with psychoactive substances in an attempt to facilitate creativity (Lapp *et al.*, 1994), this possibly contributing to the development of mental health difficulties (e.g., LSD; Vardy and Kay, 1993). Alternatively, causal pathways may vary across individuals or conditions, or may in fact be a more complex, multidirectional interaction. To inform this debate, longitudinal research is required that would allow investigators to track the development of patterns of mood, cognitive appraisal, and levels of creativity. Additionally, research techniques such as mood induction could determine whether a vulnerability to emotional lability exists in the artistically creative that might later manifest itself in terms of clinical dysfunction.

This topic brings together concepts from the diverse areas of clinical, academic, and experimental psychology. In order to more fully understand the relevant cognitive appraisal processes, there is a need for a greater level of commonality and specificity over these fields in terms of concepts and language. For example, "impulsivity" and "reduced inhibition" might appear to be similar concepts. However, in practice these have been investigated through the measurement of quite different abilities (see earlier). Ideally, relevant abilities might be dismantled through investigation into more basic components. Foci here would include the cognitive processes involved in the different concepts of creativity (such as divergent, associative, and inhibitory abilities), types of creativity (e.g., normal versus revolutionary [Sass, 2001]; scientific versus artistic), forms of psychopathology, and also protective cognitive abilities. For example, Ward (2007, p. 29) argues for greater specificity in regard to the interpretation of the testing of divergent abilities and, in so doing, begins to question the macro-level processes that might underlie participants' responses:

When a person achieves a certain fluency score on a divergent-thinking task by listing items in response to a prompt (e.g., alternate uses for a shoe), . . . the listed items may have been derived from the application of a wide range of processes, including episodic retrieval (e.g., recalling having used a shoe to kill a bug), mental imagery (e.g., scanning a mental image of a shoe, noting that it has laces, and realizing that they could serve a specific purpose), analysis of features (e.g., noting that shoes have the property of being heavy and therefore could be used as doorstops), abstraction (e.g., interpreting a shoe as a container, with the consequence that it could be used to store things), among many other possibilities.

A final challenge (which would be facilitated by a more complete understanding of common cognitive processes, as noted earlier) is associated with the development of an effective response to the distress experienced by the highly creative. Behind this intriguing phenomenon lie countless personal tragedies as well as a great loss to society. Schildkraut *et al.*'s (1994) study, which investigated the prevalence of mood disorders in a group of fifteen mid-twentieth-century, Abstract Expressionist artists, starkly illustrates this. Over 50 percent of their sample had some form of psychological difficulty and seven individuals experienced early deaths.

There are particular issues associated with the treatment of the creative. Pharmacological approaches for some conditions have been found to be unpopular because they are perceived to blunt creativity. Five of the twenty-four artists in Schou's (1979) sample of creative artists discontinued pharmacological treatment for depression for this reason. Anecdotally, some artists also have difficulty in engaging in tasks involved in CBT. Even at the outset, this form of therapy involves the use of relatively "fine-grained" appraisal tasks. For instance, as part of the assessment and induction process, sufferers are asked to consider situations when they have felt distressed. Then, within a diary task, they are asked to edit and distil from their stream of consciousness particular themes in their cognition that are likely to contribute to their low mood at these points. Therefore, these individuals may need, in some instances, more extended input in regard to various aspects of the approach or therapists may need to find ways of flexibly harnessing the individual's creativity within their contact. On a positive note, new developments in CBT have an increased emphasis upon imagery, metaphor, and also the provision of positive therapeutic experiences within sessions. In this way they may be more suited to the artistically creative (e.g., mindfulness-based CBT, Segal *et al.*, 2002; acceptance and commitment therapy, Hayes *et al.*, 2004; and compassion-focused therapy, Gilbert, 2010).

Given that differences in terms of mood and clinically related cognitive processes can be found between art students and science students as early as the eighth and ninth grades (De Moss *et al.*, 1993), this does suggest that preventive programs might be of utility within school and university settings. These would include, for example, a module that both teaches appraisal skills and also discusses their role within a mental health promotion context. Ideally, such input would allow the individual to access protective cognitive abilities without impeding creativity, enabling them to access a different mode to their thinking as and when needed. Indeed, Shure and Spivack (1979) describe a partially relevant program that is successfully delivered to kindergarten children. Such programs would benefit the artistically creative, vulnerable groups more generally, and the population at large.

References

Alloy, L. B. and Abramson, L. Y. (1979). Judgement of contingency in depressed and nondepressed students: Sadder but wiser? *Journal of Experimental Psychology: General*, 108, 441–485.

Ames, S. L. and Stacy, A. W. (1998). Implicit cognition in the prediction of substance use among drug offenders. *Psychology of Addictive Behaviors*, 12, 272–281.

Anderson, M. C., Bjork, R. A. and Bjork, E. L. (1994). Remembering can cause forgetting: Retrieval dynamics in long-term memory. *Journal of Experimental Psychology: Learning, Memory, and Cognition*, 20, 1063–1087.

Andreasen, N. J. C. (1987). Creativity and mental illness: Prevalence rates in writers and their first degree relatives. *American Journal of Psychiatry*, 144, 1288–1292.

Andreasen, N. J. C. and Canter, A. (1974). The creative writer: Psychiatric symptoms and family history. *Comprehensive Psychiatry*, 15, 123–131.

Armstrong, C. (1997). Automatic and non-automatic processing of alcohol-associations in heavy vs. light drinkers. Paper presented at the London Conference of the British Psychological Society, London.

Artazcoz, L., Benach, J., Borrell, C. and Cortès, I. (2004). Unemployment and mental health: Understanding the interactions among gender, family roles, and social class. *American Journal of Public Health*, 94, 82–88.

Barker, R. (1958). *Marcel Proust: A biography*. New York: Criterion Books.

Barron, F. and Hetherington, D. M. (1981). Creativity, intelligence, and personality. *Annual Review of Psychology*, 32, 439–476.

Beck, A. T., Rush, A. J., Shaw, B. F. and Emery, G. (1979). *Cognitive therapy of depression*. New York: Guilford Press.

Beck, A. T., Wright, F. D., Newman, C. F. and Liese, B. S. (1993). *Cognitive therapy of substance abuse*. New York: Guilford Press.

Beevers, C. G. and Miller, I. W. (2004). Depression-related negative cognition: Mood-state and trait dependent properties. *Cognitive Therapy and Research*, 28, 293–307.

Bentall, R. P., Kinderman, P. and Kaney, S. (1994). The self, attributional processes and abnormal beliefs: Towards a model of persecutory delusions. *Behaviour Research and Therapy*, 32, 331–341.

Bristol, A. S. and Viskontas, I. V. (2006). Dynamic processes within associative memory stores: Piecing together the neural basis of creative cognition. In J. C. Kaufman and J. Baer (Eds.), *Creativity, knowledge and reason*. Cambridge, UK: Cambridge University Press.

Brown, G. W. and Moran, P. M. (1997). Single mothers, poverty and depression. *Psychological Medicine*, 27, 21–33.

Carson, S. H., Peterson, J. B. and Higgins, D. M. (2003). Decreased latent inhibition is associated with increased creative achievement in high-functioning individuals. *Journal of Personality and Social Psychology*, 85, 499–506.

Chadwick, P. D. J. and Birchwood, M. J. (1994). The omnipotence of voices: A cognitive approach to hallucinations. *British Journal of Psychiatry*, 164, 190–201.

Christiansen, B. A., Smith, G. T., Roehling, P. V. and Goldman, M. S. (1989). Using alcohol expectancies to predict adolescent drinking behaviour at one year. *Journal of Consulting and Clinical Psychology*, 57, 93–99.

Clark, D. M., Layard, R., Smithies, R., Richards, D. A., Suckling, R. and Wright, B. (2009). Improving access to psychological therapy: Initial evaluation of two UK demonstration sites. *Behaviour Research and Therapy*, 47, 910–920.

Connors, G. J., Tarbox, A. R. and Faillace, L. A. (1993). Changes in alcohol expectancies and drinking behavior among treated problem drinkers. *Journal of Studies on Alcohol and Drugs*, 53, 676–683.

Dali, S. (1931). *The persistence of memory*. Oil on canvas. New York: Museum of Modern Art.

DeMoss, K., Milich, R. and DeMers, S. (1993). Gender, creativity, depression, and attributional style in adolescents with high academic ability. *Journal of Abnormal Child Psychology*, 21, 455–467.

Department of Health (1998). *Our healthier nation: A contract for health*. London: HMSO.

Dobson, D. J. G. and Dobson, K. S. (1981). Problem-solving strategies in depressed and nondepressed college students. *Cognitive Therapy and Research*, 5, 237–249.

Dudek, S. Z. (1968). Regression and creativity: A comparison of Rorschach records of successful versus unsuccessful painters and writers. *Journal of Nervous and Mental Disease*, 147, 535–546.

Dudley, R. E. J. and Over, D. E. (2003). People with delusions jump to conclusions: A theoretical account of research findings on the reasoning of people with delusions. *Clinical Psychology and Psychotherapy*, 10, 263–274.

Dykes, M. and McGhie, A. (1976). A comparative study of attentional strategies of schizophrenic and highly creative normal adults. *British Journal of Psychiatry*, 128, 50–56.

Enright, S. J. and Beech, A. R. (1993). Further evidence of reduced cognitive inhibition in obsessive-compulsive disorder. *Personality and Individual Differences*, 14, 387–395.

Freeman, D., Garety, P. A. and Phillips, M. L. (2000). An examination of hypervigilance for external threat in individuals with generalised anxiety disorder and individuals with persecutory delusions using visual scan paths. *Quarterly Journal of Experimental Psychology*, 53A, 549–567.

Freud, S. (1933). *The interpretation of dreams*. New York: Macmillan. (Originally published 1910.)

Frith, C. D. (1992). *The cognitive neuropsychology of schizophrenia*. Hove: LEA.

Garety, P. A., Fowler, D., Kuipers, E., Freeman, D., Dunn, G., Bebbington, P. E., Hadley, C. and Jones, S. (1997). The London–East Anglia randomised controlled trial of cognitive behaviour therapy for psychosis II: Predictors of outcome. *British Journal of Psychiatry*, 171, 319–327.

Garety, P. A., Hemsley, D. R. and Wessely, S. (1991). Reasoning in deluded schizophrenic and paranoid patients: Biases in performance on a probabilistic inference task. *Journal of Nervous and Mental Disease*, 179, 194–201.

Garety, P. A., Kuipers, E., Fowler, D., Freeman, D. and Bebbington, P. E. (2001). A cognitive model of the positive symptoms of psychosis. *Psychological Medicine*, 31, 189–195.

Gilbert, P. (2010). *Compassion focused therapy*. New York: Routledge.

Gotlib, I. H. and Asarnow, R. F. (1979). Interpersonal and impersonal problem-solving skills in mildly and moderately depressed university students. *Journal of Consulting and Clinical Psychology*, 47, 86–95.

Gross, T. M., Jarvik, M. E. and Rosenblatt, M. R. (1993). Nicotine abstinence produces content-specific Stroop interference. *Psychopharmacology*,
110, 333–336.

Guilford, J. P. (1967). *The nature of human intelligence*. New York: McGraw-Hill.

Halliday, J. (1950). *Mr. Carlyle my patient: A psychosomatic biography*. New York:
Grune and Stratton.

Hayes, S. C., Strosahl, K. D. and Wilson, K. G. (2004). *Acceptance and commitment therapy: An experiential approach to behaviour change*. New York: Guilford
Press.

Hemsley, D. R. (1993). A simple (or simplistic?) cognitive model for schizophrenia. *Behaviour Research and Therapy*, 31, 633–646.

Hudson, L. (1966). *Contrary imaginations: A psychological study of the young student*. New York: Schocken Books.

Huq, S. F., Garety, P. A. and Hemsley, D. R. (1988). Probabilistic judgements
in deluded and nondeluded subjects. *Quarterly Journal of Experimental Psychology*, 40A, 801–812.

Johnson, B. H., Laberg, J. C., Cox, W. M., Vaks-Dal, A. and Hugdahl, K. (1994).
Psychology of Addictive Behaviors, 8, 111–115.

Jones, B. and McMahon, J. (1996). A comparison of positive and negative alcohol
expectancy and value and their multiplicative composite as predictors of
post-treatment abstinence survivorship. *Addiction*, 91, 89–99.

Joormann, J., Yoon, K. L. and Zetsche, U. (2007). Cognitive inhibition in depression. *Applied and Preventive Psychology*, 12, 128–139.

Karlsson, J. L. (1970). Genetic association of giftedness and creativity with
schizophrenia. *Hereditas*, 66, 177–182.

Kasof, J. (1997). Creativity and breadth of attention. *Creativity Research Journal*,
10, 303–315.

Kaufman, K. C. (2001). The Sylvia Plath effect: Mental illness in eminent creative writers. *Journal of Creative Behaviour*, 35, 37–50.

Keefe, J. A. and Magaro, P. A. (1980). Creativity and schizophrenia: An equivalence of cognitive processing. *Journal of Abnormal Psychology*, 89, 390–398.

Kessler, R. C., McGonagle, K. A., Zhao, S., Nelson, C. B., Hughes, M., Eshle-
man, S., Wittchen, H. U. and Kendler, K. S. (1994). Lifetime and 12-month
prevalence of *DSM-III-R* psychiatric disorders in the United States: Results
from the National Co-morbidity Survey. *Archives of General Psychiatry*, 51,
8–19.

Koestler, A. (1964). *The act of creation*. London: Hutchinson.

Lapp, W. M., Collins, R. L. and Izzo, C. V. (1994). On the enhancement of
creativity by alcohol: Pharmacology or expectation? *American Journal of Psychology*, 107, 173–206.

Lauronen, E., Veijola, J., Isohanni, I., Jones, P. B., Nieminen, P. and Isohanni,
M. (2004). Links between creativity and mental disorder. *Psychiatry*, 67,
81–98.

Lubow, R. E., Ingberg-Sachs, Y., Zalstein-Orda, N. and Gerwitz, J. C. (1992).
Latent inhibition in low and high psychotic-prone normal subjects. *Person-
alilty and Individual Differences*, 11, 563–572.

Ludwig, A. M. (1992). Creative achievement and psychopathology: Comparison
among professions. *American Journal of Psychotherapy*, 46, 330–356.

Ludwig, A. M. (1994). Mental illness and creative activity in female writers. *American Journal of Psychiatry*, 151, 1650–1656.

Ludwig, A. M. (1995). *The price of greatness: Resolving the creativity and madness controversy*. New York: Guilford Press.

Ludwig, A. M. (1998). Method and madness in the arts and sciences. *Creativity Research Journal*, 11, 93–101.

McCrae, R. R. (1987). Creativity, divergent thinking, and openness to experience. *Journal of Personality and Social Psychology*, 52, 1258–1265.

McCusker, C. G. and Gettings, B. (1997). Automaticity of cognitive biases in addictive behaviours: Further evidence with gamblers. *British Journal of Clinical Psychology*, 36, 543–554.

McCusker, C. G., McClements, R. and McCartney, U. (1995). Cognitive bias for addiction-related stimuli in smokers and problem drinkers. *Conference Proceedings of the British Psychological Society*.

Maher, B. A. (1974). Delusional thinking and perceptual disorder. *Journal of Individual Psychology*, 30, 98–113.

Maltzman, I. (1960). On the training of originality. *Psychological Review*, 67, 229–242.

Maltzman, I. (1962). Motivation and the direction of thinking. *Psychological Bulletin*, 59, 457–467.

Mansell, W. and Lam, D. (2003). Conceptualizing a cycle of ascent into mania: A case report. *Behavioural and Cognitive Psychotherapy*, 31, 363–367.

Mansell, W., Morrison, A., Reid, G., Lowens, I. and Tai, S. (2007). The interpretation of, and responses to, changes in internal mood states: An integrative cognitive model of mood swings and bipolar disorders. *Behavioural and Cognitive Psychotherapy*, 35, 515–539.

Mednick, S. A. (1962). The associative basis of the creative process. *Psychological Review*, 69, 220–232.

Mendelsohn, G. (1976). Associative and attentional processes in creative performance. *Journal of Personality*, 44, 341–369.

Moore, M. (1951). *Collected poems*. New York: Macmillan.

Moritz, S. and Woodward, T. S. (2005). Plausibility judgement in schizophrenic patients: Evidence for a liberal acceptance bias. *German Journal of Psychiatry*, 7, 66–74.

Morrison, A. P. (2001). The interpretation of intrusions in psychosis: An integrative cognitive approach to hallucinations and delusions. *Behavioural and Cognitive Psychotherapy*, 29, 257–276.

Murphy, J. M., Monson, R. R., Oliver, D. C., Sobol, A. M., Pratt, L. A. and Leighton, A. H. (1989). Mortality risk and psychiatric disorders: Results of a general physician survey. *Social Psychiatry and Psychiatric Epidemiology*, 24, 134–142.

National Institute for Health and Clinical Excellence (NICE) (2002). *Core interventions in the treatment and management of schizophrenia in primary and secondary care*. London: NICE.

National Institute for Health and Clinical Excellence (NICE) (2005a). *The management of PTSD in adults and children in primary and secondary care*. London: NICE.

National Institute for Health and Clinical Excellence (NICE) (2005b). *Obsessive-compulsive disorder: Core interventions in the treatment of obsessive-compulsive disorder and body dysmorphic disorder*. London: NICE.

National Institute for Health and Clinical Excellence (NICE) (2007). *Anxiety: Management of anxiety (panic disorder, with or without agoraphobia, and generalised anxiety disorder) in adults in primary, secondary and community care*. London: NICE.

National Institute for Health and Clinical Excellence (NICE) (2009). *The treatment and management of depression in adults*. London: NICE.

Orbach, I., Bar-Joseph, H. and Dror, N. (1990). Styles of problem solving in suicidal individuals. *Suicide and Life Threatening Behaviour*, 20, 56–64.

Papworth, M. A. and James, I. A. (2003). Creativity and mood: Towards a model of cognitive mediation. *Journal of Creative Behavior*, 37, 1–16.

Papworth, M. A., Jordan, G., Backhouse, K., Evans, N., Kent-Lemon, N., Morris, J. and Winchester, K. J. G. (2008). Artists' vulnerability to psychopathology: An integrative cognitive perspective. *Journal of Creative Behavior*, 42, 149–163.

Peterson, C. and Seligman, M. E. P. (1984). Causal explanations as a risk factor for depression: Theory and evidence. *Psychological Review*, 91, 347–374.

Pickering, G. (1974). *Creative malady*. New York: Oxford University Press.

Platt, J. J. and Spivack, G. (1972). Problem solving thinking of psychiatric patients. *Journal of Consulting and Clinical Psychology*, 39, 148–151.

Post, F. (1994). Creativity and psychopathology: A study of 291 world-famous men. *British Journal of Psychiatry*, 165, 22–34.

Post, F. (1996). Verbal creativity, depression and alcoholism. *British Journal of Psychiatry*, 168, 545–555.

Regier, D. A., Farmer, M. E., Rae, D. S., Locke, B. Z., Keith, S. J., Judd, L. L. and Godwin, F. K. (1990). Comorbidity of mental disorders with alcohol and other drug abuse: Results from the Epidemiologic Catchment Area (ECA) Study. *Journal of the American Medical Association*, 264, 2511–2518.

Richards, R. and Kinney, D. K. (2000). "Creativity advantage," mood disorders, and what we all can learn. *Bulletin of Psychology and the Arts*, 1, 44–46.

Rothenberg, A. (1979). *The emerging goddess: The creative process in art, science, and other fields*. Chicago University Press.

Santiago, M. J. (2006). Goya, Fortuny, Van Gogh, Portinari: Lead poisoning in painters across three centuries. *Revista Clínica Española*, 206, 30–32.

Sass, L. A. (2001). Schizophrenia, modernism, and the "creative imagination": On creativity and psychopathology. *Creativity Research Journal*, 13, 55–74.

Sayette, M. A. and Hufford, M. R. (1994). Effects of cue-exposure and deprivation on cognitive resources in smokers. *Journal of Abnormal Psychology*, 103, 812–818.

Sayette, M. A., Monti, P. M., Rohsenow, D. J., Bird-Gulliver, S., Colbt, S., Sirota, A., Niaura, R. S. and Abrams, D. B. (1994). The effects of cue-exposure on attention in male alcoholics. *Journal of Studies on Alcohol*, 55, 629–634.

Schildkraut, J. J., Hirshfeld, A. J. and Murphy, J. M. (1994). Mind and mood in modern art, II: Depressive disorders, spirituality, and early deaths in the abstract expressionist artists of the New York school. *American Journal of Psychiatry*, 151, 482–488.

Schou, M. (1979). Artistic productivity and Lithium prophylaxis in manic depressive illness. *British Journal of Psychiatry*, 135, 97–103.

Schuldberg, D. (2001). Six subclinical spectrum traits in normal creativity. *Creativity Research Journal*, 13, 5–16.

Schuldberg, D., French, C., Stone, L. and Herberle, J. (1988). Creativity and schizotypal traits. *Journal of Nervous and Mental Disease*, 176, 648–657.

Segal, Z. V., Williams, J. M. G. and Teesdale, J. D. (2002). *Mindfulness-based cognitive therapy for depression: A new approach to preventing relapse*. New York: Guilford Press.

Sher, K. L., Wood, M. D., Wood, P. K. and Raskin, G. (1996). Alcohol outcome expectancies and alcohol use: A latent variable cross-lagged panel study. *Journal of Abnormal Psychology*, 105, 561–574.

Shure, M. B. and Spivack, G. (1979). Interpersonal cognitive problem solving and primary prevention: Programming for preschool and kindergarten children. *Journal of Clinical Child Psychology*, 8, 89–94.

Simpson, J. and Done, J. (2004). Analogical reasoning in schizophrenic delusions. *European Psychiatry*, 19, 344–348.

Stack, S. (1996). Gender and suicide risk among artists: A multivariate analysis. *Suicide and Life-Threatening Behavior*, 26, 374–379.

Stacy, A. W. (1997). Memory activation and expectancy as prospective predictors of alcohol and marijuana use. *Journal of Abnormal Psychology*, 106, 61–73.

Stacy, A. W., Ames, S. L., Sussman, S. and Dent, C. (1996). Implicit cognition in adolescent drug use. *Psychology of Addictive Behaviors*, 10, 190–203.

Stacy, A. W., Newcomb, M. D. and Bentler, P. M. (1991). Cognitive motivation and problem drug use: A 9-year longitudinal study. *Journal of Abnormal Psychology*, 100, 502–515.

Strakowski, S. M., Fleck, D. E., DelBello, M. P., Alder, C. M., Shear, P. K., McElroy, S. L., Keck, P. E., Moss, Q., Cerullo, M. A., Kotwal, R. and Arndt, S. (2009). Characterizing impulsivity in mania. *Bipolar Disorder*, 11, 41–51.

Stunk, D. R. and Adler, A. D. (2009). Cognitive biases in three prediction tasks: A test of the cognitive model of depression. *Behaviour Research and Therapy*, 47, 34–40.

Vardy, M. M. and Kay, S. R. (1983). LSD psychosis or LSD-induced schizophrenia? A multimethod inquiry. *Archives of General Psychiatry*, 40, 877–883.

Waddell, C. (1998). Creativity and mental illness: Is there a link? *Canadian Journal of Psychiatry*, 43, 166–172.

Walker, A. M., Koestner, R. and Hum, A. (1995). Personality correlates of depressive style in autobiographies of creative achievers. *Journal of Creative Behavior*, 29, 75–94.

Wallach, M. A. (1970). *Creativity*. In P. H. Mussen (Ed.), *Carmichael's manual of child psychology* (Vol. 1) (3rd edn.). New York: Wiley.

Wallach, M. A. (1971). *The intelligence/creativity distinction*. New York: General Learning Press.

Ward, T. B. (2007). Creative cognition as a window on creativity. *Methods*, 42, 28–37.

Weingardt, K. R., Stacy, A. W. and Leigh, B. C. (1996). Automatic activation of alcohol concepts in response to positive outcomes of alcohol use. *Alcoholism – Clinical and Experimental Research*, 20, 25–30.

Weinstein, S. and Graves, R. E. (2001). Creativity, schizotypy, and laterality. *Cognitive Neuropsychiatry*, 6, 131–146.

Williams, J. M. G. (1996). *Frontiers of cognitive therapy*. London: Guilford Press.

Zuroff, D. C., Blatt, S. J., Sanislow, C. A., III, Bondi, C. M. and Pilkonis, P. A. (1999). Vulnerability to depression: Re-examining state dependence and relative stability. *Journal of Abnormal Psychology*, 108, 76–89.

Part III

Creativity and the spectrum of mental illness

9   Creativity and the spectrum of affective and schizophrenic psychoses

Neus Barrantes-Vidal

The possible connection between madness and creativity is a highly controversial issue. This is barely surprising, because it touches upon fundamental, human nature, issues that resonate beyond the scientific arena. In a sense, the subject borders on themes that can be regarded as distributive justice (Does one need to "pay a price" for having superior gifts?), "poetic" justice (Are those cursed with mental suffering at least compensated with an easier access to the muse?), and ethics (If we could eradicate the genetics of psychosis, would we actually be removing the genetic reservoir of unique human qualities such as creativity?).

Some would consider that the question itself is fundamentally wrong for various reasons. Humanistic and positive psychology schools view it as an attempt to pathologize what is essentially a positive feature that arises in healthy and self-actualized individuals (e.g., Fromm, 1980). Others claim that the whole theme survives as a cultural myth derived from inaccurate historical reinterpretations of the association between melancholia and creativity established by Greek philosophers (e.g., Schlesinger, 2009). Finally, many have criticized the lack of "strong" methods to prove the connection, which has relied on anecdotal descriptions of mad geniuses for a long time. All of these criticisms contain grains of truth and not surprisingly are brought up when the issue is presented in terms of madness being a necessary condition for creativity or creativity leading to madness. However, as will be elaborated, the recognition of *multiple* ingredients in both creativity and madness and the addition of more sound methods challenge the simple dismissal of this topic.

Another issue is whether considering the link between creativity and madness is scientifically important or useful at all. Most would acknowledge that supporting such a connection can help to fight the stigma associated with such terribly misunderstood disorders. Indeed, this connection is positively regarded by many patients, as indicated by recent surveys reporting that, despite the strong association of bipolar disorder with social stigma and negative personal, health, and professional consequences, a large percentage of sufferers claim that the disorder provides positive associated facets such as increased creativity, sensitivity, self-awareness, and a heightened appreciation of life (Galvez et al., 2011; Parker et al., 2012). Although this is relevant enough by itself, the importance of the issue expands far beyond the desirable effects on sufferers' self-esteem and public acceptance of mental disorders. Gaining understanding of this possible connection forces us to reflect upon preconceived notions regarding the very nature of mental disorders, their relationship with normal individual variation, and models of the etiology of psychopathology.

Many authors have previously reviewed the subject from different perspectives (e.g., Barrantes-Vidal, 2004; Brod, 1997; Kaufman, 2009; Kottler, 2005; Nettle, 2001; Sawyer, 2006; Silvia and Kaufman, 2010; Simonton, 2010; Weisberg, 2006), interpreting the evidence as indicative of a strong, mild, or non-existent connection between creativity and mental disorders. The present chapter will focus specifically on the implications of our conceptualization of mental disorders for making progress in this complex area of research and will offer a selected review on studies exploring the connection with the variety of psychoses.

Conceptual issues

Temperament, personality, and mental disorder

The possible connection between creativity and mental disorder raises the paradox of assembling symptoms causing impairment with the superior mental processes and effective production necessary for creativity. This perplexing association, which has generated much of the controversy on the matter, can be satisfactorily resolved if we consider mental disorders as dimensional phenomena (Claridge and Barrantes-Vidal, 2013); that is, that they are continuously connected with "normality" or healthy functioning, as suggested by the wide margins of intermediate shades that surround the dichotomous and often artificial border between illness and health (Eysenck and Eysenck, 1976).

Psychotic disorders, characterized in their extreme by delusions, hallucinations, and loss of touch with reality, have often been linked to creativity. The *fully dimensional* view of psychoses argues that these disorders are extreme or pathological variants of otherwise *normal* personality dispositions and, as such, they can be associated with both dysfunctional and adaptive traits (Claridge, 1997). The difference between clinical psychosis and its temperamental basis, called by Eysenck "psychoticism" (in parallel to the construct of "neuroticism"), is argued to be quantitative and not qualitative, although its expression appears discontinuous in clinical populations and seems to produce qualitative changes, an observation that is considered by some to prove that psychoticism defines a discrete category or taxon and thus used to discard any connection with superior processes such as creative thinking (Claridge, 2009).

This fully dimensional view is widely accepted in pathologies such as anxiety disorders, which are readily understood as the extreme manifestations of a personality dimension (anxiety or harm avoidance) present in all people to differing degrees. Furthermore, within normal limits, anxiety has a *necessary* and *adaptive* function, such as being a vigilance mechanism that signals potential dangers and activates for a fight or flight response. However, it has been conceptually much harder for many researchers to accept that there is a personality dimension, psychoticism, that, analogous to anxiety, may have advantageous features (Claridge, 1997).

The schizophrenia and bipolar spectrums

The medical framework in which psychiatry was born imprinted the assumption that mental disorders are distinct disease entities in nature. Not surprisingly, thus, the main question in psychiatric research has been *which* disorder has a relationship to creativity, non-affective (schizophrenia) or affective psychosis (bipolar disorder) – even though the very distinction between the two families of disorders is controversial and officially bipolar disorder is outside the psychosis realm and listed as an affective disorder.

The concept of schizophrenia and bipolar *spectrums* implies that these disorders encompass a wide range of phenomenological expressions (varying in terms of severity, chronicity, and impairment) that reflect variation in levels of environmental and genetic etiological load. The fields of schizophrenia and bipolar disorders have paid increasing attention to the "soft ends" of the spectrum, which consist of lesser clinical forms (e.g., bipolar II and cyclothymia), personality disorders (mostly schizotypal), and personality traits such as schizotypy and the affective temperaments. The latter are considered to be non-clinical behavioral expressions of the genetic vulnerability towards, respectively, schizophrenia and bipolar disorders (Akiskal and Akiskal, 2007; Barrantes-Vidal *et al.*, 2002; Kwapil and Barrantes-Vidal, 2012). Schizotypy and the affective temperaments present the same heterogeneity as clinical phenotypes, but at trait level, and thus are multidimensional constructs. Both would be subsumed under the broad concept of psychoticism.

Claridge (1997) noted that the spectrum model, derived from psychiatry and not the individual differences tradition, differs conceptually from the fully dimensional model referred to earlier in ways relevant for the connection with creativity. He described the spectrum notion as *"quasi"* dimensional, because dimensionality refers to quantitative variation in *severity* within the illness domain – that is, it is qualitatively distinct from *normal* individual variation and thus not easily reconcilable with advantageous features such as creativity. The issue of spectrum versus fully dimensional models influences not only what phenotypes are investigated but also what theories and research paradigms are considered to account for a possible link between creativity and mental illness.

Theories about the connection between creativity and psychosis

The acceptance of the fully dimensional view of psychosis makes it possible to understand the connection between creativity and mental disorder. Logically, it is not the extreme variants of psychoticism (or schizotypy and affective temperaments), the psychotic *states*, that mediate the connection with creativity, but it is possible that the personality *traits* that underlie psychosis share some genetic, biological, emotional, motivational, and cognitive features with creativity. Additionally, it allows us to understand that creativity will not be related to a *single* psychological profile because, as referred to earlier, dimensionality also operates within the pathological realm as exemplified by the schizophrenia and bipolar spectrums (Claridge, 1998).

The notion of a common factor underlying the connection between creativity and psychopathology assumes that this common factor is causative, even if it is not a sufficient condition, and has overcome two alternative models (Richards, 2000–2001). One model claims that psychopathology causes creativity, either directly or indirectly. A direct relation would be, for example, that strange thoughts and bizarre perceptual processes may be vital for the creative process. For instance, so-called overinclusive thinking (Cameron, 1938), defined by the loss of the capacity to limit associative processes, is thought to contribute to creative insights when it does not reach severe forms that lead to complete incoherence. An indirect relation would be that pathology leads to cathartic writing, which, in turn, enhances the creative quality of a given work. The other model poses that creativity causes psychopathology. A direct relation would be, especially in the arts, that creativity implies facing high levels of psychic tension, leading to psychological imbalance. Rothenberg (1990) has argued that the creative thought processes employed by eminent creators and geniuses may stress mental capacities to their limits and inflict such emotional and mental strain that they result in the experience of psychosis. Various eminent writers (e.g., Virginia Woolf, Sylvia Plath) have recorded how overwhelming creative activity is, and explicitly connected it to the triggering of psychotic episodes; at the same time, many have also viewed creative endeavor as a helpful media to keep madness "at bay." Finally, an indirect relation would be that the conflicts created by creativity might result in maladaptive coping strategies such as drug abuse. Naturally, these possibilities are not mutually exclusive and most likely contribute in different degrees to the association between specific types of creativity and certain psychopathological traits.

Review of empirical studies

The empirical study of the creativity–mental disorder link suffers from methodological flaws as many authors have thoroughly described (e.g., Schlesinger, 2009; this volume). Many studies are limited by small sample sizes (although some recent reports draw on population-whole designs), there are inconsistencies in diagnostic methods, and wide disparities in creativity definitions, levels, and measurements, with few studies assessing various aspects of creativity at once. However, as now described, several approaches have been developed that complement each other and help to compensate for the limitations inherent to each specific method.

Studies on psychopathology in eminent creative people

The empirical examination of a link between creativity and mental disorder was first studied using the psychobiographical method more than one century ago. This approach consists of the systematic analysis of eminent creative individuals' biographies, autobiographies, and available clinical records in order to study the presence of psychopathology. In historiometric research (reviewed by Simonton in this volume), the historical data drawn from biographical material are subjected to objective and quantitative analyses. Obviously, these methods present numerous limitations, such as a clear selection bias imposed by the choice of the creators studied, the fact that fame is not necessarily synonymous with being highly creative and depends heavily on contextual factors such as culture (e.g., barely any women are included in such studies!), the retrospective and thus partial nature of the data, or the impossibility of contrasting the author's diagnostic judgment. However, this approach constitutes an important source of information that inspires theories for further data-driven research. Another avenue is the study of psychopathology in contemporary eminent creators, in which case standardized diagnostic measures and criteria can be applied.

The study of psychopathology in eminent creative individuals started with Lombroso (1895), who studied biographies of eminent creators and concluded that most suffered from what nowadays would be labeled as affective and schizophrenic psychosis, psychopathy, and alcoholism. The review by Becker (1978, this volume) of the psychobiographic studies published before 1950 suggested that the vast majority validated the anecdotal observation of an excess of psychopathology in eminently creative people, with two main exceptions: the work by Ellis (1904) and Bowerman (1947). Of note, Claridge *et al.* (1998/1990) pointed out that, even though both Ellis and Bowerman confirmed their *a priori* hypothesis that there was not an excess of pathology in geniuses, they acknowledged the presence of characteristic temperamental traits such as hypersensitivity, irritability, and a tendency towards melancholy and affective instability; that is, traits currently considered part of the "affective temperaments." Andreasen and Canter (1974) also noted that the selection of subjects in these studies was based upon their appearance in the *Dictionary of national biography*, which ensures public notability but not necessarily truly eminent creativity. Lange-Eichbaum (1932) first focused on studying the temporal relation between creativity and psychosis, reporting that creative work is not performed during active psychotic periods but in periods of remission, and that often psychosis follows intensely creative phases.

Andreasen (1987) compared 30 eminent American writers attending the prestigious Iowa writing workshop with 30 matched control subjects. There was an overall higher rate of affective disorders in the writers, especially bipolar forms, as well as alcoholism. Consistent with the notion of an association due to soft forms of the bipolar spectrum, bipolar II disorder (characterized by alternating episodes of hypomania and depression) was more common than the more severe bipolar I disorder (characterized by alternating episodes of mania and depression). Jamison (1989) also found a significantly higher percentage of psychopathology, especially affective disorders, in 47 contemporary British artists and writers compared with population estimates. More than one-third had received psychiatric treatment because of affective disorders. Of note, only poets had required treatment for hypomanic or manic episodes, whereas artists and the other type of writers did so for depressive phases. She also found a strikingly high rate of affective disorders, suicides, and institutionalization in the analysis of the most important British and Irish poets of the eighteenth century (Jamison, 1993). Claridge *et al.* (1998/1990) examined the biographical and medical records of ten authors (spanning from the Middle Ages to the present day, such as Margery Kempe or Sylvia Plath) who claimed to have suffered from some form of psychotic disorder.

Claridge (1998) applied several sets of operationalized diagnostic criteria to address the issue discussed earlier about the association between creativity and specific diagnoses. The results suggested that most would be diagnosable as schizophrenic or schizoaffective, with some variation depending on the diagnostic criteria used (because they vary considerably in their definition of the boundaries of schizophrenia and affective psychosis), and it was concluded that the "schizophrenic" components of psychosis were especially common in such eminent writers, with often accompanying affective features.

Some studies have examined possible differences in psychopathology based upon different *domains* of creative endeavor. Most of the literature suggests a stronger association between psychopathology and artistic creativity, especially creative writing, with a weaker or less consistent association with scientific areas. However, this remains highly debatable, because there is a scarcity of studies that have investigated multiple domains of creativity at once and most have focused specifically on writers.

Juda (1949) studied a sample of 19,000 subjects of whom 294 were highly gifted scientists and artists. It was concluded that geniuses presented a much higher incidence of psychosis and neurosis than the average population, and that schizophrenia occurred exclusively in the artists, whereas manic-depressive insanity occurred only in the scientists, in a frequency ten times the incidence of the average population.

Post (1994) selected 291 eminent and recognized creative men (visual artists, philosophers, scientists, politicians, composers, novelists, and playwrights) and found that 54 percent presented with personality disorder traits and 69 percent with at least one mental disorder. Scientists were the least affected group, a result consistent with findings from Simonton (2004). A significant proportion of novelists and playwrights had a florid history of familial psychopathology, problematic family environments during childhood, depressive episodes, drug abuse, and marital problems. Artists and intellectuals had significant psychosexual difficulties and a greater presence of alcoholism. In a replication study, Post (1996) reported that schizophrenia was less prevalent in this sample than in the general population, whereas affective disorders and alcoholism were strikingly high among writers. Poets had especially high rates of bipolar disorder.

Ludwig's (1995) study of 1,005 biographies written between 1960 and 1990 indicated a positive correlation between the presence of severe psychopathology and the magnitude of creative achievements. Overall, the study portrayed a higher incidence of mental disorders in artistic than in non-artistic professions (e.g., politics, business). Again, poets had the highest rate of mental disorders (87%), including more suicide and psychosis, whereas scientists presented with fewer problems. In another study, Ludwig (1994) again reported an increased rate of suicidal behavior in poets (18% versus 1% in the general population). He studied 59 female writers and 59 female control subjects matched on education and socioeconomic level (although not on intelligence) and found higher rates of affective, anxiety, substance use, and eating disorders.

The striking overrepresentation of psychopathology in poets has been found in other studies. In the historiometric study of 1,629 writers (including poets, novelists, playwrights, and non-fiction authors) Kaufman (2001) paid attention to gender differences and reported that *female* poets were more likely to suffer from mental disorder (as indexed by depression, suicide attempts, hospitalizations) than other types of writers (both male and female). In a second study with 520 eminent women (poets, fiction and non-fiction writers, visual artists, politicians, and actresses), poets were again found to present an excess of mental disorders. Of note, Kaufman (2005) provided evidence for the universality of such excess in poets by examining 826 Eastern European writers (fiction, non-fiction, poets, playwrights) spanning from the fourth century to the current day and replicating the increased rate of disorder in poets compared with other types of writers. In view of such a consistent pattern, Kaufman and Baer (2002) and Kaufman (2005) suggested that individuals with highly introspective, emotional profiles, and who are possibly more prone to negative moods, rumination, and depression, might feel more attracted to poetry than other forms of writing. Also, they suggested that the process of constructing a narrative is instrumental to benefiting from the possible therapeutic effects of writing (Kaufman and Sexton, 2006). Many authors have pointed out that the act of writing in verbally talented individuals can be contemplated as a way of objectifying negative emotions, organizing their experience within a narrative structure, and thus enabling the writer to gain control over despair in a disordered milieu (e.g., Ludwig, 1994; Storr, 2000–2001).

The study of other artistic areas is more limited. Schildkraut *et al.* (1994) analyzed 15 Abstract Expressionist painters from the New York School (e.g., Pollock, Rothko), a group that used the technique of psychic automatism (based on free association) in order to reveal unconscious material. Affective disorders were ten times more prevalent, and suicidal behavior was three times greater, than in the general population. In a study of 137 well-known visual artists, Ludwig (1998) reported that those with a more emotive style presented higher rates of depression and other mental disorders than those artists with more formal styles. As for musicians, Wills (2003) applied *DSM-IV* (APA, 1994) diagnoses to biographical material of 40 eminent American modern jazz musicians and found an excess of psychopathology comparable to that of other creative groups.

Family studies

The notion that both creativity and mental disorder have heritable components and might be cosegregated – that is, inherited together and thus expressed in the same individual – has prompted the investigation of the family trees of creative individuals.

In her study of eminent writers, Andreasen (1987) found that writers' first-degree relatives exceeded the relatives of the control group in their rate of affective disorders and also had more creative professions. Likewise, Jamison (1993) reported an excess of affective pathology in the family trees of the geniuses she studied (e.g., Schumann, Woolf, van Gogh, Hemingway, James). Ludwig (1994) also established the presence of high levels of psychopathology and creativity in the family members of the female writers. Of note, both personal and maternal psychopathology were significant predictors of creative performance. Furthermore, the exposure to sexual or physical abuse during childhood was also a significant predictor of creativity, suggesting a complex interaction between hereditary and environmental factors.

Studies on creativity in the schizophrenia and bipolar spectrums

Population studies   Recent work has complemented the traditional study of clinical samples and their relatives with population cohorts, in which the association between hospital diagnostic records and creativity indicators based on professional occupations avoids selection bias. However, it is important to note that these studies necessarily fail to include mild spectrum cases (which either do not require treatment or are attended to in outpatient facilities), which are hypothesized to be more likely to manifest the association.

Kyaga *et al.* (2011) conducted a nested case-control study with 300,000 individuals who had received in-patient treatment for schizophrenia, bipolar disorder, or depressive disorders, and their relatives, based on Swedish registries. Bipolar disorder patients, and even more so their siblings (as well as those of schizophrenia patients), were overrepresented in creative professions (defined as scientific or artistic occupations), and this was not accounted for by IQ (data only available for males). Schizophrenia patients were more likely to hold artistic occupations. Relatives of people with schizophrenia were overrepresented in the artistic occupations, whereas relatives of bipolar patients were overrepresented in scientific occupations. Unipolar depression patients and their siblings did not differ from controls. Among relatives, the likelihood of creative occupations was highest among first-degree relatives, and gradually decreased with increasing familial distance. Recently, Kyaga *et al.* (2013) studied a wider range of diagnoses and used a larger sample (n = 1,173,763). It was found that individuals with creative professions did not show greater levels of psychopathology than controls, except for being a literary author, which was specifically associated with higher levels of schizophrenia, bipolar disorder, unipolar depression, anxiety disorders, substance abuse, and suicide. Again, first-degree relatives of patients with schizophrenia, bipolar disorder, or anorexia nervosa, and siblings of patients with autism, had more creative professions. Finally, individuals with bipolar disorder were also disproportionately concentrated in the most creative occupations in the interview data of the epidemiological catchment area study (a US representative sample) (Tremblay *et al.*, 2010).

MacCabe *et al.* (2010) conducted a prospective whole-population cohort study of all individuals on the Swedish national school register (n = 713,876). Those with excellent school performance (particularly in humanities) had a nearly fourfold increased risk of hospital admission for bipolar disorder compared with those with average grades (the association seemed to be confined to males, although the formal test for interaction between school performance and gender was not statistically significant). In addition, those with the lowest grades had a moderately increased rate for bipolar disorder. These associations were not attributable to socioeconomic or parental education differences. MacCabe *et al.* suggest that, because IQ is only one of the factors having an impact on success in examinations, the findings may reflect that risk for bipolar disorder is driven by factors related to creativity such as intense emotion and motivation, enhanced access to sustained attention, memory, and vocabulary, and possibly social skills. On the contrary, MacCabe *et al.* (2008) reported that only low grades were associated with hospital admission for schizophrenia and schizoaffective disorder in the same sample.

Family and adoption studies   Karlsson (1970) carried out a retrospective family study in which the professional status of all first-degree relatives of psychiatric patients admitted to hospital (i.e., most likely with severe disorders like psychosis) in Iceland from 1851 to 1940 were recorded. He found that relatives had a creative profession more often than the general population, with twice as many writers than expected. Richards *et al.* (1988) found that non-affected first-degree relatives of bipolar patients obtained the highest scores on an index of lifetime everyday creativity when compared with control participants, and bipolar I and cyclothymic patients. The difference was not explained by the effects of education or intelligence. Heston (1966) showed that half of the children of schizophrenic mothers who were separated early from their biological mother and reared in adoptive families achieved an excellent adaptation, an exceptional talent on different creative fields, and, as expected, a higher risk of developing schizophrenia. Similarly, Kinney *et al.* (2000–2001) found that the adoptees with a genetic liability for schizophrenia who did not manifest the disorder were rated as more creative by blind independent researchers than demographically matched control adoptees with no family history of psychiatric hospitalization. Moreover, adoptees who showed signs of schizotypic personality were rated as even more creative.

Clinical studies   Most research has focused on either bipolar or schizophrenia spectrum populations, with fewer studies studying both of them simultaneously.

As referred to earlier, Richards *et al.* (1988) reported higher interview ratings of lifetime creativity in unaffected relatives of bipolar patients. Interestingly, they also found that cyclothymic patients obtained higher scores than bipolar I patients (who did not differ from controls). Also, Akiskal and Akiskal (1988) found that artistic occupations were present in 8 percent of those diagnosed with *soft* bipolar diagnoses compared with less than 1 percent in those receiving diagnoses of bipolar I, unipolar depression, or schizophrenia disorders. Studies focusing on severely ill populations have reported negative findings. Ghadirian *et al.* (2001) did not find differences in creative abilities comparing psychiatric inpatients, 20 with bipolar disorder and 24 with other disorders, although level of clinical severity was inversely associated with creativity scores. Eisenman (1990) also found that psychotic patients were less creative than a control group.

One line of inquiry has been to investigate possible similarities in terms of affective temperaments between bipolar spectrum patients and creative individuals. Akiskal *et al.* (2005) reported that, among psychiatric outpatients, artists and architects presented higher levels of cyclothymic temperament than physicians, lawyers, managers and executives, industrialists, and journalists. Nowakowska *et al.* (2005) reported a significant overlap between euthymic (i.e., in a normal mood) bipolar patients and graduate students in creative disciplines, characterized by higher cyclothymic temperament, openness, neuroticism, novelty seeking, and lower conscientiousness compared with healthy controls.

Most literature examining bipolar spectrum patients have used as a creativity measure the Barron–Welsh Art Scale (BWAS; Barron, 1963), where individuals express levels of like and dislike for different figures. Preference for asymmetrical and complex over symmetrical and simple figures is used as a proxy for creativity; BWAS scores have been found to be higher in visual artists and creative individuals in other disciplines (Barron, 1972) and associated with faculty and peer ratings of creativity (Gough *et al.*, 1996). Simeonova *et al.* (2005) reported increased creativity in patients with bipolar disorder and their offspring compared with healthy controls (adults and children). Also, Strong *et al.* (2007) found that a factor composed of neuroticism, cyclothymia, and dysthymia was related to dislike of simple figures, probably due to increased access to a wider range and greater changeability of affective experience, whereas an openness factor related to both creative perception and self-rated creative personality. However, none of the temperament–personality factors related to the Torrance Tests of Creative Thinking (Torrance, 1974). Also, Santosa *et al.* (2007) found that creative students and euthymic bipolar, but not unipolar, patients shared a dislike of simple figures compared with controls. Again, groups did not differ on divergent thinking. On the contrary, Rybakowski and Klonowska (2011) found that 40 bipolar patients in remission outperformed controls on a verbal "inventiveness" scale, but not on a modified version of the BWAS. Finally, Srivastava *et al.* (2010) replicated the link between the "affective" factor (cyclothymic temperament) and the BWAS dislike scores and also reported a differential association between a "cognitive" factor, composed of self-reported intuition and openness, and the BWAS preference for complex figures (shown to be less related to negative emotionality than dislike of simple figures) and self-rated components of creativity.

Soeiro-de-Souza *et al.* (2011) investigated the impact of symptoms and executive functioning on the BWAS and found that patients in manic and mixed states had higher creativity scores than those in depressed episodes (independent of intelligence). Better executive functioning was associated with higher creativity only in manic patients, even if levels of executive functioning were worse for these patients. The authors interpreted that these findings point out that, in addition to temperament traits, the association between creativity and bipolarity is also state dependent, possibly related to levels of dopaminergic functioning known to be associated with mania, creativity, and executive functioning.

Research examining clinical samples from the schizophrenia spectrum initially focused on measures of creative cognition, given the similarity between schizophrenic thought disorder and divergent thinking. The hypothesis leading this research was that there is a continuum ranging from normality through creative thinking, e.g., divergent thinking (Guilford, 1950), to pathological overinclusive thinking (Cameron, 1938) and thought disorder (Hasenfus and Magaro, 1976) (but see Rothenberg, 1990, for a criticism on the analogy between creative and psychotic thinking).

Keefe and Magaro (1980) compared divergent thinking among small samples of paranoid schizophrenics, non-paranoid schizophrenics, non-psychotic psychiatric patients, and controls. Non-paranoid schizophrenic patients obtained higher divergent thinking scores than the remaining groups. Rubenstein (2008) compared divergent thinking scores among inpatients with schizophrenia, depression, anxiety, and a mix of personality disorders. As expected, chronic schizophrenia inpatients showed the poorest level of conceptual fluency, and no differences emerged on originality levels. As the author discussed, negative symptoms of schizophrenia (which involve a diminution of thought and affect and are highly prevalent among hospitalized patients) are most likely negatively related to verbal fluency.

Rodrigue and Perkins (2012) reported that 22 outpatient schizophrenia patients had lower divergent thinking scores than university students with either normal or elevated schizotypal personality traits according to the Millon Personality Inventory. However, the "schizotypal group" was actually restricted to hypernormals with no Axis I deviance, which suggests that the group did not actually represent an intermediate level of the schizophrenia spectrum to test the hypothesized advantage of this mild condition compared with full-blown schizophrenia and controls on creative thinking. Furthermore, patients differed greatly on education and age. Of note, Millon's mania scale was related with creative scores among controls. Similarly, and not surprisingly, schizophrenia inpatients in remission obtained lower creativity scores than matched controls, a finding partially explained by deficits in executive functions (Jaracz et al., 2012). Finally, Abraham et al. (2007) compared 28 patients with chronic schizophrenia and 18 controls and showed that patients' impairment on most executive functions accounted for deficits on specific facets of creative cognition, such as fluency and relevance (which require functional goal-directed thinking), although not for originality. The authors suggested that executive and creative function is probably well represented as an inverted U, where too much executive dysfunction impairs creative cognition (also see Abraham, this volume). Thus, individuals with schizotypic traits in non-clinical populations should be able to make better use of a soft level of lower executive inhibitory control and loose associational thinking.

*Psychometric studies in non-eminent creators and
non-selected populations*

This approach consists of investigating the presence of psychotic traits in non-eminent creators or applying both personality/symptom and creativity questionnaires to non-selected populations (usually college students). A relevant aspect of the studies with non-selected populations is that, despite a narrower range of variability in psychopathology and creativity, they overcome the possible bias introduced by the role expectation of manifesting mental suffering when belonging to a creative profession (Becker, 2000–2001).

Barron (1969) described how creative individuals from a wide range of professions tended to combine elevated levels of self-reported psychological deviance on various Minnesota Multiphasic Personality Inventory (MMPI) dimensions with high scores on the positive dimension of "ego strength," which usually tends to be inversely related with psychopathology.

Pretti and Vellante (2007) found that artists reported more positive psychotic-like experiences compared with controls, which was not explained by their elevated use of substances and general distress. Nelson and Rawlings (2010) also reported elevations on positive schizotypy (other dimensions were not measured) in visual artists compared with norm data, as well as elevated openness to experience, neuroticism, and depressive but not bipolar propensity. Of note, positive schizotypy was the strongest predictor of a range of subjective experiences pertaining to creativity that overlap considerably with the central features of the "flow" type of experience, such as deep absorption, distinct shift in phenomenological experience, focus on present experience, and sense of pleasure mixed with some anxiety, suggesting a strong overlap of schizotypal and creative experience. Folley and Park (2005) also found that individuals with high global schizotypy (n = 17) had enhanced divergent thinking compared with 17 outpatients with schizophrenia and 17 controls.

Nettle (2006) compared schizotypy profiles among poets, artists, mathematicians, the general population, and psychiatric patients, and found that poets and artists had higher levels of unusual experiences (positive schizotypy) than controls, but similar levels to patients with schizophrenia. Artistic creators and psychiatric patients shared a tendency to produce unusual ideas and experiences, but creative groups were distinguished by the absence of anhedonia (inability to feel pleasure) and avolition (low scores on negative schizotypy). On the other hand, mathematicians presented the opposite pattern, with very low levels of positive schizotypy and cognitive disorganization but high levels of negative schizotypy. Nettle hypothesized the existence of a cluster of arts, unusual experiences, and affective and psychotic disorders characterized by schizotypal thought – that is, by metaphorical leaps from domain to domain, remote associations, and broad attentional set. He posited that this cluster would, in many aspects, represent the opposite tail of the features described by Baron-Cohen *et al.* (2003) as characteristic of high-functioning autism spectrum disorders: a systematizing cognitive style, defined by a drive for order and regularity, convergent thinking, and literality, which are likely found in scientists, mathematicians, and engineers. These findings were supported by Rawlings and Locarnini (2008), who found that creativity was linked to schizotypy and hypomania among artists, but this association did not emerge among scientists, for whom a mild connection was found between creativity and autistic traits.

A similar pattern has been found in college students. Weinstein and Graves (2002) found that positive but not negative schizotypy correlated with divergent thinking tasks. Claridge and McDonald (2009) reported that both negative schizotypy and autistic traits were related to convergent, but not divergent, thinking, although the connection between positive schizotypy and divergent thinking was not found, even if did emerge for impulsive non-conformity. Tsakanikos and Claridge (2005) found that decreased verbal fluency was associated with negative schizotypy, whereas increased verbal fluency was associated with positive schizotypy, which seemed to support the claim that schizophrenic-like unusual experiences, such as hallucinations, may be the product of a higher automatic spreading activation among stored lexical units. Burch *et al.* (2006) reported that visual art students scored higher on positive schizotypy and impulsive non-conformity, as well as openness and divergent thinking, compared with a non-artist group, but not on negative schizotypy.

Schuldberg *et al.* (1988) found a positive relationship among several measures of positive schizotypy and creativity tests, although a significant relationship between divergent thinking and positive schizotypy was not found. When scales of hypomanic and impulsive personality traits were added in a later study, results pointed to a stronger link between creativity and the affective/motivational sphere than with the schizotypy (Schuldberg, 1990). O'Reilly *et al.* (2001) also failed to find an association between schizotypy and divergent thinking, although schizotypy was related to engagement in creative pursuits. Miller and Tal (2007) also reported that openness and intelligence, but not schizotypy, predicted creativity in students. As the authors discuss, findings on a lack of a direct association between schizotypy and creativity may indicate that the association is due to openness to experience, which has been repeatedly associated with creativity (and with positive schizotypy), although schizotypy does not seem to be analogous to extreme openness. This issue remains controversial and, for the moment, findings are mixed.

A number of studies suggest that diminished inhibition and some asociality, as tapped by psychoticism and impulsive non-conformity scales, may facilitate the production of original responses in divergent thinking tasks. It has been suggested that impulsive or non-conformist respondents are more likely to venture responses that other people would inhibit or regard as irrelevant, which would increase the likelihood of originality of responses. Claridge and Blakey (2009) found that positive schizotypy was related to self-perceived use of creative styles but unrelated to divergent thinking, and that affective temperaments, especially hyperthymic, were related to both divergent thinking and self-perceived creativity styles in students. Also, impulsive non-conformity was related to divergent thinking, which is consistent with Schuldberg et al.'s (1988) findings indicating that those students scoring highest on impulsive non-conformity among the group of high positive schizotypy were the most creative. Among bipolar patients, Rybakowski and Klonowska (2011) reported that the schizotypy dimensions of positive, cognitive disorganization and impulsive non-conformity, but not negative schizotypy, were related to creativity measures. Impulsive non-conformity showed the strongest correlations with creativity indices, including verbal inventiveness, whereas unusual experiences were only associated with the aesthetic preference measure. Batey and Furnham (2008) found that positive schizotypy and impulsive non-conformity were related to creativity, but Batey and Furnham (2009) only found impulsive non-conformity, and not positive schizotypy, to be associated with creativity (negative schizotypy was associated with impaired creativity performance). Schuldberg (2005) found that psychoticism was associated with attitudes and activities related to creativity.

Studies on affective traits are more recent in the literature than work with schizotypy and psychoticism. Furnham et al. (2008) reported that higher scores on the hypomanic personality scale were associated with more engagement in creative daily activities, divergent thinking, fluency, and self-rated creativity in students, and that high hypomanic personality scores were the best predictor when compared with normal personality dimensions. Similarly, Vellante et al. (2011) found that undergraduates in creative fields scored higher on cyclothymic, hyperthymic, and irritable affective temperaments, but not on current psychological distress, and also reported greater involvement in creative activities than those in non-creative disciplines.

Some studies have investigated the association of schizotypy with differential aspects of creative cognition. Karimi et al. (2007) reported that high scorers on a global measure of schizotypy presented better performance in cognitive creation involved in divergent thinking as well as better performance in insight problem solving, which requires changing activated schemas and acquiring new perspectives, but not on problems asking for goal-related thinking. Comparing high versus low scorers on psychoticism, Abraham *et al.* (2005) found that high scorers performed better on measures tapping the originality/novelty dimension, but not on those tapping the practicality/usefulness dimension, lending support to the notion that the association between psychoticism and creativity is based on associative thinking and broader but weak top-down activation patterns rather than on goal-directed thinking. Abraham and Windmann (2008) compared extreme scorers on a global schizotypy measure and found that the high schizotypy group performed better than the low schizotypy group selectively on overcoming the constraining influences of examples when trying to generate original responses, but not on other creative cognition aspects, such as conceptual expansion or creative imagery. Also comparing individuals with high versus low global schizotypy, Jones *et al.* (2011) found that the high schizotypy group performed better on divergent thinking whereas the low schizotypy group performed better on convergent problem-solving tasks. Fink *et al.* (2012) reported that, compared with college students, both actors and substance abuse patients had higher originality in creative idea generation, higher psychoticism scores, and decreased latent inhibition. Also, originality of ideas (but not fluency) was associated with psychoticism in the whole sample. Finally, Fisher *et al.* (2013) found an association between creative experiences and odd beliefs and offered data suggesting that activation of semantic information (which may influence whether remote associations promote verbal creativity or interfere with verbal information processing and disrupt thought processes) in creativity and schizotypy can be differentiated by executive functioning.

Theoretical implications

Dimensionality with temperamental variation and within spectrums

The empirical literature reviewed, drawn from very diverse methods and populations, provides overall support for connections between both the schizophrenia and bipolar spectrums with diverse aspects of creativity. This is not to say, as introduced earlier when considering the possible forms of this link, that mental disorder is necessary for creativity or that creative individuals will necessarily suffer from mental disorders.

There appears to be a strong association between bipolar spectrum disorders and familial risk with lifetime creative accomplishment, engagement in creative pursuits, choice of creative occupations, and preference for complex stimuli. Also, subclinical syndromes, affective temperaments, and familial risk present a stronger and more consistent association with components of the creative process (divergent thinking, creative personality) than clinical disorder. Schizophrenia spectrum studies have focused much more on the soft end, specifically schizotypy and schizotypal personality. Many of these studies reported a positive association with divergent thinking and other variables thought to be common factors and relevant for creative outcome (e.g., openness to experience). However, there are mixed findings that indicate the need to include multiple creativity measures in order to relate specific creativity levels and components with different schizotypal features and dimensions. Studies of clinical schizophrenia are overall more mixed, which is hardly surprising given the huge heterogeneity in terms of clinical picture, chronicity, and treatments, and levels of associated impairment. Overall, studies targeting large samples, which probably allow the inclusion of neurocognitively impaired as well as intact or superior patients, find an association with lifetime creative achievements and creative pursuits; smaller clinical studies, mostly with inpatients, indicate deficits in functions necessary for cognitive cognition (e.g., flexibility). Risk for schizophrenia is positively associated with creative achievement, pursuits, and psychometric measures of creativity. Schizophrenia and schizotypy are multidimensional in nature and studies that have assessed various psychotic dimensions have generally indicated that the association is marked for the positive dimension of unusual cognitive and perceptual experiences, whereas, overall, negative schizotypy traits (anhedonia, avolition) are not related to creativity or have a negative correlation with creativity. The association of divergent thinking and non-cognitive measures of creativity with impulsive non-conformity, which has been closely related both to psychoticism and hypomanic traits, is also highly consistent across studies.

The pattern of results supports the view that the association between creativity and psychopathology is not established with outright symptoms or disorders; rather, these show a less consistent link, but with the temperamental traits, mild forms of disorder, and familial risk, a pattern summarized by Richards *et al.* (1988) as an inverted-U relationship between creativity and psychopathology. Consistent with the fully dimensional view, widely distributed genetic–temperamental variation in the population, which embeds familial liability for the psychoses, increases the likelihood of *both* developing psychotic traits (and disorders) as well as some psychological positive qualities related to creativity, given the commonality of certain dispositional features between psychoticism and creativity (as we shall return to later). This dual status would help to explain the maintenance of these putative genes in the population despite the low mating and fertility rates of individuals with schizophrenia: The genes that carry the liability for the psychoses would have been retained in human evolution because they also convey the compensatory advantage of enhanced creativity (Kinney and Matthysse, 1978; Kinney and Richards, this volume; Kinney et al., 2000–2001; Richards et al., 1988).

The severity and stability of the clinical expression of the underlying vulnerability towards psychosis (contingent upon genetic load and biological and psychosocial risk factors) would greatly impact the possibility of benefiting from the dispositional traits that favor creativity, because high symptom severity would inhibit rather than favor the creative process, although certain symptoms might be beneficial (e.g., outbursts of manic energy) if mild or limited to periods of time, a fact that might also account for some inconsistent findings when assessing diagnosed patients.

As introduced earlier, one of the main debates in psychiatry has been to establish whether creativity is related to *either* the bipolar or schizophrenia spectrum. As Sass and Schuldberg (2000–2001) point out, the connection with the schizophrenic psychoses dominated much of the twentieth century, led by the assumption that creative thinking shared features with mild thought disorder and language peculiarities, which then were ascribed to schizophrenia. However, the revival of the affective psychosis diagnoses later in that century shifted the discussion towards almost a denial of any link between creativity and schizophrenia and the assumption of a strong link with bipolar disorders. This followed from the diagnostic broadening of the affective spectrum and narrowing of the schizophrenia spectrum, the increasing importance given to emotional–motivational aspects linked to bipolarity for creativity, and the focus of recent research on a dementia-like view of schizophrenia (e.g., on neurocognitive deficits and negative symptoms), which make the possible link of schizophrenia with advantageous features even more difficult to conceive.

The literature reviewed here supports the view that the association between creativity and psychopathology is not exclusive to a single spectrum. This fits well with the fully dimensional view in which this sharp distinction within the psychoses has always been less obvious and rather embraces the unitary psychosis model, which considers that diagnostic categories reflect the relative predominance of some symptom dimensions derived from the relative weight of shared etiological factors (Claridge, 2009). The unitary psychosis model fits well with the existence of intermediate diagnoses (e.g., schizoaffective disorder), reports of elevated comorbidity rates between bipolar disorder and schizophrenia, frequent diagnostic changes, commonality in treatments, and the increasing recognition of shared common genetic factors along with specific etiological agents (Demjaha *et al.*, 2012; van Os and Kapur, 2009). Also, the fuzziness of the distinction is evidenced at the temperamental level, as positive schizotypy, hypomanic traits, and impulsive non-conformity load on a common factor when included together in factor analysis. This seems to indicate that the broader construct "psychoticism" – leaving aside the validity problems of its homonymous scale – is more accurate in reflecting the wider variety of individual differences in general and in relation to creativity in particular (Claridge, 2009).

Common and differential factors between creativity and the spectrum of psychoses

Several possible mediating mechanisms linking psychosis and creativity have been suggested, mostly referring to temperament and personality, cognition, affect, and motivation, as well as brain organization, and neurobiological and genetic factors. From a psychological perspective, personality, cognition, and affect have been the focus of most of the theories and research.

As previously noted in the description of psychometric studies, there is an overlap between temperament–personality traits that characterize creative individuals and features that define both schizotypy and affective temperaments. Consistent with Barron (1969), a meta-analysis of studies examining the personality traits of individuals in creative professions (Feist, 1998) revealed that impulsivity, low conscientiousness, and openness to experience were significant, all of which have been associated with cyclo/hyperthymic, positive schizotypy and psychoticism as reported earlier. Also, from a motivational viewpoint, the combination of high ambition and drive that characterizes creative individuals has been consistently found in the bipolar spectrum (Johnson *et al.*, 2009).

Most of the cognitive models proposed come from the schizophrenia literature and suggest that creative and psychosis-prone individuals share a neurocognitive style characterized by reduced cognitive inhibition – that is, a weak filtering of stimuli previously experienced as irrelevant during early processing (e.g., Eysenck, 1995; Hemsley, 1993; Keefe and Magaro, 1980). Although there are several theoretical models, the general idea is that such greater access to mental material usually processed below the level of conscious awareness would provide greater "raw material" that probably would be less obviously interconnected, and thus more likely to raise novel associations, as well as favor broader and more flexible associative networks. Other related characteristics that have been suggested are defocused attention (Mendelsohn, 1976) and a "flat" rather than a

more common "steep" associative hierarchy – that is, a style characterized by stimuli raising more and broad associations rather than just a few
and quite obvious ones (Martindale, 1999; Mednick, 1962). In addition,
it is hypothesized that when the filtering mechanisms become too weak
and the inhibition of irrelevant stimuli that allows efficient information
processing is too sparse, thought becomes progressively overinclusive and
ultimately can result in pathological thought disorder.

These hypotheses have received support from several experimental
paradigms, of which latent inhibition has received most attention. It refers
to a brain-gating mechanism that allows the termination of responding to stimuli that hold no apparent emotional or motivational value
(Lubow and Gewirtz, 1995). If latent inhibition is reduced, there is a
thin "screening out" of stimuli from conscious awareness independent of
their significance, and thus greater access to unfiltered stimuli. Reduced
latent inhibition has been found in both individuals with high psychosis
proneness (e.g., Baruch et al., 1988) and high creativity and openness
to experience (e.g., Peterson and Carson, 2000). Of note, dopaminergic dysregulation, which is a central neurobiological abnormality of the
schizophrenia spectrum, has been associated with reduced latent inhibition (Cassaday, 1997). Note that the association with psychosis proneness or schizotypy is most likely with the positive symptom dimension,
not negative symptoms.

The motivational and affective factors relevant for creativity seem to
be closely connected with the bipolar spectrum, as evidenced by the
close phenomenological resemblance of certain affective states with characteristics of, mostly, inspirational forms of creativity. The moderate
"hyper" side has been suggested to provide the high energy and enthusiasm necessary for sustained effort and effective production, the self-
confidence and impulsivity to pursue and express unconventional ideas,
and the increased perception, ideational association, and mental fluency
to enhance creative cognition. Additionally, two meta-analyses support
the view that positive affect is associated with an improvement in creative
cognition, especially in mood-induction paradigms (Baas et al., 2008;
Davis, 2009). Of note, findings mirror the curvilinear association found
between severity along the bipolar spectrum and creativity, because moderate levels of positive mood were more beneficial than mild levels, but
intense positive mood did not improve creativity in comparison to a moderate level. Baas et al. (2008) reported that it is the combination of positive affect and a certain degree of arousal that enhances creative cognition
(i.e., enthusiasm does, but serenity does not). Also, the beneficial effect
appeared for idea generation tasks (e.g., divergent thinking), but not for
those involving problem solving (Davis, 2009). Several mechanisms have

been proposed to account for the impact of positive affect on creative cognition. There is evidence that positive affect induces defocused attentional states, facilitates access to affectively charged material in memory (which would increase the associative range), decreases inhibitory control, raises awareness to unattended information, enhances the association of cognitively remote concepts that have an emotional resonance, and heightens the perception and processing of stimuli (see Fredrickson and Branigan, 2005; Johnson *et al.*, 2012; Russ, 2000–2001). It has been suggested that some of these effects might derive from an increased cortical activation and arousal, specifically on the prefrontal cortex and thus through executive and working memory functions (see Murray and Johnson, 2010).

On the other hand, mild depressive traits and symptoms may facilitate introspection and insight, as well as a critical pruning of the productions derived from the "hyper" exuberance (Jamison, 1993) – even though depression and negative affect do not seem to have positive effects on a variety of creativity measures in the empirical literature (e.g., Baas *et al.*, 2008; Davis, 2009). However, the relationship between mood and creativity remains to be clarified. Whereas a large number of studies report that positive mood facilitates creative problem solving, others indicate that under certain conditions positive mood may actually impair creativity, suggesting that the association is highly complex (Kaufmann, 2003). In this regard, Kaufmann (2003) proposed a model in which different moods are differentially related to various components and aspects of the creative process, such as problem definition, choice of strategy, and type of process involved, as well as requirements of task solutions. Positive mood clearly facilitates, and negative mood inhibits, ideational fluency, a critical component of the initial stages of creative thinking. However, negative mood may facilitate finding insightful and highly creative solutions to problems through, for instance, a harder strive to search for an "optimizing" rather than "satisficing" problem-solving strategy. Finally, it has been suggested that the cyclic and sometimes even juxtaposed experience of positive and negative moods and their associated cognitive and biological features may give rise to a more complex mental organization and facilitate the usage of certain forms of creative cognition (Jamison, 1993).

Naturally, the mechanisms briefly outlined here interact among themselves, delineating different combinations of both psychological make-up (i.e., the relative weight of the dimensions composing the schizophrenia and bipolar spectrums) and facilitatory effects for some specific types and levels of creativity. Presumably, a combination of these factors is necessary to ensure actual creative output, because very different ingredients are necessary for privately experiencing highly original thoughts (e.g., cognitive disinhibition), engaging in creative activities (e.g., openness to experience), or persisting and succeeding in a creative occupation (e.g., high drive and motivation).

The other side of the coin is what *differential* factors operate to keep madness at bay and facilitate a healthy outcome of the psychoses' temperamental dispositions. The presence of these traits, *per se*, would not guarantee a creative advantage; most likely many other factors need to be favorable, both from an individual (e.g., intelligence, persistence, etc.) and situational perspective (e.g., a stimulating environment, receptive sociocultural milieu, etc.).

Most models have highlighted the importance of normal-to-superior levels of intelligence, working memory, and cognitive flexibility in order to have control over the mental contents facilitated by cognitive disinhibition; thus, mental speed, ability to hold and process information, and capacity to consciously switch attentional states from one stimulus to another would allow a person to manipulate large and disparate amounts of information and establish novel connections rather than becoming overwhelmed and thought disordered (Carson, 2011; Eysenck, 1995). This notion is consistent with evidence that high IQ is a protective factor for the development of the disorder in the offspring of schizophrenic mothers, and that a substantial proportion of relatives have good neurocognition on the one hand and outstanding creative accomplishments on the other.

Besides the critical role of neurocognitive factors, environmental and personality elements also undoubtedly play a role. Interestingly, both creativity (Goertzel and Goertzel, 1962; Ludwig, 1994; Post, 1994; Runco, 1999) and increased risk for the psychoses (e.g., van Os *et al.*, 2010) have been associated with exposure to stressful environments, especially interpersonal trauma, during childhood. It is attractive to speculate that the existence of some healthy early relationship within the distressing environment allows for the development of some ego strength (or, as we shall elaborate later, some positive internal working model of the self and others), which would facilitate the channeling of vulnerability into creativity by, among other mechanisms, making the person able to trust the value of his/her own interests, ideas, and products so as to pursue them (as well as input from others), and by buffering the pernicious effects of stress on high emotional dysregulation and risk for a predominance of depressive elements (which would actually inhibit such a pursuit).

Current psychological theories of psychosis pose that the appearance of unusual cognitive and perceptual processes does not fully explain the transition into dysfunction and disorder; it is the *appraisal* of symptoms that fuels the development of clinical disorder (e.g., Garety *et al.*, 2001). A matrix that probably shapes these appraisals is made up of cognitive representations or internal working models of the self and others – that is, a template for affective responses, social cognition, and relationships that, according to attachment theory, is developed from childhood experiences with caregivers (Bowlby, 1988; Mikulincer and Shaver, 2007). The similarity between positive internal working models of the self and others (i.e., secure attachment) and ego strength (Barron, 1969) is remarkable: resourcefulness, independence, ability to cope with stress, well-being, and a proper sense of control, all of which would contribute to psychological resilience.

As suggested by Simonton (2005) and Nettle (2006), high ego strength would help to exert meta-cognitive control over symptoms, taking advantage of bizarre thoughts rather than those bizarre ideas overwhelming and controlling the individual. On the other hand, high negative emotionality, determined temperamentally as well as by distressing early interactions, is known to have a negative impact on psychological reactions towards unusual experiences, because it likely triggers an intense cascade of anxiety and rumination that amplifies their salience and the imperative need to search for an explanation, be it reasonable or delusional. Supporting this notion, Barrantes-Vidal et al. (2009) showed that self-reported unusual experiences in non-clinical young adults were more likely to be rated as clinically significant in those individuals with higher levels of neuroticism.

A complex association shaped by differences in the link between creativity domains and temperamental dispositions

As introduced earlier, part of the complexity of the association between creativity and psychopathology is based on the fact that schizophrenia and bipolar vulnerability manifest different creative advantages because of their differential, even if overlapping, personality and cognitive characteristics. Most likely, creativity requires a combination of elements from cognitive, personality, and emotional traits pertaining to both spectrums, although this depends on the specificities of different creativity domains. The notion that different creativity domains, usually oversimplified as (and restricted to) arts versus sciences, map on to different dispositional psychotic traits is a helpful organizational framework for elucidating differential mechanisms (Claridge, 1998), and helps to understand the heterogeneity that can be misinterpreted as inconsistency across studies. For example, writing has been suggested to be more closely connected with the schizophrenia spectrum because of the affinity of linguistic functions with psychotic-like thought and language (as supported by the population study by Kyaga et al., 2013).

Sass (1992) argued that the affective temperaments fit in with the emotive, inspirational features of the Romantic style, and this probably causes an overrepresentation of the affective spectrum in the artistic fields. Other kinds of creativity, such as scientific or philosophical, and artistic styles such as modernism and postmodernism, would be closer to psychological traits defining the schizophrenia spectrum. Sass (2000–2001) considered that depressive and manic traits are not a source of radical innovation, but a heightening of psychological states reasonably familiar to most who share a particular culture. On the other hand, schizotypy would be associated with traits that facilitate the development of new perspectives or frameworks, such as eccentricity, an easy engagement in states of detachment from the "given for granted" natural evidence of the world, and fragmentation of the ego, all of which have a greater affinity with the hyper self-consciousness and alienation that characterize modernism and postmodernism.

It is also likely that particular temperamental traits relate differentially with specific styles across arts and sciences (e.g., abstract versus impressionistic), and that some traits are relevant for some levels and components of creativity but not for others (e.g., generativity versus consolidation) (Murray and Johnson, 2010; Nettle, 2001; Silvia and Kaufman, 2010). For instance, as referred to earlier when describing some of the hypotheses on common mechanisms, cognitive disinhibition, positive affect, and impulsivity may facilitate divergent thinking and novelty generation; however, these traits might not necessarily be useful for creative accomplishment, which draws upon sustained effort and might benefit, for instance, from bipolar traits of high goal setting and extraversion. Relatedly, Richards (2000–2001) indicated that the bipolar spectrum is more connected with work-related than leisure-related everyday creativity, whereas the opposite is true for the schizophrenia spectrum. She suggested that the extraverted, competitive, driven, gregarious personality roots of bipolarity facilitate the display of a creative advantage in social contexts in which professional activities take place, whereas the traits of introversion, social anxiety, or awkwardness, more common in the schizophrenia spectrum, may enhance creativity that is cultivated in less socially pressured and judged environments such as leisure and avocational activities.

Summary and conclusions

This chapter focused on the implications that our conceptualization of mental disorders has for understanding the association between the psychoses and creativity. One of the main sources of controversy in this field has been the natural difficulty in reconciling the efficient cognition and production necessary for creativity with the impairing morbid traits of chaotic thinking, disconnection from reality, and erratic behavior that characterize the psychotic states. However, this puzzle can be satisfactorily resolved if we consider mental disorders, including the psychoses, as fully dimensional phenomena – that is, that these disorders are extreme or pathological variants of otherwise *normal* personality dispositions and that, as such, they can be associated with both dysfunctional *and* adaptive traits (Claridge, 1997). Logically, it is not the extreme variants of the underlying temperaments of the psychoses (schizotypy and affective temperaments), the psychotic *states*, that give rise to creativity; in fact, the severe distortion of mental processes and impaired functional capacity inherent to the psychotic states hinder creative outputs. In other words, mental disorders are not necessary for creativity and creative individuals will not necessarily suffer from mental disorders. The hypothesis presented here, which has accrued significant empirical support, is that the temperaments underlying psychosis share genetic–biological, emotional–motivational, and cognitive features with creativity; therefore, individuals with elevated schizotypy or affective temperaments are considered to be *both* more vulnerable to psychopathology and better equipped for creativity if other necessary individual and situational ingredients are also present (e.g., talent, intelligence, a stimulating milieu).

The selected literature review, drawn from diverse methods and populations, provides overall support for a connection of the temperamental traits (affective temperaments and schizotypy), mild symptoms, and familial risk for both schizophrenia and bipolar spectrums with diverse aspects of creativity. As expected, temperament, soft symptoms, and risk show a stronger and more consistent association with components of the creative process (e.g., divergent thinking, creative personality) than do full-blown clinical disorders.

Consistent with the model that dimensionality also operates within the psychoses, the literature review supports the view that the association with creativity is not exclusive to a single spectrum. Thus it is important to move beyond the debate about whether creativity is associated with schizophrenia or bipolarity, and instead consider the conceptual and empirical evidence linking creativity with both spectra. A much more useful approach is to extend the investigation of what aspects of their differential (even if overlapping) personality, emotional, and cognitive characteristics are related to different components, levels, and domains of creativity. In this sense, cognitive components, such as cognitive disinhibition (hypothesized to underlie divergent thinking), have been more closely connected with the schizophrenia spectrum because of the affinity of linguistic functions with psychotic-like thought and language, and consistently associated with creative writing. Affective and motivational components (such as high positive affect and energy), which have a close phenomenological resemblance with affective disturbances, have been associated with increased self-confidence, drive, and impulsivity to pursue and express unconventional ideas. On the other hand, some traits, such as cognitive disinhibition, positive affect, and impulsivity, may facilitate creativity components such as divergent thinking and novelty generation; however, this may not be useful for creative accomplishment, which requires sustained effort and might benefit, for instance, from bipolar traits of high goal setting and extraversion.

As described in the review, the hypothesized link between creativity and psychosis opens up a wide array of interesting conceptual and empirical possibilities. Certainly, the empirical demonstration of the creativity–psychosis link is difficult and conditioned by methodological limitations. However, it is important to note the progressive increase of hypothesis-driven and methodologically sound studies in recent years. A relevant point is the need to assemble data from diverse populations and methods to overcome the limitations inherent to each approach. Thus, it is important to map more precisely the phenomenological commonalities between certain mental states and creativity (e.g., between hypo/manic and creative cognition), which requires studying clinical and highly creative selected populations, but it is also necessary to examine the association between temperaments and different components and levels of creativity in the general population, free of biasing cultural stereotypes of the psychological profile of selected creative professions. Furthermore, future research should benefit from complementing the comparison of categorically defined group means (e.g., subtypes of bipolar disorder and SSDs) with dimensional designs in which quantitative dimensions that cut across these categories (e.g., negative affect, impulsivity, unusual perceptual experiences) are related to a wide array of creativity indices. The latter approach should decrease the level of inconsistency across studies because it avoids the noise created by the problematic validity of current categories, allows taking into consideration the existence of high heterogeneity and multidimensionality within categories, and facilitates testing out mediational hypotheses.

Obviously, it will be essential to move beyond statistical associations of creativity with psychotic traits and affective temperaments to identify the underlying mechanisms. This includes elucidating psychosocial, neurobiological, and developmental processes that give rise to creativity and mental disturbance. Clearly, complex phenotypes such as creativity and psychosis are the result of multiple, interactive biopsychosocial factors that play out across the course of development. Identifying the relevant mediational factors and their complex patterns of interactions should facilitate our understanding of creativity and psychosis, and shed light on differential pathways that lead to adaptive and pathological outcomes. In this sense, current research is identifying relevant neurocognitive factors, such as superior intelligence and working memory, which would allow the handling of large and unexpected amounts of information facilitated by cognitive disinhibition and establishing novel connections, rather than being overwhelmed and progressing into thought disorder. The study of other psychological variables that may facilitate a healthy outcome, such as the impact of positive internal working models of the self and others on stress regulation and the capacity to have metacognitive control of abnormal processes, is a necessary avenue for future research.

The clinical implications of investigating the association between creativity and psychopathology are highly relevant. The demonstration of potential advantages, and not only deficits, connected to the temperamental roots of some mental disorders, is an encouraging message that clearly contrasts with the negative and stigmatizing medical view that society has of these conditions and the demoralization, guilt, and shame felt by sufferers and families. Furthermore, it has been pointed out how important it is that clinicians familiarize themselves with the precise nature of these associations. On the one hand, it would be important that they know that symptoms actually decrease rather than favor creativity in order to confront many patients' fear that treatment may diminish creativity, which contributes to non-compliance. On the other hand, being aware of the enhancing effects that some temperamental traits and mild symptoms have for creativity should facilitate clinicians' understanding of sufferers' genuine complaints about side effects that diminish valued components of creativity (e.g., mental fluency). All of this should help in negotiating the best possible therapeutic relationship for preserving creativity, exploring treatment options, and understanding acceptable levels of symptoms and side effects. Another critical aspect is that a better understanding of how psychotic traits relate to creativity may inform preventive interventions. It is conceivable that reinforcing the engagement into creative endeavors may be an avenue to channel vulnerability traits and subclinical symptoms into adaptive, creative-promoting features, and that this should help to decrease the risk of spiraling into the pathology domain and reducing the severity of psychotic episodes. This is especially relevant in the current zeitgeist of early detection and intervention in psychopathology, in which vulnerable individuals, indexed by familial mental illness, odd personality, or subclinical manifestations, who begin to show signs of functional decline, are being targeted by the mental health system in order to prevent their transitioning into overt disorder, or to quickly minimize the severity and impairment of symptoms if they appear. However, this strategy presents the risk that, in our rush to provide early, preventive intervention, we may treat (medicate) people who are not ill, but are unconventional and creative. Furthermore, it is also obvious how dangerous it is to deal with this issue without proper information and caution, because drawing a simplistic, straightforward connection between creativity and madness can induce unrealistic expectations of creative outputs in sufferers and contribute to treatment rejection to protect a creative advantage.

References

Abraham, A. and Windmann, S. (2008). Selective information processing advantages in creative cognition as a function of schizotypy. *Creativity Research Journal*, 20, 1–6.

Abraham, A., Windmann, S., Daum, I. and Güntürkün, O. (2005). Conceptual expansion and creative imagery as a function of psychoticism. *Consciousness and Cognition*, 14, 520–534.

Abraham, A., Windmann, S., McKenna, P. and Güntürkün, O. (2007). Creative thinking in schizophrenia: The role of executive dysfunction and symptom severity. *Cognitive Neuropsychiatry*, 12(3), 235–258.

Akiskal, H. S. and Akiskal, K. (1988). Reassessing the prevalence of bipolar disorders: Clinical significance and artistic creativity. *Psychiatry and Psychobiology*, 3, 29–36.

Akiskal, K. K. and Akiskal, H. S. (2007). In search of Aristotle: Temperament, human nature, melancholia, creativity and eminence. *Journal of Affective Disorders*, 100, 1–6.

Akiskal, K. K., Savino, M. and Akiskal, H. S. (2005). Temperament profiles in physicians, lawyers, managers, industrialists, architects, journalists, and artists: A study in psychiatric outpatients. *Journal of Affective Disorders*, 85(1–2), 201–206.

American Psychiatric Association (APA) (1994). *Diagnostic and statistical manual of mental health disorders* (4th edn.). Washington DC: Author.

Andreasen, N. C. (1987). Creativity and mental illness: Prevalence rates in writers and first-degree relatives. *American Journal of Psychiatry*, 144, 1288–1292.

Andreasen, N. J. and Canter, A. (1974). The creative writer: Psychiatric symptoms and family history. *Comprehensive Psychiatry*, 15, 123–131.

Baas, M., De Dreu, C. K. W. and Nijstad, B. A. (2008). A meta-analysis of 25 years of mood creativity research: Hedonic tone, activation, or regulatory focus? *Psychological Bulletin*, 134(6), 779–806.

Baron-Cohen, S., Richler, J., Bisarya, D., Gurunathan, N. and Wheelwright, S. (2003). The systemizing quotient: An investigation of adults with Asperger syndrome or high-functioning autism, and normal sex differences.

Philosophical Transactions of the Royal Society of London Series B – Biological Sciences, 358(1430), 361–374.

Barrantes-Vidal, N. (2004). Creativity and madness revisited from current psychological perspectives. *Journal of Consciousness Studies*, 11(3–4), 58–78.

Barrantes-Vidal, N., Colom, F. and Claridge, G. (2002). Temperament and personality in bipolar affective disorders. In E. Vieta (Ed.), *Bipolar disorders: Clinical and therapeutic progress* (pp. 217–242). Madrid: Panamericana.

Barrantes-Vidal, N., Ros-Morente, A. and Kwapil, T. R. (2009). An examination of neuroticism as a moderating factor in the association of positive and negative schizotypy with psychopathology in a nonclinical sample. *Schizophrenia Research*, 115(2–3), 303–309.

Barron, F. (1963). *Barron–Welsh Art Scale: A portion of the Welsh Figure Preference Test*. Palo Alto, CA: Consulting Psychologists Press.

Barron, F. (1969). *Creative person and creative process*. New York: Holt, Rinehart & Winston.

Barron, F. (1972). *Artists in the making*. New York: Seminar.

Baruch, I., Hemsley, D. R. and Gray, J. A. (1988). Differential performance of acute and chronic schizophrenics in a latent inhibition task. *Journal of Nervous and Mental Disease*, 176, 598–606.

Batey, M. and Furnham, A. (2008). The relationship between measures of creativity and schizotypy. *Personality and Individual Differences*, 45, 816–821.

Batey, M. and Furnham, A. (2009). The relationship between creativity, schizotypy and intelligence. *Individual Differences Research*, 7(4), 272–284.

Becker, G. (1978). *The mad genius controversy: A study into the sociology of deviance*. Beverly Hills, CA: Sage.

Becker, G. (2000–2001). The association of creativity and psychopathology: Its cultural-historical origins. *Creativity Research Journal*, 13(1), 45–54.

Bowerman, W. G. (1947). *Studies in genius*. New York: Philosophical Library.

Bowlby, J. (1988). *A secure base*. New York: Basic Books.

Brod, J. H. (1997). Creativity and schizotypy: In G. Claridge (Ed.), *Schizotypy: Implications for illness and health* (pp. 274–298). Oxford: Oxford University Press.

Burch, G., Pavelis, C., Hemsley, D. and Corr, P. (2006). Schizotypy and creativity in visual artists. *British Journal of Psychology*, 97, 177–190.

Cameron, N. (1938). Reasoning, regression and communication in schizophrenics. *Psychological Monographs*, 50, 1–34.

Carson, S. H. (2011). Creativity and psychopathology: A shared vulnerability model. *Canadian Journal of Psychiatry*, 56(3), 144–153.

Cassaday, H. J. (1997). Latent inhibition: Relevance to the neural substrates of schizophrenia and schizotypy? In G. Claridge (Ed.), *Schizotypy: Implications for illness and health* (pp. 124–144). Oxford: Oxford University Press.

Claridge, G. (Ed.) (1997). *Schizotypy: Implications for illness and health*. Oxford: Oxford University Press.

Claridge, G. (1998). Creativity and madness: Clues from modern psychiatric diagnosis. In A. Steptoe (Ed.), *Genius and the mind: Studies of creativity and temperament* (pp. 226–251). New York: Oxford University Press.

Claridge, G. (2009). Personality and psychosis. In P. J. Corr and G. Matthews (Eds.), *Handbook of personality* (pp. 631–648). Cambridge: Cambridge University Press.

Claridge, G. and Barrantes-Vidal, N. (2013). Creativity: A healthy side of madness. In B. Kirkcaldy (Ed.), *Chimes of time. Wounded health professionals: Essays on recovery* (pp. 115–132). Leiden, NL: Sidestone Academic Press.

Claridge, G. and Blakey, S. (2009). Schizotypy and affective temperament: Relationships with divergent thinking and creativity styles. *Personality and Individual Differences*, 46(8), 820–826.

Claridge, G. and McDonald, A. (2009). An investigation into the relationships between convergent and divergent thinking, schizotypy, and autistic traits. *Personality and Individual Differences*, 46(8), 794–799.

Claridge, G., Pryor, R. and Watkins, G. (1998). *Sounds from the Bell Jar*. Cambridge, MA: Malor Books (reedition of the original edition, 1990).

Davis, M. A. (2009). Understanding the relationship between mood and creativity: A meta-analysis. *Organizational Behavior and Human Decision Processes*, 108(1), 25–38.

Demjaha, A., MacCabe, J. H. and Murray, R. M. (2012). How genes and environmental factors determine the different neurodevelopmental trajectories of schizophrenia and bipolar disorder. *Schizophrenia Bulletin*, 38(2), 209–214.

Eisenman, R. (1990). Creativity, preference for complexity, and physical and mental illness. *Creativity Research Journal*, 3, 231–236.

Ellis, H. (1904). *A study of British genius*. London: Hurst and Blackett.

Eysenck, H. J. (1995). *Genius: The natural history of creativity*. Cambridge: Cambridge University Press.

Eysenck, H. J. and Eysenck, S. B. G. (1976). *Psychoticism as a dimension of personality*. London: Hodder and Stoughton.

Feist, G. J. (1998). A meta-analysis of personality in scientific and artistic creativity. *Personality and Social Psychology Review*, 2(4), 290–309.

Fink, A., Slamar-Haldbedl, M., Unterrainer, H. F. and Weiss, E. M. (2012). Creativity: Genius, madness, or a combination of both. *Psychology of Aesthetics, Creativity, and the Arts*, 6(1), 11–18.

Fisher, J. E., Heller, W. and Miller, G. A. (2013). Neuropsychological differentiation of adaptive creativity and schizotypal cognition. *Personality and Individual Differences*, 54(1), 70–75.

Folley, B. S. and Park, S. (2005). Verbal creativity and schizotypal personality in relation to prefrontal hemispheric laterality: A behavioural and near-infrared optical imaging study. *Schizophrenia Research*, 80, 271–282.

Fredrickson, B. L. and Branigan, C. (2005). Positive emotions broaden the scope of attention and thought-action repertoires. *Cognition and Emotion*, 19(3), 313–332.

Fromm, E. (1980). *Greatness and limitations of Freud's thought*. New York: New American Library.

Furnham, A., Batey, M., Anand, K. and Manfield, J. (2008). Personality, hypomania, intelligence and creativity. *Personality and Individual Differences*, 44(5), 1060–1069.

Galvez, J. F., Thommi, S. and Ghaemi, S. N. (2011). Positive aspects of mental illness: A review in bipolar disorder. *Journal of Affective Disorders*, 128(3), 185–190.

Garety, P. A., Kuipers, E., Fowler, D., Freeman, D. and Bebbington, P. E. (2001). A cognitive model of the positive symptoms of psychosis. *Psychological Medicine*, 31, 189–195.

Ghadirian, A., Gregoire, P. and Kosmidis, H. (2001). Creativity and the evolution of psychopathologies. *Creativity Research Journal*, 13, 145–148.

Goertzel, V. and Goertzel, M. G. (1962). *Cradles of eminence*. Boston, MA: Little, Brown & Co.

Gough, H. G., Hall, W. B. and Bradley, P. (1996). Forty years of experience with the Barron–Welsh Art Scale. In A. Montuori (Ed.), *Unusual associates: A festschrift for Frank Barron* (pp. 252–301). Cresskill, NJ: Hampton Press, Inc.

Guilford, J. P. (1950). Creativity. *American Psychologist*, 5, 444–454.

Hasenfus, N. and Magaro, P. (1976). Creativity and schizophrenia: An equality of empirical constructs. *British Journal of Psychiatry*, 129, 346–349.

Hemsley, D. R. (1993). A simple (or simplistic?) cognitive model for schizophrenia. *Behaviour and Research Therapy*, 31, 633–645.

Heston, L. L. (1966). Psychiatric disorders in foster home reared children of schizophrenic mothers. *British Journal of Psychiatry*, 112, 819–825.

Jamison, K. R. (1989). Mood disorders and patterns of creativity in British writers and artists. *Psychiatry*, 52, 125–134.

Jamison, K. R. (1993). *Touched with fire: Manic-depressive illness and the artistic temperament*. New York: Free Press.

Jaracz, J., Patrzała, A. and Rybakowski, J. K. (2012). Creative thinking deficits in patients with schizophrenia: Neurocognitive correlates. *Journal of Nervous and Mental Disease*, 200(7), 588–593.

Johnson, S. L., Eisner, L. R. and Carver, C. S. (2009). Elevated expectancies among persons diagnosed with bipolar disorder. *British Journal of Clinical Psychology*, 48(2), 217–222.

Johnson, S. L., Murray, G., Fredrickson, B., Youngstrom, E. A., Hinshaw, S., Bass J. M. *et al.* (2012). Creativity and bipolar disorder: Touched by fire or burning with questions? *Clinical Psychology Review*, 32, 1–12.

Jones, T., Caulfield, L., Wilkinson, D. and Weller, L. (2011). The relationship between nonclinical schizotypy and handedness on divergent and convergent creative problem-solving tasks. *Creativity Research Journal*, 23(3), 222–228.

Juda, A. (1949). The relationship between highest mental capacity and psychic abnormalities. *American Journal of Psychiatry*, 106, 296–307.

Karimi, Z., Windmann, S., Güntürkün, O. and Abraham, A. (2007). Insight problem solving in individuals with high versus low schizotypy. *Journal of Research in Personality*, 41, 473–480.

Karlsson, J. L. (1970). Genetic association of giftedness and creativity with schizophrenia. *Hereditas*, 66, 177–182.

Kaufman, J. C. (2001). The Sylvia Plath effect: Mental illness in eminent creative writers. *Journal of Creative Behavior*, 35, 37–50.

Kaufman, J. C. (2005). The door that leads into madness: Eastern European poets and mental illness. *Creativity Research Journal*, 17, 99–103.

Kaufman, J. C. (2009). *Creativity 101*. New York: Springer.

Kaufman, J. C. and Baer, J. (2002). I bask in dreams of suicide: Mental illness and poetry. *Review of General Psychology*, 6(3), 271–286.

Kaufman, J. C. and Sexton, J. D. (2006). Why doesn't the writing cure help poets? *Review of General Psychology*, 10(3), 268–282.

Kaufmann, G. (2003). The effect of mood on creativity in the innovative process. In L. V. Shavinina (Ed.), *International handbook on innovation* (pp. 191–203). Mahwah, NJ: Lawrence Erlbaum Associates, Inc.

Keefe, J. A. and Magaro, P. A. (1980). Creativity and schizophrenia: An equivalence of cognitive processing. *Journal of Abnormal Psychology*, 89, 390–398.

Kinney, D. K. and Matthysse, S. (1978). Genetic transmission of schizophrenia. *Annual Review of Medicine*, 29, 459–473.

Kinney, D. K., Richards, R. R., Lowing, P. A., LeBlanc, D., Zimblaist, M. E. and Harlan, P. (2000–2001). Creativity in offspring of schizophrenic and control parents: An adoption study. *Creativity Research Journal*, 13(1), 17–26.

Kottler, J. (2005). *Divine madness*. San Francisco, CA: Jossey-Bass.

Kwapil, T. R. and Barrantes-Vidal, N. (2012). Schizotypal personality disorder: An integrative review. In T. A. Widiger (Ed.), *The Oxford handbook of personality disorders* (pp. 437–477). New York: Oxford University Press.

Kyaga, S., Landén, M., Boman, M., Hultman, C., Långström, N. and Lichtenstein, P. (2013). Mental illness, suicide and creativity: 40-year prospective total population study. *Journal of Psychiatric Research*, 47(1), 83–90.

Kyaga, S., Lichtenstein, P., Boman, M., Hultman, C., Långström, N. and Landén, M. (2011). Creativity and mental disorder: Family study of 300,000 people with severe mental disorder. *British Journal of Psychiatry*, 199(5), 373–379.

Lange-Eichbaum, W. (1932). *The problem of genius*. New York: Macmillan.

Lombroso, C. (1895). *The man of genius*. London: Walter Scott.

Lubow, R. E. and Gewirtz, J. C. (1995). Latent inhibition in humans: Data, theory, and implications for schizophrenia. *Psychological Bulletin*, 117, 87–103.

Ludwig, A. M. (1994). Mental illness and creative activity in female writers. *American Journal of Psychiatry*, 151, 1650–1656.

Ludwig, A. M. (1995). *The price of greatness*. New York: Guilford Press.

Ludwig, A. M. (1998). Method and madness in the arts and sciences. *Creativity Research Journal*, 11, 93–101.

MacCabe, J. H., Lambe, M. P., Cnattingius, S., Sham, P. C., David, A. S., Reichenberg, A. *et al.* (2010). Excellent school performance at age 16 and risk of adult bipolar disorder: National cohort study. *British Journal of Psychiatry*, 196, 109–115.

MacCabe, J. H., Lambe, M. P., Cnattingius, S., Torrång, A., Sham, P. C., David, A. S. *et al.* (2008). Scholastic achievement at age 16 and risk of schizophrenia and other psychoses: A national cohort study. *Psychological Medicine*, 38(8), 1133–1140.

Martindale, C. (1999). Biological basis of creativity. In R. J. Sternberg (Ed.), *Handbook of creativity* (pp. 137–152). New York: Cambridge University Press.

Mednick, S. A. (1962). The associative basis of the creative process. *Psychological Review*, 69, 220–232.

Mendelsohn, G. A. (1976). Associative and attentional processes in creative performance. *Journal of Personality*, 44, 341–369.

Mikulincer, M. and Shaver, P. R. (2007). *Attachment in adulthood: Structure, dynamics, and change*. New York: Guilford Press.

Miller, G. F. and Tal, I. R. (2007). Schizotypy versus openness and intelligence as predictors of creativity. *Schizophrenia Research*, 93, 317–324.

Murray, G. and Johnson, S. (2010). The clinical significance of creativity in bipolar disorder. *Clinical Psychology Review*, 30, 721–732.

Nelson, B. and Rawlings, D. (2010). Relating schizotypy and personality to the phenomenology of creativity. *Schizophrenia Bulletin*, 36(2), 388–399.

Nettle, D. (2001). *Strong imagination*. Oxford: Oxford University Press.

Nettle, D. (2006). Psychological profiles of professional actors. *Personality and Individual Differences*, 40, 375–383.

Nowakowska, C., Strong, C. M., Santosa, C. M., Wang, P. W. and Ketter, T. A. (2005). Temperamental commonalities and differences in euthymic mood disorder patients, creative controls, and healthy controls. *Journal of Affective Disorders*, 85(1–2), 207–215.

O'Reilly, T., Dunbar, R. and Bentall, R. (2001). Schizotypy and creativity: An evolutionary connection? *Personality and Individual Differences*, 31, 1067–1078.

Parker, G., Paterson, A., Fletcher, K., Blanch, B. and Graham, R. (2012). The "magic button question" for those with a mood disorder – would they wish to re-live their condition? *Journal of Affective Disorders*, 136, 419–424.

Peterson, J. B. and Carson, S. (2000). Latent inhibition and openness to experience in a high-achieving student population. *Personality and Individual Differences*, 28(2), 323–332.

Post, F. (1994). Creativity and psychopathology: A study of 291 world-famous men. *British Journal of Psychiatry*, 165, 22–34.

Post, F. (1996). Verbal creativity, depression and alcoholism: An investigation of one hundred American and British writers. *British Journal of Psychiatry*, 168, 545–555.

Pretti, A. and Vellante, M. (2007). Higher rates of psychosis proneness and nonright-handedness among creative artists compared to same age and gender peers. *Journal of Nervous and Mental Disease*, 195, 837–845.

Rawlings, D. and Locarnini, A. (2008). Dimensional schizotypy, autism, and unusual word associations in artists and scientists. *Journal of Research in Personality*, 42, 465–471.

Richards, R. (2000–2001). Creativity and schizophrenia spectrum: More and more interesting. *Creativity Research Journal*, 13(1), 111–132.

Richards, R. L., Kinney, D. K., Benet, M. and Merzel, A. P. C. (1988). Assessing everyday creativity: Characteristics of the Lifetime Creativity Scales and validation with three large samples. *Journal of Personality and Social Psychology*, 54, 476–485.

Rodrigue, A. L. and Perkins, D. R. (2012). Divergent thinking abilities across the schizophrenic spectrum and other psychological correlates. *Creativity Research Journal*, 24(2–3), 163–168.

Rothenberg, A. (1990). *Creativity and madness: New findings and old stereotypes.* Baltimore, MD: Johns Hopkins University Press.

Rubenstein, G. (2008). Are schizophrenic patients necessarily creative? A comparative study between three groups of psychiatric inpatients. *Personality and Individual Differences,* 45, 806–810.

Runco, M. A. (1999). Tension, adaptability, and creativity. In S. W. Russ (Ed.), *Affect, creative experience, and psychological adjustment* (pp. 165–194). Philadelphia, PA: Taylor & Francis.

Russ, S. W. (2000–2001). Primary-process thinking and creativity: Affect and cognition. *Creativity Research Journal,* 13, 27–35.

Rybakowski, J. K. and Klonowska, P. (2011). Bipolar mood disorder, creativity and schizotypy: An experimental study. *Psychopathology,* 44(5), 296–302.

Santosa, C. M., Strong, C. M., Nowakowska, C., Wang, P. W., Rennicke, C. M. and Ketter, T. A. (2007). Enhanced creativity in bipolar disorder patients: A controlled study. *Journal of Affective Disorders,* 100, 31–39.

Sass, L. A. (1992). *Madness and modernism: Insanity in the light of modern art, literature, and thought.* New York: Basic Books.

Sass, L. A. (2000–2001). Schizophrenia, modernism, and the "creative imagination": On creativity and psychopathology. *Creativity Research Journal,* 13(1), 55–74.

Sass, L. A. and Schuldberg, D. (2000–2001). Introduction to the Special Issue: Creativity and the schizophrenia spectrum. *Creativity Research Journal,* 13(1), 1–4.

Sawyer, R. K. (2006). *Explaining creativity: The science of human innovation.* Oxford: Oxford University Press.

Schildkraut, J. J., Hirshfeld, A. J. and Murphy, J. M. (1994). Mind and mood in modern art, II: Depressive disorders, spirituality, and early deaths in the abstract expressionist artists of the New York School. *American Journal of Psychiatry,* 151(4), 482–488.

Schlesinger, J. (2009). Creative mythconceptions: A closer look at the evidence for the "mad genius" hypothesis. *Psychology of Aesthetics, Creativity, and the Arts,* 3(2), 62–72.

Schuldberg, D. (1990). Schizotypal and hypomanic traits, creativity, and psychological health. *Creativity Research Journal,* 3, 218–230.

Schuldberg, D. (2000–2001). Six subclinical spectrum traits in normal creativity. *Creativity Research Journal,* 13(1), 5–16.

Schuldberg, D. (2005). Eysenck Personality Questionnaire scales and paper-and-pencil tests related to creativity. *Psychological Reports,* 97(1), 180–182.

Schuldberg, D., French, C., Stone, B. L. and Heberle, J. (1988). Creativity and schizotypal traits. *Journal of Nervous and Mental Disease,* 176, 648–657.

Silvia, P. and Kaufman, J. C. (2010). Creativity and mental illness. In J. C. Kaufman and R. J. Sternberg (Eds.), *The Cambridge handbook of creativity* (pp. 381–394). New York: Cambridge University Press.

Simeonova, D. I., Chang, K. D., Strong, C. and Kette, T. A. (2005). Creativity in familial bipolar disorder. *Journal of Psychiatric Research,* 39, 623–631.

Simonton, D. K. (2004). *Creativity in science: Chance, logic, genius, and zeitgeist.* New York: Cambridge University Press.

Simonton, D. K. (2005). Are genius and madness related? Contemporary answers to an ancient question. *Psychiatric Times*, 22(7), 21–22.

Simonton, D. K. (2010). So you want to become a creative genius? You must be crazy! In D. Cropley, J. C. Kaufman, A. Cropley and M. Runco (Eds.), *The dark side of creativity* (pp. 218–234). New York: Cambridge University Press.

Soeiro-de-Souza, M. G., Dias, V. V., Bio, D. S., Post, R. M. and Moreno, R. A. (2011). Creativity and executive function across manic, mixed and depressive episodes in bipolar I disorder. *Journal of Affective Disorders*, 135(1–3), 292–297.

Srivastava, S., Childers, M. E., Baek, J. H., Strong, C. M., Hill, S. J., Warsett, K. S. *et al.* (2010). Toward interaction of affective and cognitive contributors to creativity in bipolar disorders: A controlled study. *Journal of Affective Disorders*, 125, 27–34.

Storr, A. (2000–2001). Creativity and psychopathology. *Bulletin of Psychology of the Arts*, 1(2), 42–43.

Strong, C. M., Nowakowska, C., Santosa, C. M., Wang, P. W., Kraemer, H. C. and Ketter, T. A. (2007). Temperament–creativity relationships in mood disorder patients, healthy controls and highly creative individuals. *Journal of Affective Disorders*, 100, 41–48.

Torrance, E. P. (1974). *Torrance tests of creative thinking*. Lexington, MA: Personnel Press.

Tremblay, C. H., Grosskopf, S. and Yang, K. (2010). Brainstorm: Occupational choice, bipolar illness and creativity. *Economics and Human Biology*, 8, 233–241.

Tsakanikos, E. and Claridge, G. (2005). More words, less words: Verbal fluency as a function of "positive" and "negative" schizotypy. *Personality and Individual Differences*, 39(4), 705–713.

van Os, J. and Kapur, S. (2009). Schizophrenia. *Lancet*, 374, 635–645.

van Os, J., Kenis, G. and Rutten, B. P. F. (2010). The environment and schizophrenia. *Nature*, 468, 203–212.

Vellante, M., Zucca, G., Preti, A., Sisti, D., Bruno, M., Rocchi, L. *et al.* (2011). Creativity and affective temperaments in non-clinical professional artists: An empirical psychometric investigation. *Journal of Affective Disorders*, 135(1–3), 28–36.

Weinstein, S. and Graves, R. E. (2002). Are creativity and schizotypy products of a right hemisphere bias? *Brain and Cognition*, 49, 138–151.

Weisberg, R. W. (2006). *Creativity: Understanding innovation in problem solving, science, invention, and the arts*. Hoboken, NJ: Wiley.

Wills, G. I. (2003). A personality study of musicians working in the popular field. *Personality and Individual Differences*, 5, 359–360.

10 When good is bad and bad is good: mood, bipolarity, and creativity

Geir Kaufmann and Astrid Kaufmann

New meeting grounds

The meeting of affect and cognition

Arguably, one of the most significant new developments in psychological research during the last 30 years is the exploration of the interface between affect and cognition (see De Houwer and Hermans, 2010; Lewis *et al.*, 2008; Power and Dalgleish, 2008). A new perspective on the interface between emotion and cognition is emerging, in which the emphasis is on the interwoven and internal rather than the conceptually external relations between the two (e.g., Damasio, 1994). Another major emphasis has been on the constructive roles that affect can play in cognitive functions as opposed to previous conceptions, where affect was rather one-sidedly seen as detrimental to rational and effective thought (Forgas, 1995, 2008).

The meeting of affect and creativity

In the same period we have also witnessed a significant rise in research on creativity, seen as a scientifically respectable and empirically tractable phenomenon (e.g., Hennessey and Amabile, 2010; Kaufman and Sternberg, 2010). It is to be expected that these two new streams of research on affect and creativity, respectively, would interface. This has indeed happened, and we can now look back on a 25-year-long roster of research on the relationship between mood and creativity (Baas *et al.*, 2008; Rank and Frese, 2008).

Order meets disorder

Within the field of affect and creativity, we may discern two different streams of research. One treats affect and creativity as orderly phenomena in the sense that they can be operationalized and studied under controlled conditions in the laboratory. The other deals with more complex manifestations of both affect and creativity, where the focus is on the relationship between mental disorders and creativity. Here the primary emphasis has been on the case of affective disorders. It is to be expected that different streams of research may develop in parallel for long periods, without any significant interactions. However, the mental disorder–creativity and the mood-and-creativity streams of research clearly have significant overlaps in terms of the more general issues addressed. Clearly we should let these close relatives in research speak to each other to examine what the one can learn from the other. A significant limit of the former field of research is that the data are basically correlational in nature, and any causal inference will necessarily be tenuous. The strength of the latter tradition of research is to allow causal inferences. The limitation of the experimental tradition is the narrowing down of complex phenomena to make them yield to controlled experimentation.

The road ahead

Our main focus in this chapter is to review the main thrust of the findings in these two streams of research, to point to similarities and discrepancies in findings, and to offer a theory of the relationship between mood and creativity that might work as a superordinate and integrative perspective on some major findings on the more general issues at stake, that could also serve as a guide for new research.

The intricate creativity–mental disorder equation

In a television interview with the Norwegian Broadcasting Company some years ago, the up-and-coming young painter Vebjørn Sand was asked about the conditions that had been important for the development of his creativity as an artist. He pointed to a number of factors that he regarded as significant. In particular, he emphasized that he had had "two and a half depression"!

By making this statement, the artist was echoing a widely held and persistent idea that goes all the way back to Aristotle and Plato (see Becker, this volume). This is the notion that mental disorder and creativity are linked in a significant way, and that the severe pain of a disturbed mind somehow may also be a hallmark of a mind that harbors the unique qualities necessary for creativity of an exceptional kind.

Aligned with this notion comes the finding that the frequency of mental disorders, such as depression, has been conspicuously constant over time (Andrews and Thompson, 2009). If such mental disorders are just bad, and only constitute a maladaptive response to the problems of life, we should expect that such malfunctions be weeded out over time during evolution. The fact that they have not may therefore be turned into an argument that there could be an upside to these conditions that contains some adaptive functions that may work in a compensatory way. It may be argued that evolution is a mighty long process, and that we have still not had sufficient time to see decline to come. Meeting this objection, however, recent studies (e.g., Andersen *et al.*, 2011) have shown a significant *increase* rather than a decrease in the prevalence of major depressive disorder, specifically from 2.0 percent to 4.9 percent from 2000 to 2006 in the Danish population.

The affirmative answer

We may therefore legitimately ask if there is a core of truth in the proposition that genuine creativity only comes with the costly price of great suffering. Or, if not a necessary prerequisite for creativity, could it still be the case that somehow suffering mental pain and disorder may facilitate the development of ideas of a highly creative kind? This seems to be the position favored by Ludwig (1995) in his book *The price of greatness.*

Here we are confronted with something that looks like a paradox. How could something bad (mental disorder) lead to something good (creativity)? We may speculate that perhaps there is a psychological equivalent to the "creative destruction" championed by Joseph Schumpeter in the field of economics – where existing structures in the market are brutally supplanted by new structures. Perhaps similar structural forces may also be operative at the level of mental structures? Existing mental structures may come under increasing duress and stress when the individual is navigating his or her way through an ever more complex and turbulent task environment. At certain points there is disruption to the point of a breakdown resulting in mental disorders like severe affective disturbances and depression. This leads to a search for new perspectives on the complex problems facing the individual, and eventual restructuring and reframing of mental representations and knowledge structures that in turn may lead to fresh perspectives and new and creative ways of dealing with the core issues in the individual's task environment.

Another possibility on the affirmative side may be that facing serious problems in one's life, such as a particularly harsh upbringing, losing a parent, long periods of illness, harassment in school, and the like, may engender suffering of an intense kind, such as affective disorders (e.g., Amabile, 1989). But the very same conditions, we may argue, could also foster more advanced sorts of coping and flexible problem-solving skills that may increase the likelihood of creative achievements of a notable kind later in life.

The answer to the negative

Alternatively, we may argue that the proposition of the "mad genius" is a hoax that is not founded on sound empirical research, and that a thorough examination of the evidence mustered in support of the idea shows the stereotypical bias that is driving this kind of research. This is the position favored by Schlesinger (2012; see also Schlesinger, this volume) in her recently published book *The insanity hoax*. The statement by the Norwegian painter would then be seen as reflecting somewhat of a caricature of a pervasive stereotype that is endorsed by artists who use it to promote an image of themselves as belonging to an exclusive category that has reached a particularly high level of creativity.

On this account, the relationships observed between mental disorder and indices of creativity are mere appearances falsely engendered by biased research based on insufficient methodologies, where the requirements for proper controls of conditions of comparison are not met (e.g., Schlesinger, 2012). Alternatively, the correlation observed may turn out to be spurious, as proposed by Rothenberg (1990a, 1990b). On his account, the relationship between affective disorders and creativity is seen as artificial, and may reflect the operation of confounding variables such as differences in lifestyles. Unhealthy lifestyles, including alcoholism and drug abuse, alleged to occur more frequently in artistic, bohemian circles, might thus be responsible for more frequent occurrence of mental disorders involving breakdowns, anxiety, and depression.

The other way around

The causal relationship may also be turned around full circle. Here creativity is seen as the cause of mental disorders. We may appreciate the special circumstance in the existential situation of artists and others engaged in creative work. In contrast to the well-structured and predictable life of most people working in relatively stable job contexts, creative work involves living under high uncertainty in relative ill-structured problem contexts, fostering an ever-changing set of challenges and demands, along with a constant pressure to deliver something new and original. How the environment eventually will react to the work and products creative people deliver is also a matter of considerable uncertainty and unpredictability. We may therefore understand that those who are engaging in such conditions most directly and most intensely may be both the most creative and the most vulnerable to suffer nervous breakdowns, anxiety, and affective disturbances, such as depression. Here we meet our paradox in the reverse order in the sense that something good (creativity) may turn into something bad (mental disorder).

The middle ground

A third possibility has also attracted great interest and can be defended on many good grounds. This is the theory that mental disorder and creativity share some crucial common features that turn sweet in the case of creativity and sour in the case of mental disorder. Proneness towards mental disorder may also involve dispositions that somehow favor the expanding surge of new ideas. Such conditions may indeed increase the likelihood of transcending the mental status quo and lead to strikingly new insights.

A view of the empirical arena

What are we to make of the many different alternative explanations of the putative correlation between mental disorder and creativity on the basis of existing research?

The case for elevated mood

A large number of studies have addressed the core issue at stake. These studies range from qualitative studies, based on anecdotes, but also more carefully designed case studies (e.g., Goodwin and Jamison, 2007), through descriptive, epidemiological studies (e.g., Prisciandaro and Roberts, 2011) to quantitative, multivariate, and some experimental studies (e.g., Rybakowski and Klonowska, 2011; Silvia and Kimbrel, 2010).

Historically, studies by Galton, Lombroso, Nisbet, and Ellis (cited in Jamison, 1993) suggested a marked hyperfrequency of affective disorders among artists, writers, and composers. Such a link was supported in a better controlled study by Andreasen (1987). In a more recent study, Jamison (1993) examined the life histories of British poets and reported a significantly elevated frequency of manic-depressive disorder. Similarly striking findings have been obtained by Richards (1994) and Kinney and Richards (2007) and by Ludwig (1995).

The extant literature in the field has become very extensive, and is reviewed comprehensively from many different perspectives in the present volume. Here we will concentrate on identifying the major points we think can be made.

Several recent reviews of the literature (Galvez *et al.*, 2011; Johnson *et al.*, 2012; Lloyd-Evans *et al.*, 2006; Pollack-Kogan and McCabe, 2010) arrive at a consensus conclusion that there is now convincing evidence in favor of the most basic issue – that there is, indeed, a significant hyperfrequency of affective disorders among highly creative people.

A significant step in expanding and generalizing the issue was taken by Ruth Richards and her colleagues (Kinney and Richards, 2007; Richards and Kinney, 1990; Richards *et al.*, 1988) when they went beyond the high-level, eminent creativity level and examined if the relationship between mood disorder and creativity would also hold in the more general field of the everyday creativity that people engage in on the job or in their hobbies. Interestingly, the findings from a large number of such studies show that the relationship between mood disorders and creativity shines through in the more general population and is not limited to a small number of creative geniuses.

Another highly significant finding is that the relationship is stronger in the least strongly affected, like in bipolar 2 versus bipolar 1. Some findings also suggest that the higher incidence of elevated creativity is observed more clearly in normal first relatives of people with clinical diagnosis, than in the actual patients themselves (Akiskal and Akiskal, 1994; Akiskal *et al.*, 2005; Richards *et al.*, 1988). These findings are supported by the results obtained in a fresh Swedish investigation of unusual proportions. Kyaga *et al.* (2013) conducted a nested case-control study based on longitudinal Swedish total population registries involving 1,173,763 participants where the relationship between various forms of mental illness and creativity was examined. Operationally, this was done by examining the occurrence of creative occupations in patients and their non-diagnosed relatives and comparing it with that of matched population controls. Creative professions were defined as scientific and artistic occupations. A wide range of diagnoses was included, incorporating schizophrenia, schizoaffective disorder, bipolar disorder, unipolar depression, anxiety disorders, alcohol abuse, drug abuse, autism, attention-deficit/hyperactivity disorder (ADHD), anorexia nervosa, and completed suicide. A significant association between psychopathology and creative profession was found only in the case of bipolar disorder. However, a significant familial association with overall creative professions was demonstrated for schizophrenia, bipolar disorder, anorexia nervosa, and, marginally, autism.

In the case of bipolar disorders, such findings agree with results obtained in a recent study by Rybakowski and Klonowska (2011). Here, creative problem-solving performance was compared between a group of patients with bipolar disorder and a matched control group. The bipolar group was further divided into patients in remission and patients still in a depressive episode. The bipolar group scored significantly higher than the control group on a task requiring inventiveness. Within the bipolar group, those in remission performed significantly better than those still in depression.

In general, these findings may be taken to mean that milder forms of mood swings may be more conducive to creativity than the stronger, clinical manifestations, and also that individuals in a strongly depressed state score lower. Thus we may understand the recent findings of negligible relationships between anxiety and depression and various indicators of creative performance observed by Silvia and Kimbrel (2010) to mean that creativity is not readily accessible while in a highly anxious state or strongly depressed mood. Studies of this kind should therefore distinguish clearly between state and trait with respect to the pathology-oriented variables included, and also examine signs of curvilinearity.

Such findings seem to go against the theory that a collapse or breakdown may be necessary for a radical reorientation leading to markedly increased creativity. It is also difficult to reconcile with the idea that the mood-and-creativity relationship is spurious, or that the relationship manifests the consequences of navigating in highly ill-defined problem spaces and stretching creativity to the limits of a mental breakdown as a natural result. None of the interpretations discussed earlier are, however, eliminated by these findings. There may still be a significant difference between the creativity involved in everyday affairs and the creativity involved at the peak level of creative performance.

Thus the theory of a common mediator among creativity and proneness to disorder seems to be the more plausible one. What mediators should we look for that plausibly link mood disorders of a bipolar type and creativity? A prime candidate here is hypomania, or highly elevated positive mood, that by definition is a part of bipolar disorder and may reasonably be seen as the generator of creative ideation. In line with such a theory, studies reported by Jamison (1993) suggest that a mild hypomanic state of mind is conducive to high ideational fluency, speed of association, combinatorial thinking, and "loose" processing involving irrelevant intrusions in thought. In a positive sense, this cluster of cognitive characteristics may tend to facilitate originality and creativity in problem solving. In support of her hypothesis, Jamison (1993) reports a close coincidence of episodes of hypomania and reports of particularly creative periods among poets. The design of this study has been criticized as less than adequate in terms of the required controls (see Rothenberg, 1990a; Schlesinger, 2012).

In recent studies, Shapiro and Weisberg (1999) developed separate measures of hyperthymic and cyclothymic affective patterns, and argued that hyperthymia, and not cyclothymia, was responsible for the association with creativity. A significant limitation of this study, however, is that the only measure they used to tap creativity was a subjective self-rating. It is not unreasonable to think that people in an elevated positive mood may significantly overestimate their own creativity. Objective measures are needed to make the point.

In a study by Schuldberg (1990), a design was employed that was different in the sense of drawing its sample from a non-clinical and non-eminent population; it examined the relationship between pencil and paper measures of creativity and psychotic-like experiences and indicators of psychological health. Most interesting for our purpose was the finding that a measure of hypomania was seen to be significantly related to divergent thinking measures of creativity. In a recent and more comprehensive study by Furnham *et al.* (2008), a complex assessment of creativity was made, involving a self-rated, biographical inventory of creativity as well as divergent-thinking tasks. Hypomania was measured as a trait. It was shown that hypomania was significantly related to an overall index of creativity, particularly when combined with a measure of fluid intelligence.

The idea that the relationship between affect disorders and creativity may come down to the capacity of a (mild) hypomanic state to generate many and varied ideas is also favored by Kinney and Richards (2007) and Richards and Kinney (1990).

We may, however, question the idea that the observed findings are only to be accounted for by elevated positive mood. What about the depressed, negative mood side that figures so prominently on the disorder side in this kind of research? Is this only a liability that comes with the purchase, as it were? Or are there features of negative mood that also might contribute in a constructive way to creativity? And perhaps even more interesting, is there any value in the actual *swing* of mood?

The two faces of depressed mood

What good could be said about being blue in the context of creativity? In a comprehensive set of arguments, Andrews and Thomson (2009) fundamentally question the idea that depression is only to be considered a maladaptive pathology. The crux of their argument is that rumination, which figures so persistently and painfully in the depression episode, fundamentally reflects an adaptive mode of analytical thinking that could also be a most useful cognitive tool in dealing with complex problems. So one effect of sad or depressed mood could also be to promote an analytical reasoning style, where greater attention is devoted to detail, and where information is processed more systematically. We may spot this aspect in operationalized terms in insight problems, where an impasse is reached because a certain crucial piece of information in the problem definition is overlooked, or in the case where the problem presentation leads to an implicit representation of the problem that contains unnecessary constraints in the search of the problem space. An example of the last case is the "nine dot problem," where the task is to draw a line through nine dots presented as a square pattern. The problem is very difficult for most people, who seem to implicitly (and wrongly) infer that the line has to be drawn within the square configuration.

Several authors have pointed to a potential mediator role for rumination as a bridge to understanding the relationship between depression and creativity. Kaufman and Baer (2002) examined several explanations of why there is such a high prevalence of mental illness among poets, particularly among the females. One of the possibilities mentioned is that the rumination that characterizes depression may also be involved in writing poetry and may actually augment a prior vulnerability to depression. The general ideal of a "shared vulnerability" is explored in great detail by Carson and colleagues (Carson, 2011, this volume; Carson et al., 2003). More specifically, it is argued that cognitive disinhibition, which allows more stimuli into conscious awareness, is a common denominator in creativity and psychopathology. The evidence is indeed impressive, and shows that eminent creative achievers are three times as likely to have low scores on a latent inhibition test. As argued by Verhaeghen et al. (2005), the style of thinking that is manifested in rumination may be the consequence of such deficits in executive control mechanisms and may act as a two-edged sword. On the one hand, rumination may figure strongly in depression, but may also promote the development of highly original ideas.

Verhaeghen et al. (2005) put this hypothesis to the test in an empirical study that included various measures of depression (in the past versus currently), several indicators of creativity (creative interests, creative behavior, and creative ability), plus a measure of self-reflective rumination. Interestingly, the results show that rumination is related to both depression and several aspects of creativity. In a path analysis, there was no direct link between creativity and depressed mood. The authors take this to mean that the association between depression and creativity "is solely the results of rumination" (p. 226). It is not clear how we are to understand this conclusion – that is, if the relationship is spurious, or whether the relationship between depression and creativity is mediated by the tendency to engage in self-reflective rumination in both domains. Unfortunately, in this study, the required conditions for testing a mediator hypothesis were not met, because no relationship between depression and creativity was established in the first place in this particular set of data.

Flying high and low

A limitation of the multivariate studies reviewed earlier is that neither of them was designed to look separately at the potential effect of mixed mood. In a study of our own (Kaufmann and Kaufmann, 2012), with 215 participants of a diverse range in educational background and age, measures of depression, and hypomania, a diverse set of indicators of creativity (creative accomplishments, divergent thinking, and insight problems) was administered. An indicator of complex creativity was designed by combining the various indicators of creativity, and regression analysis was performed to examine the relationships between the affect variables and complex creativity. The leading hypothesis was that hypomania would predict the everyday creativity of creative accomplishments and divergent thinking, whereas bipolarity (simultaneously high on both depression and hypomania) would predict performance on the complex creativity index. We found that the lowest score on the creativity index was obtained in the category of those scoring high on depression and low on hypomania. Hypomania predicted divergent thinking and creative accomplishments, and, as posited, the simultaneous combination of high depression and high hypomania predicted complex creativity and outweighed the effect of hypomania at this level of creativity. Interestingly, those who scored high on hypomania and low on depression (hyperthymia) exhibited a mediocre-to-low performance on the complex creativity index.

We have now seen that there are good reasons to expect that a positive mood might be conducive to a varied and innovative idea production. In this capacity, elevated, positive mood may indeed function as an important mediator of both the disorderly and disturbed idea production that we can observe most clearly in manic states as well as the surge of idea production that may significantly facilitate creativity on the constructive side. But we have also seen that negative mood may contribute to creativity of a complex sort, when it is combined with an elevated, positive mood. This may come about through rapid shifts of processing styles that may increase flexibility in moving through a complex problem space that requires redefinition and new insights that involve both "loose" and "tight" thinking. We have now come to a point in our discussion where the quest for decomposition of variables and causal analysis presents itself with an ever-growing urgency. Consequently, it may be profitable to look inside the folder of the other stream of research that is overwhelmingly concerned with more controlled and experimental studies of the effect of mood on creative thinking and problem solving.

Experimental studies of mood and creativity

Theories relating to mood and creativity tend to underscore the facilitating effect of positive mood on various measures of creative task performance (Amabile *et al.*, 2005; Fredrickson, 2001; Fredrickson and Branigan, 2005; Hirt, 1999; Hirt *et al.*, 2008; Isen, 1997, 1999, 2008; Martin, 2000; Staw and Barsade, 1993). A standard explanation assertion is that positive material is more abundant, better organized, and more extensively connected in memory than is neutral and negative material (e.g., Isen, 2008). According to the mood congruence principle, positive mood triggers positive material in memory. This mechanism enables access to a broad and diverse range of associates that allows for the kind of increased cognitive flexibility held to be crucial to creative performance (Ashby *et al.*, 1999; Isen, 1997, 1999; Isen *et al.*, 1987; Isen *et al.*, 1992). A similar implication follows from Fredrickson's broaden-and-build theory of positive mood effects on cognition (Fredrickson, 2001, 2008).

In support of positive mood

In support of this notion, it has been found that induced positive mood leads to more inclusive conceptual categorizations, and more unusual associations to neutral words (Hirt, 1999; Isen and Daubman, 1984; Isen *et al.*, 1985; Murray *et al.*, 1990). Consistent with these results, Isen *et al.* (1987), in a series of four experiments, demonstrated that induced positive mood enhanced performance on a number of different creativity tasks, including an insight problem, and a remote associates task (cf. Greene and Noice, 1988). These findings are consistent with results from other studies, showing positive mood to increase fluency in divergent thinking tasks. Abele (1992a, 1992b) induced positive, negative, and neutral mood by way of autobiographical recall, and demonstrated that positive mood resulted in superior performance on ideational fluency tasks. Recently Phillips *et al.* (2002) and Hirt *et al.* (2008) replicated these findings in a positive–neutral mood contrast. Moreover, Vosburg (1998a, 1998b) recorded mood-at-arrival through an adjective checklist immediately prior to task performance and found that positive mood facilitated and negative mood inhibited fluency of idea production.

In a different approach, Martin *et al.* (1993) promoted a hedonic contingency theory of mood and information processing. A central tenet of this theory is that people strive to uphold their positive mood, and may prefer to engage in playful creative activities as part of this endeavor. Recently, Hirt *et al.* (2008) found that induced positive mood had a facilitating effect on various measures of divergent thinking. They argued that the results could best be explained in terms of a mood maintenance mechanism.

According to the cognitive tuning theory originally proposed by Schwarz (1990) and further developed by Schwarz and Bless (1991), Clore *et al.* (1994), and Schwarz and Clore (2003), the essential function of emotional states is to inform the individual about the state of the current task environment (cf. Frijda, 1986). Negative mood indicates a problematic situation, whereas positive mood signals a satisfactory state of affairs. On this theoretical premise, it was argued that individuals in negative mood will more likely be tuned to an analytic style of processing, where the situation is treated carefully and systematically, by way of what Fiedler (1988) has termed "tight" processing. In contrast, positive mood individuals will be more inclined to relax on the processing requirements, and use more "loose" processing and simplifying heuristics (Fiedler, 1988; Forgas, 2008). As part of this, they are held to be more willing to explore novel procedures and possibilities that could increase the likelihood of finding creative solutions. In the evidence reviewed by Abele (1992b), Davis (2009), Feist (1999), Fredrickson (2001), Hirt *et al.* (1996), Isen (1997, 1999, 2008), and Morris (1989), positive mood seems to fairly consistently yield facilitating effects on various indicators of exploratory, creative ideation under standard experimental laboratory conditions. Amabile *et al.* (2005) took this kind of inquiry to the field context and examined how affect is related to creativity in daily work settings. They used the daily diaries of 222 employees in 7 companies to examine the relationship between affective states and creativity. The results showed that positive affect was a consistent predictor of creativity in performing daily work tasks. However, the effects obtained were small, and the temporal, causal interpretations relied upon highly speculative ideas about mediating effects of putative incubation mechanisms.

In defiance of the singular positive mood hypothesis

Despite this mainstream trend of research on the effect of mood on creativity, it is important to recognize that significant exceptions to this pattern of findings have also been reported. Jausovec (1989) observed a confusing pattern of results, where the effect of positive mood on creative problem-solving tasks varied from task to task. In one task a facilitative effect of positive mood was obtained, but in another a detrimental effect emerged. In two other tasks no significant differences between positive and neutral mood were found. These findings call into question the results reported in the classical study by Isen *et al.* (1987), frequently cited in support of the standard positive-mood-promotes-creativity stance.

On an even more discordant note, Kaufmann and Vosburg (1997) demonstrated and replicated a reversal of the positive mood/creative problem-solving effect. In several studies, induced positive mood was found to have a detrimental effect on performance compared with both neutral and negative mood. In their theory, positive mood triggers a satisficing problem-solving strategy in these tasks, in contrast to negative mood that promotes optimizing. In deceptive insight tasks, positive mood may entice the participants to opt for quasi-solutions based on previous success in similar problems. This also accords well with the notion that positive mood promotes rapid processing based on previous experience, as conceived in the cognitive tuning model described earlier. This orientation may prevent positive mood-induced people from even detecting the impasse in these tasks (cf. Ash and Wiley, 2006). Detecting the impasse is, in turn, a necessary prerequisite to make the critical redefining maneuvers required to achieve entry to a new solution space containing high-quality, original, and insightful solutions. In contrast, negative mood would lead to extended search beyond apparent quasi-solutions, realize the impasse, and thus increase the likelihood of eventually arriving at insightful solutions. The "paradoxical" results observed by Kaufmann and Vosburg (1997) have recently been replicated in a web-based study by Verleur *et al.* (2007).

Closely related to the earlier findings, Gasper (2003) found induced positive mood, as compared to induced negative mood, to promote the classical Einstellung effect that leads to mental fixation in problem solving under conditions where the problem in question can no longer be solved by the standard rule used to solve a previous series of similar problems.

Interestingly, though, there was a tendency for positive mood to spontaneously favor a new solution under more unconstrained conditions, where both the standard and a novel procedure were possible options. In support of such findings, Vosburg (1998a, 1998b) found positive mood-at-arrival to favor unconstrained idea production. In line with all of these findings, Kaufmann and Vosburg (2002) observed a disordinal interaction, where induced positive mood facilitated idea production in early, unconstrained idea production and impeded idea production in subsequent idea production under more constrained and degraded idea production conditions. Similar findings have been observed recently by Baas *et al.* (2008), with anger and sadness as main contrasts. Anger promoted idea production in the early stages, while sadness was significantly more predictive of creativity in the later stages of idea production.

A recent study by Akinola and Mendes (2008) is particularly interesting because it represents a combination of our two streams of research on mood and creativity. They claim that low level of an adrenal steroid (dehydroepiandrosterone-sulfate, or DHEAS) has been linked to increased vulnerability for negative affect/depression. In their study, they set out to investigate the effect of induced positive and negative mood on creativity as moderated by variations in DHEAS levels among their participants. Level of DHEAS was obtained through a saliva sample prior to the experiment. Positive and negative mood were manipulated by way of positive and negative feedback on a task unrelated to the experimental task. Creativity was measured through a standardized artistic collage task developed and validated by Amabile (1982, 1996). The results showed that the negative mood manipulation had a significant facilitating effect on creativity, and that there was an interaction between DHEAS levels and creative task performance, such that those with lower DHEAS in the negative feedback condition obtained the highest score on the artistic collage task. Through a mediated moderation analysis, the authors showed that negative emotional changes mediated the link between vulnerability for negative affect and creativity for those receiving negative feedback.

In a recent series of studies conducted in a field context (George and Zhou, 2002, 2007), negative mood was also shown to be significantly related to supervisor and peer ratings of creativity, given the presence of certain, positive contextual conditions (e.g., idea and leader support).

The big picture

Recently, we have seen the publication of two meta-analyses of the complicated pattern of results obtained in the mood and creativity field. Davis (2009) concludes his meta-analysis of the literature on the mood-and-creativity relation in favor of a contingency model. Here the effect of positive mood on creativity is affirmed, but held to be moderated by a number of boundary conditions, such as type of task. The contrast between positive and negative mood was not clear. The Davis (2009) analysis suffers, however, from many serious shortcomings. Inclusion criteria were designed in such a way that several findings favoring negative mood as facilitative of creativity were excluded. Indeed, many published findings in this category that did meet the inclusion criteria were also missing in the analysis. In addition to these limitations, clear mistakes in the classification of tasks were made, where, for instance, remote association tasks were labeled idea production tasks, rather than insight tasks, which is the standard way of categorization. Reclassification of these tasks will probably have a significant impact on the general conclusions that can be drawn from this meta-analysis.

The other meta-analysis was conducted by Baas *et al.* (2008). This is a much more comprehensive and inclusive analysis, where the results of the past previous 25 years of research in the field are reported and analyzed. Baas *et al.* (2008) conclude by joining forces with other reviewers of the literature who argue for a more balanced view on the relationship between mood and creativity (e.g., Kaufmann, 2003). Interestingly, Baas *et al.* (2008) advocate a dual-track model, where positive mood favors cognitive flexibility (crossing categories in idea production) and negative mood triggers the persistence in solution search efforts within a more narrowly and strategically defined area of the problem space. Persistence in search of a solution is often seen as a core requirement in creative thinking (e.g., Newell *et al.*, 1979). Another significant moderator of the valence effect of mood on creativity is, according to Baas *et al.* (2008), the significance of level of activation. They argue that the effects of positive and negative mood may occur only at high activation levels.

Mixed mood and creativity

So far we have considered positive and negative mood separately. But there is also the possibility that a state of mixed mood may incrementally influence creativity, particularly under the condition of complex creativity, as evidenced in our finding of the independent effect of a combination of elevated and depressed mood. In a laboratory context, this issue has been addressed in an interesting way by Fong (2006). She argues that a mixed mood (i.e., a simultaneous experience of both positive and negative mood) is much more frequently occurring than laymen, and also researchers in the field, believe (cf. Larsen *et al.*, 2001). Here she reviews a large number of experiments that show that people frequently report experiencing mixed moods, but when asked to recall their mood at a later stage they tend to fall down on reporting either positive or negative mood. The interpretation is that mixed mood is real, and occurs frequently, but that this experience is incongruent with our schematic conceptions of mood experiences – in other words, that they fall discretely into the two moods of positive and negative, and hardly occur as integrated companion components in our emotional experiences (see Barrett and Russell [1999] for a review of this debate).

From a cognitive tuning perspective, Fong (2006) argues that the experience of an ambivalent mood will naturally lead to the experience of the current situation, or task at hand, as unusual, anomalous, and atypical. The implication of this conception of the task environment is, according to Fong, to open up the problem space to allow for more unusual associations. In two experiments, this core hypothesis was tested by way of inducing positive, negative, neutral, and mixed mood through autobiographical recall and specially designed film clips. Creativity was measured by performance on the Remote Associates Test. The results showed that it was indeed possible to induce an ambivalent mood that could be distinguished from positive, negative, and neutral. Moreover, the results also showed that the ambivalent mood conditions yielded higher creativity performance than the comparison mood conditions.

From laboratory to the field on the mixed mood note

In a new study, George and Zhou (2007) observed a dual-mood effect of mood on creativity, where creativity was highest under the conditions of both high positive and negative mood, given high leader support. They also concluded by favoring a dual-track model of the effect of mood and creativity.

In a recent study, To *et al.* (2011) took as its point of departure the more elaborate dual-track models proposed earlier and examined the effect of mood in the more complex, real-life situation of doctoral and post-doctoral students working on their theses. A within-subjects experience sampling methodology was used where the participants frequently reported their moods. Creativity scores were obtained by way of a standardized method for measuring creative process engagement (CPE), as well as supervisory ratings. The results showed that both activating-positive and activating-negative moods were related to concurrent CPE. Deactivating positive and negative moods were both negatively related to CPE. Activating negative moods had a significant lagged effect on creativity, whereas activating positive moods did not. Interestingly, these findings stand in direct contradiction to the findings reported by Amabile *et al.* (2005), cited earlier.

Coordinating the pictures from the two streams of research on mood and creativity

We have now seen a picture emerge from the experimental literature on the effects of mood on creativity that is very much in line with the one painted by the mental/affective disorder and creativity literature. Positive mood seems to enhance idea production and flexibility in the sense of allowing cross-categorization of ideas. But there is also a place for negative mood. According to Baas *et al.* (2008, 2011), this effect is due to increased persistence in targeted search for a solution. This is clearly in line with the theory offered by Kaufmann (2003) and George and Zhou (2007) who favor an interpretation along the lines of satisficing and optimizing, where satisficing may easily lead up to unconstrained idea development, and optimizing may favor the persistent and more constrained search in a more targeted area of the problem space. Last, but not least, there is also evidence in both streams of research to the effect that ambiguous or mixed mood may be a distinct condition that also can favor creativity.

Dual mood and dual thought

The theories described earlier may be said to offer important hints at a new framework to understand the complexities in navigating through the more general mood-and-creativity maze. However, it is also clear that such models offer only crude approximations of what is needed to get on top of the extensive research findings in the field. As already pointed out, our mission here is to focus only on the issues of how to deal with the relationship between mood and creativity from a cognitive perspective, not disregarding that many other important dimensions from fields like personality, biological, developmental, and social psychology are involved in the more comprehensive analysis of the mood-and-creativity equation.

What kind of theory may cognitive psychology have to offer that could lend itself to resolving the issues, square the many seemingly paradoxical findings, and offer an overarching theory that has the power to integrate the major findings, and also to provide more specific suggestions for productive, future lines of empirical research? A theory that has generated a lot of research and offers integrative perspectives in the field of thinking and reasoning is the dual-process theory of reasoning. As pointed out by Evans (2008), we should rather speak of dual-process *theories*, because there are many versions of this model, where the relative focus is on different aspects of thinking. Thus, these theories are often subsumed under the more general scheme of System 1 and System 2 thinking (e.g., Kahneman, 2011). Core features of System 1 are that it is fast, automatic (un-/preconscious), implicit, heuristic, associative, and intuitive, in the sense of responding to hunches and impressions, and relies heavily on past experience. System 2 is slow, deliberate, conscious, explicit, analytical–logical, and systematic–methodical, and relies on logical rules of inference.

It is often assumed, implicitly and explicitly, that creative thinking belongs to System 1, where "loose" and intuitive thinking is prevalent. Along with such assumptions, we see that a bulk of the research conducted within the experimental mood-and-creativity research has used some sort of divergent idea production as a measure of creativity. These are contentions that are highly fallible for a number of reasons. As pointed out by many researchers in the field, most of the thinking that meets the criteria for creativity needs to draw on both types of processes in order to be successful (e.g., Allen and Thomas, 2011; Dreyfus, 2009; Hélie and Sun, 2010). At best, only a half-baked account of what is minimally involved in creative thought can be delivered by idea production tasks of the divergent thinking type, as pointed out by Zeng *et al.* (2011). This is not about "ecological validity." It is about minimal construct validity. So what is missing in the idea production paradigm for measuring creativity? Zeng *et al.* (2011) claim that, at least, the two criteria of novelty and appropriateness (value) have to be met by a valid operationalization of creativity. In the standard tests of idea production normally used in the field, there is a fundamental lack of taking into account the crucial element of appropriateness. Furthermore, to arrive at creative solutions to problems, there has to be an integration of the processing involved in problem definition, development of ideas, and deciding on a solution that fully meets the constraints of the task. Such integrated processing may be tapped through insight problems, but it is not to a minimal degree captured through the idea production tasks. This latter point is made forcibly in a new theory of creative problem solving offered by Hélie and Sun (2010). They distinguish between implicit and explicit thinking processes, and place creativity at the intersection of the integration of the results of both implicit and explicit processes. They highlight conditions where implicit and explicit thinking are on a collision course and yield different outcomes. Solving such conflicts is often crucial to arriving at new and insightful solutions to complex creative problems (cf. Allen and Thomas, 2011).

Theories of the dual-process kind have largely been developed within the reasoning tradition dealing with various sorts of logical thinking tasks. This is a somewhat closed domain, compared with the domain of creative thinking that can be more fully understood from a perspective of problem solving. In order to cast the net a little wider and also to put some more meat on the bones, we will now describe a theory of mood and creativity based on original formulations suggested by Kaufmann (2003), which could be regarded as a problem-solving variant of a dual-process theory.

A theory of mood effects on creative problem solving

A theory of mood effects on creative problem solving needs to be anchored in a more general theoretical perspective on the functions of emotions, particularly with respect to their role in cognition.

In general, we agree with Frijda's (1986) functionalist account of emotions, where emotions are seen as basically having a signal, or heuristic cue function (cf. Kaufmann, 2003; Vosburg and Kaufmann, 1999). More specifically, we agree with the basic premise behind the cognitive tuning theory developed by Clore *et al.* (1994; see also Schwarz, 2000). Here a positive emotional state signals a satisfactory state in the task environment, whereas a negative emotional state signals that the task environment is problematic. Thus, mood may induce a "frame of mind" (cf. Morris, 1989) that serves as a mental backdrop for choosing a particular strategy to deal with the task at hand.

The principles stated earlier may now be applied more specifically to different aspects of problem solving, and testable hypotheses may be derived. Different levels of abstraction may be chosen for the development of a theory in this field. For the present purpose, we will focus on four general dimensions of problem solving. These are: (1) *Problem perception* – how the problem is represented to the individual in general terms; (2) *Solution requirements* – what the criteria are for an adequate solution to the problem; (3) *Process* – what type of processing of problem information is most adequate to deal with the problem at hand; and (4) *Strategy* – what kind of general method or tactic of solving the problem is required.

Mood and problem perception

Fundamental to problem perception is the question of whether we will or can understand the existing task environment in terms of familiar schemas that need only modifications within a familiar frame, or if the current situation represents a more fundamental restructuring and redefinition in order to be handled appropriately. In the first case we are talking about what Piaget called assimilation, and in the second we are dealing with accommodation. It is interesting to note here that accommodation was Piaget's mechanism for creative thinking, where deeper and more far-reaching restructuring or re-ordering of schemata was required (e.g., Furth, 1969).

Here we can clearly see how tenets from the cognitive tuning theory can be applied. A positive mood is supposed to elicit the frame of the current situation as satisfying and straightforward. Thus we should expect positive mood to make the problem solver bent on an assimilative style of problem perception. This will work fine when the conditions of familiarity are met, and result in rapid and highly effective processing and problem solving. When these conditions are not met, however, and the conditions are such that a major reorganizing of existing schemata or scripts is required, it becomes necessary to take a closer look at the crucial elements that are discrepant. We have to slow down processing to a more detailed and careful examination of the critical elements that make the situation not fit into a ready-made category, with well-known procedures to handle it sufficiently. A System 2 type of handling now becomes apt, and may even be essential. System 2 is generally assumed to come alive when a situation surpasses a critical threshold of novelty and stands in need of an accommodative approach to meet requirements. We see clearly that negative mood may come in handy here, and provide the relevant cue for framing the situation as problematic, uncertain, and in need of accommodative Type 2 processing in order to move forward in the task environment. The theory then claims that positive mood encourages an assimilative mode of problem perception and negative mood triggers an accommodative framing of the problem. Here we may also add a note on what Guilford (1967) reminded us when he pointed to the crucial importance of *problem sensitivity* in creativity. Being able to see that the present situation does indeed represent a problem may be crucial in anticipating proactive, necessary adjustments of an innovative kind (see Kaufmann, 2004).

Mood and solution requirements

There are many different considerations to be made in describing the requirements for a good or appropriate solution. A cardinal considera-tion may, however, be said to reside in the distinction between optimizing versus satisficing criteria originally proposed by Simon (e.g., 1956) and further developed by Simon (1977) and March (1994). Rather than view-ing these criteria as distinct categories, we have previously argued that it is more convenient to regard them as opposite, extreme points on a con-tinuum (Kaufmann, 2003; Kaufmann and Vosburg, 1997; Vosburg and Kaufmann, 1999). At the satisficing end of this continuum, the individ-ual is held to construct a simplified mental model of the solution space, and accept the first solution that meets the corresponding aspiration level for an adequate solution. At the optimizing end of the continuum, the individual will attempt to perform an exhaustive search and rational evaluation of the expected utilities of all alternative solutions available. Kaufmann and Vosburg (1997) posited that positive mood would pro-mote a satisficing strategy of solution finding, whereas negative mood would be more appropriate under optimizing conditions. In their exper-iments testing these notions, the tasks employed ranked extremely high in solution requirements (ingenious and highly unconventional solutions were required to fulfill all the solution requirements). They explained their findings that positive mood was detrimental and negative mood facilitative of finding the ingenious, "ideal" solutions with reference to the hypothesis that positive mood promotes a satisficing and negative mood an optimizing solution strategy.

One important determinant of solution criteria along this continuum is the degree to which the task environment is perceived as satisfactory or problematical. Carrying this argument a step further, we may also argue that satisficing versus optimizing criteria will be applied in the course of solving a problem, and that different individuals may settle for solutions of highly different quality. From the theory presented earlier, it follows that being in a positive mood will lead to perceiving a task as less requiring of high-quality solutions than when being in a negative mood, when a stricter criterion for an acceptable solution is more likely to be upheld, and extended search required.

We may now posit the general principle that positive mood will promote a satisficing strategy of solution finding, whereas negative mood will be more appropriate under optimizing conditions. The former is a System 1 and the latter is a System 2 type of thinking.

Mood and type of process

In cognitive information-processing theory, kind of process is often distinguished in terms of level of processing and breadth of processing (Anderson, 1990).

Level of processing refers to the question of whether processing occurs at a surface level, such as the sensory level, or at a deeper level, such as the semantic level, where information is further processed in terms of meaning and organizational structure in memory. Breadth of processing refers to the distance between informational units that are related during processing.

As we have seen earlier, the breadth dimension has been particularly targeted by mood theories (e.g., Baas et al., 2008; Isen and Daubman, 1984; Isen et al., 1985). One possible explanation is that positive material is more richly interconnected than negative material, and that positive mood may provide a retrieval cue for linking information at a broader level, as suggested by Isen and Daubman (1984). This hypothesis also entails, however, that positive material is better organized than negative material. We should then expect that positive mood promotes both higher level and broader information processing than negative mood. In our theory, however, positive mood is linked to broader information processing on the premise that positive mood promotes a less problematic perception of the task, and possibly also to overconfidence in ability to handle the task in question. Thus, positive mood may lead to a less cautious approach to the task than negative mood. The downside of this attitude is that it may also lead to a more superficial processing. More precisely, our theory implies that positive mood promotes broad and shallow processing, whereas negative mood leads to narrower but deeper processing. This may be an advantage in a task that requires the generation of new ideas, but it may be detrimental when a task requires careful consideration and deeper processing. In line with this idea, Elsbach and Barr (1999) set out to observe the effect of induced positive and negative mood on the cognitive processing of information in a structured decision protocol. Here the subjects were given the task of assessing and weighing information in a complex case involving the core issue of whether a racing team should participate in an upcoming race. Negative mood subjects made much more careful and elaborate considerations than the positive mood subjects who were more prone to rely upon superficial, "holistic" judgment without going into the depth and details of the available information. Broad and shallow processing here are regarded as System 1, whereas narrow and deep processing are held to be the System 2 type of processing.

Mood and strategy

This is probably the dimension that has received the most attention in dual-process theories as well as in discussion of the effects of mood on problem-solving behavior. As stated earlier, several theorists claim that positive mood increases the likelihood of employing heuristic–intuitive strategies, whereas negative mood promotes the use of controlled, systematic, and analytic information-processing methods.

A hallmark of a heuristic strategy is, of course, simplification. Analytic strategies are costly in terms of cognitive economy, and often the problem solver has to resort to cruder and more general strategies in dealing with a fairly complex task. Choice of strategy may, however, also be determined by the general assessment of the structure of the task, and the individual's confidence in his or her ability to solve the problem. It follows, then, that positive mood would increase the likelihood of employing heuristic, shortcut strategies, whereas negative mood should lead to more cautious, analytic, and systematic methods of dealing with the task at hand. As we have argued earlier, System 2 also includes the kind of sustained analysis of problem spaces that resembles rumination, which also involves extensive use of counterfactual thinking, shown to be favorable to creative thought (e.g., Markman et al., 2007).

Mixed mood and mixed thought

We have now seen that there are ample grounds to expect that the effect of mood on creative thought is not just a matter of positive mood releasing a brainstorming kind of idea production. This may be an important and, indeed, vital component of the process, but it does not cover the whole territory to justify sweeping and one-sided claims that "positive mood promotes creativity" (e.g., Isen, 2008; Johnson *et al.*, 2012). On the contrary, we have seen that there are very good theoretical reasons to expect that, under important conditions, negative mood may provide the best mental context for the kind of processing that is required to achieve insightful solutions to complex problems. And, indeed, positive mood may be expected to have negative consequences under such conditions, in the same way as a negative mood may work strongly against the kind of loose, icebreaker type of processing that is most often required in tasks of creative thinking.

Mood swings, bipolarity, ambivalence, and creative thinking

The empirical evidence described and discussed earlier shows many examples where there is a separate, independent effect of a mixed mood on creativity, which is incremental to the separate effects of positive or negative mood, and also applies when we take level of activation into account. It is therefore likely that a comprehensive theory of mood effects on creativity must also provide a conceptual space for such effects. It is important too to address the question of what is meant specifically by a "mixed mood." It could be rapid swings from one mood to the other, or the simultaneous experience of both a positive and a negative mood. These different versions of mixed mood could indeed turn out to have different kinds of effect on creative problem solving. Rapid shifts, we expect, could lead to enhanced flexibility in shifting between different modes of thinking, as described in System 1 and System 2 models. A simultaneous experience of both positive and negative mood could lead, as posited by Fong (2006), to the perception of the existing situation as atypical and anomalous, which in turn may lead to opening up the problem space to incorporate unusual associations and lead to new insights.

Mood effects across domains and professional fields

It is a well-established finding that the relationship between mood disorders and creativity is strongest in the artistic field and among writers, in particular poets. It is present also in architects, but less so, and least among scientists (Feist, 1998). Many interesting explanations have been offered for the existence of this particular pattern (e.g., Simonton, this volume). It can be argued that there is also a piece of the puzzle that can be added, and should be explored, based on the cognitive perspective we have adopted here. The hypothesis we would like to offer is that the extent of a mood swing conducive to creative thinking may depend on the extent to which the domain requires high-level uses of and extensive shifts between System 1 and System 2 types of thinking. Ludwig (1998) pointed out that creative people in domains that require extensive logical and formal processes and experiences show less psychopathology than highly creative people in fields that require more intuitive and "emotive" engagements and expressions. In our terminology, we can understand this as a reflection of differential operations of System 1 and System 2 processes. Such a view accords well with findings showing more psychopathology among eminent social scientists than in the natural sciences. Particularly interesting is also the higher incidence of psychopathology in "paradigm-breaking" (innovator) versus "paradigm-preserving" (adaptor) oriented scientists demonstrated by Ko and Kim (2008). Such findings are consistent with the hypothesis we have advanced earlier to the effect that mixed moods may be particularly congenial to creativity of a more complex nature.

Conclusion

We have argued that the framework we have presented here may indeed address both streams of research and serve as an integrative theory to understand the kind of mood effects observed in the two research streams in the mood-and-creativity field.

Positive and negative mood effects show themselves in both streams of research in a theory-consistent way, as does mixed mood as an experiential frame of mind for complex creative thought. Thus there is also a significant place for mood volatility in the understanding of the manifold of findings in both streams of research. The theory focuses on the effect of mood on creativity and not on the effect of disorder. The most productive cases may indeed be those where the stronger kind of mood swings and aberrations are not rampant, and where the individual may be able to keep an "unquiet mind" (Jamison, 1995) within the outer limits of what is profitable in order to achieve high levels of creativity. It is important to identify mitigating conditions that are relevant here, such as the high level of working memory capacity suggested and shown by Carson (2011; also in this volume) and Carson et al. (2003).

References

Abele, A. (1992a). Positive and negative mood influences on creativity: Evidence for asymmetrical effects. *Polish Psychological Bulletin*, 23, 203–221.

Abele, A. (1992b). Positive versus negative mood influences on problem solving: A review. *Polish Psychological Bulletin*, 23, 187–202.

Akinola, M. and Mendes, W. B. (2008). The dark side of creativity: Biological vulnerability and negative emotions lead to greater artistic creativity. *Personality and Social Psychology Bulletin*, 34, 1677–1686.

Akiskal, H. S. and Akiskal, K. K. (1994). Temperaments et humeur des musiciens de blues [Temperament and mood blues musicians]. *Nervure*, 8, 28–204.

Akiskal, K. K., Savino, M. and Akiskal, H. S. (2005). Temperament profiles in physicians, lawyers, managers, industrialists, architects, journalists, and artists: A study in psychiatric outpatients. *Journal of Affective Disorders*, 85, 201–206.

Allen, A. P. and Thomas, K. B. (2011). A dual process account of creative thinking. *Creativity Research Journal*, 23(2), 109–118.

Amabile, T. M. (1982). Social psychology of creativity: A consensual assessment technique. *Journal of Personality and Social Psychology*, 43, 997–1013.

Amabile, T. M. (1989). *Growing up creative*. Norwalk, CT: Crown House Publishing.

Amabile, T. M. (1996). *Creativity in context*. Boulder, CO: Westview Press.

Amabile, T. M., Barsade, S. G., Mueller, J. S. and Staw, B. M. (2005). Affect and creativity at work. *Administrative Science Quarterly*, 50, 367–403.

Andersen, I., Thielen, K., Bech, P. and Diderichsen, F. (2011). Increasing prevalence of depression from 2000 to 2006. *Scandinavian Journal of Public Health*, 39, 857–863.

Anderson, J. R. (1990). *Cognitive psychology and its implications* (3rd edn.). New York: Freeman.

Andreasen, N. C. (1987). Creativity and mental illness: Prevalence rates in writers and their first-degree relatives. *American Journal of Psychiatry*, 144, 1288–1292.

Andrews, P. W. and Thomson, J. A. (2009). The bright side of being blue: Depression as an adaptation for analyzing complex problems. *Psychological Review*, 116, 620–654.

Ash, I. K. and Wiley, J. (2006). The nature of restructuring in insight: An individual-differences approach. *Psychonomic Bulletin Review*, 13(1), 66–73.

Ashby, F. G., Isen, A. M. and Turken, A. U. (1999). A neuropsychological theory of positive affect and its influence on cognition. *Psychological Review*, 106, 529–550.

Baas, M., De Dreu, C. K. W. and Nijstad, B. A. (2008). A meta-analysis of 25 years of mood-creativity research: Hedonic tone, activation, or regulatory focus? *Psychological Bulletin*, 6, 779–806.

Baas, M., De Dreu, C. K. W. and Nijstad, B. A. (2011). Creative production by angry people peaks early on, decreases over time, and is relatively unstructured. *Journal of Experimental Psychology*, 47, 1107–1115.

Barrett, L. F. and Russell, J. A. (1999). The structure of current affect: Controversies and emerging consensus. *Current Directions in Psychological Science*, 8, 10–14.

Carson, S. H. (2011). Creativity and psychopathology: A shared vulnerability model. *Canadian Journal of Psychiatry*, 56, 144–153.

Carson, S. H., Peterson, J. B. and Higgins, D. M. (2003). Decreased latent inhibition is associated with increased creative achievement in high-functioning individuals. *Journal of Personality and Social Psychology*, 85, 499–506.

Clore, L., Schwarz, N. and Conway, M. (1994). Affective causes and consequences of social information processing. In R. S. Wyer, Jr. and T. K. Srull (Eds.), *Handbook of social cognition: Vol. 1. Basic processes* (2nd edn.) (pp. 323–417). Hillsdale, NJ: Erlbaum.

Damasio, A. R. (1994). *Descartes' error: Emotion, reason, and the human brain.* New York: Grosset/Putnam.

Davis, M. A. (2009). Understanding the relationship between mood and creativity: A meta-analysis. *Organizational Behavior and Human Decision Processes*, 108, 25–38.

De Houwer, J. and Hermans, D. (2010). *Cognition and emotion: Reviews of current research and theories.* New York: Psychology Press.

Dreyfus, S. E. (2009). A modern perspective on creative cognition. *Bulletin of Science, Technology and Society*, 29, 3–8.

Duncker, K. (1945). *Psychological Monographs*, 5 (Whole No. 270).

Elsbach, K. E. and Barr, P. S. (1999). The effect of moods on individuals' use of structured decision processes. *Organization Science*, 10, 181–189.

Evans, J. St. B.T. (2008). Dual-processing accounts of reasoning, judgment, and social cognition. *Annual Review of Psychology*, 59, 255–278.

Feist, G. J. (1998). A meta-analysis of personality in scientific and artistic creativity. *Personality and Social Psychology Review*, 2, 290–309.

Feist, G. J. (1999). The influence of personality on artistic and scientific creativity. In R. J. Sternberg (Ed.), *Handbook of creativity* (pp. 273–296). Cambridge, UK: Cambridge University Press.

Fiedler, K. (1988). Emotional mood, cognitive style, and behavior regulation. In K. Fiedler and J. Forgas (Eds.), *Affect, cognition and social behavior* (pp. 100–119). Göttingen: Hofgrefe.

Fong, C. T. (2006). The effects of emotional ambivalence on creativity. *Academy of Management Journal*, 49, 1016–1030.

Forgas, J. P. (1995). Mood and judgment: The affect infusion model. *Psychological Bulletin*, 117, 39–66.

Forgas, J. P. (2008). Affect and cognition. *Perspectives on Psychological Science*, 3, 94–101.

Fredrickson, B. L. (2001). The role of positive emotions in positive psychology: The broaden-and-build theory of positive emotions. *American Psychologist*, 56, 218–226.

Fredrickson, B. L. and Branigan, C. (2005). Positive emotions broaden the scope of attention and thought-action repertoires. *Cognition and Emotion*, 19, 313–332.

Fredrickson, B. L., Cohn, M. A., Coffey, K. A., Pek, J. and Finkel, S. M. (2008). Open hearts build lives: Positive emotions, induced through loving-kindness meditation, build consequential personal resources. *Journal of Personality and Social Psychology*, 95, 1045–1062.

Frijda, N. H. (1986). The laws of emotion. *American Psychologist*, 43, 349–358.

Furnham, A., Batey, M., Anand, K. and Manfield, J. (2008). Personality, hypomania, intelligence and creativity. *Personality and Individual Differences*, 44, 1060–1069.

Furth, H. G. (1969). *Piaget and knowledge: Theoretical foundations*. University of Chicago.

Galvez, J. F., Thommi, S. and Ghaemi, S. N. (2011). Positive aspects of mental illness: A review in bipolar disorder. *Journal of Affective Disorders*, 128, 185–190.

Gasper, K. (2003). When necessity is the mother of invention: Mood and problem solving. *Journal of Experimental Social Psychology*, 39, 248–262.

George, J. M. and Zhou, J. (2002). Understanding when bad moods foster creativity and good ones don't: The role of context and clarity of feelings. *Journal of Applied Psychology*, 87, 687–697.

George, J. M. and Zhou, J. (2007). Dual tuning in a supportive context: Joint contributions of positive mood, negative mood, and supervisory behaviors to employee creativity. *Academy of Management Journal*, 50, 605–622.

Goodwin, F. K. and Jamison, K. R. (2007). *Manic-depressive illness: Bipolar disorders and recurrent depression*. New York: Oxford University Press.

Greene, T. R. and Noice, H. (1988). Influence of positive affect upon creative thinking and problem solving in children. *Psychological Reports*, 63, 895–898.

Guilford, J. P. (1967). *The nature of human intelligence*. New York: McGraw-Hill.

Hélie, S. and Sun, R. (2010). Incubation, insight, and creative problem solving: A unified theory and a connectionist model. *Psychological Review*, 117, 994–1024.

Hennessey, B. A. and Amabile, T. M. (2010). Creativity. *Annual Review of Psychology*, 61, 569–598.

Hirt, E. R. (1999). Mood. In M. A. Runco and S. R. Pritzker (Eds.), *Encyclopedia of creativity* (Vol. 2) (pp. 241–250). San Diego, CA: Academic Press.

Hirt, E. R., Dreyers, E. T. and McCrae, S. M. (2008). I want to be creative: Exploring the role of hedonic contingency theory in the positive mood–cognitive flexibility link. *Journal of Personality and Social Psychology*, 94, 214–230.

Hirt, E. R., McDonald, H. E. and Melton, R. J. (1996). Processing goals and the affect–performance link: Mood as main effect or mood as input? In L. L. Martin and A. Tesser (Eds.), *Striving and feeling: Interactions among goals, affect, and self-regulation* (pp. 303–328). Mahwah, NJ: Erlbaum.

Isen, A. M. (1997). Positive affect and decision making. In W. M. Goldstein and R. A. Hogarth (Eds.), *Research on judgment and decision making* (pp. 509–534). Cambridge, UK: Cambridge University Press.

Isen, A. M. (1999). On the relationship between affect and creative problem solving. In S. W. Russ (Ed.), *Affect, creative experience and psychological adjustments* (pp. 3–17). Philadelphia, PA: Brunner/Mazel.

Isen, A. M. (2008). Some ways in which positive affect influences decision making and problem solving. In M. Lewis, J. M. Haviland-Jones and L. F. Barrett (Eds.), *Handbook of emotions* (pp. 548–573). New York: Guilford Press.

Isen, A. M. and Daubman, K. A. (1984). The influence of affect on categorization. *Journal of Personality and Social Psychology*, 47, 1206–1217.

Isen, A. M., Daubman, K. A. and Nowicki, G. P. (1987). Positive affect facilitates creative problem solving. *Journal of Personality and Social Psychology*, 52, 1122–1131.

Isen, A. M., Johnson, M. M. S., Mertz, E. and Robinson, G. (1985). The influence of positive affect on the unusualness of word associations. *Journal of Personality and Social Psychology*, 48, 1413–1426.

Isen, A. M., Niedenthal, P. and Cantor, N. (1992). An influence of positive affect on social categorization. *Motivation and Emotion*, 16, 65–78.

Jamison, K. R. (1993). *Touched with fire: Manic-depressive illness and the artistic temperament*. New York: Free Press.

Jamison, K. R. (1995). *An unquiet mind*. New York: Random House.

Jausovec, N. (1989). Affect in analogical transfer. *Creativity Research Journal*, 2, 255–266.

Johnson, S. L., Murray, G., Fredrickson, B., Youngstrom, E. A., Hinshaw, S., Bass Malbranchcq, J. *et al.* (2012). The effect of emotion inductions on creative thinking. Creativity and bipolar disorder: Touched by fire or burning with questions? *Clinical Psychology Review*, 32, 1–12.

Kahneman, D. (2011). *Thinking, fast and slow*. New York: Farrar, Straus and Giroux.

Kaufman, J. C. and Baer, J. (2002). I bask in dreams of suicide: Mental illness, poetry, and women. *Review of General Psychology*, 6, 271–286.

Kaufman, J. C. and Sternberg, R. J. (2010). *The Cambridge handbook of creativity*. New York: Cambridge University Press.

Kaufmann, G. (1993). The content and logical structure of creativity concepts: An inquiry into the conceptual foundations of creativity research. In S. G. Isaksen, M. C. Murdock, R. L. Firestien and D. J. Treffinger (Eds.), *Understanding and recognizing creativity: The emergence of a discipline* (pp. 141–157). Norwood, NJ: Ablex.

Kaufmann, G. (2003). The effect of mood on creativity in the innovative process. In L. Shavinina (Ed.), *International handbook on innovation* (pp. 191–203). New York: Erlbaum.

Kaufmann, G. (2004). Two kinds of creativity: But which ones? *Creativity and Innovation Management*, 13, 154–165.

Kaufmann, G. and Kaufmann, A. (2012). *Bipolarity adds to hypomania in predicting complex creativity*. Unpublished manuscript.

Kaufmann, G. and Vosburg, S. K. (1997). "Paradoxical" mood effects on creative problem solving. *Cognition and Emotion*, 11, 151–170.

Kaufmann, G. and Vosburg, S. K. (2002). The effects of mood on early and late idea production. *Creativity Research Journal*, 14, 317–330.

Kinney, D. K. and Richards, R. L. (2007). Artistic creativity and affective disorders: Are they connected? In C. Martindale, P. Locher and V. M. Petrov (Eds.), *Evolutionary and neurocognitive approaches to aesthetics, creativity and the arts* (pp. 225–237). Amityville, NY: Baywood Publishing Co.

Ko, Y. and Kim, J. (2008). Scientific geniuses' psychopathology as a moderator in the relation between creative contribution types and eminence. *Creativity Research Journal*, 20, 251–261.

Kyaga, S., Landén, M., Boman, M., Hultman, C. M. and Långström, N. (2013). Mental illness, suicide and creativity: 40-year prospective total population study. *Journal of Psychiatric Research*, 47, 83–90.

Larsen, J. T., McGraw, A. P. and Cacioppo, J. (2001). Can people feel happy and sad at the same time? *Journal of Personality and Social Psychology*, 81, 684–696.

Lewis, M., Haviland-Jones, J. M. and Barrett, L. F. (2008). *Handbook of emotions* (3rd edn.). New York: Guilford Press.

Lloyd-Evans, R., Batey, M. and Furnham, A. (2006). Bipolar disorder and creativity: Investigating a possible link. In A. Columbus (Ed.), *Advances in psychology research*, 40. New York: Nova Press.

Ludwig, A. M. (1995). *The price of greatness: Resolving the creativity and madness controversy*. New York: Guilford Press.

Ludwig, A. M. (1998). Method and madness in the arts and sciences. *Creativity Research Journal*, 11, 93–101.

March, J. (1994). *A primer of decision making*. New York: Simon & Schuster.

Markman, K. D., Lindberg, M. J., Kray, L. J. and Gralinsky, A. D. (2007). Implications of counterfactual structure for creative generation and analytical problem-solving. *Personality and Social Psychology Bulletin*, 33, 312–324.

Martin, L. L. (2000). Moods do not convey information: Moods in context do. In J. P. Forgas (Ed.), *Feeling and thinking: The role of affect in social cognition* (pp. 153–177). New York: Cambridge University Press.

Martin, L. L., Ward, D. W., Achee, J. W. and Wyer, R. S. (1993). Mood as input: People have to interpret the motivational implications of their moods. *Journal of Personality and Social Psychology*, 64, 317–326.

Morris, W. N. (1989). *Mood: The frame of mind*. New York: Springer.

Murray, N., Sujan, H., Hirt, E. R. and Sujan, M. (1990). The influence of mood on categorization: A cognitive flexibility interpretation. *Journal of Personality and Social Psychology*, 59, 411–425.

Newell, A., Shaw, J. C. and Simon, H. A. (1979). The processes of creative thinking. In H. A. Simon (Ed.), *Models of thought* (Vol. 1) (pp. 144–174). New Haven, CT: Yale University Press.

Phillips, L. H., Louise, H., Bull, R., Adams, E. and Fraser, L. (2002). Positive mood and executive function: Evidence from Stroop tasks. *Emotion*, 2, 12–22.

Pollack-Kagan, S. and McCabe, R. C. (2010). Mood disorders and creativity. In P. C. McCabe and S. R. Shaw (Eds.), *Psychiatric disorders* (pp. 41–49). Thousand Oaks, CA: Sage.

Power, M. and Dalgleish, T. (2008). *Cognition and emotion: From order to disorder* (2nd edn.). New York: Psychology Press.

Prisciandaro, J. J. and Roberts, J. E. (2011). Evidence for the continuous latent structure of mania in the epidemiologic catchment area from multiple latent structure and construct validation methodologies. *Psychological Medicine*, 41, 575–588.

Rank, J. and Frese, M. (2008). The impact of emotions, moods and other affect-related variables on creativity, innovation and initiative. In N. M. Ashkanasy and C. L. Cooper (Eds.), *Research companion to emotions in organizations* (pp. 103–119). Cheltenham, UK: Edward Elgar Publishing.

Richards, R. L. (1994). Creativity and bipolar mood swings: Why the association? In M. P. Shaw and M. A. Runco (Eds.), *Creativity and affect* (pp. 44–72). Norwood, NJ: Ablex.

Richards, R. L. and Kinney, D. K. (1990). Mood swings and creativity. *Creativity Research Journal*, 3, 202–217.

Richards, R. L., Kinney, D. K., Benet, M. and Merzel, A. (1988). Assessing everyday creativity. *Journal of Personality and Social Psychology*, 54, 476–485.

Rothenberg, A. (1990a). *Creativity and madness: New findings and old stereotypes.* Baltimore, MD: Johns Hopkins University Press.

Rothenberg, A. (1990b). Creativity, mental health and alcoholism. *Creativity Research Journal*, 3, 179–201.

Rybakowski, J. K. and Klonowska, P. (2011). Bipolar mood disorder, creativity and schizotypy: An experimental study. *Psychopathology*, 44, 296–302.

Schlesinger, J. (2012). *The insanity hoax: Exposing the myth of the mad genius.* New York: Ardsley-on-Hudson.

Schuldberg, D. (1990). Schizotypical and hypomanic traits, creativity, and psychological health. *Creativity Research Journal*, 3, 218–230.

Schwarz, N. (1990). Feelings as information: Informational and motivational functions of affective states. In E. T. Higgins and R. Sorrentino (Eds.), *Handbook of motivation and cognition: Foundations of social behavior* (Vol. 2) (pp. 527–561). New York: Guilford Press.

Schwarz, N. (2000). Emotion, cognition and decision making. *Cognition and Emotion*, 14, 433–440.

Schwarz, N. and Bless, H. (1991). Happy and mindless, but sad and smart? The impact of affective states on analytic reasoning. In J. Forgas (Ed.), *Emotion and social judgement* (pp. 55–71). Oxford: Pergamon.

Schwarz, N. and Clore, G. L. (2003). Mood as information: 20 years later. *Psychological Inquiry*, 14, 296–303.

Shapiro, P. J. and Weisberg, R. W. (1999). Creativity and bipolar diathesis: Common behavioral and cognitive components. *Cognition & Emotion*, 13, 741–762.

Silvia, P. J. and Kimbrel, N. A. (2010). A dimensional analysis of creativity and mental illness: Do anxiety and depression symptoms predict creative cognition, creative accomplishments, and creative self-concepts? *Psychology of Aesthetics, Creativity, and the Arts*, 4, 2–10.

Simon, H. A. (1956). Rational choice and the structure of the environment. *Psychological Review*, 63, 129–138.

Simon, H. A. (1977). *The new science of management decision.* Englewood Cliffs, NJ: Prentice-Hall.

Simon, H. A. (1979). *Models of thought.* New Haven, CT: Yale University Press.

Staw, B. M. and Barsade, S. G. (1993). Affect and managerial performance: A test of the sadder-but-wiser vs. happier-and-smarter hypotheses. *Administrative Science Quarterly*, 38, 304–331.

To, M. L., Fisher, C. D., Ashkanasy, N. M. and Rowe, P. A. (2011). Within-person relationships between mood and creativity. *Journal of Applied Psychology*. doi:10.1037/a0026097

Verhaeghen, P., Joormann, J. and Khan, R. (2005). Why we sing the blues: The relation between self-reflective rumination, mood and creativity. *Emotion*, 5, 226–232.

Verleur, R., Verhagen, P. W. and Heuvelman, A. (2007). Can mood-inducing videos affect problem solving in a web-based environment? *British Journal of Technology*, 38, 1010–1019.

Vosburg, S. K. (1998a). The effects of positive and negative mood on divergent-thinking performance. *Creativity Research Journal*, 11, 165–172.

Vosburg, S. K. (1998b). Mood and the quantity and quality of ideas. *Creativity Research Journal*, 11, 315–324.

Vosburg, S. and Kaufmann, G. (1999). Mood and creativity research: The view from a conceptual organizing perspective. In S. W. Russ (Ed.), *Affect, creative experience, and psychological adjustment* (pp. 19–39). Philadelphia, PA: Brunner/Mazel.

Zeng, L., Proctor, R. W. and Salvendy, G. (2011). Can traditional divergent thinking tests be trusted in measuring and predicting real-world creativity? *Creativity Research Journal*, 23, 24–37.

11 Attention-deficit/hyperactivity disorder and creativity: ever the twain shall meet?

Dione Healey

Attention-deficit/hyperactivity disorder (ADHD) is the existing label for one of the most prevalent and vigorously studied conditions in child psychology. It is seen as a developmental neurocognitive disorder where the core symptoms include extreme inattention and hyperactive/impulsive behavior, which cause significant impairment in functioning. It is conservatively estimated to occur in 3–6 percent of children from varied cultures and geographical regions, with an overrepresentation of boys by approximately three to one (APA, 2000). ADHD affects individuals throughout the life span, although there are age- and gender-related changes in its manifestation (Barkley, 1998; Tannock, 1998; Weiss and Hechtman, 1993).

Similarities between children with ADHD and those who are creative

Some authors have argued that there are distinct similarities between children who are diagnosed with ADHD and those who are creative (Cramond, 1994; Guenther, 1995; Leroux and Levitt-Perlman, 2000; Lovecky, 1994; Shaw and Brown, 1991). For instance, Guenther (1995) noted that many of the features of ADHD, such as inattention, hyperactivity, impulsivity, difficult temperament, deficient social skills, and academic underachievement, are also found in children who are creative. In accordance with this, Dawson (1997) found that teachers rated the following traits as typical of a creative child: "makes up the rules as he or she goes along," "is impulsive," "is a non-conformist," and "is emotional." The traits seen as least typical of the creative child were "is tolerant," "is practical," "is reliable," and "is good natured"; similar ratings have been given in regard to children with ADHD. There is, however, often a distinct difference in the description of these similar behaviors across the two bodies of literature. In the ADHD literature, each characteristic is generally described with negative connotations, whereas in the creative literature the same characteristic is often described with positive connotations (Cramond, 1995). When describing inattention, children with ADHD are depicted as easily distracted, often failing to complete tasks, and frequently changing activities (Lahey et al., 1988); and creative children are depicted as having a broad range of interests, showing a tendency to play with ideas, and sometimes losing interest in one idea to take up another (Cramond, 1995). When describing hyperactivity, children with ADHD are depicted as fidgeting excessively, having difficulty staying seated, running and climbing excessively, and having difficulty playing quietly (McBurnett et al., 1993); and creative children are depicted as radiating vitality, having high energy levels, and showing psychomotor overexcitability (Daniels and Piechowski, 2009; Davis, 1986; Ochse, 1990; Piechowski, 1986). When describing impulsivity, children with ADHD are depicted as frequently calling out in class, acting without thinking, engaging in dangerous activities without considering the outcome, and having difficulty waiting their turn (McBurnett et al., 1993); and creative children are depicted as risk taking, thrill seeking, and with an innate temperamental trait of sensation seeking (Barron, 1988; Cramond, 1995; Healey and Rucklidge, 2006b).

In addition to the primary symptoms of ADHD (i.e., hyperactivity, impulsivity, and inattention), other characteristics of the disorder include difficult temperament, deficient social skills, and academic underachievement – all of which are seen among creative children as well (Kerr, 1985; Ochse, 1990; Sternberg, 1988). With regard to temperament, similar personality traits have been mentioned in the two bodies of literature, particularly in relation to risk-taking behavior. Children with ADHD often engage in physically dangerous activities without considering the possible consequences (APA, 2000). Creative children have been described as willing to take chances (Barron, 1988) and having Type T personality, a personality dimension that characterizes individuals along a continuum ranging from those who are excited by risk taking, stimulation seeking, and thrill seeking (Big T) to those who avoid risk, stimulation, and thrills (Little t) (Knutson and Farley, 1995). Shaw and Giambra (1993) noted that the inborn temperament of sensation seeking has been linked to both ADHD and creativity. Children with ADHD have a low sensory threshold and strong reactions to sensory stimuli (Barkley, 1998); and the same has been said about creative individuals (Bachtold, 1980). Children with ADHD have also been observed to have quick and drastic mood changes, and to exhibit a difficult temperament (Werry et al., 1987). Similarly, creative children seem to experience deep emotions (Sternberg, 1988) and to be emotionally unstable (Ochse, 1990). Additionally, many creative and ADHD children are reported to suffer from anxiety, depression, or bipolar disorder (Carlsson et al., 2000; Cox, 1999; Hershman and

Lieb, 1988; Jamison, 1993; Waskowic and Cramer, 1999; Weinberg and Ernslie, 1990).

Socially, children with ADHD have been reported to experience numerous difficulties in interacting with their peers (Barkley, 1998; Werry *et al.*, 1987). However, the findings in relation to social functioning in creative children are variable. It has been noted in the creativity literature that these children have difficulty with, or little interest in, establishing warm interpersonal relationships (Ochse, 1990); however, other studies have shown that creative children are seen as the most popular in a group (Aranha, 1997; Lau and Li, 1996). The conflicting literature on the social acceptance of highly creative children may be due to the fact that there are two basic types of creative children: (1) those who have behaviors very similar to children with ADHD, which have an impact on their social functioning; and (2) those who do not, and therefore are socially accepted. This would explain why not all of the creative children in past studies have exhibited elevations in ADHD symptomatology (Cramond, 1994; Healey and Rucklidge, 2006a).

With regard to academic functioning, children with ADHD struggle both within the classroom setting, because they are often very disruptive, and in keeping up with their academic work (Barkley, 1998). Similarly, highly creative children have been found to struggle to function well within traditional school environments (Amabile, 1989), and many are thought of as "gifted underachievers" (Kim, 2008).

The nature of the relationship between ADHD and creativity

Considering the many similarities between ADHD and creativity, the next step is to look at the nature of the relationship between these two phenomena. As mentioned earlier, not all creative children exhibit high levels of ADHD-like behaviors and not all children who have ADHD are creative (Cramond, 1994; Healey and Rucklidge, 2005); therefore, it is important to examine what may distinguish children with ADHD who are not creative from those who are; as well as from children who are creative and exhibit symptoms of ADHD, but do not meet the criteria for a diagnosis; and from those creative children who do not display any symptoms of ADHD. A growing body of literature has begun to try and unpack these issues across a range of areas – behavioral, psychosocial, temperamental, and cognitive.

Behavior

Shaw and Brown (1991) examined levels of creativity in children presenting with behaviors characteristic of ADHD and found that they used more imagery in problem solving than did normal control children, and attained much higher scores on a figural creativity test than did controls. They suggested that children with ADHD might generate novel or unusual ideas (i.e., show creativity) as a function of the different knowledge bases that they have acquired through their less focused interactions with their environments. However, a significant weakness of this study is that the children were all of high IQ (i.e., scores of 115 and above) and not formally diagnosed with ADHD; in fact, they were all "functioning adequately in ordinary schools" (p. 15), suggesting that they may not have met the impairment requirements for a diagnosis of ADHD. Cramond (1994) conducted a similar study where she tested a group of children with ADHD for creativity using the Torrance Tests of Creative Thinking and found that 32 percent scored high enough to have qualified for a creative scholars' program. She also tested a group of creative children for ADHD and found that 26 percent displayed significantly elevated symptoms of ADHD according to their self-reports. These percentages were significantly larger than what you would expect in the general population (Cramond, 1994). This research showed that there is definitely an overlap in the symptoms of ADHD and creativity, but, as in Shaw and Brown's (1991) study, there are two main flaws in this one – first, those in the ADHD group were not formally diagnosed: they were classified based on self-report; and, second, the IQs of the children in the ADHD group were high. ADHD samples usually have lower IQs than typically developing children and therefore the sample in this study is likely to have been biased. A third study looked at rates of ADHD diagnoses within gifted children and found that 9.4 percent of their gifted sample met the criteria for ADHD based on parent and teacher ratings and performance on a continuous performance task. However, it is not clear whether and how the authors assessed impairment in these children, nor how creative these gifted children were (Chae *et al.*, 2003).

To address some of these issues, Healey and Rucklidge (2005) compared the creative abilities of a group of 6–12-year-old children formally diagnosed with ADHD with those of a group of typically developing children. They found no group differences on their measures of creativity, which included the Torrance Tests of Creative Thinking and Maier's Two-String Problem. The authors concluded that, although children with ADHD can also be creative, they are no more likely to be creative than typically developing children, and therefore it is unlikely that creativity is a positive aspect for many or all children with ADHD. The key strength of this study was that the children went through a rigorous diagnostic process to confirm that they met the formal *DSM-IV* (APA, 2000) criteria for the disorder. In another study (Healey and Rucklidge, 2006a), the same authors examined the rates of formal ADHD diagnosis in a group of highly creative children and found that 40 percent of them were rated as displaying clinically elevated levels of ADHD symptomatology by parents on a standardized ADHD rating scale. This percentage was four times higher than would be expected within the general population, because the cut-off used to identify these children was 1.5 standard deviations above the mean, where one would expect approximately 9 percent of children in the general population to fall. However, despite clinically elevated symptoms, none of these creative children met the full diagnostic criteria for the disorder, mostly because they were not rated highly by teachers and were not exhibiting significant impairment in their functioning as a result of their symptoms (Healey and Rucklidge, 2006a). A diagnosis of ADHD requires the presence of symptoms across two or more settings *and* the symptoms need to cause significant impairment in functioning (APA, 2000). In relation to the types of symptoms displayed by the creative children in Healey and Rucklidge's (2006a) study, all but one child displayed elevated symptoms of inattention only, with the exception displaying symptoms of both inattention and hyperactivity/impulsivity.

Psychosocial functioning

Children with ADHD are well known to exhibit a wide array of comorbid disorders and to suffer from low self-esteem (Biederman *et al.*, 2004; Topolski *et al.*, 2004). The literature on the psychosocial functioning of creative children is less clear, with many discrepant findings reported. For example, Hershman and Lieb (1998) and Papworth and James (2003) both found that creative individuals experience high rates of low mood, yet Sitton and Hughes (1995) found no correlation between creativity and current depressive state (see Kaufmann and Kaufmann, this volume, for more on creativity and mood). The same patterns have been found in relation to self-esteem, with some studies reporting higher self-esteem in creative individuals (Goldsmith and Matherly, 1988; Kemple *et al.*, 1996) while others found no difference in the self-esteem of creative and non-creative individuals (Williams *et al.*, 1977). Additionally, some studies have shown higher rates of anxiety in creative children (Carlsson, 2002; Carlsson *et al.*, 2000) while others have found lower rates than in controls (Asthana, 1993; Matejik *et al.*, 1988). Finally, in relation to social functioning, on the one hand creative children have been described as lacking interest in others and displaying a low level of warmth in interpersonal relationships (Ochse, 1990); and on the other hand they have been found to be equally as sociable as controls (Smith and Moran, 1990), and described as the most popular in a group (Aranha, 1997; Lau and Li, 1996).

A possible explanation for these discrepant findings is that there are two types of creative children – those who display symptoms of ADHD and experience similar difficulties in psychosocial functioning to children diagnosed with ADHD; and those who do not exhibit any symptoms of ADHD and therefore do not experience any of the related psychosocial difficulties. In an attempt to examine whether this may be the case, Healey and Rucklidge (2006b) compared the psychosocial functioning of four groups of 6–12-year-old children: (1) diagnosed with ADHD but not creative; (2) creative and displaying elevated ADHD symptomatology, but not meeting diagnostic criteria for ADHD (CA); (3) creative without symptoms of ADHD (CNA); and (4) controls (NC). They found that, for parent ratings on the Child Behavior Checklist (CBCL), there were no significant differences between the ADHD and CA groups' Withdrawn and Anxious/Depressed scores, with both groups' scores significantly higher than the CNA and NC groups, who did not differ. Additionally, the children with ADHD had significantly higher Social Problems scores than the other three groups, with the CA group having significantly higher scores than the CNA and NC groups, who did not differ. Similarly, for teacher ratings of these three subscales on the CBCL, there were no differences between the ADHD and CA groups, but both differed significantly from the CNA and NC groups.

These findings are in line with those of Chae *et al.* (2003) who compared the social skills of gifted children with and without a diagnosis of ADHD and non-gifted children. They found that as a group the gifted children had significantly poorer social skills than the non-gifted children; and when they compared the gifted children with and without ADHD, those with ADHD had significantly poorer social skills than those without, indicating that the presence of ADHD symptoms is linked to the social skills deficits seen within gifted populations. Thus, in summary, it seems that those creative children who display symptoms of ADHD experience similar psychosocial difficulties to children with ADHD; and that those children who do not exhibit any ADHD symptoms seem to function similarly to typically developing children of their age.

Temperament

As with the behavioral and psychosocial findings, there are many similarities in the reported temperaments of children with ADHD and those who are creative. In particular, they are both seen as sensation seeking and rebellious (Barron, 1988; Farley, 1985; Runco and Sakamoto, 1996; Shaw and Giambra, 1993; Werry *et al.*, 1987). In their examination of similarities and differences between children with ADHD and those who are creative, Healey and Rucklidge (2006b – described earlier) also compared the temperaments of their four groups: ADHD, CA, CNA, and NC. They found that the CA and ADHD groups had very similar temperaments; and that their temperaments were significantly different from the CNA and NC groups, who also had similar temperaments. In particular, they found that for Persistence and Cooperativeness the ADHD and CA groups did not differ, and both had significantly lower scores than the CNA and NC groups, who also did not differ. Similarly, for Novelty Seeking, the ADHD and CA groups did not differ, and scored higher than the CNA and NC groups. Finally, for Self-directedness the ADHD group scored significantly lower than the CA, CNA, and NC groups; and the CA group scored significantly lower than the CNA and NC groups – indicating that, while the ADHD group scored the lowest, the CA group still had significantly lower scores than the CNA and NC groups, who did not differ. Thus, in tying the results together, this study showed a clear pattern whereby the ADHD group had the most extreme scores, and the CA group's scores tended to fall somewhere between the ADHD and the CNA and NC groups. Therefore, just like for behavioral and psychosocial functioning, there is a continuum where the CA group's scores fall in between those in the ADHD group and those in the CNA and NC groups, and are generally more similar to the ADHD than the CNA and NC groups.

Cognitive functioning

Although the literature shows that both ADHD and creative children may display very similar behavioral and emotional manifestations, there has only been one study directly comparing their cognitive functioning. Healey and Rucklidge (2006a) suggested that, given that creativity is seen as a unique problem-solving ability, one would assume that creative children have intact executive functioning abilities, and that this may be a key differential between the two groups. Children with ADHD are believed to have difficulties with executive functions, which are theorized as being manifested in the behavioral symptoms of ADHD (Barkley, 1998); and thus the question arises as to whether the creative children displaying ADHD-like behavior have similar executive functioning deficits, or whether the mechanisms underlying their behavioral manifestations are different from those potentially underlying ADHD.

In examining models of executive functioning and creativity Healey and Rucklidge (2006a) found distinct similarities between the two. Zelazo et al. (1997) proposed a problem-solving model of executive functions. The model divides problem solving into four separate stages where each stage involves the mastery of different executive functions. Zelazo et al.'s

Table 11.1 *Table showing the cognitive processes involved in each stage of Wallas' (1926) model of the creative process and Zelazo et al.'s (1997) model of the problem-solving process*

Wallas (1926)	Zelazo *et al.* (1997)
Preparation Involves motivation, knowledge, remembering, integration, learning, and flexibility.	**Problem representation** Involves set creation, selective attention, and flexible use of scale models.
Incubation Involves convergent thinking, motivation, and problem-finding skills.	**Planning** Involves finding a problem space, event planning, logical search, sequencing, planning to remember, and social planning.
Illumination Involves divergent thinking, openness, tolerance for ambiguity, rule use, and a willingness to take risks.	**Execution** Involves intending, and rule use.
Verification Involves familiarity with norms and conventions, and evaluation of configurations of novelty.	**Evaluation** Involves termination, error detection, and error correction.

model appears to parallel Wallas' (1926) model of the creative process involving the four stages of preparation, incubation, illumination, and verification. Table 11.1 depicts the two models, highlighting their similarities.

Based on the similarity of these models, one would predict a positive relationship between executive functioning ability and creative ability. No studies to date seem to have looked at this correlation, but Healey and Rucklidge (2006a) compared their four groups (ADHD, CA, CNA, and NC) on a range of cognitive tasks including IQ, Working Memory, Processing and Naming Speed, Reaction Time, Inhibitory Control, and Executive Functioning. They found that on measures of IQ, Working Memory, and Executive Functioning the ADHD group performed significantly worse than both of the creative groups, who did not differ. These findings fit with the similarities between creativity and executive functioning because these are all measures of higher-order cognitive functioning and, therefore, based on the models, creative children would be expected to do well on these measures. However, on measures of Processing Speed, Naming Speed, and Reaction Time, the CA group's scores consistently fell in between those of the ADHD and CNA groups, suggesting that the CA group was somewhat impaired on tasks involving quick responses. This was confirmed by the significant positive relations between inattention and Reaction Time, and the significant negative relations between inattention and both Processing and Naming Speed within the combined creative groups. Furthermore, there were no significant relations between inattention and IQ or executive functions, suggesting that CA children display high levels of inattention and process information more slowly, but that this does not affect their more general cognitive abilities. These findings are in line with those of Chae *et al.* (2003) who compared the cognitive functioning of gifted children with ADHD and non-gifted children with ADHD. They found significant differences in omission and commission errors and response sensitivity on the continuous performance task, such that gifted children with ADHD made few errors and showed higher sensitivity than children with ADHD who were not gifted. Similarly, when comparing the IQ scores of gifted children with and without ADHD, they found only one significant difference and that was on the Coding subset of the Wechsler Intelligence Scale for Children (WISC), which is a speeded task requiring attention and motor control. Furthermore, when comparing the reaction times and response variability of the gifted children with ADHD with the non-gifted children with ADHD, there were no significant differences. These findings highlight the link between ADHD symptoms and deficits on speeded tasks, even in children with high IQs who are otherwise performing very well cognitively.

Answering the question: attention-deficit/hyperactivity disorder and creativity, ever the twain shall meet?

So far this chapter has reviewed literature on the similarities and differences between ADHD and creativity, but the question still remains... *ever the twain shall meet?* I have demonstrated that, although there are many similarities between ADHD and creativity, they certainly are not the same thing! But are they a similar thing? Now this is where things become a little trickier. My answer would be – *sometimes*. There appear to be two distinct groups of creative children – those displaying symptoms of ADHD and those who are not. It is quite clear in the literature that those who are not displaying symptoms of ADHD are very different from children with ADHD across the board because they do significantly better on IQ, executive functioning, processing speed, social functioning, and emotional functioning than do children diagnosed with ADHD. The waters begin to get muddied when we examine creative children who exhibit elevated symptoms of ADHD. It seems that many of the researchers who have looked at rates of ADHD diagnoses within creative samples have not used comprehensive and rigorous diagnostic measures, and therefore their estimates of the rates of ADHD within creative samples are most likely inflated. Healey and Rucklidge (2006a) are the only authors to have reported formal diagnoses made by a clinical psychologist and they found that, although 40 percent of their creative group displayed elevated ADHD symptomatology, none of them met the full criteria for a diagnosis of ADHD. Thus, this one study suggests that rates of formal diagnoses of ADHD do not appear to be higher (and may even be lower than expected) within creative samples; but of course these results need to be replicated before we can be confident that this is the case. Likewise, when examining the rates of creativity within a sample diagnosed with ADHD, Healey and Rucklidge (2005) found that children with ADHD were no more likely to be creative than typically developing children.

So if creative children are not more likely to have ADHD, and children with ADHD are no more likely to be creative than typically developing children – then why is there so much talk about how the two are related? The reason is that the distinction between the groups is not all black and white – there are many shades of gray. Researchers have repeatedly found higher than expected rates of ADHD symptomatology within creative samples; and therefore, while they may not have the disorder, there is little doubt that many creative individuals fall high on the continuum of ADHD traits. Thus the question remains as to whether these behaviors have the same or different underlying mechanisms. The literature on this is sparse, but at this early stage it seems that there are more similarities than differences. Those creative children who exhibit ADHD symptoms appear to have very similar temperaments to children with ADHD, and different temperaments from those creative children who do not display symptoms of ADHD. Likewise their psychosocial functioning is similar to those with ADHD, and different from creative children without ADHD symptoms. Therefore, when looking at their behavioral and psychosocial functioning, there are many similarities between children with a diagnosis of ADHD and creative children who display elevations in ADHD symptomatology; although across the board their behaviors and psychosocial difficulties are less severe than those of children who are diagnosed with ADHD.

The one area that may distinguish creative children with ADHD symptomatology from children who are diagnosed with ADHD is their cognitive functioning. Creative children displaying symptoms of ADHD outperformed those with a diagnosis of ADHD who were not creative on measures of IQ, working memory, and executive functioning. Interestingly these results were the same in a sample of children who had both a diagnosis of ADHD and were gifted, suggesting that giftedness/creativity is associated with higher cognitive functioning, even in the presence of ADHD symptoms or diagnosis. Having said that, there is an even more interesting consistent finding, which is that, despite their superior general cognitive functioning, creative and gifted children displaying symptoms of ADHD have consistently exhibited poorer processing speed, with their scores on speed-based tasks being similar to those of children diagnosed with ADHD but who are not creative.

Therefore, in closing, it seems that **YES, ADHD and creativity shall meet** and likely meet again and again. The picture is still murky at this point but it seems that those creative children who exhibit symptoms of ADHD experience many of the same difficulties as children with ADHD, even if they do not meet the criteria for a diagnosis of ADHD. Their IQs and executive functioning abilities, however, do not appear to be affected by or related to their ADHD symptomatology.

However, one question that has not yet been addressed is whether those creative and gifted children who present with symptoms of ADHD are the ones most likely to be "gifted underachievers"? Gifted underachievers/school drop-outs have been characterized as willing to take risks, rebellious, talkative, expressive, non-conformist, estranged from peers, at risk of emotional problems, and highly sensitive to negative feedback (Kim, 2008; Reis and McCoach, 2000). Based on Healey and Rucklidge's (2006a, 2006b) comparisons of temperaments and behavioral and psychosocial functioning of creative children who do and don't exhibit symptoms of ADHD, it seems likely that those exhibiting ADHD symptoms are more likely to underachieve.

Most creative children probably do not have ADHD, and most children with ADHD will not be notably more creative. However, those creative children displaying elevated symptoms of the disorder are a high-risk group who may warrant interventions even if their symptoms do not reach the level of diagnosis. Such interventions would be aimed at assisting them in regulating their behavior, improving their psychosocial functioning, and managing their difficulties in performing speed-based tasks in order to ensure that they are able to reach their potential, engage well socially, and reduce the likelihood of early school dropout/underachievement. Every effort needs to be made to enable these children to realize their full potential. While labeling and stigmatization is something we always want to avoid, we also need to identify those children at risk of adverse outcomes and ensure that we intervene early and extensively to give them every opportunity for success.

References

Akande, A. (1997). Creativity: The caregiver's secret weapon. *Early Childhood Development and Care*, 134, 89–101.

Amabile, T. M. (1989). *Growing up creative: Nurturing a lifetime of creativity.* Williston, VT: Crown House.

American Psychiatric Association (APA) (2000). *Diagnostic and statistical manual of mental disorders: DSM-IV-TR* (4th edn). Washington, DC: Author.

Aranha, M. (1997). Creativity in students and its relation to intelligence and peer perception. *Interamerican Journal of Psychology*. 31, 309–313.

Asthana, M. (1993). A study of anxiety among high creative and low creative girls in relation to socio-economic status. *Indian Journal of Behavior*, 17, 1–5.

Bachtold, L. M. (1980). Speculation on a theory of creativity: A physiological basis. *Perceptual and Motor Skills*, 50, 699–702.

Barkley, R. A. (1998). *Attention-deficit hyperactivity disorder: A handbook for diagnosis and treatment* (2nd edn.). New York: Guilford Press.

Barron, F. (1988). Putting creativity to work. In R. J. Sternberg (Ed.), *The nature of creativity* (pp. 76–98). New York: Guilford Press.

Biederman, J., Faraone, S. V., Monuteaux, M. C., Bober, M. and Cadogen, E. (2004). Gender effects on attention-deficit/hyperactivity disorder in adults, revisited. *Biological Psychiatry*, 55, 692–700.

Carlsson, I. (2002). Anxiety and flexibility of defence related to high or low creativity. *Creativity Research Journal*, 14, 341–349.

Carlsson, I., Wendt, P. E. and Risberg, J. (2000). On the neurobiology of creativity: Differences in frontal lobe activity between high and low creative subjects. *Neuropsychologia*, 38, 873–885.

Chae, P. K., Kim, J. and Noh, K. (2003). Diagnosis of ADHD among gifted children in relation to KEDI-WISC and T.O.V.A. performance. *Gifted Child Quarterly*, 47(3), 192–201.

Cox, A. J. (1999). Psychological vulnerability and the creative disposition: Etiological factors associated with psychopathology in visual artists. *Dissertation Abstracts International. Section B: The Sciences and Engineering*, 60 (1–B).

Cramond, B. (1994). *The relationship between attention-deficit hyperactivity disorder and creativity*. Paper presented at the meeting of the American Educational Research Association, New Orleans, LA.

Cramond, B. (1995). The coincidence of attention-deficit hyperactivity disorder and creativity. *Attention Deficit Disorder Research-Based Decision Making Series 9508*.

Daniels, S. and Piechowski, M. (Eds.) (2009). *Living with intensity: Understanding the sensitivity, excitability, and emotional development of gifted children, adolescents, and adults.* Scottsdale, AZ: Great Potential Press.

Davis, G. A. (1986). *Creativity is forever* (2nd edn.). Dubuque, IA: Kendall/Hunt.

Dawson, V. L. (1997). In search of the wild bohemian: Challenges in the identification of the creatively gifted. *Roeper Review*, 19, 148–152.

Farley, F. H. (1985). Psychobiology and cognition: An individual-differences model. In F. H. Farley, F. J. Strelau and A. Gale (Eds.), *The biological bases of personality and behavior: Theories, measurement techniques, and development* (pp. 61–73). Washington, DC: Hemisphere Publishing Corporation.

Goldsmith, R. E. and Matherly, T. A. (1988). Creativity and self-esteem: A multiple operationalization validity study. *Journal of Psychology*, 122, 47–56.

Guenther, A. (1995). *What educators and parents need to know about... ADHD, creativity, and gifted students*. Practitioners' guide A9814. The National Center on the Gifted and Talented, University of Connecticut.

Healey, D. and Rucklidge, J. J. (2005). An exploration into the creative abilities of children with ADHD. *Journal of Attention Disorders*, 8, 88–95.

Healey, D. and Rucklidge, J. J. (2006a). An investigation into the relationship among ADHD, creativity, and neuropsychological functioning in children. *Child Neuropsychology*, 12, 421–438.

Healey, D. and Rucklidge, J. J. (2006b). An investigation into the psychosocial functioning of creative children: The impact of ADHD symptomatology. *Journal of Creative Behavior*, 40, 243–264.

Hershman, D. J. and Lieb, J. (1998). *Manic depression and creativity*. New York: Prometheus Books.

Jamison, K. R. (1993). *Touched with fire: Manic-depressive illness and the artistic temperament*. New York: Free Press.

Kemple, K. M., David, G. M. and Wang, Y. (1996). Preschoolers' creativity, shyness and self-esteem. *Creativity Research Journal*, 9, 317–326.

Kerr, B. (1985). *Smart girls, gifted women*. Columbus, OH: Ohio Psychological Association.

Kim, K. H. (2008). Underachievement and creativity: Are gifted underachievers highly creative? *Creativity Research Journal*, 20, 234–242.

Knutson, K. A. and Farley, F. (1995). *Type T personality and learning strategies*. Paper presented at the annual meeting of the American Educational Research Association (San Francisco, CA, April 18–22, 1995).

Lahey, B. B., Pelham, W. E., Schaugnency, E. A., Atkins, M. S., Murphy, H. A., Hynd, G. *et al.* (1988). Dimensions and types of attention deficit disorder. *Journal of the American Academy of Child and Adolescent Psychiatry*, 27, 330–335.

Lau, S. and Li, W. L. (1996). Peer status and perceived creativity: Are popular children viewed by peers and teachers as creative? *Creativity-Research-Journal*, 9, 347–352.

Leroux, J. A. and Levitt-Perlman, M. (2000). The gifted child with attention deficit disorder: An identification and intervention challenge. *Roeper Review*, 22, 171–176.

Lovecky, D. V. (1994). Gifted children with attention deficit disorder. In L. K. Silverman (Ed.). *Understanding our gifted*, 6, issue 5.

McBurnett, K., Lahey, B. B. and Pfiffner, L. J. (1993). Diagnosis of attention deficit disorders in *DSM-IV*: Scientific basis and implications for education. *Exceptional Children*, 60, 108–117.

Matejik, M., Kovac, T. and Kondas, O. (1988). The creativity–anxiety relationships in pupils. *Studia Psychologica*, 30, 25–30.

Ochse, R. (1990). *Before the gates of excellence: The determinants of creative genius*. New York: Cambridge University Press.

Papworth, M. A. and James, I. A. (2003). Creativity and mood: Towards a model of cognitive mediation. *Journal of Creative Behavior*, 37, 1–16.

Piechowski, M. M. (1986). The concept of developmental potential. *Roeper Review*, 8, 190–197.

Reiss, S. M. and McCoach, D. B. (2000). The underachievement of gifted students: What do we know and where do we go? *Gifted Child Quarterly*, 44(3), 152–170.

Runco, M. A. and Sakamoto, S. O. (1996). Optimization as a guiding principle in research on creative problem solving. In T. Helstrup, G. Kaufmann and K. H. Teigen (Eds.), *Problem solving and cognitive processes: Essays in honour of Kjell Raaheim* (pp. 119–144). Bergen, Norway: Fagbokforlaget Vigmostad & Bjorke.

Shaw, G. A. and Brown, G. (1991). Laterality, implicit memory and attention disorder. *Educational Studies*, 17, 15–23.

Shaw, G. A. and Giambra, L. (1993). Task-unrelated thoughts of college students diagnosed as hyperactive in childhood. *Developmental Neuropsychology*, 9, 17–30.

Sitton, S. C. and Hughes, R. B. (1995). Creativity, depression and circannual variation. *Psychological Reports*, 77, 907–910.

Smith, D. E. and Moran, J. D. (1990). Socioemotional functioning of creative preschoolers. *Perceptual and Motor Skills*, 71, 267–273.

Sternberg, R. J. (1988). A three-facet model of creativity. In R. J. Sternberg (Ed.), *The nature of creativity* (pp. 125–147). New York: Cambridge University Press.

Tannock, R. (1998). Attention deficit hyperactivity disorder: Advances in cognitive, neurobiological and genetic research. *Journal of Child Psychology and Psychiatry*, 39, 65–99.

Topolski, T. D., Edwards, T. C., Patrick, D. L., Varley, P., Way, M. E. and Buesching, D. P. (2004). Quality of life of adolescent males with attention-deficit hyperactivity disorder. *Journal of Attention Disorders*, 7, 163–173.

Wallas, G. (1926). *The art of thought*. New York: Harcourt, Brace.

Waskowic, T. and Cramer, K. M. (1999). Relation between preference for solitude scale and social functioning. *Psychological Reports*, 85 (3, part 1), 1045–1050.

Weinberg, W. A. and Ernslie, G. J. (1990). *Attention deficit hyperactivity disorder: The differential diagnosis*. Paper presented at the Annual Conference of the Learning Disabilities Association of America, Anaheim, CA.

Weiss, G. and Hechtman, L. T. (1993). *Hyperactive children grown up: ADHD in children, adolescents, and adults*. New York: Guilford Press.

Werry, J. S., Reeves, J. C. and Elkind, G. S. (1987). Attention deficit, conduct, oppositional and anxiety disorders in children: A review of research on differentiating characteristics. *Journal of the American Academy of Child and Adolescent Psychiatry*, 26, 133–143.

Williams, A. J., Poole, M. E. and Lett, W. R. (1977). The creativity/self-concept relationship reviewed: An Australian longitudinal perspective. *Australian Psychologist*, 12, 313–317.

Zelazo, P. D., Carter, A., Reznick, J. S. and Frye, D. (1997). Early development of executive function: A problem solving framework. *Review of General Psychology*, 1, 198–226.

Part IV

Creativity and mental illness:
possible commonalities

12   The shared vulnerability model of creativity and psychopathology

Shelley Carson

Creative individuals frequently describe the creative process as irrational. Even those luminaries who are in the most rational and logic-driven of fields, such as physics and mathematics, attest to the irrational and illogical nature of creative accomplishments. The empiricist Karl Popper, for example, wrote that "every discovery contains 'an irrational element' or 'a creative intuition'" (Popper, 1959/2005, p. 8). The mathematician Poincaré suggested that "logic has very little to do with discovery or invention" (cited in Beveridge, 1957, p. 85). Regarding scientific creativity, Einstein wrote that "there is no logical way to the discovery of these elemental laws. There is only the way of intuition" (Einstein, 1952, p. 10).

Given that there is often a perceived illogical or irrational component to creative work (an intuitive leap, so to speak), it is reasonable to suggest that cognitive states that allow access to intuitive or irrational thought processes might promote creative ideation. Psychopathological brain states, which are often characterized by irrational thought processes, may act as doorways into the chaotic and irrational aspects of thought that can inspire intuitive leaps of imagination and creative ideas (see Jamison, 1993; Norlander, 1999; Prentky, 1989, 2000–2001).

However, psychopathological states as such are not necessarily creative. Some connection with rational thought appears necessary in order to allow the creative individual to fashion an original idea out of the material gleaned from the descent into irrational thought. Koestler (1990), in *The act of creation*, likens this process to a skin-diver who explores the underwater depths while still being connected to the surface by a breathing tube. "The capacity to regress," he wrote, "more or less at will, to the games of the underground, without losing contact with the surface, seems to be the essence of the poetic, and of other forms of creativity" (Koestler, 1990, p. 317). The creative person is able to access and utilize both nonrational and rational brain states.

In this chapter, I will describe and expand upon a shared vulnerability model of the relationship between creativity and psychopathology that was first introduced elsewhere (Carson, 2011). The model will provide a framework for explaining both the irrational aspects of creative thought (Koestler's descent to the "mental underground") and the rational and adaptive aspects of creative thought (Koestler's "contact with the surface"). The model will also account for the intrinsic motivation and perseverance in the face of obstacles that often accompany creative effort. Before introducing the model, I will review research that indicates there is, indeed, an association between creativity and psychopathology. I will then describe cognitive factors that may characterize both high levels of creative thought and certain types of psychopathology. This description will include some preliminary molecular biology findings that support the model. Finally, I will describe cognitive strengths that may allow the creative individual to remain in "contact with the surface." Understanding the nature of the creativity/psychopathology association may have broad implications for both the treatment of mental disorders and for the enhancement of creativity, a human faculty that is important for the survival and enrichment of our species.

Is there an association between creativity and psychopathology?

Creativity is typically described as the ability to manifest a product or idea that is both novel or original and adaptive or useful (Barron, 1969). The ability to be creative appears to have evolved gradually across epochs of the Homo lineage (Gabora and Kaufman, 2010), culminating in the great artistic, scientific, and architectural work produced by Homo sapiens. Creativity doubtless acted as a survival mechanism for our ancestors, who were not as fast or strong as potential predators but who were able to gain the evolutionary edge through the creative work of fashioning weapons, tools, shelters, and cultivatable food sources (Carson, 2010).

Clearly, creativity has been, and will continue to be, important for the survival, comfort, and progress of humans as a species. At the individual level, creative activity has been associated with enrichment, personal fulfillment, and peak experience (Csikszentmihalyi, 1996; Maslow, 1970), and even with certain health benefits (Cohen, 2006). The importance of creativity is not confined to artists, writers, musicians, and scientists; it has also been demonstrated in an array of human occupations. It is a sought-after trait in corporate chief executive officers (IBM Corporation, 2010) and athletes (Memmert and Roth, 2007), as well as in potential life mates and sex partners (Buss and Barnes, 1986; Nettle and Clegg, 2006). While the benefits of creativity have been well documented on the one hand, the costs of mental illness – both in terms of financial burden and human suffering – have also been well documented on the other hand (World Health Organization, 2001). Is it possible that these two seemingly contradictory human characteristics – creativity and mental illness – are connected in some meaningful way?

Indeed, certain types of mental illness, including mood disorders, schizospectrum symptoms, and substance abuse disorders, seem to flourish in the ranks of highly creative individuals (see, for example, Andreasen, 1987; Post, 1996; Prentky, 1989). Although the potential connection between creativity and psychopathology has been questioned (see Sawyer, 2012; Schlesinger, 2009; Weisberg, 1994), suggestions of such a connection have been noted at least since the time of the ancient Greeks. Plato, for instance, proposed that poets, philosophers, and dramatists tended to display "divine madness," one of the four types of madness described in his dialogue *Phaedrus* (Plato, 360 BCE). Aristotle, Plato's protégé, may have been the first to suggest a connection between creative individuals and depression when he asked in *Problem XXX* why it is that men who have become outstanding in poetry and the arts tend to be melancholic (Aristotle, 1984). The ancients also expressed a tendency to find creative inspiration in the use of substances, particularly alcohol, because, as the Roman poet Horace wrote, "No poems can please for long or live that are written by water drinkers" (as cited in Goodwin, 1992, p. 425). Thus began a long history of associating creativity with specific types of psychopathology (see Becker, 2001, and this volume, for an historical overview).

Two studies in the mid-twentieth century provided some of the first empirical evidence for the creativity/psychopathology connection. Heston (1966) studied the adopted-away offspring of mothers with and without schizophrenia and found that a subset of the children of schizophrenic mothers were more likely to have creative jobs and hobbies, as well as more musical ability, than the children of the control mothers. Shortly after this study was published, Karlsson (1970) published a study that examined males born in Iceland between 1881 and 1910, and reported that those individuals who had a psychotic relative were nearly three times as likely as those without psychosis in the family to be registered in *Who's Who* for accomplishments in creative fields such as creative writing, painting, composing, and performing. Karlsson (1970) concluded that "some type of mental stimulation is associated with a genetic relationship to psychotic persons" (p. 180). These intriguing findings spurred further interest in examining the mental illness pedigrees of creative individuals, and ushered in a new wave of research on the topic.

Creativity and rates of mood disorders

There are numerous names associated with both high levels of creativity and depressive episodes. Vincent van Gogh lost his ear while in a state of mental desperation. Virginia Woolf, entering an episode of psychotic depression, left a note to her husband stating that "I feel we can't go through another of those terrible times" before she filled her pocket with stones and drowned herself (Rose, 1979, p. 243). Several studies in the late 1980s examined creativity in the context of mood disorders. In 1987, Andreasen, a noted schizophrenia researcher, compared thirty writers in residence at the prestigious Iowa writers' workshop and their first-degree relatives with a matched control group and their relatives. Based on the earlier studies by Heston (1966) and Karlsson (1970), Andreasen had expected to find elevated rates of schizophrenia in the relatives of the writers. She found no instances of schizophrenia. Instead, she found that 80 percent of the writers had suffered from a mood disorder, and that the writers were four times more likely to suffer from bipolar disorder than the controls. She also found that both mood disorders and creativity tended to run in families, and concluded that "affective disorder may be both a 'hereditary taint' and a hereditary gift" (Andreasen, 1987, p. 1292). This study has been criticized because Andreasen herself conducted all of the diagnostic interviews and thus was not blind to the creativity status of each of the participants. Further, the criteria Andreasen used for determining bipolar pathology may have been fairly vague (Schlesinger, 2009).

In a second study, Jamison (1989) reported rates of mental illness, mood disorders, and creative productivity in forty-seven British artists and poets. Jamison found that 38 percent of these award-winning subjects had been treated for mood disorders, and 6.4 percent had been treated for bipolar disorder. Poets (55.2%) and novelists (62.5%) were especially prone to mood disorders. These rates are substantially higher than the 20.8 percent rate for mood disorders found in the general public (Kessler et al., 2005). Jamison further found that rates of creative productivity were temporally associated with upswings in mood (going from depressive to normal or normal to hypomanic mood). Mood elevations, she concluded, may lead to increased activation of associational networks and enhanced sensory experience, both of which are important for creative work. These conclusions are in accord with findings from non-clinical groups that suggest upswings in positive emotions are associated with cognitive changes such as broadened attention and increased divergent thinking (see Ashby et al., 1999; Frederickson, 2001). As with the Andreasen study, Jamison's report has been criticized for methodological issues (Schlesinger, 2009), including the lack of a control group and the possibility of investigator bias in the hand-picking of subjects.

Despite methodological flaws in the Andreasen and Jamison studies, evidence for higher rates of mood disorder in creative professions continued to accrue. Ludwig (1994) compared fifty-nine female writers in the University of Kentucky National Women Writers' Conference with controls who had been matched for age and education. The writers' rates of both depression (56%) and mania (19%) were significantly higher than in the controls. In a doctoral dissertation study, Colvin (1995) compared forty advanced conservatory students training for careers as classical performing musicians with forty matched controls who were training for careers outside the creative arts. Again, rates of mood disorders were significantly higher in the creative group (60%) than in the control group (20%).

Researchers also examined mood disorders in deceased creative luminaries, based on available biographical sources. Post (1994) studied the lives of 291 world-famous men from various creative professional categories and provided evidence for post-mortem psychiatric diagnoses based on *DSM-III-R* (APA, 1987) criteria. Compared with general population morbidity rates, Post found that subjects in all creative professional categories demonstrated higher rates of mood disorder; however, these rates were particularly high in writers. Ludwig (1992, 1995) gathered data on psychiatric symptoms from biographical sources of more than 1,000 deceased luminaries whose biographies had been reviewed in the *New York Times* book review section between 1960 and 1990. He reported significantly higher rates of mood disorders among persons in the creative arts (artists, musical composers and performers, and writers) than among persons in other professions. Wills (2003) studied forty deceased jazz musicians who were considered to have made major creative contributions to their field between 1945 and 1960. He awarded them provisional diagnoses based on information from biographical sources. Twenty-nine percent of the sample qualified for a mood disorder diagnosis based on *DSM-IV* (APA, 1994) criteria.

Finally, in the largest study looking at creativity and psychopathology that has been undertaken to date, Kyaga and colleagues (2012) examined professional data and psychiatric histories of over one million citizens listed in Swedish national registers. They found that individuals in creative professions (scientific and artistic occupations) had higher rates of bipolar disorder than those in non-creative professions, although rates of other types of mental illness were not elevated in the creative group. However, they found that individuals identified as writers had higher rates of unipolar depression (as well as other forms of psychopathology) than non-writers. First-degree relatives of persons with bipolar disorder and several other psychiatric diagnoses were more likely to be in creative professions than persons without this psychiatric family history.

The results of these empirical investigations suggest that individuals in the creative professions (especially artists, writers, and musicians) are at greater risk for mood disorders than are members of the general population. Creativity and mood disorders also often appear to run in families (Andreasen, 1987; Jamison, 1993; Kyaga *et al.*, 2012).

Creativity and schizospectrum symptoms

The schizophrenia spectrum of symptoms extends from eccentric behavior through to full-blown psychosis. There are numerous accounts of the eccentric and even psychotic behavior of creative luminaries. The composer Robert Schumann reported that Beethoven and Mendelssohn were channeling musical compositions to him from their tombs (Jensen, 2001; Lombroso, 1891/1976). The creative visionary William Blake believed that many of his poems and paintings were channeled to him through spirits who often jostled him to get his attention. He also believed that an etching technique he developed was sent to him by his dead brother (Galvin, 2004). Nobel Prize winner John Forbes Nash believed that supernatural beings from outer space were recruiting him to save the world (Nasar, 1998), and Nikola Tesla, the scientist credited with discovering alternating current, composed love letters to pigeons, as well as suffering from auditory and visual hallucinations (Pickover, 1998).

In addition to anecdotal reports, researchers at the University of California, Berkeley's famed Institute of Personality Assessment and Research (IPAR) reported that eminent creative writers and architects had elevated scores on the Minnesota Multiphasic Personality Inventory (MMPI) scales of schizophrenia and paranoia (Barron, 1955; MacKinnon, 1962). These writers and architects reported odd mystical experiences as well as unusual perceptual occurrences (Barron, 1969). Other researchers of the same period noted that creative individuals scored high on a personality measure they called "schizothymia," a tendency to experience elements of schizophrenia but without the same depth of psychotic disturbance (Cattell and Drevdahl, 1955; Drevdahl and Cattell, 1958).

Robert Prentky (1979) suggested a theory that highly creative individuals might share a common cognitive style with persons who suffered from schizophrenia. This cognitive style is characterized by a relatively broad band of attentional focus in which information is processed at a relatively shallow level. This is in contrast to a more typical cognitive style characterized by a narrow attentional focus in which information is processed with more depth and detail. Some evidence for this theory was provided by findings that subjects with schizophrenia tend to score higher on divergent thinking tasks than normal control subjects

(Keefe and Magaro, 1980). Divergent thinking tasks have traditionally been used as measures of trait creativity (McCrae, 1987). It seems that both creative individuals and people with schizophrenia have a thinking style that favors making *loose* and non-obvious associations between objects and concepts rather than more apparent and logical associations (Maher, 1972).

As the early studies by Heston (1966) and Karlsson (1970) suggested, elevated indicators of creativity are more likely to be found in the first-degree relatives of people with schizophrenia than in schizophrenics themselves. Relatives of schizophrenics often display a set of subclinical (or less severe) symptoms referred to as *schizotypal personality*. Schizotypal personality – or schizotypy – is an indicator of a predisposition to psychosis, existing on a continuum between normal experience and schizophrenia (Claridge, 1997). Symptoms of schizotypy include unusual perceptual experiences (such as hearing voices in the wind), magical thinking (such as believing you can communicate with others through telepathy), impulsive non-conformity (such as urges to violate rules or social standards), cognitive disorganization (such as trouble concentrating or paying attention), and mild social anhedonia (such as not needing or desiring close friends) (Mason *et al.*, 2005). Schizotypy is considered to be disordered when it leads to distress or dysfunction; however, rather high levels of schizotypy are also often found in high-functioning non-disordered individuals (Claridge, 1997).

A considerable body of research has linked schizotypy and creativity (Brod, 1987; Cox and Leon, 1999; Green and Williams, 1999; Poreh *et al.*, 1994; Schuldberg *et al.*, 1988). Recent studies have distinguished between *positive* and *negative* schizotypy. Positive schizotypy, or psychosis-proneness, includes unusual perceptual experiences and magical thinking. These symptoms are subclinical associates of hallucinations and delusions, which are considered the *positive* signs of schizophrenia. Negative schizotypy includes social anhedonia and cognitive disorganization, symptoms that resemble subclinical variants of the *negative* signs of schizophrenia (Mason and Claridge, 2006).

In general, research indicates that creative people in arts-related professions endorse higher rates of positive schizotypy than non-arts professionals, while scientists and mathematicians endorse higher rates of negative schizotypy. British art students are featured in two separate studies (Burch *et al.*, 2006; O'Reilly *et al.*, 2001). O'Reilly *et al.* (2001) compared 50 students who were studying for a performance/visual arts degree with 50 students who were studying for conventional degrees in the humanities. They found that the arts degree students had significantly higher scores on measures of creativity and on a measure of positive schizotypy than the humanities students. In a similar study, Burch *et al.* (2006) found that visual art students at the University of London had higher scores on measures of positive schizotypy and creativity than did students in non-art-related fields.

Two studies compared subjects in arts-related fields with those in STEM fields (science, technology, engineering, and math). Nettle (2006) examined a group of 501 subjects from a combined community and university sample. Subjects included individuals who had been diagnosed with schizophrenia and bipolar disorder, as well as subjects who were classified as poets, artists, or mathematicians. Poets, artists, and psychiatric patients had elevated levels of positive schizotypal traits, while mathematicians had elevated levels of negative schizotypal traits. In another study, Rawlings and Locarnini (2008) found that professional artists and musicians scored higher on measures of positive schizotypy and hypomania than biologists and mathematicians, who in turn scored higher on symptoms related to negative schizotypy. In our Harvard lab, we have also found that high creative achievers in the fields of art, music, and creative writing have significantly higher positive schizotypy scores than low achievers, matched for IQ, in those fields. High achievers in scientific fields, however, actually scored lower on a measure of positive schizotypy than low creative achievers (Carson, 2001).

In sum, the research on schizotypal pathology and creativity supports an elevated level of schizotypy or psychosis-proneness in divergent thinkers and creative individuals (e.g., Brod, 1987; Burch *et al.*, 2006; Schuldberg *et al.*, 1988). However, the type of schizotypal symptoms may vary depending on the domain in which the creative individual works (Nettle, 2006; Rawlings and Locarnini, 2008).

Creativity and alcoholism

The use of alcohol has been associated with great works of art and literature since the time of Homer and Seneca (Pritzker, 1999). Aristophanes, in his play *The Knights*, had the character of Demosthenes say, "Come, bring hither quick a flagon of wine, that I may soak my brain and get an ingenious idea" (Aristophanes, 424 BCE, [92]), suggesting that even 2,000 years ago creative inspiration was associated with wine consumption. There seems to be an expectation, especially among writers, that alcohol can summon the muse and jumpstart creative output (Ludwig, 1990). Novelist William Styron, for example, described alcohol as "the magical conduit to fantasy and euphoria, and to the enhancement of the imagination" (Styron, 1990, p. 40). If creative individuals have expectations that alcohol will enhance creativity, then it is likely that they will experience heightened risk for alcohol-related disorders. Indeed, research that has examined this issue suggests that there is a greater prevalence of alcoholism in creative professions than in the general population (Andreasen, 1987; Dardis, 1989; Ludwig, 1992; Post, 1994).

Thirty percent of the writers that Andreasen (1987) studied from the Iowa writers' workshop suffered from alcoholism, compared with 7 percent from the control group. Post (1994), in his biographical review of famous men from a variety of professions, found that 28 percent of writers, 29 percent of artists, and 21 percent of composers met diagnostic criteria for alcoholism. This far exceeds the 5.4 percent lifetime risk for dependence that is found in the general public (Kessler *et al.*, 2005). The *DSM-IV* (APA, 1994) drew distinctions between alcohol dependence (alcoholism), which is typically characterized by tolerance and withdrawal symptoms, and alcohol abuse, which involves using alcohol despite dangerous or dysfunctional consequences (although the *DSM-V* has dropped this distinction [APA, 2013]). The lifetime rate of alcohol abuse in the United States is 13.2 percent (Kessler *et al.*, 2005). Ludwig (1992) reported an elevated mean level of alcohol abuse among creative professions. Artists (22%), composers (21%), musical performers (40%), actors (60%), fiction writers (37%), and poets (30%) had substantially higher rates of alcohol abuse than the population norms, but natural scientists (1–2%) had lower-than-normal rates. Levels of alcoholism and alcohol abuse are particularly elevated among fiction writers. Of the eight American novelists who have won the Nobel Prize, five have suffered from alcoholism, a rate of 62.5 percent (Dardis, 1989).

It is of interest that risk for alcoholism is elevated among the bipolar and the schizospectrum populations as well (Kessler *et al.*, 1995). The heightened risk of alcoholism in creative individuals and also in those who suffer from related forms of psychopathology suggests an underlying shared vulnerability.

Creativity and psychopathology: a dose-dependent relationship

While creative individuals may experience greater risk for some forms of psychopathology than members of the general public, there is substantial evidence that creative work is not enhanced by severe forms of these disorders; in fact, creative work seems virtually impossible during episodes of full-blown mental illness. For example, despite having higher overall levels of mood disorders than control subjects, the writers from Andreasen's (1987) writers' workshop reported that depressive episodes actually interfered with their writing by decreasing cognitive fluency and energy. They

also reported that manic episodes led to distractibility and disorganization, decreasing their ability to work effectively (Andreasen, 2008).

Likewise, meaningful creative work is difficult, if not impossible, during active episodes of schizophrenia and psychosis. Most research that
has examined psychosis and creativity has found that subclinical manifestations of psychotic symptoms in the form of unusual perceptual
experiences and magical beliefs (rather than actual hallucinations and
delusions) are more often characteristic of creative individuals (Brod,
1987; Claridge, 1997). Even when creative individuals have been diagnosed with actual schizophrenia, as in the case of John Forbes Nash
who completed his Nobel-Prize-winning theories very early in his career
(Nasar, 1998), their creative work has typically been accomplished before
the onset of the disorder (Prentky, 1989).

Researchers Ruth Richards, Dennis Kinney, and their colleagues provided empirical evidence for the beneficial effects of attenuated forms
of mental illness on creativity (Kinney and Richards, this volume). In a
series of studies, they looked at the relationship of both bipolar spectrum
disorders and schizophrenia spectrum symptoms to creativity. In their
first study of this relationship (Richards et al., 1988), they found that levels of creative activity, interest, and achievement were higher in subjects
with cyclothymia and in the first-degree relatives of bipolar probands
than in either control subjects or subjects with actual bipolar disorder.
The authors concluded that a mild version of bipolar disorder or a predisposition to the disorder was beneficial to creativity, but the full-blown
manifestation of the illness was not a benefit. This conclusion suggests an
inverted "U" relationship between creativity and psychopathology, with
the highest levels of creativity occurring with mild symptoms, and lower
levels of creativity associated with either no symptoms or with severe
symptoms (Richards et al., 1988).

This "inverted-U" pattern of creativity and psychopathology was also
replicated in subjects with schizotypal symptoms. Kinney, Richards, and
colleagues (Kinney et al., 2000–2001) examined creativity in the adopted-
away offspring of individuals with schizophrenia and a matched control
group adopted away from parents with no history of psychological disorder. The researchers found that schizotypal traits tended to run in families. They also found that creativity levels were higher in subjects who
had schizotypal personality disorder or at least two schizotypal symptoms
(such as magical ideation or illusion experiences) than in subjects with
no schizotypal symptoms or with full-blown schizophrenia. This study
again highlights the creative benefit of a "little" psychopathology.

As with other disorders, there seems to be an "inverted-U" association
between alcoholism and creativity (Dardis, 1989; Ludwig, 1990). A small
dose of alcohol may disinhibit mental blocks to creativity; however, those

who drink on a regular basis to summon the muse run the risk of developing substance dependence. Biographical information from the lives of creative writers suggests that drinking may have facilitated creativity early in their careers (or at least the writers may have perceived that it did): F. Scott Fitzgerald stated that "Writing heightens feelings" (cited in Goodwin, 1992, p. 427), and E. B. White insisted that he needed a martini to "get up the courage" to write (cited in Goodwin, 1992, p. 424). However, later in their careers, progressive alcoholism diminished both the quality and quantity of creative work in many writers such as Hemingway, Poe, and Fitzgerald (Dardis, 1989). Although creative individuals may believe that drinking inspires creativity, full-blown alcoholism appears to be detrimental to creative efforts. Ludwig (1990) reviewed the effects of alcohol on the creative work of 34 heavy drinkers in the fields of art, creative writing, and musical composition. He found that 59 percent of the sample believed that alcohol facilitated their creativity either directly or indirectly during the early phases of their drinking. However, most of the sample (75%) believed that alcohol ultimately had a direct negative effect on their work in the later phases of their drinking careers.

Both biographical and empirical evidence suggests, then, that the relationship between creativity and psychopathology is curvilinear. A small amount of psychopathology in the form of either mild symptoms or a biological predisposition to a disorder may be beneficial to an individual's creativity. However, moderate-to-severe psychopathology appears to be detrimental to creative efforts.

Thus far, I have provided a considerable body of evidence that there is an elevated risk for certain types of psychopathology among the population of highly creative individuals. While some of the supporting research contains methodological flaws, the preponderance of both anecdotal and empirical evidence supports this finding. I have also suggested that certain symptoms of psychopathology may enhance aspects of creative cognition. In addition, I have reviewed the evidence that attenuated psychopathology (in the form of either subclinical levels of symptoms or genetic risk for mental illness) is more conducive to creative enhancement than severe illness. The shared vulnerability model suggests a framework for understanding this body of evidence.

The shared vulnerability model of creativity and psychopathology

The shared vulnerability model suggests that psychopathology and creativity may share genetic components that are expressed as either pathology or creativity depending upon the presence or absence of other moderating factors (Berenbaum and Fujita, 1994; Carson, 2011). This model accounts for the elevated numbers of creative individuals who suffer from specific forms of psychopathology while also explaining why not all highly creative individuals express psychopathology and, conversely, why not all mentally ill individuals express unusual creativity. It also accounts for the findings of increased creativity in the first-degree relatives of individuals with serious psychopathology. The model potentially accounts for one of the mysteries of evolutionary psychology: the stable maintenance rates of serious pathologies such as schizophrenia and bipolar disorder in the population, despite their maladaptive consequences. Because creativity is so important in maintaining the adaptability of the species, it may provide a reproductive advantage for the transmission of at least some factors associated with the genotypes of severe psychopathologies (Crow, 1997).

The current shared vulnerability model is a work in progress. It includes several cognitive vulnerability factors that are common to both creativity and the forms of psychopathology that are associated with creativity – namely, mood disorders, schizotypal symptoms, and alcohol dependence. It also includes several cognitive protective factors that may interact with vulnerability factors to allow creative thought processes rather than psychopathology to flourish.

Evidence from molecular biology research indicates that there is a heritable component to both creativity and the disorders in question, and that the nature of that component is polygenetic (Berrettini, 2000; Whitfield *et al.*, 1988). In order for the full maladaptive force of a disorder such as schizophrenia to be expressed in the phenotype, a constellation of genetic variations, many of which have not yet been identified, must be in place. However, it is possible that individuals with various subsets of these genetic variations may express only attenuated symptoms of the disorder, or they may express more benign, or even adaptive, phenotypic behaviors. This latter possibility may be aided by gene/gene interactions between vulnerability and protective genetic variants.

Recall that in Koestler's (1990) analogy of a skin diver, the successful diver descends into the dark unexplored regions of the unconscious but retains a lifeline connected to the surface. Using accounts of the creative process as reported by creative luminaries as well as findings from neuroimaging and genetic studies as a basis, I propose a set of vulnerability factors common to both creativity and psychopathology, which acts to increase access and attention to material normally processed below the level of conscious awareness. I also propose a set of protective cognitive factors that allow for executive monitoring and control of such enhanced access. These protective factors, like the diver's lifeline to the surface, would allow creative individuals to exert meta-cognitive

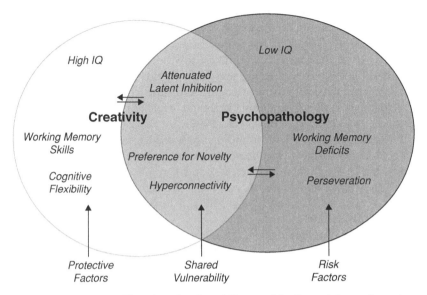

Figure 12.1 The shared vulnerability model of creativity and psychopathology (with permission from Carson [2011])

control over bizarre or unusual thoughts and enable them to take creative advantage of such thoughts without being overwhelmed by them (Carson *et al.*, 2003; Simonton, 2005). The set of vulnerability factors includes attenuated latent inhibition, increased novelty seeking, and neural hyperconnectivity. The set of protective factors includes high IQ, enhanced working memory capacity, and cognitive flexibility (see Figure 12.1). The number of factors will expand as our knowledge of the functioning of the human brain progresses.

Attenuated latent inhibition as a shared vulnerability factor

Latent inhibition (LI) is the capacity to screen from conscious awareness stimuli previously experienced as irrelevant. It is an adaptive selective attention mechanism that effectively limits and filters information entering the cognitive workspace, thus allowing an individual to focus on the current task at hand. The LI mechanism also makes it more difficult to detect connections between suppressed "irrelevant" stimuli and potential solutions to problems. For example, if you found the constant chiming of a clock down the hall to be irrelevant to your work, LI would allow you (after a number of exposures to the chimes) to suppress attention to that sound so you could concentrate on your work. However, if you found that your watch had stopped, you might then be less likely to realize that you could tell the time by listening to the chimes. When LI is attenuated, on the other hand, stimuli that would typically be categorized as irrelevant are allowed into conscious awareness (Lubow and Gewirtz, 1995). Attenuated or reduced LI, a form of cognitive disinhibition, has been found in individuals with schizophrenia and high levels of psychosis-proneness (Baruch et al., 1988b; Lubow et al., 1992).

In our labs at Harvard, we found that reduced LI is also correlated with the personality variable openness to experience, a trait that characterizes highly creative individuals (Peterson and Carson, 2000). Further, we found that reduced LI was characteristic of high creative achievers of above-average IQ (Carson et al., 2003), a finding that has since been replicated (Kéri, 2011).

According to Mednick's (1962) association theory, creativity is dependent upon finding unusual associations between disparate elements, then combining, synthesizing, or organizing these elements in novel ways to serve a purpose. Reduced LI may enhance creativity by increasing the inventory of unfiltered elements available for recombination in conscious awareness. While this increased inventory of stimuli has the potential to overwhelm and overload the information-processing system, it may also increase the odds that novel and original combinations of elements may be synthesized into productive and useful ideas or concepts (Carson et al., 2003).

Reduced LI appears to be associated with elevated levels of dopamine in the mesolimbic pathways of the brain. Agonists that increase dopamine in this area have been shown to increase symptoms of schizophrenia and reduce LI (Weiner, 2003). While it appears that dopamine dysregulation is involved in reduced LI, to date, no studies have linked LI to genes directly associated with dopamine transmission. However, another gene, neuregulin 1 (NRG-1), has often been identified as one of the candidate genes for susceptibility to schizophrenia (Tosato et al., 2005), and mice with a mutation of the NRG-1 gene have demonstrated reduced LI (Rimer et al., 2005). NRG-1 has also been shown to alter dopamine function in conjunction with psychiatric disorders (Roy et al., 2007). Kéri (2009) has shown that the T/T genotype of the promoter region of the NRG-1 gene is prevalent in high creative achievers with high IQs. This genotype has also been related to risk for psychosis and altered prefrontal cortical functioning. According to Kéri (2009), this genotype may be related to reduced LI. Although the findings concerning the NRG-1 gene and creativity need to be replicated, they support the reduced LI phenomenon as a candidate for shared vulnerability between creativity and psychopathology.

Novelty-seeking as a shared vulnerability factor

Novelty-seeking is a personality trait associated with a preference for exploring novel aspects of ideas, objects, or aspects of one's environment. Creative individuals are generally high in novelty-seeking and prefer novel or complex stimuli over familiar or simple stimuli (McCrae, 1993; Reuter *et al.*, 1995). The person who is high in novelty-seeking receives internal rewards via the dopaminergic reward system for attending to novel or unexpected stimuli. Novelty-seeking may benefit creativity in several ways. First, it enhances intellectual curiosity (which is the drive to attend to new or unfamiliar intellectual material). Second, it provides motivation for creative work. The most creative outcomes are accomplished by individuals who pursue their work for its own sake (intrinsic motivation) rather than for some outside reward (Amabile, 1996). Because novelty-seeking activates the internal reward system, it provides the constant intrinsic motivation in the form of internal rewards to attend to novel ideas and creative projects (Schweizer, 2006). Novelty-seekers, through this sensitized reward system, may also be motivated to keep working on a novel project in the face of obstacles or criticism.

However, there is a downside to novelty-seeking. It is also associated with alcohol abuse and addiction (Grucza *et al.*, 2006), which hijack the internal reward system. Novelty-seeking is also associated with the hypomanic and manic phases of bipolar disorder and may be especially prevalent in individuals with comorbid alcoholism and bipolar disorder (Frye and Salloum, 2006). Novelty-seeking is thus both a motivator for creative work and a risk factor for the types of psychopathology we have associated with creativity, making it a suitable shared vulnerability factor.

Novelty-seeking is associated with dopaminergic activity in the reward system of the brain, and it is no surprise that molecular biology research has tied it to variations in dopamine-related genes. The A1+ allele of the TAQ 1A polymorphism of the DRD2 (D2 dopamine receptor) gene has been linked to novelty-seeking, as well as to schizophrenia and addiction (Golimbet *et al.*, 2003; Noble, 2000; Reuter *et al.*, 2006b). The A1+ allele has also been linked to creativity in a sample of German university students (Reuter *et al.*, 2006a). Additional genes involved in dopamine functioning have been linked to risk for schizophrenia and bipolar disorder. These include the DRD4 dopamine D4 receptor gene (DRD4) and the dopamine transporter gene (SLC6A3) (Serretti and Mandelli, 2008). These genes are also involved in novelty-seeking (Ekelund *et al.*, 1999). Variations in novelty-seeking, determined by the availability of dopamine in reward-sensitive regions of the brain, seem to provide another area of shared vulnerability between creativity and the associated forms of psychopathology.

Neural hyperconnectivity as a shared vulnerability factor

A third potential shared vulnerability factor, neural hyperconnectivity, is characterized by abnormal neural linking of brain areas that are not functionally connected. There is some evidence that unusual patterns of cortical connections may be associated with artistic, writing, and scientific achievements (McCrea, 2008). This would allow for a rapid and broad activation of associational networks that could ultimately enhance the ability to make unusual associations, a hallmark of creative ideation (Mednick, 1962).

Hyperconnectivity has been noted in neuroimaging studies of synesthesia, which is the tendency to make cross-modal sensory associations such as hearing colors or smelling musical notes (Hubbard and Ramachandran, 2005). The condition of synesthesia is seven to eight times more prevalent among highly creative individuals than in the general population (Ramachandran and Hubbard, 2001). Hyperconnectivity may also be evidenced by simultaneous activation of cortical areas. Brain imaging studies have reported more alpha synchronization, both within and across hemispheres, in the brains of high creative versus less creative subjects during creativity tasks, suggesting unusual patterns of connectivity (Fink and Benedek, 2013; Fink *et al.*, 2009). Ramachandran and Hubbard (2001) have speculated that hyperconnectivity may form the basis of metaphorical thinking, which is also important in creative cognition.

Hyperconnectivity may allow an individual to make unusual connections between disparate ideas (as is the case in metaphorical thinking), leading to the emergence of original and creative ideas. However, hyperconnectivity has a downside as well. One theory of schizophrenia suggests that clinical manifestations of the disease are the result of abnormal neural connections throughout the brain, perhaps caused by faulty synaptic pruning during development (Feinberg, 1982). Hyperconnectivity has been noted in post-mortem investigations in both schizophrenics and their first-degree relatives. These unusual connectivity patterns may be linked to the bizarre associations often reported by schizophrenics (Whitfield-Gabrieli *et al.*, 2009). Bipolar disorder has also been associated with hyperconnectivity between specific regions of the brain (McCrea, 2008). In fact, white matter diffusion tensor imaging studies have revealed enough anomalies in the connectivity of bipolar brains that McCrea (2008) has suggested that bipolar disorder may be a "complex disorder of connectivity" (p. 1129).

Brang and Ramachandran (2007) theorized that the HTR2A (serotonin transporter) gene may underlie the expression of synesthesia and may therefore be implicated in anomalous neural connectivity. This gene has also been associated with schizotypy and the risk for schizophrenia, although there is debate about which alleles confer this risk (Abdolmaleky *et al.*, 2004). The study of hyperconnectivity is relatively new and much more work needs to be done before the genetic basis of this factor can be determined. However, unusual patterns of neural connectivity may constitute a shared vulnerability factor between the ability to connect disparate stimuli to form novel and creative ideas and the risk for bipolar disorder and psychosis.

High IQ as a protective factor

High IQ is a known protective factor for a variety of mental disorders (Barnett *et al.*, 2006). Low IQ, on the other hand, has consistently been identified as a risk factor for disorders such as schizophrenia (Woodberry *et al.*, 2008). While the relationship between creativity and IQ has been disputed, there does seem to be a minimum IQ below which creative thought is difficult; in fact, low IQ individuals are underrepresented in the ranks of creative luminaries. A threshold of IQ 120 has been posited as necessary but not sufficient for fluid creative ideation (Sternberg and O'Hara, 1999), although that threshold may fluctuate depending upon the domain of the creative work. It would make sense, for instance, for a lower IQ threshold to be necessary for work in the visual arts compared with the field of theoretical physics. Because high (or at least adequate) IQ seems to be necessary for creative work, and because high IQ has previously been shown to be protective against psychotic disorders, high IQ is a reasonable choice for a protective factor that promotes creativity in individuals who display signs of vulnerability to mental disorders.

Me and my colleagues Jordan Peterson and Daniel Higgins hypothesized that if reduced LI increased the amount of stimuli available in conscious awareness, then high IQ might allow for the processing and manipulation of the additional stimuli in ways that lead to creative associations. The combination of low IQ combined with attenuated LI had already been linked to increased risk for psychosis, and we suggested that this was due in part to the inability of the low IQ brain to cope with the influx of additional stimuli introduced by cognitive disinhibition. We conducted a series of studies using high-functioning subjects and found that the combination of attenuated LI and high IQ predicted up to 30 percent of the variance in creative achievement scores (Carson *et al.*, 2003; see Figure 12.2).

These results suggest that high IQ acts as a protective factor when combined with reduced LI (a shared vulnerability factor), while low IQ is an additional risk factor for psychosis.

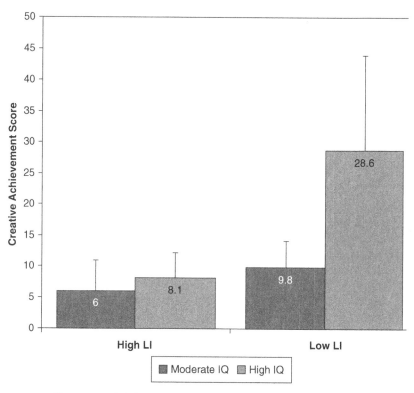

Figure 12.2 High IQ and attenuated latent inhibition predict creative achievement in eminent achievers and controls (with permission from Carson *et al.* [2003])

Enhanced working memory capacity as a protective factor

Working memory capacity is generally considered to be a facet of IQ. Because working memory is the mechanism through which we hold "in mind" bits of information that we wish to manipulate (Baddeley, 1986), a higher capacity of working memory may allow for the advantageous processing of additional stimuli in conscious awareness due to reduced LI.

My colleagues and I provided support for this hypothesis in a study of high-achieving student writers, composers, and artists at Harvard. In this study, attenuated LI and high scores on a measure of working memory for abstract forms predicted over 25 percent of the variance in creative achievement scores (Carson, 2001). In another study of college students, high working memory capacity for abstract forms predicted the ability to solve insight problems – a type of creativity task (DeYoung *et al.*, 2008).

Because creative ideas may arise from combining and rearranging bits of information that are only remotely associated with each other (Mednick, 1962), the ability to hold and process a large number of bits of information simultaneously without becoming confused or overwhelmed should predispose the individual to creative rather than disordered cognition. High working memory capacity may act as a protective factor in individuals who must process unusually large stimuli loads due to attenuated latent inhibition or hyperconnectivity.

Cognitive flexibility as a protective factor

Cognitive flexibility is the ability to disengage attention from one stimulus or concept and deliberately refocus it on another stimulus through conscious mental control. Individuals with schizophrenia often lack this ability, and instead lock onto a stimulus (a state called *perseveration*) (Waford and Lewine, 2010). Cognitive flexibility may allow a person at risk for psychosis the ability to change perspectives and disengage from unusual thoughts or perceptions, instead of interpreting those perceptions in a psychotic manner (O'Connor, 2009). Thus, cognitive flexibility may act as a protective factor for persons who also display shared vulnerability factors.

Cognitive flexibility may also offer creative individuals the ability to switch from focused to defocused attentional states. Dietrich (2003) has suggested that creative individuals have the ability to modulate attentional systems in the brain to allow for temporary cognitive disinhibition (or reduced LI). Cognitive flexibility is dependent upon dopamine availability in the prefrontal cortex (Darvis and Palmiter, 2011). Prefrontal dopamine pathways control the availability of dopamine in the mesolimbic pathway (Davis *et al.*, 1991). This is the pathway that is implicated in both reduced LI and psychosis-proneness (Lubow and Gewirtz, 1995; Woodward *et al.*, 2011). Creative individuals may be able to use cognitive flexibility to achieve alternating states of reduced LI and conscious executive control of attention. This may allow unusual and creative ideas to make their way into consciousness awareness, while also allowing for the deliberate and rational evaluation and elaboration of these ideas. Cognitive flexibility appears to be a protective factor in preventing information-processing overload in vulnerable individuals, while also enhancing the creative process.

Conclusions

Creativity is a desired and important human trait. The artistic and scientific achievements of creative individuals inspire, give comfort, and improve the quality of life and the adaptability of humanity. However, despite these profound benefits of creativity, a review of research indicates that creative individuals are at greater risk for certain forms of psychopathology than are members of the general public, including mood disorders, schizospectrum disorders, and alcohol abuse and dependence. I have attempted to account for this paradox by presenting a shared vulnerability model of creativity and psychopathology.

Creative individuals appear to share cognitive vulnerabilities also found in certain forms of mental pathology. These may include attenuated LI, novelty-seeking, and neural hyperconnectivity. These vulnerabilities may facilitate access to disinhibited states of consciousness, increase motivation to attend to novel aspects of the inner and outer environment, and promote novel associations through unusual patterns of neural connectivity. Cognitive strengths, including high IQ, expanded working memory capacity, and cognitive flexibility, may interact with these vulnerabilities to promote creativity and to act as protective factors against severe forms of psychopathology.

The current shared vulnerability model is only a preliminary framework for understanding risk and protective factors associated with creativity and psychopathology. It focuses only on neurocognitive mechanisms for which there is currently some corroborating support from brain imaging and molecular biology research. However, there are likely additional shared vulnerabilities and protective factors that warrant inclusion. The model has thus far only considered factors that exist within the person. However, current research trends emphasize the interaction of genetic risk and environmental factors. An example of this gene/environment interaction was recently reported by Kéri (2011), who demonstrated that social networks (an established protective factor for many mental disorders) may interact with genetically mediated neurocognitive factors (such as attenuated LI) to predict creative achievement. Social support and other environmental factors may be important additions to future iterations of the shared vulnerability model.

Clearly the voice of the muse may call to some who descend into the "mental underground" described by Koestler (1990, p. 317). However, the inner demons associated with psychopathology may accost those who remain in the mental underground too long. Genetically mediated protective factors may provide Koestler's "contact with the surface" that allows the creative individual to make that descent underground and return at will with a treasure of novel material. Our knowledge of these protective factors and the shared vulnerabilities of creativity and psychopathology will, it is hoped, allow us to understand more fully the creative processes that are important to the enrichment, survival, and progress of the human species. This understanding may also suggest areas of focus to help those who suffer from psychopathology to bolster protective mechanisms. There is a long history of suffering associated with great artistic and scientific achievement. The individuals who pay the price for this achievement through increased vulnerability to mental illness are worthy and deserving of our investigatory resources and our gratitude.

References

Abdolmaleky, H. M., Faraone, S. V., Glatt, S. J. and Tsuang, M. T. (2004). Meta-analysis of association between the T102C polymorphism of the 5HT2a receptor gene and schizophrenia. *Schizophrenia Research*, 67, 53–62.

Amabile, T. M. (1996). *Creativity in context*. Boulder, CO: Westview Press.

American Psychiatric Association (APA) (1987). *Diagnostic and statistical manual of mental disorders* (3rd edn.). Washington, DC: Author.

American Psychiatric Association (APA) (1994). *Diagnostic and statistical manual of mental disorders* (4th edn.). Washington, DC: Author.

American Psychiatric Association (APA) (2013). *Diagnostic and statistical manual of mental disorders* (5th edn.). Arlington, VA: American Psychiatric Publishing.

Andreasen, N. (1987). Creativity and mental illness: Prevalence rates in writers and their first-degree relatives. *American Journal of Psychiatry*, 144, 1288–1292.

Andreasen, N. (2008). Creativity and mood disorders. *Dialogues in Clinical Neuroscience*, 10, 252–255.

Aristophanes (424 BCE). *The knights*. http://classics.mit.edu/Aristophanes/knights.pl.txt, last accessed March 18, 2014.

Aristotle (1984). Problems. In J. Barnes (Ed.), *The complete works of Aristotle: The revised Oxford translation* (Vol. 2) (pp. 1319–1527). Princeton University Press.

Ashby, F. G., Isen, A. M. and Turken, A. U. (1999). A neuropsychological theory of positive affect and its influence on cognition. *Psychological Review*, 106, 529–550.

Baddeley, A. (1986). *Working memory*. Oxford: Clarendon Press.

Barnett, G. H., Salmond, G. H., Jones, P. B. and Sahakian, B. J. (2006). Cognitive reserve in neuropsychiatry. *Psychological Medicine*, 36, 1053–1064.

Barron, F. (1955). The disposition toward originality. *Journal of Abnormal and Social Psychology*, 51, 478–485.

Barron, F. (1969). *Creative person and creative process*. New York: Holt, Rinehart & Winston.

Baruch, I., Hemsley, D. R. and Gray, J. A. (1988a). Differential performance of acute and chronic schizophrenics in a latent inhibition task. *Journal of Nervous and Mental Disease*, 176, 598–606.

Baruch, I., Hemsley, D. R. and Gray, J. A. (1988b). Latent inhibition and "psychotic proneness" in normal subjects. *Personality and Individual Differences*, 9, 777–783.

Becker, G. (2001). The association of creativity and psychopathology: Its cultural-historical origins. *Creativity Research Journal*, 13, 45–53.

Berenbaum, H. and Fujita, F. (1994). Schizophrenia and personality: Exploring the boundaries and connections between vulnerability and outcome. *Journal of Abnormal Psychology*, 103, 148–158.

Berrettini, W. H. (2000). Susceptibility loci for bipolar disorder: Overlap with inherited vulnerability to schizophrenia. *Biological Psychiatry*, 47, 245–251.

Beveridge, W. I. B. (1957). *The art of scientific investigation*. New York: W.W. Norton & Co.

Brang, D. and Ramachandran, V. S. (2007). Psychopharmacology of synesthesia: The role of serotonin S2a receptor activation. *Medical Hypotheses*, 70, 903–904.

Brod, J. H. (1987). Creativity and schizotypy. In G. Claridge (Ed.), *Schizotypy: Implications for illness and health* (pp. 274–298). Oxford: Oxford University Press.

Burch, G. St. J., Pavelis, C., Hemsley, D. R. and Corr, P. J. (2006). Schizotypy and creativity in visual artists. *British Journal of Psychology*, 97, 177–190.

Buss, D. and Barnes, M. (1986). Preferences in human mate selection. *Journal of Personality and Social Psychology*, 50, 559–570.

Carson, S. H. (2001). *Demons and muses: An exploration of cognitive features and vulnerability to psychosis in creative individuals*. Retrieved from dissertations and theses database, Harvard University, AAT3011334.

Carson, S. H. (2010). *Your creative brain: Seven steps to maximize imagination, productivity, and innovation in your life*. San Francisco, CA: Jossey-Bass.

Carson, S. H. (2011). Creativity and psychopathology: A genetic shared-vulnerability model. *Canadian Journal of Psychiatry*, 56, 144–153.

Carson, S. H., Peterson, J. B. and Higgins, D. M. (2003). Decreased latent inhibition is associated with increased creative achievement in high-functioning individuals. *Journal of Personality and Social Psychology*, 85, 499–506.

Cattell, R. B. and Drevdahl, J. E. (1955). A comparison of the personality profile (16PF) of eminent researchers with that of eminent teachers and administrators, and of the general populations. *British Journal of Psychology*, 46, 248–261.

Claridge, G. (Ed.) (1997). *Schizotypy: Implications for illness and health*. New York: Oxford University Press.

Cohen, G. D. (2006). Research on creativity and aging: The positive impact of the arts on health and illness. *Generations*, 30(1), 7–15.

Colvin, K. (1995). Mood disorders and symbolic function: An investigation of object relations and ego development in classical musicians. *Dissertation Abstracts International. Section B: The Sciences and Engineering*, 55(11-B), 5062.

Cox, A. J. and Leon, J. L. (1999). Negative schizotypal traits in the relation of creativity to psychopathology. *Creativity Research Journal*, 12, 25–36.

Crow, T. J. (1997). Is schizophrenia the price that Homo sapiens pays for language? *Schizophrenia Research*, 28, 127–141.

Csikszentmihalyi, M. (1996). *Creativity: Flow and the psychology of discovery and invention*. New York: HarperCollins.

Dardis, T. (1989). *The thirsty muse: Alcohol and the American writer*. New York: Tichnor & Fields.

Darvis, M. and Palmiter, R. D. (2011). Contributions of striatal dopamine signaling to the modulation of cognitive flexibility. *Biological Psychiatry*, 69, 704–707.

Davis, K. L., Kahn, R. S., Ko, G. and Davidson, M. (1991). Dopamine in schizophrenia: A review and reconceptualization. *American Journal of Psychiatry*, 148, 1474–1486.

DeYoung, C. G., Flanders, J. L. and Peterson, J. B. (2008). Cognitive abilities involved in insight problem solving: an individual differences model. *Creativity Research Journal*, 20, 278–290.

Dietrich, A. (2003). Functional neuroanatomy of altered states of consciousness: The transient hypofrontality hypothesis. *Consciousness & Cognition*, 12, 231–256.

Drevdahl, J. E. and Cattell, R. B. (1958). Personality and creativity in artists and writers. *Journal of Clinical Personality*, 14, 107–111.

Einstein, A. (1952). Preface. In M. Planck, *Where is science going?* New York: W.W. Norton & Co.

Ekelund, J., Lichtermann, D., Jarvelin, M. R. and Peltonen, L. (1999). Association between novelty seeking and the type 4 dopamine receptor gene in a large Finnish cohort sample. *American Journal of Psychiatry*, 156, 1453–1455.

Feinberg, I. (1982). Schizophrenia: Caused by a fault in programmed synaptic elimination during adolescence? *Journal of Psychiatric Research*, 17, 319–334.

Fink, A. and Benedek, M. (2013). The creative brain: Brain correlates underlying the generation of original ideas. In O. Vartanian, A. S. Bristol and J. C. Kaufman (Eds.), *The neuroscience of creativity* (pp. 207–231). Cambridge, MA: MIT Press.

Fink, A., Grabner, R. H., Benedek, M., Reishofer, G., Hauswirth, V., Fally, M. *et al.* (2009). The creative brain: Investigation of brain activity during creative problem solving by means of EEG and fMRI. *Human Brain Mapping*, 30, 734–748.

Frederickson, B. (2001). The role of positive emotions in positive psychology: The Broaden-and-Build Theory of positive emotions. *American Psychologist*, 56(3), 218–226.

Frye, M. A. and Salloum, I. M. (2006). Bipolar disorder and comorbid alcoholism: Prevalence rate and treatment considerations. *Bipolar Disorder*, 8, 677–685.

Gabora, L. and Kaufman, S. B. (2010). Evolutionary approaches to creativity. In J. C. Kaufman and R. J. Sternberg (Eds.), *The Cambridge handbook of creativity* (pp. 279–300). New York: Cambridge University Press.

Galvin, R. (2004). William Blake: Visions and verses. *Humanities*, 25, 16–20.

Golimbet, V. E., Aksenova, M. G., Nosikov, V. V., Orlova, V. A. and Kaleda, V. G. (2003). Analysis of the linkage of the Taq1A and Taq1B loci of the dopamine D2 receptor gene with schizophrenia in patients and their siblings. *Neuroscience and Behavioral Physiology*, 33, 223–225.

Goodwin, D. W. (1992). Alcohol as muse. *American Journal of Psychotherapy*, 46, 422–433.

Green, M. J. and Williams, L. M. (1999). Schizotypy and creativity as effects of reduced cognitive inhibition. *Personality and Individual Differences*, 27, 263–276.

Grucza, R. A., Cloninger, C. R., Bucholz, K. K., Constantino, J. N., Schuckit, M. I., Dick, D. M. *et al.* (2006). Novelty seeking as a moderator of familial risk for alcohol dependence. *Alcoholism: Clinical and Experimental Research*, 30, 1176–1183.

Heston, L. L. (1966). Psychiatric disorders in foster home reared children of schizophrenic mothers. *British Journal of Psychiatry*, 112, 819–825.

Hubbard, E. M. and Ramachandran, V. S. (2005). Neurocognitive mechanisms of synaesthesia. *Neuron*, 48, 509–520.

IBM Corporation (2010). *2010 Global Chief Executive Officer Study*. Somers, NY: IBM Global Business Services.

Jamison, K. (1989). Mood disorders and patterns of creativity in British writers and artists. *Psychiatry*, 52, 125–134.

Jamison, K. (1993). *Touched with fire: Manic-depressive illness and the artistic temperament*. New York: Free Press.

Jensen, E. F. (2001). *Schumann*. New York: Oxford University Press.

Karlsson, J. L. (1970). Genetic association of giftedness and creativity with schizophrenia. *Hereditas*, 66, 177–182.

Keefe, J. A. and Magaro, P. A. (1980). Creativity and schizophrenia: An equivalence of cognitive processing. *Journal of Abnormal Psychology*, 89, 390–398.

Kéri, S. (2009). Genes for psychosis and creativity: A promoter polymorphism of the neuregulin 1 gene is related to creativity in people with high intellectual achievement. *Psychological Science*, 20, 1070–1073.

Kéri, S. (2011). Solitary minds and social capital: Latent inhibition, general intellectual functions and social network size predict creative achievements. *Psychology of Aesthetics, Creativity, and the Arts*, 5, 215–221.

Kessler, R. C., Berglund, P., Demler, O., Jin, R., Merikangas, K. R. and Walters, E. E. (2005). Lifetime prevalence and age-of-onset distribution of *DSM-IV* disorders in the National Comorbidity Survey replication. *Archives of General Psychiatry*, 62, 593–602.

Kinney, D. K., Richards, R., Lowing, P. A., LeBlanc, D., Zimbalist, M. E. and Harlan, P. (2000–2001). Creativity in offspring of schizophrenic and control parents: An adoption study. *Creativity Research Journal*, 13, 17–25.

Koestler, A. (1990). *The act of creation*. London: Penguin Arkana.

Kyaga, S., Landén, M., Boman, M., Hultman, C. M., Långström, N. and Lichtenstein, P. (2012). Mental illness, suicide and creativity: 40-year prospective total population study. *Journal of Psychiatric Research*, 47(1), 83–90.

Lombroso, C. (1891/1976). *The man of genius*. London: Walter Scott.

Lubow, R. E. and Gewirtz, J. C. (1995). Latent inhibition in humans: Data, theory, and implications for schizophrenia. *Psychological Bulletin*, 117, 87–103.

Lubow, R. E., Ingberg-Sachs, Y., Zalstein-Orda, N. and Gewirtz, J. C. (1992). Latent inhibition in low and high "psychotic-prone" normal subjects. *Personality and Individual Differences*, 13, 563–572.

Ludwig, A. (1990). Alcohol input and creative output. *British Journal of Addiction*, 85, 953–963.

Ludwig, A. (1992). Creative achievement and psychopathology: Comparison among professions. *American Journal of Psychotherapy*, 46, 330–354.

Ludwig, A. (1994). Mental illness and creative activity in female writers. *American Journal of Psychiatry*, 151, 1650–1656.

Ludwig, A. (1995). *The price of greatness: Resolving the creativity and madness controversy*. New York: Guilford Press.

McCrae, R. R. (1987). Creativity, divergent thinking, and openness to experience. *Journal of Personality and Social Psychology*, 52(6), 1258–1265.

McCrae, R. R. (1993). Openness to experience as a basic dimension of personality. *Imagination, Cognition and Personality*, 13, 39–55.

McCrea, S. M. (2008). Bipolar disorder and neurophysiologic mechanisms. *Neuropsychiatric Disease and Treatment*, 4(6), 1129–1153.

MacKinnon, D. W. (1962). The nature and nurture of creative talent. *American Psychologist*, 17, 484–495.

Maher, B. (1972). The language of schizophrenia: A review and interpretation. *British Journal of Psychiatry*, 120, 3–17.

Maslow, A. H. (1970). *Motivation and personality* (2nd edn.). New York: Harper & Row.

Mason, O. and Claridge, G. (2006). The Oxford–Liverpool inventory of feelings and experiences (O-LIFE): Further description and extended norms. *Schizophrenia Research*, 82, 203–211.

Mason, O., Linney, Y. and Claridge, G. (2005). Short scales for measuring schizotypy. *Schizophrenia Research*, 78, 293–296.

Mednick, S. (1962). The associative basis of the creative process. *Psychological Review*, 69, 220–232.

Memmert, D. and Roth, K. (2007). The effects of non-specific and specific concepts on tactical creativity in team ball sports. *Journal of Sports Sciences*, 25(12), 1423–1432.

Nasar, S. (1998). *A beautiful mind: The life of mathematical genius and Nobel Laureate John Nash*. New York: Simon & Schuster.

Nettle, D. (2006). Schizotypy and mental health amongst poets, visual artists, and mathematicians. *Journal of Research in Personality*, 40, 876–890.

Nettle, D. and Clegg, H. (2006). Schizotypy, creativity and mating success in humans. *Proceedings of the Royal Society, B. Biological Sciences*, 273, 611–615.

Noble, E. P. (2000). Addiction and its reward process through polymorphisms of the D2 dopamine receptor gene: A review. *European Psychiatry*, 15, 79–89.

Norlander, T. (1999). Inebriation and inspiration? A review of the research on alcohol and creativity. *Journal of Creative Behavior*, 33, 22–44.

O'Connor, K. (2009). Cognitive and meta-cognitive dimensions of psychoses. *Canadian Journal of Psychiatry*, 54, 152–159.

O'Reilly, T., Dunbar, R. and Bentall, R. (2001). Schizotypy and creativity: An evolutionary connection. *Personality and Individual Differences*, 31, 1067–1078.

Peterson, J. B. and Carson, S. (2000). Latent inhibition and openness to experience in a high-achieving student population. *Personality and Individual Differences*, 28, 323–332.

Pickover, C. A. (1998). *Strange brains and genius*. New York: Plenum Press.

Plato (360 BCE) *Phaedrus*. MIT internet classics. http://classics.mit.edu/Plato/phaedrus.html, last accessed March 19, 2014.

Popper, K. (1959/2005). *The logic of scientific discovery*. London: Routledge.

Poreh, A. M., Whitman, D. R. and Ross, T. P. (1994). Creative thinking abilities and hemispheric asymmetry in schizotypal college students. *Current Psychology: Developmental, Learning, Personality, Social*, 12, 344–352.

Post, F. (1994). Creativity and psychopathology: A study of 291world-famous men. *British Journal of Psychiatry*, 165, 22–34.

Post, F. (1996). Verbal creativity, depression and alcoholism: An investigation of one hundred American and British writers. *British Journal of Psychiatry*, 168, 545–555.

Prentky, R. A. (1979). Creativity and psychopathology: A neurocognitive perspective. In B. Maher (Ed.), *Progress in experimental personality research* (Vol. 9) (pp. 1–39). New York: Academic Press.

Prentky, R. A. (1989). Creativity and psychopathology: Gamboling at the seat of madness. In J. A. Glover, R. R. Ronning and C. R. Reynolds (Eds.), *Handbook of creativity* (pp. 243–270). New York: Plenum Press.

Prentky, R. A. (2000–2001). Mental illness and roots of genius. *Creativity Research Journal*, 13(1), 95–104.

Pritzker, S. A. (1999). Alcohol and creativity. In M. A. Runco and S. R. Pritzker (Eds.), *Encyclopedia of creativity* (Vol. 1) (pp. 53–57). San Diego: Academic Press.

Ramachandran, V. S. and Hubbard, E. M. (2001). Synaesthesia – a window into perception, thought and language. *Journal of Consciousness Studies*, 8, 3–34.

Rawlings, D. and Locarnini, A. (2008). Dimensional schizotypy, autism, and unusual word associations in artists and scientists. *Journal of Research in Personality*, 42, 465–471.

Reuter, M., Panksepp, J., Schnabel, N., Kellerhoff, N., Kempel, P. and Hennig, J. (1995). Personality and biological markers of creativity. *European Journal of Personality*, 19, 83–95.

Reuter, M., Roth, S., Holve, K. and Hennig, J. (2006a). Identification of first genes for creativity: A pilot study. *Brain Research*, 1069, 190–197.

Reuter, M., Schmitz, A., Corr, P. and Hennig, J. (2006b). Molecular genetics support Gray's personality theory: The interaction of COMT and DRD2 polymorphisms predicts the behavioural approach system. *International Journal of Neuropsychopharmacology*, 9, 155–166.

Richards, R., Kinney, D. K., Lunde, I., Benet, M. and Merzel, A. P. C. (1988). Creativity in manic-depressives, cyclothymes, their normal relatives, and control subjects. *Journal of Abnormal Psychology*, 97, 281–288.

Rimer, M., Barrett, D. W., Maldonado, M. A., Vock, V. M and Gonzalez-Lima, F. (2005). Neuregulin-1 immunoglobulin-like domain mutant mice: Clozapine sensitivity and impaired latent inhibition. *NeuroReport*, 16, 271–275.

Rose, P. (1979). *Woman of letters: Life of Virginia Woolf.* London: Routledge & Kegan Paul.

Roy, K., Murtie, J. C., El-Khodor, B. F., Edgar, N., Sardi, S. P., Hooks, B. M. et al. (2007). Loss of erbB signaling in oligodendrocytes alters myelin and dopaminergic function, a potential mechanism for neuropsychiatric disorders. *Proceedings of the National Academy of Sciences USA*, 104, 8131–8136.

Sawyer, K. (2012). *Explaining creativity: The science of human innovation* (2nd edn.). New York: Oxford University Press.

Schlesinger, J. (2009). Creative mythconceptions: A closer look at the evidence for the "mad genius" hypothesis. *Psychology of Aesthetics, Creativity, and the Arts*, 3(2), 62–72.

Schuldberg, D., French, C., Stone, B. L. and Heberle, J. (1988). Creativity and schizotypal traits: Creativity test scores and perceptual aberration, magical ideation, and impulsive nonconformity. *Journal of Nervous and Mental Disease*, 176, 648–657.

Schweizer, T. J. (2006). The psychology of novelty-seeking, creativity and innovation: Neurocognitive aspects within a work–psychological perspective. *Creativity and Innovation Management*, 15, 164–172.

Serretti, A. and Mandelli, L. (2008). The genetics of bipolar disorder: Genome "hot regions," genes, new potential candidates and future directions. *Molecular Psychiatry*, 13, 742–771.

Simonton, D. K. (2005). Are genius and madness related? Contemporary answers to an ancient question. *Psychiatric Times*, 22, 21–22.

Sternberg, R. J. and O'Hara, L. A. (1999). Creativity and intelligence. In R. J. Sternberg (Ed.), *Handbook of creativity* (pp. 251–272). New York: Cambridge University Press.

Styron, W. (1990). *Darkness visible: A memoir of madness.* New York: Random House.

Tosato, S., Dazzan, P. and Collier, D. (2005). Association between the neuregulin 1 gene and schizophrenia: A systematic review. *Schizophrenia Bulletin*, 31, 613–617.

Waford, R. N. and Lewine, R. (2010). Is perseveration uniquely characteristic of schizophrenia? *Schizophrenia Research*, 118, 128–133.

Weiner, I. (2003). The "two-headed" latent inhibition model of schizophrenia: Modeling positive and negative symptoms and their treatment. *Psychopharmacology*, 169, 257–297.

Weisberg, R. W. (1994). Genius and madness? A quasi-experimental test of the hypothesis that manic-depression increases creativity. *Psychological Science*, 5(6), 361–367.

Whitfield, J. B., Nightingale, B. N., O'Brien, M. E., Heath, A. C., Birley, A. J. and Martin, N. G. (1998). Molecular biology of alcohol dependence, a complex polygenic disorder. *Clinical Chemistry and Laboratory Medicine*, 36, 633–636.

Whitfield-Gabrieli, S., Thermenos, H. W., Milanovic, S., Tsuang, M. T., Faraone, S. V., McCarley, R. W. et al. (2009). Hyperactivity and hyperconnectivity of the default network in schizophrenia and in first-degree relatives of persons with schizophrenia. *Proceedings of the National Academy of Science USA*, 106, 1279–1284.

Wills, G. I. (2003). Forty lives in the bebop business: Mental health in a group of eminent jazz musicians. *British Journal of Psychiatry*, 183, 255–259.

Woodberry, K. A., Giuliano, A. J. and Seidman, L. J. (2008). Premorbid IQ in schizophrenia: A meta-analytic review. *American Journal of Psychiatry*, 165, 579–587.

Woodward, N. D., Cowan, R. L., Park, S., Ansari, M. S., Baldwin, R. M., Li, R. *et al.* (2011). Correlation of individual differences in schizotypal personality traits with amphetamine-induced dopamine release in striatal and extrastriatal brain regions. *American Journal of Psychiatry*, 168, 418–426.

World Health Organization (2001). *Mental health: New understanding, new hope.* Geneva: Author.

13   On the fragility of the artist: art's precarious triad

Maja Djikic and Keith Oatley

Beauty is truth, truth beauty, – that is all
Ye know on earth, and all ye need to know.

– John Keats

When Amy Winehouse, a 27-year-old British singer, died in her London flat in July of 2011, few were surprised. While her musical talent was prodigious (her singing was compared to that of Billy Holiday), her battle with alcohol and drug addiction also attracted public attention. Her breakout song was entitled "Rehab." Was she not another artist sacrificed at the altar of the muses?

Are we not tripped, here, by a stereotype (Kaufman *et al.*, 2006), seduced by an availability heuristic? After all, how many alcoholics perish quietly out of the public eye? And given that we are unable to calculate conditional probabilities for this kind of case, we may wonder whether the chance of Amy Winehouse overdosing on alcohol would have been the same if she had not been an accomplished songwriter and singer (Silvia and Kaufman, 2010).

An argument of the kind that can follow from assuming causal connections between artistic creativity and mental illness has been made by Currie (2011). He drew on a study by Post (1994) who made psychiatric diagnoses of 291 famous men from biographies. Post found that 48 percent of writers had severe psychopathology, whereas rates of psychopathology in scientists, statesmen, and thinkers were lower. On the basis of these and similar data, Currie argues that we cannot expect to learn anything useful from people who are as crazy as many writers seem to be. In this argument, Currie accepts that correlation means causality; that mental illness contributes to the writer's art; and he assumes that the illnesses of the writers were permanent. Therefore, he concludes, one should not take the writers seriously. He also makes no comparison with levels of mental illness in the ordinary community. The best recent study of psychiatric disorder in the community is by Moffitt *et al.* (2010), who found in a prospective study that the proportion of people who had suffered an anxiety disorder during their lives was 49.5 percent, the proportion who had suffered from depression was 41.4 percent, and the proportion who had experienced alcohol dependence was 31.8 percent (a substantial proportion of people had more than one disorder). So it is not clear how different the fiction writers in Post's study were in their rates of disorder from members of the ordinary population. One may also remark that most mental disorders (anxiety and depression being the most common) do not start because of something wrong in people's brains. More usually they start because something has gone wrong in their lives (Brown and Harris, 1978; Oatley and Bolton, 1985).

The questions of whether mental illness might contribute to artistic creativity, and whether artistic creativity might drive people into mental illness, are empirical. They have been tackled by many researchers (for research reviews, see Kaufman, 2009; Weisberg, 2006). But as Silvia and Kaufman (2010) stress, the data are correlational. They suffer from the problem known in statistics as the third variable, which here means that creativity and mental illness might co-occur because they are both related to one or more other variables. In other words, arguments of the kind proposed by Currie can be spurious because literary creativity and mental illness may not be related directly; both could derive from one or more third variables. It is this possibility we explore here. As Silvia and Kaufman point out, although there are many studies of relationships between artistic creativity and mental illness, very few of them include measures of third variables. A rare example of a study that did so was by Miller and Tal (2006). They measured creativity by means of verbal and visual tests in 225 students, and also measured schizotypy (unusual thinking and experience of the kind that occurs in schizophrenia), Big Five personality traits (which conceive of personality as consisting of five basic traits: Extraversion, Neuroticism, Openness, Conscientiousness, and Agreeableness [McCrae and Costa, 2003]), and intelligence. When they performed a first-order correlation, schizotypy was associated with creativity, but when, in regression tests, the third variable of the personality trait of Openness and the factor of intelligence were controlled for, the correlation disappeared. It was Openness and intelligence that predicted creativity, not schizotypy.

In this chapter, we suggest a route to understanding the connection between art and mental illness that considers possible third variables. We propose a theoretical framework about what characteristics artists need – given what we know about art – and how these characteristics might also relate to mental illness. We hope this approach gives a useful perspective to the difficult-to-disentangle problem surrounding the vision of the "mad artist." In this approach, although we started our paper with a stereotype (an addicted artist), we abide by Silvia and Kaufman's (2010) cautions, and make no further appeal to specific cases.

In this chapter, much of our discussion is in terms of traits of personality, because it is with this concept that the relationship between artist and mental illness has usually been framed. But along the way we propose that situational factors, as well as factors specific to the production of art, are important. We propose that three qualities need to coexist in an artist, and are necessary for successful works of art to be made: sensitivity, emotion-driven preoccupation with exploration within a particular medium of expression (which we call "artistic compulsion"), and lack of self-deception. We argue that each of these factors separately provides a necessary, but not sufficient, contribution to artistic personality, while the three in combination may be both necessary and sufficient for the kind of personality required for artistic production. Because of the propinquity of these qualities with risk factors that can indeed contribute to mental illness, these qualities can also, we suggest, place artists in a precarious position.

Sensitivity

Many people take it for granted that artists are more sensitive than others. There are two ways in which this may be true. From the perceptual perspective, for example in the field of tone recognition, a more sensitive person can perceive the difference between the two tones more accurately than a less sensitive person. This means that, to a more perceptually sensitive person, the world is more differentiated and contains more things. The objects of perception, of course, need not be only external; they may be internal as well. Perceptions themselves, as well as emotions and thoughts, are subject to the sensitivity of the artist.

The second way in which artists can be called sensitive belongs to the modern field of personality. Of particular interest among the "Big Five" traits mentioned earlier is Neuroticism, which usually connotes proneness to negative emotions and emotional instability (McCrae and Costa, 2003). Neuroticism is unfortunately named, because it has its own stereotypic power in relation to the personality of artists, and it is useful to examine it more carefully. At one end, this dimension has come to be synonymous with poor adjustment and malfunction; at the other end, it is known as Emotional Stability. From the perspective of the Big Five model, Neuroticism describes people who are easily stressed, often upset, and moody. It is one trait, but has two components that are distinguishable. The first component is simply sensitivity of the emotional system to events: the point at which a person perceives a meaningful difference that engages the emotional system (Eysenck, 1970). The second component is response to these meaningful events. From the Big Five perspective, someone high on the scale of Neuroticism is someone who both perceives something (perhaps barely perceptible to others) and also responds by being caught up in its negative aspects – for instance, by becoming moody, worried, irritable, or dejected about it. This kind of person, in other words, is adversely affected by the negativity of events and their aspects of danger, loss, and defeat. This kind of person's life as a whole tends to be marked by the negativity bias of feeling oppressed, threatened, and depressed, rather than by enjoyment of positive aspects.

From the perspective of the model that we are building for our artist, it is only the component of Sensitivity that is required. Sensitive individuals experience keenly both positive and negative aspects of reality, which makes them liable to be emotionally more volatile. Emotional volatility is perhaps a better dimensional opposite to Emotional Stability than is Neuroticism. Unless issues that cause emotions are explored and resolved, the emotional volatility can easily tip into depression, anxiety, or mania. For artists, the intensity of emotional life both serves as a fuel to their artistic production and leaves them more vulnerable to the potential of mental illness.

The factor of Sensitivity shares meaningful similarity with the factor of low latent inhibition, which is a part of Carson's (2011) shared vulnerability model of creativity and psychopathology. According to this model, low latent inhibition – low capacity to screen from conscious awareness stimuli that are irrelevant – is one of the qualities that contributes both to general creativity and to mental illness by enabling more unfiltered stimuli to be available in conscious awareness. From the perspective of our model, however, a perception that might seem irrelevant (or invisible) to another would enter conscious awareness because it has been deemed relevant to self. So while a physicist with low latent inhibition might get an influx of seemingly irrelevant data that she may then use to create a more complex or novel theory (if she is intelligent enough to systematize the information in a meaningful way and so not slide into schizophrenia or psychosis), a highly sensitive writer may get an influx of stimuli she perceives are relevant to self, and may struggle to maintain emotional equilibrium without succumbing to depression or bipolar disorder.

Here, then, is a way in which a common factor – Sensitivity – can account both for an aspect of artistic activity and for susceptibility to mental illness, but without the art causing illness or the illness causing art.

Artistic compulsion (or emotion-driven preoccupation with exploration through some artistic medium)

The second factor we propose can co-occur naturally with Sensitivity is emotion-impelled compulsion to create. Emotions are important in psychology and art because they are neither inherent (like aspects of personality) nor external (like objects of perception). They are uniquely important because they signal meetings between inward concerns (or goals) and events. They are our best, most informative signposts to significance in the human world. Emotional signals (most of which indicate discrepancy between what one implicitly or explicitly believes or wants the world to be and the way the world turns out) provide individuals with energy and impetus to deal with the often problematic issues at hand (Frijda, 2007). We argue that artists require the trait whereby the impetus caused by emotion feeds preoccupation with exploring the issue through some artistic medium. The issue can be a unique, personal one, or as insoluble as "love" or "death," or a political issue, such as the oppression of certain kinds of people in society. The lasting nature of artistic media allows one to explore experiences at length and in depth, to lift them from the ephemeral to the lasting.

Our formulation is related to, but different from, the one proposed by Collingwood (1938). He thought that art proper could be understood as an exploration of emotion, expressed in a language. Imagine, he says, a man as follows:

At first he is conscious of having an emotion, but not conscious of what this emotion is. All he is conscious of is a perturbation or excitement, which he feels going on within him, but of whose nature he is ignorant. While in this state, all he can say about his emotion is: "I feel . . . I don't know how I feel." From this helpless and oppressed condition, he extricates himself by doing something which we call expressing himself. This is an activity which has something to do with the thing we call language: he expresses himself by speaking. It also has something to do with consciousness: the emotion expressed is the emotion of whose nature the person who feels it is no longer unconscious. (Collingwood, 1938, pp. 109–110)

Collingwood says that the language may be of words, of painting, of music, or of some other artistic medium. We agree with the importance of emotion for the production of art, but we would like to extend Collingwood's idea by suggesting that art does not necessarily need to focus on the emotion as such; the focus could for instance be on some state of society, an aspect of inequality, for example. The subject of art may, indeed, be any aspect of experience that perturbs, and seems to impel exploration, because it is not yet understood. Our modification is that, although we propose art is impelled by an emotion, the focus of a work of art need not itself be an emotion. The result is that, while emotion has often been the subject examined under the artist's magnifying glass, this need not always be so.

The emotions of artists are not different from those of other people. Rather, artists seek to transform the experience and the exploration of the issue prompted by the emotions into an external object (in their chosen language of writing, painting, music, or whatever it might be) to try and understand it. As Hyde (1983) suggests, this externalization may then be offered as a gift to others who can themselves take part in the art by bringing it alive for themselves. Readers, viewers, and audience members are not passive. They do not merely receive art. In their engagement with art, people themselves may become artists and not necessarily in ways that the original artist intended.

As with the case of Sensitivity and Neuroticism, one can see that there is likely to be an association between artistic compulsion in the exploration of inner experience of the world and such disorders as the painful shyness of introversion, and/or an undue Openness to sensation seeking, and/or the obsessional side of Conscientiousness, because the element of emotionally sustained preoccupation can also be related to these. Engagement in one's inner life is not, however, the same as painful shyness that drains social confidence and leads to social phobia. Being compelled by emotions does not mean that one is driven to seek out emotional thrills. And being obsessed with certain problems in the production of art in a certain medium is not the same as having an obsessive–compulsive disorder.

If you are a reader of fiction, you may recognize that you have an interest in novels of a particular kind, perhaps love stories, perhaps stories of conflicts in families, perhaps depictions of how wrongs are righted, or perhaps adventures. An interest in a certain kind of theme is sometimes called a fantasy. So, for instance, Radway (1984) and Vivanco and Kramer (2010) have depicted important elements of the fantasies involved in love stories. Often, the term "fantasy" comes with a sneer. But this should not be so. The real meaning of fantasy in this context is an inner structure with which an externalized work of art can resonate: a mental schema derived from experiences of life that have been important, perhaps from childhood, perhaps from momentous events later in life, or perhaps with lovers. Such experiences can leave a residue of concentration in the mind, a focus or nexus, to which a person can return in a somewhat obsessional way, a template to which later experience can be assimilated. One might call this a theme rather than a fantasy.

Corresponding with the fantasies or themes of readers and audience members are the fantasies or themes of artists, including writers, who

work on them in ways that they hope will resonate with the inner structures of readers and audience members. In other words, each artist tends
to have certain emotion-driven issues at which they work, first from one
angle and then from another. With any such theme, an inner schema
is maintained from which new experience can be developed, and with
which – inexhaustibly – a motivation for further exploration can be
derived. In each artist, therefore, a certain set of issues tends to pervade
their works, sometimes explicitly as, for instance, with writers who focus
on heterosexual or homosexual love themes, or with writers who focus
on ravages of post-colonialism, although sometimes the themes may be
more difficult to recognize.

In clinical psychology, preoccupation with a particular emotion-driven
experience, with compulsions to return to it and to make it central to
mental life, is known as rumination (Joormann *et al.*, 2006; Nolen-
Hoeksema *et al.*, 2008). Rumination has been shown to be related to
depression, and also to anxiety states. After a severe life event such as a
loss, failure, or threat, the feature of rumination that makes it pathological
is a lack of working through, a dwelling in the anguish of the state itself.
Artists are vulnerable to tipping into rumination and anxiety instead of
active exploration, but so are non-artists who have a preoccupation with
the inner world.

You may ask whether or not this trait – artistic compulsion – can be
applied to anyone but artists. Are we making a meaningless distinction?
We think not. One can be writing one's novel every night for 10 years,
but unless one has both the sensitivity to perceive things that may be less
clear to others (and sometimes oneself) and the truthfulness to address
the issue at hand without self-deception, one will never write a novel that
should be called art. So, a person may be considered an artist, have thirst
for creating art, and make artistic efforts, but without our third quality
she will, in the end, not succeed in creating a work of real art.

Lack of self-deception

The idea of psychological defense has a long history in personality psychology. Freud described many defenses that help individuals deal with
the realities of their life by distorting them (Freud, 1933/1991). Denial,
rationalization, projection, and so on all function to maintain an image
of the self and the world by distorting information that challenges this
image. By "image" we do not just mean "impression offered to others,"
but a deep sense of reality. The defenses are not meant just for impression management (to induce other people to have a particular belief
about qualities of the self), but a mechanism for psychological survival.

An umbrella term that we will use in this chapter for cognitively based defenses is self-deception. Self-deception can be any self-defense that distorts perception and comprehension of reality to protect the psychological stability of self (Peterson, 1999). For example, Djikic et al. (2005) found that self-deceiving individuals among undergraduates experience distortion in memory within 15 minutes of being exposed to negative information relevant to self. Distorting incoming information to fit one's own conceptual scheme appears to be universal; it becomes pathological only when it is used extensively to ward off perception and comprehension of unwanted reality (Ramachandran, 1996).

A relative lack of self-deception is the third quality that we claim to be important to artists. We claim that, for art to be created, it is necessary for artists to be truthful, not self-deceptive, in that specific aspect of the self related to the domain of their art. If they are unable to be truthful within this domain, their art will be of no use to them. Even more important, it would be of no significant interest to anyone else, because it would represent merely a self-absorbed quirk of the person who produced it, not sufficient to communicate usefully to others.

According to our model, an artist could be self-deceptive about aspects of the self and world that are not related to her art (and this is a difficult distinction to maintain), or while not creating art (or good art, if we may make this distinction). Why is this quality necessary for artists? In the previous section, we argued that art is based on a certain fantasy, a metaphorical description of a truthful experience at a certain level of abstraction. The scientist studies the laws of the world, and artists the laws of human nature as this nature confronts the world. A primary source for the model of self and the world (and other selves in the world) can be nothing other than the artist herself. Motivated distortion in perception and comprehension in this sense is bound to kill the truth, or, as Keats would have it, the beauty, of art.

Self-deception is most often reflected in an unwillingness to confront negative aspects of life experience. If artists are less self-deceptive, they should be more willing to face and explore the negative aspects of their experience. We have taken this as a hypothesis and tested some aspects of it. For instance, in a study of distinguished fiction writers and distinguished scientists (Djikic et al., 2006), we used Pennebaker's Linguistic Inquiry Word Count (LIWC), a computerized text analysis program that Pennebaker and his colleagues had developed to analyze the ways in which people use language, and what that use reveals about their psychological states (Pennebaker and Ireland, 2011). We found that the fiction writers were more preoccupied with negative experiences (using more negative emotion words) than were the scientists. This does not mean they were more depressed – we excluded that possibility empirically. While the support this finding offers for our proposal is limited, it hints at artists' seemingly unusual willingness to confront the negative in their experience. Furthermore, factors such as IQ and cognitive flexibility, which are considered protective from the general creativity perspective (Carson, 2011), may be dangerous to self-deceivers, who could use their intelligence and ability to see matters from various perspectives to defend and fortify their self-deceptions.

Lack of self-deception, however, has its dangers. One useful way to conceptualize self-deception is to think of it as a mental form of a human endorphin system (Goleman, 1985). Endorphins protect us against pain during stress, but they can then leave us to the pain so that we might address its source once the situation is less urgent. In a similar way, self-deception protects the psychological system of self against psychological pain until we feel ready to address its source. Physical and psychological pain share underlying neurological mechanisms (MacDonald and Leary, 2005). Just as one might continue using painkillers after a back problem is solved, so self-deception, which reduces psychological pain, can become addictive. This may be a reason why individuals who are lacking in self-deception, who need protection against psychological pain, are likely to use, and perhaps even abuse, substances such as alcohol and drugs, and thereby put themselves into the category of the mentally ill. Again: the processes that are necessary for art share aspects with those that can drive people towards psychopathology, in this case the psychopathology of addiction.

Like sensitivity and artistic compulsion, lack of self-deception is a necessary but not sufficient condition for the artistic personality. There are plenty of people who are not self-deceptive who do not create art; they, too, suffer vulnerability toward various addictions. However, we argue that the combination of sensitivity, artistic compulsion, and lack of self-deception are traits both necessary and sufficient for our Platonic ideal of artistic personality.

Sensitivity + artistic compulsion + lack of self-deception

An important interaction is likely to happen when factors of sensitivity, artistic compulsion, and lack of self-deception coexist in a person. We suggest that this coexistence is necessary for works of art to be created, and, because of it, artists' psychological vulnerabilities, the proneness to anxiety, depression, mania, rumination, and addiction that may result in their psychological fragility, do not just add, but multiply. So, we propose, correlations have been found between being an artist and being mentally ill not because art causes illness, and not because mental illness makes for creativity in the arts, but because both can share these "third variables."

Consider, for instance, the relationship between art, sensitivity, and addiction with which we began this chapter, in our brief depiction of an apparently stereotypical addicted artist. Sensitive people may be more likely to use defenses for an issue that is important to them simply because they might perceive more things to be defensive about. If a person perceives that she has been cruel to her partner, she might concoct a defense such as justification or rationalization to protect herself against having to admit she has non-admirable qualities among her characteristics. If she does not perceive it, she generally does not need the defense, although she may need it if her partner perceives it and confronts her about it. While there may exist a variety of responses to sensitivity – including the non-optimal ones of falling into depression, mania, anxiety disorder, substance abuse, etc. – we may assume that at least some sensitive people protect themselves by cognitive means: self-deception. It is not unreasonable to believe that the more sensitive the people are, the more likely they would be to need psychological defenses. What sensitive artists may do, in contrast, because they are motivated to create art, is to avoid cognitive distortion not in all their life, but in the specific domain of their art. With cognitive defenses stripped away in this domain, an artist can confront negative emotions by means of exploration and externalization. This result is an unusual situation, whereby an artist may need protection but cannot create art if he or she indulges in the protection. This may then lead to substance addiction. This is how the third-variable problem can manifest itself: a sensitivity spreads from the domain of art into the rest of life in a way that may seem unbearable, and may prompt a person towards self-medication with addictive drugs.

In the end, the three qualities – sensitivity, artistic compulsion, and lack of self-deception – which together can prompt the person towards works of art, can each bring their own vulnerabilities, which further multiply when combined. Although they are vulnerable, artists are not doomed to mental illness, and they are not creative because they are mentally ill. An artist can be fragile without being broken, psychologically. If broken, she will no longer be fragile enough (or even alive enough) to create art.

Three provisos

In making our proposal about art and artists, we need to stress three provisos. First, what we propose does not apply to creativity in sciences or creativity in everyday life. Both the stereotype with which we started and the account of artistic qualities that we have offered are specific to artists. An award-winning microbiologist or a brilliant gardener might go on nightly drug binges, but the theory presented in this chapter will not enlighten us about any relation between such a person's creativity and their binges.

A second proviso is that, despite the definition of personality as a stable and characteristic way of thinking, emoting, and behaving, personality traits do change – both normatively (in the entire population as it ages), and uniquely (for some individuals due to their specific life experiences). This happens even to most basic personality traits, even those that are generally seen as mostly biologically determined (Roberts *et al.*, 2006). What this means is that the qualities the artist has during the time she is making art need not be the ones she has while in repose. If we talk of "artistic personality," we need to restrict it to the time when the artist is active. Our exercise, of trying to infer what qualities artists need to have, given what we know about art, works only if the artists are actually in the process of working on their art. Otherwise, the constraints that art production necessitates need not hold. This distinction might also serve to challenge the stereotype of an unchanging artistic personality. It might be unpleasant to challenge the title of an artist in a person who created actively for 10 years, and spent another 30 doing other things – but such a distinction is necessary to understand what qualities a person needs to have while making art.

Furthermore, qualities that we describe range in terms of their likelihood of change over the life span. Sensitivity seems least likely to change. Artistic compulsion seems to come and go at different periods in artists' lives. Self-deception seems most likely to change unpredictably.

Our third proviso is that we do not conceive of personality qualities as dichotomous (e.g., extraverted versus introverted); they lie on distributions. When we talk of an extraverted person, we are pointing toward people who score higher than average on a particular quality. The lack of dichotomous qualities is also applied to "artist" and "art." There is no quintessential artist, no quintessential piece of art, yet for the sake of argument we have talked about them in this way. So in the hypothesis we offer of artistic personality, we hold in the back of our mind that we are using "artist" and "art" to refer to continuous variables.

Conclusion

The hypothesis of artistic personality that we have proposed here has been focused on the vulnerability of artists to mental illnesses, including addiction. Starting with the idea that sensitivity, artistic compulsion, and lack of self-deception are together necessary and sufficient personality conditions for creating art, among interesting next steps would be to start making measurements of these components, in artists and others, to test the theory. One approach would be to use technologies like the LIWC (Pennebaker and Ireland, 2011). We made a start in this direction when we used it in a study of the emotional preoccupations of fiction writers and scientists (Djikic *et al.*, 2006, mentioned earlier). The kind of question that could perhaps be answered with this method is how the language of artists might indicate underlying qualities that make them vulnerable. Other questions, requiring different methods, include how artists usually cope with their sensitivity, their emotion-driven compulsion to create, and their lack of self-deception. What kind of resilience might lead them to negotiate and survive the combination of characteristics that can be so troublesome, and for some, like Amy Winehouse, fatal?

References

Brown, G. W. and Harris, T. O. (1978). *Social origins of depression: A study of psychiatric disorder in women*. London: Tavistock.

Carson, S. H. (2011). Creativity and psychopathology: A shared vulnerability model. *Canadian Journal of Psychiatry*, 56(3), 144–153.

Collingwood, R. G. (1938). *The principles of art*. Oxford: Clarendon Press.

Currie, G. (2011). Let's pretend: Literature and the psychology lab. *Times Literary Supplement*, September 2, 14–15.

Djikic, M., Oatley, K. and Peterson, J. B. (2006). The bitter-sweet labor of emoting: The linguistic comparison of writers and physicists. *Creativity Research Journal*, 18(2), 195–201.

Djikic, M., Peterson, J. B. and Zelazo, P. D. (2005). Attentional biases and memory distortions in self-enhancers. *Personality and Individual Differences*, 38, 559–568.

Eysenck, H. J. (1970). *The structure of human personality* (3rd edn.). New York: Methuen.

Freud, S. (1933/1991). *New introductory lectures on psychoanalysis*. New York: Penguin Books.

Frijda, N. H. (2007). *The laws of emotion*. Mahwah, NJ: Erlbaum.

Goleman, D. (1985). *Vital lies, simple truths: The psychology of self-deception*. London: Bloomsbury.

Hyde, L. (1983). *The gift: Imagination and the erotic life of property*. New York: Vintage.

Joormann, J., Dkane, M. and Gotlib, I. H. (2006). Adaptive and maladaptive components of rumination? Diagnostic specificity and relation to depressive biases. *Behavior Therapy*, 37, 269–280.

Kaufman, J. C. (2009). *Creativity 101*. New York: Springer.

Kaufman, J. C., Bromley, M. L. and Cole, J. C. (2006). Insane, poetic, lovable: Creativity and endorsement of the "Mad Genius" stereotype. *Imagination, Cognition and Personality*, 26, 149–161.

McCrae, R. R. and Costa, P. T. (2003). *Personality in adulthood: A five-factor perspective* (2nd edn.). New York: Guilford Press.

MacDonald, G. and Leary, M. R. (2005). Why does social exclusion hurt? The relationship between social and physical pain. *Psychological Bulletin*, 130, 202–223.

Mar, R. A., Oatley, K., Hirsh, J., dela Paz, J. and Peterson, J. B. (2006). Bookworms versus nerds: Exposure to fiction versus non-fiction, divergent associations with social ability, and the simulation of fictional social worlds. *Journal of Research in Personality*, 40, 694–712.

Mar, R. A., Oatley, K. and Peterson, J. B. (2009). Exploring the link between reading fiction and empathy: Ruling out individual differences and examining outcomes. *Communications: The European Journal of Communication*, 34, 407–428.

Miller, G. F. and Tal, I. (2006). Schizotypy versus openness and intelligence as predictors of creativity. *Schizophrenia Research*, 93, 317–324.

Moffitt, T. E., Caspi, A., Taylor, A., Kokaua, J., Milne, B. J., Polanczyk, G. et al. (2010). How common are common mental disorders? Evidence that lifetime prevalence rates are doubled by prospective versus retrospective ascertainment. *Psychological Medicine*, 40, 899–909.

Nolen-Hoeksema, S., Wisco, B. E. and Lyubomirsky, S. (2008). Rethinking rumination. *Perspectives on Psychological Science*, 3, 400–424.

Oatley, K. (2003). Creative expression and communication of emotion in the visual and narrative arts. In R. J. Davidson, K. R. Scherer and H. H. Goldsmith (Eds.), *Handbook of affective sciences* (pp. 481–502). New York: Oxford University Press.

Oatley, K. and Bolton, W. (1985). A social-cognitive theory of depression in reaction to life events. *Psychological Review*, 92, 372–388.

Pennebaker, J. W. and Ireland, M. E. (2011). Using literature to understand authors: The case for computerized text analysis. *Scientific Study of Literature*, 1(1), 34–48.

Peterson, J. B. (1999). *Maps of meaning: The architecture of belief*. New York: Routledge.

Post, F. (1994). Creativity and psychopathology: A study of 291 famous men. *British Journal of Psychiatry*, 165, 22–34.

Radway, J. A. (1984). *Reading the romance: Women, patriarchy, and popular literature*. Chapel Hill: University of North Carolina Press.

Ramachandran, V. S. (1996). The evolutionary biology of self-deception, laughter, dreaming, and depression: Some clues from anosognosia. *Medical Hypotheses*, 47, 347–362.

Roberts, B. W., Walton, K. E. and Viechtbauer, W. (2006). Patterns of mean-level change in personality traits across the life course: A meta-analysis of longitudinal studies. *Psychological Bulletin*, 132, 1–25.

Silvia, P. J. and Kaufman, J. C. (2010). Creativity and mental illness. In J. C. Kaufman and R. J. Sternberg (Eds.), *The Cambridge handbook of creativity* (pp. 381–394). New York: Cambridge University Press.

Vivanco, L. and Kramer, K. (2010). There are six bodies in this relationship: An anthropological approach to the romance genre. *Journal of Popular Romance Studies*, 1 (online August 4). www.jprstudies.org, last accessed March 17, 2014.

Weisberg, R. W. (2006). Creativity: Understanding innovation in problem solving, science, inventions, and the arts. Hoboken, NJ: Wiley.

14　Creativity as "compensatory advantage": bipolar and schizophrenic liability, the inverted-U hypothesis, and practical implications

Dennis K. Kinney and Ruth Richards

The idea that creativity is somehow associated with major mental illness is an ancient one that goes back at least as far as Aristotle, who wrote that all of the creative geniuses of his time were "inclined toward insanity" (see Becker, this volume). The notion that creative genius and "madness" are linked is still a popular one, stoked in part by the famous examples of eminent artists, such as van Gogh, and the Nobel-prizewinning mathematician and economist John Nash, who was hospitalized for schizophrenia and was the subject of the film, *A Beautiful Mind*.

While this "mad genius stereotype," as Silvia and Kaufman (2010) put it, is widely held, the research we will review in this chapter suggests that the stereotype gives a misleading impression of the actual relations between creativity and psychopathology. *This research suggests that psychotic symptoms actually tend to hinder creativity, and that it is the presence of other psychological characteristics associated with genetic liability or susceptibility to certain mental illnesses that actually aid creativity (Kinney and Richards, 2011).*

Understanding the relationship between creativity and mental illness is of great practical, as well as theoretical, interest. A correct understanding of this relationship may lead, for example, to improved treatment and prevention of some of the most serious mental disorders. This understanding may also provide important clues for how to identify and nurture unusually great creative potential. This is a vitally important issue, because creative genius is a vital resource for developing the innovative solutions urgently needed for many seemingly intractable economic, environmental, and political problems – problems that, if not solved, threaten potentially catastrophic consequences for humankind.

Until relatively recently in human history, the issue of whether creativity and mental illness were in fact linked has remained a matter of clinical observation, historical anecdotes, and theoretical speculation. Since the mid-twentieth century, however, the issue has been the subject of a growing body of scientific research, with some clear and converging findings (e.g., Glicksohn, 2011; Jamison, 1990; Kinney and Richards, 2011; Richards, 1981, 2010; Richards, Kinney, Lunde *et al.*, 1988; Runco and Richards, 1997; Silvia and Kaufman, 2010). A variety of convergent findings suggest, increasingly, that it is the *better functioning* individuals who carry genetic liability for certain major mental disorders who tend to have a creative advantage. Moreover, in the case of those particularly gifted creators who *do* have a history of severe mental illness, their most creative periods tend to occur at times when they experience either mild symptoms or no clinical symptoms at all.

These findings suggest that enhanced creativity in individuals with a personal or family history of mental illness tends to involve unconventional ways of thinking about the world that are sources of inspiration and novel ideas, combined with strong executive functions that make adaptive use of this creative ideation. The creativity–psychopathology relationship, as we will see later, may thus really be less about madness than about *health*.

Key questions about creativity and psychopathology

In this chapter, we will review some of the most important available scientific evidence that bears on several key questions about creativity and mental illness, or liability for such illness.

1. Are certain forms of major mental illness more prevalent in *creative geniuses* than in the general population?
2. If this is true – as several lines of research we will summarize suggests it is – *what accounts for it?*
3. Is the association between creativity and mental illness limited to a small number of eminent creators in the fine arts – or does it extend to *non-eminent* forms of creativity in a *wide range* of *vocational and avocational activities?*
4. Does the association between creativity and liability for mental illness extend to the *healthier* biological relatives of individuals with certain mental disorders?
5. Are the suffering and disability that accompany the most severe forms of mental illness a necessary "price" that individuals must "pay" in order to achieve great creativity – or does severe mental illness actually tend to inhibit creativity?

6. If – as research we will also review indicates – severe psychiatric symptoms actually tend to impede creativity, then *what processes actually produce the association* between creative genius and mental illness?
7. May associations between creativity and liability for mental illness have *implications for important social and clinical issues*, such as increasing the self-esteem and morale of patients and their families, or reducing the stigma and discrimination with which many patients must deal?
8. What practical and clinical implications do research findings have for the *treatment and prevention of mental illness*, and for the *identification – and nurturing – of creative potential*?

The focus of this chapter is on the relation of creativity to liability for two types of illness – *mood disorders and schizophrenia* – and their respective "spectrums" of milder, but genetically related, disorders. This focus reflects the fact that empirical research to date suggests that the evidence for a relation with creativity is strongest for these mental disorders and associated liability.

Are certain mental illnesses more prevalent in eminent creators in the arts?

Biographies of individual creative geniuses, as well as surveys of biographies of eminent creators, have identified many striking examples of creative geniuses in the arts who have had what appear to be major mental illnesses – especially major depression and bipolar disorder. Jamison (1990, 1993), for example, has used biographical reports to compile an impressive array of cases of mood disorders among some of history's most eminent writers, composers, and visual artists. Hemingway, Virginia Woolf, Edgar Alan Poe, Coleridge, and Byron are only a few of the examples that Jamison lists – and just among novelists and poets.

However, such biographical surveys have significant limitations. For example, the accuracy of the diagnoses can be questioned, because they are often not based on current diagnostic criteria. Moreover, the sampling of cases has typically not been systematic or representative, so it is difficult to demonstrate convincingly that the prevalence of the disorders is actually higher among the eminent creators than among the general population.

In a monograph that rigorously reviewed many older studies on this issue, along with related features and models, Richards (1981) found elevated levels of psychopathology among socially recognized creators compared with the population at large, and familial (perhaps genetic) patterns of creativity–psychopathology association. The potential for an association of enhanced creativity with milder forms of mental illness, or familial liability for such illness, was also noted. An elevated prevalence of so-called "affective psychosis" in eminent creators was prominent across studies. However, design problems and differences among these earlier studies limited the conclusions that could be drawn from them. Furthermore, certain psychiatric diagnoses might be framed differently today (including individuals then called schizophrenic who might now fall on the affective spectrum). Possible factors that might lead to a creative advantage for patients and their relatives were proposed in three areas: *cognitive*, *affective*, and *motivational*. Potential causal pathways through which creativity and psychology might influence one another were described within a five-part framework of direct and indirect causation (see Kinney and Richards, 2011, and Richards, 2010, for current examples).

Psychiatrist Arnold Ludwig (1996) later conducted a highly ambitious, and systematic, study of the relationship between eminent creativity and mental illness, based on biographical information. He reviewed the biographies of more than one thousand eminent individuals in 18 different professions whose biographies had been reviewed in the book review sections of the *New York Times*. Ludwig found episodes of depression were reported in 40–66 percent of writers, visual artists, and musical composers, with the highest rates in poets. Manic episodes were reported in 5–13 percent of several artistic groups, with the highest rate again among poets. These rates are striking for several reasons. First, the rates are much higher than rates in the general population (which are about 1 percent for bipolar disorder, and 10 percent for major depression). Second, the true rates among these eminent creators are very likely much higher than those reported in the biographies, because most people with major mood disorders don't receive proper diagnosis. Third, biographers may not always be aware of the subjects' psychiatric histories (and newspaper reviews may not always mention them, even if reported in a biography). Fourth, the eminent non-artists in the study showed markedly less psychopathology than the artists (or possibly, the non-artists had milder forms of dysfunction that were not noted in these archival sources).

Ludwig's study is impressive for its breadth and large number of subjects. However, it also has some important limitations, such as the fact that those diagnoses that were noted in biographies did not consistently involve application of standard research diagnostic criteria.

In the past two decades, several more systematic, interview-based studies – led by different investigators in three different geographic areas – have been conducted on the prevalence of major mental disorders in eminent creators in the arts. These studies showed significant advances in their methods, such as identifying more complete, well-defined samples of artistic eminent creators, and then diagnosing mental illness in the creators based on information collected in direct interviews with the creators, with the current, widely used diagnostic criteria then being applied to make the diagnoses.

In the United States, psychologist Nancy Andreasen (1987) interviewed thirty of the country's most eminent creative writers who had taught at the University of Iowa's famous workshop for writers. She found that 80 percent of these writers had had a major mood disorder, with over half of those affected having had either full bipolar disorder with a history of mania ("type I" bipolar disorder) or a milder form in which episodes of hypomania alternate with major depression ("type II" bipolar disorder).

Kay Redfield Jamison (1989) interviewed forty-seven of the most eminent artists and writers in the British Isles, and she asked them about their treatment for mental illness and their mental states during their most creative periods. Thirty-eight percent reported that they had been treated for a mental disorder, most often for a mood disorder. The actual proportion who had a history of mood disorder is probably much higher; Jamison estimated that only about one in three people with mood disorder would actually seek professional help. Even more striking was the finding that a full 89 percent of the eminent creators in this study reported "intense creative episodes," with a modal length of 2 weeks. These creative episodes involved many signs and symptoms that are characteristic of hypomania.

In Continental Europe, Akiskal and his colleagues (Akiskal, 2007; Akiskal and Akiskal, 1988) studied several dozen eminent artists, writers, and composers. These investigators also found that these eminent creators had mood disorders at rates considerably higher than in the general population. In addition, the research revealed that artistic creativity and eminence were more likely to be characterized by the milder, type-II bipolar disorder (rather than the full-blown type-I disorder), and by cyclothymic and hyperthymic temperaments that may represent a "dilute temperamental form of bipolarity" (Akiskal, 2007, p. 3). Similar results have also been reported in other studies, such as Post's (1996) findings with writers, or Kaufman's (2005) results with Eastern European poets.

Thus, results from a number of more recent and rigorous studies have found that there is indeed a markedly increased prevalence of major mood disorders, as well as of substance abuse and some personality disorders, in eminent creators in literature, music, and the visual arts. These studies raise the question of whether this creativity–psychopathology link is limited to a small number of eminent creators in the arts, or applies much more broadly.

Do creativity–psychopathology links extend to non-eminent creativity, diverse fields, and patients' healthier relatives?

Creativity as "compensatory advantage" to bipolar liability: evidence for an "inverted-U" hypothesis

Several studies have investigated these questions, using samples of mental patients and their relatives. The inclusion of patients' relatives is important because of extensive evidence from many studies that genetic factors have a powerful influence on risk for major mental disorders (e.g., Kendler *et al.*, 1994). In the case of mood disorders, Richards, Kinney, Lunde *et al.* (1988) designed a study to investigate these issues, including the question of whether creativity–psychopathology associations arise (a) because creativity is somehow facilitated by the *experience of having had severe moods* – or, instead, (b) because creativity is fostered by *psychological traits associated with genetic liability for mood disorders*.

To study these issues in a scientifically rigorous manner, the investigators conducted a study distinguished by several features. First, the investigators developed and validated a new instrument – the *Lifetime Creativity Scales* (LCS) – for assessing a broad range of real-life creativity in general population samples (Richards, Kinney, Benet *et al.*, 1988). The LCS provide guidelines and anchored rating scales for assessing everyday creative accomplishments in a variety of real-life vocational and avocational activities, including different levels of non-eminent creativity. Several studies using the LCS have produced good evidence for their reliability and validity.

This study's methods also had several other important strengths. For instance: (a) psychiatric diagnoses and ratings of creativity were done independently of one another – to avoid raters' knowledge of one variable biasing ratings of the other – using established research criteria for diagnostic and creativity assessment; (b) good inter-rater agreement was obtained for both the diagnoses and the creativity ratings; (c) the information on both psychiatric symptoms and creative activities was obtained from direct semi-structured interviews with subjects, supplemented by family history information; (d) the creativity ratings were based on applying the creativity scales to information on subjects' avocational, as well as vocational, activities (which turns out to be particularly important for schizophrenia); and (e) finally, controls for other variables, such as subjects' education and intelligence, were included in the data analyses.

This study's research design complemented those used in the earlier studies in that in this study, unlike in the earlier ones, the samples were identified based on the subjects' diagnostic status (or family relationship to patients), with the *creativity* of each group then being the *dependent* variable. This is a key design difference, creating a quite different type of study. The earlier interview-based studies, which involved relatively small groups of eminent creators in the arts, tell us little about the average creativity (broadly defined) of individuals in the general population who carry a certain psychiatric diagnosis. Nor does a study focused exclusively on eminent creators tap – at all – the many and varied ways in which non-eminent creativity (in this case, assessed using the dual criteria of *originality* and *meaningfulness*) may emerge.

The research design used in the study by Richards, Kinney, Benet *et al.* (1988) defined groups of subjects by their personal or family histories of mental illness. This design makes it possible to generalize findings about creativity–psychopathology relationships beyond a small group of exceptionally creative people in artistic fields. Indeed, the result using this kind of research design may potentially apply to millions of psychiatric patients and family members. Silvia and Kaufman (2010) have written quite eloquently about the importance of these directional design issues for the conclusions one can draw from research.

The design of the study by Richards, Kinney, Lunde *et al.* (1988) involved 77 Danish subjects in five groups: (a) patients with bipolar disorder, (b) patients with cyclothymia, (c) the healthy first-degree biological relatives of these first two groups, (d) control subjects with no personal history of mental disorder and no family history of mood disorders, and (e) subjects with psychiatric disorders other than mood disorders or psychotic disorders.

The investigators proposed and tested an *"inverted-U" hypothesis* of the relation between creativity and liability for bipolar disorder. This curvilinear relationship was suggested by the possibility of a "compensatory advantage" to genes that increase one's liability (susceptibility) for developing bipolar disorder. That is, the inverted-U hypothesis proposes that increasing levels of genetic liability for bipolar disorders – and increasing levels of psychological traits that are likely to be associated with this liability – will tend to facilitate creativity, but only up to a certain point, beyond which further increases in liability will actually begin to interfere with creativity.

In fact, the study found that the pooled index subjects (bipolars, cyclothymes, and their normal biological relatives) were significantly higher in their mean overall "peak" creativity rating than the control subjects combined. The "peak" measure was regarded as the most important for testing the hypothesis because it was based on an individual's most creative major accomplishment over his or her entire adult lifetime, in either a vocational or avocational sphere. (Peak creativity was regarded as a better estimate of a person's creative potential than measures of the "extent," or number of years of creativity activity, which could be more subject to environmental factors that could obstruct or aid creative productivity.)

Most notably, and consistent with an inverted-U hypothesis, within this pooled group of index subjects it was the *normal* relatives of the bipolar and cyclothymic patients – that is, those with the mildest manifestation of bipolar risk – who had the highest mean creativity rating. Thus, in this study, it was neither bipolar illness nor mental health *per se* that was associated with being most creative, but rather being a more psychologically healthy person with a biological family history of bipolar disorder. Thus an inverted-U relationship was observed, consistent with the theory that enhanced creativity acts as a compensatory advantage to genes that increase liability for bipolar disorder – and the serious disadvantages for health that the disorder carries.

A second study using parallel methods with Danish subjects (Richards et al., 1992) examined whether the association with increased creativity was specific to bipolar mood disorders, or also extended to unipolar *depression*. This second study applied the LCS to rate the creativity of depressed patients with, versus without, a family history of bipolar disorder, as well as of controls with no personal or family history of mood disorders. In fact, mean creativity was found to be significantly higher in the depressed patients – but only if the patients had a family history of bipolar disorder. This is an important finding – first, because it means family as well as personal history of mood disorders must be considered, and, second, because it suggests that patients with unipolar depression may still carry a bipolar "compensatory advantage." The mood elevations in such depressed patients might not be recognized because the elevation is at subclinical levels. Consistent with this interpretation are the findings of Akiskal and his colleagues (Akiskal et al., 2006) from a national study in France, involving over 15 sites and more than 500 people with major depressive episodes. That study found that 65 percent of depressed patients actually fell within the *bipolar* spectrum, when the spectrum was broadly defined.

Many studies indicate that genetic factors are important etiological factors in both bipolar disorders and schizophrenia (e.g., Jamison, 1990;

Kety *et al.*, 1994; Kinney and Matthysse, 1978). The idea that *creativity* could be a *"compensatory advantage"* for these strong genetic liabilities for bipolar disorder and schizophrenia has a *precedent* in the classic medical textbook example of *sickle cell anemia*. In this devastating genetic medical disorder, an individual who inherits a copy of a recessive gene from each parent is unable to produce a normal form of the hemoglobin molecule and, as a result, usually develops serious and painful medical crises that often cause death at a young age. The puzzle of why this inherited disorder has been maintained at remarkably high population rates in many regions of the world was solved when it was discovered that individuals who inherit only one copy of the gene tend to avoid more serious medical complications while gaining the benefit of greatly increased resistance to malaria. This increased genetic resistance is an extremely important advantage in geographic regions where malaria is a leading cause of mortality. In places where malaria is endemic, this advantage compensates for the disadvantages of the severe medical illness in homozygotes who inherit two copies of the sickle-cell gene. In these regions, this compensatory advantage maintains sickle cell anemia and the gene that causes it at high levels in the population.

The example of sickle cell anemia suggests that it is plausible to investigate whether genes that increase liability for certain major psychiatric disorders may also carry an analogous compensatory advantage for patients or their relatives – advantages that could have kept such genes and their associated disorders from being selected out of the population and instead perpetuated them down through the generations (Kinney and Matthysse, 1978; Richards, Kinney, Lunde *et al.*, 1988). Akiskal (2007, p. 1), in fact, suggests that affective disorders "serve as the genetic reservoir for adaptive temperaments and the genes for genius."

However, despite the multiple strengths in their methods, including samples of mood-disordered patients and relatives, these creativity studies of Richards, Kinney, Lunde *et al.* (1988) did have some notable limitations. For example, the samples were modest in size, and they were not representative of the general population.

These latter two limitations were addressed in a recent, complementary Swedish study conducted by Kyaga *et al.* (2012). Those investigators carried out a population-based investigation of the prevalence of creative professions in subjects with bipolar disorder, unipolar depression, or schizophrenia, as well as their respective relatives, compared with control subjects without such disorders and those control subjects' own relatives.

Notably, the study made use of the total population registers available in Sweden, which made it possible to access information on all patients with in-patient discharge diagnoses for the three disorders, and then link that information with data on the patients' biological relatives. These datasets were in turn linked to (a) self-report information on subjects' occupations (information provided as part of mandatory census questionnaires), as well as to (b) data on IQ collected on all men, as part of mandatory conscription into the armed services. These datasets were integrated and anonymized by Statistics Sweden before being given to the investigators.

Thus, this study's analyses were based on samples that were at once much larger and more representative than any previous studies of creativity and psychopathology. (For example, there were nearly 30,000 subjects with a diagnosis of bipolar disorder, 54,000 with schizophrenia, and 218,000 with depression.)

For their analyses, Kyaga and colleagues considered artistic and scientific occupations to be more creative. The artistic professions included both visual artists (including, e.g., photographers and designers) and non-visual artists (e.g., authors, composers, musicians, and performing artists). The scientists were individuals who taught or did research at a university level. To examine the specificity of any association with creative professions, the investigators also considered accountants and auditors, occupations considered to be less creative on average.

Individuals with a diagnosis of bipolar disorder were found to be significantly overrepresented in creative professions (by roughly 35%); this effect was largely due to an overrepresentation in *both* visual and non-visual artistic occupations. The bipolar patients' close relatives – first degree (parents, siblings, and offspring) – also reported significantly higher rates of creative professions (siblings had the highest rate). However, for the relatives, unlike the patients, this increase was actually greater for *scientific* than for artistic professions. For more distant, second- and third-degree relatives (e.g., half-siblings, cousins), the increases were smaller and/or non-significant.

The pattern of results for *unipolar depression* was quite different: depressed patients were slightly but significantly *less* likely than controls to report a creative occupation. A similar tendency was reported for most of the depressed patients' *relatives*, with the exception of their parents, aunts, and nephews, who were slightly more likely to report creative occupations.

It is notable that, for both bipolar and unipolar patients and their relatives, these associations seemed to be specific to creative professions. That is, there were no significant associations involving professionals such as accountants and auditors.

Creativity as a "compensatory advantage" in the schizophrenia
spectrum: evidence for another "inverted-U" relationship

Parallel studies have investigated the relation of creativity to *schizophrenia* and genetic liability for that disorder. This includes the spectrum of disorders (particularly schizotypal personality disorder) that are genetically related to schizophrenia, and hence part of familial risk, but display milder symptoms.

As in the case of mood disorders, there are some marked anecdotal reports of schizophrenia-related psychopathology in some of the world's most famous creative geniuses. Moreover, as was the case for mood disorders, the strongest association with increased creativity appears to be with *milder* forms of schizophrenia spectrum disorders and symptoms, or with genetic *liability* for the disorder in individuals who themselves may have robust psychological health.

It is striking, for example, that Albert Einstein and James Joyce – the two figures widely viewed as, respectively, the twentieth century's most creative scientist and novelist – each had a child who was hospitalized for many years with a diagnosis of schizophrenia. The great Irish poet, William Butler Yeats, and Alan Turing, the eccentric British mathematician who is regarded by many as the father of modern computer science and whose work in breaking the Nazi's secret code played a pivotal role in the Allied victory in World War II, are examples of creative geniuses who may have had schizotypal personality disorder. In parallel to Jamison's impressive long lists of eminent creators in the fine arts who had mood disorders, Louis Sass (2000–2001) has published an impressive list of eminent writers and philosophers who appeared to have had, not frank schizophrenia, but rather milder forms of schizophrenia-spectrum disorders. However, as noted earlier in our discussion of mood disorders, such lists do not provide conclusive evidence for a causal relation between mental illness and creativity. Other studies, using different research strategies, are needed.

In fact, the results of other studies do also suggest that the healthier biological relatives of patients with schizophrenia may tend to be more creative than control subjects with no family history of mental illness. Thus, for example, both Heston (1966) and Kaufman *et al.* (1979) reported serendipitously discovering unusually great creativity in subgroups of the non-schizophrenic offspring of biological mothers who had been diagnosed with schizophrenia. In both studies, the authors were surprised to find that a subgroup of the schizophrenic mothers' children was not only psychologically quite healthy, but also had more creative jobs or hobbies than almost any of the control subjects whose biological mothers had no history of mental illness. Heston's study was particularly interesting because his index and control subjects had been adopted away from their biological mothers at an early age, suggesting that the association between maternal schizophrenia and offspring creativity was mediated by genetic factors rather than ones in the rearing environment.

As striking as their findings were, however, these studies had important limitations. As both Heston and Kaufmann et al. noted, their findings were unexpected and serendipitous, were based on clinical observations and subjective impressions of subjects' creative activities, and used post-hoc analyses. Moreover, the studies' samples were modest in size, and the investigators were potentially biased by their knowledge of subjects' mental status. The studies also used older diagnostic criteria.

Kinney et al. (2000–2001) addressed these issues, using a research design and methods parallel to those noted in the study of mood disorders and creativity described earlier. They hypothesized that, as in the case of mood disorders, there is an inverted-U relationship between creativity and liability for schizophrenia. That is, a milder degree of genetic liability and associated symptoms along a schizophrenia spectrum would tend to facilitate creativity, because unconventional modes of thinking and perceiving would tend to produce more novel ideas and associations that could in turn serve as the basis for creative products, theories, and works of art. However, if these cognitive tendencies become too extreme and develop into psychotic symptoms such as hallucinations, delusions, and severe thought disorder, then they will tend to impair, rather than aid, creative processes.

This study of creativity and schizophrenia by Kinney et al. had many of the same methodological strengths noted earlier for the mood disorder study by Richards, Kinney, Lunde et al. (1988). These strengths included use of the LCS (Richards, Kinney, Benet et al., 1988) to rate subjects' creativity, creativity and diagnostic evaluations that were done blindly with respect to each other, use of established research criteria, and evidence of adequate reliability for both diagnostic and creativity assessments. There were 27 wide-spectrum cases versus 44 non-spectrum controls.

The results of this study showed similarities to those noted earlier for mood disorders (Richards, Kinney, Lunde et al., 1988). Thus, adoptees who did not have schizophrenia but *did* have milder symptoms that other research suggests are linked to genetic liability for schizophrenia (Kendler et al., 1994; Kety et al., 1994) – either schizotypal personality disorder or multiple schizotypal signs – had a mean overall peak creativity rating that was significantly higher than that in subjects who had neither schizotypal signs nor a family history of schizophrenia. The "inverted-U" relationship between symptomatology and creativity peaked at about two schizotypal signs. Creativity was most strongly associated with "positive" schizotypal traits, such as magical thinking, recurrent illusions, and odd speech. The strongest association with schizotypal signs was for leisure or avocational (rather than vocational) creativity. Interestingly, the opposite was found for the bipolar spectrum (Richards, Kinney, Lunde *et al.*, 1988) where evidence for enhanced creativity was most evident in vocational, or work-related, activities.

Thus, the findings of the Kinney *et al.* (2000–2001) study on schizophrenia-spectrum traits resembled those found for the bipolar spectrum. That is, there was an "inverted-U" relation between creativity and apparent degree of liability for the illness. The limitations of the Kinney *et al.* study paralleled those noted earlier for the Richards, Kinney, Lunde *et al.* study of creativity and mood disorders.

These limitations were again addressed in the Swedish study by Kyaga *et al.* (2012), which, as noted earlier, involved parallel analyses on the association of occupational creativity to personal and family history of schizophrenia. Kyaga *et al.* found that patients with schizophrenia were significantly more likely than controls to report having an artistic profession, but patients were significantly *less* likely to report having a scientific one. The schizophrenia patients' parents, siblings, and aunts and uncles were also significantly more likely to report having creative occupations – but for these relatives, these occupations included *scientific* as well as artistic ones. For the other types of relatives, the associations were not significant.

As Kyaga *et al.* (2012) pointed out, it is noteworthy that, for both schizophrenia and bipolar disorder, the likelihood of reporting a creative profession was greatest for the *healthy* first-degree relatives of the patients. It is also notable that for men (the group for whom IQ data were available), when IQ was controlled for in the analyses, the associations with creative occupations were actually strengthened. Moreover, there was specificity to the associations with creative professions, because no significant associations were found for accounting and auditing – two professions that also typically require considerable education and professional expertise, but tend to involve less creativity.

This study by Kyaga *et al.*, however, also clearly had its own limitations. Thus, the creativity of their subjects could not be independently assessed, and the assessment depended on the subjects' accurately reporting their professions. This may have been more of a problem for reports of artistic occupations, for which it may have been easier to claim a professional identity than it is in the case of a university appointment. Reporting accuracy may have been particularly problematic for the schizophrenia patients, for whom only 45 percent reported an occupational status. (Increased reports of artistic occupations, though, may at least indicate an increased interest in, or aspiration for, such occupations.) A related limitation is that the study had no data on avocational creativity, which studies described earlier (e.g., Heston, 1966; Kinney *et al.*, 2000–2001) suggest may be most elevated in the relatives of patients with schizophrenia. The best creativity data on schizophrenic patients and their relatives may therefore have been missed.

On balance, though, the results of Kyaga and colleagues dovetail nicely with findings from most of the studies cited earlier. Overall, complementary results have been obtained from many studies, involving a variety of different time periods, investigators, research designs, samples, and countries. These converging lines of evidence provide substantial – and growing – support for the inverted-U hypothesis of the relation between creativity and liability for schizophrenia and bipolar disorder. This evidence warrants further research to test the hypothesis more thoroughly.

Compensatory advantage: what psychological processes mediate associations of creativity with liability for mental illness?

Mental processes, creativity, and liability for bipolar disorder

Several lines of research support the hypothesis that mild, or subclinical, levels of mood elevation are most conducive to creativity. The studies' finding that creativity tends to be elevated, on average, in bipolar patients and their relatives – but not in depressed patients and their relatives (unless there is a family history of bipolar disorder) – suggests that there is something about mood *elevation* (or at least alternations between milder mood elevation and depression), rather than depressed mood, by itself, that facilitates creativity. The finding that creativity tends to be elevated in depressed patients with, but not those without, a family history of bipolar disorder (Richards *et al.*, 1992) further supports this idea that there is something about moderately elevated mood that facilitates creativity. At times the facilitating elevation in mood may even be subclinical. In the mental health field, clinicians often look for what is going wrong; they may not look often enough for what is going right.

Biographical accounts of eminent creators such as Vincent van Gogh and the composer Franz Schumann have reported that enormous bursts of creative output tend to occur during periods of mood elevation, whereas depressed moods tend to occur during periods of little or no creative output. Complementary evidence comes from studies that asked people to indicate their mood when they were most creative. For example, when Jamison (1989) asked her sample of eminent creators to describe their psychological state when they were most creative, they tended to describe psychological characteristics typically found during episodes of elevated mood, or even of hypomania.

Other studies (Jamison et al., 1980; Richards and Kinney, 1990) asked non-eminent patients with mood disorders to describe their mood when they tended to be most creative. These patients commonly reported that milder mood elevation was most conducive to creativity; episodes of extreme mood elevation or full-blown mania, by contrast, tended to interfere with creativity. It is interesting in this regard that, in college students heading for an artistic career versus a non-artistic career, there is a prominence in the artistically oriented group of cyclothymic and hyperthymic temperaments (Vellante et al., 2011).

Srivastava et al. (2010) found that bipolar patients and highly creative controls, when compared with depressed patients and less creative control subjects, tended to have higher Myers-Briggs intuition preference types, as well as higher cyclothymia scores. One should note as well the decrease in latent inhibition that has not only been linked with psychopathology, but also with openness, and significantly with "faith in intuition" in high-achieving college students (Kaufman, 2009).

What is it about moderate mood elevation that tends to be optimal for creativity? The inverted-U hypothesis proposes that a number of psychological states are increased in an optimal amount by elevated mood and can serve as a "compensatory advantage" to genes for bipolar disorder. These states may facilitate creativity – but only up to a certain point, beyond which further increases begin to disrupt creativity.

Elevated mood tends to be associated with increased access to ideas, including many unusual ideas, associations, and combinations of ideas. These novel ideas can serve as the kernels for creative products, provided the person is able to assess the potential of these embryonic ideas, winnow the good from the bad, and go further in refining, developing, and testing the better ideas. By contrast, in full-blown mania, this tendency may result in a fire-hose rush of thoughts, an uncontrolled flight of ideas, a loss of judgment, an inability to evaluate the worth of ideas, and even flagrantly psychotic symptoms. Similarly, in a fuller affective spectrum, an increased sensitivity to feelings may be helpful in many creative endeavors, if one doesn't get swept away by intense emotions. This is where the balance is needed – where the right dose of inspiration is needed and where appropriate regulation by executive functions may be required to achieve creative outcomes.

Similarly, a moderate increase in self-confidence and willingness to take risks, which often accompanies milder mood elevation, can help motivate one to persist in developing creative ideas – despite the criticism and rejection often provoked by ideas that challenge conventional wisdom – and to work to sell one's ideas to skeptical "gatekeepers." However, in mania, this tendency may balloon into frank grandiosity and reckless, even dangerous, actions that are inimical to creativity. Moderate mood elevation may also produce increased energy and ambition, which help one summon the extraordinary levels of focus, time, and commitment often needed to develop a novel idea into a meaningful invention or work of art. Taken to an extreme during mania, however, even this tendency can lead to agitation, frenetic activity, and severe sleep deprivation, all of which are dysfunctional.

Complementary results come from a large body of research conducted by Philip Holzman and his colleagues on cognitive styles and thought disorder in patients with bipolar disorder or schizophrenia, their respective biological relatives, and controls (e.g., Shenton *et al.*, 1989). This research found that the relatives of patients with bipolar disorder often show milder variants of the unusual cognitive patterns found during mania, variants that have traditionally been labeled as thought disorder by clinicians. One type of thought disorder characteristically observed in bipolar patients is the generation of a profusion of ideas, which can diverge wildly from the appropriate topic of a task or conversation (e.g., being asked to describe clearly and logically what one sees in an inkblot). Manic subjects are also likely to bring different ideas or percepts together in incongruous, fanciful, and fabulized combinations – a tendency that these investigators concluded was a form of thought disorder characteristic of mania.

Interestingly, the healthy relatives of bipolar patients also tend to show this tendency, but to a much milder, more controlled degree. Holzman and colleagues viewed this milder tendency as a form of thought disorder too, albeit a less severe one. One could, however, also consider this tendency a cognitive style that – if properly channeled, used judiciously, and controlled by adaptive executive functions – could facilitate the generation of creative ideas. The most marked creative breakthroughs, after all, often involve combining different ideas in extremely novel ways – ways that often initially seem bizarre, outlandish, or even "crazy," to most other people. Thus in the case of liability for bipolar disorders, research suggests that a compensatory advantage may involve aspects of cognition, as well as affect and motivation.

Mental processes, creativity, and liability for schizophrenia

By contrast, thought disorder in *schizophrenic* patients tends to take somewhat different forms, often involving thinking that is impoverished, illogical, or circumstantial. What about patients' relatives? In the adoption studies of schizophrenia noted earlier, the *biological* (but not the adoptive) *relatives* of adoptees with schizophrenia were several times more likely than controls to have schizotypal personality disorder and/or to display multiple schizotypal signs. Some of these signs – such as odd speech, magical thinking, and recurrent illusions or unusual perceptual experiences – may tend to facilitate the generation of novel ideas, as some findings are now suggesting (Kinney *et al.*, 2000–2001).

If these unusual modes of perceiving and thinking about the world balloon into full-blown hallucinations and delusions, as they often do in psychotic episodes experienced by patients with schizophrenia, then they are likely to interfere with creativity. Milder, more controlled levels of this unconventional cognition, however, could allow individuals to evaluate their novel ideas and use them to develop creative products.

Note that it was the biological, rather than the adoptive, relatives of schizophrenic adoptees who showed these schizotypal traits. This suggests that the link to creativity involves genetic liability for the illness – to a "compensatory advantage" to genes for the illness. That is, the increased creative potential that may tend to be associated with these genes provides an advantage that offsets the increased risk for mental illness that these genes also confer. At the right level, this genetic liability provides a compensatory advantage in the form of increased creative potential – a potential that may be realized if given a nurturing rearing environment.

This interpretation is consistent with other research noted earlier, such as the finding of Kyaga *et al.* (2012) that the offspring of a schizophrenic biological parent were not more likely to report a creative profession, whereas in Heston's (1966) adoption study adoptees who were separated at an early age from their schizophrenic biological mothers were more likely than control adoptees to have developed creative jobs and hobbies. These results suggest that genes that increase susceptibility for schizophrenia may tend to facilitate unconventional modes of cognition, which in turn can lead to creative outcomes, provided that they develop in the context of a supportive, nurturing rearing environment. It may be more difficult for parents to provide such an environment if they are themselves struggling with the social, economic, and psychological difficulties that often burden patients with schizophrenia. In addition, in these strongly familial illnesses, the young person may not be the only person in the family dealing with major psychopathology.

In research involving *non*-clinical populations, such as college students, many studies have also found support for the inverted-U hypothesis in the schizophrenia spectrum and the bipolar spectrum (though some studies have not found strong relationships; e.g., Armstrong, 2012; Rodrigue and Perkins, 2012). In a notable program of research, Schuldberg (2000–2001) and colleagues administered multiple measures of creativity to student samples, together with measures of clinical and *subclinical* psychological traits that are associated with bipolar and schizophrenia spectra. Higher scores on the creativity measures were positively and significantly correlated with indicators of both hypomania and schizotypal signs.

One mental process that may help mediate associations between creativity and liability for schizophrenia is latent inhibition, which tends to be reduced in schizophrenia and may make it easier to be open to the intrusion of unusual mental content, providing a highly functioning creative person who has strong executive controls with access to an unusually rich flow of novel ideas (e.g., Kaufman, 2009). It is noteworthy that Kaufman (2009) found that a low level of latent inhibition was associated with increased openness to new ideas and with "faith in intuition" in high-achieving college students. How interesting, then, that Fink *et al.* (2012) found significant correlations between low levels of latent inhibition and high levels of originality.

Parallel lines of research are not only providing additional support for an inverted-U relationship between creativity and liability for schizophrenia, but are also beginning to discover neurological bases for this association. Folley and Park (2005), for example, found significantly higher creativity scores on divergent thinking tests of creativity in subjects with schizotypal personality disorder than in demographically similar control subjects. Moreover, brain-imaging measures, involving infrared optical spectroscopy, found higher prefrontal cortex (PFC) activation during periods of more creative thinking, and particularly strong *right prefrontal* activation during creative activity in the schizotypal subjects.

Research in the late 1990s by Martindale (1999) also found associations between patterns of electroencephalography (EEG) activity and creative functioning, linked to defocused attention, associative thought, and many simultaneous representations on verbal report (see Martindale, 1999; Richards, 2010). This earlier work is now linked to recent research by Kounios, Jung-Beeman, and associates with functional magnetic resonance imaging (fMRI) and EEG, showing not only signature brain patterns for *insight versus analytic strategies* in creative problem solving (e.g., Kounios *et al.*, 2008; Subramaniam *et al.*, 2008), but also indicating that highly creative people are able to turn the insight pattern on *ahead of time.*

There is obviously much work that needs to be done in order to understand these phenomena. It seems clear, however, that *there are important relationships between creativity and liabilities for schizophrenia and bipolar disorder.* Furthermore, there is a large and growing body of evidence for a "compensatory advantage" in enhanced creative potential, which follows an inverted-U-type pattern in its relationships to both bipolar and schizophrenia liability. Other genetic and environmental factors may also be needed to create the right conditions for this creative potential to be realized, but further research on this issue holds great promise.

Clinical and social implications for stigma, treatment, counseling, and nurturing of creative potential

The multiple lines of evidence for the association between increased creative potential and liability for schizophrenia and bipolar disorder have some important potential clinical and social implications (e.g., Kinney, 1992; Richards, 1997, 2007, 2010). These include the potential for creative coping, empowerment, increased self-esteem, and resilient response – even being able to move from Maslow's "deficiency creativity" to the much healthier and outward-focused "being creativity" (Rhodes, 1997). With each new creative breakthrough, many people can benefit. For example, stigma, discrimination, and demoralization are major problems faced by many patients and their families.

Evidence for an association between enhanced creativity and liability for these illnesses may help reduce stigma and prejudice, and boost the morale of patients and their relatives. Evidence for the creativity link may also enhance patients' compliance with treatment regimes. The myth that the suffering and disability associated with psychosis and extreme moods somehow aid creativity – and are even a "price" that eminent creators must "pay" for their genius – is still widely believed. The research we have reviewed strongly suggests that this view is wrong, and that *appropriate treatment is likely to enhance, rather than diminish, patients' creativity.*

The importance of patients receiving such treatment is underscored by evidence that more than half of all patients with bipolar disorder have stopped taking their prescribed medication in the 6 months before being hospitalized, and that most patients also stop following prescribed treatment within 6 months following discharge from the hospital. There is thus every reason to get, and to continue, treatment. One of the most motivating factors for increasing treatment compliance may be recognition that appropriate treatment may actually enhance creativity.

The evidence for unusual creative potential in individuals who carry genetic *liability* for schizophrenia and bipolar disorder also has other implications for these individuals, as well as for people in the helping professions, such as educators, counselors, and therapists. These professionals often have the opportunity to be "muses" who help patients and their relatives manage or avoid symptoms that prevent them from realizing their potential (Kinney, 1992). Such professionals are also often in positions to help students and others with such genetic liability to explore educational and career paths that may enable them to develop their unusual creative potential – to the benefit not just of the individuals themselves, but also society as a whole.

References

Akiskal, H. S. (2007). In search of Aristotle: Temperament, human nature, melancholia, creativity and eminence. *Journal of Affective Disorders*, 100, 1–6.

Akiskal, H. S. and Akiskal, K. K. (1988). Reassessing the prevalence of bipolar disorders: Clinical significance and artistic creativity. *Psychiatry and Psychobiology*, 3, 29–36.

Akiskal, H. S., Akiskal, K. K., Lancrenon, S., Hantouche, E. G., Fraud, J. P., Gury, C. and Allilaire, J. F. (2006). Validating the bipolar spectrum in the French National EPIDEP Study: Overview of the phenomenology and relative prevalence of its clinical prototypes. *Journal of Affective Disorders*, 96(3), 197–205.

Andreasen, N. C. (1987). Creativity and mental illness: Prevalence rates in writers and their first-degree relatives. *The American Journal of Psychiatry*, 144(10), 1288–1292.

Armstrong, D. (2012). The contributions of creative cognition and schizotypal symptoms to creative achievement. *Creativity Research Journal*, 24(2–3), 177–190.

Fink, A., Slamar-Halbedl, M., Unterrainer, H. F. and Weiss, E. M. (2012). Creativity: Genius, madness, or a combination of both? *Psychology of Aesthetics, Creativity, and the Arts*, 6(1), 11–18.

Folley, B. S. and Park, S. (2005). Verbal creativity and schizotypal personality in relation to prefrontal hemispheric laterality: A behavioral and near-infrared optical imaging study. *Schizophrenia Research*, 80, 271–282.

Glicksohn, J. (2011). Schizophrenia and psychosis. In M. Runco and S. Pritzker (Eds.), *Encyclopedia of creativity* (2nd edn.) (pp. 325–330). San Diego, CA: Academic Press.

Heston, L. L. (1966). Psychiatric disorders in foster home reared children of schizophrenic mothers. *British Journal of Psychiatry*, 112, 819–825.

Jamison, K. R. (1989). Mood disorders and patterns of creativity in British writers and artists. *Psychiatry*, 52, 125–134.

Jamison, K. R. (1990). Manic-depressive illness and accomplishment: Creativity, leadership, and social class. In F. K. Goodwin and K. R. Jamison (Eds.), *Manic-depressive illness*. Oxford: Oxford University Press.

Jamison, K. R. (1993). *Touched with fire: Manic-depressive illness and the artistic temperament.* New York: Free Press.

Jamison, K. R., Gerner, R. H., Hammen, C. and Padesky, C. (1980). Clouds and silver linings: Positive experiences associated with the primary affective disorders. *American Journal of Psychiatry,* 137, 198–202.

Kauffman, C., Grunebaum, H., Cohler, B. and Gamer, E. (1979). Superkids: Competent children of psychotic mothers. *American Journal of Psychiatry,* 136, 1398–1402.

Kaufman, J. C. (2005). The door that leads into madness: Eastern European poets and mental illness. *Creativity Research Journal,* 17(1), 99–103.

Kaufman, S. B. (2009). Faith in intuition is associated with decreased latent inhibition in a sample of high-achieving adolescents. *Psychology of Aesthetics, Creativity, and the Arts,* 3(1), 28–34.

Kendler, K. S., Gruenberg, A. M. and Kinney, D. K. (1994). Independent diagnoses of adoptees and relatives as defined by *DSM-III* in the provincial and national samples of the Danish Adoption Study of Schizophrenia. *Archives of General Psychiatry,* 51(6), 456–468.

Kety, S. S., Wender, P. H., Jacobsen, B., Ingraham, L. J., Jansson, L., Faber, B. *et al.* (1994). Mental illness in the biological and adoptive relatives of schizophrenic adoptees: Replication of the Copenhagen Study in the rest of Denmark. *Archives of General Psychiatry,* 51(6), 442–455.

Kinney, D. K. (1992). The therapist as muse: Greater roles for clinicians in fostering innovation. *American Journal of Psychotherapy,* 46(3), 434–453.

Kinney, D. K. and Matthysse, S. (1978). Genetic transmission of schizophrenia. *Annual Review of Medicine,* 29, 459–473.

Kinney, D. K. and Richards, R. (2011). Bipolar mood disorders. In M. Runco and S. R. Pritzker (Eds.), *Encyclopedia of creativity* (2nd edn.) (pp. 140–148). San Diego, CA: Academic Press.

Kinney, D. K., Richards, R., Lowing, P. A., LeBlanc, D., Zimbalist, M. E. and Harlan, P. (2000–2001). Creativity in offspring of schizophrenic and control parents: An adoption study. *Creativity Research Journal,* 13(1), 17–25.

Kounios, J., Fleck, J., Green, D. L., Payne, L., Stevenson, J., Bowden, E. *et al.* (2008). The origins of insight in resting brain activity. *Neuropsychologia,* 46(1), 281–291.

Kyaga, S., Lichtenstein, P., Borman, M., Hultman, C., Langstrom, N. and Landen, M. (2012). Creativity and mental disorder: Family study of 300,000 people with severe mental disorder. *British Journal of Psychiatry,* 199(5), 373–379.

Ludwig, A. M. (1996). *The price of greatness: Resolving the creativity and madness controversy.* New York: Guilford Press.

Martindale, C. (1999). Biological bases of creativity. In R. Sternberg (Ed.), *Handbook of creativity* (pp. 137–152). New York: Cambridge University Press.

Post, F. (1996). Verbal creativity, depression, and alcoholism: An investigation of one hundred American and British writers. *British Journal of Psychiatry,* 168(5), 545–555.

Rhodes, C. (1997). Growth from deficiency creativity to being creativity. In M. Runco and R. Richards (Eds.), *Eminent creativity, everyday creativity, and health* (pp. 247–263). Stamford, CT: Ablex.

Richards, R. (1981). Relationships between creativity and psychopathology: An evaluation and interpretation of the evidence. *Genetic Psychology Monographs*, 103, 261–324.

Richards, R. (1997). When illness yields creativity. In M. Runco and R. Richards (Eds.), *Eminent creativity, everyday creativity, and health* (pp. 485–540). Stamford, CT: Ablex.

Richards, R. (Ed.) (2007). *Everyday creativity and new views of human nature.* Washington, DC: American Psychological Association.

Richards, R. (2010). Everyday creativity: Process and way of life – four key issues. In J. C. Kaufman and R. J. Sternberg (Eds.), *The Cambridge handbook of creativity* (pp. 189–215). New York: Cambridge University Press.

Richards, R. and Kinney, D. K. (1990). Mood swings and everyday creativity. *Creativity Research Journal*, 3(3), 202–217.

Richards, R., Kinney, D. K., Benet, M. and Merzel, A. P. C. (1988). Assessing everyday creativity: Characteristics of the Lifetime Creativity Scales and validation with three large samples. *Journal of Personality and Social Psychology*, 54, 476–485.

Richards, R., Kinney, D. K., Daniels, H. and Linkins, K. (1992). Everyday creativity and bipolar and unipolar affective disorder: Preliminary study of personal and family history. *European Psychiatry*, 2, 49–52.

Richards, R., Kinney, D. K., Lunde, I., Benet, M. and Merzel, A. P. (1988). Creativity in manic-depressives, cyclothymes, their normal relatives, and control subjects. *Journal of Abnormal Psychology*, 97(3), 281–288.

Rodrigue, A. L. and Perkins, D. R. (2012). Divergent thinking abilities across the schizophrenic spectrum and other psychological correlates. *Creativity Research Journal*, 24(2–3), 163–168.

Runco, M. and Richards, R. (Eds.) (1997). *Eminent creativity, everyday creativity, and health.* Stamford, CT: Ablex.

Sass, L. (2000–2001). Schizophrenia, modernism, and the "creative imagination": On creativity and psychopathology. *Creativity Research Journal*, 13(1), 55–74.

Schuldberg, D. (2000–2001). Six subclinical spectrum traits in normal creativity. *Creativity Research Journal*, 13(1), 5–16.

Shenton, M. E., Solovay, M. R., Holzman, P. S., Coleman, M. and Gale, H. J. (1989). Thought disorder in the relatives of psychotic patients. *Archives of General Psychiatry*, 46(10), 897–901.

Silvia, P. J. and Kaufman, J. C. (2010). Creativity and mental illness. In J. C. Kaufman and R. J. Sternberg (Eds.), *The Cambridge handbook of creativity* (pp. 381–394). New York: Cambridge University Press.

Srivastava, S., Childers, M. E., Baek, J. H., Strong, C. M., Hill, S. J., Warsett, K. S. *et al.* (2010). Toward interaction of affective and cognitive contributors to creativity in bipolar disorders: A controlled study. *Journal of Affective Disorders*, 125(1–3), 27–34.

Subramaniam, K., Kounios, J., Parrish, T. B. and Jung-Beeman, M. (2008). A brain mechanism for facilitation of insight by positive affect. *Journal of Cognitive Neuroscience*, 21(3), 415–432.

Vellante, M., Zucca, G., Preti, A., Sisti, D., Rocchi, M. B., Akiskal, K. K. *et al.* (2011). Creativity and affective temperaments in non-clinical professional artists: An empirical psychometric investigation. *Journal of Affective Disorders*, 135(1–3), 28–36.

Part V

Creativity and mental health

15 Bringing the whole universe to order: creativity, healing, and posttraumatic growth[1]

Marie J. C. Forgeard, Anne C. Mecklenburg, Justin J. Lacasse, and Eranda Jayawickreme

Past research and anecdotal accounts suggest that individuals pursuing creative work (especially in artistic fields) tend to report higher-than-average levels of challenging life circumstances, including experiencing adverse life events (Simonton, 1994) and psychological disorders (for reviews, see Jamison, 1993, Johnson *et al.*, 2012; Kaufman, 2009; Ludwig, 1995). One explanation for these findings is the possibility, noted by researchers, creators, and laypeople alike, that creative work and activities confer benefits for the well-being of individuals who engage in them (Cropley, 1990, 1997; Winner, 1982). By engaging in creative work, individuals are given the opportunity to heal and grow from the challenges that have befallen them. Anecdotal accounts from eminent creative individuals suggest that engaging in creative activities – defined as activities that generate novel and useful ideas or products (Sternberg and Lubart, 1999) – appears to have therapeutic benefits. In her diary, the writer Virginia Woolf commented:

Odd how the creative power at once brings the whole universe to order. I can see the day whole, proportioned – even after a long flutter of the brain such as I've had this morning[;] it must be a physical, moral, mental necessity, like setting the engine off. (Woolf, 1934/2003, p. 213)

Woolf, known to suffer from bipolar disorder (Caramagno, 1992), expressed her belief that writing was essential to her well-being. Other eminent artists echoed a similar feeling with regards to either physical or psychological health. For example, the painter Paul Klee, who suffered from a severe autoimmune disorder, explained during the last stages of his disease: "I create – in order not to cry" (Sandblom, 1997, p. 187).

[1] This chapter was made possible through the support of a grant from the John Templeton Foundation. The opinions expressed in this chapter are those of the authors and do not necessarily reflect the views of the John Templeton Foundation. Additional funding for this project was generously provided by Eva Kedar, PhD.

321

The novelist and screenwriter Graham Greene, who also suffered from bipolar disorder, called writing "a form of therapy" (p. 37), and the confessional poet Anne Sexton, having composed verse based on the advice of her therapist, famously wrote that "poetry led me by the hand out of madness" (Jamison, 1993, p. 122). Finally, the French writer Antonin Artaud, who suffered from clinical depression, chronic pain, and addiction to opiates throughout his life (Rowlands, 2004), commented that "No one has ever written, painted, sculpted, modeled, built, or invented except literally to get out of hell" (Jamison, 1993, p. 121).

The purpose of this chapter is to summarize current scientific knowledge on the healing powers of creative work and activities. This review mostly addresses the benefits of artistic creativity, because – to the best of our knowledge – the evidence on the benefits of creative activities in other fields has not yet been explored. We begin by reviewing research on the effectiveness of art therapy and expressive writing, which suggests that these creative activities do indeed confer benefits for the well-being of those who engage in them. Second, we review and extend the literature on the mechanisms explaining the therapeutic effects of creativity. We discuss past research on the role of catharsis, positive affect, and meaning making as the active ingredients of creative involvement. In addition, we discuss the results of recent research suggesting that meaning making through creative work may lead to posttraumatic growth, defined as "the experience of positive change that occurs as a result of the struggle with highly challenging life crises" (Tedeschi and Calhoun, 2004, p. 1). The chapter concludes by discussing the strengths and limitations of current scientific knowledge on the healing and growth-inducing potential of creative work and activities, and outlines future directions for research in this area.

The therapeutic benefits of creativity

Two main bodies of literature – research on art therapy and expressive writing – have sought to establish the extent to which creative work and activities can decrease psychopathology and increase well-being.

Art therapy

Investigations of the relationship between creativity and psychological disorders date as far back as Plato (e.g., Becker, this volume), though the figure of the "mad genius" became especially popular during the Romantic period of the late eighteenth and early nineteenth centuries – for example, in 1812, Benjamin Rush described patients who had discovered hidden artistic talents upon developing a psychiatric illness (Beveridge, 2001). The promotion of creative activities as part of clinical, therapeutic practice, however, came into being relatively recently in the mid-twentieth century (Vick, 2003). Although originally born out of the psychoanalytic tradition, the field of art therapy now encompasses a range of theoretical approaches, and most art therapists primarily define their practice as "eclectic" rather than aligning themselves with any specific therapeutic discipline or technique (Vick, 2003). The present review discusses art therapy in its broadest form. According to the American Art Therapy Association (AATA), the practice of art therapy "is based on the belief that the creative process involved in artistic self-expression helps people to resolve conflicts and problems, develop interpersonal skills, manage behavior, reduce stress, increase self-esteem and self-awareness, and achieve insight" (AATA, 2011, para. 7). In practice, clients often engage in both art therapy (used as an adjunctive) and traditional ("talk") therapy simultaneously, though reflection and discussion are often significant components of art therapy as well (Malchiodi, 2003).

Art therapy frequently takes place in a group setting, and can therefore focus more specifically on building relationships between the client, therapist, and other members of the group (Crawford et al., 2012; Gussak, 2006). In addition, art therapy is thought to facilitate self-expression and growth (Fisher and Specht, 1999). By using and creating concrete images (or other creative media such as music or dance), individuals can explore difficult thoughts and emotions in a pleasurable, nonthreatening manner (Malchiodi, 2003). Art therapy has been used to treat a variety of conditions including (but not limited to) eating disorders (Frisch et al., 2006), learning disabilities (Safran, 2003), or addiction (Wilson, 2003). Art therapy may also be particularly beneficial for individuals whose disorders cause them to have difficulty communicating verbally (e.g., schizophrenia) and would therefore benefit from the non-verbal communication tools used in art therapy (Crawford and Patterson, 2007; Richardson et al., 2007).

Art therapy appears to be useful for individuals of all ages. Art therapy interventions have, for example, been designed for older individuals as an integral part of successful aging (Fisher and Specht, 1999). In addition, children may respond well to art therapy, because they may be more willing to engage in imaginative, creative exercises than adults, and may also benefit from using non-verbal forms of communication (Malchiodi, 2003). Art therapy may be especially helpful for children who have experienced a trauma (Eaton et al., 2007; Ottarsdottir, 2010). Like cognitive–behavioral interventions, art therapy focuses on reducing excessive arousal, exploring cognitions, and using real or imagined sensory experiences (in art therapy, the physical experience of drawing the trauma) to gain control over physiological reactions and traumatic memories, and to reduce symptoms of posttraumatic stress (Lyshak-Stelzer et al., 2007; Sarid and Huss, 2010).

Among hospitalized adults, art therapy has been found to lead to improved clinical outcomes as manifested by better vital signs and reduced hospital stays (Stuckey and Nobel, 2010). Art therapy has also been found to be as effective as verbal psychotherapy for women suffering from depression (Thyme et al., 2007). In addition, art therapy has been demonstrated to decrease depression and anxiety and increase quality of life for patients diagnosed with cancer (Geue et al., 2010) as well as for prison inmates (Gussak, 2006, 2007, 2009). Art therapy may also help create positive attitudes towards therapy in general and retain clients (Pizarro, 2004). In keeping with this, researchers have noted that participants enjoy art therapy more, and are more likely to attend sessions, relative to traditional therapy (e.g., Crawford et al., 2012).

While these results are encouraging, much more research is needed in order to establish art therapy as an effective, empirically supported form of treatment (Holmkvist and Persson, 2012; Kaplan, 2000; Ruddy and Milnes, 2005). Few trials of art therapy, for example, follow established clinical guidelines (e.g., Chambless and Hollon, 1998). Instead, some art therapists have argued for the use of different standards of evidence for this discipline (e.g., Gilroy, 1996), which may unfortunately lead to skepticism from other researchers. A recent review of research on the effectiveness of art therapy including 35 papers nevertheless found that art therapy (most often using visual arts media) overall leads to small but usually statistically significant improvements on a range of psychological measures (Slayton et al., 2010). In addition, many people who engage in art therapy subjectively report being able to better express their emotions and engage in adaptive coping strategies (Geue et al., 2010), as well as experiencing an increased sense of purpose and engagement with others (Fisher and Specht, 1999).

Expressive writing

In addition to empirical work on the benefits of art therapy, researchers have looked at the usefulness of writing for psychological and physical health. Clinicians working with psychiatric populations, for example, have noted that participating in creative writing groups has a number of benefits, including providing an opportunity to remember, process, and externalize painful but also positive feelings, increasing self-esteem, and helping with concentration and orientation in time (Phillips et al., 1999). Beyond anecdotal or qualitative reports, a large number of quantitative studies have documented the benefits of writing (Pennebaker, 1997; Sexton and Pennebaker, 2009). These studies have usually followed the expressive writing paradigm put forward by Pennebaker and colleagues. In a typical expressive writing study, participants are asked to write about an emotionally salient topic for 15–20-minute sessions over the course of several days or weeks. They are then compared with a control condition in which participants are asked to write about a non-emotional topic. Overall, engaging in expressive writing has been shown to improve outcomes in a wide range of domains such as physical health (including blood pressure, medication use, or recovery time from medical procedures), psychological health (including depression and rumination), occupational outcomes (including work attendance and shorter periods of unemployment), and cognitive outcomes (such as working memory) (for a review, see Sexton and Pennebaker, 2009). Although expressive writing does not resemble typical creative writing activities, because the main focus of the writing is on real past events, participants are nonetheless asked to write about these events in a way that allows for the expression of original ideas. Thus, it is possible that writing done in this paradigm falls on a continuum of creativity, depending on the degree to which writers express novel and useful insights about their experiences.

A number of meta-analyses have been conducted in order to draw reliable conclusions from this large body of literature. These have yielded somewhat contradictory results regarding the overall effectiveness and usefulness of expressive writing: one meta-analysis indicated that writing has a reliable and moderate effect on outcomes (Smyth, 1998); another evidenced a reliable but small effect on outcomes (Frattaroli, 2006); and finally, yet another meta-analysis found insufficient evidence to suggest a reliable effect of expressive writing (Meads and Nouwen, 2005). In light of these inconsistent findings, a more fruitful approach has been to look for the conditions under which expressive writing exerts its most beneficial effects. Expressive writing, for example, seems to reduce the utilization of health-care services mostly in healthy samples, but not in a sample characterized by preexisting medical or psychological problems (Harris, 2006). In addition, expressive writing appears to be most beneficial in samples with higher proportions of males, in samples of individuals having experienced a recent traumatic event, in samples that engaged in longer and more frequent writing sessions, and in samples that wrote at home rather than in the lab (Frattaroli, 2006).

Finally, recent research has explored whether the benefits of expressive writing are limited to dealing with past negative events or illnesses. Some studies have found that writing is particularly beneficial when it focuses on negative experiences (Lyubomirsky *et al.*, 2006), whereas others have found that writing about good experiences may also be helpful (Burton and King, 2004, 2008; King, 2001). In addition, some research suggests that one need not have experienced important events directly in order to benefit from writing. Greenberg *et al.* (1996), for example, found that writing about the emotional experience brought about by a real or imaginary trauma led to comparable positive health outcomes including fewer illness visits (which represented an improvement over a control group who wrote about trivial events). In addition, the imaginary trauma group displayed less symptoms of ill-being (depression, fatigue, avoidance) than the real trauma group. This finding has important implications for creative writers, whose work consists of writing about important but imaginary events.

The effect of the medium employed

The effect of creative activities on psychological and physical health may be moderated by the creative medium used, although little research to date has investigated this important question. Some evidence suggests that visual art therapy promotes positive emotion in the short term, while expressive writing may produce short-term negative emotion but long-term health benefits (Drake *et al.*, 2011; Pennebaker and Beall, 1986; Pizarro, 2004). Because of these short-term effects, participants may find art therapy more immediately rewarding than other therapies, and some studies have found that art therapy promoted better attendance and engagement than traditional therapy (Crawford *et al.*, 2012). As a result of these encouraging findings on the usefulness of both visual art and writing activities, some researchers have argued for a combination of visual art and writing therapy in clinical practice (e.g., Pizarro, 2004).

Mechanisms underlying the therapeutic effects of creative work and activities

Several mechanisms have been proposed and investigated to explain the therapeutic benefits of creative activities, including engagement and flow, catharsis, increases in positive affect, and meaning making.

Engagement and flow

Engagement in creative activities may promote well-being by promoting experiences of absorption with the task at hand. Csikszentmihalyi's (1990) concept of flow provides one mechanism explaining how creativity may increase well-being. Csikszentmihalyi developed the construct of flow in the 1960s as a result of observing artists paint (Csikszentmihalyi, 2000). Flow is a psychological state defined by the presence of both high skills and high challenges, giving individuals a sense of control over the activity at hand. It is characterized by intense focus and concentration, a merging of action and awareness, the feeling that the passage of time may be distorted in some way, and intrinsic reward. The experience of flow helps explain how creative involvement may benefit various facets of psychological well-being including a sense of personal competence, accomplishment, positive emotion, and meaning in life (Csikszentmihalyi, 1996; Forgeard and Eichner, in press).

Catharsis

The concept of catharsis, from the Greek for "cleansing" or "purging," was first used by Aristotle and refers to the emotional release one gets by expending pent-up negative energy, thoughts, and emotions, allowing the human soul to be purged of its "excessive passions" (Lucas, 1928, p. 24). Creative activities may therefore give individuals a vehicle through which to express their painful emotions (DePetrillo and Winner, 2005; Sloan and Marx, 2004). As an illustration, Virginia Woolf reported that writing the novel *To the lighthouse* (Woolf, 1927) allowed her to express her feelings about, and recover from, losing her mother, who died when Woolf was 13:

> I wrote the book very quickly; and when it was written, I ceased to be obsessed with my mother. I no longer hear her voice; I do not see her. I suppose that I did for myself what psycho-analysts do for their patients. I expressed some very long felt and deeply felt emotions. And in expressing it I explained it and then laid it to rest. (Woolf, 1985, p. 81)

As noted later, however, little empirical research supports the notion that creative activities increase well-being by promoting catharsis (Dalebroux et al., 2008).

Distraction and positive emotion

In contrast, creative activities may promote healing by simply distracting individuals and engaging them in an enjoyable activity that promotes the expression of positive emotions. Drawing on Fredrickson's (1998, 2001) "broaden-and-build" model, activities that increase positive emotions (such as creative activities, which are often reported to be intrinsically enjoyable) produce a broadening of attention that allows individuals to "pursue novel, creative, and often unscripted paths of thought and action" (1998, p. 304). Experiences of positive emotion and creativity may therefore reinforce each other in a virtuous "broaden-and-build" cycle, in which engaging in a pleasurable creative activity encourages individuals to think of new ways to understand and deal with their psychological symptoms. The positive emotions induced by creative activities may also ameliorate the deleterious health effects of negative emotions and stress on the cardiovascular and immune systems (Fredrickson, 1998, 2001; Salovey *et al.*, 2000). By distracting individuals from negative emotions and promoting novel ways of thinking, creative activities and positive emotions may work hand-in-hand to promote healing. During the painter's stay in a psychiatric hospital in the South of France, Van Gogh (1889) wrote in a letter to his brother Theo: "Work distracts me infinitely better than anything else, and if I could once really throw myself into it with all my energy that might possibly be the best remedy."

A few studies have compared the effects of creative activities that promote either catharsis or positive emotion. Dalebroux *et al.* (2008) found that an artistic activity that focused on the expression of positive feelings was more effective at repairing short-term negative mood, induced by watching a sad movie clip, than an equivalent artistic activity that focused on the expression of negative feelings (catharsis). In support of this conclusion, other studies have shown that distracting individuals from their negative emotional states may alleviate symptoms of depression (Nolen-Hoeksema, 1991) and effectively repair short-term negative moods (Drake *et al.*, 2011). In addition, the promotion of positive emotions may strengthen individuals' resilience for future stressful events (Keltner and Bonanno, 1997; Tugade and Fredrickson, 2007).

Meaning making

In addition to promoting flow experiences, catharsis, and positive emotion, creative activities may also promote healing by engaging individuals in a process of making meaning out of difficult experiences. The Irish writer Colm Toibin, for example, described the writer's need to build a coherent narrative to make sense of one's experience in the following terms:

It seems that the essential impulse in working at all is to rehaunt your own house, or to allow what haunts you to have a voice, to chart what is deeply private and etched on the soul, and find form and structure for it. (Eugenides and Toibin, 2011, para. 7)

The hypothesis that creative activities help create meaning for painful experiences has primarily been investigated with regards to expressive writing, although meaning making may certainly occur with other forms of creative expression. The benefits of creative activities may result from the fact that these activities do not just entail recording or expressing ideas, but also interacting with them, leading one's thinking to evolve as a direct result of the creative activity. Writing may constitute an especially beneficial form of creativity, because it provides clear opportunities for self-disclosure, self-expression, and problem resolution (Runco, 2009). In particular, the formation of a narrative may assist individuals in making meaning out of their experiences by shifting perspectives and restructuring their cognitions around difficult events (Sexton and Pennebaker, 2009). In keeping with this, the beneficial effects of writing have been related to the degree to which participants use cognitive words (e.g., "know," "understand") (Pennebaker and Seagal, 1999).

Beyond healing: creativity and posttraumatic growth

In addition to promoting healing through catharsis, distraction, positive emotion, and meaning making, creative work and activities may also promote positive functioning after adversity by fostering psychological growth, above and beyond recovery and return to baseline levels of functioning. Psychological disorders constitute an important kind of adversity, and disorders with sudden and acute onsets can be experienced as traumatic. Psychologists have become increasingly interested in studying the positive life changes that people report in the aftermath of highly stressful life events (including, but by no means limited to, being diagnosed with a chronic or terminal illness, bereavement, and sexual assault). This phenomenon is most commonly referred to by scientists as *posttraumatic growth* (the term used in the present review), *growth through adversity*, *stress-related growth*, or *benefit finding*, among other terms (Jayawickreme *et al.*, 2012; Joseph and Linley, 2005; Tedeschi *et al.*, 1998). Research in this field has evidenced at least five domains of growth following stressful life experiences: interpersonal relations, the identification of new possibilities for one's life, personal strength, spirituality, and appreciation of life. While researchers have noted that creativity may also constitute a way in which posttraumatic growth is expressed (Aldwin and Sutton, 1998; Bloom, 1998), little research has been conducted to date in order to investigate this hypothesis, although some evidence suggests that reminders of one's mortality (as present in some psychological disorders) can enhance creativity under certain conditions (e.g., Routledge *et al.*, 2008). In addition, the identification of new possibilities for one's life after an adverse experience is closely related to openness to experience (Tedeschi and Calhoun, 1996), the personality trait most predictive of creativity (Feist, 1998; King *et al.*, 1996; McCrae, 1987). Creative work may therefore constitute one such "new possibility."

Theoretical background

A number of theoretical approaches have attempted to explain the processes associated with posttraumatic growth. We review the main approaches that can inform the scientific understanding of how creativity relates to posttraumatic growth (for other perspectives, see Aldwin *et al.*, 1996; Meichenbaum, 1985; Seery, 2011). First, *organismic valuing theory* (Joseph and Linley, 2006) posits that humans have an innate tendency to integrate their experiences (including adverse experiences) into a unified sense of self. Positive or negative outcomes may result according to how information about adverse experiences is integrated. An individual can either "assimilate" (p. 268) this information by integrating the experience into beliefs or worldviews they held before the event (leading them to recover but perhaps not grow), or they can "accommodate" (p. 268) this information by modifying their prior worldviews in light of their experience. If an individual accommodates information in a positive way and modifies their prior worldview appropriately (e.g., "Life is unpredictable, so it should be lived to the fullest"), they can experience psychological growth, which may manifest itself in increased creativity, especially when such events occur during childhood and adolescence (Joseph and Linley, 2005; Simonton, 2000). Second, and related to organismic valuing theory, *assumptive world theory* (Janoff-Bulman, 1992, 2006; Tedeschi and Calhoun, 2004) proposed that adverse experiences act as "a psychologically seismic event" (Tedeschi and Calhoun, 2004, p. 5) capable of shaking one's deeply held beliefs about oneself and the world. Importantly, adverse events can lead individuals to question and reconsider their belief in the benevolence, predictability, and controllability of the world. Individuals faced with such seismic events must then rebuild new beliefs by engaging in cognitive processing, a process through which growth or depreciation may occur. Individuals may take part in two main forms of cognitive processing (either in sequence, or simultaneously): they may engage with unwanted or unsolicited thoughts about the event (intrusive rumination), or they may engage in a more voluntary and purposeful thinking process about the impact of the event on their lives (Calhoun *et al.*, 2010; Tedeschi and Calhoun, 2004). Although intrusive rumination may precede and lead to deliberate rumination, it is more closely linked to posttraumatic depreciation (i.e., negative changes), while deliberate rumination is more closely linked to growth (Cann *et al.*, 2011).

In parallel to findings showing that deliberate rumination fosters growth after adverse experiences, research on creativity has also begun to examine the contribution of ruminative processes to creativity. One body of research shows that rumination focused on one's negative emotional states (as is common, for example, in depression) leads to poorer creative problem-solving performance (Davis and Nolen-Hoeksema, 2000; Lyubomirsky et al., 1999). In contrast, rumination that does not focus on one's negative feelings positively predicts creative thinking outcomes (Cohen and Ferrari, 2010). Related to this, eminent authors known to have suffered from depression appear to be more likely to use cognitive words reflective of repetitive thinking processes (e.g., "know," "understand," etc.) in their fictional works than other authors (Forgeard, 2008). In addition, research on the relationship between depression and creativity has evidenced that it is not depression itself that is associated with enhanced creative performance, but rather the repetitive thinking processes associated with depression that promote fluency as well as seriousness for one's creative activities (Verhaeghen et al., 2005).

Research on the processes at play in posttraumatic growth has therefore begun to explain how adverse events may promote creativity by enabling individuals to think about new possibilities for their lives, and leading them to engage in sustained, deep, and potentially productive cognitive processing regarding their beliefs about themselves and the world. Other theoretical perspectives have, however, advanced the possibility that posttraumatic growth primarily reflects a subjective coping mechanism rather than a genuine reflection of psychological growth. For example, according to *cognitive adaptation theory* (Taylor, 1983), stressful and threatening life events challenge an individual's self-esteem, sense of personal control, and optimism about the future. Successful adaptation to threatening experiences is then based on the individual's ability to develop and maintain a set of positive illusions that protect them from the potentially deleterious effects of adversity. In light of this possibility, Maercker and Zoellner (2004) have argued for a Janus-faced (two-faced) model of posttraumatic growth, in which a constructive, strength-based side of growth coexists with a negative, maladaptive, and self-deceptive side (e.g., Hobfoll et al., 2006). The Janus-faced model suggests that posttraumatic growth may not be associated with positive effects, depending on the side being manifested.

Empirical evidence

To the best of our knowledge, only one study to date has looked at the relationship between creativity and posttraumatic growth. Forgeard (2012) asked a sample of 373 web users from the United States to report the kinds of adverse events (e.g., disaster, illness, accident, assault, etc.) they had previously experienced in their lives. In addition, participants reported which of these events had had the greatest impact on their lives. Results of the study indicated that the level of distress experienced during the most impactful adverse event reported by each participant predicted increased levels of self-reported creative growth (assessed using a brief scale designed for the purpose of the study), a relationship mediated by specific domains of posttraumatic growth and depreciation. Following assumptive world theory (Calhoun *et al.*, 2010; Tedeschi and Calhoun, 2004), distress at the time of the event predicted the amount of intrusive and deliberate rumination participants engaged in after the event. In turn, intrusive rumination predicted all five domains of posttraumatic depreciation (but not posttraumatic growth). Of these domains, negative changes in the perception of new possibilities for one's life predicted decreased self-reported creative growth. In contrast, negative changes in interpersonal relationships predicted increased self-reported creative growth. Conversely, deliberate rumination predicted all five domains of posttraumatic growth (but not posttraumatic depreciation). Of these domains, positive changes in relationships and in the perception of new possibilities for one's life both predicted increased self-reported creative growth. In this study, self-reported creative growth did not differ according to the domain of creativity considered, using the domains proposed by Kaufman *et al.* (2009) (entrepreneur, artistic/verbal, artistic/visual, math/science, performance, interpersonal, and problem solving).

Results of this study unexpectedly suggested that both positive and negative changes in interpersonal relationships lead to increases in perceived creativity. This finding initially seems contradictory, but makes sense considering that artistic works frequently draw on both happy and unhappy relational events for subject matter. For example, Tennessee Williams' plays such as *The glass menagerie* (1944) are widely thought to be modeled on his own dysfunctional family, whereas Louisa May Alcott took her strong bond with her three sisters as inspiration for the novel *Little women* (1868). In contrast, the role of perceiving new possibilities for one's life is not surprising given that, as explained earlier, this facet of posttraumatic growth has been linked to openness to experience, the personality trait most closely linked to creativity (Feist, 1998; King *et al.*, 1996; McCrae, 1987). Openness to experience may therefore allow individuals to think creatively about future opportunities for their lives and for their work. In keeping with this, a qualitative study of the biographies of eminent painters having suffered from physical illnesses (e.g., Botticelli, Monet, Munch) suggested that the experience of illness may lead to the emergence of new possibilities for one's art by breaking habits, provoking disequilibrium, and forcing artists to come up with new ways to fulfill their creative goals (Zausner, 1998, 2007).

Universality of the phenomenon

Much work remains to be done to clarify the precise role of creativity in the process of growing from adversity, and one challenge for this research is to establish the extent to which these findings represent a universal or culturally bound phenomenon by examining, for example, whether findings generalize to an international sample. In preparation for future studies investigating this question, we recently completed an exploratory pilot study focused on a Rwandan sample exposed to the traumatic events of the 1994 genocide. Having come to local clinics seeking mental health services, participants ($N = 100$) were asked to indicate the degree to which they perceived that their creativity had increased since the genocide (using a 7-point Likert Scale), and to give a qualitative description of the reported changes. The mean level of creative growth reported was 2.26 (standard deviation $= 1.77$). Frequencies of scores, however, evidenced a bimodal distribution in which 61 percent of participants reported no change at all in creativity (score of 1 out of 7), while the second largest group of 25 percent of participants reported a moderate increase in creativity (score of 4 out of 7) (all other scores were endorsed by 3–5 percent of participants). Thus, increased creativity appeared to be an important subjective change linked to adversity for a subset of participants only, and future research should investigate moderators explaining why some individuals but not others report experiencing creative growth. Qualitative responses given by participants also provided insights into the domains of creative growth endorsed. Approximately half of respondents who acknowledged creative growth referred to the domain of music or singing (and in particular, composing love songs). The remaining domains of creative growth reported by participants belonged mainly to the arts and included creative writing, poetry, dancing, crafts, artisan skills, and the more general ability to come up with new ideas or projects. Although a significant proportion of participants reported no change in growth, it is possible that this pilot sample may have underreported growth in creative domains other than art as a result of the non-specific nature of instructions. Further research is needed to investigate how culture relates to posttraumatic growth as well as to creative manifestations of such growth. These findings, however, continue to lend credence to the notion that increases in perceived creativity may, at least in a subset of individuals, follow from the experience of adversity, and that this phenomenon may not be limited to the United States.

Future directions

The main limitation of research on the extent to which creativity may constitute a form of posttraumatic growth is the paucity of current empirical evidence. In addition, and mirroring limitations of empirical research on posttraumatic growth as a whole, researchers need to move beyond cross-sectional and self-report data in order to more firmly establish the nature of the growth that occurs following adversity. Current research assesses growth retrospectively, which requires sophisticated cognitive accounting on the part of participants – for this reason, people have been shown to be inaccurate in their perceptions of change over time (Ford et al., 2008). One solution that has been recommended consists of using multiple measures of constructs as well as informant corroboration in order to increase the reliability and validity of assessments of growth (Helgeson, 2010).

In addition, because past research on posttraumatic growth has tended to collect data at one point in time only, past studies have not been able to investigate the causal nature of the association between adversity and self-reported positive changes. For example, it is unclear whether adversity causes positive changes (including creative growth), or whether people who are currently doing well are more likely to retrospectively perceive benefits in adversity. Alternatively, a third variable (e.g., coping style) may explain perceiving benefits in adversity in addition to doing well. For example, intelligent individuals, or individuals who are more creative and/or more open to experience, may also be more likely to perceive growth over time and report greater well-being. This important question can only be addressed using longitudinal studies that collect information from participants at different points over time (e.g., Frazier et al., 2009). Furthermore, the subjective nature of the positive changes examined in past research (including measures of creative growth) may or may not be associated with concurrent positive behavioral changes.

One of three pictures may emerge from future studies on the nature of creative growth, using both prospective designs as well as combinations of subjective and behavioral measures of creative growth. First, and in line with cognitive adaptation theory, it is possible that subjective positive changes in creativity merely constitute a coping mechanism (Taylor, 1983) or the result of derogating the past (i.e., seeing the past as worse than it really was) rather than from real changes that occurred from past to present (McFarland and Alvaro, 2000). Second, creative growth may be primarily psychological in nature and not always observable through behavioral measures. We agree with Tedeschi *et al.* (2007) that such psychological growth is itself valuable and important in its own right. Third, psychological growth may be accompanied by observable changes in creative behavior and performance. Future research using rigorous methods is therefore highly needed in order to tease out the exact nature and adaptive value of creative growth following adversity.

Discussion and conclusions

This chapter reviewed the current state of scientific knowledge on the therapeutic and growth-promoting properties of creative activities and work. Overall, research findings in the area of art therapy and expressive writing suggest that creative activities have the potential to decrease psychopathological symptoms and increase well-being by engaging individuals and fostering positive emotion, meaning making, and psychological growth. Much more research is needed to investigate exciting new questions in this area. First, are the benefits of creative activities limited to creativity in the arts, or might creativity in other fields (e.g., science, business, etc.) also promote healing and growth? Second, are there other possible mechanisms explaining why creative activities and work decrease psychopathological symptoms and increase well-being? For example, among other possible mechanisms, the role of mastery and self-efficacy in the relationship between creativity and psychological well-being deserves further investigation: by engaging in creative activities, individuals may gain a sense of control over their own lives as well as increased confidence in their own ability to succeed, psychological processes that have been linked to well-being, anxiety, and depression (Bandura *et al.*, 1999; Chorpita *et al.*, 1998). Finally, future research needs to further explore the possibility that increased creativity constitutes an important way in which individuals grow in the aftermath of adversity. Future investigations should build on existing research on the phenomenon of posttraumatic growth by using prospective designs to move beyond retrospective assessments, as well as combinations of subjective and behavioral measures of creativity in order to tease out the exact nature of creative growth following adversity. By continuing to expand our scientific knowledge about these important questions, researchers can play their part in helping individuals to not only cope effectively with their symptoms, but also to grow and fulfill their creative potential.

References

Alcott, L. M. (1868). *Little women*. Boston, MA: Roberts Brothers.

Aldwin, C. M. and Sutton, K. J. (1998). A developmental perspective on post-traumatic growth. In R. G. Tedeschi, C. L. Park and L. G. Calhoun (Eds.), *Posttraumatic growth: Positive changes in the aftermath of crisis* (pp. 43–64). Mahwah, NJ: Erlbaum.

Aldwin, C. M., Sutton, K. J. and Lachman, M. (1996). The development of coping resources in adulthood. *Journal of Personality*, 64, 837–871.

American Art Therapy Association (2011). *History and background*. www.arttherapy.org/aata-history-background.html, last accessed March 17, 2014.

Bandura, A., Pastorelli, C., Barbaranelli, C. and Caprara, G. V. (1999). Self-efficacy pathways to childhood depression. *Journal of Personality and Social Psychology*, 79, 258–269.

Beveridge, A. (2001). A disquieting feeling of strangeness? The art of the mentally ill. *Journal of the Royal Society of Medicine*, 94, 595–599.

Bloom, S. L. (1998). By the crowd they have been broken, by the crowd they shall be healed: The social transformation of trauma. In R. G. Tedeschi, C. L. Park and L. G. Calhoun (Eds.), *Posttraumatic growth: Positive changes in the aftermath of crisis* (pp. 173–208). Mahwah, NJ: Erlbaum.

Burton, C. M. and King, L. A. (2004). The health benefits of writing about intensely positive experiences. *Journal of Research in Personality*, 38, 150–163.

Burton, C. M. and King, L. A. (2008). Effects of (very) brief writing on health: The two-minute miracle. *British Journal of Health Psychology*, 13, 9–14.

Calhoun, L. G., Cann, A. and Tedeschi, R. G. (2010). The posttraumatic growth model: Sociocultural considerations. In T. Weiss and R. Berger (Eds.), *Posttraumatic growth and culturally competent practice* (pp. 1–14). Hoboken, NJ: Wiley & Sons.

Cann, A., Calhoun, L. G., Tedeschi, R. G., Triplett, K. N., Vishnevsky, T. and Lindstrom, C. M. (2011). Assessing posttraumatic cognitive processes: The Event Related Rumination Inventory. *Anxiety, Stress and Coping*, 24, 137–156.

Caramagno, T. C. (1992). *The flight of the mind: Virginia Woolf's art and manic-depressive illness*. Los Angeles: University of California Press.

Chambless, D. and Hollon, S. (1998). Defining empirically supported therapies. *Journal of Consulting and Clinical Psychology*, 66, 7–18.

Chorpita, B. F., Brown, T. A. and Barlow, D. H. (1998). Perceived control as a mediator of family environment in etiological models of childhood anxiety. *Behavior Therapy*, 29, 457–476.

Cohen, J. R. and Ferrari, J. R. (2010). Take some time to think this over: The relation between rumination, indecision, and creativity. *Creativity Research Journal*, 22, 68–73.

Crawford, M. J. and Patterson, S. (2007). Arts therapies for people with schizophrenia: An emerging evidence base. *Evidence-Based Mental Health*, 10, 69–70.

Crawford, M. J., Killaspy, H., Barnes, T. R., Barrett, B., Byford, S., Clayton, K. *et al.* (2012). Group art therapy as an adjunctive treatment for people with schizophrenia: A randomised controlled trial (MATISSE). *Health Technology Assessment*, 16, 1–76.

Cropley, A. J. (1990). Creativity and mental health. *Creativity Research Journal*, 3, 167–178.

Cropley, A. J. (1997). Creativity and mental health in everyday life. In M. A. Runco and R. Richards (Eds.), *Eminent creativity, everyday creativity, and health*. Stamford, CT: Ablex.

Csikszentmihalyi, M. (1990). *Flow: The psychology of optimal experience*. New York: Harper & Row.

Csikszentmihalyi, M. (1996). *Creativity: Flow and the psychology of discovery and invention*. New York: HarperCollins Publishers.

Csikszentmihalyi, M. (2000). *Beyond boredom and anxiety* (2nd edn.). San Francisco, CA: Jossey-Bass.

Dalebroux, A., Goldstein, T. R. and Winner, E. (2008). Short-term mood repair through art-making: Positive emotion is more effective than venting. *Motivation and Emotion*, 32, 288–295.

Davis, R. N. and Nolen-Hoeksema, S. (2000). Cognitive inflexibility among ruminators and non-ruminators. *Cognitive Therapy and Research*, 24, 699–711.

De, L. and Winner, E. (2005). Does art improve mood? A test of a key assumption underlying art therapy. *Art Therapy: Journal of the American Art Therapy Association*, 22(4), 205–212.

Drake, J. F., Coleman, K. and Winner, E. (2011). Short-term mood repair through art: Effects of medium and strategy. *Art Therapy: Journal of the American Art Therapy Association*, 28, 26–33.

Eaton, L. G., Doherty, K. L. and Widrick, R. M. (2007). A review of research and methods used to establish art therapy as an effective treatment method for traumatized children. *The Arts in Psychotherapy*, 34, 256–262.

Eugenides, J. and Toibin, C. (2011). The stuff that won't go away. *New York Times*, October 1.

Feist, G. J. (1998). A meta-analysis of personality in scientific and artistic creativity. *Personality and Social Psychology Review*, 2, 290–309.

Fisher, B. J. and Specht, D. K. (1999). Successful aging and creativity in later life. *Journal of Aging Studies*, 13, 457–472.

Ford, J. D., Tennen, H. and Albert, D. (2008). A contrarian view of growth following adversity. In S. Joseph and P. A. Linley (Eds.), *Trauma, recovery, and growth: Positive psychological perspectives on posttraumatic stress* (pp. 297–324). Hoboken, NJ: John Wiley & Sons.

Forgeard, M. J. C. (2008). Linguistic styles of eminent writers suffering from unipolar and bipolar mood disorder. *Creativity Research Journal*, 20, 81–92.

Forgeard, M. J. C. (2012). *Finding benefits after adversity: Perceived creativity constitutes a manifestation of posttraumatic growth*. Manuscript submitted for publication.

Forgeard, M. J. C. and Eichner, K. V. (in press). Creativity as a target and tool for positive interventions. In A. C. Parks and S. M. Schueller (Eds.), *Handbook of positive psychological interventions*. Oxford: Wiley-Blackwell.

Frattaroli, J. (2006). Experimental disclosure and its moderators: A meta-analysis. *Psychological Bulletin*, 132, 823–865.

Frazier, P., Tennen, H., Gavian, M., Park, C., Tomich, P. and Tashiro, T. (2009). Does self-reported posttraumatic growth reflect genuine positive change? *Psychological Science*, 20, 912–919.

Fredrickson, B. L. (1998). What good are positive emotions? *Review of General Psychology*, 2, 300–319.

Fredrickson, B. L. (2001). The role of positive emotions in positive psychology: The broaden-and-build theory of positive emotions. *American Psychologist*, 56, 218–226.

Frisch, M. J., Franko, D. L. and Herzog, D. B. (2006). Arts-based therapies in the treatment of eating disorders. *Eating Disorders*, 14, 131–142.

Geue, K., Goetze, H., Buttstaedt, M., Kleinert, E., Richter, D. and Singer, S. (2010). An overview of art therapy interventions for cancer patients and the results of research. *Complementary Therapies in Medicine*, 18, 160–170.

Gilroy, A. (2006). *Art therapy, research, and evidence-based practice*. London: Sage Publications.

Greenberg, M. A., Wortman, C. B. and Stone, A. A. (1996). Emotional expression and physical health: Revising traumatic memories or fostering self-regulation? *Journal of Personality and Social Psychology*, 71, 588–602.

Gussak, D. (2006). Effects of art therapy with prison inmates: A follow-up study. *The Arts in Psychotherapy*, 33, 188–198.

Gussak, D. (2007). The effectiveness of art therapy in reducing depression in prison populations. *International Journal of Offender Therapy and Comparative Criminology*, 51, 444–460.

Gussak, D. (2009). The effects of art therapy on male and female inmates: Advancing the research base. *The Arts in Psychotherapy*, 36, 5–12.

Harris, A. H. S. (2006). Does expressive writing reduce health care utilization? A meta-analysis of randomized trials. *Journal of Consulting and Clinical Psychology*, 74, 243–252.

Helgeson, V. S. (2010). Corroboration of growth following breast cancer: 10 years later. *Journal of Social and Clinical Psychology*, 29, 546–574.

Hobfoll, S. E., Canetti-Nisim, D. and Johnson, R. J. (2006). Exposure to terrorism, stress-related mental health symptoms, and defensive coping among Jews and Arabs in Israel. *Journal of Consulting and Clinical Psychology*, 74, 207–218.

Hobfoll, S. E., Hall, B. J., Canetti-Nisim, D., Galea, S., Johnson, R. J. and Palmieri, P. A. (2007). Refining our understanding of traumatic growth in the face of terrorism: Moving from meaning cognitions to doing what is meaningful. *Applied Psychology: An International Review*, 56, 345–366.

Holmkvist, G. and Persson, C. L. (2012). Is there evidence for the use of art therapy in treatment of psychosomatic disorders, eating disorders, and crisis? A comparative study of two different systems for evaluation. *Scandinavian Journal of Psychology*, 53, 47–53.

Jamison, K. R. (1993). *Touched with fire: Manic-depressive illness and the artistic temperament*. New York: Free Press.

Janoff-Bulman, R. (1992). *Shattered assumptions*. New York: Free Press.

Janoff-Bulman, R. (2006). Schema-change perspectives on posttraumatic growth. In L. G. Calhoun and R. G. Tedeschi (Eds.), *Handbook of posttraumatic growth* (pp. 81–99). Mahwah, NJ: Erlbaum.

Jayawickreme, E., Jayawickreme, N. and Seligman, M. E. P. (2012). From victims to survivors: The positive psychology of refugee mental health. In K. M. Gow and M. J. Celinski (Eds.), *Mass trauma: Impact and recovery issues* (pp. 313–330). New York: Nova Science Publishers.

Johnson, S. L., Murray, G., Fredrickson, B., Youngstrom, E. A., Hinshaw, S., Malbrancq Bass, J. *et al.* (2012). Creativity and bipolar disorder: Touched by fire or burning with questions? *Clinical Psychology Review*, 32, 1–12.

Joseph, S. and Linley, A. P. (2005). Positive adjustment to threatening events: An organismic valuing theory of growth through adversity. *Review of General Psychology*, 9, 262–280.

Kaplan, F. F. (2000). *Art, science, and art therapy*. London: Jessica Kingsley.

Kaufman, J. C. (2009). *Creativity 101*. New York: Springer.

Kaufman, J. C., Cole, J. C. and Baer, J. (2009). The construct of creativity: Structural model for self-reported creativity ratings. *Journal of Creative Behavior*, 43, 119–134.

Keltner, D. and Bonanno, G. A. (1997). A study of laughter and dissociation: Distinct correlates of laughter and smiling during bereavement. *Journal of Personality and Social Psychology*, 73, 687–702.

King, L. A. (2001). The health benefits of writing about life goals. *Personality and Social Psychology Bulletin*, 27, 798–807.

King, L. A., Walker, L. M. and Broyles, S. J. (1996). Creativity and the five-factor model. *Journal of Research in Personality*, 30, 189–203.

Lucas, F. L. (1928). *Tragedy in relation to Aristotle's Poetics*. New York: Harcourt, Brace, and Company.

Ludwig, A. M. (1995). *The price of greatness: Resolving the creativity and madness controversy*. New York: Guilford Press.

Lyshak-Stelzer, F., Singer, P., John, P. S. and Chemtob, C. M. (2007). Art therapy for adolescents with posttraumatic stress disorder symptoms: A pilot study. *Art Therapy: Journal of the American Art Therapy Association*, 24, 163–169.

Lyubomirsky, S., Sousa, L. and Dickerhoof, R. (2006). The costs and benefits of writing, talking, and thinking about life's triumphs and defeats. *Journal of Personality and Social Psychology*, 90, 692–708.

Lyubomirsky, S., Tucker, K. L., Caldwell, N. D. and Berg, K. (1999). Why ruminators are poor problem solvers: Clues from the phenomenology of dysphoric rumination. *Journal of Personality and Social Psychology*, 77, 1041–1060.

McCrae, R. R. (1987). Creativity, divergent thinking, and openness to experience. *Journal of Personality and Social Psychology*, 52, 1258–1265.

McFarland, C. and Alvaro, C. (2000). The impact of motivation on temporal comparison: Coping with traumatic events by perceiving personal growth. *Journal of Personality and Social Psychology*, 79, 327–343.

Maercker, A. and Zoellner, T. (2004). The Janus face of self-perceived growth: Toward a two component model of posttraumatic growth. *Psychological Inquiry*, 15, 41–48.

Malchiodi, C. A. (Ed.) (2003). *Handbook of art therapy*. New York: Guilford Press.

Meads, C. and Nouwen, A. (2005). Does emotional disclosure have any effects? A systematic review of the literature with meta-analyses. *International Journal of Technology Assessment in Health Care*, 21, 153–164.

Meichenbaum, D. (1985). *Stress inoculation training*. New York: Pergamon.

Nolen-Hoeksema, S. (1991). Responses to depression and their effects on the duration of depressive episodes. *Journal of Abnormal Psychology*, 100, 569–582.

Ottarsdottir, U. (2010). Art therapy in education for children with specific learning difficulties who have experienced stress and/or trauma. In V. Karkou (Ed.), *Arts therapies in schools: Research and practice* (pp. 145–160). Philadelphia, PA: Jessica Kingsley.

Pennebaker, J. W. (1997). Writing about emotional experiences as a therapeutic process. *Psychological Science*, 8, 162–166.

Pennebaker, J. W. and Beall, S. K. (1986). Confronting a traumatic event: Toward an understanding of inhibition and disease. *Journal of Abnormal Psychology*, 95, 274–281.

Pennebaker, J. W. and Seagal, J. D. (1999). Forming a story: The health benefits of narrative. *Journal of Clinical Psychology*, 55, 1243–1254.

Philips, D., Linington, L. and Penman, D. (1999). *Writing well: Creative writing and mental health*. Philadelphia, PA: Jessica Kingsley.

Pizarro, J. (2004). The efficacy of art and writing therapies: Increasing positive mental health outcomes and participant retention after exposure to traumatic experience. *Art Therapy: Journal of the American Art Therapy Association*, 21, 5–12.

Richardson, P., Jones, K., Evans, C., Stevens, P. and Rowe, A. (2007). Exploratory RCT of art therapy as an adjunctive treatment in schizophrenia. *Journal of Mental Health*, 16, 483–491.

Routledge, C., Arndt, J., Vess, M. and Sheldon, K. M. (2008). The life and death of creativity: The effects of mortality salience on self versus social-directed creative expression. *Motivation and Emotion*, 32, 331–338.

Rowlands, E. (2004). *Redefining resistance: The poetic wartime discourses of Francis Ponge, Benjamin Péret, Henri Michaux, and Antonin Artaud*. New York: Rodopi BV.

Ruddy, R. and Milnes, D. (2005). Art therapy for schizophrenia or schizophrenia-like illnesses (review). *Cochrane Database of Systematic Reviews*, 4, CD003728.

Runco, M. A. (2009). Writing as an interaction with ideas. In S. B. Kaufman and J. C. Kaufman (Eds.), *The psychology of creative writing* (pp. 180–195). New York: Cambridge University Press.

Safran, D. S. (2003). An art therapy approach to attention-deficit/hyperactivity disorder. In C. A. Malchiodi (Ed.), *Handbook of art therapy* (pp. 181–192). New York: Guilford Press.

Salovey, P., Rothman, A. J., Detweiler, J. B. and Steward, W. T. (2000). Emotional states and physical health. *American Psychologist*, 55, 110–121.

Sandblom, P. (1997). *Creativity and disease: How illness affects literature, art and music*. New York: Marion Boyars.

Sarid, O. and Huss, E. (2010). Trauma and acute stress disorder: A comparison between cognitive behavioral intervention and art therapy. *The Arts in Psychotherapy*, 37, 8–12.

Seery, M. D. (2011). Resilience: A silver lining to experiencing adverse life events. *Current Directions in Psychological Science*, 20, 390–394.

Sexton, J. D. and Pennebaker, J. W. (2009). The healing powers of expressive writing. In S. B. Kaufman and J. C. Kaufman (Eds.), *The psychology of creative writing* (pp. 264–273). New York: Cambridge University Press.

Simonton, D. K. (1994). *Greatness: Who makes history and why*. New York: Guilford Press.

Simonton, D. K. (2000). The positive repercussions of traumatic events and experiences: The life lessons of historic geniuses. In P. A. Linley (Ed.), *Psychological trauma and its positive adaptations* (pp. 21–23). Leicester: British Psychological Society.

Slayton, S. C., D'Archer, J. and Kaplan, F. (2010). Outcome studies on the efficacy of art therapy: A review of findings. *Art Therapy: Journal of the American Art Therapy Association*, 27, 108–119.

Sloan, D. M. and Marx, B. P. (2004). Taking pen to hand: Evaluating theories underlying the written disclosure paradigm. *Clinical Psychology: Science and Practice*, 11, 121–137.

Smyth, J. M. (1998). Written emotional expression: Effect sizes, outcome types, and moderating variables. *Journal of Consulting and Clinical Psychology*, 66, 174–184.

Sternberg, R. J. and Lubart, T. I. (1999). The concept of creativity: Prospects and paradigms. In R. J. Sternberg (Ed.), *Handbook of creativity* (pp. 3–15). Cambridge, UK: Cambridge University Press.

Stuckey, H. L. and Nobel, J. (2010). The connection between art, healing, and public health: A review of current literature. *American Journal of Public Health*, 100, 254–263.

Taylor, S. E. (1983). Adjustment to threatening events: A theory of cognitive adaptation. *American Psychologist*, 38, 1161–1173.

Tedeschi, R. G. and Calhoun, L. G. (1996). The Posttraumatic Growth Inventory: Measuring the positive legacy of trauma. *Journal of Traumatic Stress*, 9, 455–471.

Tedeschi, R. G. and Calhoun, L. G. (2004). Posttraumatic growth: Conceptual foundations and empirical evidence. *Psychological Inquiry*, 15, 1–18.

Tedeschi, R. G., Calhoun, L. G. and Cann, A. (2007). Evaluating resource gain: Understanding and misunderstanding posttraumatic growth. *Applied Psychology: An International Review*, 56, 396–406.

Tedeschi, R. G., Park, C. L. and Calhoun, L. G. (1998). *Posttraumatic growth: Positive changes in the aftermath of crisis*. Mahwah, NJ: Erlbaum.

Thyme, K. E., Sundin, E. C., Stahlberg, G., Lindstrom, B., Eklof, H. and Wiberg, B. (2007). The outcome of short-term psychodynamic art therapy compared to short-term psychodynamic verbal therapy for depressed women. *Psychoanalytic Psychotherapy*, 21, 250–264.

Tugade, M. M. and Fredrickson, B. L. (2007). Regulation of positive emotions: Emotion regulation strategies that promote resilience. *Journal of Happiness Studies*, 8, 311–333.

Van Gogh, V. (1889). *Letter to Theo*. http://vangoghletters.org/vg/letters/let798/letter.html, last accessed March 17, 2014.

Verhaeghen, P., Joorman, J. and Khan, R. (2005). Why we sing the blues: The relation between self-reflective rumination, mood, and creativity. *Emotion*, 5, 226–232.

Vick, R. M. (2003). A brief history of art therapy. In C. A. Malchiodi (Ed.), *Handbook of art therapy* (pp. 5–15). New York: Guilford Press.

Williams, T. (1944). *The glass menagerie*. New York: Random House.

Wilson, M. (2003). Art therapy in addictions treatment: Creativity and shame reduction. In C. A. Malchiodi (Ed.), *Handbook of art therapy* (pp. 281–293). New York: Guilford Press.

Winner, E. (1982). *Invented worlds: The psychology of the arts*. Cambridge, MA: Harvard University Press.

Woolf, V. (1927). *To the lighthouse*. London: Hogarth.

Woolf, V. (1934/2003). Friday, July 27th 1934. In L. Woolf (Ed.), *A writer's diary* (p. 213). Orlando, FL: Harcourt.

Woolf, V. (1985). *Moments of being: A collection of autobiographical writing* (2nd edn.; J. Schulkind, Ed.). Orlando, FL: Harcourt.

Zausner, T. (1998). When walls become doorways: Creativity, chaos theory, and physical illness. *Creativity Research Journal*, 11, 21–28.

Zausner, T. (2007). *When walls become doorways: Creativity and the transforming illness*. New York: Crown Archetype.

16 Inspiration and the creative process[1]

Todd M. Thrash, Emil G. Moldovan, Amanda K. Fuller, and John T. Dombrowski

During his self-narrated journey through Purgatory in Part II of *Divine comedy*, Dante encounters a fellow poet, Donati Ferese, who ingratiates Dante with the following greeting: "[T]ell me if I see here the one who drew forth the new rhymes, beginning, 'Ladies who have intellect of Love'?" Dante replies, "I in myself am one who, when Love breathes within me, takes note, and to that measure which he dictates within, I go signifying." Ferese continues, "O my brother, now I see the knot that held Notary and Guittone and me back on this side of the sweet new style I hear. I see well how your pens follow close behind him who dictates, which with ours certainly did not happen" (Alighieri, 2003, Canto 24, p. 403).

It would be difficult to find in the literary canon a pithier portrayal of the role of inspiration in the creative process. Dante's description of inspiration conveys its hallmark features – passive evocation ("when Love breathes within me"), transcendent awakening ("I . . . take note"), and motivation to express the content of the new awareness in concrete form ("I go signifying"). This passage also puts forth a provocative thesis: without inspiration, the writer produces a work of inferior quality. Although not universal, the belief that inspiration plays an important role in the creative process is widely held among writers and other creators (Fehrman, 1980; Harding, 1948). However, scientists traditionally have not invoked the inspiration concept in their theories or investigations of the creative process. In fact, some scientists (e.g., Sawyer, 2006) have portrayed inspiration as an outmoded explanation of creativity, a supernatural account that originated in ancient times and that has been perpetuated by Romantic poets and other creators.

Our aim in this chapter is to separate what is mythical about inspiration from what is real. Muses are not real; nevertheless, something real and important is happening when Dante personifies the source of his

[1] The writing of this chapter was supported by Grant #SBE-0830366 from the National Science Foundation, Science of Science and Innovation Policy.

inspiration as Love that breathes into him. To dismiss inspiration as a myth on the grounds that poets personify its cause is to confuse the poet's craft with the scientist's. In the following, we carry out our scientific craft by offering a scientifically tractable conceptualization of inspiration and reviewing the empirical literature on inspiration and creativity.

Conceptualization of the inspiration construct

The term "inspiration" has been used in numerous ways within the scientific literature on creativity. Among these many usages are the following: (1) an external stimulus (e.g., a sunset) that evokes a creative state (Weisberg, 1993); (2) the process – called *illumination* hereafter – through which an idea emerges into awareness or the associated subjective experience (Martindale, 1989; Simonton, 1995; Weisberg, 1993); (3) the content of the idea that emerges during illumination (Abra, 1988); (4) a diffuse mode of thought posited to facilitate illumination (Kris, 1952; Martindale and Hasenfus, 1978); (5) a motivational state that leads to creative activity (Piirto, 2005); and (6) creativity *per se* (Chamorro-Premuzic, 2006; Schuler, 1994). Further complicating matters, researchers tend to use the term "inspiration" informally without defining it, and often it is unclear which meaning is intended. In the absence of a firm foundation for the inspiration construct within the creativity literature, our strategy has been to apply a domain-general conceptualization of inspiration (Thrash and Elliot, 2003, 2004), which is grounded in scholarship from diverse disciplines and content areas (e.g., Abrams, 1953; Bradley, 1929; Harding, 1948; Kris, 1952), to the specific case of inspiration to create. In the following, we review our general conceptualization, and we then discuss how to apply this general conceptualization to the context of creative activity.

The first step in defining a construct is to identify the central noun of the definition – what sort of thing is it? The inspiration construct does not fall into traditional construct categories, such as emotion, motive, or attitude. Accordingly, we begin with a few generic but serviceable nouns. Most precisely, inspiration is an *episode* that unfolds across time. One may also conceptualize inspiration as a *state* that is elevated during episodes of inspiration and that varies in intensity across time and across individuals. Finally, because individuals differ in the frequency and intensity of inspiration episodes, one may conceptualize inspiration as a *trait*. The term "trait" has a variety of connotations, but we use the expression "trait inspiration" to refer to nothing more than individual differences in the frequency and intensity of inspiration. Whether inspiration is best viewed as an episode, state, or trait depends on the research context.

The next task in defining inspiration is to constrain its meaning, so that it may be distinguished from other episodes, states, and traits. To date, Thrash and colleagues have offered three complementary ways to conceptualize the inspiration construct – in terms of (a) its core characteristics (Thrash and Elliot, 2003), (b) the component processes that compose episodes of inspiration (Thrash and Elliot, 2004), and (c) the broader theoretical function of inspiration (Thrash, Maruskin *et al.*, 2010). In the following, we discuss each in turn.

Tripartite conceptualization

Thrash and Elliot (2003) proposed that three core characteristics are necessary and collectively sufficient to define inspiration in a way that distinguishes it from other constructs: transcendence, evocation, and approach motivation. *Transcendence* refers to gaining an awareness of better possibilities. *Evocation* refers to the passive manner by which inspiration occurs; one does not feel directly responsible for becoming inspired and ascribes responsibility to something beyond one's own will. Finally, inspiration involves *approach motivation*, in which one feels compelled to transmit, express, or actualize one's new idea or vision. Thrash and Elliot (2003) referred to this set of three core characteristics as the *tripartite conceptualization* of inspiration.

Component processes

Thrash and Elliot (2004) subsequently argued that an episode of inspiration may be broken down into two conceptually and functionally distinct component processes: being inspired *by* and being inspired *to*. Being inspired *by* refers to being moved by the perceived intrinsic value of an eliciting object (e.g., a role model, a creative idea, or a spiritual revelation). Being inspired *to* refers to the motivation to transmit or extend the inspiring qualities exemplified in the evocative object. These processes are posited to give rise to the core characteristics of inspiration, such that being inspired *by* involves transcendence and evocation, whereas being inspired *to* involves approach motivation.

The incremental value of the component process conceptualization above and beyond the tripartite definition is two-fold. On the one hand, it clarifies the fact that transcendence and evocation are intertwined as two aspects of the same process. As Thrash and Elliot (2004) put it, one cannot actively awaken oneself to better possibilities through an act of will any more than one can awaken oneself from sleep; transcendence requires evocation. On the other hand, the component process model emphasizes that the process responsible for transcendence and evocation is separable from the motivational process to which it gives rise. Indeed, the process of being inspired *by* is most potent when one's appreciation of the evocative object is most disinterested. Nevertheless, disinterested *appreciation* of the evocative object (i.e., being inspired *by*) often sparks a non-disinterested *motivation* to transmit the inspiring qualities exemplified in the evocative object (i.e., being inspired *to*), and if such a desire is sparked then a full episode of inspiration is present.

Transmission model

Thrash and colleagues' third conceptualization of inspiration specifies its function and embeds it in the context of antecedents and consequences. Specifically, inspiration is posited to motivate transmission of the perceived intrinsic value exemplified in the evocative object (Thrash, Maruskin *et al.*, 2010). From a statistical modeling standpoint, transmission implies a mediational process; intrinsically valued qualities of an elicitor object evoke inspiration, which, in turn, compels the individual to extend the intrinsically valued properties to a new object. The transmission process may take a variety of forms – for instance, one may emulate a role model's virtue, record the content of a spiritual revelation, or actualize a creative idea (Shiota *et al.*, 2014; Thrash, Maruskin *et al.*, 2010).

Thrash, Maruskin *et al.* (2010) identified this third case – actualization of a creative idea – as the prototypical form of inspiration within the context of creative activity. In this case, inspiration is stimulated by a creative idea or insight and compels the individual to bring the idea to fruition. Because this conceptualization was derived from the general conceptualization, it is consistent with usage of the inspiration construct in other literatures and disciplines. For instance, although it may seem counterintuitive to conceptualize inspiration as a response to creative insight rather than as its cause, this perspective is consistent with usage of the inspiration construct in theology – theologians regard inspiration not as a source of spiritual revelation, but rather as a response to revelation (Geisler and Nix, 1986). Moreover, because inspiration is conceptualized as a response to creative ideas and not as their source, critiques of inspiration as a mysterious or magical source of creativity (e.g., Sawyer, 2006) – although applicable to the muse myth – do not apply to the scientific construct of inspiration. Inspiration is posited to explain the actualization, not the origin, of creative ideas.

We, like Thrash, Maruskin *et al.* (2010), embrace actualization of creative ideas as the prototypical form of inspiration within the context of creative activity. Nevertheless, we note that actualization of ideas is not the only form of inspired transmission that occurs during creative activity, and actualization may occur outside the context of creative activity *per se*. In the following section, we explore more fully the ways in which the general inspiration construct may be differentiated and contextualized within and beyond the creative process.

Differentiation of the inspiration construct

A number of theorists have grappled with the problem of how to differentiate the general inspiration construct into specific types (e.g., Bradley, 1929; Hart, 1998; Hymer, 1990; Kris, 1952; Schwöbel, 1987; Thrash and Elliot, 2003). Most often, types of inspiration are distinguished in terms of broad content domains, such as creative, interpersonal/self, and religious inspiration. Although useful from a descriptive standpoint, content domains tend not to be precisely defined or mutually exclusive and therefore may not provide the most theoretically useful means of carving nature at its joints. Building on Thrash, Maruskin *et al.* (2010), we propose that three forms of transmission – replication, actualization, and expression – are applicable across content domains and provide a useful basis of construct differentiation. In the following, we describe each and offer examples from the domains of creative activity, interpersonal/self, and religion. In order to keep these domains distinct for illustrative purposes, we hereafter use the phrase "creativity domain" to refer narrowly to activities in which creativity tends to be a central and salient goal (e.g., artistic creation, invention, and scientific innovation).

In the case of *replication*, one is inspired by the qualities of a preexisting object (e.g., person, thing, concept) in the external environment, and one seeks to reproduce these qualities in a new object. Examples within the creativity, interpersonal/self, and religion domains are shown in the first row of Table 16.1. Within the creativity domain, if a novelist or screenwriter is moved by his or her father's poignant life story, this story could serve as the basis of a novel or screenplay. Within the interpersonal/self domain, one might seek to model a future self, as opposed to a protagonist, after one's father. Within the religion domain, one may seek to model oneself after a religious figure such as Christ. *Emulation*, in which one seeks to transmit characteristics specifically from a person to a future self, as in these latter two examples, may be viewed as a specific variety of replication.

Whereas replication is a response to the qualities of an existing object in the environment, *actualization* is a response to the qualities of a seminal idea, which often arises from the unconscious and enters awareness

Table 16.1 *Examples of three forms of transmission within three content domains*

Form of transmission	Type of evocative object	Content domain		
		Creativity	Interpersonal/ Self	Religion
Replication	Exemplar in environment	Modeling a protagonist after one's father	Modeling oneself after one's father	Modeling oneself after Christ
Actualization	Seminal idea/insight	Bringing an idea for an invention into fruition	Bringing an idea for a career path into fruition	Bringing one's calling into fruition
Expression	Well-formed, modality-fitting mental prototype	Recording insights as poetry	Recording insights as diary entries	Recording revelation as scripture

during a moment of illumination or insight. This seminal idea is compelling, and the individual is energized by the prospect of bringing the idea into fruition. Examples are shown in the second row of Table 16.1. Within the creativity domain, an individual may get an idea for a new invention or poem and become motivated to bring the invention or poem to life. Within the interpersonal/self domain, the individual may gain insight about a career path and feel compelled to pursue this new vision. Within the religion domain, the individual may have an epiphany regarding his or her purpose in life and feel moved to fulfill this calling.

The third form of transmission, *expression*, resembles actualization in that it is prompted by a compelling idea that arises through unconscious processes. However, in this case, transmission requires little more than expression or articulation, because the idea is already well formed when it enters awareness and exists in an immediately actionable sensory or kinesthetic modality. Examples are shown in the third row of Table 16.1. Within the creativity domain, a master poet may record verse that comes to mind spontaneously, as if merely transcribing content that has been delivered by a muse; the passage from *Divine comedy* at the beginning of this chapter provides an illustration. Within the interpersonal/self domain, one may feel moved to capture one's insights about life in a diary or journal. In the religion domain, a prophet may record a revelation or the word of God in the form of scripture or sacred writings. These three examples all involve writing, and in such cases the more specific term *transcription* could also be used (in a figurative sense). We have suggested the more general term "expression," which encompasses not only transcription but also the inspired communications of, say, an orator or dancer.

One benefit of differentiating the inspiration construct in terms of forms of transmission is that this approach accounts for patterns of homogeneity across content domain. For instance, consider examples of inspired expression within the domains of creative activity and religion – the act of expressing a creative insight as poetry resembles the act of expressing revelation as scripture (Heschel, 2001). Differences in content and origin aside, these instances of inspiration are likely to involve similar cognitive, emotional, motivational, and physiological processes. (Acknowledgment of such similarities does not require a position on divine underpinning of spiritual texts. As others have argued [e.g., James, 1902; Laski, 1961], if such divine underpinning exists, it likely operates through standard psychological processes.) A second benefit is that the forms of transmission help account for heterogeneity within a given content domain. For example, consider the difference between inspired replication and inspired expression within the domain of creative activity. In the case of replication, the processes of being inspired *by* and being inspired *to* may be only loosely coupled; being moved by one's father's life history could occur decades before his story serves as the raw material for a screenplay. Indeed, if one is not a screenwriter, this *to* process would likely never occur. With inspired expression, in contrast, the *by* and *to* processes are so tightly integrated that there may be little gap between them. Indeed, in the most extreme case, these component processes may fuse into a single integrated process, such that inspiration is experienced as "channeling" one's muse or serving as its mouthpiece.

From the perspective of the 3×3 matrix of inspiration experiences in Table 16.1, most empirical research on the relation between inspiration and creativity has focused either on the general inspiration construct (in which content domains and forms of transmission are not distinguished), or more specifically on inspiration experiences that involve actualization of ideas within the domain of creative activity. We now turn to the empirical literatures on these general and specific inspiration constructs. We first discuss construct validation studies, followed by studies of the relation between inspiration and creativity.

Validation of the inspiration construct

Most construct validation research has focused on general trait inspiration, general state inspiration, or state inspiration within the context of idea actualization (specifically, as part of the writing process). We review these literatures in the following subsections.

General trait inspiration

Thrash and Elliot (2003) developed an eight-item questionnaire, the Inspiration Scale, that assesses general trait inspiration – that is, individual differences in the frequency and intensity of inspiration, regardless of content domain or form of transmission. This measure consists of four stem statements (e.g., "I feel inspired"), each of which is rated in terms of both frequency and intensity using seven-point Likert scales. The frequency and intensity subscales tend to be highly correlated and may be combined into an overall index of inspiration.

The Inspiration Scale has been found to have excellent psychometric properties (Thrash and Elliot, 2003). The measure consistently shows the expected two-factor (frequency, intensity) structure. The Inspiration Scale converges with an alternative measure of inspiration (the content of which is based on the *Oxford English Dictionary*'s definition of "inspiration"), and the inspiration construct is factorially distinct from activated positive affect, the strongest-known correlate of inspiration to date. The frequency and intensity subscales, as well as the overall inspiration index, are internally consistent, with Cronbach's αs equal to or greater than .90. Scores on the frequency and intensity subscales predict inspiration frequency and intensity, respectively, as assessed using daily diary methods. Two-month test–retest reliabilities are high, r = .77, for both subscales. On the basis of stringent means-and-covariance-structures analysis, the Inspiration Scale has been found to have invariant measurement properties (e.g., factor structure, loadings, and intercepts) across time (2 months), as well as across populations (patent holders, university alumni). Thus, the Inspiration Scale assesses comparable constructs on different occasions and in groups of participants with very different backgrounds.

The Inspiration Scale is flexible and adaptable because of its brevity and modular design. Particular items may be used to measure the component processes of being inspired *by* and being inspired *to* (Thrash and Elliot, 2004); the instructions may be adapted for assessment of inspiration over specified time periods, such as the prior week (Thrash, Maruskin *et al.*, 2010) or half-day (Thrash, Elliot *et al.*, 2010); and they may be altered in order to assess inspiration in particular domains, such as stages of the creative process (Thrash, Maruskin *et al.*, 2010).

Trait inspiration, as assessed by the Inspiration Scale, has been found to converge meaningfully with a variety of individual difference variables. Regarding the Big Five traits, Thrash and Elliot (2003) theorized that trait inspiration would converge with Openness to Experience and Extraversion. Openness to Experience was posited to promote the process of being inspired *by*, whereas Extraversion, an indicator of approach temperament (Elliot and Thrash, 2002), was posited to promote the process of being inspired *to*. Because approach and avoidance processes tend to be largely independent, inspiration was expected to be unrelated to Neuroticism, an indicator of avoidance temperament (Elliot and Thrash, 2002). As expected, Openness to Experience and Extraversion have consistently emerged as significant and robust predictors of trait inspiration (Milyavskaya *et al.*, 2012; Thrash and Elliot, 2003; Thrash, Elliot *et al.*, 2010), whereas Neuroticism has consistently failed to predict inspiration. Conscientiousness and Agreeableness have shown weak and sporadic relations to inspiration.

Other correlates, aside from the Big Five traits, paint a broader portrait of the inspired individual. Those higher in trait inspiration are also higher in intrinsic motivation, behavioral activation system (BAS) strength, absorption, work-mastery motivation, activated positive affect, optimism, perceived competence, self-esteem, and self-determination (Thrash and Elliot, 2003). Students higher in trait inspiration are more likely than those lower in trait inspiration to pursue majors in the humanities, and they pursue more majors simultaneously (Thrash and Elliot, 2003).

General state inspiration

Whereas Thrash and Elliot (2003) validated the general inspiration construct at the trait level, Thrash and Elliot (2004) validated the inspiration construct at the state level by contrasting the state of inspiration with other states. In one study, participants were asked to write about an occasion when they were inspired. Participants were also asked to write about a representative experience from their lives, thus providing a baseline for comparison. Supporting the tripartite conceptualization, inspiration experiences were found to involve elevated levels of variables representing transcendence (e.g., spirituality), evocation (e.g., passive self), and approach motivation (e.g., activated positive affect). In subsequent studies, Thrash and Elliot (2004) contrasted inspiration with another appetitive state: activated positive affect. As expected, inspiration involved a comparable level of approach motivation but higher levels of transcendence and evocation. Thrash (2007) provided additional evidence of the discriminant validity of inspiration and activated positive affect by documenting different distributions of these states across days of the week. Whereas activated positive affect was relatively stable across days of the week, inspiration declined on weekends. This divergence was most pronounced on Fridays; the TGIF attitude appears to be more conducive to fun and leisure than to embodying virtue or channeling one's muse.

Thrash and Elliot (2004) also provided evidence in support of the component process conceptualization. On the basis of a confirmatory factor analysis of inspiration intensity items, being inspired *by* and being inspired *to* were found to converge as indicators of a general inspiration construct, but they were also found to have discriminant relations to indicators of evocation, transcendence, and motivation. Being inspired *by* was uniquely positively related to evocation and transcendence, whereas being inspired *to* was uniquely negatively related to evocation and transcendence and uniquely positively related to approach motivation.

Studies of the trait antecedents of state inspiration also provide support for the *by–to* distinction. Thrash and Elliot (2004) proposed that the antecedents of inspiration are different from those of other appetitive states (e.g., activated positive affect), because inspiration, unlike other motivations, begins the epistemic process of being inspired *by*. As predicted, Thrash and Elliot (2004) found that the tendency to become inspired in daily life was predicted proximally by the experience of illumination (and not by reward salience) and distally by openness-related traits (and not by approach temperament). The tendency to experience activated positive affect in daily life showed the opposite pattern; it was predicted proximally by reward salience and distally by approach temperament. Although approach temperament did not predispose individuals to become inspired, it predicted inspiration intensity and motivation strength during episodes of inspiration. In sum, consistent with the *by–to* distinction, openness-related traits predispose individuals to the illumination experiences that precede inspiration; once the individual is inspired *by*, the approach temperament system is recruited to support motivation and action.

State inspiration within the writing process

Thrash, Maruskin *et al.* (2010) sought to apply the tripartite conceptualization to the specific case of inspiration during the writing process. The study designs were optimized for the study of the idea actualization process. In one study, inspiration was assessed with items specific to evocation (e.g., "These ideas came to me unexpectedly or spontaneously"), transcendence (e.g., "I saw some deep truths as I wrote this"), or approach motivation (e.g., "I was highly motivated to capture these ideas on paper"). In addition, non-specific face-valid items that included the forms of the word "inspired" were also administered (e.g., "I felt inspired while writing this"), as were effort items (e.g., "I worked hard in writing this"). A principal components analysis indicated that evocation, transcendence, approach motivation, and face-valid inspiration items all loaded on the same component, thus providing evidence of convergent validity. Equally important, effort items loaded on a separate component, thus providing evidence of discriminant validity. These findings support the tripartite conceptualization within the context of the creative process.

Research on the relation between inspiration and creativity

Before turning to the empirical literature on the relation between inspiration and creativity, we comment briefly on why an association between inspiration and creativity would be expected. Regarding the specific case of idea actualization in the context of creative activity (e.g., the writing process), the rationale is straightforward: a creative idea or insight is expected to inspire, because it satisfies the criteria of transcendence (i.e., the idea is novel), evocation (i.e., the idea arises from the unconscious), and approach motivation (i.e., actualization of the idea provides a course of action). If creative ideas inspire and if inspiration motivates actualization of those ideas, then inspiration should predict the creativity of the resulting product.

However, it is likely that creativity is predicted by inspiration more generally – that is, for forms of transmission other than actualization and in content domains other than creative activity. Idea actualization is fundamentally the same process, whether it occurs in the so-called creativity domain or in some other context; one may write creatively, but one may also live creatively and embody one's religion creatively. Moreover, all forms of transmission, rather than idea actualization distinctively, are fundamentally constructive processes in which new entities (e.g., creative products, future selves, or a spiritual life) are created as a result of stimulation from the environment or unconscious processes. We therefore expect inspiration to predict indicators of creativity, regardless of whether inspiration is operationalized using general or specific measures. We restrict our literature review to quantitative studies in which both inspiration and creativity were assessed. For a review of other studies and indirect evidence, see Thrash, Maruskin *et al.* (2010).

General trait and state inspiration

Findings from a number of studies confirm a relation between general trait or state inspiration and creativity. In two studies, Thrash and Elliot (2003) found that trait inspiration was positively related to creative self-concept; that is, individuals higher in trait inspiration tend to regard themselves as more creative. In a daily diary study, inspiration and creativity covaried positively not only between persons, but also within persons across days; that is, a typical individual feels more creative on days when he or she is more inspired. In this same study, trait inspiration predicted mean levels of creativity in daily life, even when creative self-concept was controlled, suggesting that inspiration influences subsequent creativity. A limitation of these studies is that creativity was assessed by self-report, which is subject to self-presentation biases.

Thrash and Elliot (2003) addressed this limitation in a different study by examining an objective indicator of creative output: receipt of US patents. Among a sample of inventors who had received at least one patent, trait inspiration frequency was found to be positively related to the number of patents held. In addition, the inventors, as a group, experienced inspiration more frequently and intensely than individuals from a matched comparison sample. In sum, the general inspiration construct has been found to predict both subjective and objective indicators of creativity.

State inspiration within the writing process

In three studies of undergraduate writers by Thrash, Maruskin *et al.* (2010), inspiration during the writing process was found to predict expert ratings of the creativity of the completed written products. These findings held regardless of the type of writing (scientific writing, poetry, fiction), research context (naturalistic, laboratory), and level of analysis (e.g., across persons, across written pages). Moreover, the findings were robust when a variety of covariates was controlled, including aptitude (e.g., SAT verbal scores), traits (e.g., openness), states (e.g., positive affect), writing behaviors (e.g., deletion), and other aspects of writing quality (e.g., technical merit).

Thrash, Maruskin *et al.* (2010) also conducted the first direct tests of the hypothesis that inspiration mediates transmission (actualization) of creative ideas. In a cross-lagged analysis of data from a 4-week panel study, Thrash, Maruskin *et al.* (2010) found that creative ideation in a given week predicts inspiration during the following week, whereas inspiration does not predict subsequent creative ideation. In the context of the writing process, inspiration was found to mediate the relation between the creativity of the seminal idea and the creativity of the completed product. Covariates of inspiration (effort, awe, activated positive affect) did not mediate transmission of creativity, suggesting that the transmission function is unique to inspiration. Regarding individual differences, and building on the trait findings of Thrash and Elliot (2004) discussed earlier, the trait of Openness (specifically, openness to aesthetics) predicted the creativity of individuals' seminal ideas; in contrast, approach temperament (specifically, BAS strength) moderated the effect of idea creativity on inspiration, such that idea creativity was a strong predictor of inspiration among individuals high in approach temperament and a weak predictor among individuals low in approach temperament. These findings support the transmission model and show how different parts of the idea actualization process are facilitated by different personality traits.

Further situating the inspiration construct

In this final section, we broaden our focus in an effort to explicate more fully the place of the inspiration construct within the creativity literature, as well as the place of the inspiration experience within the life of the creator. We focus on four questions that have frequently been posed in the literature but that have generally not been answered clearly.

How does inspiration differ from insight?

Insight is generally conceptualized as a cognitive event – the "aha!" or eureka moment when a novel solution enters awareness (Sternberg and Davidson, 1995). From the perspective of the tripartite conceptualization of inspiration, insight shares with inspiration the qualities of transcendence and evocation, but it lacks a motivational component. Nevertheless, insight may give rise to inspiration, in which case the content of the insight becomes the object of the inspired *by* component process; the idea grips the individual, who then seeks to actualize the idea as part of the inspired *to* component process.

If insight and inspiration always co-occurred, one might question the need for both constructs on the grounds of parsimony. However, both insight and inspiration may occur without the other. Consider, first, the case of insight without inspiration. Insights that do not involve actionable ideas are unlikely to give rise to inspiration. Moreover, as noted earlier, Thrash, Maruskin *et al.* (2010) found that creative ideas are inspiring for some individuals (those with a strong approach temperament) but not others (those with a weak approach temperament). We wonder how many individuals have had creative insights regarding solutions to societal problems but have not become sufficiently motivated to communicate or implement their ideas, whether due to personality or other factors. From this perspective, it is difficult to overstate the importance of investigating inspiration and the idea actualization process. Unfortunately, however, most creativity researchers operationalize creativity using tests of creative insight (e.g., Remote Associates Test, or "alternative uses for a common object"). Although well suited for the study of creative cognition, these tests do not allow participants to carry out ideas. Reliance on such tests precludes the investigation – and perhaps serious consideration – of inspiration and idea actualization.

Consider, next, the case of inspiration without insight. We suspect that discrete eureka moments are common in instances of inspired actualization and expression. However, they may be less common in instances of replication, because external sources of inspiration (e.g., one's father) are not necessarily encountered or appreciated abruptly.

Is inspiration a stage of the creative process?

The term "inspiration" is sometimes used to refer to a particular stage of the creative process (e.g., Kris, 1952). Most often, the term "inspiration" is used as a synonym for the illumination or insight stage identified by Wallas (1926), which is preceded by preparation and incubation stages and followed by a verification stage.

We do not identify inspiration with the illumination stage of Wallas' model for the same reasons that we do not equate inspiration with insight. More generally, we do not conceptualize inspiration as a stage. Stages tend to be defined in terms of characteristic behaviors (e.g., preparation) or events (e.g., illumination), whereas motivation constructs such as inspiration are conceptually orthogonal to particular behaviors and events (Thrash and Hurst, 2008); a given behavior may be undergirded by a variety of possible motivations, and a given motivation may give rise to any of a variety of possible behaviors (see also Elliot and Church, 1997; Frenkel-Brunswik, 1942; McClelland, 1951). Although, on average, inspiration may tend to be higher in some stages (e.g., illumination) than others (e.g., preparation), any stage that involves behavior could involve high or low levels of inspiration for particular individuals or on particular occasions.

One reason that inspiration could occur at a variety of stages is that a preliminary version of the core idea for a project could inspire preparatory behavior, a more refined version of the idea could inspire creative production, and a highly refined version of the idea could inspire revision. Moreover, different forms of transmission could occur at different stages of the creative process. Consider, for instance, the following example, which involves all three forms of transmission: Hearing a song with an infectious bass line inspires a composer to undertake the act of song writing (i.e., replication). While experimenting with the bass line, the composer experiences a more acute feeling of inspiration in response to the insight that a variant of the bass line would provide an interesting complement to a song that is otherwise quite different in style (i.e., actualization). While the composer develops this idea, melodies begin to present themselves (i.e., expression). Even during subsequent revision, the composer may seek to remain true to one or more of the three muses: the spirit of the original bass line, the appealing juxtaposition of distinct styles, and the authenticity of the melodies that flowed out automatically during the peak of the composition process.

Is creativity 99 percent perspiration?

Some readers may object that inspiration does not just happen out of the blue; it is preceded by a lot of practice and hard work. Indeed, the importance of inspiration has often been challenged on the grounds that creative individuals tend to be extremely hard working (e.g., Fehrman, 1980; Martindale, 1989; Rothenberg, 1970). Creativity researchers frequently quote Edison's claim that genius is 1 percent inspiration and 99 percent perspiration (e.g., Abra, 1997; Martindale, 1989, 2001; Sawyer, 2006; Schuler, 1994; Simonton, 1994). Indeed, Martindale (1989) suggested that "the 1 percent versus 99 percent partitioning of the 'variance' in creativity is probably close to the mark" (p. 213), and Martindale (2001) and Sawyer (2006) suggested that Edison's claim has been undisputed among scientists. We suspect that some of the researchers who have made such claims used the term "inspiration" differently from the way we do. Regardless, discussion of the relation of effort to inspiration and creativity appears to be called for.

We note, first of all, that inspiration and effort (or, similarly, work-mastery motivation) are positively correlated at both between-person and within-person levels of analysis, and this holds true whether or not these processes are investigated within the specific context of creative activity (Thrash and Elliot, 2003; Thrash, Maruskin et al., 2010). Moreover, inspiration while writing is positively related to objective indicators of productivity and efficiency (Thrash, Maruskin et al., 2010); thus, individuals who are more inspired do more work in an objective sense. Because inspiration and effort-related variables are positively rather than negatively related, the argument that creative individuals are hard working supports rather than refutes the possible importance of inspiration to creativity (for details, see Thrash, Maruskin et al., 2010).

Second, although work-mastery motivation leads to an increase in (general) inspiration (Thrash and Elliot, 2003), it is also true that (general) inspiration leads to an increase in work-mastery motivation (Thrash and Elliot, 2003; see also Milyavskaya *et al.*, 2012). Both of these effects have been documented at two distinct levels of analysis. Because inspiration and perspiration appear to be reciprocally reinforcing motivations, we question the wisdom of singling out one of these as important and the other as unimportant.

Third, the available studies in which inspiration, effort, and creativity were all assessed (Thrash, Maruskin *et al.*, 2010) have indicated that inspiration predicts creativity and that effort does not. Across three writing studies, inspiration was consistently a positive predictor of creativity, whereas effort consistently failed to predict creativity. Objective effort-related variables also failed to predict creativity. These findings are difficult to reconcile with the claim that creativity is 1 percent inspiration and 99 percent perspiration.

Finally, whereas the inspiration–perspiration debate pits inspiration and effort against one another in a single predictive validity contest, it may be more constructive to explore the distinct contributions of each to the creative product and process. Indeed, findings from Thrash, Maruskin *et al.* (2010) indicate that inspiration and effort have very different nomological nets. Whereas inspiration predicted the creativity of scientific writing, poetry, and fiction, effort predicted the technical merit of scientific writing and use of rhyme in poetry. In the fiction-writing study, inspiration predicted the number of words typed, whereas effort predicted the number of words deleted. Inspiration predicted less time pausing, whereas effort predicted more time pausing (presumably for planning) and less time off task. In sum, inspiration and effort predict different aspects of the quality of the product (e.g., creativity and technical merit, respectively) and appear to play distinct roles in the creative process (e.g., automatic/generative processes, and controlled/regulatory processes, respectively).

Is inspiration related to well-being or psychopathology?

To date, there has been much discussion but little quantitative research on the relation between inspiration and clinical psychopathologies, such as depression or bipolar disorder. However, increasing evidence suggests that inspiration contributes in important ways to non-clinical indicators of subjective or psychological well-being. In fact, Straume and Vittersø (2012) argued that inspiration is itself an indicator of well-being; specifically, they argued that inspiration is an indicator of eudaimonic well-being, which is growth-oriented, as opposed to hedonic well-being, which involves pleasure or satisfaction. Although it is reasonable to use inspiration as an indicator of eudaimonic well-being, we focus here on the relation between inspiration and other variables that have more traditionally been conceptualized as well-being variables.

Thrash, Elliot et al. (2010) proposed that inspiration leads to improvements in both eudaimonic and hedonic well-being, as a result of two mediating processes: purpose in life and gratitude. These mediating processes correspond roughly to the inspired to and inspired by component processes, respectively. Inspiration was posited to promote purpose in life, because the transmission process involves the deeply meaningful process of channeling something beyond the self. Inspiration was also posited to promote gratitude, because inspiration experiences are attributed partially or wholly to the source of inspiration. In turn, purpose in life and gratitude were posited to promote eudaimonic and hedonic well-being, as has been established in past research.

A series of studies by Thrash, Elliot et al. (2010), which included an experiment, two cross-lagged panel studies, and a diary study, provided support for these predictions. Inspiration consistently predicted improvements in a variety of hedonic and eudaimonic well-being variables, including activated positive affect, life satisfaction, vitality, and self-actualization. In most studies, inspiration did not lead to improvements (decreases) in activated negative affect (NA). In the diary study, both purpose in life and gratitude were documented as simultaneous mediators of improvements in well-being across the course of a given day. Milyavskaya et al. (2012) recently reported that trait inspiration predicts greater progress toward personal goals, and they proposed that goal progress may serve as an additional mediator of the relation between inspiration and well-being.

Although these studies concerned general inspiration (trait, state, and personal goal inspiration), we suspect that similar findings would apply to inspiration within the context of creative activity. Indeed, mediating between the muse and the masses is the fulfillment of the creator's calling. As Williams (1997) stated, the function served by poets is to obey "the dictates of their internal Muse, to mediate on behalf of the rest of society and draw the culture forward towards more complex and thoughtful values" (p. 34).

When Dante and other poets speak of muses, they are not perpetuating myths about magical influences. Rather, they are employing the poetic device of personification to convey gratitude for the inspiring influences that imbue their work with purpose and significance. They are grateful for the opportunity to express something that is deeper, more authentic, and more timeless than the ideas they manufacture during their less inspired moments.

References

Abra, J. (1988). *Assaulting Parnassus: Theoretical views of creativity*. Lanham, NY: University Press of America.

Abra, J. (1997). *The motives for creative work: An inquiry with speculations about sports and religion*. Cresskill, NJ: Hampton Press.

Abrams, M. H. (1953). *The mirror and the lamp: Romantic theory and the critical tradition*. New York: Oxford University Press.

Alighieri, D. (2003). *The divine comedy of Dante Alighieri, Volume 2: Purgatorio* (R. M. During, Trans.). Cary, NC: Oxford University Press.

Bradley, A. C. (1929). *A miscellany*. London: Macmillan.

Chamorro-Premuzic, T. (2006). Creativity versus conscientiousness: Which is a better predictor of student performance? *Applied Cognitive Psychology*, 20, 521–531.

Elliot, A. J. and Church, M. A. (1997). A hierarchical model of approach and avoidance achievement motivation. *Journal of Personality and Social Psychology*, 72, 218–232.

Elliot, A. J. and Thrash, T. M. (2002). Approach-avoidance motivation in personality: Approach and avoidance temperaments and goals. *Journal of Personality and Social Psychology*, 82, 804–818.

Fehrman, C. (1980). *Poetic creation: Inspiration or craft*. Minneapolis, MN: University of Minnesota Press.

Frenkel-Brunswik, E. (1942). Motivation and behavior. *Genetic Psychology Monographs*, 26, 121–265.

Geisler, N. L. and Nix, W. E. (1986). *A general introduction to the Bible* (revised and expanded edition). Chicago, IL: Moody Press.

Harding, R. E. M. (1948). *An anatomy of inspiration*. Cambridge, UK: W. Heffer & Sons.

Hart, T. (1998). Inspiration: Exploring the experience and its meaning. *Journal of Humanistic Psychology*, 38, 7–35.

Heschel, A. J. (2001). *The prophets*. New York: HarperCollins.

Hymer, S. (1990). On inspiration. *Psychotherapy Patient*, 6, 17–38.

James, W. (1902). *The varieties of religious experience*. London: Longmans, Green and Co.

Kris, E. (1952). *Psychoanalytic explorations in art*. New York: Schocken Books.

Laski, M. (1961). *Ecstasy in secular and religious experiences*. Los Angeles, CA: Tarcher.

McClelland, D. C. (1951). *Personality*. New York: Sloane.

Martindale, C. (1989). Personality, situation, and creativity. In J. A. Glover, R. R. Ronning and C. R. Reynolds (Eds.), *Handbook of creativity* (pp. 211–228). New York: Plenum.

Martindale, C. (2001). Oscillations and analogies. *American Psychologist*, 56, 342–345.

Martindale, C. and Hasenfus, N. (1978). EEG differences as a function of creativity, stage of the creative process, and effort to be original. *Biological Psychology*, 6, 157–167.

Milyavskaya, M., Ianakieva, I., Foxen-Craft, E., Colantuoni, A. and Koestner, R. (2012). Inspired to get there: The effects of trait and goal inspiration on goal progress. *Personality and Individual Differences*, 52, 56–60.

Piirto, J. (2005). The creative process in poets. In J. C. Kaufman and J. Baer (Eds.), *Creativity across domains: Faces of the muse* (pp. 1–22). Mahwah, NJ: Lawrence Erlbaum Associates.

Rothenberg, A. (1970). Inspiration, insight and the creative process in poetry. *College English*, 32, 172–183.

Sawyer, R. K. (2006). *Explaining creativity: The science of human innovation*. New York: Oxford.

Schuler, H. (1994). Communication rather than inspiration and perspiration? On performance requirements in highly qualified occupations. In K. A. Heller and E. A. Hany (Eds.), *Competence and responsibility* (Vol. 2) (pp. 112–116). Ashland, OH: Hogrefe & Huber.

Schwöbel, C. (1987). Divine agency and providence. *Modern Theology*, 3, 225–244.

Shiota, M. N., Thrash, T. M., Danvers, A. F. and Dombrowski, J. T. (2014). Transcending the self: Awe, elevation, and inspiration. In M. M. Tugade, M. N. Shiota and L. D. Kirby (Eds.), *Handbook of positive emotions* (pp. 362–377). New York: Guilford Press.

Simonton, D. K. (1994). *Greatness: Who makes history and why*. New York: Guilford Press.

Simonton, D. K. (1995). Foresight in insight? A Darwinian answer. In R. J. Sternberg and J. E. Davidson (Eds.), *The nature of insight* (pp. 465–494). Cambridge, MA: MIT Press.

Sternberg, R. J. and Davidson, J. E. (Eds.) (1995). *The nature of insight*. Cambridge, MA: MIT Press.

Straume, L. V. and Vittersø, J. (2012). Happiness, inspiration and the fully functioning person: Separating hedonic and eudaimonic well-being in the workplace. *The Journal of Positive Psychology*, 7, 387–398.

Thrash, T. M. (2007). Differentiation of the distributions of inspiration and positive affect across days of the week: An application of logistic multi-level modeling. In A. D. Ong and M. Van Dulmen (Eds.), *Oxford handbook of methods in positive psychology* (pp. 515–529). Oxford University Press.

Thrash, T. M. and Elliot, A. J. (2003). Inspiration as a psychological construct. *Journal of Personality and Social Psychology*, 84, 871–889.

Thrash, T. M. and Elliot, A. J. (2004). Inspiration: Core characteristics, component processes, antecedents, and function. *Journal of Personality and Social Psychology*, 87, 957–973.

Thrash, T. M. and Hurst, A. L. (2008). Approach and avoidance motivation in the achievement domain: Integrating achievement motive and achievement goal traditions. In A. J. Elliot (Ed.), *Handbook of approach and avoidance motivation* (pp. 215–231). New York: LEA.

Thrash, T. M., Elliot, A. J., Maruskin, L. A. and Cassidy, S. E. (2010). Inspiration and the promotion of well-being: Tests of causality and mediation. *Journal of Personality and Social Psychology*, 98, 488–506.

Thrash, T. M., Maruskin, L. A., Cassidy, S. E., Fryer, J. W. and Ryan, R. M. (2010). Mediating between the muse and the masses: Inspiration and the actualization of creative ideas. *Journal of Personality and Social Psychology,* 98, 469–487.

Wallas, G. (1926). *The art of thought.* New York: Harcourt Brace.

Weisberg, R. W. (1993). *Creativity: Beyond the myth of genius.* New York: Freeman.

Williams, M. H. (1997). Inspiration: A psychoanalytic and aesthetic concept. *British Journal of Psychotherapy,* 14, 33–43.

17 King Solomon and psychoneuroimmunology: creativity and life coping

Michael J. Lowis

What is psychoneuroimmunology?

King Solomon reigned from about 971 to 932 before the Christian era, and he is credited with writing most if not all of the biblical Old Testament book *Proverbs*. In Chapter 17, verse 22, we read "a cheerful heart is good medicine, but a crushed spirit dries up the bones" (*New International Version*). One can imagine the wise king keenly observing what was going on around him, and noting that those people who seemed to be happy and cheerful also appeared to be physically well. Conversely, those who invariably looked unhappy and miserable often also seemed to be ill. A brilliant observation, and the sort of deduction that today spawns scientific research in order to confirm the hypothesis and, if successful, to investigate the variables that may be responsible. Solomon did, however, make one assumption that, if untested, would make today's researchers frown, that being the implied causality: "... a crushed spirit *dries up* the bones." In reality, does being miserable lead to ill health, or does ill health lead a person to be miserable? Conversely, is there another factor that leads people to be both miserable and unhealthy? To confirm directionality, a controlled experiment is usually required, but then it would be a bold ethics committee that sanctioned a study designed to deliberately make people miserable to see if they then become unhealthy!

Although Solomon did not know it at the time, he was actually referring to the science of psychoneuroimmunology (PNI) – the study of the link between psychological processes such as the emotions, brain function, and the immune response that play a significant role in physical illness. Perhaps the directionality question can be resolved by looking more deeply into the mechanisms of PNI. The specific term was first used by Ader and Cohen (1975), but the origins of the modern understanding of PNI can be traced back to earlier observations on physical changes that accompany emotional states. For example, Walter Cannon (1929) found that stomach movement had ceased in experimental animals that had experienced emotional changes such as anxiety or distress.

While other researchers contributed to the understanding of the PNI relationship, a more complete explanation was advanced by Hans Seyle (1956) with his description of the process he called the "general adaptation syndrome." Seyle found that, in response to physical or psychological stress, the hypothalamus mediates the secretion of the adrenocorticotropic hormone (ACTH) by the pituitary, which in turn results in the adrenal gland releasing adrenal corticoids. This leads to the person becoming more active and able to react to the stressor: This is sometimes referred to as the "freeze, fight, or flight reaction." However, if the problem persists, the heightened alert condition may be prolonged and lead to impairment of the body's immune system, and a range of serious physical conditions including atrophy of various organs, gastric ulcerations, proneness to infections, slow wound healing, and ultimately even death. There has been much recent interest in the precise mechanisms of PNI and the role of neural and endocrine links, and the reader can consult the latest academic publications for fuller explanations that are outside the scope of the present chapter.

Although the earlier brief résumé may seem to imply that PNI is only concerned with the adverse effect of the emotions on physical health ("a crushed spirit *dries up* the bones"), the mechanisms also can work in the opposite direction ("a cheerful heart is *good medicine*"), and most of the remainder of this chapter will be devoted to discussing how some activities are linked to a healthy and happy lifestyle. Before continuing, however, on the question of directionality, it seems from PNI research that the emotional response to an event can trigger a physical reaction; this suggests the following pathway:

Event → emotion → physical health

This causal direction would be in keeping with the phrasing given in *Proverbs* 17:22. But what determines the nature and severity of an emotional reaction to an event? Some people are very tense, and others are chronic worriers, but we also see people who seem to remain cheerful whatever happens to them – the laid-back, *laissez faire* individuals. These character traits will be determined by a person's unique personality, and how personality develops is a complex mixture of nature and nurture. Thus, there is a third factor in the equation: personality, which underpins King Solomon's astute link between mind and body, so perhaps directionality is not such a simple matter after all. Whether or not personality can be changed is a debated point, but behavior can be changed, and this might ultimately have an impact on personality itself. This topic will be revisited when humor training is discussed.

Humor, health, and life coping

The term "humor" was first used in a different way than it is today, but even then it had a strong health-related connection. Hippocrates (460–c.370 BCE), the founder of "modern" medicine, described what he called the four essential "humors" of life and their association with mood or disposition. These were black bile (associated with melancholia and sadness), yellow bile (choleric and angry), phlegm (phlegmatic and unemotional), and blood (sanguine and optimistic). The physician treated the patient in order to bring these humors back into balance, resulting in "good humor" or well-being.

The earliest-recorded direct reference to a topic related to humor is generally accredited to Aristotle (384–322 BCE), with his comment in *Poetics* that comedy had already acquired its (then) present features, and that Homer was the first to use the techniques of making a story out of the laughable (Bambrough, 1963). Although references to various aspects of humor appear in literature throughout the ages, it was Sigmund Freud who made a significant contribution to the understanding of all things funny. Freud (1905/1976) stated that "humor" takes its place in the great series of methods devised by an individual for evading the compulsion to suffer. He differentiated between "wit" (jokes intentionally contrived and used in a social situation), "the comic" (an observation by one person of something unintended in another – e.g., a character trait), and "humor" (an attitude within an individual regarding his or her situation). In the 1960s, there was a surge of interest called the "Humor Movement," with the realization that humor and laughter serve important roles in enhancing and maintaining quality of life (Korotkov, 1991).

What makes humor so interesting and potentially useful is its link with creativity. As noted by Earleywine (2011), a good sense of humor can correlate with creative flair. He added that this does not necessarily imply cause and effect, and both traits can be influenced by other aspects of personality and intelligence. Although specific features of creativity are discussed later under "Benefits of humor," in general terms the construct may be thought of as an ability to see beyond common logic and traditional ideas in order to create novel associations and ideas. Put another way, creativity requires divergent rather than convergent thinking – the ability to "think out of the box." As will be discussed later, such an ability is required not only to create and appreciate humor, but also to cope successfully with the problems of life.

It is speculated that laughter originated from a primitive "roar of triumph" of the victor in an ancient jungle duel. Not only did this release accumulated energy but it also expressed the victor's superiority and it communicated to others, who may have been in hiding, that it was now safe to come out (Raskin, 1985). Thus, from the earliest times, people laughed because they were (or felt they were) superior and could look down on those whom they considered inferior; today this is reflected in jokes that are told at the expense of others. By contrast, Lockard et al. (1977) thought that the smile stemmed from the submissive grimace, or expression of appeasement, of the loser in that jungle duel: an indication that the individual was no longer a threat, that later became a mark of social interaction and greeting.

Laughter is often thought of as purely a reaction to something perceived as amusing, but there are many other reasons why we laugh. These include tickling, nervousness, tension relief, defensiveness, ignorance, embarrassment, surprise, high spirits, and play (Fridlund and Loftis, 1990; Keith-Spiegel, 1972), and are in addition to forced laughter that conceals true feelings, and certain pathological conditions. It is important to do as Freud suggested and separate the physical expression of "laughter" from the personality trait of "humor," because both can have an impact on health and well-being, but in significantly different ways. Whereas laughter is an emotional reaction to a stimulus, humor has been described as an attitude, disposition, or personality trait that influences the way we look at, and cope with, life. Some say that it has survival value and is a "mature" defense mechanism (Lowis and Nieuwoudt, 1993; Vaillant et al., 1986). The benefits of laughter and humor will now be considered under separate headings.

Benefits of laughter

Is laughter the best medicine, as the popular saying goes? Keith-Spiegel (1972) summarized the views of earlier writers in stating that laughter "restores homeostasis, stabilizes blood pressure, oxygenates the blood, massages the vital organs, stimulates circulation [, and] facilitates digestion" (p. 15). In addition to these physical benefits, laughing facilitates the release of a number of health-giving hormones. These include catecholamines, which improve alertness, stimulate memory, and reduce inflammation; endorphins, the body's natural opiates that enhance positive mood, control pain, and stimulate the immune system; and immunoglobulin "A," which protects against upper respiratory tract infections. Also, the activity of white blood cells and T-cells is increased, thus enhancing the ability to fight infections (Holden, 1993; Lally, 1991).

Does this mean that all we have to do to promote our good health is to laugh as much as possible? Laughter clinics exist in various parts of the world, where humorous material is presented and overt mirth encouraged. Santhanam (2000) stated that there are 70 laughter clubs in Mumbai, India, founded by Dr. Madan Kataria, and more than 400 throughout the country. In Amsterdam, Holland, there is "the center in favor of laughter" that is run by Dr. Dhyan Sutorius who describes laughter as a "transforming force," and, in the United States, Dr. Hunter Adams became known to a wider audience through the film *Patch Adams* (1998, directed by Tom Shadyac, Universal Studios). Adams is quoted as saying that the best therapy is being happy, and that all the other things that doctors can do are, at best, aids (Holden, 1993).

While certainly acknowledging the very important health benefits of laughter, the present writer is of the view that laughter therapy alone can be seen to parallel, for example, taking an analgesic for a headache: it treats the symptoms but is unlikely to address the cause or provide long-term immunity. Dr. Kataria of Mumbai was obviously aware of this when he was quoted as saying that no claims are made for the cure of long-standing ailments by laughter therapy, but that it is mainly an anti-stress measure and a supplementary and preventative therapy (Santhanam, 2000).

Benefits of humor

In contrast to the largely short-term physical benefits of laughter is the personal disposition of humor that can strengthen the psychological resistance to negative affect and address the cause. There are many reports on humor being useful for aspects such as social facilitation and control (Overholser, 1992), teaching and education (Dolce, 1984; Rutkaus, 1981), expression of veiled aggression, and mediation of behavior (Benton, 1988; Haig, 1988). It is, however, for its value as an aid to coping with life's difficulties that is of greatest interest here. The key to understanding how this operates can be seen in the power of *creativity*. Although different brain areas work together for most tasks and functions, either directly or through cross-linkages, at a simplistic level the left hemisphere plays the dominant role in reasoning and logic, while the right hemisphere is the main region for creative and artistic activities (Nolen-Hoeksema and Fredrickson, 2008). Humor requires a creative ability to decipher the punch line of a joke, because this is not a logical end to the story. A joke can be a coherent narrative that is not strictly sensible in everyday terms – instead, it makes *non*-sense.

As an example, consider the following joke (origin unknown):

A parent phones the doctor and says, "Come quickly, my baby has swallowed a pen." The doctor replies, "I'll come right over. What are you doing in the meantime?" The parent says, "Using a pencil."

If we had no sense of humor, this might be seen as quite a rational story; the parent gave a logical answer – one needs something to write with! However, we quickly realize that something is not quite right and conclude that the parent's response was not socially acceptable, because the main concern should have been (and no doubt would be if this were a true life story) with the welfare of the baby. Thus, while the response "using a pencil" might have been logical in itself, it was not what was expected and would be unlikely to happen in reality. The joke has deliberately led us astray. On this realization, we might permit ourselves some relief from the mental effort through laughter. There are several mechanisms through which humor can aid life coping, including the following.

Multiple perspectives

The creative search for the resolution of a joke is a skill parallel to that of searching for the resolution to real-life problems. Instead of just going for one, obvious explanation for a difficult or unhappy situation, and adopting an equally single-track solution, the ability to identify many possible explanations *and solutions* for a problem provides insight and puts a person back in charge of his or her life, rather than being at the mercy of events deemed out of one's control. Lefcourt and Martin (1986) found from their own research that people who coped best with traumatic life events appeared to use humor in stressful as well as non-stressful circumstances. They noted that such individuals were able to bring multiple perspectives to bear on their problematic situations, in the same way that multiple solutions have to be considered in order to resolve the punch line of a joke. It is not that personal problems are reduced to trivia but, when they can be viewed from different angles, a variety of solutions usually present themselves. This increases the potential for a successful resolution, and the pleasure of cognitive mastery that accompanies it is enhanced. It follows that exercises in creativity and humor production can enhance skills that can be transferred to help cope with real-life issues.

Ego mastery

Adopting a humorous attitude helps a person be more capable of overcoming fears and tolerating distress: it can relieve anxiety and re-assert ego mastery (Levine, 1977). By "whistling in the dark," an individual who may be experiencing anxiety now introduces a non-serious activity into the situation. The original negative affect has difficulty competing with this jocularity, with the result that the anxiety is usually dispelled. The point here is that it is not the circumstances that change, but rather the attitude toward them: introducing an element of humor makes the situation seem less threatening and helps a person maintain control. As so neatly put by Berger (1976), we "cock a snook" (i.e., ignore it, or divert to something else, to show that we are not concerned) at (negative) events as a sign of transcending adversity.

Accepting ambiguity

Sometimes we are confronted with situations that are ambiguous or uncertain and trying to understand, accept, or resolve them through logic and reasoning alone is likely to be unsuccessful. Because humor requires creative skills to produce and understand it, these same processes can be used to help cope with "illogical" life events (Linstead, 1988). The "just world theory" (Lerner and Miller, 1978) holds that people have an inherent need to believe that the world is an orderly, predictable, and just place. With such a belief, people can confront their physical and social environments as though they were stable and orderly. Without this, it would be difficult to commit to long-range goals or even the socially regulated behavior of everyday life.

When some disaster strikes and innocent people are victims of crimes and perhaps even lose their lives, the core belief that the world is a just place is threatened. This can lead susceptible individuals to experience cognitive dissonance and difficulty in coping with life, because the world no longer seems to be predictable. However, people are very reluctant to relinquish the worldview that has sustained them up to this point. In order to try and restore consonance and provide evidence to reinforce the just world belief, blame may be apportioned to the victim with the thought that he or she might not have been as innocent as it seemed on first glance, and could have either invited the violation or deserved it. The just world theory is sometimes cited as the explanation for why the victims of crime may receive little sympathy from the law courts, and criminals such as rapists are sometimes not given the punishment that they seem to deserve.

There is, however, at least one other way that the cognitive dissonance caused by threats to the just world belief can be dissipated, and that is by the creative use of humor as a defense mechanism. Humor originated in a cruel environment, and often stemmed from feelings of superiority by the perpetrator and disparagement of those deemed to be less fortunate. While present-day politeness and political correctness may curb the inclination to laugh directly at the deformities or misfortunes of others, nevertheless mirth at someone else's expense is very much alive and well. For example, one of the most common joke forms is the three-part format, where an action by two "sensible" people is followed by something foolish by a third person. Unkind as it may seem to be, most countries have a social group that can be cited as the butt of the joke (La Fave *et al.*, 1976; Lowis and Nieuwoudt, 1993; Zillerman and Cantor, 1976).

Evidence that people turn to humor to help them cope with disasters that defy logic, and which seriously question that the world is a just place, can be seen by the speed that jokes are circulated following major catastrophes. For just two examples from jokes posted on the internet, selected for their relative mildness compared with many examples that are there, consider first one that followed the Asian tsunami of December 29, 2004:

Bob Geldof has got musicians together for "Flood Aid." So far Muddy Waters, The Drifters, Wet Wet Wet, and the Beach Boys have agreed to sing "The tide is high." (www.laughline.com, last accessed March 17, 2014)

The second example refers to the attacks on the World Trade Center in New York, September 19, 2001:

Did you hear the one about American Airlines' new deal? They'll fly you straight from the airport to the office. (www.ooze.com, last accessed March 17, 2014)

Jokes like these, which can be deemed examples of "black humor," are a way of trying to make light of serious situations and assert mastery over death. They can seem very tactless and cruel for those who are victims, or friends and relatives of victims, who have actually suffered as a result of the disaster. Other examples that are easily accessed on the World Wide Web seem to demonstrate an utterly sick and callous disregard for the immense hardship, injury, and loss of life that result from major catastrophes. It is, however, unlikely that they were usually created with this cruel intention in mind, but were rather attempts to distance (or escape) the fear of death by joking about it, or to cope with something we simply cannot understand. The absence of such a psychological defense mechanism would leave many individuals unable to cope with the sheer horror of these tragic events, resulting in panic, anxiety, and eventual breakdown.

While the examples used earlier concern major events that have affected the lives of many, the same principle applies to less serious but still worrying problems experienced by the individual: if you can joke about it, then you are exercising mastery over it; you are putting it in perspective and remaining in control of your life.

Summary of humor as a coping aid

Humor (as opposed to laughter) helps us to cope with our own problems, and tragic life events, through the use of creativity rather than, or
in addition to, logic and reasoning. Freud (1928/1952) wrote that the
defense mechanism of humor comes about when we would normally be
tempted to release a distressing emotion. Instead, humor withdraws the
painful affect from conscious attention, thus bringing about a saving in
expenditure of effort. The energy thereby set free is discharged as laughter. Humor is unique among Freud's triad (wit, the comic, and humor)
in that it does not necessarily require the presence of another person –
pleasure can be derived by contemplating a real or imaginary situation
(Freud, 1905/1976).

By adopting the creative processes used to produce and appreciate
humor, we can bring multiple perspectives to bear on the situation, we
can strengthen our egos and remain positive and in control, and we can
cope with ambiguity and events that seem to disconfirm our belief that
the world is basically a just place. To these can be added the ability of
humor to allow us to step back and see a problem in perspective, to ask if
we and others are perhaps behaving too seriously (is the situation really
so bad?), to defuse a difficult situation with a joke (you cannot be cross
with somebody you laugh with), and to afford the opportunity to break
away from stress for a while and seek some comic relief while we recharge
our mental batteries. Some people might believe that they have no sense
of humor, and that they would find difficulty using humor as a coping
mechanism in the ways just outlined. The next question is, therefore, can
people be trained to make better use of humor as a defense?

Can coping through humor be trained?

While it may be difficult or impossible to change a person's personality, it is possible to change behavior and this does have an impact on the
individual's personality. It has been said that some people are born comedians, while others may be seen to have little or no sense of humor. While
it is likely that nurture plays a dominant role in humor development, a
personality disposition, perhaps involving traits such as extraversion or
aggression, may help the process, especially with those comedians who
perform in public. Freud (1928/1952) stated that humorists are able to
regard stressful situations as simply "child's play," and Morreall (1991)
noted that humor can be thought of as a kind of play, and that a playful
attitude toward problems can result in creative solutions. In an attempt
to consolidate existing knowledge and formulate a definition of humor,

Lowis and Nieuwoudt (1993) concluded that there are three interlinking processes involved in a sense of humor – namely, creativity (the divergent thinking aspect), playfulness, and a sufficient experience of life to be able to recognize when reality is being accidentally distorted (e.g., coincidences, extremes, unintended errors) or deliberately manipulated as in contrived jokes.

Just how much of this can be trained? The life experience component has to be regarded as a given; by the time one attains 16 years it is possible to relate many events in a joke to personal experiences, and enjoy adult-type humor (Barnhart, 1989; Sheppard, 1977). However, the more diverse experiences one has had, then the more life events there will be to relate to – for example, marriage, children, the workplace, or hospitals. Playfulness can be encouraged, perhaps with the help of relaxation or stress management exercises, but is maybe difficult to teach in a formal way. The third component, creativity, can be taught through appropriate exercises, as will be described shortly. Earleywine (2011) noted that experimental studies have revealed that exposure to humor increases scores on creativity tests. Just as beauty is in the eye of the beholder (a true artist does not have to look very far for something to paint), so humor is in the perception and cognition of the observer. It surrounds us virtually all the time, waiting to be interpreted as such by those receptive to its cues (Lowis and Nieuwoudt, 1993). With a little training and practice, most people are able to develop their skills in observing the world around them with a twinkle in their eye, and have fun doing it.

The writer of this chapter developed a workshop program to see if participants could be trained to improve their coping skills by making more use of humor (Lowis, 1997). It draws on the work of others, including Lefcourt and Martin (1986), Linstead (1988), McGhee (1979), and Overholser (1992). In addition, a useful reference point is the 20-year retrospective review on humor in counseling and psychotherapy presented by Shaughnessy and Wadsworth (1992). The program is designed as five 2-hour sessions, the first four being held at weekly intervals but with the final session being scheduled for a month later. The 1- and 4-week intervals between sessions allow time for applying in real-life situations some of the strategies learned, and for completing homework assignments. The program comprises a blend of information and theory, practical exercises and role plays, techniques of humor construction, homework tasks, and discussion on attempts to use coping humor during the previous week.

Two components of the workshop are particularly important, and first and foremost is creativity. It was stated earlier that, at a simplistic level, the left hemisphere plays the dominant role in reasoning and logic, while the right hemisphere is the main region for creative and artistic activities.

In the technological age in which we live, for many people much of their daily activities requires logic and reasoning, and therefore most use is made of the left cerebral hemisphere. The artistic and creative right hemisphere is thus relatively neglected, even though it can help us to deal with ambiguous and other situations that cannot be resolved through logic and reasoning alone. Any biological component that is underutilized tends to atrophy, but fortunately, just like a neglected muscle, the right brain can be invigorated through appropriate exercise. Many creativity exercises are available, and a useful starting point is "brainstorming" whereby participants shout out as many uses they can think of for a simple object. A common example is an empty soda can; using logic alone a group of people are fortunate to reach double figures but, once creative skills click in, up to 50 uses are readily achievable. The breakthrough usually occurs when participants realize that the container can be broken open to create a sheet of metal, which then can be used to fabricate a great many useful objects such as a knife, plate, or mirror. Such exercises are used throughout the workshop sessions, and it is not uncommon to see that performance on these improves with practice (Lowis, 1997).

Another component of the humor workshop is the joke construction technique. The uninitiated may wonder just how comedians think up their jokes. There are many influences, such as the ability to observe real life in a quirky way ("the world is child's play, the very thing to jest about" [Freud, 1928/1952]), a creative ability to make novel links between seemingly unrelated events or phenomena, but also knowledge of how jokes are constructed. A two-stage theory of incongruity–resolution was proposed by Suls (1972), which holds that a joke or cartoon is intentionally constructed so as to lead the recipient astray and then produce a punch line that violates expectations. An elaboration of this was given by Mulkay (1988) who stated that standard jokes often make use of a three-part sequence: the first acts as a guide for what is to come in the second, while the third breaks the pattern established by the first two. This includes the joke format based on three people, with the third being the "fall guy." Another trick that comedians have is to keep a small number of "standard" jokes that can be adapted for any occasion by simply switching either the set-up (e.g., location), punch line, concept, or time frame (Iapoce, 1988).

During the workshop sessions, it is rewarding to observe how a combination of creativity exercises and application of joke construction techniques can lead to participants, who originally claimed that they had no sense of humor, compiling a list of original jokes and sharing them with the rest of the group. Once such skills have been developed, participants are encouraged to adopt the same principles to coping with everyday life stress – for example, by searching for multiple causes and solutions, by making jokes about situations that may initially seem daunting, and by interacting with family and work colleagues in ways that create a happy atmosphere and the joy of laughing together, rather than remaining tense and grumpy. It is surprising how much more easily tasks are accomplished and problems solved when this state is achieved.

When the workshops were first facilitated, quantitative and qualitative assessments were carried out to see if any behavioral changes had occurred. Statistical analysis of the scores from a Coping Humor Scale (Martin and Lefcourt, 1984) showed a significant increase from the first to the fifth session ($N = 22$, $t = 1.922$, $p = .031$). This finding reinforced a majority of the qualitative comments made, in that participants said they were using the knowledge and skills gained during the workshop to help them cope with problematic life situations. Others mentioned that, while still needing more practice at initiating humor to help them cope, they were now better able to distance themselves from the emotional impact of difficult circumstances. A few participants did not admit to obtaining any increase in coping skills, but nevertheless stated that they still found the sessions enjoyable. From observations of the group interactions, these individuals participated well and already seemed to possess good ego strength and coping ability. It may be concluded that at least some degree of behavior change had occurred with the majority of participants, which addresses the question that was posed earlier regarding PNI on whether or not people can be encouraged to exploit the link between state of mind and physical health in a positive way.

Music

The mechanisms that are responsible for the health-giving properties of humor can equally apply to other activities. In fact anything that is enjoyable and gives pleasure (chemical addictions excluded) is likely to be good for you, and lead to the secretion of useful hormones and the physical relaxation that allows the "doctor within" to go about its healing processes, without being restricted by physical and mental inner tensions. In this section, the question of why music is so universally popular and can give such profound pleasure to so many people will be addressed.

What is music?

Music is universally enjoyed, and there is archaeological evidence that it has survived since the dawn of civilization. In his book *The singing Neanderthals*, Mithen (2006) explored the thesis that music is a fundamental aspect of the human condition, encoded in the human genome during the evolutionary history of our species. Music was described by Leonard Bernstein (1976) as energy in vibrating motion, which is produced by beating, blowing, plucking, striking, or frictionalizing with a bow. He added that, unlike random "noise," music is structured into time and space, forming the components of melody, rhythm, tone color (timbre), and harmony. What qualifies as music (and particularly harmony) has changed over the years, and is subject to the whims of taste, fashion, culture, and social context; what is an unbearable cacophony of noise to one person might be a sublime musical experience to another.

Music is a non-verbal form of communication, associated with emotions and feelings, although the neurological processes involved are complex and can vary. Music is processed predominantly in the creative right cerebral hemisphere (Garland and Kuhn, 1995), especially in the case of naïve or casual listeners, but the left hemisphere also becomes involved with more sophisticated listeners such as trained musicians (Lerdahl and Jackendoff, 1983). Also, as demonstrated by Petsche and colleagues (1993), electroencephalogram studies have shown that hemispheric laterality can change when listening to different styles of music. By contrast, speech, which communicates facts and ideas, is mainly processed in the left hemisphere. Melodies with rising contours and high pitches tend to be associated with cheerfulness, sprightliness, and humor, whereas falling contours and low pitches suggest sadness and dignity (Shutter-Dyson and Gabriel, 1981). Sloboda (1991) noted that appoggiatura, descending fifths, earlier-than-expected changes in harmony, and unexpected variations or tensions can be responsible for producing in the listener what have been variously called "chills," "thrills," or "shivers." Additionally, research has indicated that major musical modes tend to convey feelings of happiness, merriness, and playfulness, whereas minor modes are more likely to suggest sadness, dreaminess, tenderness, and yearning (Dowling and Harwood, 1986). Time signature can also influence the feelings that music can generate, with triple time (3/4) indicating smooth-flowing and relaxed, but with duple (2/2) and quadruple (4/4) time suggesting controlled or firm, and said to be more sacred and serious (Bruner, 1990). Hughes and Lowis (2002) investigated the response to hymns in different modalities, and found that those in triple time received the highest scores for emotional/spiritual impact, and that there was a trend for minor modes to rate higher on this than major.

It was back in 1962 that Abraham Maslow first described *peak* (emotional) *experiences* that can occur in practically everyone, and could manifest as moments of great awe, a feeling of oneness in the world, seeing the ultimate truth, satisfaction of vague, unsatisfied yearnings, stepping into heaven, or being detached from time and place. Others have subsequently used more succinct definitions such as altered states of consciousness, but the emotional impact needs to be much more profound than just great pleasure or enjoyment for it to qualify as a *peak*. Maslow said that aesthetic events, particularly music, could act as triggers for these events, and that some individuals could rely on certain pieces of music to help bring them about.

Lowis and Touchin (2002) investigated whether or not music could be shown to produce "peak experiences" in a laboratory setting. Under controlled conditions, they exposed participants to 30-minute selections of classical music recordings, some being upbeat pieces and others more gentle. The participants had to press a button each time they experienced a peak conforming to a pre-defined description. The researchers found that some 77 percent of participants pressed the button at least once during the two trials, with the maximum number of pressings for any individual being 42. They then scrutinized the scores of the music to try to identify specific moments or aspects of the pieces that coincided with the main clusters of peaks. Only a few such musical items were identified with any certainty – for example, at the start of a solo passage, where one instrument takes over from another, at a fortissimo, at percussive impacts, at crescendos, and at a full-blooded climax.

It is interesting to ponder just why music can have such profound emotional effects on listeners. One factor that has been suggested is arousal. Back in 1971, Berlyne noted that aesthetic patterns (including music) "may give pleasure both through arousal increase and closely followed by arousal reduction" (p. 92). He added that arousal could be raised by properties such as novelty, surprise, complexity, ambiguity, and puzzlement. Trehub and Schellenberg (1995) mentioned that music contains tensions and resolutions – the ebb and flow of feeling – while North and Hargreaves (1996) suggested that the relationship between musical complexity and listening pleasure followed an inverted-U pattern of intensity, but that this was dependent upon the listener's level of musical sophistication and training. This notion of arousal is in keeping with observations that physical and psychological manifestations such as increased blood pressure, respiration, and pulse rates, along with tears, shivers, tingles, and lumps in the throat, can occur during significant moments in music (Aldridge, 1996; Sloboda, 1991; Storr, 1993). Similar reactions were reported by some of the participants in the Lowis and Touchin (2002) study.

While arousal theory might account for some of the "peak experiences" found by Lowis and Touchin, especially in the case of upbeat and rousing music, it is likely that other factors could also be involved, particularly in the case of gentle music that can impart a dreamy or even hypnotic state in the listener, and which also resulted in the peak button being pressed by participants. During the earlier discussion on the benefits of humor, it was stated that laughter stimulates *inter alia* the production of endorphins, the body's natural opiates that enhance positive mood, control pain, and stimulate the immune system. It has been suggested that music listening can also encourage the release of endorphins that in turn elicit emotional responses and buffer the production of stress-induced hormones. Goldstein (1980) held the view that the tingling sensations or thrills that some listeners experience in response to music might be mediated by endogenous opioids. Several years later, McKinney and colleagues (1997) found that β-endorphin levels tended to increase in their participants over a two-hour period of listening to classical music, compared with a control group where the levels decreased, although in both cases the changes were below the level of significance usually adopted by the social sciences.

Thus, increased levels of hormones such as endorphins might help to account for the feelings of pleasure that can be experienced when listening to music, especially with more gentle pieces where arousal is less likely. There are, however, other factors. Music is able to evoke memories of association, especially if it was being played at the time of an earlier event, and even more so if that event was an emotional one such as a wedding, funeral, or the first meeting of a future marriage partner (the "darling, they are playing our tune" syndrome). This could either generate an emotional response in the listener that was not specifically intended by the composer, or enhance an emotion that was so intended, in an individual sensitized by a previous experience. Sometimes this effect is sufficiently strong to stimulate mental imagery of the earlier occasion. Daniel Levitin (2006) has delved deeply into the biological processes underlying how humans experience music, and why it plays such a unique role in our lives. He concluded that our brains are hardwired for music and that our musical preferences begin to form even before we are born. Rather than music being just an addition to our lives, Levitin is convinced that it is an obsession at the heart of human nature.

Music therapy

Music therapy is an established health profession that aims to help people who have difficulties with social, physical, mental, and emotional functions such as communication, cognitive functioning, learning difficulties, autism, dementia, and depression. Because music is such a powerful communication medium, it can sometimes be used to interact with a client when attempts to do so through words alone have failed. After an assessment of the client's needs, the music therapist, who is a skilled and experienced musician, will use a range of musical styles including improvisation to try and establish rapport with, and obtain responses from, the client. The music that is successful may provide an indication of the client's prevailing mood. The practitioner can then manipulate the music to facilitate mood improvement, confidence, and other positive outcomes, and encourage transfer of these to other aspects of the client's life. Song writing, singing, or other musical performances may be introduced as part of the procedure, and the therapy can be individual or group based. The fact that music therapy is successful serves to confirm the important role that music can play in the lives of many people.

The Mozart effect

In 1995, great interest was generated by the publication of research by Frances Rauscher and her colleagues, which claimed that listening to 10 minutes of Mozart's *Sonata for two pianos in D major* resulted in a short-term (10 to 15 minutes) improvement in scores on a spatial-temporal problem-solving test. In attempting to explain this phenomenon, the authors built on an earlier notion that similar neurons fired when either listening to music or performing spatial tasks, and they proposed that hearing the right type of music might "warm up" neurons before completing this type of test. Another suggested explanation is that appropriate music, including Mozart compositions, stabilizes arousal level by either raising one that is too sedentary for efficient operation, or reducing excessive arousal that might be caused by anxiety or hyperactivity, so that the level of concentration for addressing the task is optimal for good performance. Thompson *et al.* (2001) conducted a controlled experiment with a Mozart composition and another piece, measuring enjoyment, arousal, and mood in addition to performance on a test of spatial abilities. Their evidence from statistical analyses of the outcomes was that the Mozart effect is an artifact of arousal and mood.

In a partly successful attempt to identify just one aspect of classical music that could enhance performance, this time on verbal as well as spatial tasks, Sutton and Lewis (2008) digitally manipulated a piece of music composed by Handel to create two identical versions, except that one was now in the key of F-major and the other in F-minor. The major mode version was rated by participants as emotionally more positive than was the minor, and performance on verbal tasks by females was enhanced by listening to this version. Such conflicting and inconsistent research findings on the ability of music to enhance task performance, including the so-called "Mozart effect," rather than suggesting that all such claims are spurious and not to be taken seriously, instead merit even more carefully controlled trials. A particularly interesting theory on why specifically Mozart's music might have beneficial effects, but one now difficult to prove, is that Mozart himself suffered from Tourette's syndrome, and instinctively created compositions that were therapeutic for his own condition (Kammer, 2007). If this was in fact the case, and the calming effects of his music can be passed on to the listener, then Mozart did not suffer in vain.

Other health benefits

Further uses or benefits of music include social aspects such as the promotion of group solidarity, cultural identity, trust, and cooperation brought about by playing or singing in groups. Such benefits are of particular advantage to the physical and mental health of the elderly, including those with various stages of dementia. Because music is a medium of communication, as well as having the power to evoke memories, appropriate musical selections enable people to maintain links with the real world, even when verbal communication and facial recognition become difficult. Likewise, music may sometimes be the only way that communication can be made with people who are neurologically impaired through birth defects or injury. Some researchers have claimed that certain biological rhythms can become synchronized with the rhythmic contour of music being played, and that this can help the recovery of cardiovascular or stroke patients, or even help to prevent such events.

Laura Mitchell and colleagues (2008) investigated what they called "audioanalgesia," that being the use of music for pain control, either by distracting attention from the discomfort through emotional engagement with the music, or by creating a feeling of control over the pain by having a technique to decrease its severity. Their studies made use of the participants' own choices of music (compared with the common practice of imposing classical selections), and many were of contemporary vocal tracks. The pain administered was a cold water vessel into which the participant plunged his or her hand, and the measure was the length of time that could be tolerated. Results showed that listening to the preferred music led to significantly longer pain tolerance, and a greater perceived control, compared with the control conditions. Familiarity with the music, and a combination of anticipation and tension release from within the music structure, plus being able to sing along with the lyrics (silently or audibly), were considered to be contributory factors to these outcomes.

Findings such as these have far-reaching clinical implications, such as in recovery from, or tolerance of, pain of surgery, childbirth, accidents, or other medically related conditions, and music is already being used in these contexts. To cite just one example, Paul Robertson (1996) describes studies on the benefits of music in a clinical setting that were carried out in a German hospital by Dr. Ralph Spintge; it was found that just 15 minutes of soothing music allowed the dosage of sedatives and anesthetic drugs used to control the pain of operations to be reduced by 50 percent.

Education

Because of the likely relationship between musical skills and creativity in other spheres, could musical training enhance the learning process *per se*? Weinberger (1999) reviewed some research evidence, including a study where high school music students were compared with non-music students on a measure of creativity involving devising unusual uses for common objects. A significant correlational effect was found between music involvement and creative ability. Another research study used a participant pool of schoolchildren in the first grade. One group received 30 minutes of music instruction per day for a full year, while a control group did not. Those receiving the music education scored significantly higher on creativity tests and in perceptual-motor skills than did the control group. Weinberger also reports on a similar trial carried out in Hungary, but this time involving pre-school children, and the results also demonstrated an increase in creative ability. Interestingly, however, there was no parallel increase in intelligence quotient, showing that the effect of the music education on creativity was quite specific.

A different aspect of this relationship was investigated in Israel by Ziv and Keydar (2009). The researchers were interested in the degree of complexity of musical selections that creative individuals prefer. They subjected their participants to a range of music of differing complexity, and then measured their preferences, liking, and perceived complexity of the selections, in addition to administering a test of creative potential. As hypothesized, a positive and significant relationship was found between creative potential and preference for (but not necessarily enjoyment of) the more complex musical pieces administered, although musical tastes and familiarity with specific musical styles were also relevant factors.

The conclusion from studies such as these does point to the power of music to enhance other cognitive and creative skills, and this should be regarded as an important factor for all those involved in the education sector.

Other artistic pursuits

In addition to music, already discussed, the literature is replete with reports on the benefits of engaging with other art forms (Stuckey and Nobel, 2010), and, like music, they have been used by trained therapists. Some examples were summarized by Lowis et al. (2011). These included the statement by Luschei (1995) that literature therapy is an in-depth, psychotherapeutic modality based on the reading and discussion of imaginative or informative literature, and Lowe's (2006) view that undertaking expressive writing had resulted in improved health and well-being, even to the extent of reducing the severity of symptoms in arthritis and asthma sufferers. For the visual arts, Weir (2010) reported that visiting art galleries can challenge our thinking and emotions, and reveal something about the way we explain events in the world, while Stuckey and Nobel (2010) noted that the way a person draws pictures about his or her illness is insightful and informs how the particular medical condition is visualized. Sculpture therapy was reported by Goodman (2004) to improve the self-concept and behavior of the blind, while molding in clay can be a powerful way to help people express emotions associated with illness, through tactile involvement at a somatic level (Stuckey and Nobel, 2010).

Lowis et al.'s (2011) review also noted that similar benefits have been cited for the performing arts. These include the reports by Landy (2007, 2010) that drama therapy is an aesthetic healing process that proceeds as one takes on a role and tells a story in that role. Landy added that, at a safe distance, a real-life traumatic event can be replayed in the mind and/or body, and a way discerned to cope with the consequences. Stuckey and Nobel (2010) noted that dance and movement, apart from the benefits of motor activity, facilitate physical forms of expression as psychotherapeutic tools that help to relieve stress and anxiety. Finally, a literature review by Hunter (1999) revealed consistent support for the physical and psychological health benefits of singing, while Bungay et al. (2010) found that members of a Silver Song Club confirmed that singing made them feel good and imparted a sense of well-being. Further evidence for the therapeutic benefits of engaging in creative, artistic activities is presented in Chapter 15, "Bringing the whole universe to order: creativity, healing, and posttraumatic growth," by Marie Forgeard et al., this volume.

For their own study, Lowis and colleagues (2011) surveyed a sample of 102 older adults (mean age = 77.42, standard deviation = 8.94) and asked their level of interest in each of six common forms of artistic activities: painting, sculpture and similar objets d'art, theatre and ballet, instrumental music, singing, and literature. In each case, one question

Table 17.1 *Interest in the arts*

Rank	Artistic pursuit	Mean score	Standard deviation
1	Reading books, poems, and other literature	3.80	0.54
2	Listening to music	3.55	0.69
3	Listening to people singing	3.20	0.75
4	Visiting theatre or ballet	2.93	0.82
5	Looking at paintings, visiting galleries	2.83	0.85
6	Looking at sculpture, fine pottery/objets d'art	2.79	0.86
7	Singing in groups, choirs, solo	1.63	0.93
8	Writing stories, books, poems, plays	1.48	0.87
9	Playing a musical instrument	1.47	0.74
10	Painting and drawing	1.46	0.74
11	Making sculptures, pottery, glassware	1.14	0.61
12	Acting, performing, dancing	1.23	0.71

Note. Table reproduced by permission of the Editor, *Journal of Applied Arts and Health.*

concerned "passive" interest (e.g., watching or listening) and another "active" interest (actually taking part). It was clear from the results that there was a divide between "passive" and "active" pursuits, with literature being the highest-ranked passive interest (mean score = 3.80 out of a possible 4) and singing being ranked first among the active (mean score = 1.63).

See Table 17.1 for mean scores for all pursuits. If the related pairs of active and passive interests are totaled (maximum score 8), then interest in literature emerges as the most frequent (combined mean score 5.28), followed by instrumental music (5.02).

The arts, creativity, and aging

The findings revealed in the previous section suggest that interest in the arts, particularly at a more passive level, is popular within the older age group surveyed, and quite possibly also across a wider age range. It can probably be assumed that such voluntary participation is both pleasurable and has health benefits. Thus, the use of the arts in various forms of therapy would seem to be justified. However, the question needs asking: why should participation in the arts be enjoyed by so many people? Perhaps a pertinent factor is the link between such activities and creativity.

It was mentioned earlier that the right cerebral hemisphere is the main region for processing creative and artistic activities (Nolen-Hoeksema and Fredrickson, 2008) and that, for many people, several of their daily activities require logic and reasoning that predominantly involve the left cerebral hemisphere. The creative right hemisphere is thus relatively neglected, and so the opportunity to exercise this through artistic hobbies during the increased leisure time afforded by retirement is both pleasurable and intrinsically rewarding. For example, engagement with literature, the highest-ranked activity in total, can allow the reader to relate their own emotional experiences and creative fantasies to those portrayed in the prose or poetry (Lowe, 2006).

The benefits of engaging with music have already been reviewed in detail in this chapter. Of particular note (excuse the pun!) were the findings from studies carried out in schools where the inclusion of music lessons was accompanied by increases in scores on creative ability tests. While the findings on the Mozart effect may be regarded by some researchers as still unconfirmed, the original results did indicate an improvement on spatial-temporal problem-solving tests following exposure to Mozart's music. The results of the research on engagement with the arts indicate that singing was rated first in the list of active pursuits; in addition to the benefits that will result from the musical component *per se*, singing has the added advantages of community involvement and shared creative experience.

Humor has already been discussed at length in this chapter, and it was suggested that the benefits of engaging in it can be largely attributed to the fact that production of, and appreciation of, humor is very much a creative right-hemisphere activity. It follows that exercising one's creative ability through humor is likely to have the considerable benefit of enhancing one's life coping skills in general, whatever one's age or status. The humor workshops showed that participants significantly increased their scores on a coping humor scale, and most also gave positive feedback on how they were now suffering less stress at home and in the workplace. This shows that working with humor has the potential to enhance creative ability for everyone. There are surely worse ways to set about improving one's ability to cope with life's adversities, reduce stress, and enjoy life to the full.

A happiness formula?

In this chapter, a number of topics have been discussed that can have a profound positive influence on physical and mental health, happiness, and well-being via the phenomenon of psychoneuroimmunology. Would it be possible to construct a formula that would summarize all the main components that contribute to the feeling of happiness, and thus encourage the "doctor within" to go about its healing work through the mechanism of PNI? Much has been written on this aspect of positive psychology, including the famous "right to the pursuit of happiness" included in the American Declaration of Independence, but many people still seem unable to achieve it. Is pursuing happiness like chasing the proverbial end of the rainbow – a goal that evades capture? Can we, and should we, be happy all the time, or is it a matter of contrasting the ups and downs of life and not achieving the gain without the pain?

Peterson and Park (2009) wrote that acquiring new possessions, new jobs, or new loves usually brings happiness; we hope that this will last forever, but invariably the magic wears off before too long. Seeking pleasure through acquisitiveness is thus doomed to failure. In fact, actually doing things with the aim of making yourself happy is unlikely to be successful, and this is nicely expressed by philosopher Simon Blackburn (1998) as the "paradox of hedonism." Blackburn took as his starting point the oft-heard dictum that we should always act on the principle of maximizing our own expected utility, but that this did not always lead to happiness. His response to this was that the more you concentrate on happiness, the more you worry about it, and the less likely you are to be happy. According to Peterson and Park (2009), however, there are two simple exercises that one can do that, surprisingly, have been shown to improve sense of well-being and happiness. They are:

1. Spend 10 minutes before you go to bed writing down three things that went well today, no matter how small. Then against each one, try to explain why.

2. Identify what you think are your five main positive character strengths – for example, humor, creativity, or kindness. Then each day make a point of using at least one of them in a way that you have not done before.

Ed Diener has written extensively on the topic of happiness (see, for example, Diener and Biswas-Diener, 2008), and has devised a simple self-rating questionnaire to measure happiness levels. He concludes that happiness is good for health and even longevity, but advocates an optimal level rather than seeking euphoria, along with the recognition that some negative emotions are an integral part of a happy life.

Is there a formula which, if followed, will lead to happiness? The present author has trawled various writings and suggestions on this, and now presents his own personal conclusions. No doubt there will be many other views, and the reader might wish to create his or her own version.

(a) Health: Many will claim that this is the most important contribution to happiness. If we feel unwell and believe that our health is threatened, we will be unhappy. Some people moan all the time about their health problems, which actually may be relatively minor.

Others, who could have quite severe disabilities, nevertheless are always cheerful and try to live life to the full. Perhaps we can think of these as "cup half full" people compared with the miseries who are "cup half empty." Being prepared to carry on regardless, adapt to changing circumstances and continue to do things that give pleasure, plus having a good laugh whenever possible, is no doubt an important component of the happiness formula.

(b) Activities: These include full-time, part-time, and voluntary work, as well as being a homemaker, parent, or grandparent. If we enjoy doing these things, and feel that what we do is meaningful and satisfying, then this will make us happy. However, we do need an activity level that is *just right* because, if we are too busy with the things we must do, or if we are bored with having too little to do, then this will negate some or all of the happiness.

(c) Social relationships: We are a gregarious species, not a solitary one, and we obtain much pleasure from mixing with others and being part of the greater whole of humanity where we can give and receive love. If we are lonely, then we will be unhappy. However, like most aspects of life, we can sometimes have too much of a good thing, and maybe also need some time to ourselves. Thus, we do not want either too much or too little socializing, but what is just right for each of us.

(d) Meaning in life: For many people it is important to feel a connection with something larger than oneself. Although this may often be linked to religion or spirituality, it does not have to be. For example, some will feel happy that they are part of a greater humanity and have a faith in the basic goodness of human nature. If we cannot see any meaning in life, we will find it difficult to be happy. It is important that we are able to look back on a life lived so far, and believe that we have few regrets and that we mostly did what was right at the time, as stated by Erikson (1963) in his description of ego-integrity in later life. It is equally important to be able to look forward, try to understand our place in the universe, and use our mind to explore the spiritual gifts yet to come.

(e) Freedom: In most developed countries people will take the freedom they have for granted. In some parts of the world, however, people are oppressed and so curtailed by poverty and corrupt government that they cannot even contemplate the freedom that many others enjoy. Of course, all countries have jails and it is clearly a punishment to have one's freedom taken away through incarceration. It is difficult to contemplate a worse deprivation than being imprisoned in Auschwitz during World War II, yet one of the inmates there, Viktor Frankl, survived by always being able to find meaning in life no matter how terrible things were. After the war he became a leading psychologist of the Humanist school, and drew on his experiences to develop the technique of logotherapy (Frankl, 1946/2006).

(f) Money: Much has been written on the role of money in the pursuit of happiness, and many might be embarrassed to admit giving this a prominent place in their formula. The popular song of yesteryear "Money is the root of all evil" reflects the view that money can bring the downfall of people, and that it does not result in happiness. However, we cannot deny that we live in an almost universally capitalist society, so can we do without money? As commented by Li-Ping Tang (2007), maybe it is not so much money itself that can reduce quality of life, but rather the *love* of it, and how we feel about the money that we do have. (See also the biblical reference "For the love of money is the root of all evil" [1 Timothy 6:10].) Having too little money to survive and provide the necessities of life certainly causes unhappiness. Once the poverty threshold is crossed, however, and we can afford a home, food, and clothing, then the joy of receiving additional income is often short-lived and may just be prompted by wanting to go one better than our neighbors!

Economic psychologist Dr. Chris Boyce of Warwick University, UK, was asked by a British newspaper to comment on the likelihood of happiness resulting from winning what was then a record lottery prize of £56 million (about $84 million) (*Daily Mail*, UK, February 17, 2010). He wrote that, in the long run, it would not make the husband and wife winners happy. Such wealth would change relationships with friends and neighbors, and would probably result in a house move to an unfamiliar, expensive location where it might be difficult to fit in and make new friends. The couple would no doubt give up their jobs and familiar routine, so they would then reorganize how they would spend their days. Their lives might soon lack purpose, and buying expensive cars or boats would not remedy the situation. Depression and despair were likely eventual outcomes. Giving money away and engaging in voluntary work was the main advice that Dr. Boyce offered, but this could still lead to arguments and family jealousies.

Taking all this into consideration, a suggested happiness formula is:

HEALTH (good enough to be able to do pleasurable things)

+

ACTIVITIES (a range that is just right)

+

SOCIALIZATION (enough friends and family to share love and social activities)

+

MEANING (a belief that our life is meaningful, and an awareness of something greater than our self)

+

FREEDOM (to be free to be able to accomplish all these things)

+

MONEY (enough to feel secure, warm, fed, and clothed)

=

HAPPINESS!

No doubt there are many other factors, and different individuals will probably create their own formula based on their life experiences and philosophies. If attempting to concoct a formula for happiness seems rather trite, perhaps we would do better just reminding ourselves of the "paradox of hedonism" and not even deliberately try to be happy. Even better, maybe we would be more successful if we instead concentrated our efforts on helping other people to achieve happiness. Happiness achieved vicariously through making other people happy is the epitome of altruism, and is far more satisfying and desirable than the pursuit of personal gain. Ultimate and permanent happiness is probably unachievable (at least on this earth) and, as Diener and Biswas-Diener (2008) stated, it is more about a way of traveling than simply being a destination.

References

Ader, R. and Cohen, N. (1975). Behaviorally conditioned immunosuppression. *Psychosomatic Medicine*, 37(4), 333–340.

Aldridge, D. (1996). *Music therapy research and practice in medicine*. London: Jessica Kingsley.

Bambrough, R. (Ed.). *The philosophy of Aristotle*. New York: New American Library.

Barnhart, N. C. (1989). Humor: An art in itself. *Delta-Kappa Gamma Bulletin*, 55, 9–12.

Benton, G. (1988). The origins of the political joke. In C. Powell and G. E. Patton (Eds.), *Humor in society: Resistance and control* (pp. 33–55). New York: St. Martin's.

Berger, A. A. (1976). Anatomy of a joke. *Journal of Communication*, 1, 113–116.

Berlyne, D. E. (1971). *Aesthetics and psychobiology*. New York: Appleton-Century-Crofts.

Bernstein, L. (1976). *The unanswered question*. Cambridge, MA: Harvard University Press.

Blackburn, S. (1998). *Ruling passions*. Oxford: Clarendon Press.

Bruner, G. C. (1990). Music, mood, and marketing. *Journal of Marketing*, 54(4), 94–104.

Bungay, H., Clift, S. and Skingley, A. (2010). The Silver Song Club project: A sense of well-being through participatory singing. *Journal of Applied Arts and Health*, 1(2), 165–178.

Cannon, W. B. (1929). *Bodily changes in pain, hunger, fear and rage*. New York: Appleton-Century-Crofts.

Diener, E. and Biswas-Diener, R. (2008). *Happiness: Unlocking the mysteries of psychological wealth*. Malden, MA: Blackwell Publishing.

Dolce, R. (1984). Being a teacher of the behaviour disordered. *Education*, 105(2), 155–161.

Dowling, W. J. and Harwood, D. L. (1986). *Music cognition*. Orlando, FL: Academic Press.

Earleywine, M. (2011). *Humor 101*. New York: Springer.

Erikson, E. H. (1963). *Childhood and society* (2nd edn.). New York: Norton.

Frankl, V. (1946/2006). *Man's search for meaning*. Boston, MA: Beacon Press.

Freud, S. (1905/1976). Jokes and their relation to the unconscious. In J. Strachey (Ed. and Trans.) and A. Richards (Ed.), *The Pelican Freud library* (Vol. 6). Harmondsworth: Penguin.

Freud, S. (1928/1952). Humour. In J. Strachey (Ed.), *Sigmund Freud, collected papers* (pp. 215–221). London: Hogarth.

Fridlund, A. J. and Loftis, J. M. (1990). Relations between tickling and humorous laughter: Preliminary support for the Darwin-Hecker hypothesis. *Biological Psychology*, 30, 141–150.

Garland, T. H. and Kuhn, C. V. (1995). *Math and music harmonious connections*. New Jersey: Dale Seymour Publications.

Goldstein, A. (1980). Thrills in response to music and other stimuli. *Physiological Psychology*, 8(1), 126–129.

Goodman, L. (2004). The influence of sculpture therapy upon the self-concept and behaviours of older blind individuals. *Dissertation Abstracts International. Section B: The Sciences and Engineering*, 65, 6–B, 3159.

Haig, R. (1988). Some socio-cultural aspects of humour. *Australian and New Zealand Journal of Psychiatry*, 22(4), 418–422.

Holden, R. (1993). *Laughter is the best medicine*. London: HarperCollins.

Hughes, A. G. and Lowis, M. J. (2002). The role of rhythm and mode in emotional response to hymn tunes. *The Mankind Quarterly*, 42(4), 441–454.

Hunter, B. C. (1999). Singing as a therapeutic agent, in *The Etude*, 1891–1949. *Journal of Music Therapy*, 36(2), 125–143.

Iapoce, M. (1988). *A funny thing happened on the way to the boardroom*. New York: Wiley.

Kammer, T. (2007). Mozart in the neurological department – who has the tic? In J. Bogousslavsky and M. G. Hennerici (Eds.), *Neurological disorders in famous artists – Part 2* (pp. 184–192). Basel, Switzerland: Karger.

Keith-Spiegel, P. (1972). Early conceptions of humour: Varieties and issues. In J. H. Goldstein and P. E. McGhee (Eds.), *The psychology of humour* (pp. 3–35). New York: Academic Press.

Korotkov, D. (1991). An exploratory factor analysis of the sense of humour personality construct: A pilot project. *Personality and Individual Differences*, 12(5), 395–397.

La Fave, L., Haddad, J. and Maesen, W. A. (1976). Superiority, enhanced self-esteem, and perceived incongruity humour theory. In A. J. Chapman and H. C. Foot (Eds.), *Humour and laughter: Theory, research and applications* (pp. 63–91). London: Wiley.

Lally, S. (1991). Laugh your stress away. *Prevention*, 43, 50–52.

Landy, R. J. (2007). Drama therapy: Past, present, and future. In I. A. Serlin, J. Sonke-Henderson, R. Brandman and J. Graham-Pole (Eds.), *Whole person healthcare (Vol. 3: The arts and health)* (pp. 143–163). Westport, CT: Praeger.

Landy, R. J. (2010). Drama as a means of preventing post-traumatic stress following trauma within a community. *Journal of Applied Arts and Health*, 1(1), 7–18.

Lefcourt, H. M. and Martin, R. A. (1986). *Humour and life stress: Antidote to adversity*. New York: Springer.

Lerner, M. J. and Miller, D. T. (1978). Just world research and the attribution process: Looking back and ahead. *Psychological Bulletin*, 85, 1030–1051.

Levine, J. (1977). Humour as a form of therapy: Introduction to symposium. In A. J. Chapman and H. C. Foot (Eds.), *It's a funny thing, humour* (pp. 127–137). Oxford: Pergamon.

Levitin, D. J. (2006). *This is your brain on music: The science of human obsession*. New York: Dutton/Penguin Books.

Li-Ping Tang, T. (2007). Income and quality of life: Does the love of money make a difference? *Journal of Business Ethics*, 72, 375–393.

Linstead, S. (1988). Jokers wild: Humour in organisational culture. In C. Powell and G. E. Paton (Eds.), *Humour in society* (pp. 123–146). New York: St. Martin's.

Lockard, J. S., Fahrenbruch, C. E., Smith, J. L. and Morgan, C. J. (1977). Smiling and laughter: Different phyletic origins? *Bulletin of the Psychonomic Society*, 10(3), 183–186.

Lowe, G. (2006). Health-related effects of creative and expressive writing. *Health Education*, 106(1), 60–70.

Lowis, M. J. (1997). A humour workshop program to aid coping with life stress. *The Mankind Quarterly*, 38, 25–38.

Lowis, M. J. and Nieuwoudt, J. M. (1993). The humour phenomenon: A theoretical perspective. *The Mankind Quarterly*, 33(4), 409–422.

Lowis, M. J. and Touchin, C. (2002). An analysis of the properties of music found to trigger peak emotional experiences. *British Journal of Music Therapy*, 16(1), 35–45.

Lowis, M. J., Jewell, A. J. and Jackson, M. I. (2011). Engagement in the arts and well-being and health in later adulthood: An empirical study. *Journal of Applied Arts and Health*, 2(1), 25–36.

Luschei, D. K. (1995). Integrated treatment or addictions. A comprehensive program based on literature therapy: An innovative approach to recovery. *Dissertation Abstracts International. Section B: The Sciences and Engineering*, 55, 11–B, 5077.

McGhee, P. E. (1979). *Humour, its origin and development*. San Francisco, CA: Freeman.

McKinney, C. H., Tims, F. C., Kumar, A. M. and Kumar, M. (1997). The effect of selected classical music and spontaneous imagery on plasma β-endorphin. *Journal of Behavioural Medicine*, 20(1), 85–99.

Martin, R. A. and Lefcourt, H. M. (1984). Situational Humour Response Questionnaire: Quantitative measure of sense of humour. *Journal of Personality and Social Psychology*, 47(1), 145–155.

Maslow, A. H. (1962). Lessons from peak experiences. *Journal of Humanistic Psychology*, 2(2), 9–18.

Mitchell, L. A., MacDonald, A. R. and Knussen, C. (2008). An investigation of the effects of music and art on pain perception. *Psychology of Aesthetics, Creativity, and the Arts*, 2(3), 162–170.

Mithen, S. (2006). *The singing Neanderthals: The origins of music, language, mind and body*. Cambridge, MA: Harvard University Press.

Morreall, J. (1991). Humour at work. *Humour*, 4(3/4), 359–373.

Mulkay, M. (1988). *On humour: Its nature and place in modern society*. Oxford: Polity Press.

Nolen-Hoeksema, S. and Fredrickson, B. (2008). *Atkinson and Hilgard's introduction to psychology* (15th edn.). London: Cenage Learning.

North, A. C. and Hargreaves, D. J. (1996). *Liking for music in every-day life*. Paper presented at the British Association Annual Festival of Science. University of Birmingham, September.

Overholser, J. C. (1992). Sense of humour when coping with life stress. *Personality and Individual Differences*, 13(7), 799–804.

Peterson, C. and Park, N. (2009). Classifying and measuring strengths of character. In S. J. Lopez and C. R. Snyder (Eds.), *Oxford handbook of positive psychology* (2nd edn.) (pp. 25–33). New York: Oxford University Press.

Petsche, H., Richter, P., von Stein, A., Etlinger, S. C. and Filz, O. (1993). EEG coherence and musical thinking. *Music Perception*, 11, 117–151.

Raskin, V. (1985). *Semantic mechanism of humour*. Dordrecht: Reidel.

Rauscher, F. H., Shaw, G. L. and Ky, K. N. (1995). Listening to Mozart enhances spatial-temporal reasoning: Toward a neurological basis. *Neuroscience Letters*, 185, 44–47.

Robertson, P. (1996). *Music and the mind*. London: Channel 4 Television.

Rutkaus, M. (1981). Use of humour in instruction. *Performance and Instruction*, 20, 8, 17–19.

Santhanam, K. (2000). Laugh and be well. *The Hindu*, www.hindu.com/folio/fo0003/00030440.htm, last accessed March 17, 2014.

Seyle, H. H. B. (1956). *The stress of life*. New York: McGraw-Hill.

Shaughnessy, M. F. and Wadsworth, T. M. (1992). Humour in counseling and psychotherapy: A 20-year retrospective. *Psychological Reports*, 70, 755–762.

Sheppard, A. (1977). Developmental levels in explanations of humour from childhood to late adolescence. In A. J. Chapman and H. C. Foot (Eds.), *It's a funny thing, humour* (pp. 225–228). Oxford: Pergamon.

Shutter-Dyson, R. and Gabriel, C. (1981). *The psychology of musical ability* (2nd edn.). London: Methuen.

Sloboda, J. A. (1991). Musical structure and emotional responses: Some empirical findings. *Psychology of Music*, 19, 110–120.

Storr, A. (1993). *Music and the mind*. London: HarperCollins.

Stuckey, H. L. and Nobel, J. (2010). The connection between art, healing, and public health: A review of current literature. *American Journal of Public Health*, 100(2), 254–263.

Suls, J. M. (1972). A two-stage model for appreciation of jokes and cartoons: An information-processing analysis. In J. H. Goldstein and P. E. McGhee (Eds.), *The psychology of humour* (pp. 81–100). New York: Academic Press.

Suls, J. M. (1977). Cognitive and disparagement theories of humour: A theoretical and empirical analysis. In A. J. Chapman and H. C. Foot (Eds.), *It's a funny thing, humour* (pp. 41–45). Oxford: Pergamon.

Sutton, C. J. C. and Lowis, M. J. (2008). The effect of musical mode on verbal and spatial task performance. *Creativity Research Journal*, 20(4), 420–426.

Thompson, W. F., Schellenberg, E. G. and Husain, G. (2001). Arousal, mood, and the Mozart Effect. *Psychological Science*, 12(3), 248–251.

Trehub, S. E. and Schellenberg, E. G. (1995). Music: Its relevance to infants. *Annals of Child Development*, 11, 1–24.

Vaillant, G. E., Bond, M. and Vaillant, C. O. (1986). An empirically validated hierarchy of defence mechanisms. *Archives of General Psychology*, 43, 786–794.

Weinberger, N. M. (1999). Music research at the turn of the millennium. *Musica Research Notes V1*, 3, 298–316.

Weir, H. (2010). You don't have to like them: Art, Tate Modern and learning. *Journal of Applied Arts and Health*, 1(1), 93–110.

Zillerman, D. and Cantor, J. R. (1976). A disposition theory of humour and mirth. In A. J. Chapman and H. C. Foot (Eds.), *Humour and laughter: Theory, research and applications*. London: Wiley.

Ziv, N. and Keydar, E. (2009). The relationship between creative potential, aesthetic responses to music, and musical preferences. *Creativity Research Journal*, 21(1), 125–133.

Part VI

Creativity and mental illness: what now?

18 Ruminating about mental illness and creativity

Emily C. Nusbaum, Roger E. Beaty, and Paul J. Silvia

Ruminating about mental illness and creativity

Although a popular one, the question of whether mental illness is good for creativity is not new. As Becker discusses in his chapter, the ancient Greeks were speculating about "madness" and how it relates to creative genius long before the Renaissance-era artists thought to paint portraits of Italian emperors as piles of twigs and gourds (see Giuseppe Arcimboldo, sixteenth century), or the Romanticists composed paintings of grown men eating babies (Francisco Goya – *Saturn devouring his son*, c.1819) and people biting one another to steal each other's identities (William-Adolphe Bouguereau – *Dante and Virgil in Hell*, 1850). In fact, Socrates, Plato, and Aristotle carried on a philosophical tradition of questioning the "divine madness" of inspiration. It was thought in ancient Greece that the greatness of poets and prophets was a gift bestowed upon people in an altered state of awareness by the gods (or demons, depending on whom we're asking). Periodically since then, artists, poets, and philosophers were thought to be able to create because of divine demonic intervention, "melancholia," disease, drug use, or the like. And we, as researchers, are left to sift through the madness (or lack thereof) in search of evidence that this relationship actually exists (or doesn't).

In this chapter, we offer some reflections – or ruminations, as befits the occasion – on creativity and mental illness. These ideas are abstracted from and inspired by this interesting batch of chapters. We'll ponder a few topics: whether mental illness is specific to a few creative domains, why links exist when they are found, and what to take away from this large and sprawling literature.

Is mental illness particularly prevalent in certain creative domains?

Take almost any biography of a great writer, thinker, or artist, and somewhere in that book you are bound to find at least some mention of an extreme ritual or habit that the subject embraced. For instance, it's been alleged that Ernest Hemingway would begin the day's work by meticulously sharpening twenty pencils. And perhaps even more radically, it has been rumored that Edith Sitwell used to begin her day by lying in a coffin, as a means of inspiring her poetry. But are these rituals or superstitions ever responsible for the greatness of these eminent creators? It's possible that an odd habit here and there may make up a small part of great creators' daily routines, but incredibly unlikely that saying good morning to the pots and pans (as Carl Jung was rumored to do) and other such fanciful strategies result in spontaneous inspiration for high-caliber creative ideas.

Perhaps only *some types* of creative thinkers benefit from odd habits and eccentricities that are characteristic of psychopathologies. Indeed, historical evidence seems to suggest this. Simonton (this volume) discusses research surrounding this perception of madness and creative genius through a historiometric perspective. Earlier studies of the creativity/madness relationship found that only between 4 and 8 percent of the studied creative geniuses displayed signs of some sort of mental illness (Ellis, 1904). But more contemporary research found that breaking creative thinkers into groups based on discipline leads to a more detailed picture of the relationship between psychopathology and creativity. Post (1994) collected information about a large group of eminent creators and divided them into subcategories based on their expertise. Strikingly, what Post found when he divided his sample of "greats" into categories was that eminent writers and composers were markedly more likely than great thinkers, politicians, or scientists to display signs of psychopathologies. Likewise, Ludwig (1995) also found that great poets, writers, and composers had far higher lifetime prevalence of mental illnesses than great military leaders or politicians. It seems, then, that perhaps only *certain types* of creative achievements are fueled by aberrant functioning.

Indeed, certain domains of creative achievement seem plagued by psychopathology. For instance, there's some evidence (albeit outdated and controversial, as other authors in this volume point out) that great works of fiction and poetry were likely drafted by an alcoholic author (Andreasen, 1987). Famous ballerinas are more likely than the rest of us to have an eating disorder (Ravaldi *et al.*, 2003). Poets die younger and have hard and tormented lives (Kaufman, 2001, 2003, 2005). And much of the most influential and best-loved music was written or played by drug-addled musicians (Ludwig, 1995). But scientific discoveries and political and military coups, it seems, do not share this same affinity for psychopathology; in fact, Ludwig (1998) found that creative geniuses in domains like science and politics – domains that require logical thinking and formal expression of ideas – experience less psychopathology than creative geniuses operating in any other domain. (Except maybe for Joseph Goldberger, who – in an attempt to prove that pellagra was not an infectious disease – ate the scabs from the rashes of pellagra sufferers.)

Are certain mental illnesses particularly associated with creative greatness?

The range of mental illnesses is vast, as an afternoon browsing through the *Diagnostic and statistical manual of mental disorders* (*DSM*; APA, 2013) and *International classification of diseases* (*ICD*; World Health Organization, 2010) will attest, but only a small handful of disorders consistently appears in research, and the evidence is stronger for some disorders than others. In her chapter, Healey (this volume) dissects the research on creativity and attention-deficit/hyperactivity disorder (ADHD) in children. In the literature, disordered children and creative children are often described similarly in terms of temperament, activity, and social skills (Guenther, 1995). But Healey points out that, although the behaviors exhibited by children with ADHD resemble behaviors also exhibited by children who are skilled at creative thinking, the two are more distinctive than first glance may let on. Where children with ADHD often leap from idea to idea without a guiding theme, children who are creative thinkers can be more selective, controlled, and structured in recruiting and combining ideas. A seal and a sea lion may look like the same animal, but, like ADHD and creative thinking, they're entirely different species.

For other disorders, however, as several chapters in this volume point out (Abraham; Carson; Kaufmann and Kaufmann; Kinney and Richards; Kozbelt *et al.*), perhaps we should not be so skeptical of the slew of biographies (Jamison, 1993), epidemiological studies (Goodwin and Jamison, 2007), and recent reviews (Galvez *et al.*, 2011; Johnson *et al.*, 2012; Lloyd-Evans *et al.*, 2006; Pollack-Kagan and McCabe, 2010) indicating that there is indeed a higher incidence of psychopathology in creative thinkers. There's enough evidence associated with some disorders – depression; mania and the bipolar spectrum; and the schizophrenia spectrum – to suggest that some disorders have some associations with some creative domains.

Several authors suggest that rather than disorders being the cause of creativity, creativity and certain features of disorders may be linked to similar neurological and genetic processes (see chapters by Beaussart *et al.*; Kinney and Richards). For instance, while both hypomania and bipolar disorder are associated with prolonged periods of increased energy, rapid thinking, less need for sleep, and more positive attitudes, only people affected by the less intense hypomanic mood swings are able to harness the motivating positive energy in order to increase productivity while still filtering out the grandiose, impractical ideas. In the same vein, people experiencing a major depressive episode are often plagued by ruminating negative thoughts, but people experiencing a less intense dysthymic episode are able to use the rumination adaptively to channel insight.

Adaptationism as an explanation for creativity and mental illness

An intriguing idea found in several chapters is that some mental illnesses are passed down because they convey creativity as an adaptive feature (see chapters by Carson and Kozbelt *et al.*). Positive schizotypal symptoms, for example, might be dysfunctional, but they foster creative ideas that can serve adaptive functions. This argument has a certain appeal – it tackles the hard problem of how mental illnesses persist, and celebrates creativity as a positive resource – but we're ultimately unconvinced.

First, the associations between some disorders and creativity are not large enough or consistent enough, in our opinion, to be compelling. Bipolar disorder, for example, isn't so strongly related to creativity, and creativity isn't so strongly related to reproductive success, that bipolar could persist solely because of an incidental effect on creativity. Second, "heritability" and "adaptiveness," themselves slippery concepts, become even more slippery when applied to sociocultural concepts such as creativity and psychopathology.

And, finally, we wonder if these ideas reflect hubris on the part of creativity researchers, who naturally see creativity as tremendously important and a driving force in individual and cultural achievement. We would encourage researchers to consider bipolar disorder and schizophrenia from the lens of people with these disorders, their parents, and their children. Are we really to believe that disorders like depression, bipolar, and schizophrenia – disorders that are crippling and disabling, that disrupt relationships and social networks, and that cause self-harm and suicide – persist because they have weak effects on creativity in some cultural domains? The implications of this idea feel vulgar and sound wrong.

The big picture of mental illness and creativity

Stepping back to look at the literature as a whole, what can we conclude? It seems obvious to us from research discussed in the preceding chapters that creativity and mental illness are less related than common stereotypes would have us believe. We're thus sympathetic to Schlesinger (this volume), who denounces the "mad genius stereotype" as an empty stereotype. We agree that this idea has been seriously oversold. Like no other research problem, this one can drive creativity researchers to madness and melancholia: the amount of evidence in support of such links is disproportionate to the amount of popular interest in the problem and to the contentiousness of the issue in professional circles. Nevertheless, we take away from these chapters a sense that, for some severity levels of some disorders, and for some domains, one can reasonably conclude that creativity and mental illness are linked.

As Abraham, Carson, Healey, Kinney and Richards, Papworth, and others in this volume point out, there are some interesting insights found in the creativity–mental illness literature. As discussed by Papworth (this volume), we find that across mental illnesses researchers incorporate two prevalent patterns of disordered thinking into their models of psychopathologies. The first, *maintaining cognitive biases*, leads to people interpreting information, thoughts, feelings, and sensations as particularly meaningful or representative of skewed expectations and beliefs. The second, *lacking cognitive inhibition*, leads to a reduction in filtering out seemingly irrelevant cognitive input. Although these patterns are strongly associated with maladaptive thought processes – like rumination, impulsivity, hearing voices, and catastrophizing, for example – and with disorders such as major depression, generalized anxiety, and schizophrenia, they are also strongly associated with the normal cognitive functions that people elect to engage in when coming up with creative ideas. People who are able to think creatively often have diverse associations, uninhibited generation, and divergent problem-solving strategies – in other words, they are able to selectively turn off and on the same thinking patterns that consistently plague people with persistent psychopathologies.

Likewise, many chapters in this volume acknowledge that there is a lot of murkiness in the study of creativity and mental illness. In this literature – more so than in any other recent creativity research – the concept of creativity is loose, poorly defined, and ill-suited for serious, quantitative research. This presents two problems for researchers. First, as Simonton (this volume) points out, the looser a domain's constraints are for defining what is creative, the more we tend to find instances of people with various psychoses operating "creatively" within that domain. And second, as Abraham and others, Carson, Kinney and Richards, Schlesinger (all this volume) discuss, there seems to be a shared vulnerability or "third variable" that is associated with the thinking styles of the mentally ill and the thinking styles that lead to creative ideas. But because "creativity" isdifferent across different studies, it's difficult to say just which commonalities are driving the relationship between the two thinking styles.

In short, it is admittedly fascinating that people who develop or are genetically predisposed to developing mental illness are often more creative. But as we've seen in chapters throughout this volume, the connection between mental illness and creativity is tenuous, at best, and likely perpetuated by romanticized and mystical conceptions of artists as tortured souls. Artists, writers, and creative thinkers are no more tortured than the rest of us though – more realistically, they just seem to embrace the unconventional thinking strategies that we tend to associate with affective and schizotypal disorders, yet maintain intact executive functions that are advantageous (and probably necessary) for creative thinking (see Beaty and Silvia, 2012, 2013; Nusbaum and Silvia, 2011; Silvia and Beaty, 2012). Researchers ought to focus on demystifying the creativity–psychopathology relationship by examining the specific, functional ways in which disordered thoughts are similar to creative thoughts. For example, as Kinney and Richards point out (this volume), disordered eminent creators are often disordered in the direction of unhealthy positive moods – and as Baas *et al.*'s (2008) comprehensive meta-analysis of mood and creativity finds, positive mood is, in general, conducive for creative thinking because it increases fluency and flexibility, two important cognitive abilities that contribute to creative ideation.

One take-home message, we think, is that creativity science should invest more heavily in understanding the basic processes of normal creativity. This strategy is more likely to yield theories that can be translated to the problem of how creativity works in disorders and pathological samples. The other route – using disordered samples as a lens through which to understand creativity more generally – seems less fertile, if only because it hasn't moved our basic-science understanding of creativity very far thus far. The best way to understand the few links that exist between creativity and mental illness might therefore be to step back from this contentious problem and work out the foundational cognitive, biological, and social processes that foster creative ideas in normal populations.

References

American Psychiatric Association (APA) (2013). *Diagnostic and statistical manual of mental health disorders* (5th edn.). Washington, DC: Author.

Andreasen, N. C. (1987). Creativity and mental illness: Prevalence rates in writers and their first degree relatives. *American Journal of Psychiatry*, 144, 1288–1292.

Baas, M., De Dreu, C. and Nijstad, B. (2008). A meta-analysis of 25 years of mood-creativity research: Hedonic tone, activation, or regulatory focus? *Psychological Bulletin*, 134, 779–806.

Beaty, R. E. and Silvia, P. J. (2012). Why do ideas get more creative across time? An executive interpretation of the serial order effect in divergent thinking tasks. *Psychology of Aesthetics, Creativity, and the Arts*, 6, 309–319.

Beaty, R. E. and Silvia, P. J. (2013). Metaphorically speaking: Cognitive abilities and the production of figurative language. *Memory and Cognition*, 41, 255–267.

Ellis, H. (1904). *A study of British genius*. London: Hurst & Blackett.

Galvez, J. F., Thommi, S. and Ghaemi, S. N. (2011). Positive aspects of mental illness: A review in bipolar disorder. *Journal of Affective Disorders*, 128, 185–190.

Goodwin, F. K. and Jamison, K. R. (2007). *Manic-depressive illness: Bipolar disorders and recurrent depression*. New York: Oxford University Press.

Guenther, A. (1995). *What educators and parents need to know about ADHD, creativity, and gifted students*. Practitioners' guide A9814. The National Center on the Gifted and Talented, University of Connecticut.

Jamison, K. R. (1993). *Touched with fire: Manic-depressive illness and the artistic temperament*. New York: Free Press.

Johnson, S. L., Murray, G., Fredrickson, B., Youngstrom, E. A., Hinshaw, S., Bass, J. M. et al. (2012). Creativity and bipolar disorder: Touched by fire or burning with questions? *Clinical Psychology Review*, 32, 1–12.

Kaufman, J. C. (2001). The Sylvia Plath effect: Mental illness in eminent creative writers. *Journal of Creative Behavior*, 35, 37–50.

Kaufman, J. C. (2003). The cost of the muse: Poets die young. *Death Studies*, 27, 813–821.

Kaufman, J. C. (2005). The door that leads into madness: Eastern European poets and mental illness. *Creativity Research Journal*, 17, 99–103.

Lloyd-Evans, R., Batey, M. and Furnham, A. (2006). Bipolar disorder and creativity: Investigating a possible link. In A. Columbus (Ed.), *Advances in psychology research*, 40. New York: Nova Press.

Ludwig, A. M. (1995). *The price of greatness: Resolving the creativity and madness controversy*. New York: Guilford Press.

Ludwig, A. M. (1998). Method and madness in the arts and sciences. *Creativity Research Journal*, 11, 93–101.

Nusbaum, E. C. and Silvia, P. J. (2011). Are intelligence and creativity really so different? Fluid intelligence, executive processes, and strategy use in divergent thinking. *Intelligence*, 39, 36–45.

Pollack-Kagan, S. and McCabe, R. C. (2010). Mood disorders and creativity. In P. C. McCabe and S. R. Shaw (Eds.), *Psychiatric disorders* (pp. 41–49). Thousand Oaks, CA: Sage.

Post, F. (1994). Creativity and psychopathology: A study of 291 world-famous men. *British Journal of Psychiatry*, 165, 22–34.

Ravaldi, C., Vannacci, A., Zucchi, T., Mannucci, E., Cabras, P. L., Boldrini, M. et al. (2003). Eating disorders and body image disturbances among ballet dancers, gymnasium users and body builders. *Psychopathology*, 36, 247–254.

Silvia, P. J. and Beaty, R. E. (2012). Making creative metaphors: The importance of fluid intelligence for creative thought. *Intelligence*, 40, 343–351.

World Health Organization (2010). *International statistical classification of diseases and related health problems* (10th revision). Geneva, Switzerland. http://apps. who.int/classifications/icd10/browse/Help/en, last accessed March 17, 2014.

19 Creativity and mental illness: reasons to care and beware

James C. Kaufman

As I was finishing up this project, a colleague asked me a question that stuck with me – Why exactly was I doing this book? I ask myself that question every time I am in the final stages of an edited project, as I track down the last chapters and begin the marketing questionnaires. But, of course, this question was a bit deeper. Why creativity and mental illness? Why study it?

Some would argue the topic has been done to death. There have been hundreds and hundreds of studies, most of them analyzing one small piece of the puzzle. Small effects or mixed results are overstated – or consistent patterns are minimized. The benchmark papers are flawed and, even if perfectly executed, would only shed light on one aspect of the question. The analogy of the blind men and the elephant (all touching a different part of the creature and reaching quite distinct assumptions about its essence) is overused but particularly apt in this field.

Part of me is ready for this question with two quotes. One is from my favorite play, Tom Stoppard's *Arcadia*. The quote is spoken by an academic; her first sentence refers to her friends' different research interests in mathematics, history, and English literature:

It's all trivial – your grouse, my hermit, Bernard's Byron. Comparing what we're looking for misses the point. It's wanting to know that makes us matter . . . If the answers are in the back of the book I can wait, but what a drag. Better to struggle on knowing that failure is final. (Stoppard, 1993, pp. 75–76)

Some find the passage depressing (the idea of being doomed to eternal failure); I find it inspiring – the joy is in the hunt.

The other quote is from one of my favorite musicals, *1776*. As the members of the continental congress bandy about the idea of independence, there is a vote called about whether official debate can begin. The tie-breaking vote is left to Rhode Island's Stephen Hopkins. He says:

So it's up to me, is it? Well, I tell y', in all my years I never heard, seen nor smelled an issue that was so dangerous that it couldn't be talked about. Hell yes, I'm for debatin' anything – Rhode Island says Yea! (Stone and Edwards, 1976, p. 38)

But another part of me believes in the WGASA factor. I have discussed this before (Kaufman, 2009); to recap . . . The WGASA factor is named after the (now sadly defunct) WGASA Bush Line at the Wild Animal Park in San Diego. Years ago, the park held a contest to name the monorail. After some fruitless discussion, one executive amended a memo to say WGASA. What did that mean? The official line is it stands for "World's Greatest Animal Show Anywhere." According to legend (which I hope is true), it stands for something much simpler: "Who Gives a S**t Anyway?"

So much of scholarship doesn't pass the WGASA test (who actually cares?). It also doesn't pass the WGASA corollary, which is that research should ideally lead to more positive outcomes than negative ones. We can't all cure cancer, but ideally we aren't teaching little cancer cells to reproduce more effectively.[1]

So where does that leave creativity and mental illness? My main empirical contribution to the field (so far) has been the "Sylvia Plath effect" (Kaufman, 2001b). It came from a large project I embarked on about creative writers and their life histories. Put quite simply, in the first study for the paper, I found that, among eminent writers, female poets were more likely than other writers (male novelists, male poets, male playwrights, male journalists, female novelists, female playwrights, and female journalists) to have experienced mental illness in their life. In the second study for the paper, I found that, among eminent women, poets were more likely to have experienced mental illness than actors, politicians, artists, novelists, and journalists. It initially came out with little fanfare. I followed up with some theory papers (Kaufman and Baer, 2002; Kaufman and Sexton, 2006) and some empirical studies that mostly found further evidence that poets were more likely to die young or have poor mental health (Kaufman, 2001a, 2003, 2005). An odd confluence of events led the press to treat these findings as news in 2004, and they became blogger-fodder (and have remained so since). I noticed that, aside from the usual signal-noise issues, there were some strong feelings emerging.

Some people were pissed off:

The globally morbid interest in these women and their choices to die, as well as the manners in which they chose to die has been perpetuated by Kaufman. By portraying their creativity as hysterical and intrinsically linked to mental illness, he has belittled their literary output and the artistic influence it has had. Other women writers also said to suffer from The Sylvia Plath Effect include Sara Teasdale, Anne Sexton and Sarah Kane, who all committed suicide, leaving

---

[1] I wrote this sentence without factoring in the case of Henrietta Lacks, whose cancer cells were used to save lives (Skloot, 2010). So even metaphors are complicated.

behind them great volumes of writing brushed idly aside by the fame [of] their dramatic deaths. Kaufman is peddling tabloid drama that surely fails to override the great output of these women and the intellectual contributions they have made... To reduce these women's lives to mere spectacle is surely to belittle their art. (Pelling, 2013)

Others embraced the idea:

I wouldn't call it the Plath effect. I mean, LOTS of creative people are alcoholics, drug abusers, etc. Plenty of writers have suffered with addiction, mental illnesses, etc. It's also shown that addictive personalities and creative minds are almost interlinked. I suffer gladly for my imagination. I myself am bipolar, with an addictive personality, and I use substances to turn the monsters off in my head. Oh, to be normal... not really. Normal is boring. I couldn't imagine not having the ability to create and destroy whenever I inclined. (mollymillions, 2013)

And others were self-reflective:

How do we not self-destruct? How do we, as master's artists, be we poets, painters, musicians, belly-dancers, keep from isolating ourselves and fashioning our own pine boxes? I would like to say, I am no longer in the dark dangerous place. But sometimes I wonder. I have to fight to enter into community. It is tough to drag myself even to my cyber gatherings at times, because I grapple with the difficult circumstances of life and the ever-present rejection of the "industry." It is hard to hold my head up sometimes even when I know my work is blessed, some have even said, anointed. But then I struggle with all the polishing... I get down about it all. (siouxsiepoet, 2004)

Unlike so much of academic scholarship, people care about this topic. Creative individuals *particularly* care (Kaufman *et al.*, 2006). And the researchers care. The topic of creativity and mental illness can be emotional – people tend to study things that are important to them, and both constructs are highly personal. It is also an area of popular interest, which can mean sudden attention from journalists. I can only speak for myself, but it is far too easy to make grand conclusions or pronouncements in conversation and then see them in print and think, "Uh oh." I have never been misquoted, but I have said some mighty stupid things. Finally, it is a romantic subject – there are all sorts of poems and paintings that can inspire the type of hyperbolizing that is less appropriate in science. We can sometimes get carried away. I imagine that it is less tempting for a proctologist to begin a research article with an epigram by someone like Oscar Wilde or Dorothy Parker.

In addition, research on creativity and mental illness – and the public interpretation of such work – may have an impact on how the average person views those who are creative. Right now, creative people are not viewed in a particularly positive light. Teachers may show unconscious biases against creative students (Aljughaiman and Mowrer-Reynolds, 2005; Westby and Dawson, 1995). Workers show similar biases about whether or not creativity is a positive trait for potential leaders (Mueller *et al.*, 2011). Even people who expressed positive or neutral explicit views of creativity demonstrated implicit biases against creativity when primed to be intolerant of uncertainty (Mueller *et al.*, 2012). The concept that creativity is linked with mental illness (which is itself subject to a strong stigma, e.g., Ben-Zeev *et al.*, 2010) likely does not help make public perceptions any more favorable.

So what comes next? The cliché ending of a research paper is "More research is needed." Well, I wouldn't necessarily say that *more* research is needed – there is plenty of research out there (and much of it has been discussed, summarized, and critiqued within these pages). But I'd like to see work that is precise about what part of the elephant is being studied, and then keeps the discussion firmly focused on that piece. Examining anxiety in ballet dancers is different from looking at how schizophrenics perform on a divergent-thinking test, which is itself different from an analysis of hypomania and poetry writing in college students.

As I believe the essays in this book demonstrate, we have come a long way. We can (and should) approach the question with new perspectives (such as neuroscience) and new (and more specific) definitions of creativity and mental illness. But we should also take care when presenting our research, both in academic and popular circles. To quote from Stoppard's *Arcadia* one last time, "One does not aim at poetry with pistols. At poets, perhaps" (1993, p. 41).

References

Aljughaiman, A. and Mowrer-Reynolds, E. (2005). Teachers' conceptions of creativity and creative students. *Journal of Creative Behavior*, 39, 17–34.

Ben-Zeev, D., Young, M. and Corrigan, P. (2010). *DSM-V* and the stigma of mental illness. *Journal of Mental Health*, 19, 318–327.

Kaufman, J. C. (2001a). Genius, lunatics, and poets: Mental illness in prize-winning authors. *Imagination, Cognition, and Personality*, 20, 305–314.

Kaufman, J. C. (2001b). The Sylvia Plath effect: Mental illness in eminent creative writers. *Journal of Creative Behavior*, 35, 37–50.

Kaufman, J. C. (2003). The cost of the muse: Poets die young. *Death Studies*, 27, 813–822.

Kaufman, J. C. (2005). The door that leads into madness: Eastern European poets and mental illness. *Creativity Research Journal*, 17, 99–103.

Kaufman, J. C. (2009). *Creativity 101*. New York: Springer.

Kaufman, J. C. and Baer, J. (2002). I bask in dreams of suicide: Mental illness and poetry. *Review of General Psychology*, 6, 271–286.

Kaufman, J. C. and Sexton, J. D. (2006). Why doesn't the writing cure help poets? *Review of General Psychology*, 10, 268–282.

Kaufman, J. C., Bromley, M. L. and Cole, J. C. (2006). Insane, poetic, lovable: Creativity and endorsement of the "Mad Genius" stereotype. *Imagination, Cognition, and Personality*, 26, 149–161.

mollymillions (2013). *Sylvia Plath effect*. http://mollymillions.tumblr.com/post/3560417697/sylvia-plath-effect, last accessed May 3, 2013 (website defunct but content active at http://fleurdelanuit.tumblr.com/post/3560666135/sylvia-plath-effect).

Mueller, J. S., Goncalo, J. A. and Kamdar, D. (2011). Recognizing creative leadership: Can creative idea expression negatively relate to perceptions of leadership potential? *Journal of Experimental Social Psychology*, 47, 494–498.

Mueller, J. S., Melwani, S. and Goncalo, J. A. (2012). The bias against creativity: Why people desire but reject creative ideas. *Psychological Science*, 23, 13–17.

Pelling, M. (2013, January 24). *Remembering the Sylvia Plath effect on Orwell Day*. www.kettlemag.com/article/remembering-sylvia-plath-effect-orwell-day, last accessed May 3, 2013.

siouxsiepoet (2004, June 19). *Self-destructive tendencies*. http://themastersartist.blogspot.com/2004/06/self-destructive-tendencies-tonight-as.html, last accessed July 17, 2004.

Skloot, R. (2010). *The immortal life of Henrietta Lacks*. New York: Crown.

Stone, P. and Edwards, S. (1976). *1776*. New York: Penguin Books.

Stoppard, T. (1993). *Arcadia*. London: Faber and Faber.

Westby, E. L. and Dawson, V. L. (1995). Creativity: Asset or burden in the classroom? *Creativity Research Journal*, 8, 1–10.

Index

Lightning Source UK Ltd.
Milton Keynes UK
UKOW06n1459170515

251694UK00001B/5/P